Teach Yourself FrontPage 2000 VISUALLY™

IDG's 3-D Visual™ Series

IDG Books Worldwide, Inc.
An International Data Group Company
Foster City, CA • Indianapolis • Chicago • New York

Teach Yourself FrontPage 2000 VISUALLY™

Published by
IDG Books Worldwide, Inc.
An International Data Group Company
919 E. Hillsdale Blvd., Suite 400
Foster City, CA 94404

Library of Congress Catalog Card No.: 00-102152

ISBN: 0-7645-3451-3

Printed in the United States of America
10 9 8 7 6 5 4 3 2 1

Distributed in the United States by IDG Books Worldwide, Inc.

Distributed by CDG Books Canada Inc. for Canada; by Transworld Publishers Limited in the United Kingdom; by IDG Norge Books for Norway; by IDG Sweden Books for Sweden; by IDG Books Australia Publishing Corporation Pty. Ltd. for Australia and New Zealand; by TransQuest Publishers Pte Ltd. for Singapore, Malaysia, Thailand, Indonesia, and Hong Kong; by Gotop Information Inc. for Taiwan; by ICG Muse, Inc. for Japan; by Intersoft for South Africa; by Eyrolles for France; by International Thomson Publishing for Germany, Austria and Switzerland; by Distribuidora Cuspide for Argentina; by LR International for Brazil; by Galileo Libros for Chile; by Ediciones ZETA S.C.R. Ltda. for Peru; by WS Computer Publishing Corporation, Inc. for the Philippines; by Contemporanea de Ediciones for Venezuela; by Express Computer Distributors for the Caribbean and West Indies; by Micronesia Media Distributor, Inc. for Micronesia; by Chips Computadoras S.A. de C.V. for Mexico; by Editorial Norma de Panama S.A. for Panama; by American Bookshops for Finland.
For corporate orders, please call maranGraphics at 800-469-6616.
For general information on IDG Books Worldwide's books in the U.S., please call our Consumer Customer Service department at 800-762-2974.
For reseller information, including discounts and premium sales, please call our Reseller Customer Service department at 800-434-3422.
For information on where to purchase IDG Books Worldwide's books outside the U.S., please contact our International Sales department at 317-572-3993 or fax 317-572-4002.
For consumer information on foreign language translations, please contact our Customer Service department at 800-434-3422, fax 800-550-2747, or e-mail rights@idgbooks.com.
For information on licensing foreign or domestic rights, please phone 650-653-7000 of fax 650-653-7500.
For sales inquiries and special prices for bulk quantities, please contact our Sales department at 650-655-3200.
For information on using IDG Books Worldwide's books in the classroom or for ordering examination copies, please contact our Educational Sales department at 800-434-2086 or fax 317-572-4005.
For press review copies, author interviews, or other publicity information, please contact our Public Relations department at 650-653-7000 or fax 650-653-7500.
For authorization to photocopy items for corporate, personal, or educational use, please contact maranGraphics at 800-469-6616.

Trademark Acknowledgments

maranGraphics Inc. has attempted to include trademark information for products, services and companies referred to in this guide. Although maranGraphics Inc. has made reasonable efforts in gathering this information, it cannot guarantee its accuracy.

All brand names and product names used in this book are trade names, service marks, trademarks, or registered trademarks of their respective owners. IDG Books Worldwide and maranGraphics Inc. are not associated with any product or vendor mentioned in this book.

FOR PURPOSES OF ILLUSTRATING THE CONCEPTS AND TECHNIQUES DESCRIBED IN THIS BOOK, THE AUTHOR HAS CREATED VARIOUS NAMES, COMPANY NAMES, MAILING ADDRESSES, E-MAIL ADDRESSES AND PHONE NUMBERS, ALL OF WHICH ARE FICTITIOUS. ANY RESEMBLANCE OF THESE FICTITIOUS NAMES, COMPANY NAMES, MAILING ADDRESSES, E-MAIL ADDRESSES AND PHONE NUMBERS TO ANY ACTUAL PERSON, COMPANY AND/OR ORGANIZATION IS UNINTENTIONAL AND PURELY COINCIDENTAL.

maranGraphics has used their best efforts in preparing this book. As Web sites are constantly changing, some of the Web site addresses in this book may have moved or no longer exist. maranGraphics does not accept responsibility nor liability for losses or damages resulting from the information contained in this book. maranGraphics also does not support the views expressed in the Web sites contained in this book.

Permissions

Microsoft
Screen shots reprinted with permission from Microsoft Corporation.

Netscape
Copyright 1999 Netscape Communications Corporation. All rights reserved.

Permissions Granted
Sunkist

The 3-D illustrations are the copyright of maranGraphics, Inc.

U.S. Corporate Sales	**U.S. Trade Sales**
Contact maranGraphics at (800) 469-6616 or Fax (905) 890-9434.	Contact IDG Books at (800) 434-3422 or (650) 655-3000.

ABOUT IDG BOOKS WORLDWIDE

Welcome to the world of IDG Books Worldwide.

IDG Books Worldwide, Inc., is a subsidiary of International Data Group, the world's largest publisher of computer-related information and the leading global provider of information services on information technology. IDG was founded more than 30 years ago by Patrick J. McGovern and now employs more than 9,000 people worldwide. IDG publishes more than 290 computer publications in over 75 countries. More than 90 million people read one or more IDG publications each month.

Launched in 1990, IDG Books Worldwide is today the #1 publisher of best-selling computer books in the United States. We are proud to have received eight awards from the Computer Press Association in recognition of editorial excellence and three from Computer Currents' First Annual Readers' Choice Awards. Our best-selling *...For Dummies®* series has more than 50 million copies in print with translations in 31 languages. IDG Books Worldwide, through a joint venture with IDG's Hi-Tech Beijing, became the first U.S. publisher to publish a computer book in the People's Republic of China. In record time, IDG Books Worldwide has become the first choice for millions of readers around the world who want to learn how to better manage their businesses.

Our mission is simple: Every one of our books is designed to bring extra value and skill-building instructions to the reader. Our books are written by experts who understand and care about our readers. The knowledge base of our editorial staff comes from years of experience in publishing, education, and journalism — experience we use to produce books to carry us into the new millennium. In short, we care about books, so we attract the best people. We devote special attention to details such as audience, interior design, use of icons, and illustrations. And because we use an efficient process of authoring, editing, and desktop publishing our books electronically, we can spend more time ensuring superior content and less time on the technicalities of making books.

You can count on our commitment to deliver high-quality books at competitive prices on topics you want to read about. At IDG Books Worldwide, we continue in the IDG tradition of delivering quality for more than 30 years. You'll find no better book on a subject than one from IDG Books Worldwide.

John Kilcullen
Chairman and CEO
IDG Books Worldwide, Inc.

Eighth Annual Computer Press Awards 1992

Ninth Annual Computer Press Awards 1993

Tenth Annual Computer Press Awards 1994

Eleventh Annual Computer Press Awards 1995

IDG is the world's leading IT media, research and exposition company. Founded in 1964, IDG had 1997 revenues of $2.05 billion and has more than 9,000 employees worldwide. IDG offers the widest range of media options that reach IT buyers in 75 countries representing 95% of worldwide IT spending. IDG's diverse product and services portfolio spans six key areas including print publishing, online publishing, expositions and conferences, market research, education and training, and global marketing services. More than 90 million people read one or more of IDG's 290 magazines and newspapers, including IDG's leading global brands — Computerworld, PC World, Network World, Macworld and the Channel World family of publications. IDG Books Worldwide is one of the fastest-growing computer book publishers in the world, with more than 700 titles in 36 languages. The "...For Dummies®" series alone has more than 50 million copies in print. IDG offers online users the largest network of technology-specific Web sites around the world through IDG.net (http://www.idg.net), which comprises more than 225 targeted Web sites in 55 countries worldwide. International Data Corporation (IDC) is the world's largest provider of information technology data, analysis and consulting, with research centers in over 41 countries and more than 400 research analysts worldwide. IDG World Expo is a leading producer of more than 168 globally branded conferences and expositions in 35 countries including E3 (Electronic Entertainment Expo), Macworld Expo, ComNet, Windows World Expo, ICE (Internet Commerce Expo), Agenda, DEMO, and Spotlight. IDG's training subsidiary, ExecuTrain, is the world's largest computer training company, with more than 230 locations worldwide and 785 training courses. IDG Marketing Services helps industry-leading IT companies build international brand recognition by developing global integrated marketing programs via IDG's print, online and exposition products worldwide. Further information about the company can be found at www.idg.com.
1/26/00

maranGraphics is a family-run business located near Toronto, Canada.

At **maranGraphics**, we believe in producing great computer books–one book at a time.

Each maranGraphics book uses the award-winning communication process that we have been developing over the last 25 years. Using this process, we organize screen shots, text and illustrations in a way that makes it easy for you to learn new concepts and tasks.

We spend hours deciding the best way to perform each task, so you don't have to! Our clear, easy-to-follow screen shots and instructions walk you through each task from beginning to end.

Our detailed illustrations go hand-in-hand with the text to help reinforce the information. Each illustration is a labor of love–some take up to a week to draw!

We want to thank you for purchasing what we feel are the best computer books money can buy. We hope you enjoy using this book as much as we enjoyed creating it!

Sincerely,

The Maran Family

Please visit us on the Web at:

www.maran.com

CREDITS

Author:
Ruth Maran

Technical Consultant:
Paul Whitehead

Copy Editors:
Raquel Scott
Jill Maran
Roxanne Van Damme

Project Manager:
Judy Maran

Editors:
Janice Boyer
Stacey Morrison

Screen Captures:
James Menzies

Layout Designer:
Treena Lees

Illustrators:
Russ Marini
Sean Johannesen
Steven Schaerer
Ted Sheppard

Screen Artist & Illustrator:
Jimmy Tam

Indexer:
Janice Boyer

Post Production:
Robert Maran

Senior Vice President, Technology Publishing IDG Books Worldwide:
Richard Swadley

Editorial Support IDG Books Worldwide:
Barry Pruett
Martine Edwards

ACKNOWLEDGMENTS

Thanks to the dedicated staff of maranGraphics, including Jennifer Amaral, Cathy Benn, Janice Boyer, Sean Johannesen, Eric Kramer, Usha Krishnan, Wanda Lawrie, Treena Lees, Jill Maran, Judy Maran, Robert Maran, Sherry Maran, Russ Marini, James Menzies, Stacey Morrison, Teri Lynn Pinsent, Steven Schaerer, Raquel Scott, Ted Sheppard, Jimmy Tam, Roxanne Van Damme, Paul Whitehead and Kelleigh Wing.

Finally, to Richard Maran who originated the easy-to-use graphic format of this guide. Thank you for your inspiration and guidance.

TABLE OF CONTENTS

Chapter 1 GETTING STARTED

Chapter 2 FRONTPAGE BASICS

Chapter 3 WORK WITH WEB PAGES

Chapter 4

EDIT TEXT

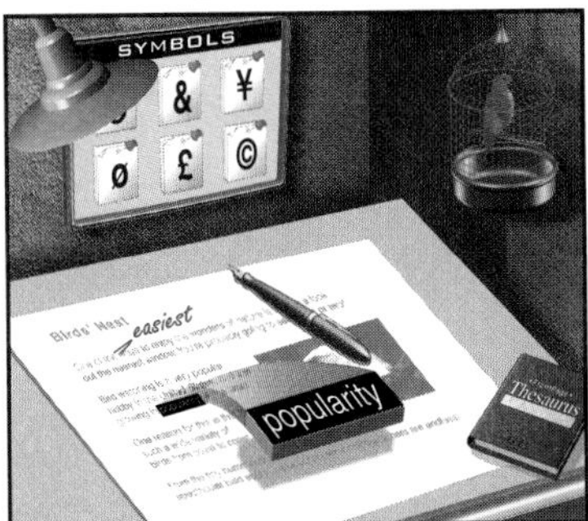

Chapter 5

FORMAT WEB PAGES

TABLE OF CONTENTS

Chapter 6 ADD IMAGES

Chapter 7 CUSTOMIZE IMAGES

Chapter 8 CREATE LINKS

Chapter 9 CREATE TABLES

Chapter 10 WORK WITH NAVIGATIONAL STRUCTURE

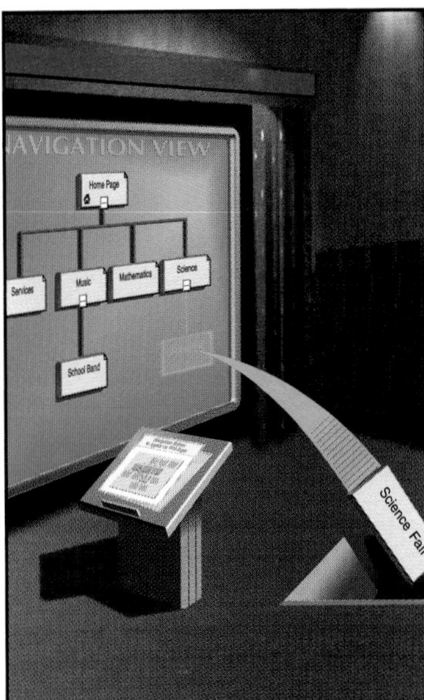

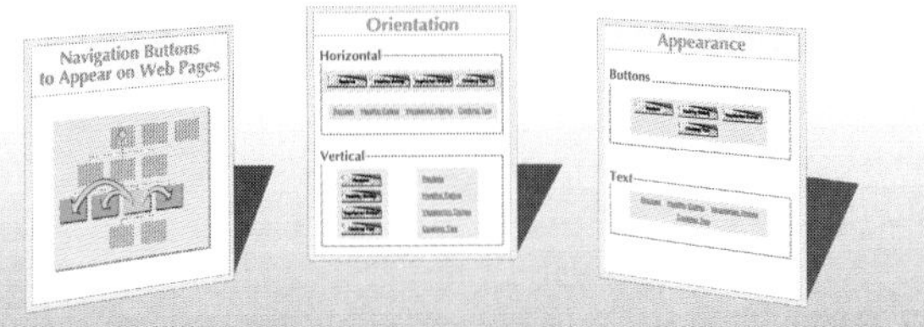

TABLE OF CONTENTS

Chapter 11 CREATE FRAMES

Chapter 12 CREATE FORMS

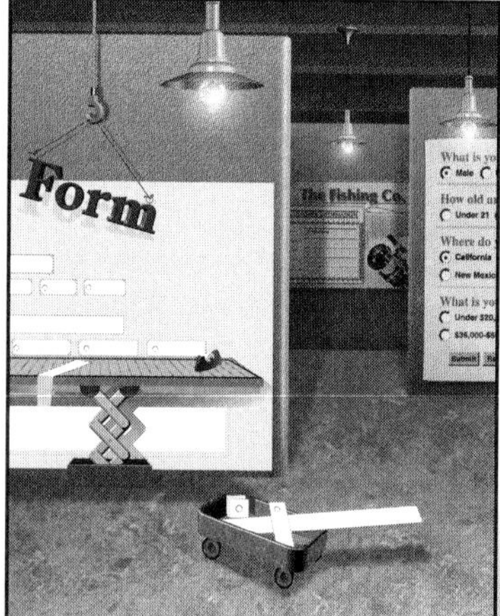

Chapter 13 ADD WEB PAGE EFFECTS

Chapter 14 MANAGE WEB PAGES

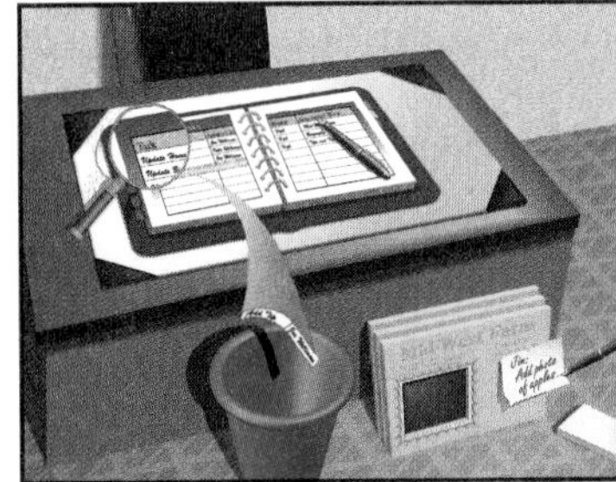

Chapter 15 PUBLISH WEB PAGES

FRONTPAGE
Ink

CHAPTER 1

Getting Started

Are you thinking about creating Web pages? This chapter will help you get started.

INTRODUCTION TO FRONTPAGE

FrontPage allows you to create, edit, manage and publish Web pages.

EDIT AND FORMAT TEXT

FrontPage offers many features that help you edit and format text on your Web pages. You can add, delete and rearrange text as well as check your Web pages for spelling errors. You can enhance or emphasize information by using various fonts, styles and colors or apply a theme to instantly give your Web pages a professional look.

ADD IMAGES

You can add images to illustrate concepts or enhance the appearance of your Web pages. You can add images such as drawings, paintings, photographs, charts and diagrams. FrontPage offers many ways to customize images, such as adding a border to an image.

CREATE LINKS

You can create links to connect a word, phrase or image on a Web page to another page in your own Web site or on the Web. You can also create links that readers can select to send you an e-mail message.

CREATE TABLES

You can create a table to neatly display a list of information on a Web page. Tables are also useful for controlling the placement of text and images on a Web page.

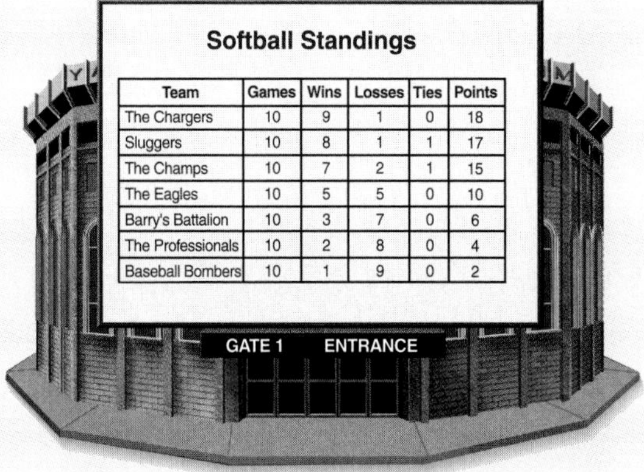

Softball Standings

Team	Games	Wins	Losses	Ties	Points
The Chargers	10	9	1	0	18
Sluggers	10	8	1	1	17
The Champs	10	7	2	1	15
The Eagles	10	5	5	0	10
Barry's Battalion	10	3	7	0	6
The Professionals	10	2	8	0	4
Baseball Bombers	10	1	9	0	2

CREATE FRAMES

You can create frames to divide a Web browser window into sections. Each section will display a different Web page. Frames allow you to display information such as a company logo or navigational tools that will remain on the screen while readers browse through your Web pages.

CREATE FORMS

Forms allow you to gather information from readers who visit your Web pages. You can create forms that let readers send you questions or comments about your Web pages. You can also create forms that allow readers to purchase your products and services on the Web.

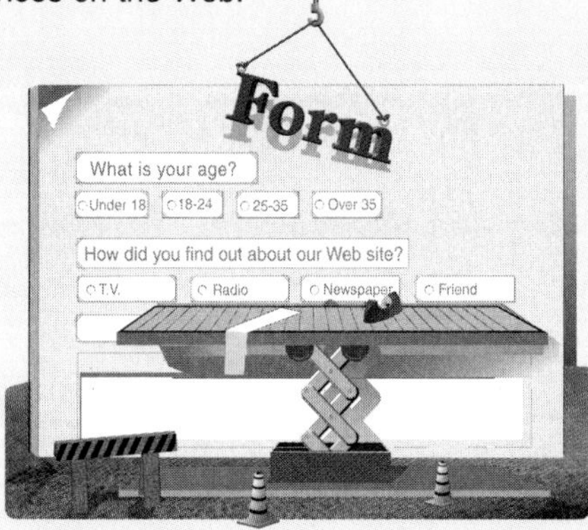

PUBLISH WEB PAGES

When you finish creating your Web pages, FrontPage helps you transfer the pages to a Web server to make the pages available on the Web. Web servers are computers on the Internet that store, monitor and control access to Web pages.

INTRODUCTION TO THE WEB

The World Wide Web is part of the Internet and consists of a huge collection of documents stored on computers around the world.

The World Wide Web is also called the Web.

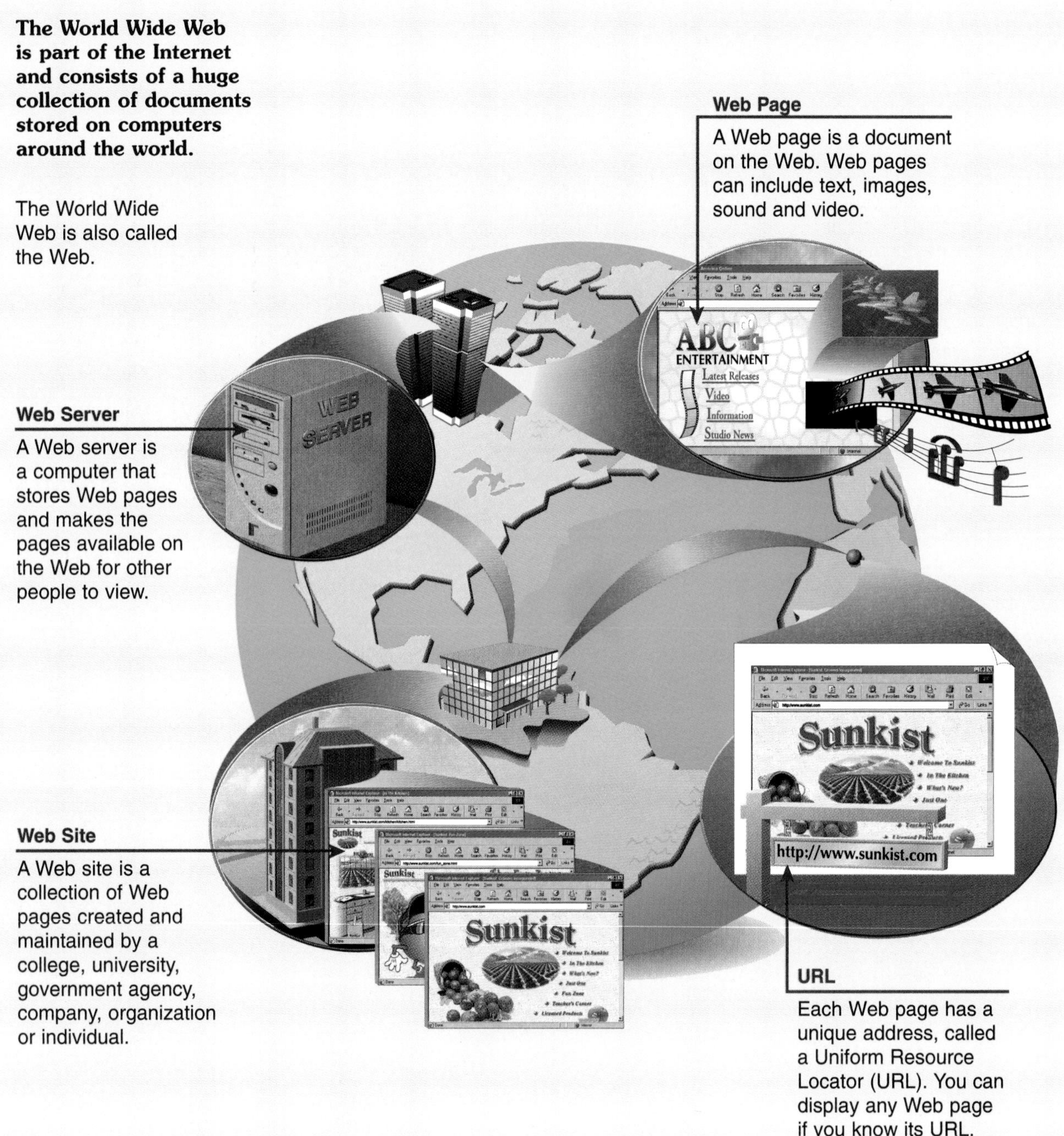

Web Page

A Web page is a document on the Web. Web pages can include text, images, sound and video.

Web Server

A Web server is a computer that stores Web pages and makes the pages available on the Web for other people to view.

Web Site

A Web site is a collection of Web pages created and maintained by a college, university, government agency, company, organization or individual.

URL

Each Web page has a unique address, called a Uniform Resource Locator (URL). You can display any Web page if you know its URL.

LINKS

Web pages contain links, which are highlighted text or images on a Web page that connect to other pages on the Web. You can select a link to display a Web page located on the same computer or on a computer across the city, country or world.

Links allow you to easily navigate through a vast amount of information by jumping from one Web page to another. Links are also known as hyperlinks.

WEB BROWSERS

A Web browser is a program that allows you to view and explore information on the Web.

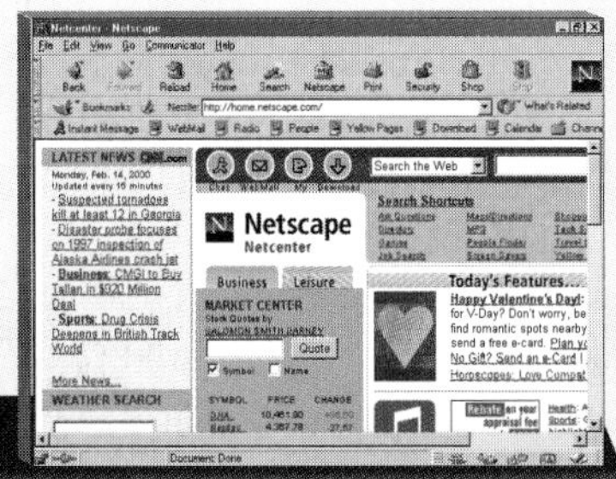

Microsoft Internet Explorer

Microsoft Internet Explorer is a popular Web browser that comes with the latest versions of Windows. You can also obtain Microsoft Internet Explorer at the www.microsoft.com/windows/ie Web site.

Netscape Navigator

Netscape Navigator is a popular Web browser that you can obtain at the www.netscape.com Web site or at computer stores.

HTML

HyperText Markup Language (HTML) is a computer language used to create Web pages. Web pages are HTML documents that consist of text and special instructions called tags. A Web browser interprets the tags in an HTML document and displays the document as a Web page. FrontPage hides the tags when you create a Web page.

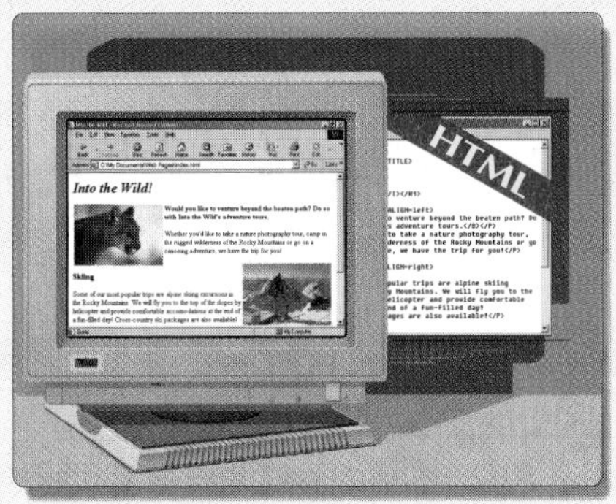

REASONS FOR CREATING WEB PAGES

PERSONAL

SHARE PERSONAL INFORMATION

Many people create Web pages to share information about their families, pets, vacations or favorite hobbies. Some people create Web pages to present a résumé to potential employers.

SHARE KNOWLEDGE

Many scientists and business professionals make their work available on the Web. If you are experienced in an area that many people want to learn more about, you can create Web pages to share your knowledge.

ENTERTAIN READERS

Many people create Web pages to display collections of jokes or humorous stories. You can also create Web pages to display information, pictures, sound clips and videos about a favorite celebrity, sports team or TV show.

PROMOTE INTERESTS

You can create Web pages to display information about an organization or club that you belong to. You can include a schedule of upcoming events and detailed information about the goals of the organization.

COMMERCIAL

PROVIDE INFORMATION

Companies often place pages on the Web to provide information about their business and the products and services they offer. Companies can use Web pages to keep the public informed about new products and interesting news. Many companies display their press releases on the Web.

SHOPPING

Many companies create Web pages that allow readers to order products and services over the Internet. Companies can display descriptions and pictures of products to help readers determine which products they want to purchase.

JOB LISTINGS

Many companies use Web pages to advertise jobs that are available within the company. Some companies allow readers to submit résumés on their Web sites.

CONTACT INFORMATION

Companies can display their office addresses, e-mail addresses and phone numbers on their Web pages. This helps readers contact the company to ask questions and express opinions.

WEB PAGE CONTENT CONSIDERATIONS

PROOFREAD INFORMATION

Carefully check your Web pages for spelling and grammar errors. Spelling mistakes can make readers think that the information on your Web pages is inaccurate. You may want to print your Web pages to help you proofread the pages.

PUT IMPORTANT INFORMATION FIRST

Always display the most important information at the top of each Web page. Some readers may not scroll through a Web page to read all the information. These readers will miss important information if you do not display the information at the top of the page.

PAGE LENGTH

Web pages should not be too short or too long. If a Web page is shorter than half a screen of information, try to combine the information with another page. If a Web page is longer than five screens, try to break up the page into several shorter pages.

PROVIDE A FAQ

A FAQ is a list of Frequently Asked Questions about a topic. A FAQ can help answer questions that people have about your Web pages and can help prevent people from sending you e-mail messages asking the same questions repeatedly.

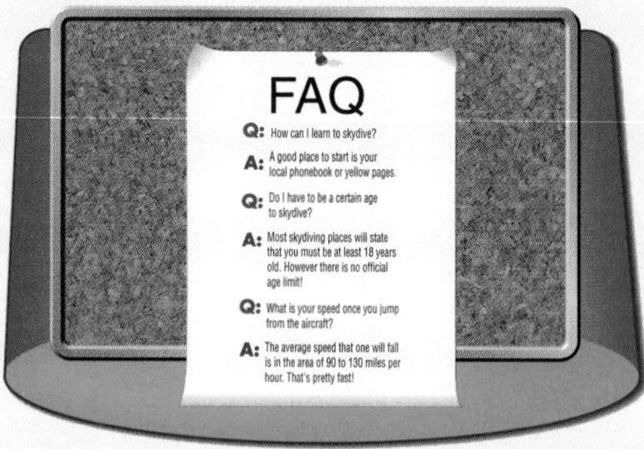

COPYRIGHT CONSIDERATIONS

If you plan to use information or images you did not create, make sure the information or images are not copyrighted. Many pages on the Web offer information and images that do not have copyright restrictions.

UPDATE INFORMATION

You should update your Web pages on a regular basis. If the information on your Web pages never changes, people may read the pages only once and may not revisit them in the future. You should include the date on your Web pages to let readers know when you last updated the pages.

TRANSFER SPEED

When creating your Web pages, try to keep the file size of the pages and images as small as possible. This will speed up the display of your Web pages by reducing the time it takes for the information to transfer.

INCLUDE CONTACT INFORMATION

Always include your name and e-mail address on Web pages you create. This allows readers to contact you if they have questions or comments.

PLAN A HOME PAGE

The home page is the main Web page in a Web site. The home page is the first page people will see when they visit a Web site.

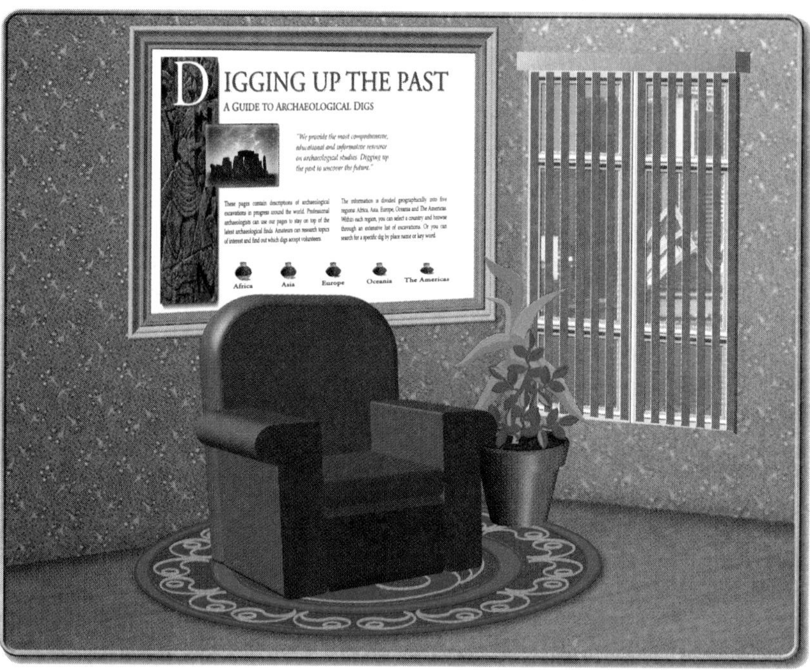

DIGGING UP THE PAST
A GUIDE TO ARCHAEOLOGICAL DIGS
Africa
Asia
Europe
Oceania
The Americas

When you create a Web site, FrontPage automatically names your home page index.htm.

SUMMARY

Always include a brief summary of your Web pages on your home page. You should state the purpose of your Web pages, such as whether you want to entertain or inform readers. You should not assume that readers will understand the purpose of your Web pages just by reading the title.

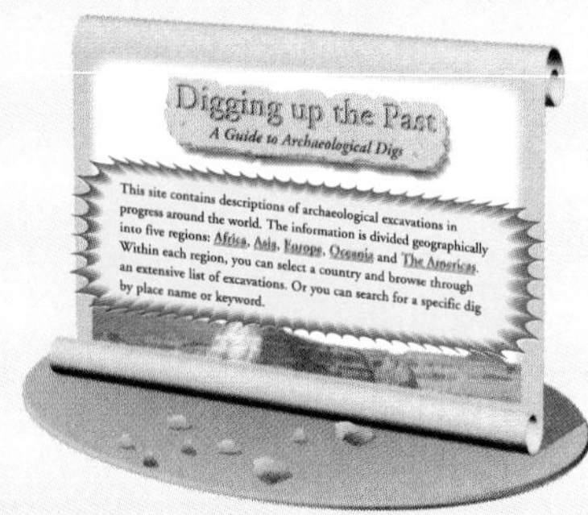

Digging up the Past
A Guide to Archaeological Digs
This site contains descriptions of archaeological excavations in progress around the world. The information is divided geographically into five regions: Africa, Asia, Europe, Oceania and The Americas. Within each region, you can select a country and browse through an extensive list of excavations. Or you can search for a specific dig by place name or keyword.

TABLE OF CONTENTS

Your home page can include a table of contents that lists the information contained in your Web site. You can include links that allow readers to quickly access information of interest.

Welcome to
The Classical Music Pages!
Table of Contents:
1. Introduction to Classical Music
2. Composer Biographies
3. Sound Files
4. CD Reviews

BOOKMARK REMINDER

Web browsers have a feature called bookmarks or favorites that allows people to store the addresses of Web pages they visit. You can include an image or phrase on your home page to remind readers to bookmark your Web page. This allows readers to quickly return to your Web site.

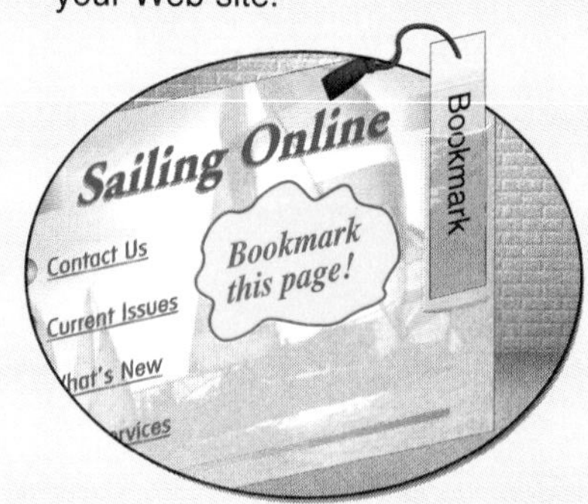

Sailing Online
Contact Us
Current Issues
Bookmark this page!
Bookmark

USING THE MOUSE

A mouse is a handheld device that lets you select and move items on your screen.

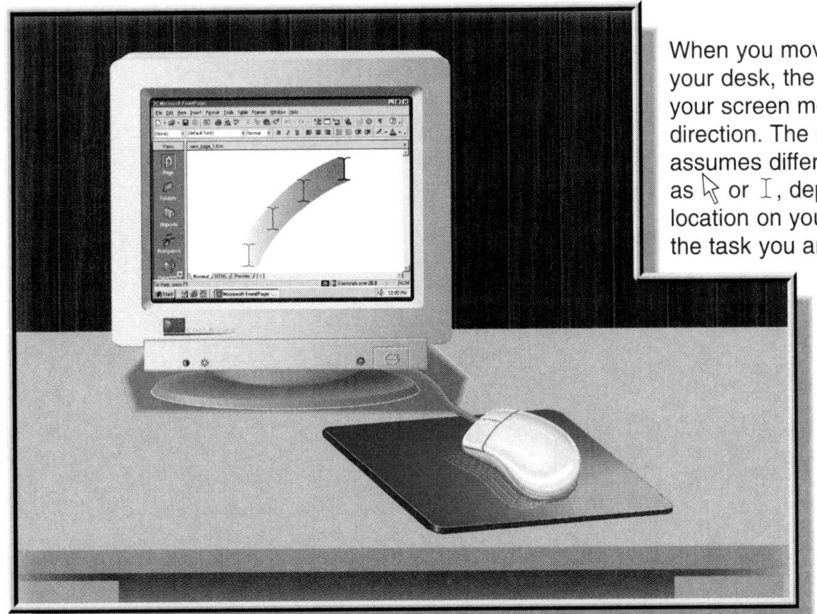

When you move the mouse on your desk, the mouse pointer on your screen moves in the same direction. The mouse pointer assumes different shapes, such as ⇖ or I, depending on its location on your screen and the task you are performing.

Resting your hand on the mouse, use your thumb and two rightmost fingers to move the mouse on your desk. Use your two remaining fingers to press the mouse buttons.

MOUSE ACTIONS

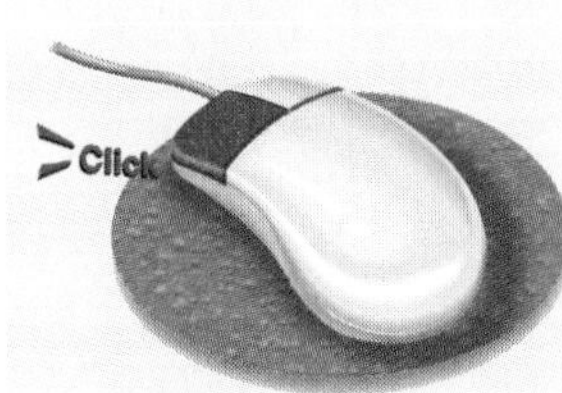

Click

Press and release the left mouse button.

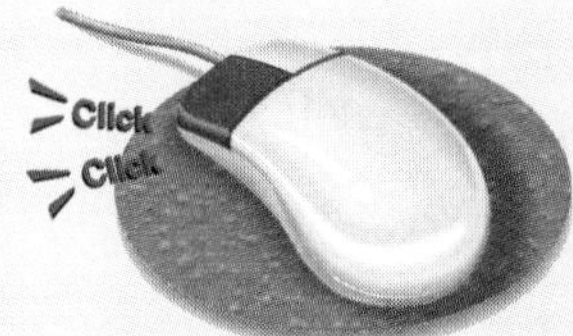

Double-click

Quickly press and release the left mouse button twice.

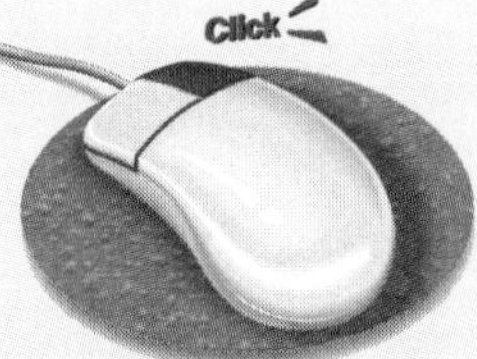

Right-click

Press and release the right mouse button.

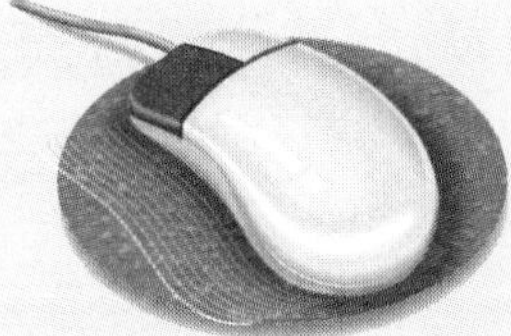

Drag

Position the mouse pointer (⇖) over an object on your screen and then press and hold down the left mouse button as you move the mouse to where you want to place the object. Then release the button.

START FRONTPAGE

You can start FrontPage to create Web pages that you can publish on the Web.

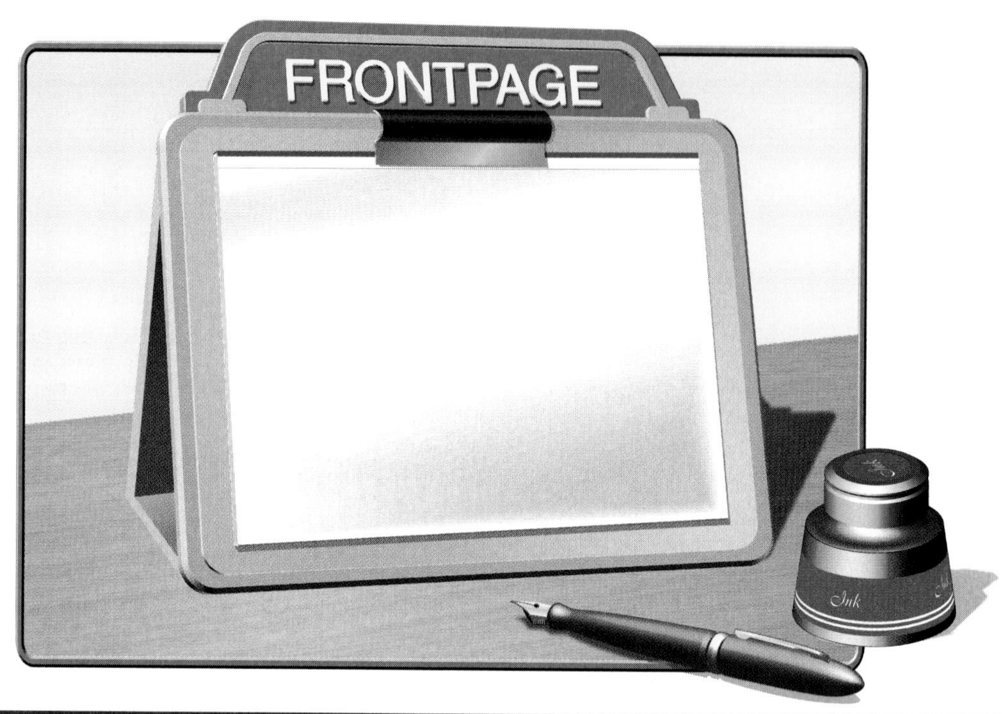

START FRONTPAGE

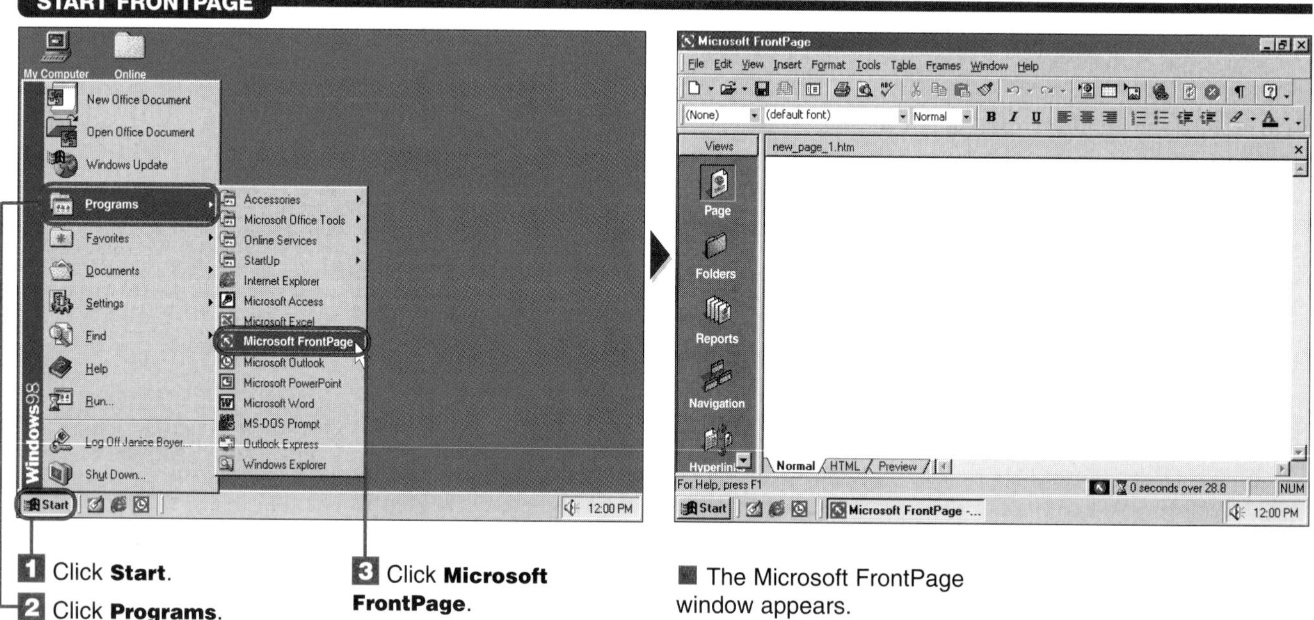

1 Click **Start**.

2 Click **Programs**.

3 Click **Microsoft FrontPage**.

■ The Microsoft FrontPage window appears.

THE FRONTPAGE WINDOW

The FrontPage window displays many items to help you use FrontPage.

WEB SITE NAME

Shows the location and name of the displayed Web site.

MENU BAR

Provides access to lists of commands available in FrontPage.

STANDARD TOOLBAR

Contains buttons to help you select common commands, such as Save and Print.

FORMATTING TOOLBAR

Contains buttons to help you select common formatting commands, such as Bold and Italic.

WEB PAGE NAME

Shows the name of the displayed Web page.

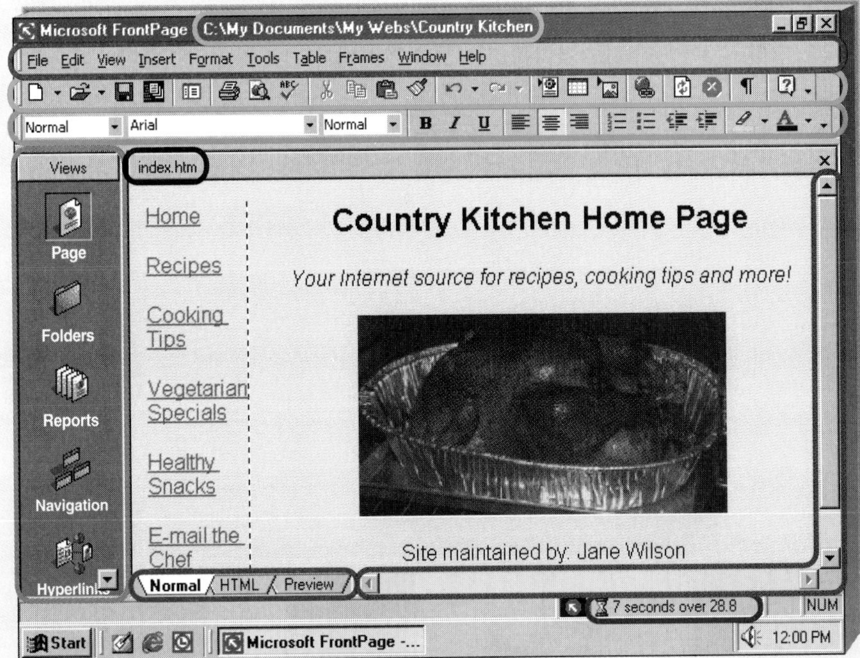

VIEWS BAR

Provides access to six different views of your Web site that you can use to create and organize your Web pages.

PAGE VIEW TABS

Provides access to three different views of your Web page.

SCROLL BARS

Allow you to browse through a Web page.

ESTIMATED DOWNLOAD TIME

Indicates how many seconds the displayed Web page will take to transfer to a reader's computer when using a 28.8 Kb/s modem.

If you do not know how to perform a task in FrontPage, you can search for help information on the task.

GETTING HELP

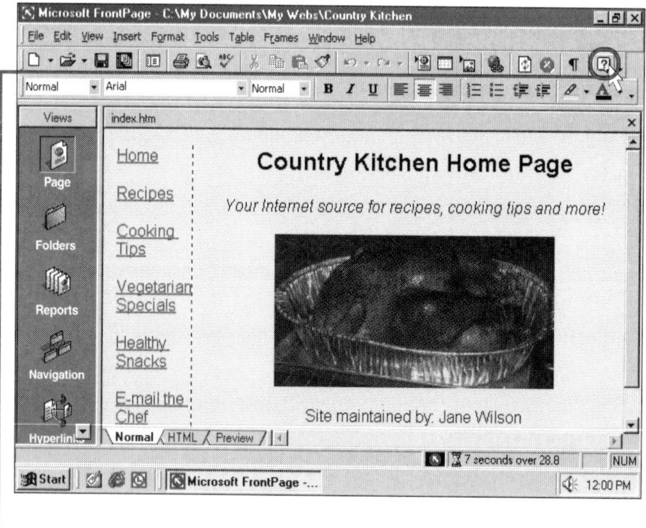

1 Click [?] to get help information on a specific task.

■ The Microsoft FrontPage Help window appears.

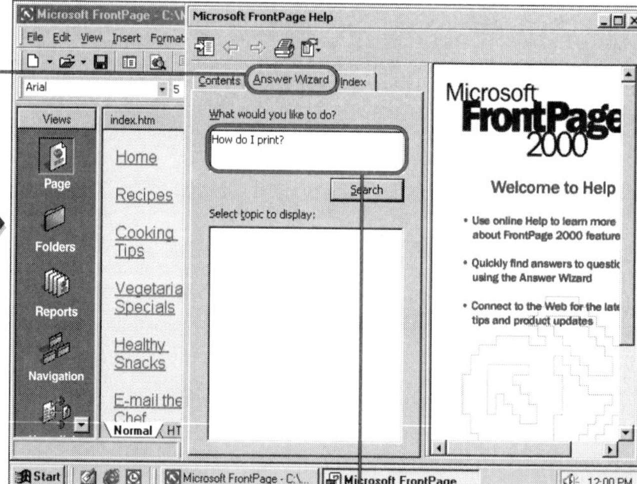

2 Click the **Answer Wizard** tab.

3 To select the text in this area, drag the mouse I over the text until you highlight all the text.

4 Type your question and then press the Enter key.

Why do some words in the Microsoft FrontPage Help window appear blue and underlined?

Words or phrases that appear blue and underlined are links that will display help topics related to the help information you are currently viewing. To display a related help topic, click the highlighted word or phrase.

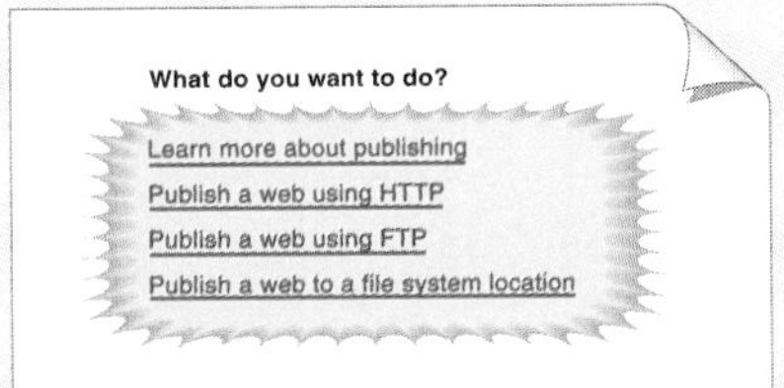

How can I determine the function of a toolbar button?

When you position the mouse over a button on a toolbar, the name of the button appears in a yellow box. This information can help you determine what task the button allows you to perform.

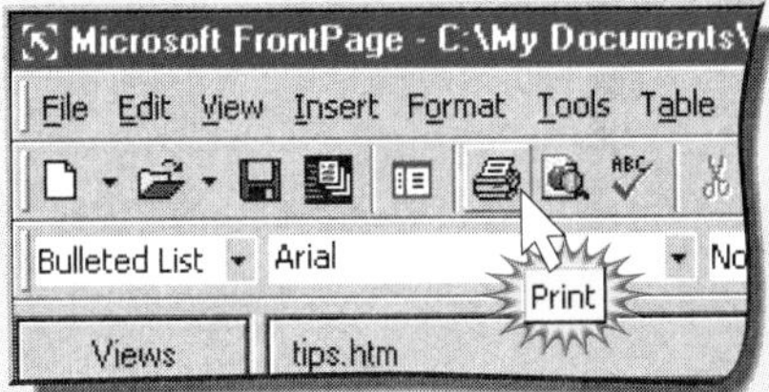

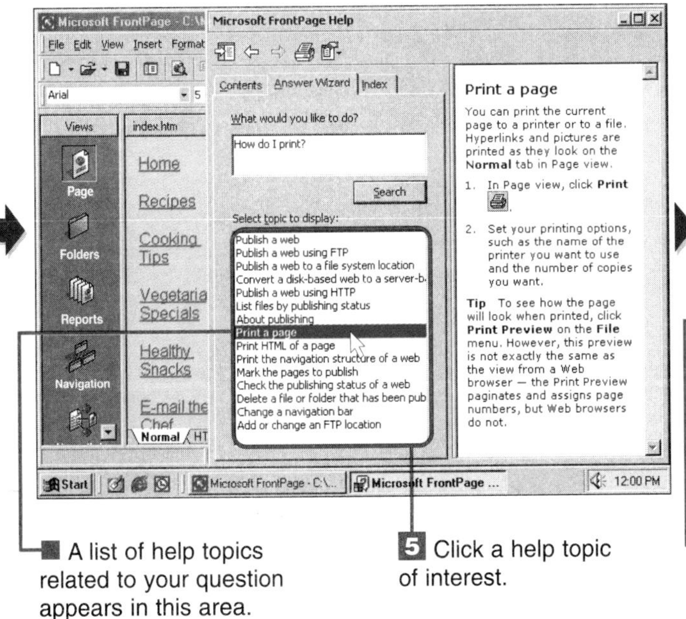

■ A list of help topics related to your question appears in this area.

5 Click a help topic of interest.

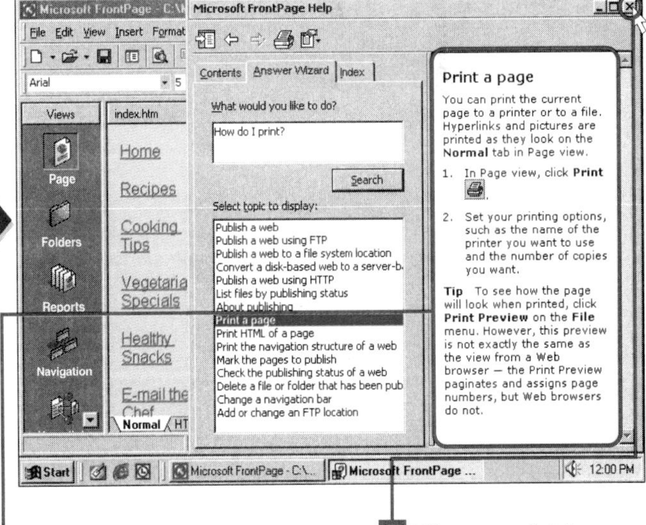

■ Information about the help topic you selected appears in this area.

6 When you finish reviewing the help information, click ☒ to close the Microsoft FrontPage Help window.

Wonderful World
of Sailing

Sailing for Beginners
Purchasing a Sailboat
Online Sailing Clubs
Sailboat Maintenance and Repair
Sailing Competitions
Sailing Stories
E-mail
Places to Sail

Welcome to my sailing Web site on the World Wide Web. I have been a sailing enthusiast for many years, and this Web site is designed so I can share my knowledge of sailing with others!
Whether you have been sailing for many years, or are interested in taking up this wonderful hobby, you will find all the information you need on my Web site!
If you have any questions or suggestions for the Web site, please e-mail me.
This Web site will help you learn how to sail safely, and maintain and repair your sailboat so you don't get stranded.
You will also be able to share your sailing experiences with others and learn about some of the best sailing destinations in the world!
Be sure to read about my personal sailing adventures, which will be sure to excite even the most experienced sailors.

CHAPTER 2

Are you ready to begin creating your Web pages? This chapter will provide you with the basics you need to get started.

CREATE A NEW WEB SITE

You can use a template or wizard to create a new Web site. Templates and wizards provide the layout and design for your Web site.

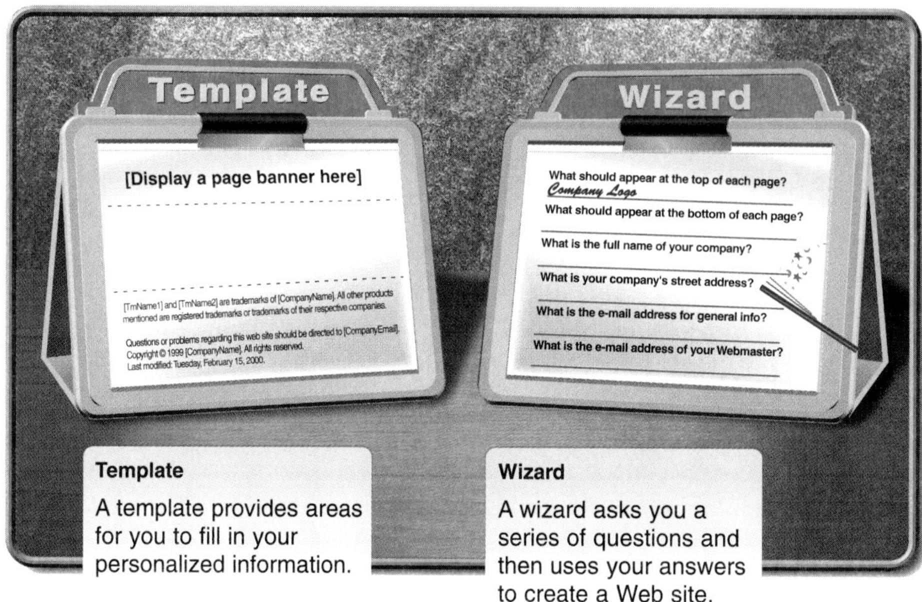

Template

A template provides areas for you to fill in your personalized information.

Wizard

A wizard asks you a series of questions and then uses your answers to create a Web site.

A Web site is a collection of Web pages.

CREATE A NEW WEB SITE

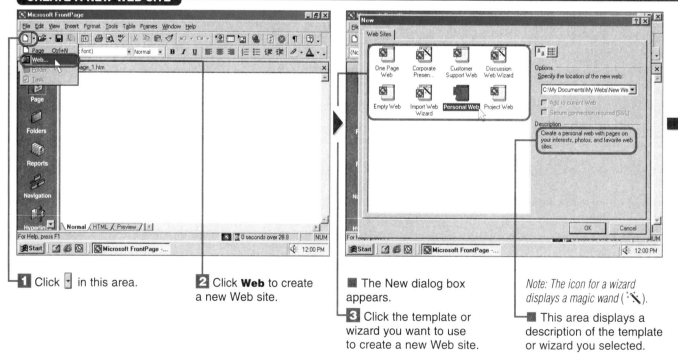

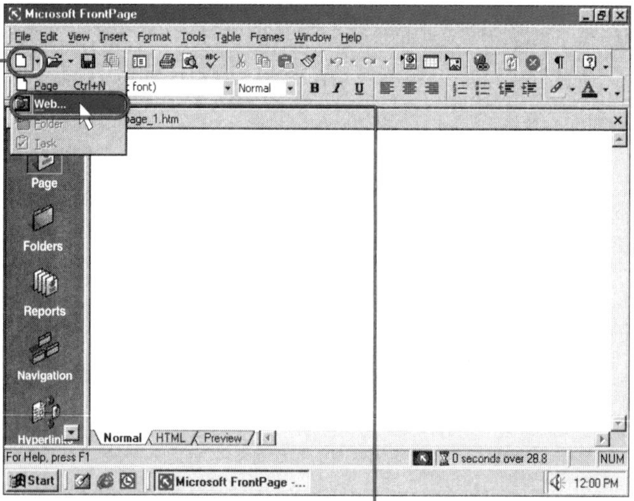

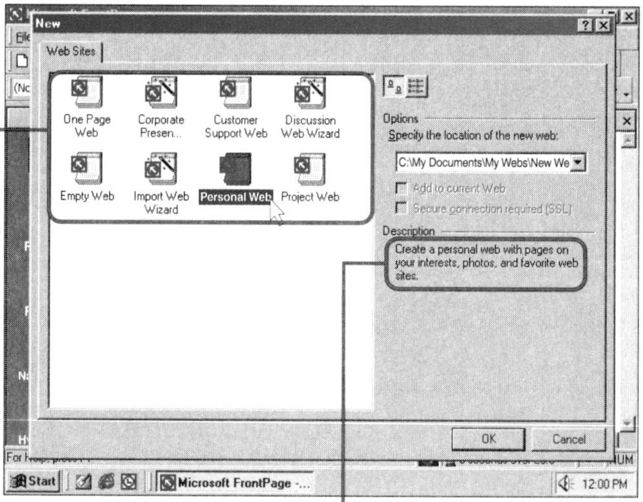

1 Click ▾ in this area.

2 Click **Web** to create a new Web site.

■ The New dialog box appears.

3 Click the template or wizard you want to use to create a new Web site.

Note: The icon for a wizard displays a magic wand ( ).

■ This area displays a description of the template or wizard you selected.

How can I create a blank Web site?

You can use one of the following templates to create a blank Web site. A blank Web site gives you the most flexibility and control.

The **One Page Web** template creates a Web site containing one blank Web page.

The **Empty Web** template creates an empty Web site that contains no Web pages. You can add the Web pages you need.

Where will FrontPage store my Web sites?

When you installed FrontPage on your computer, a folder called "My Webs" was automatically created in the My Documents folder. FrontPage stores your Web sites in this folder.

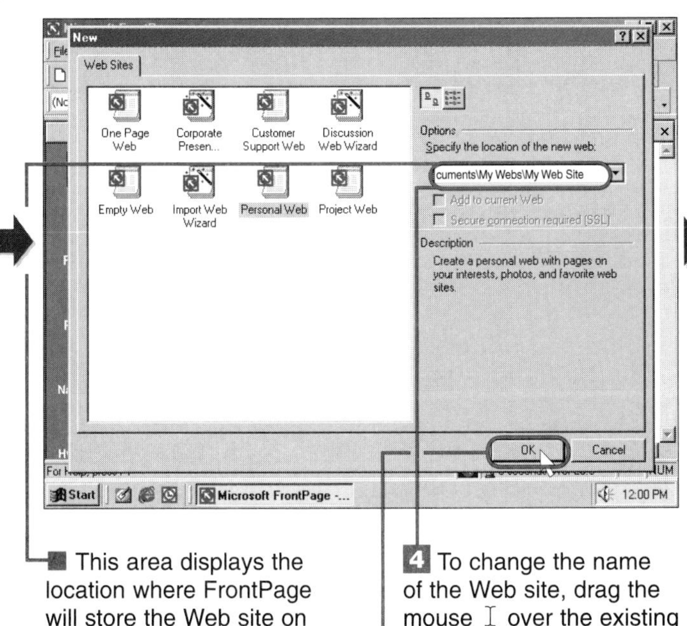

■ This area displays the location where FrontPage will store the Web site on your computer and the name of the Web site.

4 To change the name of the Web site, drag the mouse I over the existing name and then type a new name.

5 Click **OK** to create the Web site.

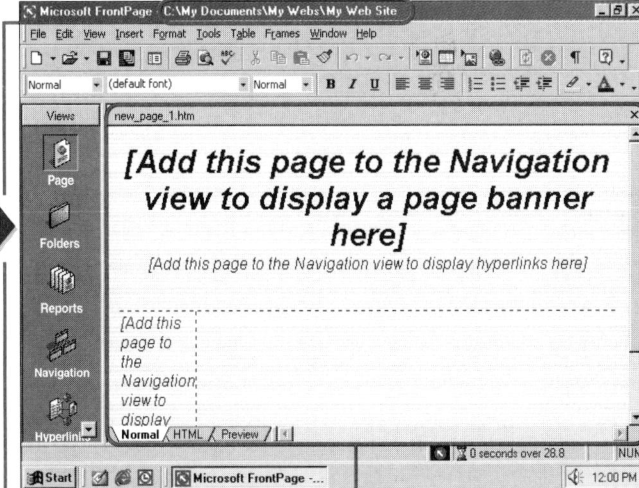

■ FrontPage creates the Web site.

*Note: If you selected a wizard in step **3**, FrontPage will ask you a series of questions before creating the Web site.*

■ This area displays the location and name of the Web site.

■ This area displays a page in the Web site. You can add your personalized information to the appropriate areas to complete each Web page.

HIDE OR DISPLAY THE FOLDER LIST

You can hide or display a list of all the folders and Web pages in your Web site.

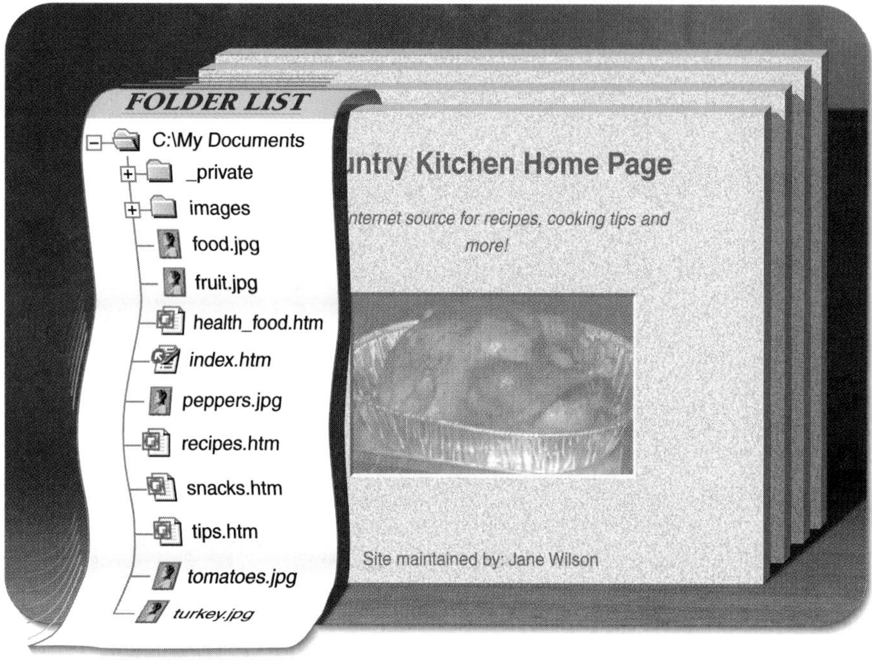

Hiding the Folder List will give you a larger and less cluttered working area.

HIDE OR DISPLAY THE FOLDER LIST

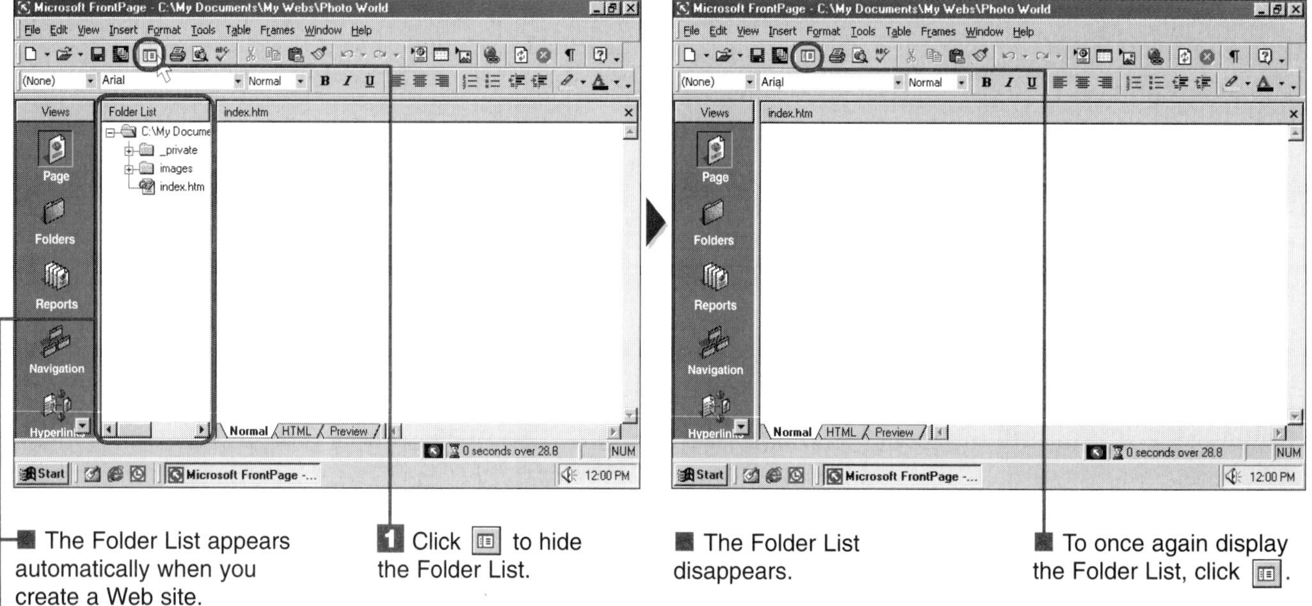

■ The Folder List appears automatically when you create a Web site.

■ The Folder List displays all the folders ( ) and Web pages ( ) in your Web site.

1 Click to hide the Folder List.

■ The Folder List disappears.

■ To once again display the Folder List, click .

ENTER TEXT

FrontPage allows you to type text into your Web page quickly and easily.

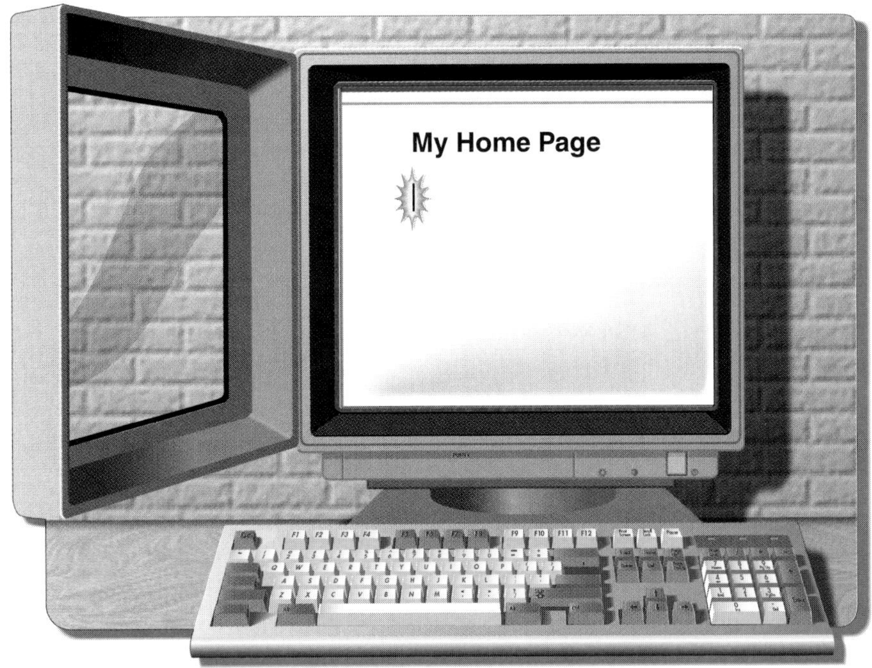

ENTER TEXT

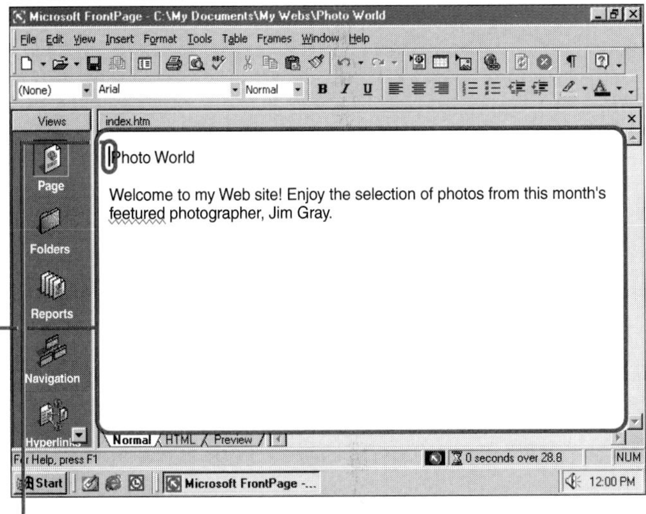

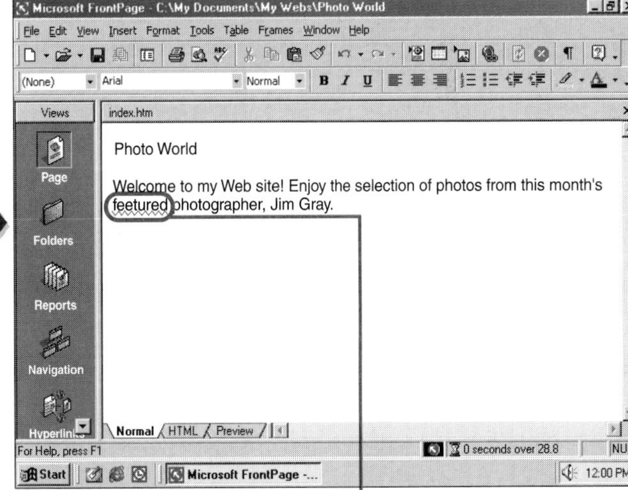

■ The text you type will appear where the insertion point flashes on your screen.

1 Type the text you want to display on your Web page.

Note: In this book, the font of text was changed to Arial to make the Web page examples easier to read. To change the font of text, see page 74.

■ When the text you type reaches the end of a line, FrontPage automatically wraps the text to the next line. You need to press the Enter key only when you want to start a new paragraph.

■ FrontPage automatically underlines misspelled words in red. The underlines will not appear when you publish your Web page. To correct misspelled words, see page 64.

START A NEW LINE OF TEXT

When typing the text on your Web page, you can specify where you want a new line of text to begin.

Starting a new line of text is useful for separating short lines of text, such as text in a mailing address or poem.

START A NEW LINE OF TEXT

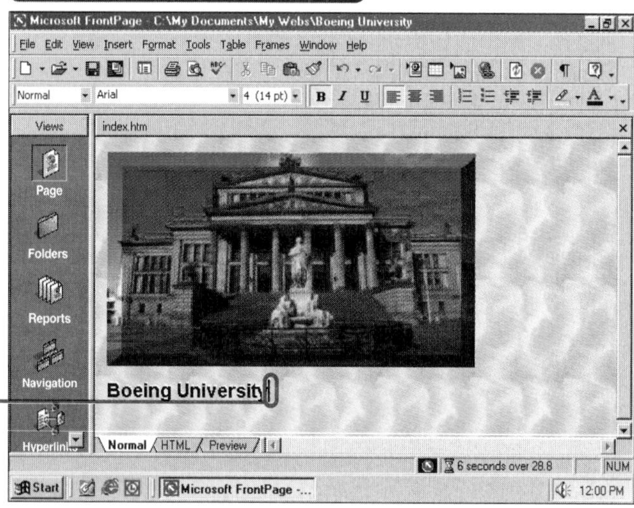

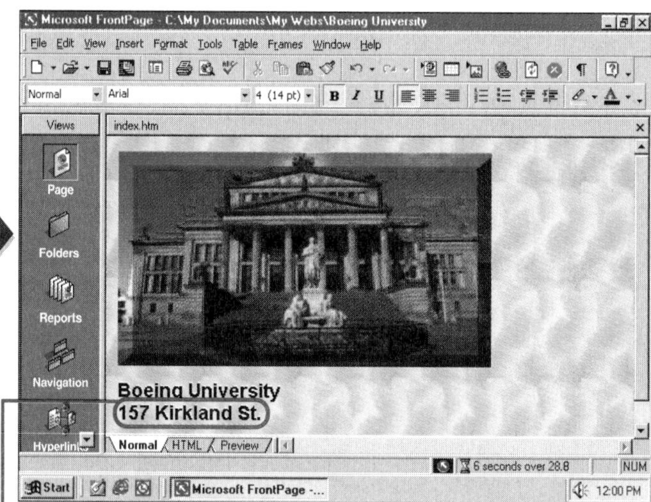

1 Click the location where you want to start a new line of text without creating a new paragraph.

2 Press and hold down the Shift key as you press the Enter key.

■ The flashing insertion point appears on the next line. You can now type the text you want to appear on the new line.

Note: When you start a new line of text, no space appears between the lines. When you use only the Enter key, a blank line appears between the lines of text.

CREATE A BLANK WEB PAGE

You can add a blank Web page to discuss a new topic in your Web site.

CREATE A BLANK WEB PAGE

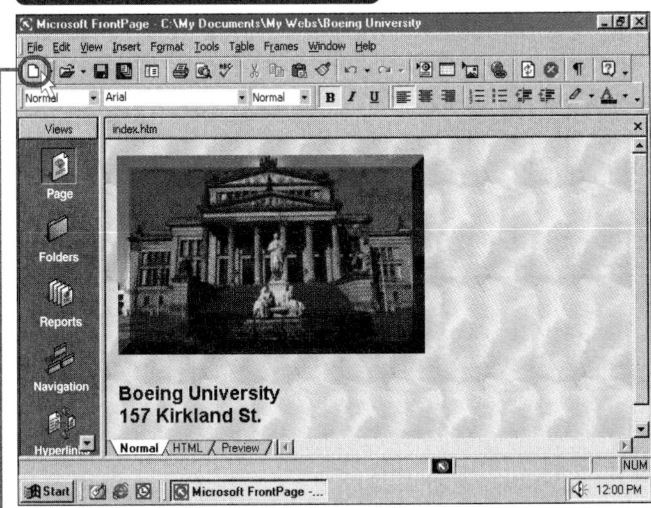

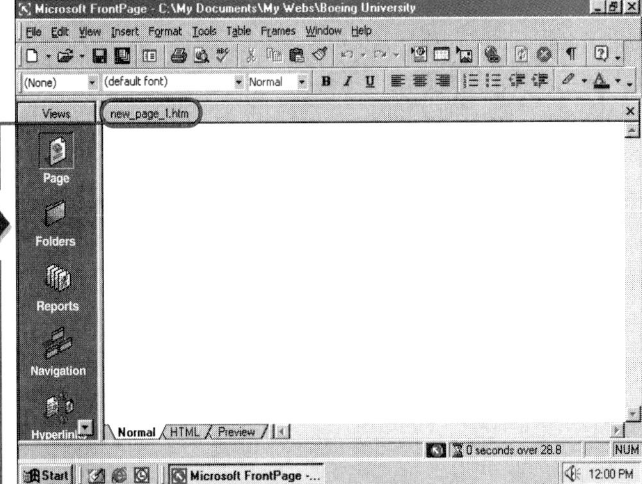

1 Click [new page icon] to create a blank Web page.

- A blank Web page appears.
- This area displays a temporary name for the Web page. To save and name the Web page, see page 28.

- You can immediately add information to the Web page.

CREATE A WEB PAGE USING A TEMPLATE

You can use a template to save time when creating a new Web page. A template provides you with the layout and design for a Web page.

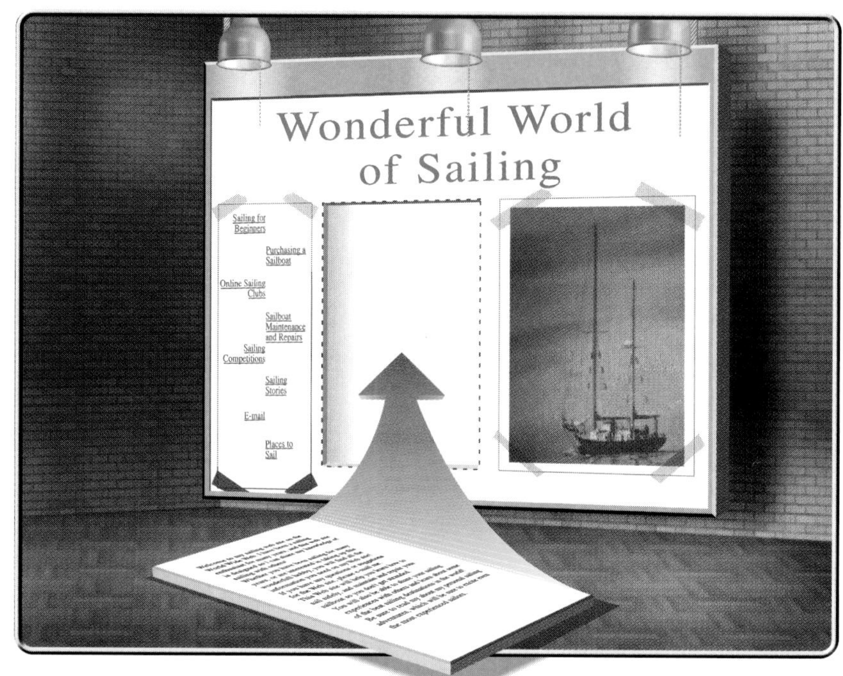

CREATE A WEB PAGE USING A TEMPLATE

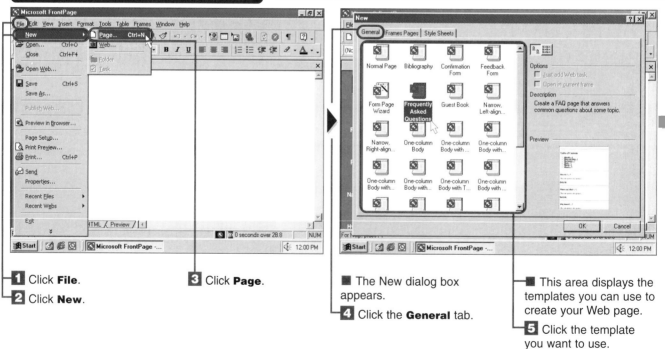

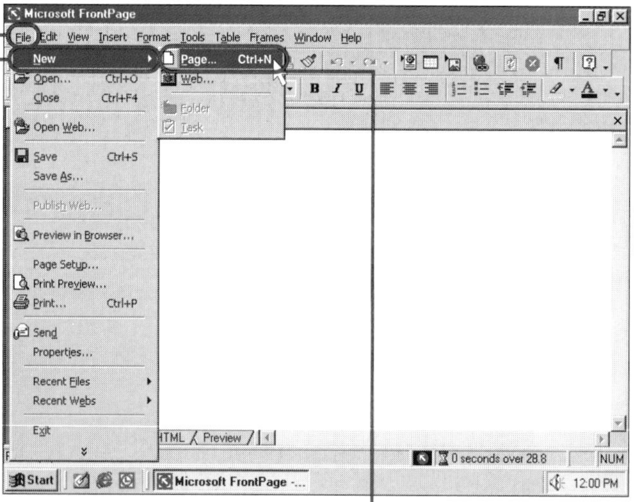

1 Click **File**.

2 Click **New**.

3 Click **Page**.

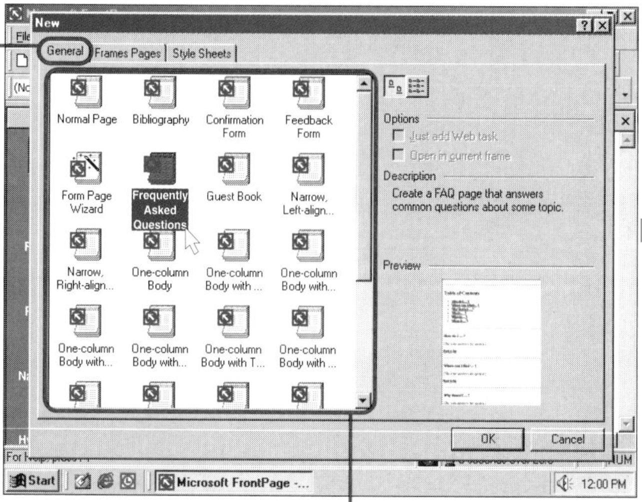

■ The New dialog box appears.

4 Click the **General** tab.

■ This area displays the templates you can use to create your Web page.

5 Click the template you want to use.

?

Why would I use a template to create a new Web page?

If you are new to creating Web pages, templates can provide a good starting point for the layout and design of your Web pages. Templates also provide sample text that can help you determine what text you should include on your Web pages. You can replace the sample text with your own personalized information. FrontPage offers a variety of templates, such as a bibliography, feedback form, guest book and table of contents.

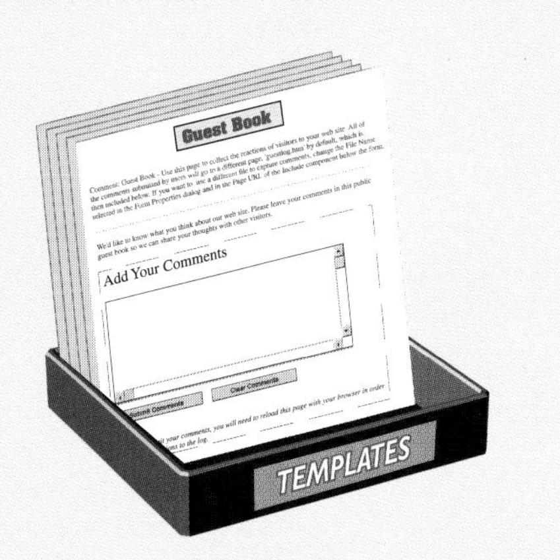

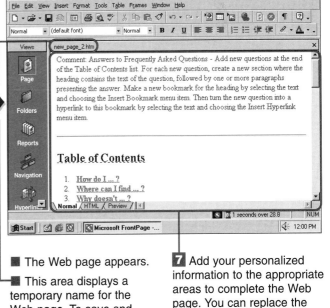

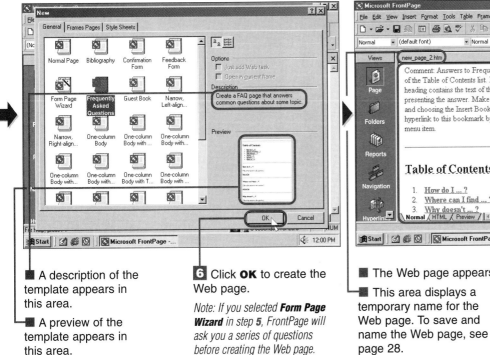

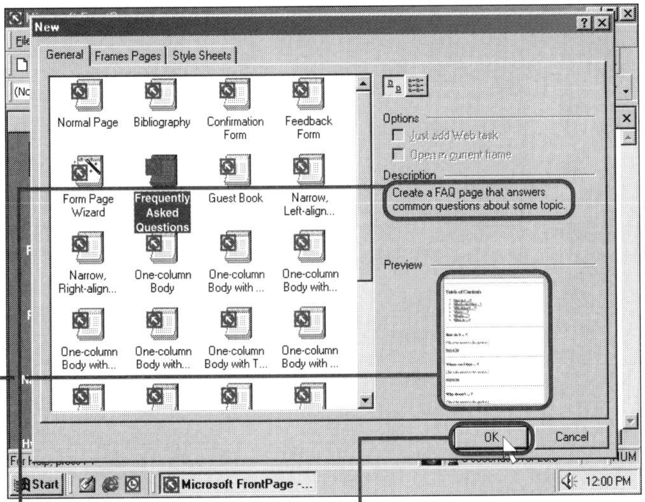

■ A description of the template appears in this area.

■ A preview of the template appears in this area.

6 Click **OK** to create the Web page.

*Note: If you selected **Form Page Wizard** in step **5**, FrontPage will ask you a series of questions before creating the Web page.*

■ The Web page appears.

■ This area displays a temporary name for the Web page. To save and name the Web page, see page 28.

7 Add your personalized information to the appropriate areas to complete the Web page. You can replace the existing text and images with your own information.

SAVE A WEB PAGE

You should save your Web page to store the page for future use. This lets you later review and edit the Web page.

If your Web page contains images, FrontPage will ask you to save the images when you save the Web page.

You should regularly save changes you make to a Web page to avoid losing your work.

SAVE A WEB PAGE

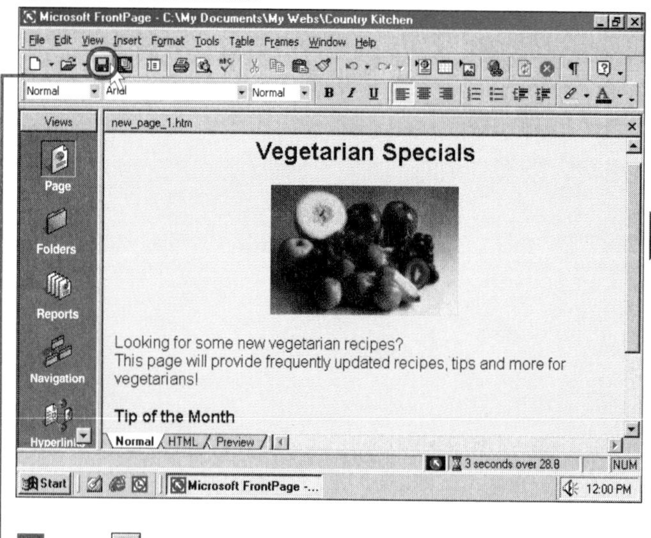

1 Click [save icon] to save your Web page.

■ The Save As dialog box appears.

Note: If you previously saved the Web page, the Save As dialog box will not appear since you have already named the page.

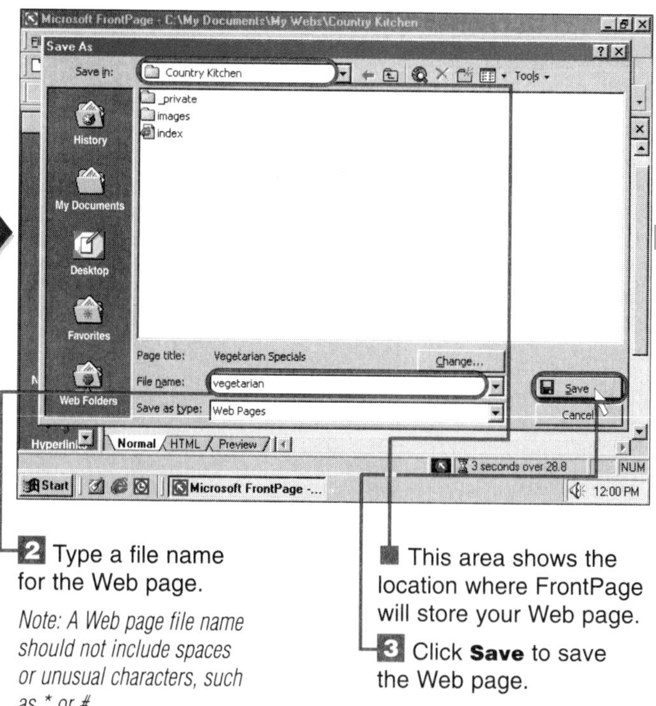

2 Type a file name for the Web page.

*Note: A Web page file name should not include spaces or unusual characters, such as * or #.*

■ This area shows the location where FrontPage will store your Web page.

3 Click **Save** to save the Web page.

Where will FrontPage store a Web page on my computer?

When you installed FrontPage on your computer, a folder called "My Webs" was automatically created in the My Documents folder. The My Webs folder contains a separate folder for each Web site you create. FrontPage will store a new Web page in the folder for the current Web site.

When I save a Web page, why do I need to save the images displayed on the page?

When you add an image to a Web page, you must save the image as part of your Web site. A copy of the image will be stored in the same folder that stores all the Web pages for your Web site. This ensures the image will transfer with your Web site when you publish your Web pages.

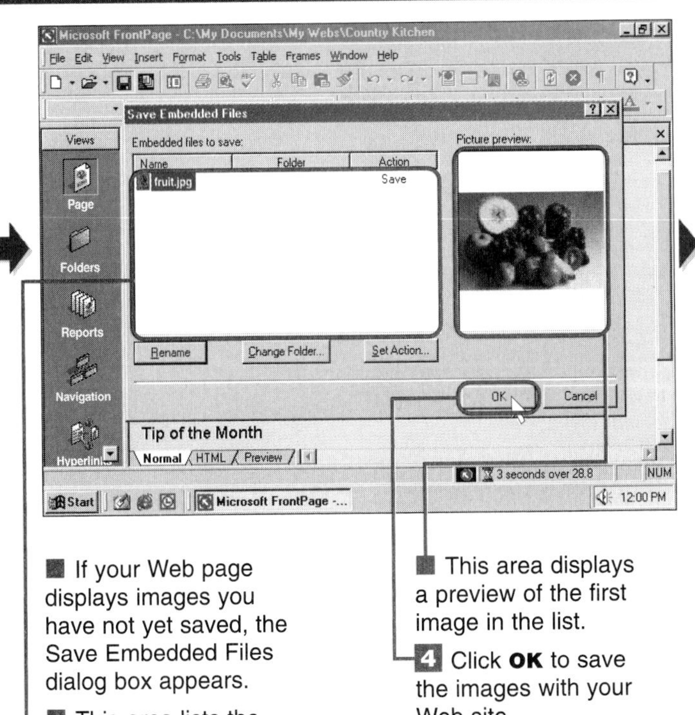

■ If your Web page displays images you have not yet saved, the Save Embedded Files dialog box appears.

■ This area lists the images displayed on the Web page.

■ This area displays a preview of the first image in the list.

4 Click **OK** to save the images with your Web site.

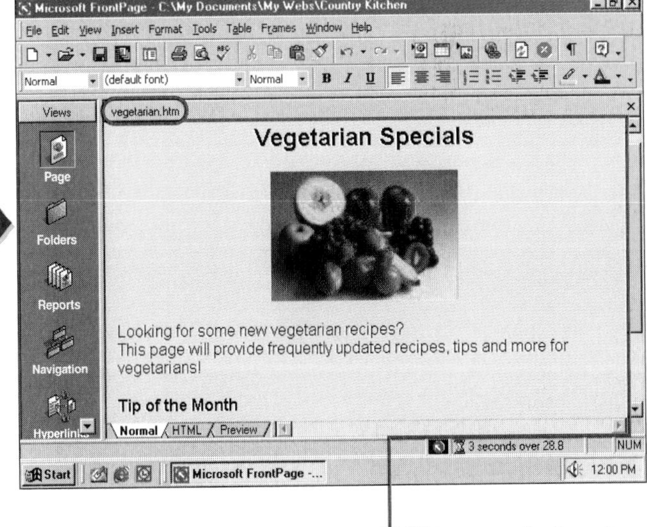

■ FrontPage saves your Web page and the images displayed on the page.

■ This area displays the name of the Web page.

DISPLAY OR HIDE A TOOLBAR

FrontPage offers several toolbars that you can display or hide at any time. Each toolbar contains buttons that help you quickly perform common tasks.

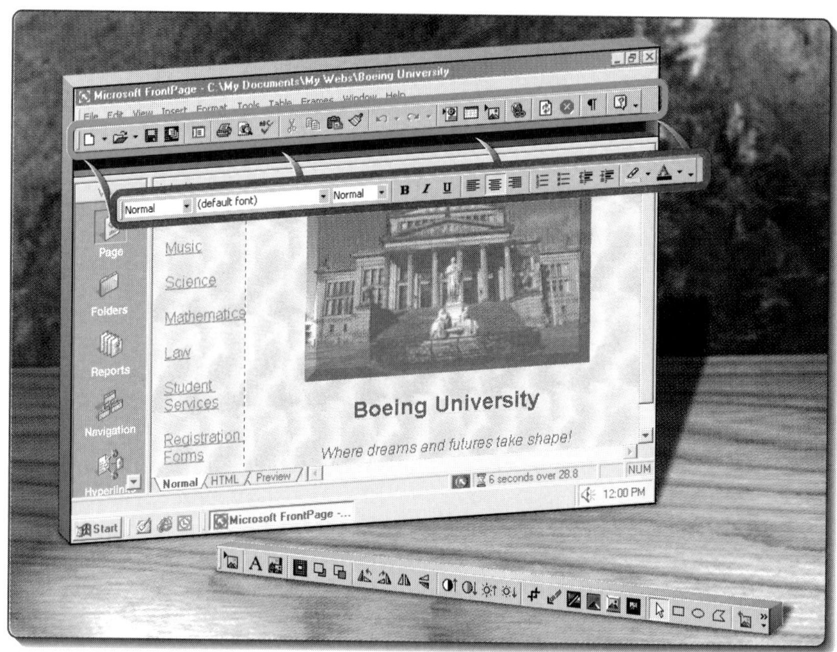

When you first start FrontPage, the Standard and Formatting toolbars appear on your screen.

Standard

Formatting

DISPLAY OR HIDE A TOOLBAR

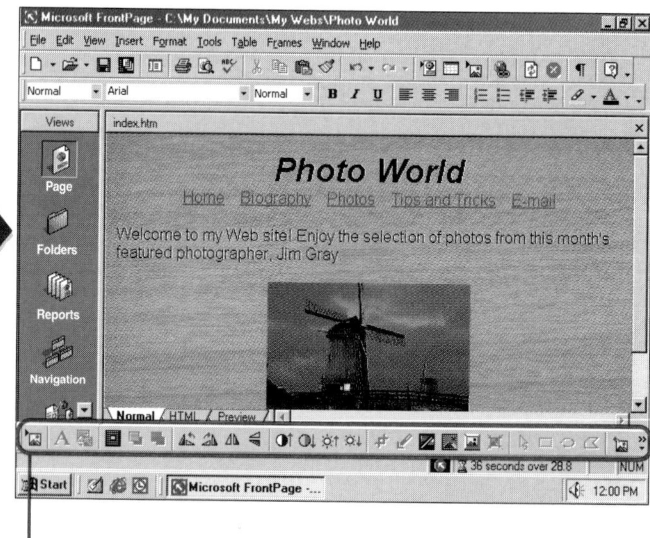

1 Click **View**.

2 Click **Toolbars**.

■ A list of toolbars appears. A check mark (✔) beside a toolbar name tells you the toolbar is currently displayed.

3 Click the name of the toolbar you want to display or hide.

■ FrontPage displays or hides the toolbar you selected.

Note: A screen displaying fewer toolbars provides a larger and less cluttered working area.

EXIT FRONTPAGE

When you finish using FrontPage, you can exit the program.

You should always exit FrontPage and all other programs before turning off your computer.

EXIT FRONTPAGE

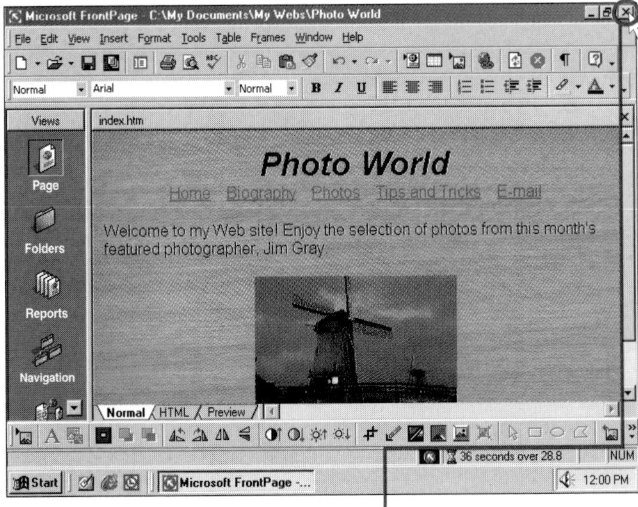

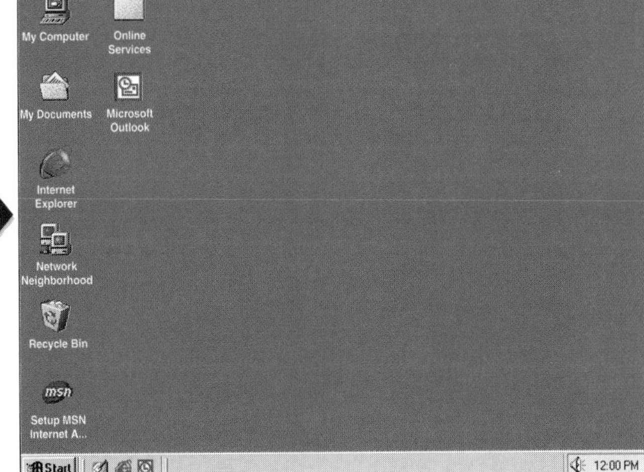

■ Before exiting FrontPage, you should save all the Web pages in your Web site. To save a Web page, see page 28.

1 Click ☒ to exit FrontPage.

■ The Microsoft FrontPage window disappears from your screen.

■ If you have more than one Web site open, you need to repeat step 1 for each Web site.

OPEN A WEB SITE

You can open a Web site you previously saved. This allows you to review and make changes to the Web site.

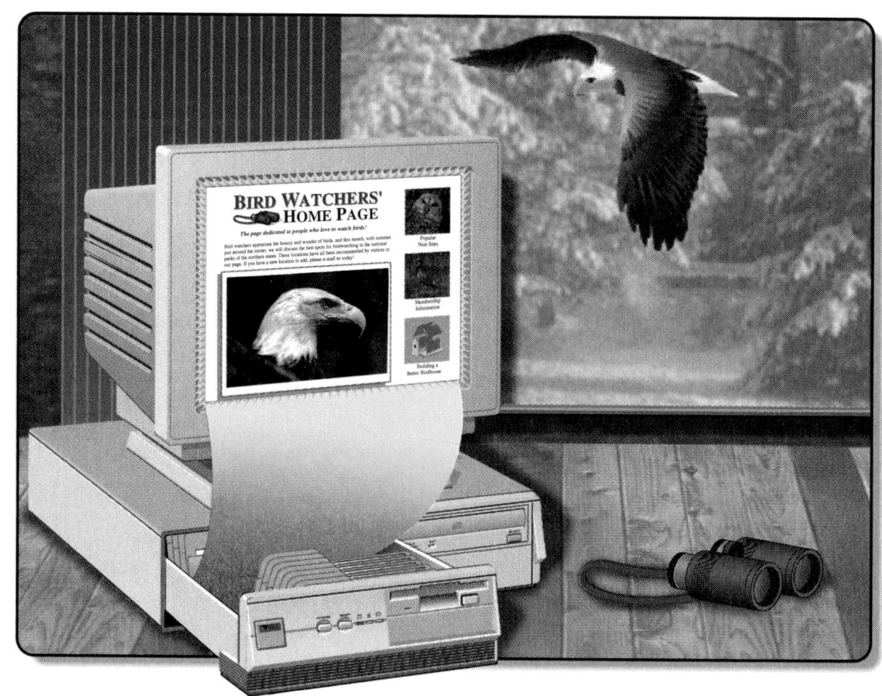

OPEN A WEB SITE

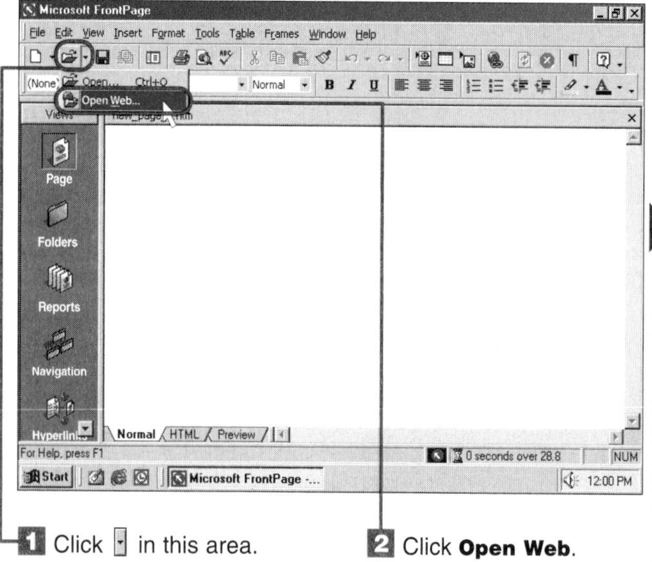

1 Click ▾ in this area.

2 Click **Open Web**.

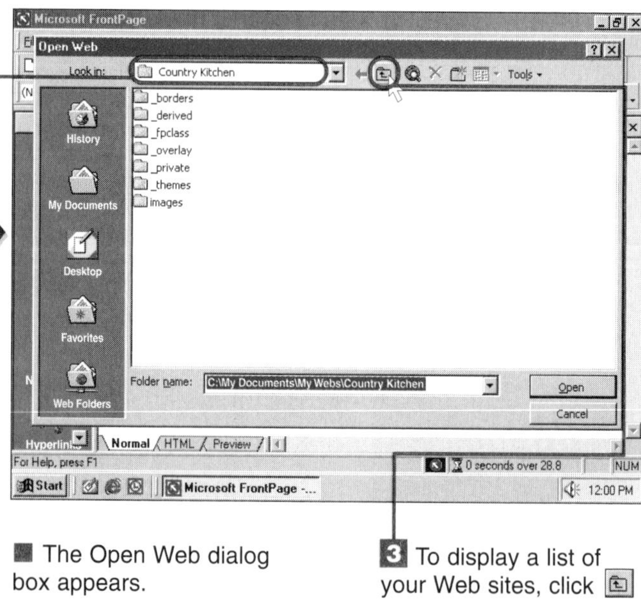

■ The Open Web dialog box appears.

■ This area shows the location of the displayed folders.

3 To display a list of your Web sites, click ▣ to display the contents of the My Webs folder.

Note: FrontPage automatically stores your Web sites in the My Webs folder.

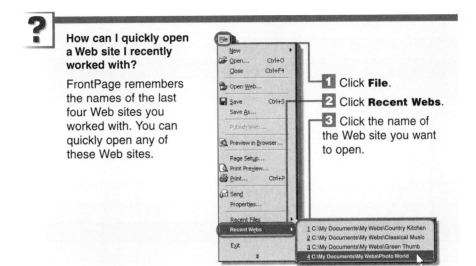

How can I quickly open a Web site I recently worked with?

FrontPage remembers the names of the last four Web sites you worked with. You can quickly open any of these Web sites.

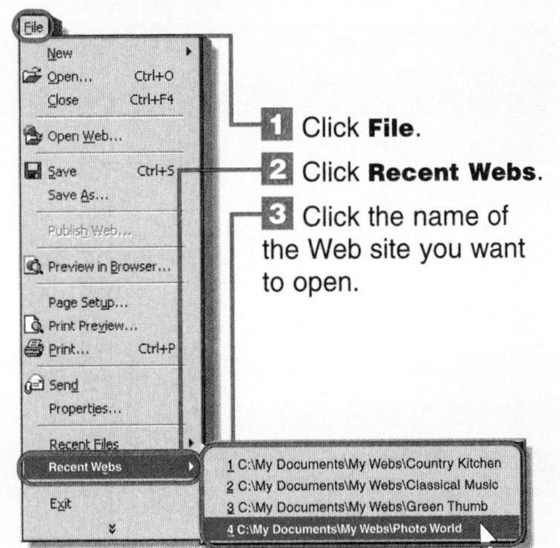

1 Click **File**.

2 Click **Recent Webs**.

3 Click the name of the Web site you want to open.

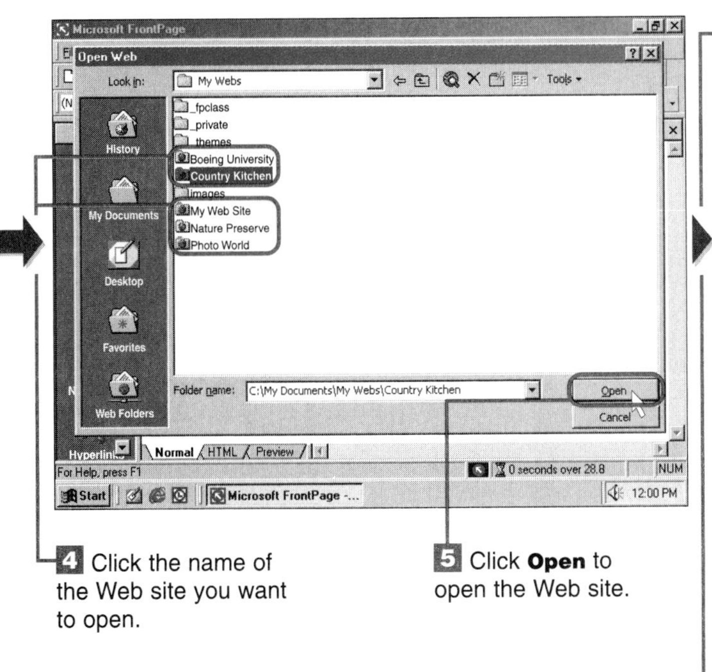

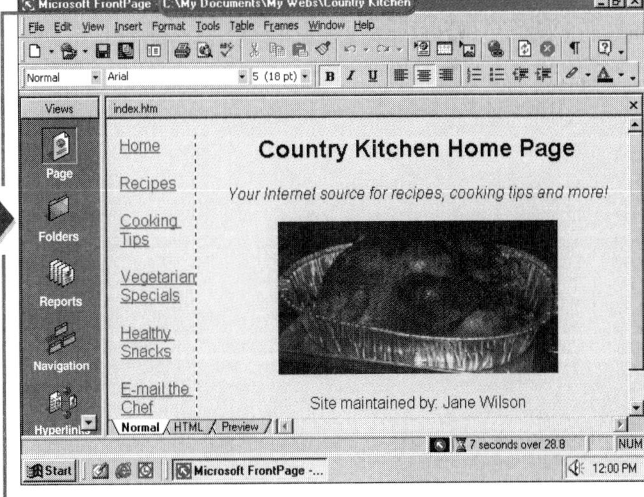

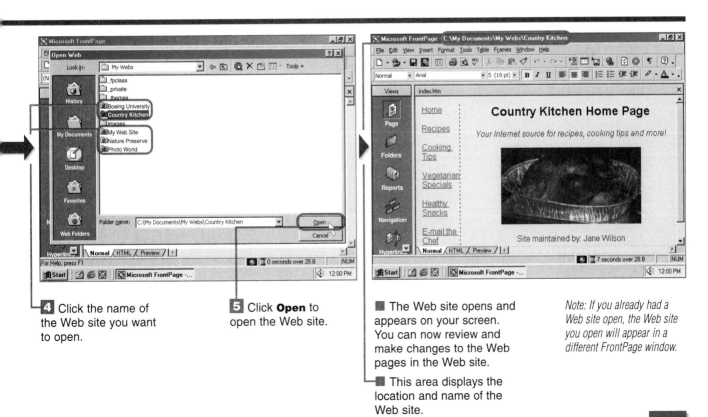

4 Click the name of the Web site you want to open.

5 Click **Open** to open the Web site.

■ The Web site opens and appears on your screen. You can now review and make changes to the Web pages in the Web site.

■ This area displays the location and name of the Web site.

Note: If you already had a Web site open, the Web site you open will appear in a different FrontPage window.

Nature Paradises
Cats' Corner
The Nature Preserve
Join us for a journey through the World Wild Web!
Home
Cats' Corner
Birds' Nest
Nature Paradises
Nature Preserve
The Nature Preserve
Join us for a journey through the World Wild Web!
Home
Cats' Corner
Birds' Nest
Nature Paradises
Page 1

CHAPTER 3

Work With Web Pages

Would you like to work effectively with your Web pages? This chapter shows you how to print, rename, delete Web pages and more.

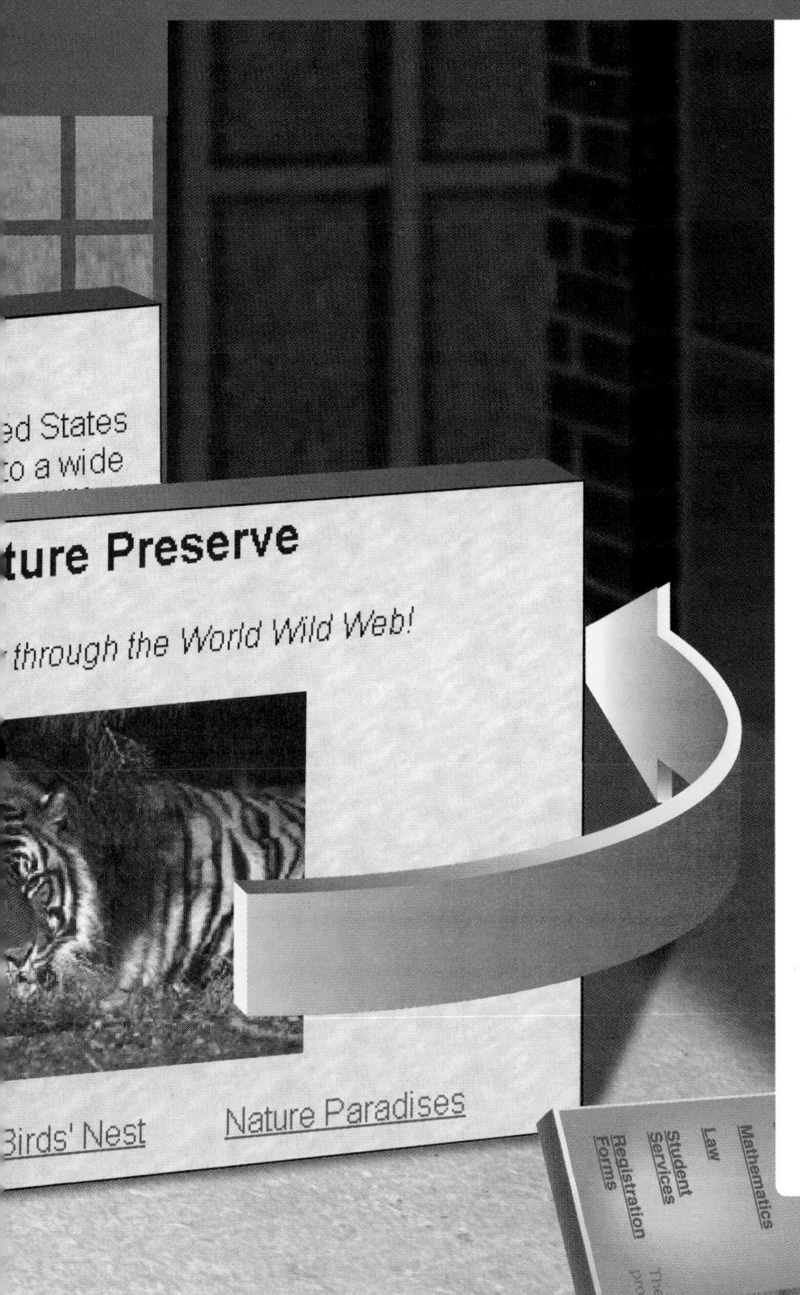

SCROLL THROUGH A WEB PAGE

You can use the scroll bar to browse through the information on your Web page.

SCROLL THROUGH A WEB PAGE

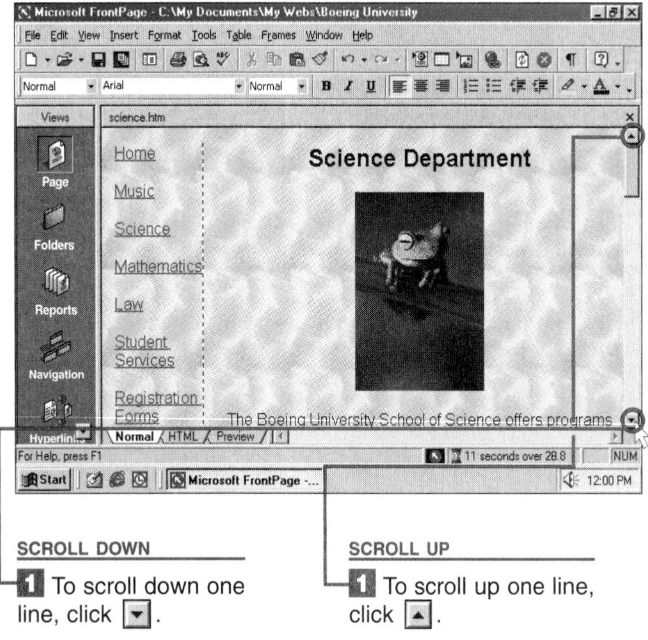

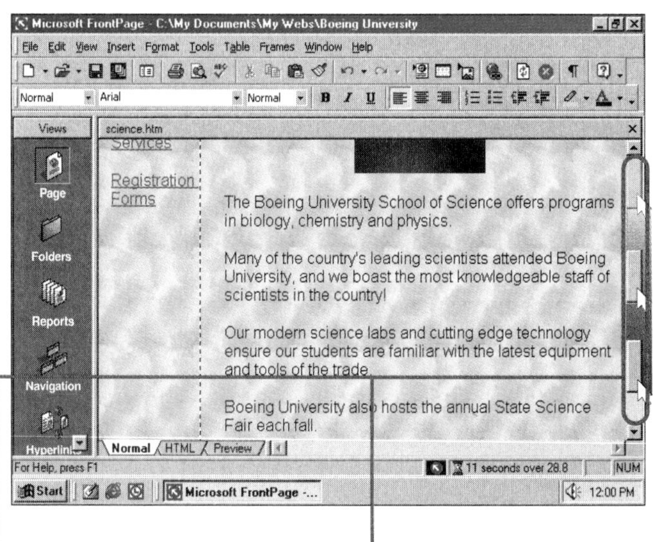

SCROLL DOWN

1 To scroll down one line, click ▼.

SCROLL UP

1 To scroll up one line, click ▲.

SCROLL TO ANY POSITION

1 Drag the scroll box along the scroll bar until the information you want to view appears.

■ The location of the scroll box indicates which part of the Web page you are viewing. To view the middle of the Web page, drag the scroll box halfway down the scroll bar.

PRINT A WEB PAGE

You can produce a paper copy of the Web page displayed on your screen. This is useful for reviewing and editing the Web page.

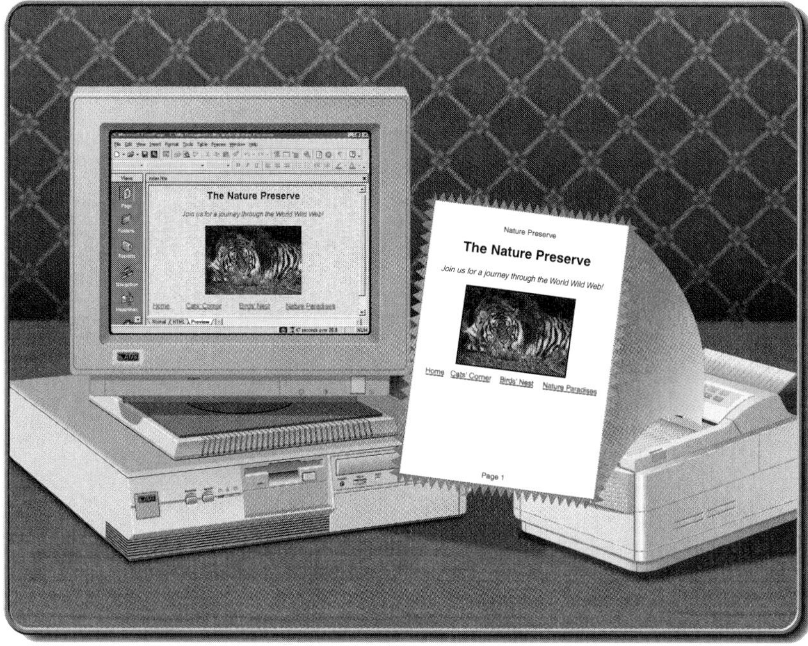

Before printing your Web page, make sure your printer is turned on and contains paper.

PRINT A WEB PAGE

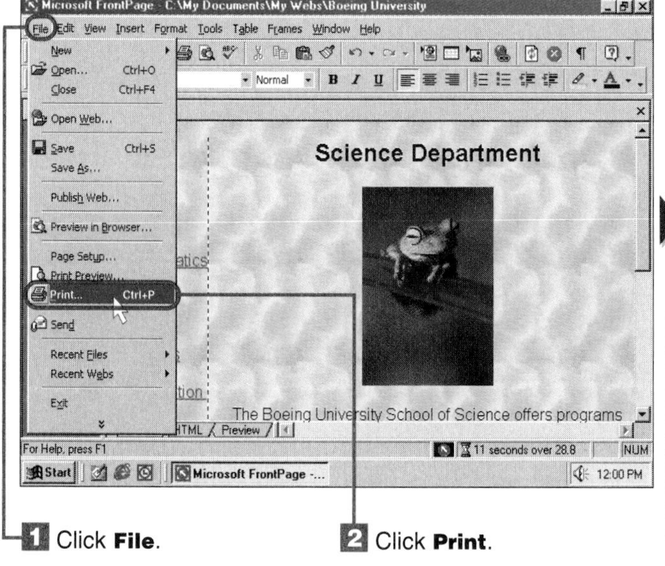

1 Click **File**.

2 Click **Print**.

■ The Print dialog box appears.

3 Click the print option you want to use (○ changes to ⊙).

All
Prints every page of the Web page.

Pages
Prints the pages you specify.

4 If you selected **Pages** in step **3**, type the first page you want to print. Press the Tab key and then type the last page you want to print.

5 Click **OK**.

SWITCH BETWEEN WEB PAGES

You can easily switch between the Web pages in your Web site. This allows you to review and edit more than one Web page at a time.

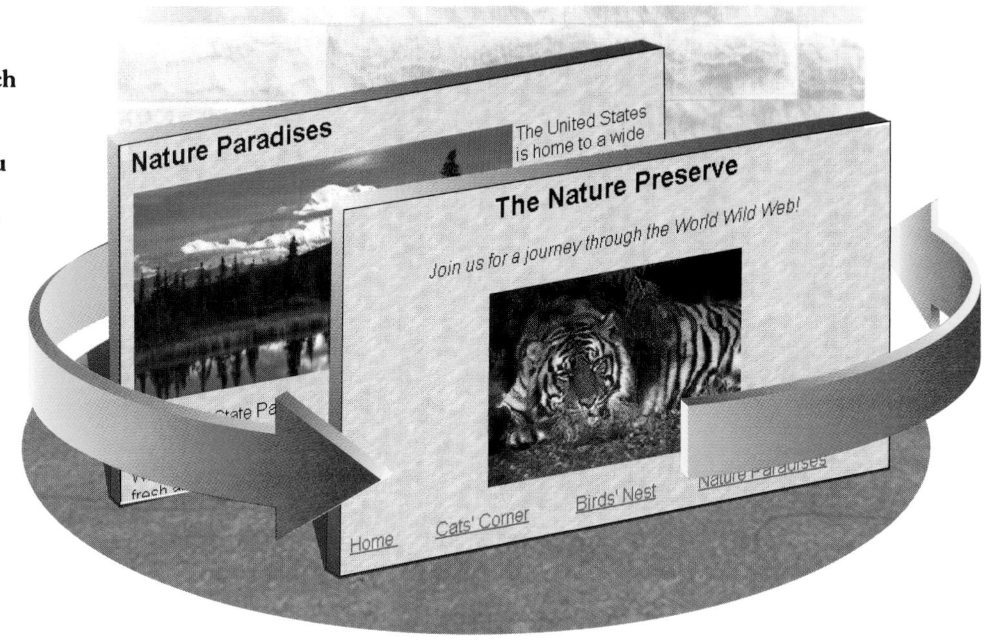

USING THE FOLDER LIST

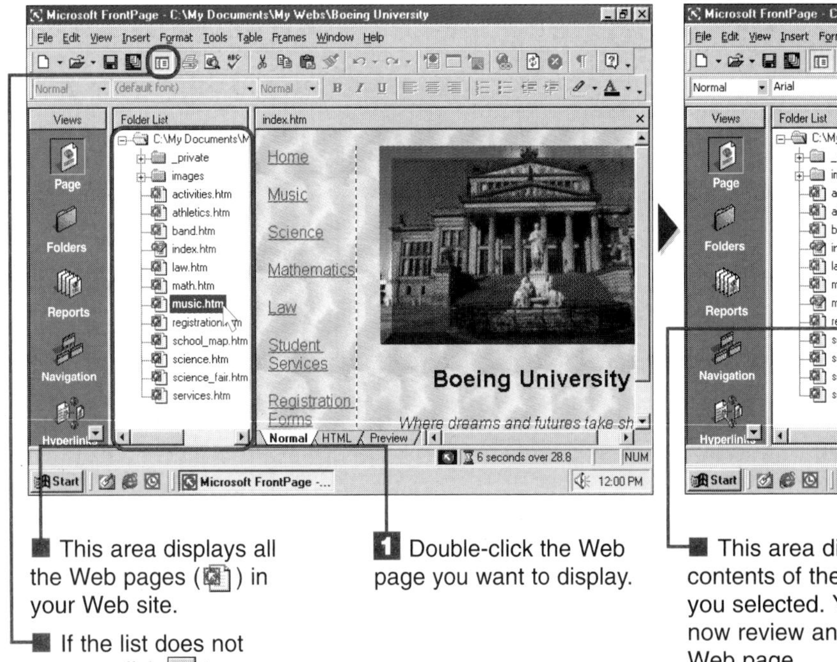

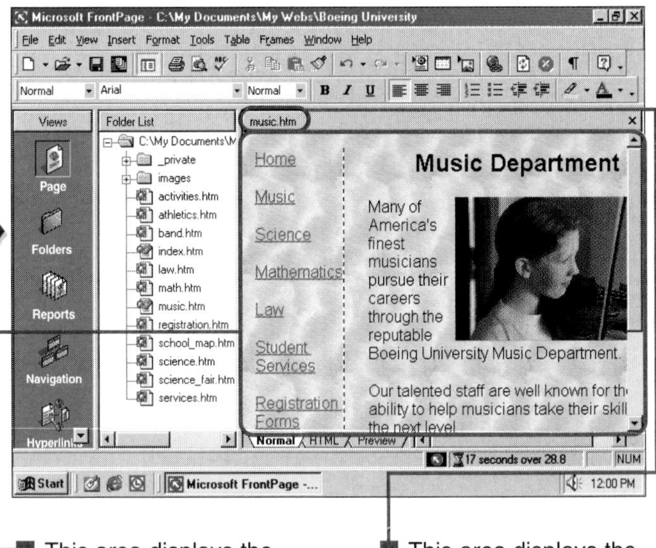

■ This area displays all the Web pages (▣) in your Web site.

■ If the list does not appear, click ▣ to display the list.

1 Double-click the Web page you want to display.

■ This area displays the contents of the Web page you selected. You can now review and edit the Web page.

■ This area displays the name of the Web page.

What is the difference between the way the Folder List and the Window menu display Web pages?

Folder List

✔ Displays all the Web pages in your Web site.

✔ Displays only the Web pages you have saved.

✔ A pencil (✎) appears in the icon for Web pages that are currently open.

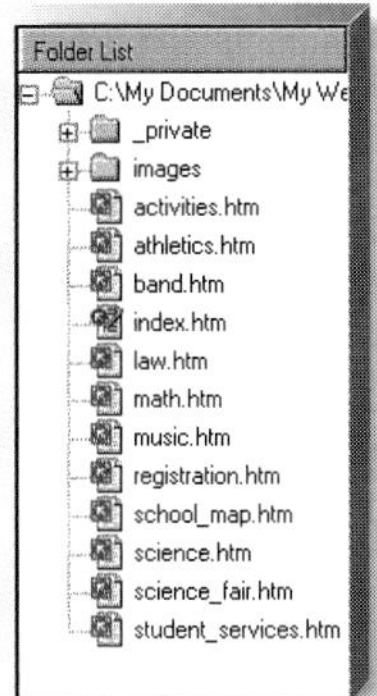

Window Menu

✔ Displays up to nine Web pages that are currently open in your Web site.

✔ Displays saved and unsaved Web pages.

✔ A star (*) appears beside Web pages that you have changed but have not yet saved.

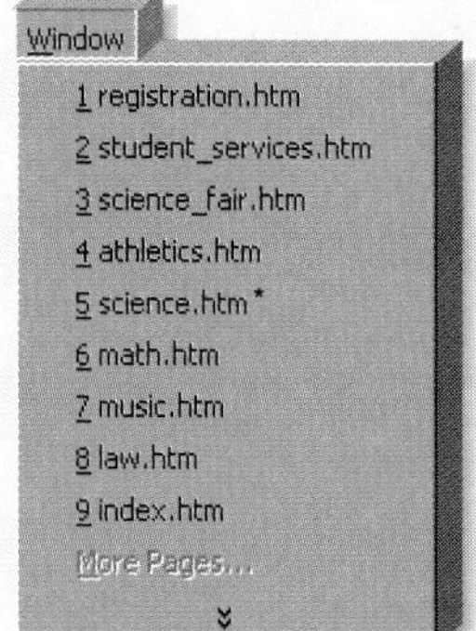

USING THE WINDOW MENU

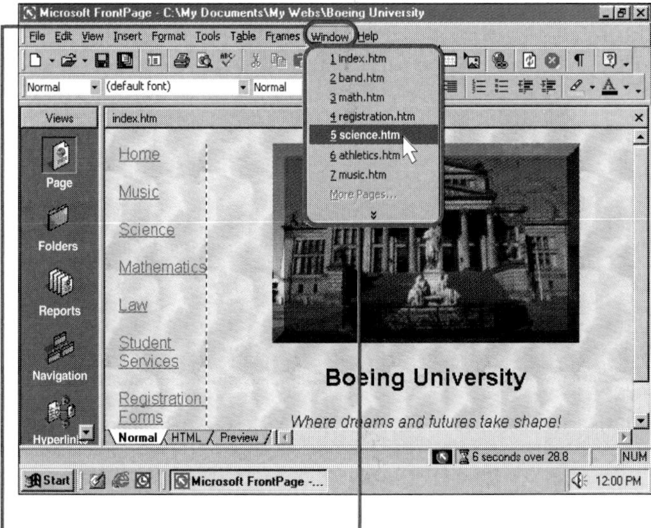

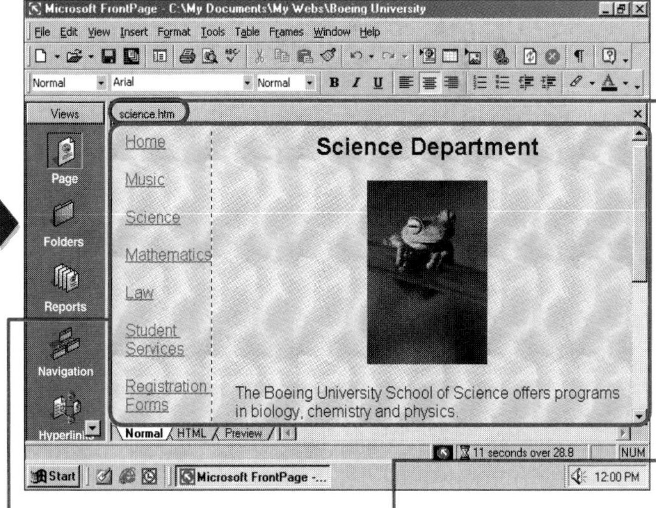

1 Click **Window** to display a list of Web pages that are currently open in your Web site.

■ The Web page you are currently working with appears at the top of the list.

2 Click the Web page you want to display.

■ This area displays the contents of the Web page you selected. You can now review and edit the Web page.

■ This area displays the name of the Web page.

CLOSE A WEB PAGE

When you finish working with a Web page, you can close the page to remove it from your screen.

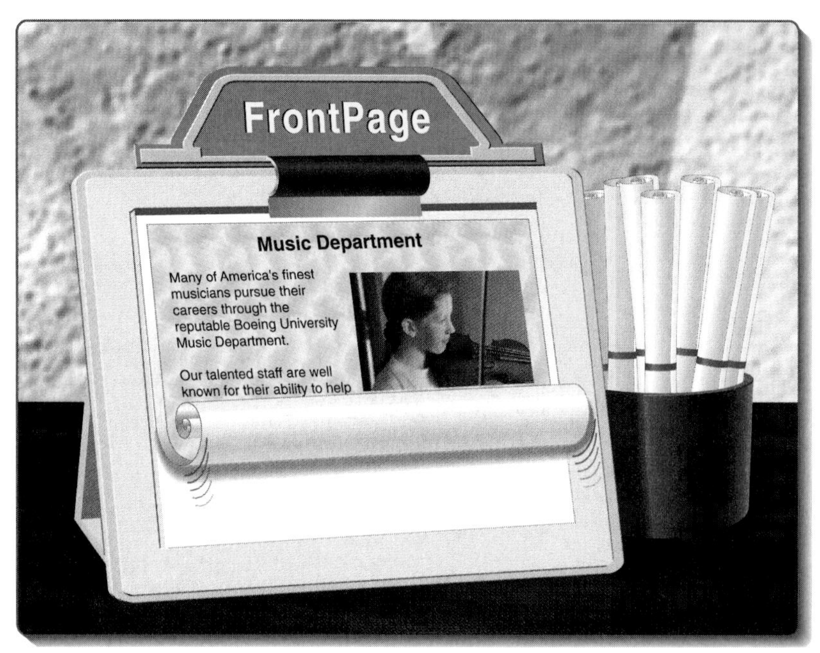

When you close a Web page, you do not exit the FrontPage program. You can continue to work with other Web pages in the Web site.

CLOSE A WEB PAGE

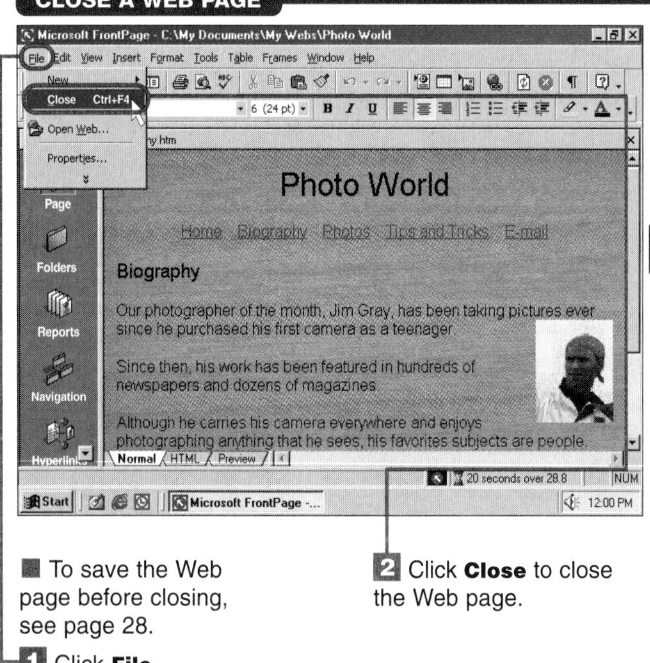

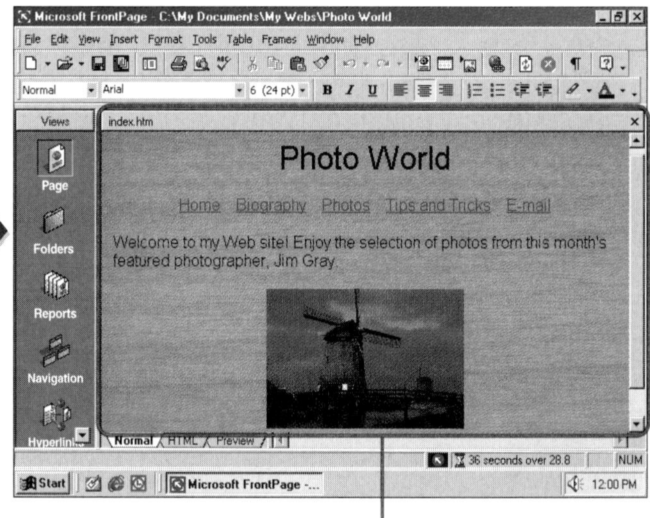

■ To save the Web page before closing, see page 28.

1 Click **File**.

2 Click **Close** to close the Web page.

■ The Web page disappears from your screen.

■ If you have more than one Web page open, another Web page that you previously opened appears on your screen.

DISPLAY WEB PAGE DOWNLOAD TIME

FrontPage can display the estimated amount of time a Web page will take to transfer to a reader's computer.

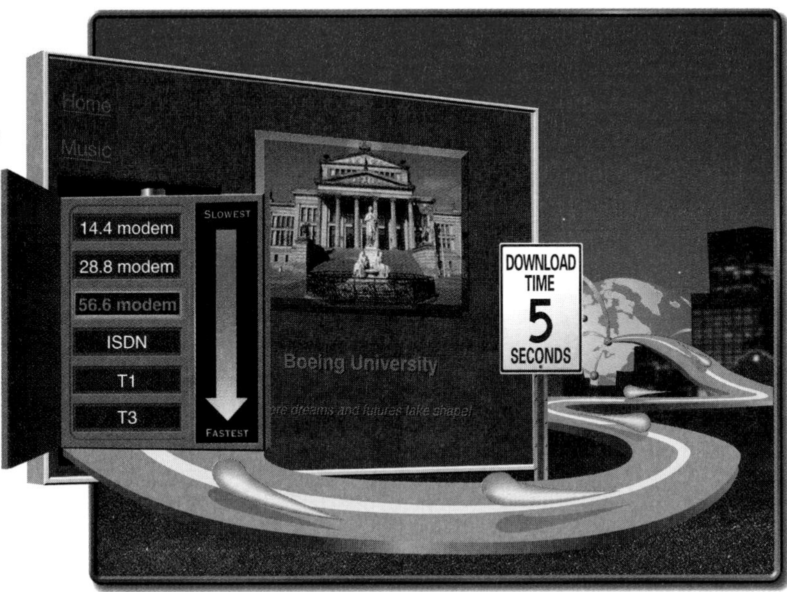

You can display the estimated download time at various connection speeds. Faster connection speeds will download a Web page more quickly.

DISPLAY WEB PAGE DOWNLOAD TIME

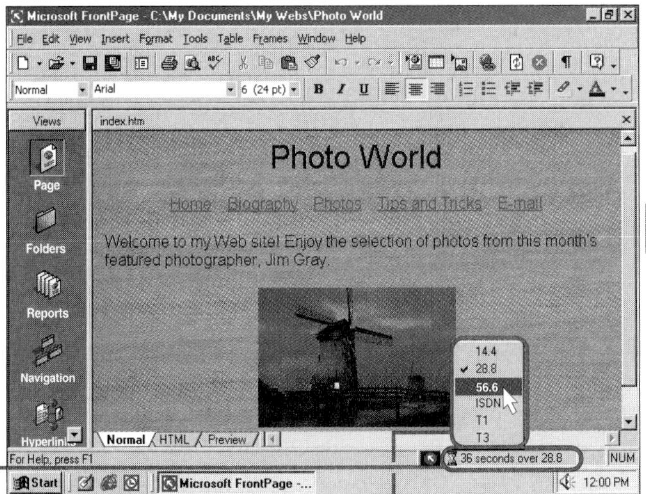

■ This area indicates the estimated amount of time the displayed Web page will take to transfer to a reader's computer using a 28.8 modem.

1 To view the estimated amount of time for another connection speed, click the area. A list of connection speeds appears.

2 Click the connection speed of interest.

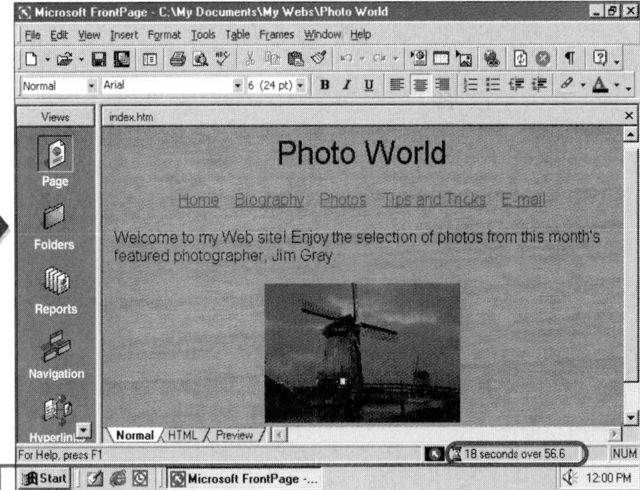

■ This area displays the estimated amount of time the Web page will take to transfer to a reader's computer at the connection speed you selected.

Note: Web pages with more text, images and other items will take longer to transfer to a reader's computer.

USING THE PAGE VIEWS

FrontPage offers three different ways that you can view your Web page.

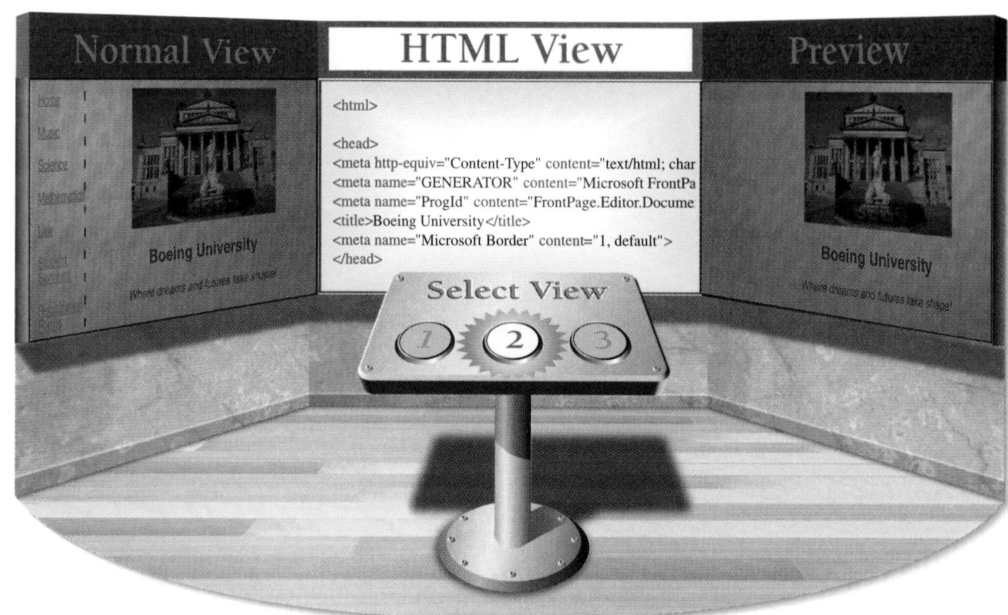

USING THE PAGE VIEWS

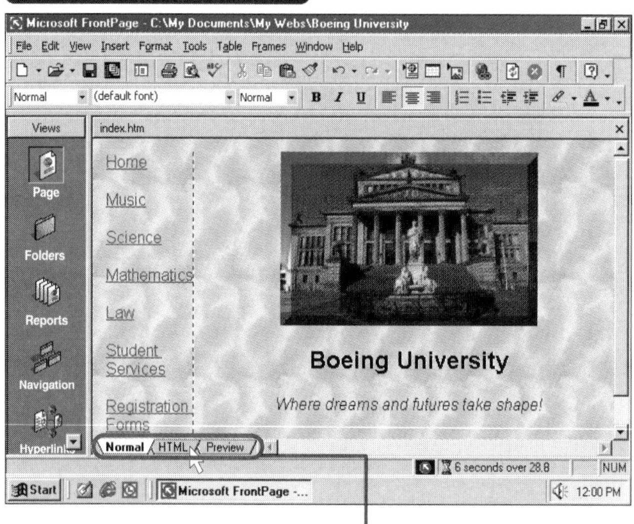

■ By default, the Web page appears in the Normal view.

1 Click a tab to display the Web page in a different view.

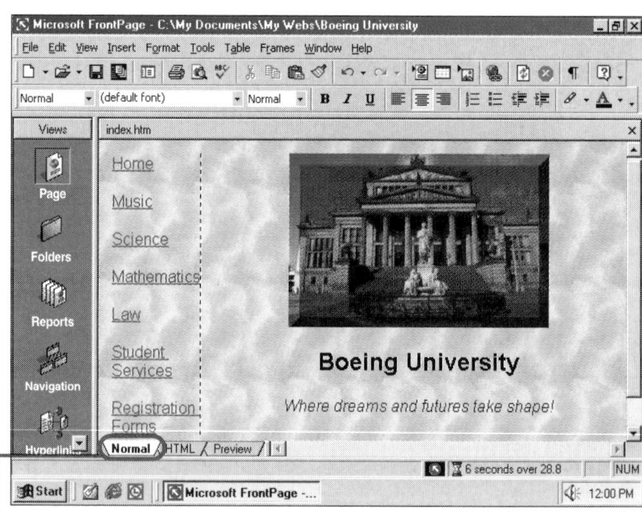

NORMAL

■ The Normal view allows you to enter, edit and format the information on your Web page.

How are HTML tags used to create a Web page?

Each tag gives a specific instruction and is surrounded by angle brackets < >. Most tags have an opening tag and a closing tag that affect the text between the tags. The closing tag has a forward slash (/). Some tags have only an opening tag. Here are some common tags.

Tag	Description
<b>	Bolds text
<blockquote>	Separates a section of text from the main text
<body>	Identifies the main content of a Web page
<i>	Italicizes text
<p>	Starts a new paragraph
<title>	Creates a title for a Web page

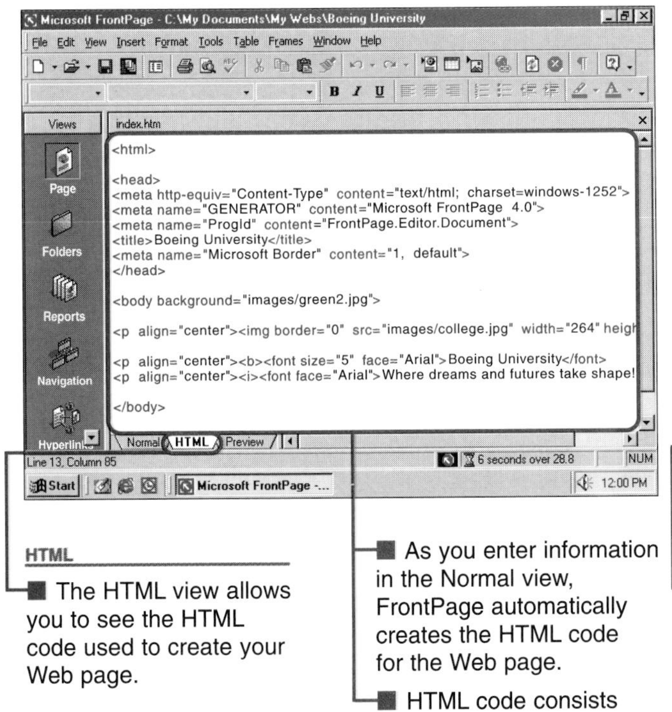

HTML

■ The HTML view allows you to see the HTML code used to create your Web page.

■ As you enter information in the Normal view, FrontPage automatically creates the HTML code for the Web page.

■ HTML code consists of text and special instructions called tags. Each tag is shown in blue.

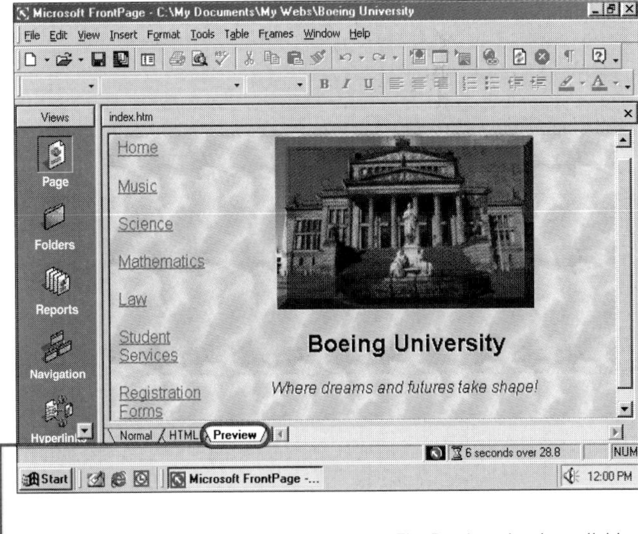

PREVIEW

■ The Preview view allows you to see how your Web page will appear on the Web.

Note: The Preview view is available only if you have the Microsoft Internet Explorer Web browser installed on your computer.

DISPLAY A WEB PAGE IN A WEB BROWSER

You can display your Web page in a Web browser to see how the page will appear on the Web.

A Web browser is a program that allows you to view and explore information on the Web.

DISPLAY A WEB PAGE IN A WEB BROWSER

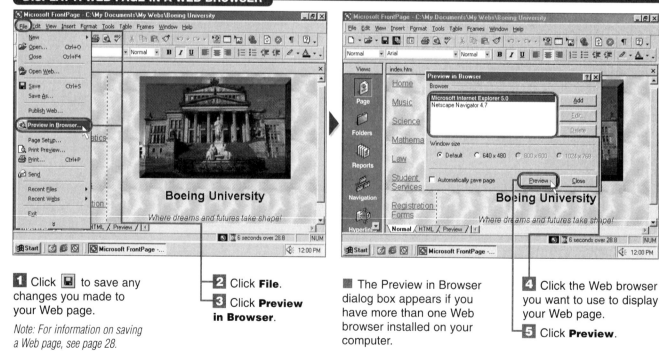

1 Click 💾 to save any changes you made to your Web page.

Note: For information on saving a Web page, see page 28.

2 Click **File**.

3 Click **Preview in Browser**.

■ The Preview in Browser dialog box appears if you have more than one Web browser installed on your computer.

4 Click the Web browser you want to use to display your Web page.

5 Click **Preview**.

Should I display my Web page in more than one Web browser?

You should display your Web page in several Web browsers so you can see how each browser will display your Web page. Each Web browser will display your Web page in a slightly different way. The most popular Web browsers are Microsoft Internet Explorer and Netscape Navigator.

Microsoft Internet Explorer

Microsoft Internet Explorer comes with the latest versions of Windows. You can also obtain Internet Explorer at the www.microsoft.com/windows/ie Web page.

Netscape Navigator

You can obtain Netscape Navigator at the www.netscape.com Web site or at computer stores.

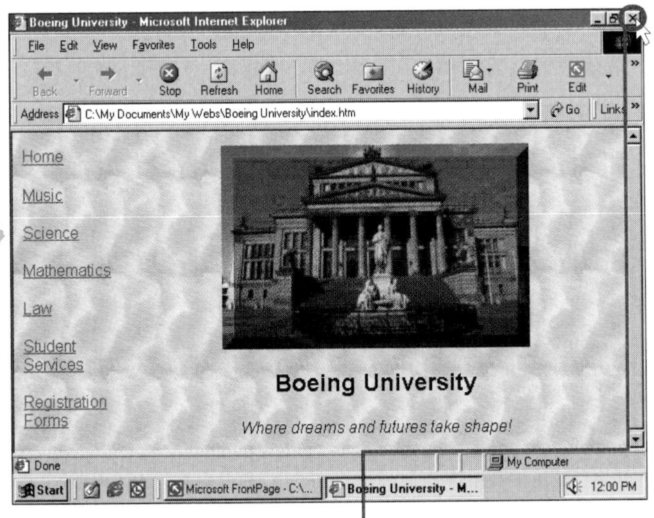

■ The Web browser opens and displays the Web page.

6 When you finish reviewing the Web page, click ☒ to close the Web browser window.

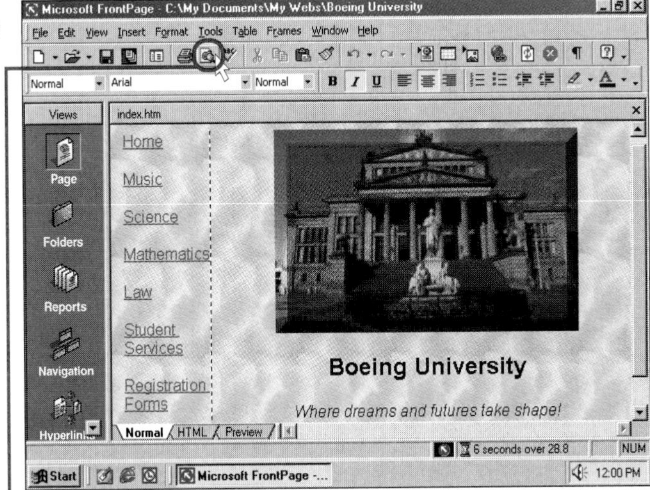

QUICKLY DISPLAY A WEB PAGE IN A WEB BROWSER

1 Click 🔍 to quickly display a Web page in a Web browser.

■ The Web page will appear in the Web browser you last used to display a Web page.

CHANGE THE VIEW OF A WEB SITE

FrontPage offers six different views of your Web site that you can use to create and organize your Web pages.

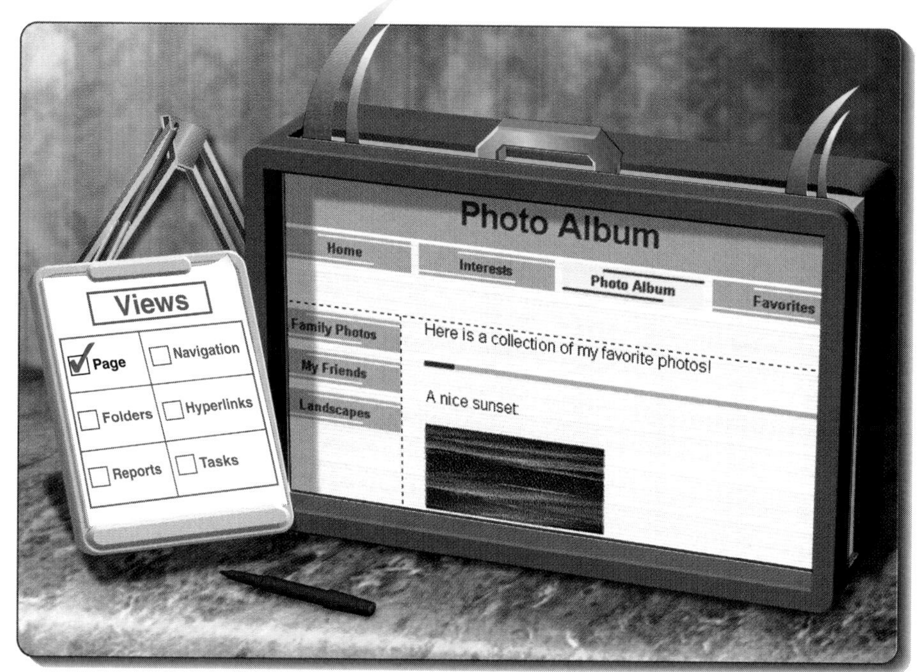

CHANGE THE VIEW OF A WEB SITE

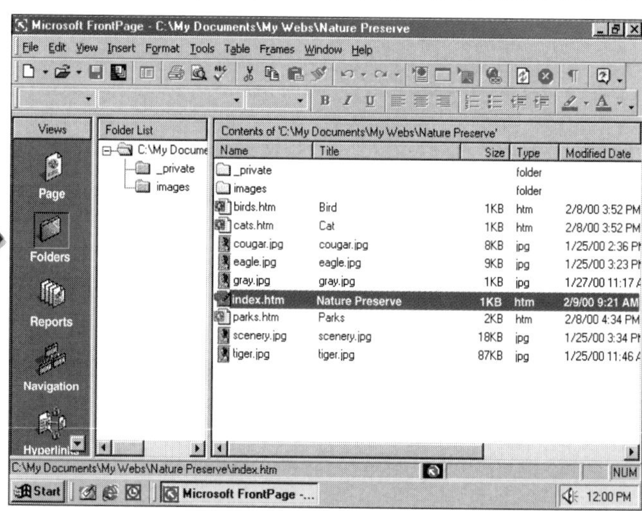

■ When you first start FrontPage, your Web site appears in the Page view.

1 To change the view, click the icon for the view you want to use.

■ You can click ▼ to browse through the views.

■ Your Web site appears in the view you selected.

THE WEB SITE VIEWS

PAGE

The Page view allows you to enter, edit and format the information on your Web pages.

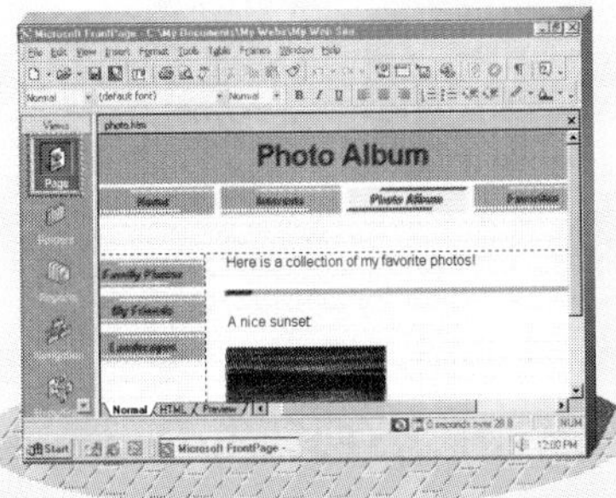

FOLDERS

The Folders view displays the folder structure of your Web site and lists information about the Web pages, images and other files in your Web site.

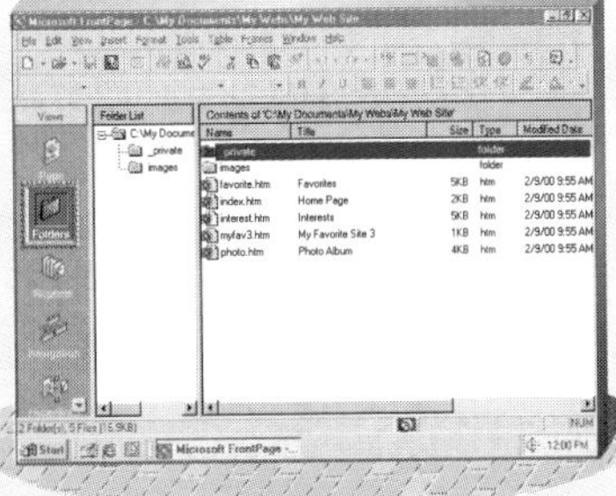

REPORTS

The Reports view allows you to display various reports that analyze and summarize information about your Web site.

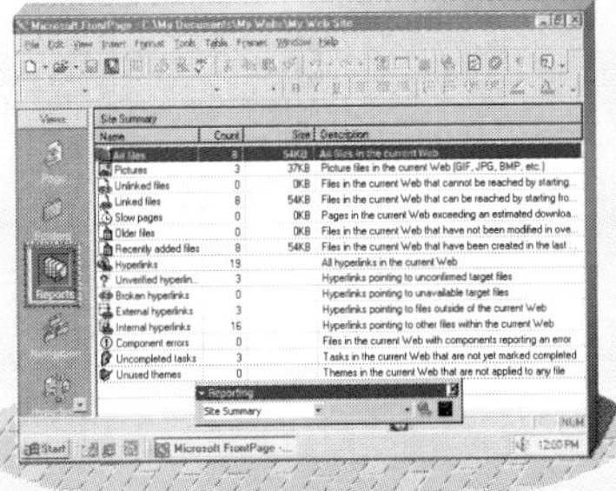

NAVIGATION

The Navigation view allows you to view and work with the navigational structure of the Web pages in your Web site.

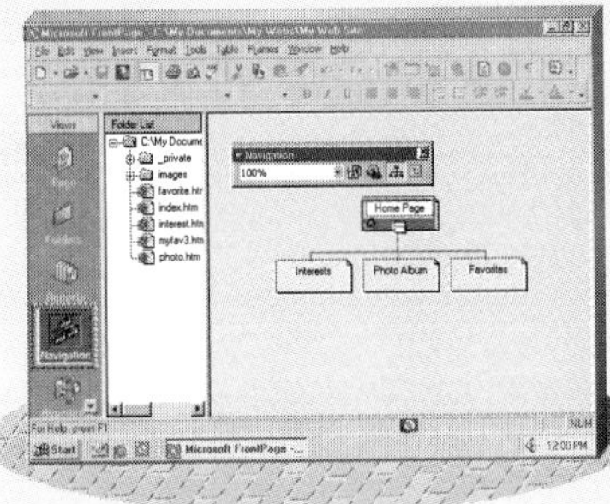

HYPERLINKS

The Hyperlinks view allows you to view the links that connect each Web page to other pages in your Web site.

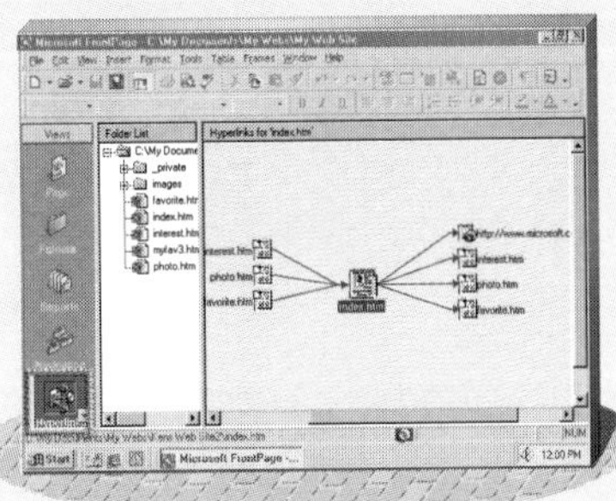

TASKS

The Tasks view allows you to create a to-do list to keep track of tasks you need to accomplish to complete your Web site.

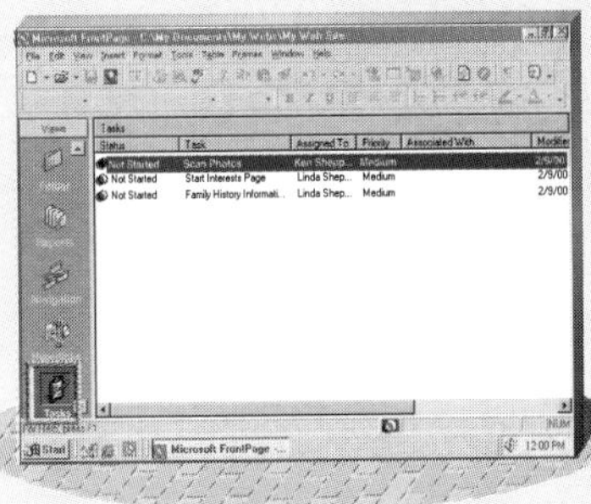

USING THE FOLDERS VIEW

You can use the Folders view to display information about the Web pages, images and other files in your Web site.

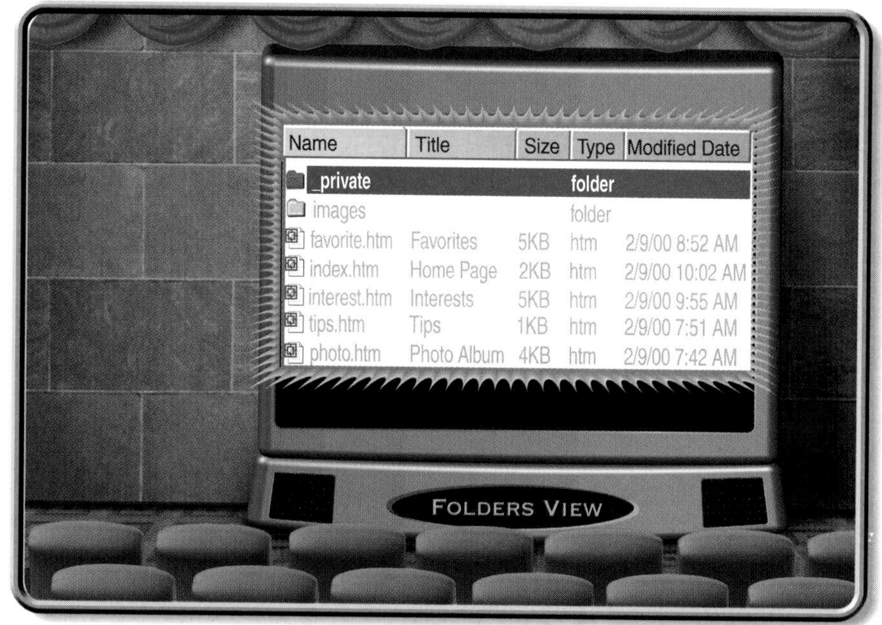

USING THE FOLDERS VIEW

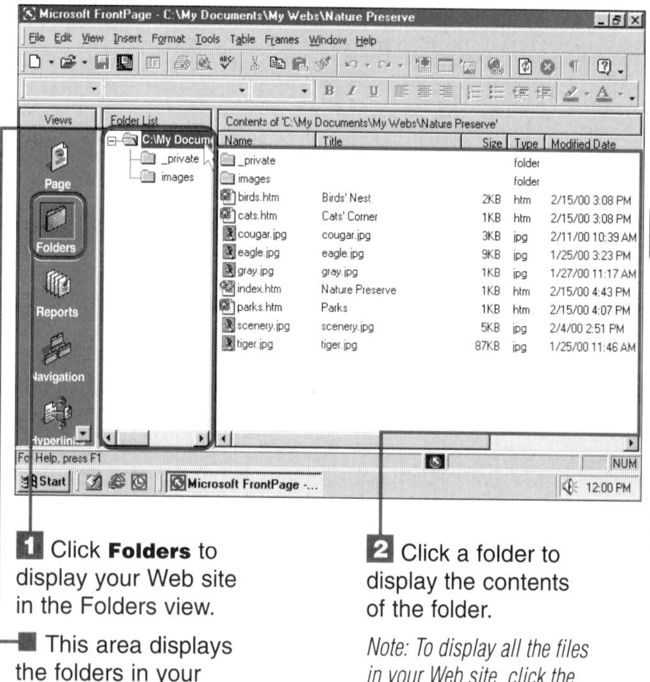

1 Click **Folders** to display your Web site in the Folders view.

■ This area displays the folders in your Web site.

2 Click a folder to display the contents of the folder.

Note: To display all the files in your Web site, click the top folder.

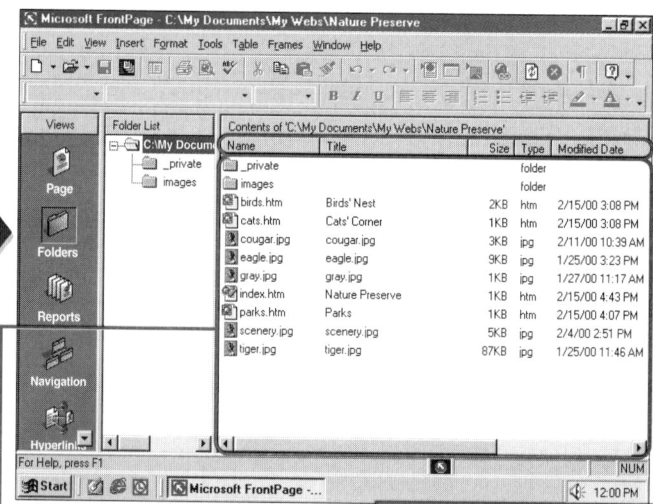

■ This area displays the contents of the folder you selected. FrontPage displays information about the Web pages (), images () and other files in your Web site.

■ To view the files in a different order, click the heading of the column you want to use to sort the files.

Note: You can click the heading of the column again to sort the files in the opposite order.

CHANGE THE TITLE OF A WEB PAGE

You can give a Web page a title that describes the contents of the page. The title appears at the top of a Web browser window.

If you do not specify a title for your Web page, FrontPage will use the first line of text as your title.

You should use a brief, descriptive title that will interest people in reading your Web page. Use a title such as "Favorite Golf Getaways" rather than a less descriptive title such as "My Home Page."

CHANGE THE TITLE OF A WEB PAGE

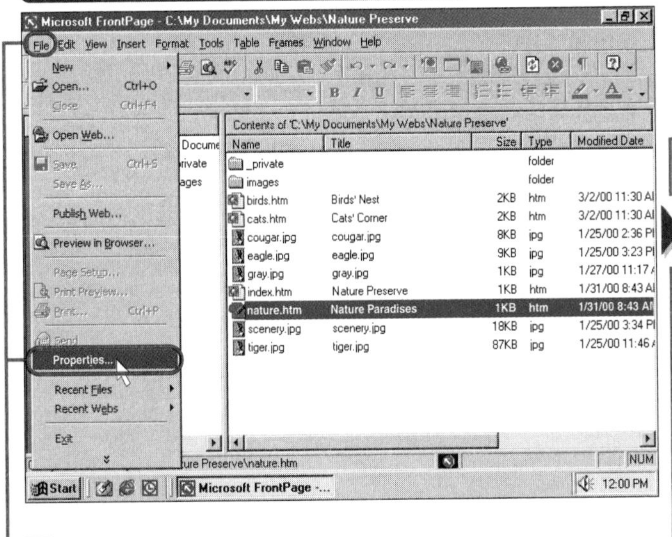

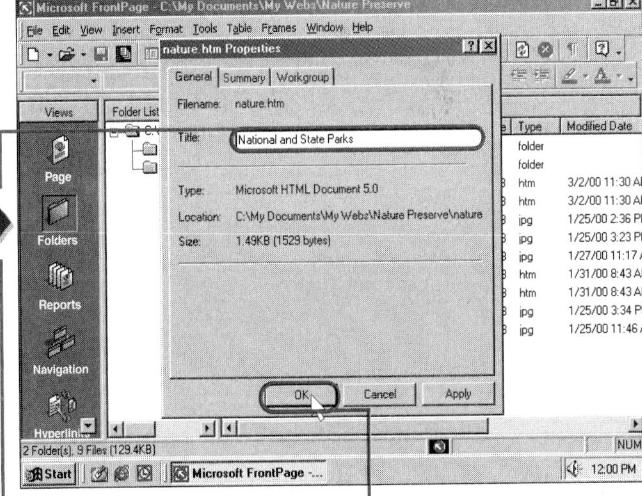

1 Click **File**.

2 Click **Properties**.

Note: If Properties does not appear on the menu, position the mouse over the bottom of the menu to display all the menu commands.

■ The Properties dialog box appears.

3 Type a title for the Web page.

4 Click **OK** to confirm the information you entered.

■ When a reader displays the Web page, the title will appear at the top of the Web browser window. To preview a Web page in a Web browser, see page 44.

RENAME A WEB PAGE

You can rename a Web page to better describe the contents of the page.

You should not rename the Web page named index.htm since this is your home page. If you rename this Web page, readers may get an error message when they visit your Web site.

RENAME A WEB PAGE

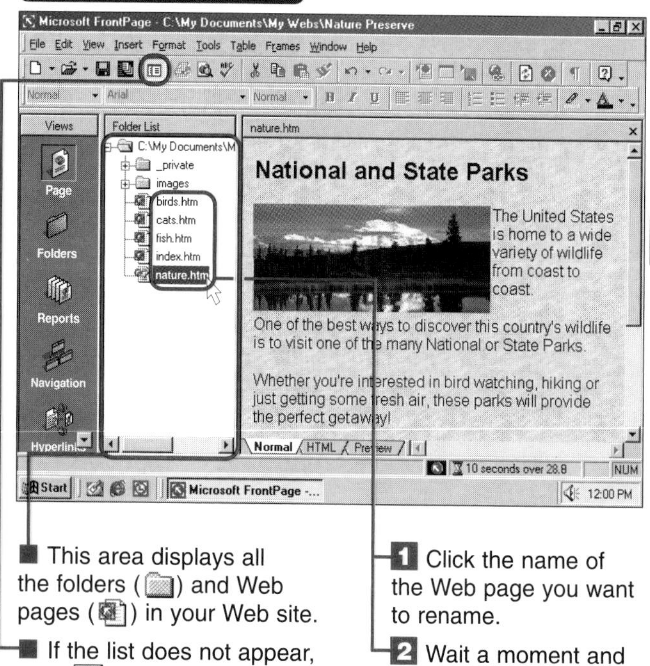

■ This area displays all the folders (▭) and Web pages (▭) in your Web site.

■ If the list does not appear, click ▭ to display the list.

1 Click the name of the Web page you want to rename.

2 Wait a moment and then click the name of the Web page again.

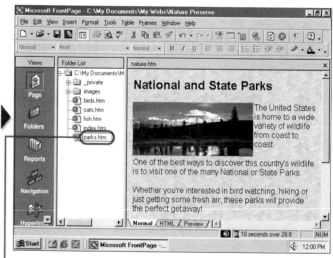

■ The name of the Web page appears in a box.

3 Type a new name for the Web page and then press the Enter key. Make sure you add the **.htm** extension to the end of the Web page name.

*Note: A dialog box will appear if the Web page is linked to other Web pages in your Web site. Click **Yes** to have FrontPage automatically update the linked pages.*

DELETE A WEB PAGE

You can delete a Web page you no longer want to include in your Web site.

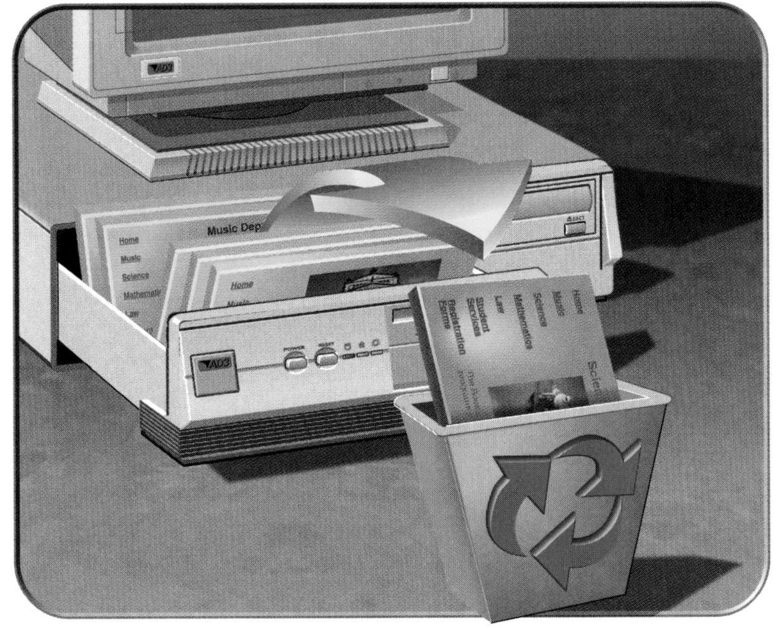

Before you delete any Web pages, consider the value of your work. Do not delete a Web page unless you are certain you no longer need the page.

You should not delete the Web page named index.htm since this is your home page. If you delete this Web page, readers may get an error message when they visit your Web site.

DELETE A WEB PAGE

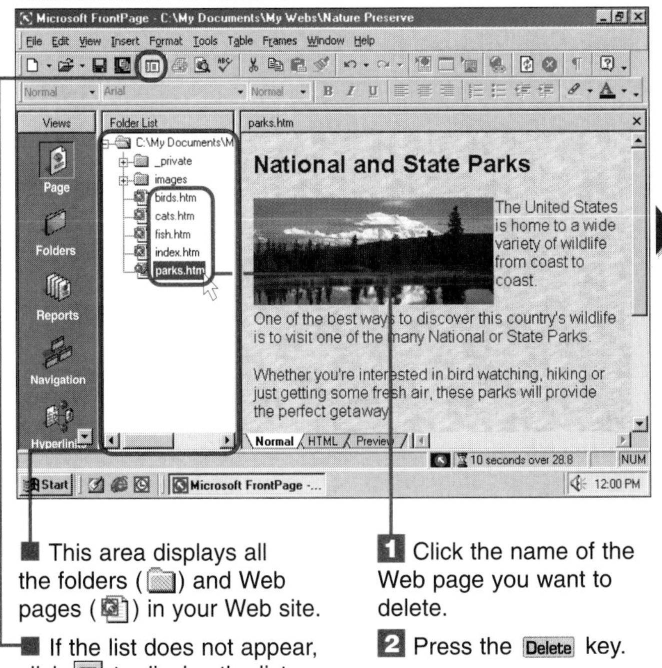

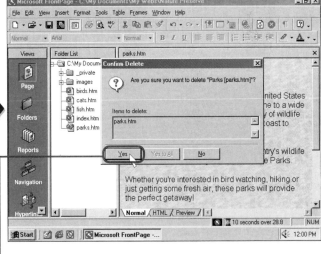

■ This area displays all the folders ( ) and Web pages ( ) in your Web site.

■ If the list does not appear, click to display the list.

1 Click the name of the Web page you want to delete.

2 Press the Delete key.

■ A confirmation dialog box appears.

3 Click **Yes** to delete the Web page.

■ FrontPage deletes the Web page.

SYMBOLS
&
¥
ø
£
©
Birds' Nest
easiest
One of the ways to enjoy the wonders of nature is
a look
out the nearest window. You're probably going to se
or two!
Bird watching is a very popular
hobby in the United States, and it is
growing in popularity all the time!
One reason for this is that
such a wide variety of
coast to coast.
popularity

CHAPTER 4

Edit Text

Would you like to edit the text in your Web pages or check your Web pages for spelling errors? This chapter teaches you how.

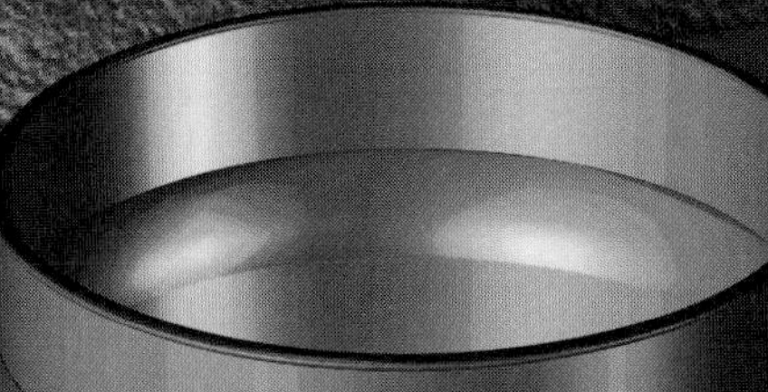

SELECT TEXT

Before performing many tasks in FrontPage, you must select the text you want to work with. Selected text appears highlighted on your screen.

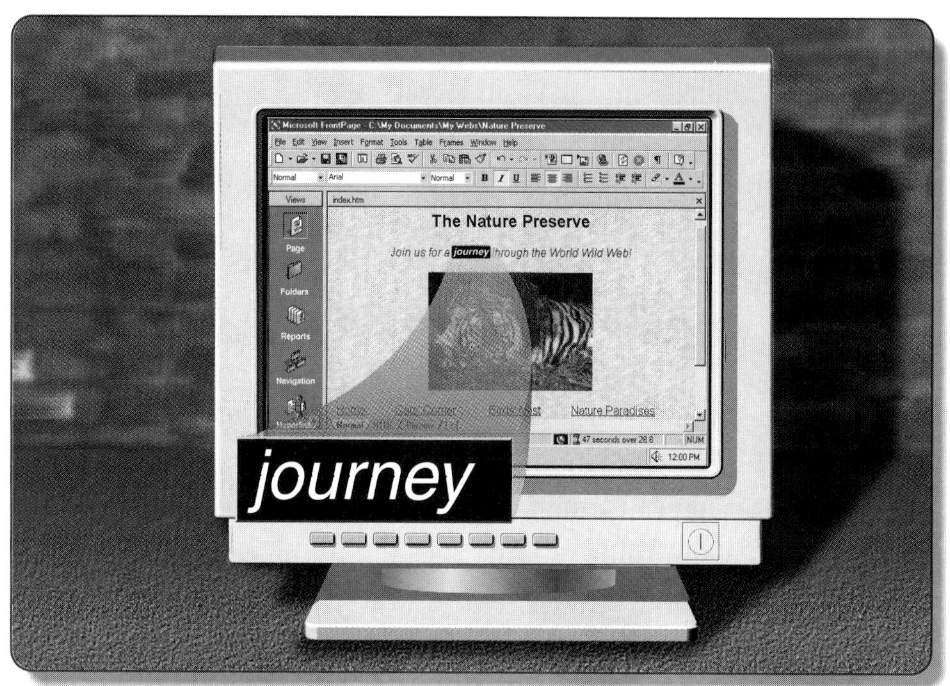

SELECT TEXT

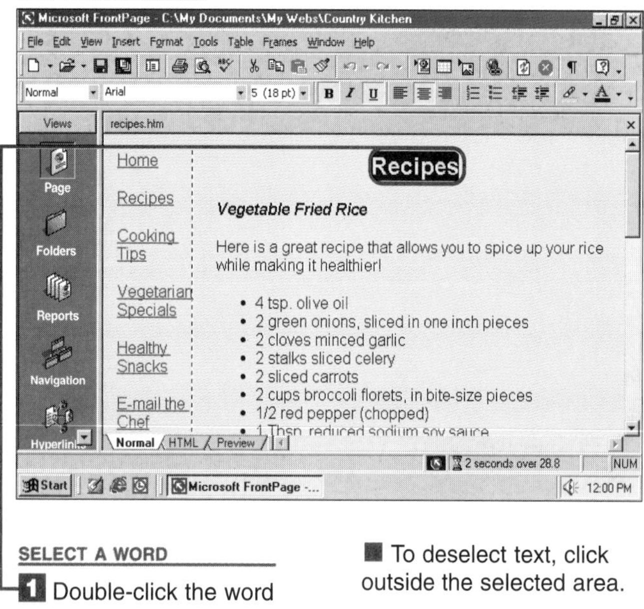

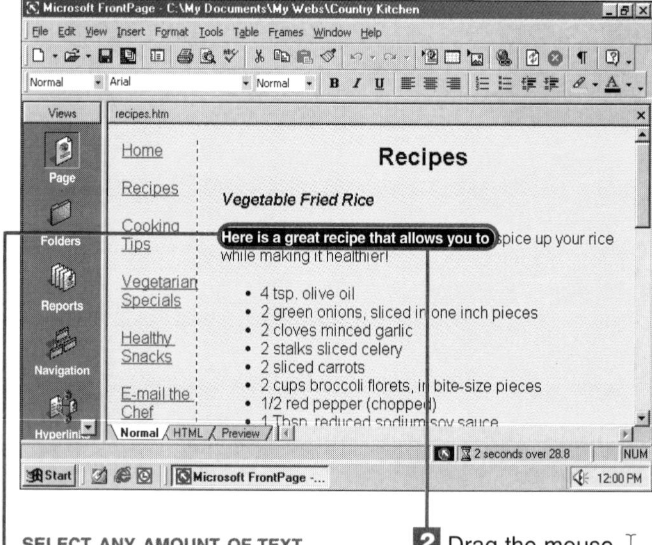

SELECT A WORD

1 Double-click the word you want to select.

■ To deselect text, click outside the selected area.

SELECT ANY AMOUNT OF TEXT

1 Position the mouse I to the left of the first word you want to select.

2 Drag the mouse I over the text until you highlight all the text you want to select.

UNDO CHANGES

FrontPage remembers the last changes you made to your Web page. If you regret these changes, you can cancel them by using the Undo feature.

The Undo feature can cancel up to 30 of your last editing and formatting changes.

UNDO CHANGES

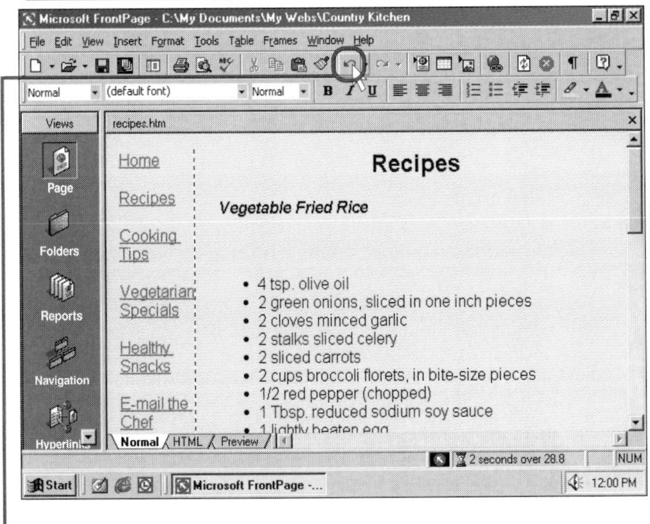

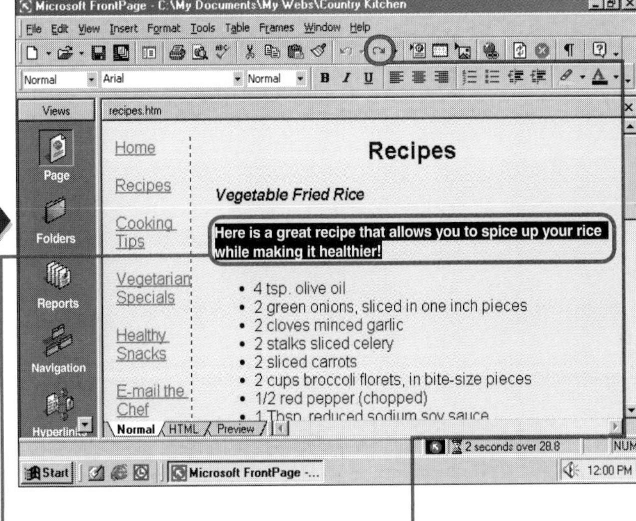

1 Click [Undo] to undo the last change you made to your Web page.

■ FrontPage cancels the last change you made to your Web page.

■ You can repeat step 1 to cancel previous changes you made.

■ To reverse the results of using the Undo feature, click [Redo].

INSERT AND DELETE TEXT

You can add new text to your Web page and remove text you no longer need.

INSERT TEXT

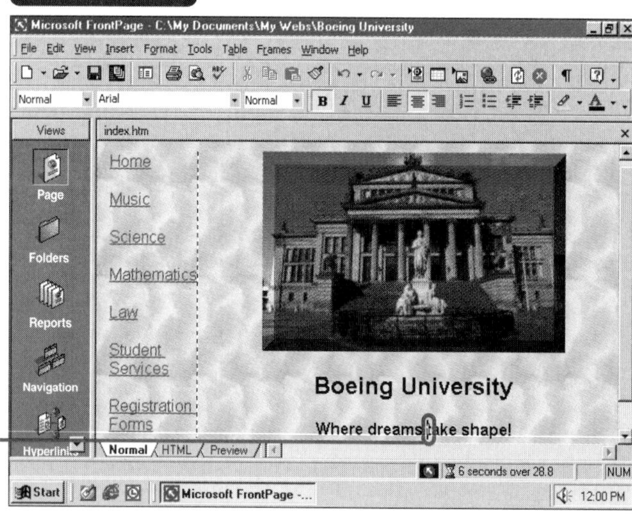

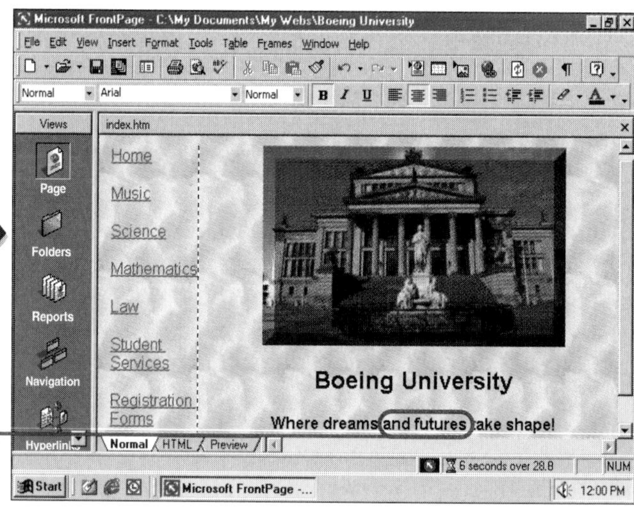

1 Click the location where you want to insert the new text.

■ The text you type will appear where the insertion point flashes on your screen.

Note: You can press the ←, →, ↑ or ↓ key to move the insertion point.

2 Type the text you want to insert. To insert a blank space, press the **Spacebar**.

■ The words to the right of the new text move forward.

How can I easily enter numbers on my Web page?

When **NUM** appears at the bottom of your screen, you can use the number keys on the right side of your keyboard to enter numbers. To turn the display of **NUM** on or off, press the Num Lock key.

How can I use the keyboard to quickly move the insertion point?

To move the insertion point	Press
To the end of a line	End
To the beginning of a line	Home
To the end of a paragraph	Ctrl and ↓ at the same time
To the beginning of a paragraph	Ctrl and ↑ at the same time
One screen down	Page Down
One screen up	Page Up

DELETE TEXT

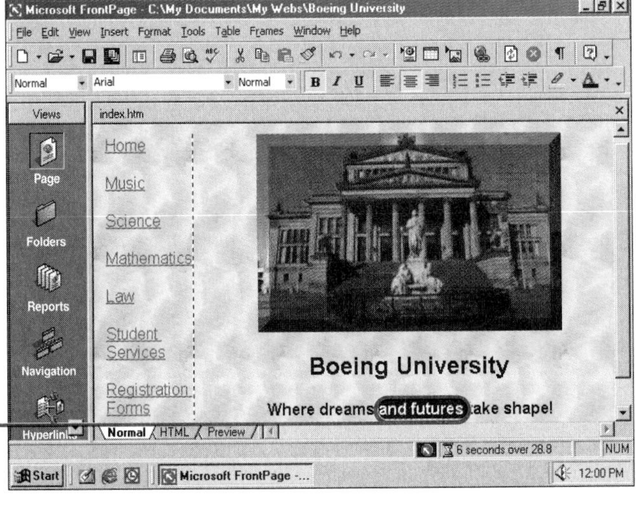

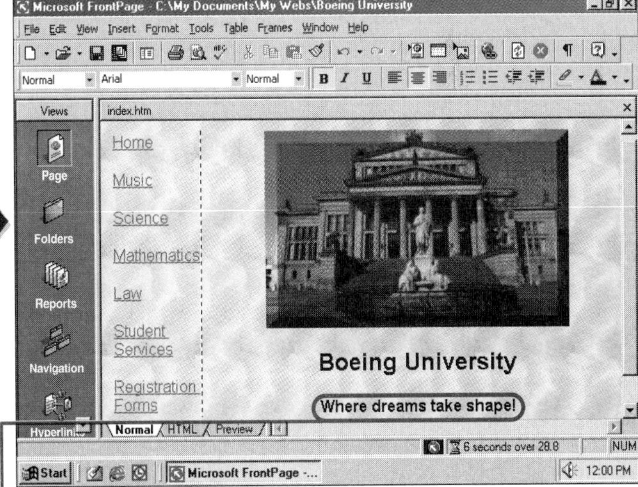

1 Select the text you want to delete. To select text, see page 54.

2 Press the Delete key to remove the text.

■ The text disappears. The remaining text moves to fill the empty space.

■ To delete a single character, click to the right of the character you want to delete and then press the ←Backspace key. FrontPage deletes the character to the left of the flashing insertion point.

MOVE OR COPY TEXT

You can move or copy text to a new location on your Web page.

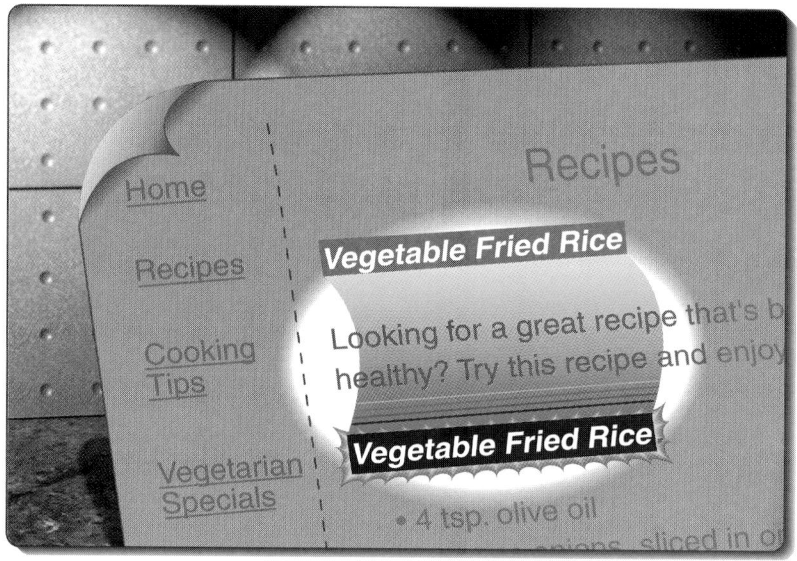

Moving text allows you to rearrange text on your Web page. When you move text, the text disappears from its original location.

Copying text allows you to repeat information on your Web page without having to retype the text. When you copy text, the text appears in both the original and new locations.

MOVE OR COPY TEXT

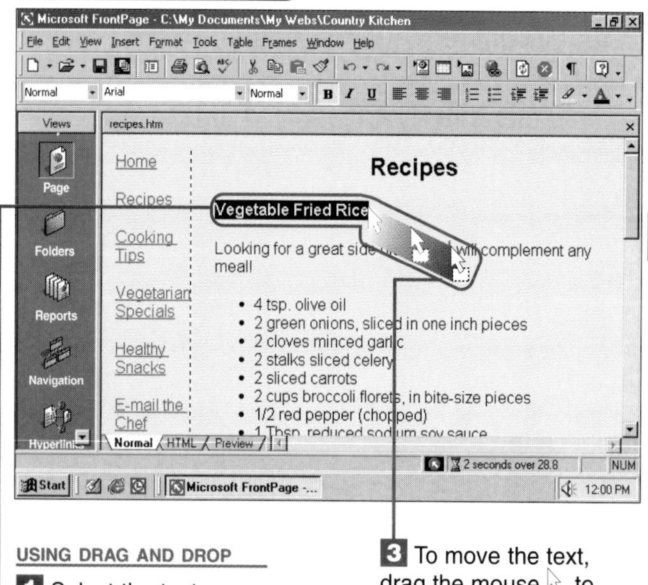

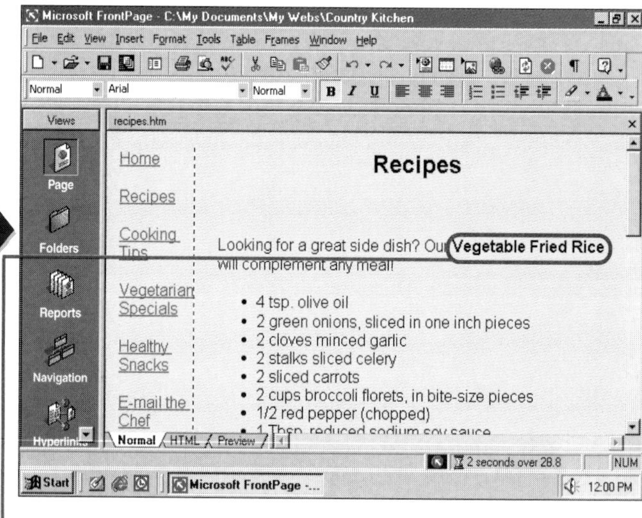

USING DRAG AND DROP

1 Select the text you want to move. To select text, see page 54.

2 Position the mouse I over the selected text (I changes to ↖).

3 To move the text, drag the mouse to where you want to place the text.

Note: The text will appear where you position the dotted insertion point on your screen.

■ The text moves to the new location.

■ To copy text, perform steps **1** to **3**, except press and hold down the **Ctrl** key as you perform step **3**.

How can copying text help me edit my Web page?

If you plan to make major changes to a paragraph, you may want to copy the paragraph before you begin. This gives you two copies of the paragraph–the original paragraph and a paragraph with all the changes.

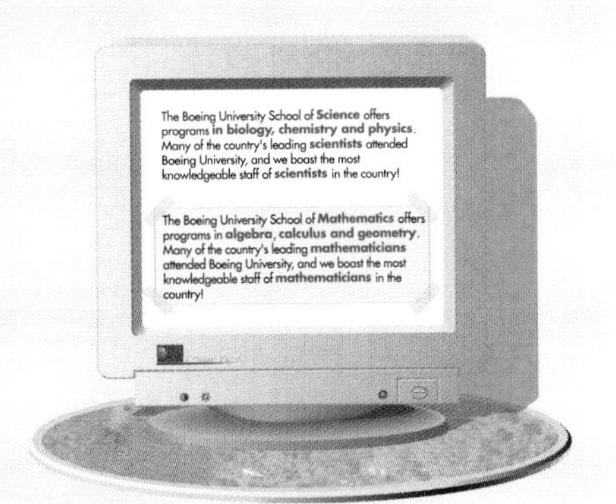

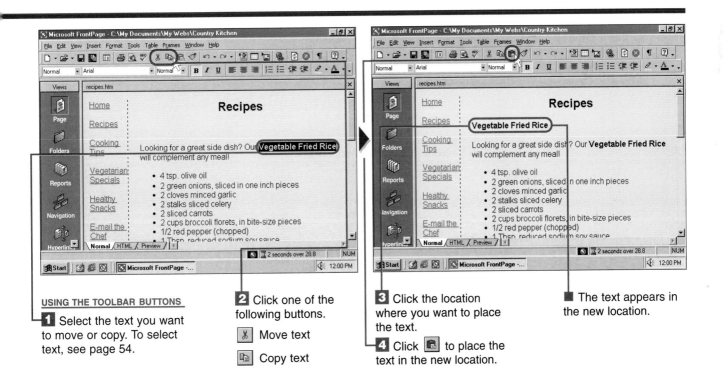

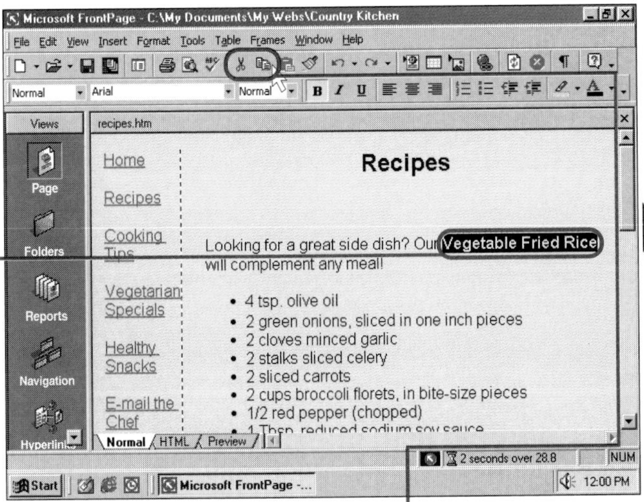

USING THE TOOLBAR BUTTONS

1 Select the text you want to move or copy. To select text, see page 54.

2 Click one of the following buttons.

- Move text
- Copy text

3 Click the location where you want to place the text.

4 Click to place the text in the new location.

■ The text appears in the new location.

ADD SYMBOLS

You can add symbols or special characters that do not appear on your keyboard to your Web page.

ADD SYMBOLS

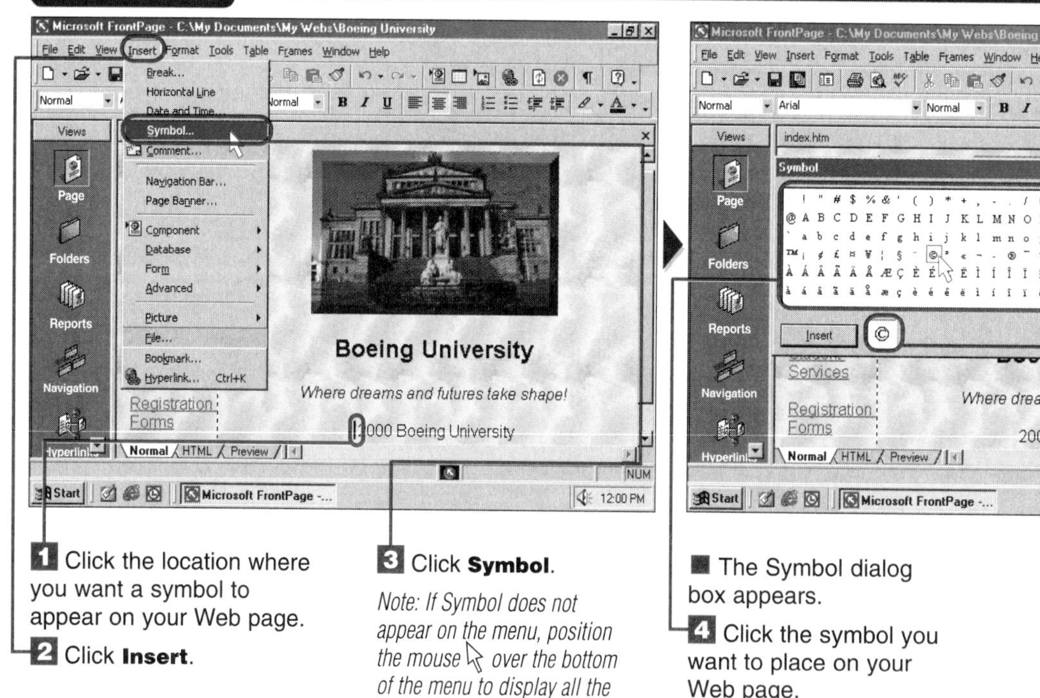

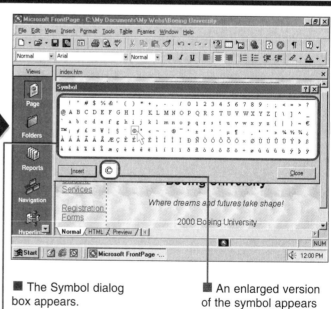

1 Click the location where you want a symbol to appear on your Web page.

2 Click **Insert**.

3 Click **Symbol**.

Note: If Symbol does not appear on the menu, position the mouse over the bottom of the menu to display all the menu commands.

■ The Symbol dialog box appears.

4 Click the symbol you want to place on your Web page.

■ An enlarged version of the symbol appears in this area.

How can I quickly add a symbol to many locations on my Web page?

After you add a symbol, you can copy the symbol to various locations on your Web page. This is useful if you need to add a symbol such as ™ next to each instance of your company name. For information on copying text, see page 58.

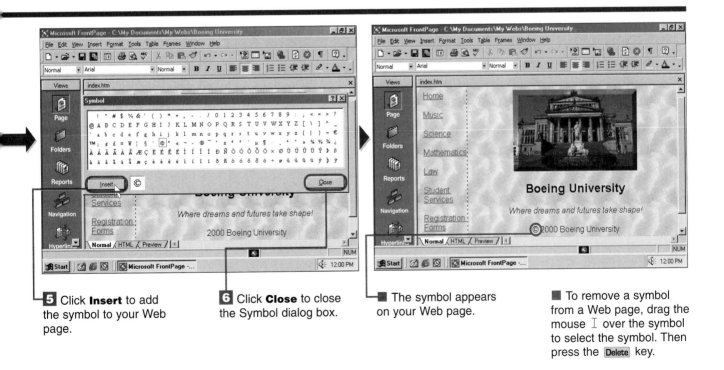

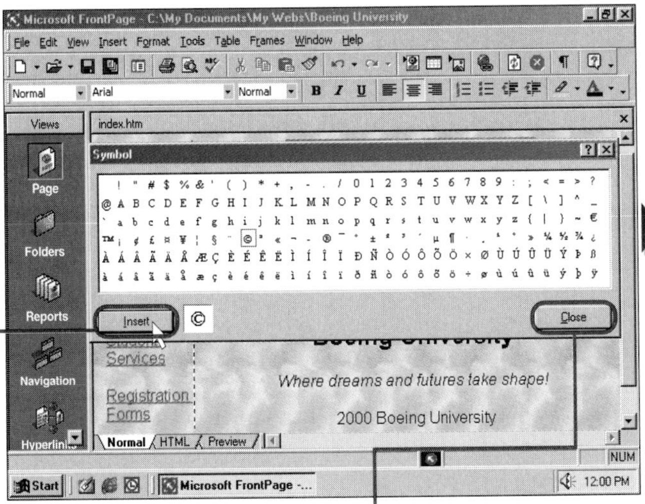

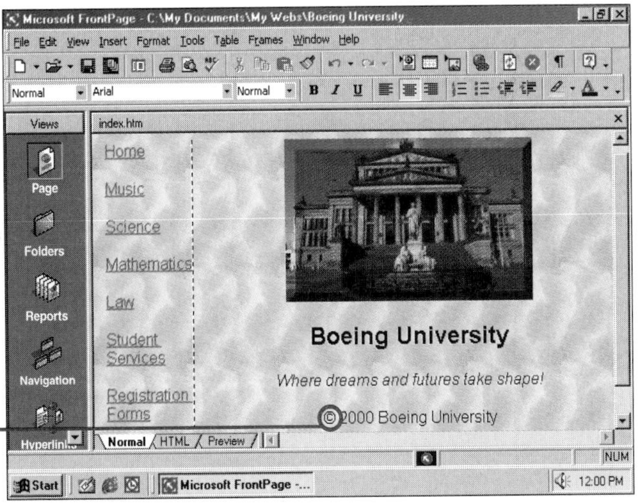

5 Click **Insert** to add the symbol to your Web page.

6 Click **Close** to close the Symbol dialog box.

■ The symbol appears on your Web page.

■ To remove a symbol from a Web page, drag the mouse I over the symbol to select the symbol. Then press the Delete key.

ADD THE DATE AND TIME

You can add the date and time to a Web page to let readers know when you last updated the page.

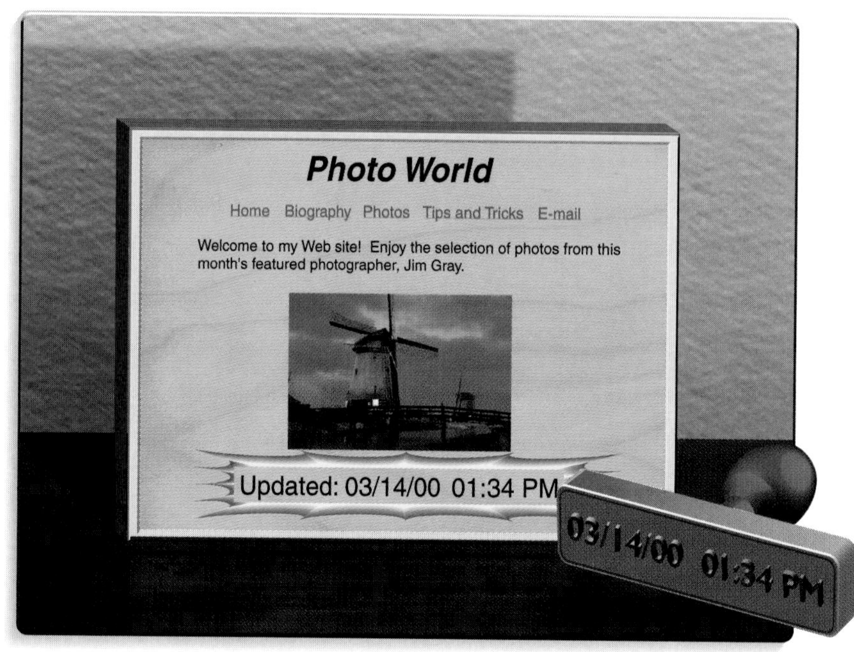

FrontPage will automatically update the date and time each time you open the Web page.

ADD THE DATE AND TIME

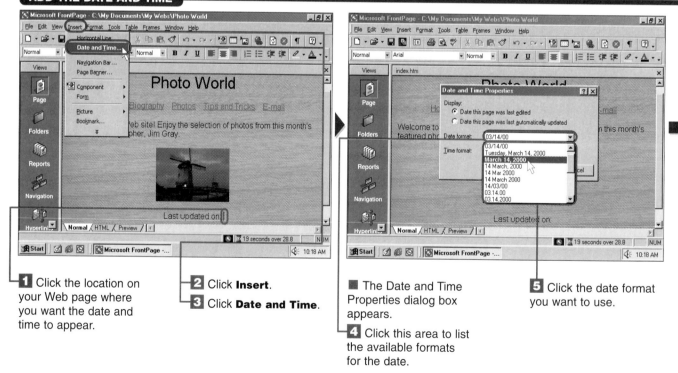

1 Click the location on your Web page where you want the date and time to appear.

2 Click **Insert**.

3 Click **Date and Time**.

■ The Date and Time Properties dialog box appears.

4 Click this area to list the available formats for the date.

5 Click the date format you want to use.

Why did FrontPage add the wrong date and time to my Web page?

FrontPage uses your computer's built-in clock to determine the current date and time. If FrontPage adds the wrong date and time to your Web page, you must change the date and time set in your computer. To change the date and time set in your computer, refer to your Windows manual.

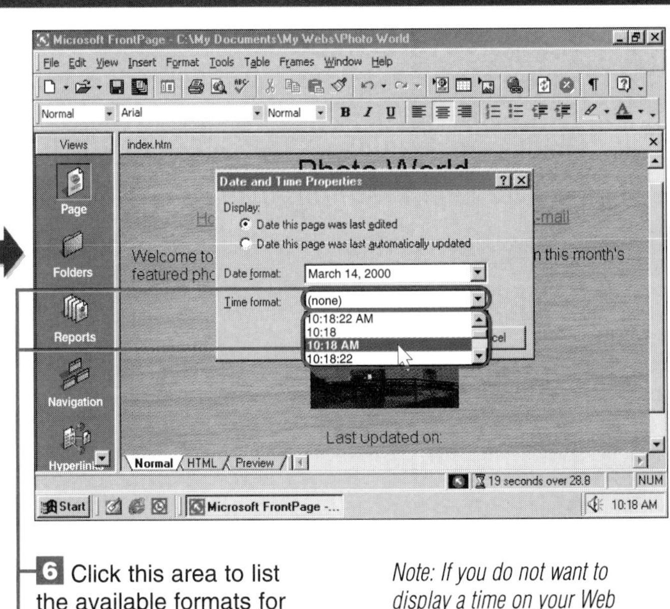

6 Click this area to list the available formats for the time.

7 Click the time format you want to use.

*Note: If you do not want to display a time on your Web page, click **(none)**.*

8 Press the Enter key to add the date and time to your Web page.

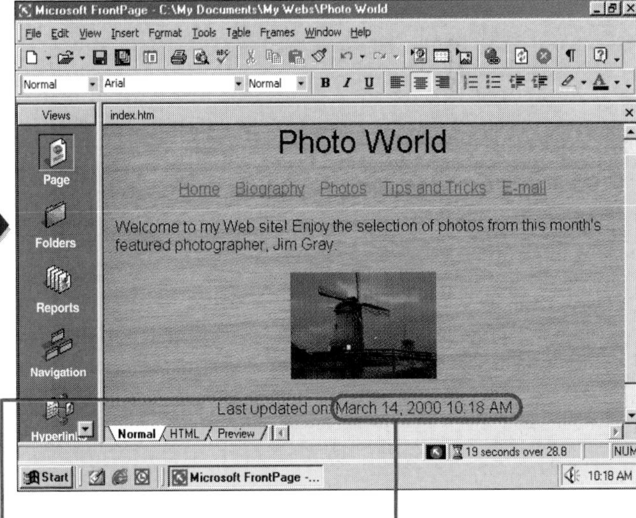

■ The date and time appears on your Web page.

■ To remove the date and time, click the date and time and then press the Delete key.

CHECK SPELLING

You can quickly find and correct all the spelling errors on your Web page.

CHECK SPELLING

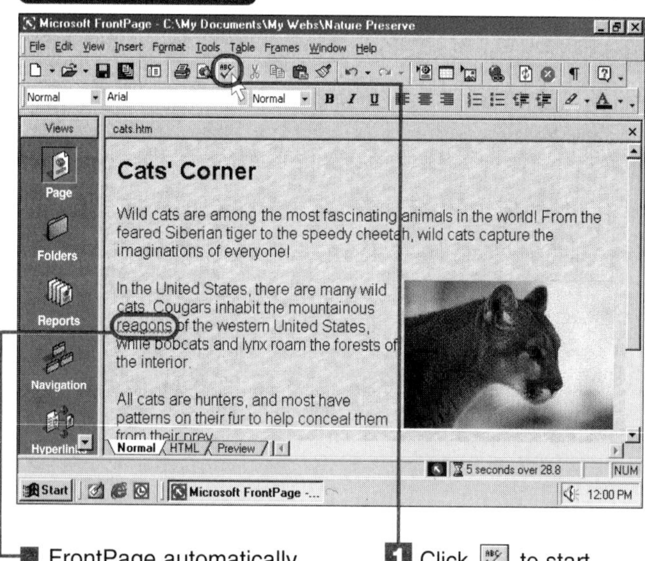

■ FrontPage automatically checks your Web page for spelling errors as you type. Misspelled words display a red, wavy underline. The underlines will not appear when you publish your Web page.

1 Click the spelling button to start the spell check.

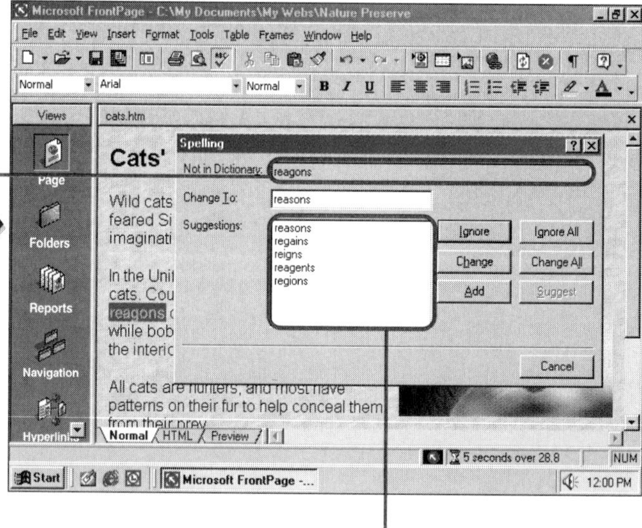

■ The Spelling dialog box appears if FrontPage finds a misspelled word on your Web page.

■ This area displays the misspelled word.

■ This area displays suggestions for correcting the word.

?

How does FrontPage find spelling errors on my Web page?

FrontPage compares every word on your Web page to words in its own dictionary. If a word does not exist in the dictionary, the word is considered misspelled.

FrontPage will not find a correctly spelled word used in the wrong context, such as "My niece is **sit** years old." You should carefully reread your Web page to find this type of error.

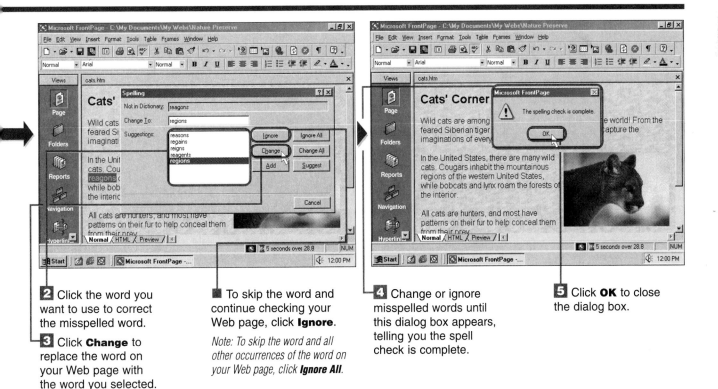

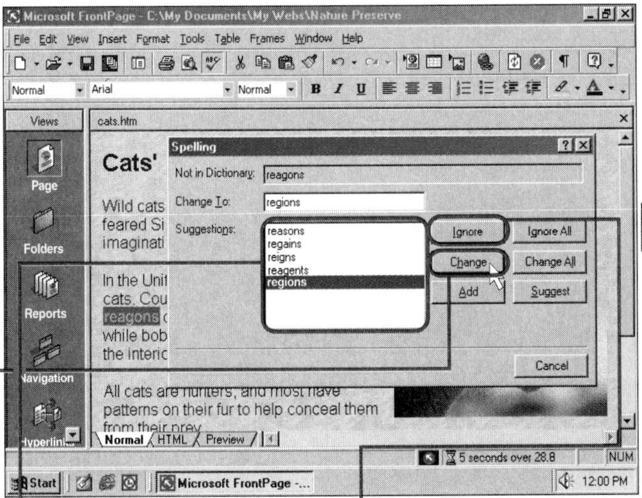

2 Click the word you want to use to correct the misspelled word.

3 Click **Change** to replace the word on your Web page with the word you selected.

■ To skip the word and continue checking your Web page, click **Ignore**.

*Note: To skip the word and all other occurrences of the word on your Web page, click **Ignore All**.*

4 Change or ignore misspelled words until this dialog box appears, telling you the spell check is complete.

5 Click **OK** to close the dialog box.

USING THE THESAURUS

You can use the thesaurus to replace a word on your Web page with a word that is more suitable.

USING THE THESAURUS

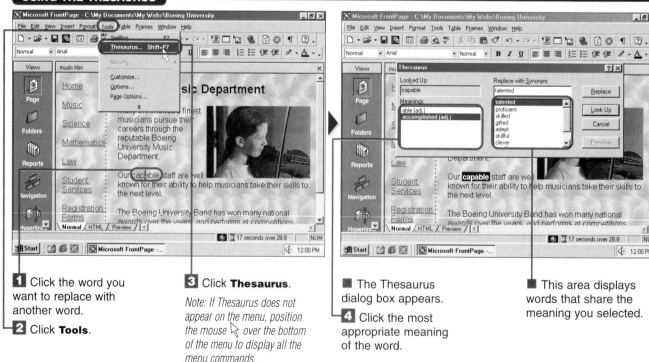

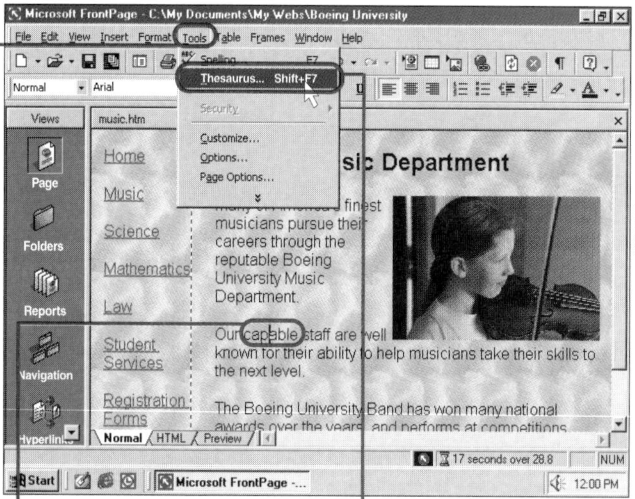

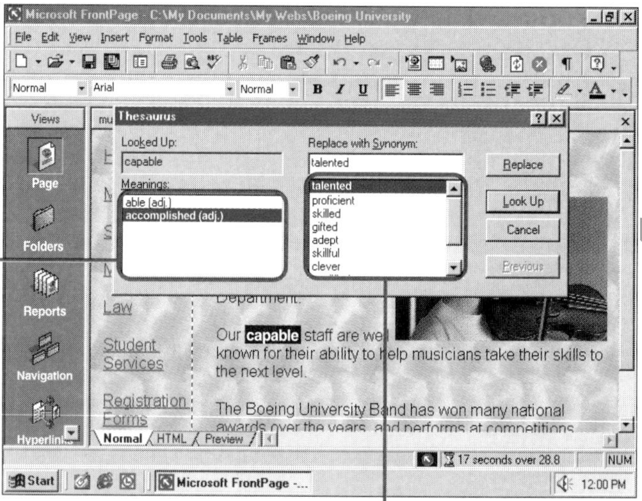

1 Click the word you want to replace with another word.

2 Click **Tools**.

3 Click **Thesaurus**.

Note: If Thesaurus does not appear on the menu, position the mouse over the bottom of the menu to display all the menu commands.

■ The Thesaurus dialog box appears.

4 Click the most appropriate meaning of the word.

■ This area displays words that share the meaning you selected.

?

How can the thesaurus help me?

Many people use the thesaurus to replace a word that appears repeatedly on a Web page. Replacing repeatedly used words can help add variety to your writing. Using the thesaurus included with FrontPage is faster and more convenient than searching through a printed thesaurus.

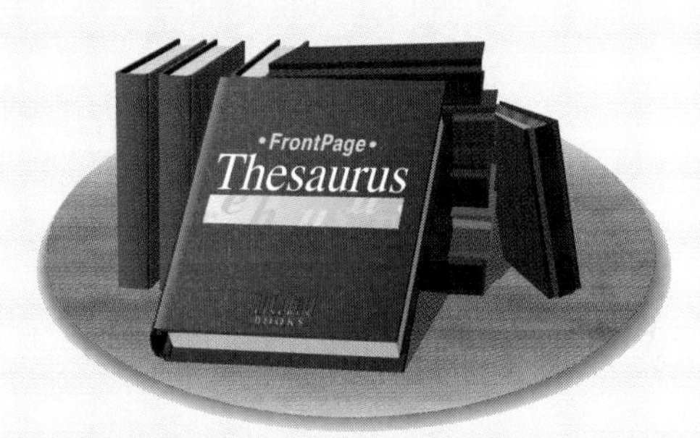

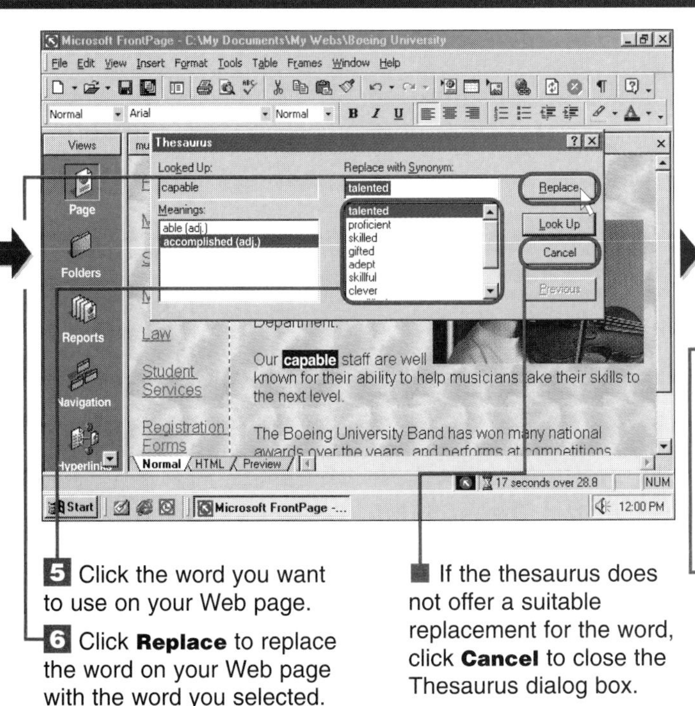

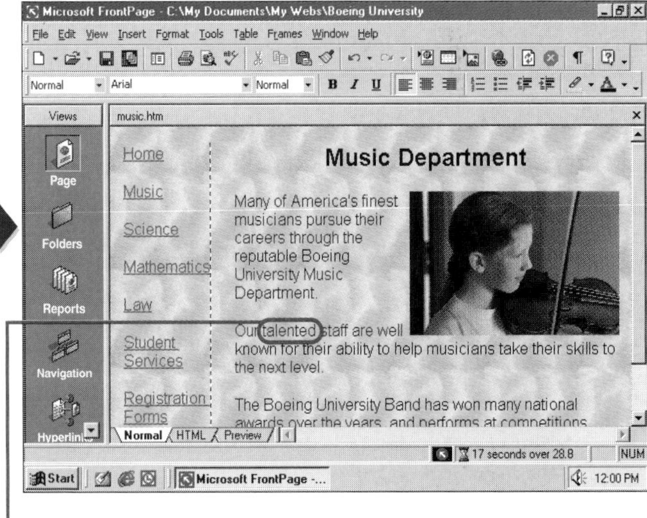

5 Click the word you want to use on your Web page.

6 Click **Replace** to replace the word on your Web page with the word you selected.

■ If the thesaurus does not offer a suitable replacement for the word, click **Cancel** to close the Thesaurus dialog box.

■ The word you selected replaces the word on your Web page.

■ To deselect text, click outside the selected area.

FIND AND REPLACE TEXT

You can find and replace every occurrence of a word or phrase on a Web page. This is useful if you have frequently misspelled a name.

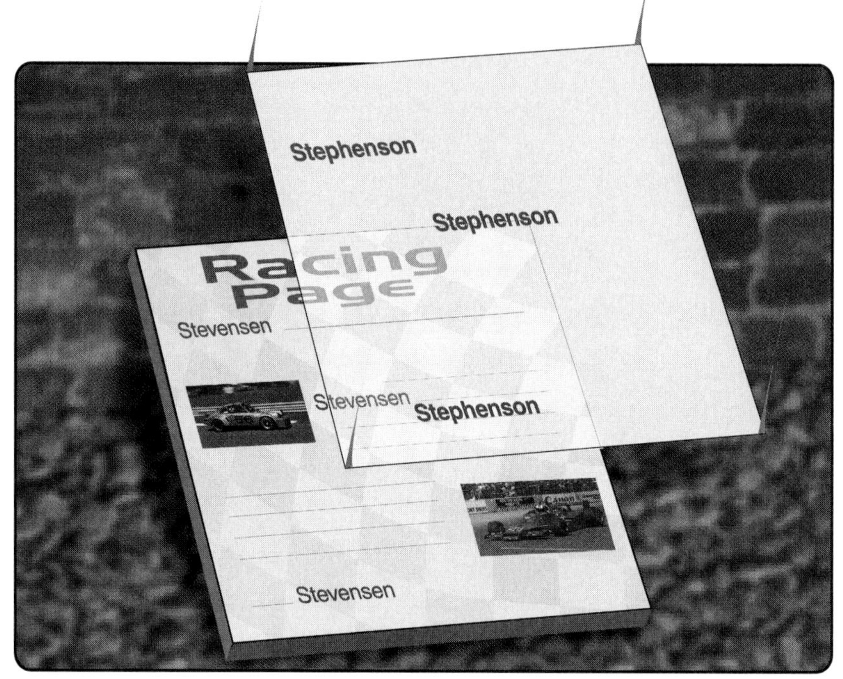

FIND AND REPLACE TEXT

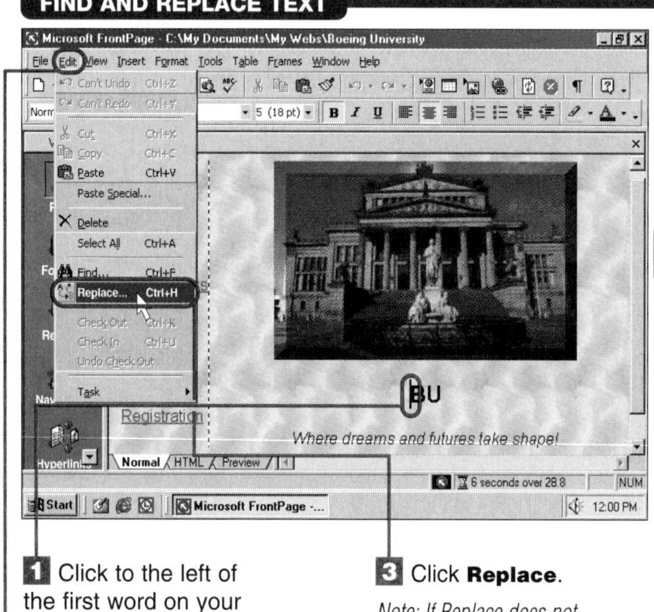

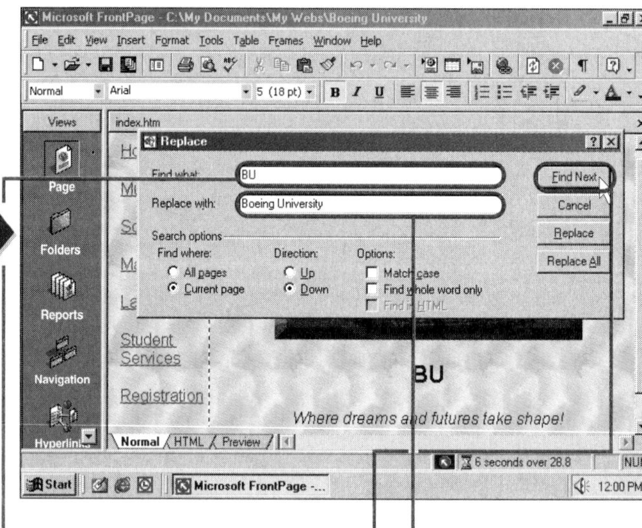

1 Click to the left of the first word on your Web page to search the entire page.

2 Click **Edit**.

3 Click **Replace**.

Note: If Replace does not appear on the menu, position the mouse over the bottom of the menu to display all the menu commands.

■ The Replace dialog box appears.

4 Type the text you want to find.

5 Click this area and type the text you want to replace the text that FrontPage finds.

6 Click **Find Next** to start the search.

Can I use the Replace feature to quickly enter text?

The Replace feature is useful when you have to type a long word or phrase, such as University of Massachusetts, many times on a Web page.

You can type a short form of the word or phrase, such as UM, throughout your Web page and then have FrontPage replace the short form with the full word or phrase.

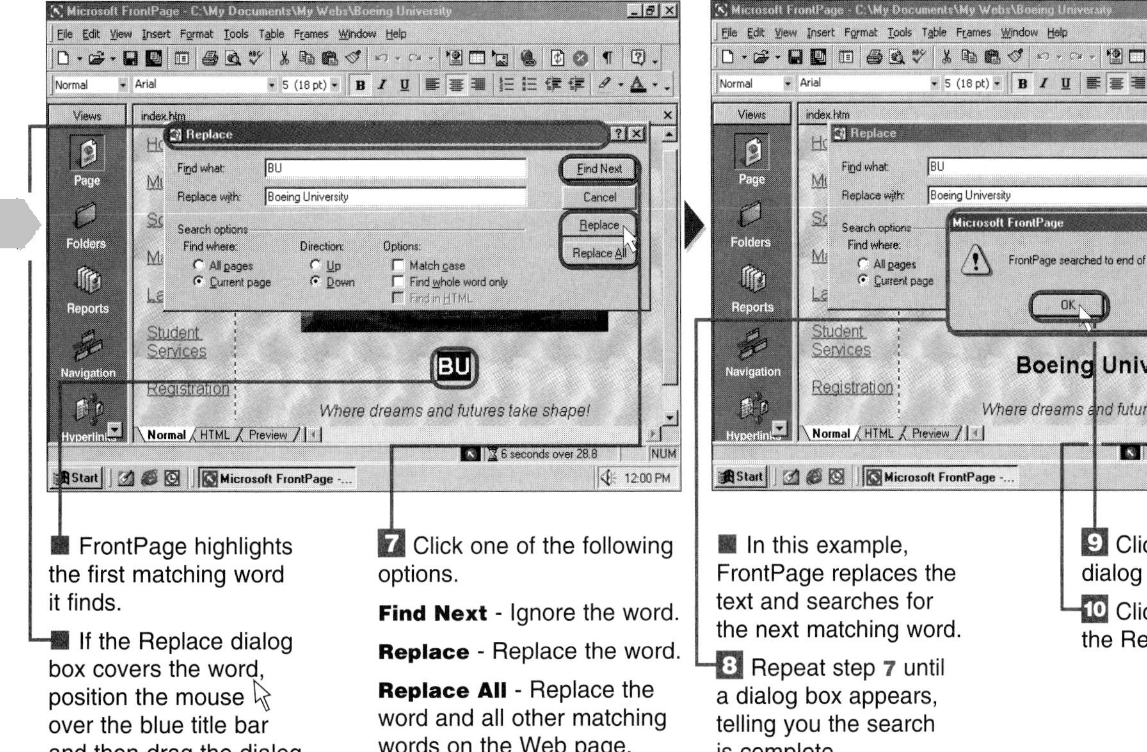

■ FrontPage highlights the first matching word it finds.

■ If the Replace dialog box covers the word, position the mouse over the blue title bar and then drag the dialog box to a new location.

7 Click one of the following options.

Find Next - Ignore the word.

Replace - Replace the word.

Replace All - Replace the word and all other matching words on the Web page.

■ In this example, FrontPage replaces the text and searches for the next matching word.

8 Repeat step **7** until a dialog box appears, telling you the search is complete.

9 Click **OK** to close the dialog box.

10 Click **Cancel** to close the Replace dialog box.

Sunshine VACATIONS
Reservations
Schedules
HEADING 1
About Sunshine Vacations
At Sunshine Vacations, we make all your vacations memorable ones. Call us today to plan your next trip!
TEXT

CHAPTER 5

Format Web Pages

Do you want to change the appearance of text on your Web pages? This chapter will show you how to change the size and color of text, create lists, apply a theme and much more.

BOLD, ITALICIZE OR UNDERLINE TEXT

You can bold, italicize or underline text to emphasize information on your Web page.

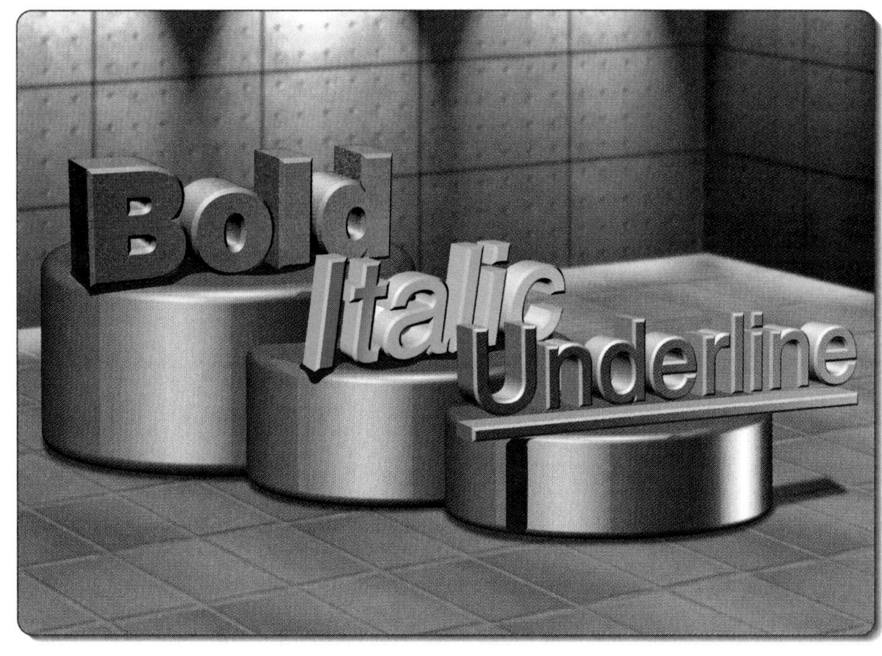

Be careful when underlining text, since readers may think the text is a link. For information on links, see pages 132 to 149.

BOLD, ITALICIZE OR UNDERLINE TEXT

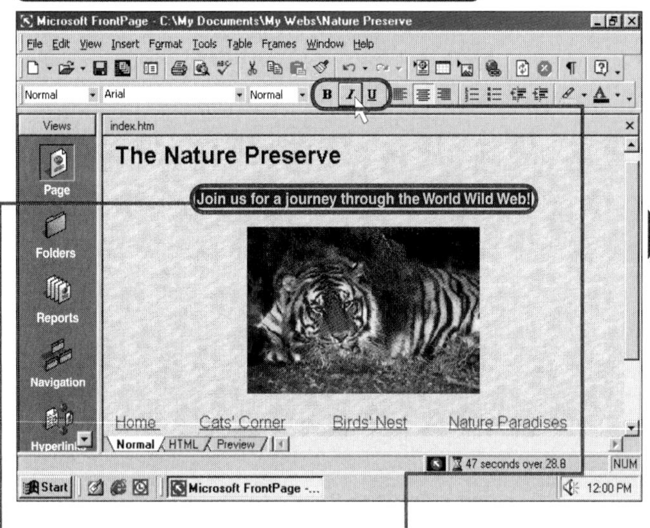

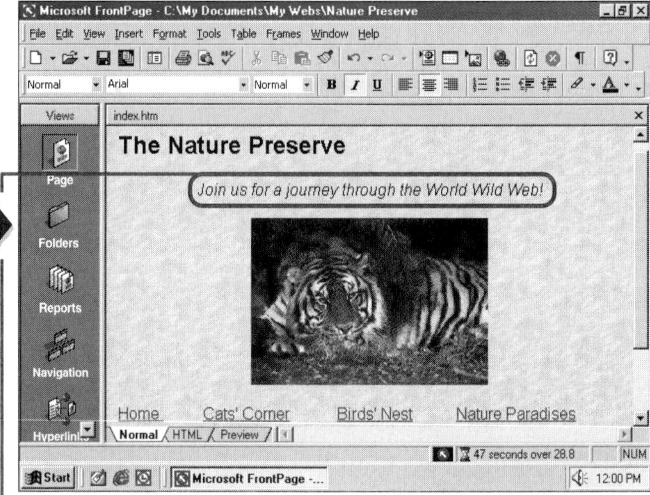

1 Select the text you want to change to a new style. To select text, see page 54.

2 Click one of the following options.

- **B** Bold
- *I* Italic
- U Underline

■ The text you selected appears in the new style.

■ To deselect text, click outside the selected area.

■ To remove a bold, italic or underline style, repeat steps **1** and **2**.

CHANGE ALIGNMENT OF TEXT

You can enhance the appearance of your Web page by aligning text in different ways.

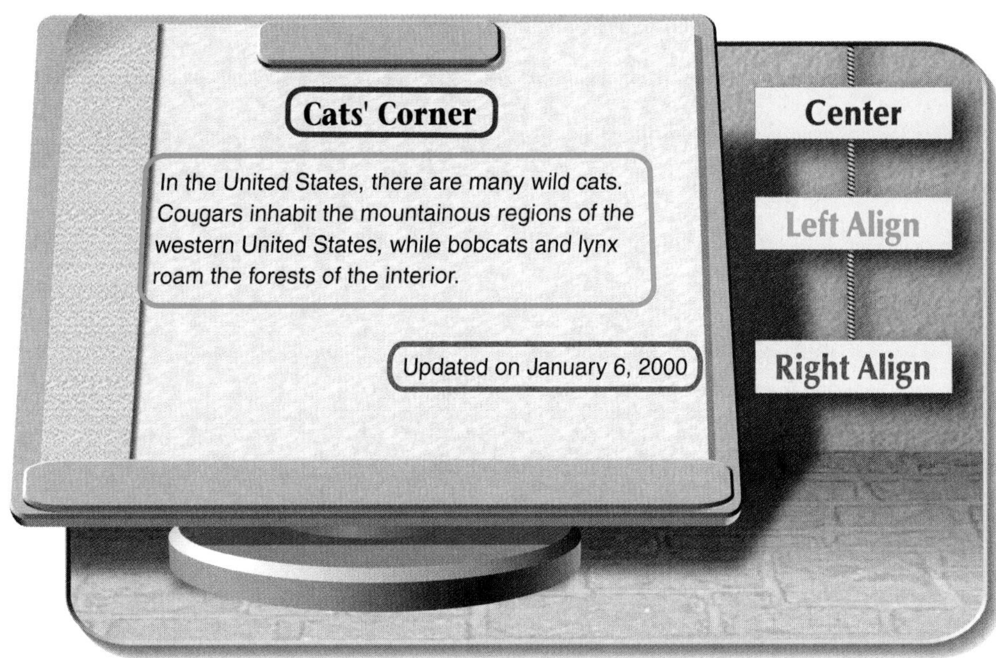

CHANGE ALIGNMENT OF TEXT

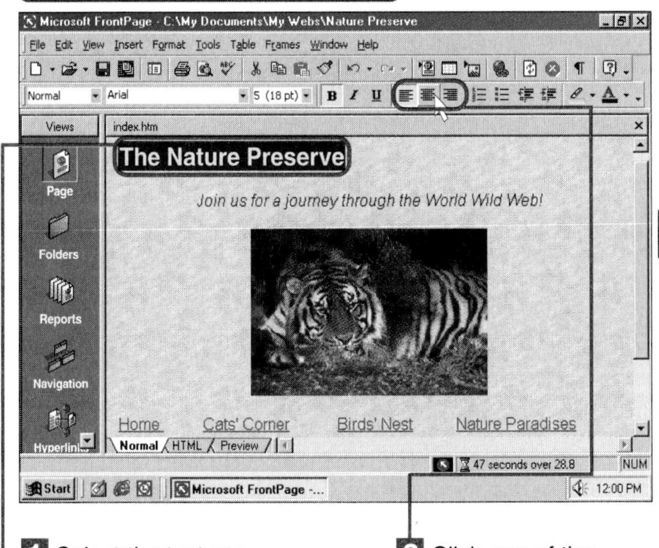

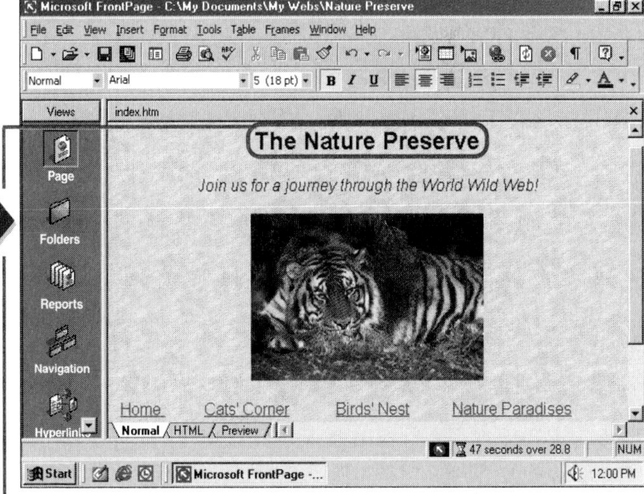

1 Select the text you want to align differently. To select text, see page 54.

2 Click one of the following options.

- Left align
- Center
- Right align

■ The text appears in the new alignment.

■ To deselect text, click outside the selected area.

CHANGE FONT OF TEXT

You can change the font of text to enhance the appearance of your Web page.

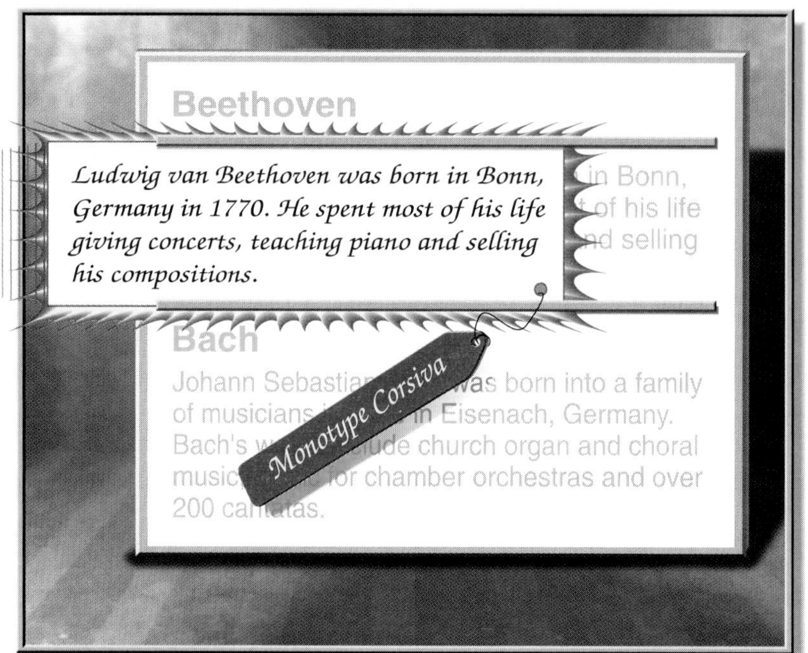

You should choose common fonts for your Web page, such as Arial or Times New Roman. If a font you choose is not available on a reader's computer, the Web browser will use a different font and your text may not appear the way you expected.

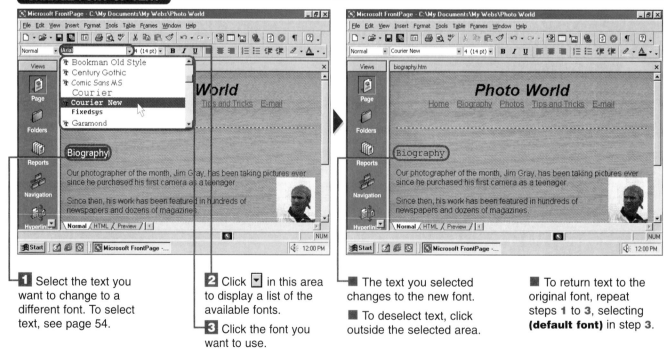

CHANGE FONT OF TEXT

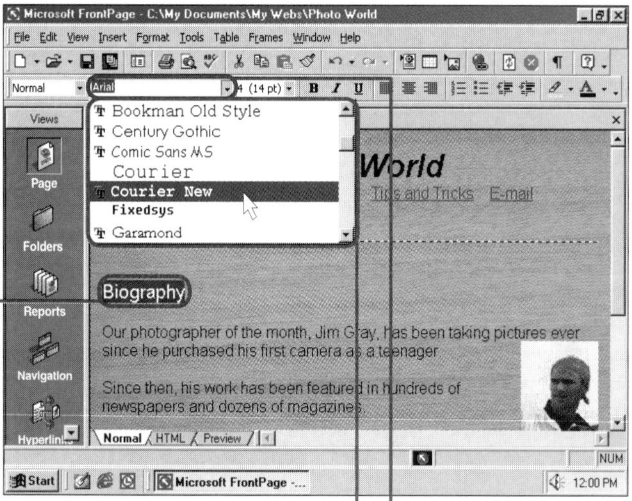

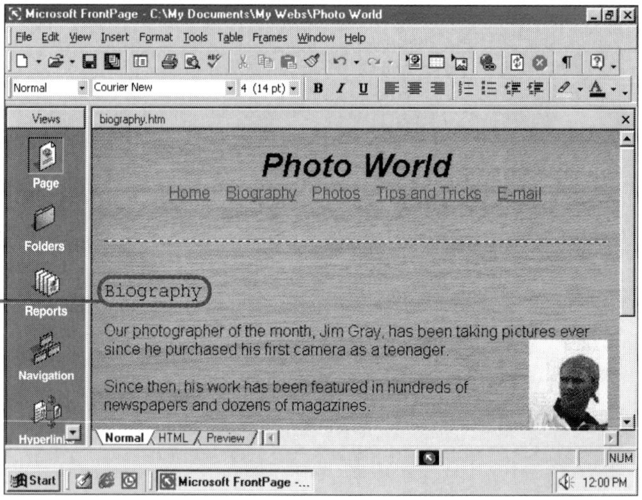

1 Select the text you want to change to a different font. To select text, see page 54.

2 Click ▾ in this area to display a list of the available fonts.

3 Click the font you want to use.

■ The text you selected changes to the new font.

■ To deselect text, click outside the selected area.

■ To return text to the original font, repeat steps **1** to **3**, selecting **(default font)** in step **3**.

CHANGE SIZE OF TEXT

You can increase or decrease the size of text on your Web page.

Larger text is easier to read, but smaller text allows you to fit more information on a screen.

CHANGE SIZE OF TEXT

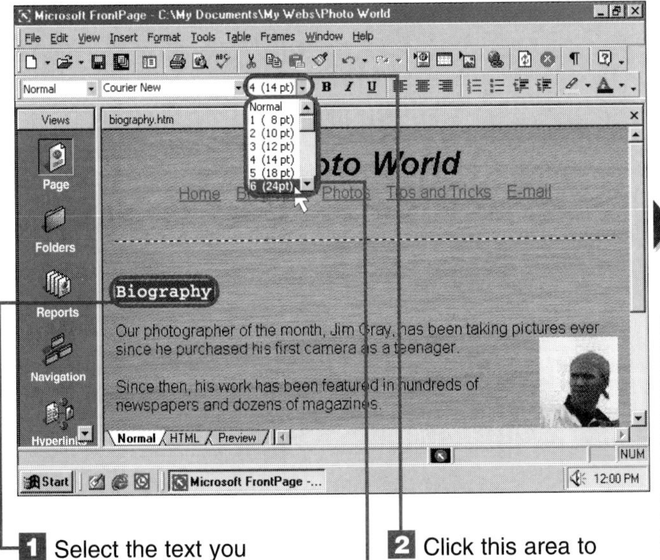

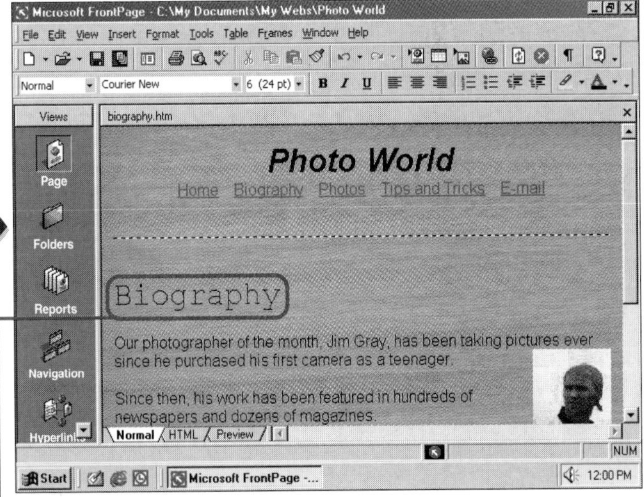

1 Select the text you want to change to a new size. To select text, see page 54.

2 Click this area to display a list of the available sizes.

3 Click the size you want to use.

■ The text you selected changes to the new size.

■ To deselect text, click outside the selected area.

■ To return text to the original size, repeat steps **1** to **3**, selecting **Normal** in step **3**.

CHANGE COLOR OF TEXT

You can change the color of text to draw attention to headings or important information on your Web page.

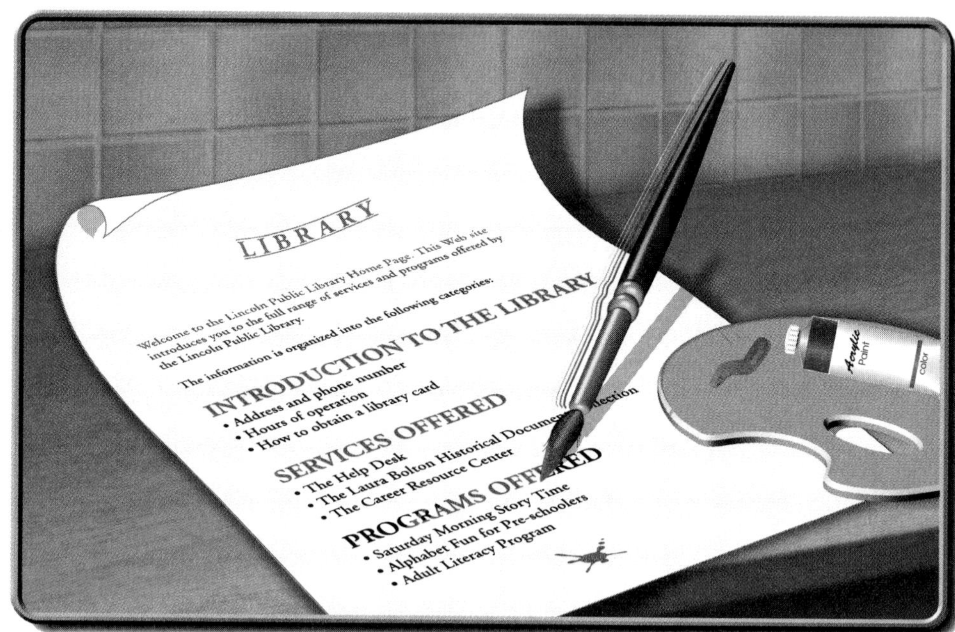

CHANGE COLOR OF TEXT

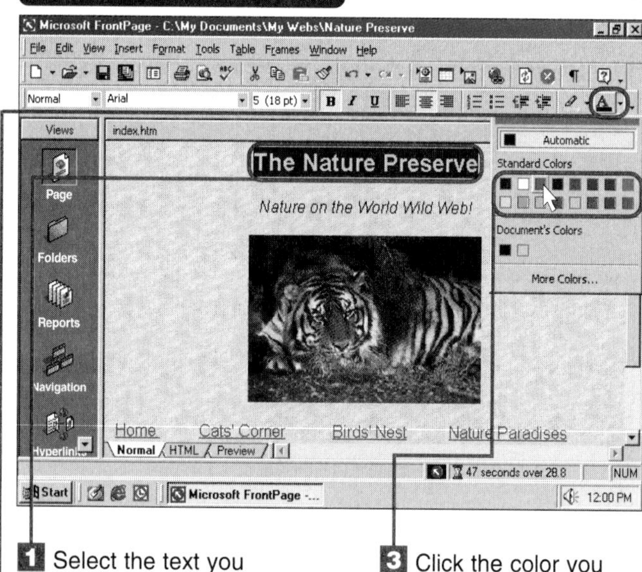

1 Select the text you want to change to a different color. To select text, see page 54.

2 Click ▾ in this area to display the available colors.

3 Click the color you want to use.

■ The text appears in the color you selected.

■ To deselect text, click outside the selected area.

■ To return text to its original color, repeat steps **1** to **3**, selecting **Automatic** in step **3**.

HIGHLIGHT TEXT

You can highlight text you want to stand out on your Web page.

Highlighting text is also useful for marking information you want to review or verify later.

HIGHLIGHT TEXT

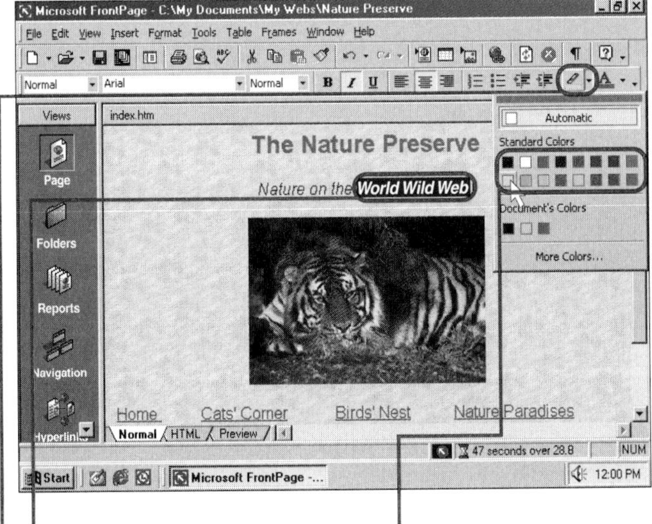

1 Select the text you want to highlight. To select text, see page 54.

2 Click ▾ in this area to display the available highlight colors.

3 Click the highlight color you want to use.

■ The text appears highlighted in the color you selected.

■ To deselect text, click outside the selected area.

■ To remove a highlight, repeat steps **1** to **3**, selecting **Automatic** in step **3**.

CHANGE STYLE OF TEXT

You can change the style of text on your Web page. FrontPage offers many styles that you can choose from.

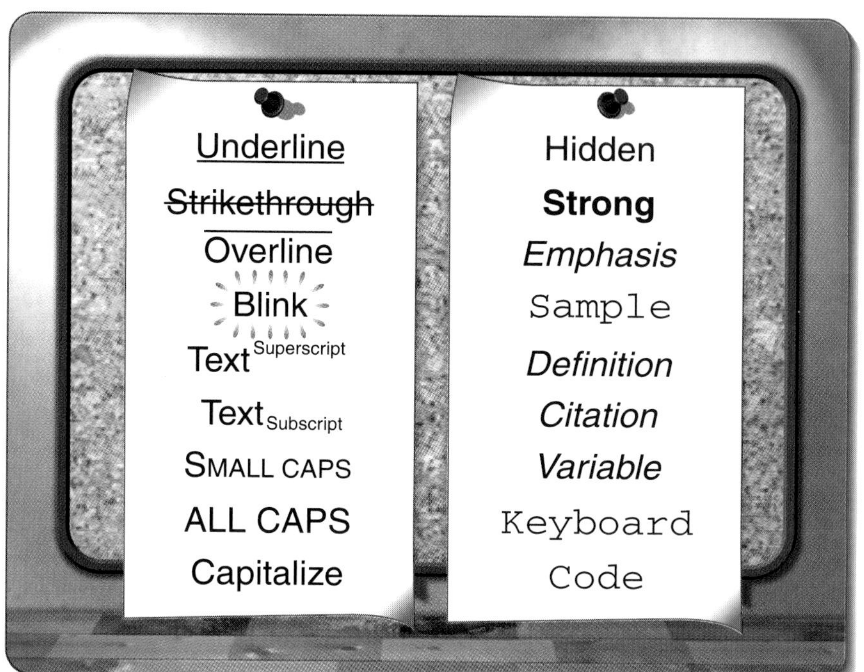

CHANGE STYLE OF TEXT

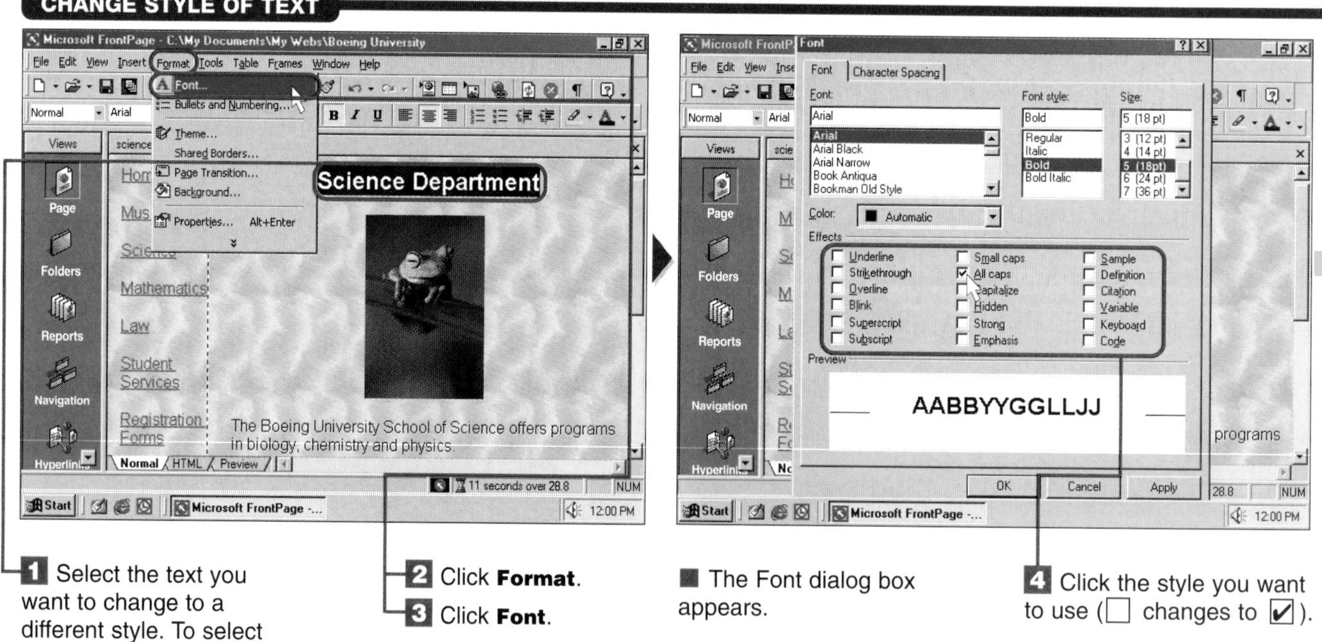

1 Select the text you want to change to a different style. To select text, see page 54.

2 Click **Format**.

3 Click **Font**.

■ The Font dialog box appears.

4 Click the style you want to use (☐ changes to ☑).

?

What should I consider when changing the style of text on my Web page?

Here are some factors you should consider before changing the style of text on your Web page.

Underline

Try to avoid using this style since readers may think the text is a link.

Strikethrough

This style places a line through text. Companies often use this style to strike out old prices to show that new prices are lower.

Blink

This style blinks text on and off. Many readers may find this style distracting. The Internet Explorer Web browser cannot display blinking text.

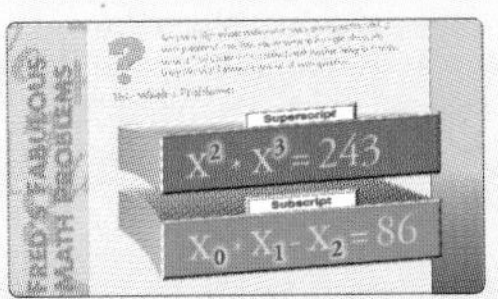

Superscript and Subscript

These styles place text or numbers slightly above or below text on a Web page. These styles are useful for displaying mathematical equations.

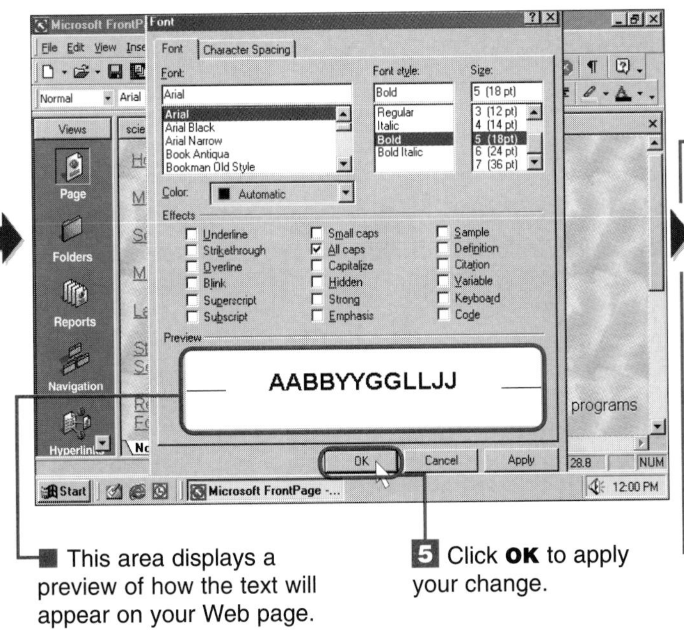

■ This area displays a preview of how the text will appear on your Web page.

5 Click **OK** to apply your change.

■ The text you selected displays the change.

■ To deselect text, click outside the selected area.

■ To return the text to its original appearance, repeat steps **1** to **5** (☑ changes to ☐ in step **4**).

ADD A HEADING

You can use headings to help organize the information on your Web page.

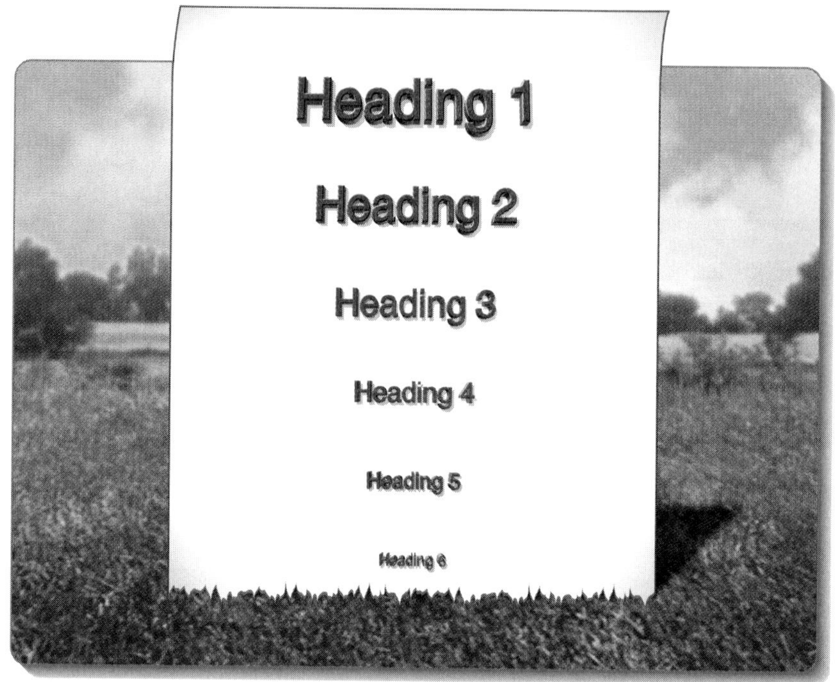

There are six heading sizes you can use.

ADD A HEADING

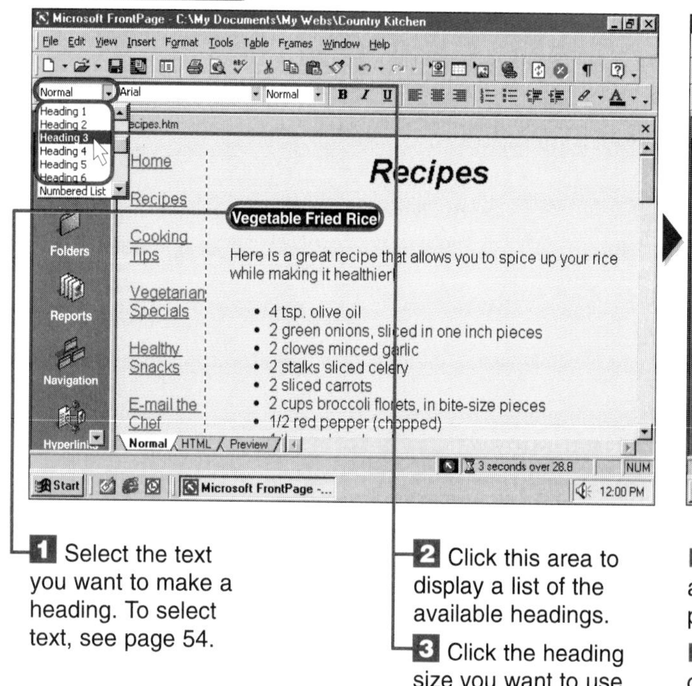

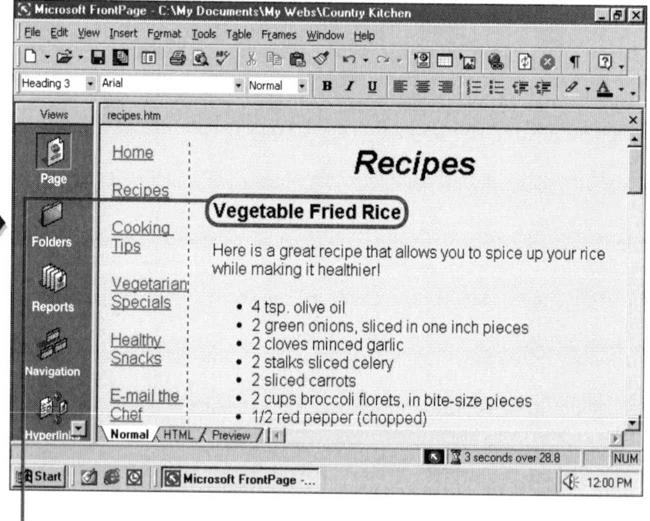

1 Select the text you want to make a heading. To select text, see page 54.

2 Click this area to display a list of the available headings.

3 Click the heading size you want to use.

■ The text appears as a heading on your Web page.

■ To deselect text, click outside the selected area.

■ To remove the heading formatting from text, repeat steps **1** to **3**, selecting **Normal** in step **3**.

HEADING CONSIDERATIONS

PROVIDE AN OUTLINE

You can use headings to provide an outline of the Web page for your readers. By scanning the headings, a reader should get a general overview of the information covered on the Web page and be able to quickly locate topics of interest.

USE HEADINGS CONSISTENTLY

Make sure you use headings consistently on a Web page to help readers understand the relative importance of information. Use the same heading size for all headings of equal importance.

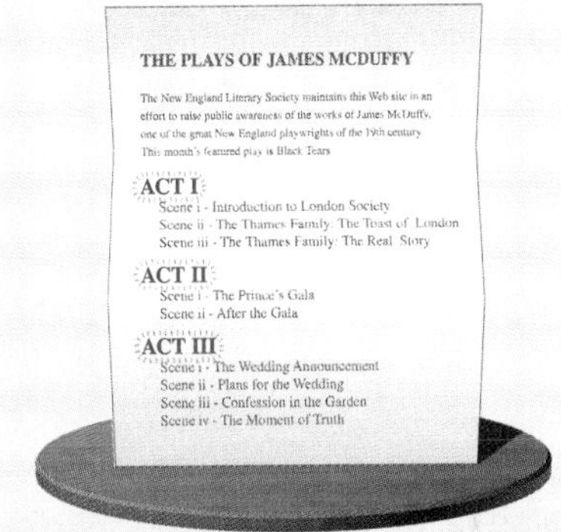

PROPER USE OF HEADINGS

Use headings to signify the importance of information on your Web page. Do not use headings to add a certain look or style to text. Since different Web browsers display headings in slightly different ways, you cannot predict exactly how a heading will look to readers.

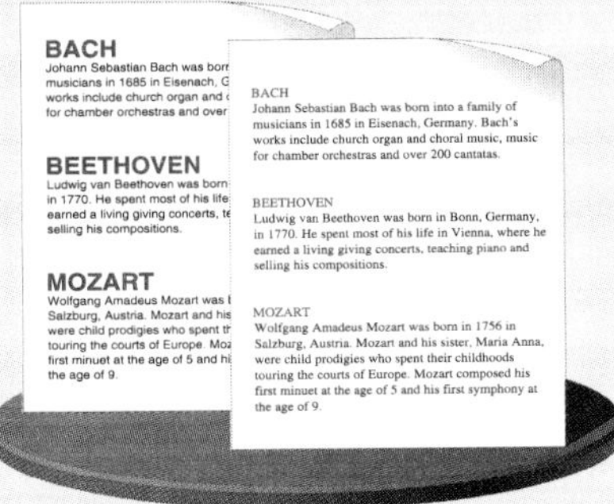

SUBHEADINGS

When creating subheadings, do not skip heading sizes. For example, a size 2 heading should be followed by a size 3 subheading.

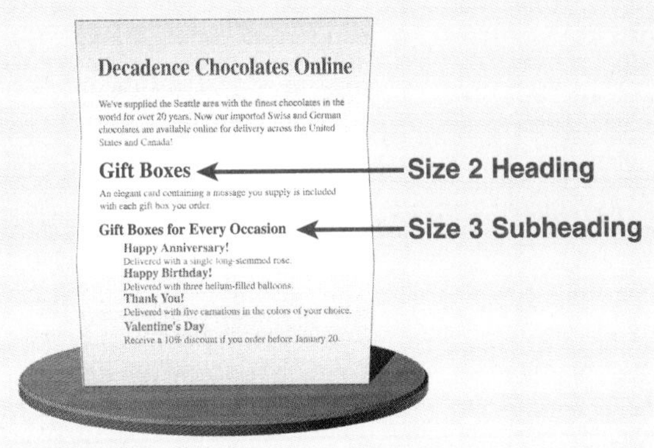

COPY FORMATTING

You can make one area of text on your Web page look exactly like another.

COPY FORMATTING

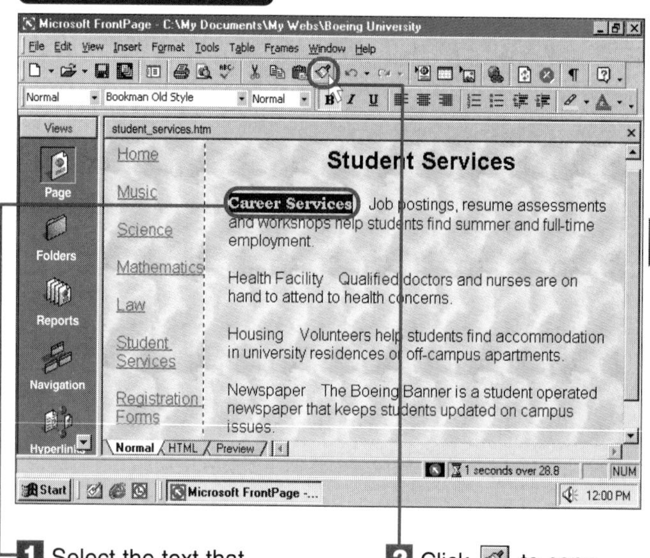

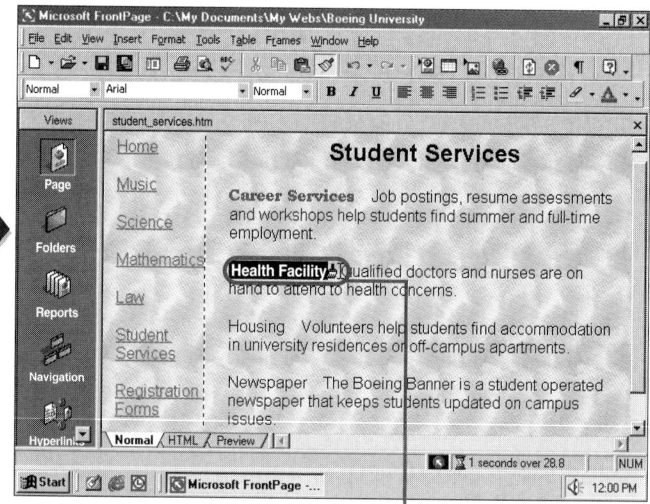

1 Select the text that displays the formatting you want to copy. To select text, see page 54.

2 Click the Format Painter button to copy the formatting.

■ The mouse pointer changes to the Format Painter pointer when over your Web page.

3 Select the text you want to display the same formatting.

Why would I want to copy the formatting of text?

You may want to copy the formatting of text to make all the headings or important words on your Web page look the same. This will give your Web page a consistent appearance.

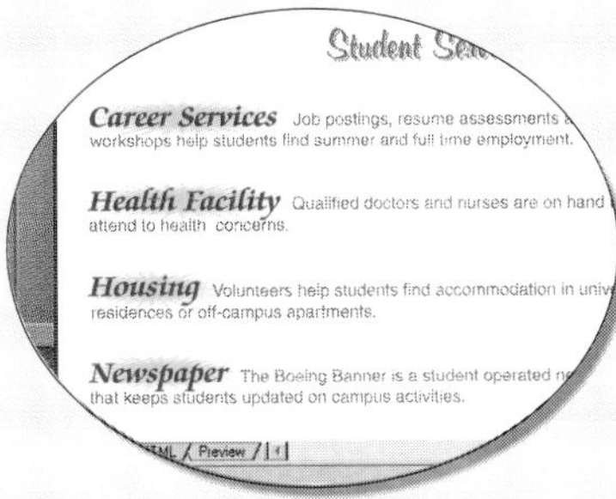

Can I copy the formatting of a link?

You can copy the formatting of a link to another word or phrase on your Web page. The text you copy the formatting to will link to the same destination as the original text.

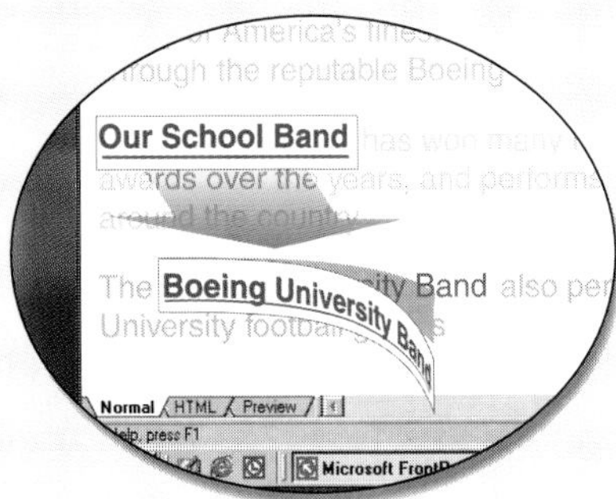

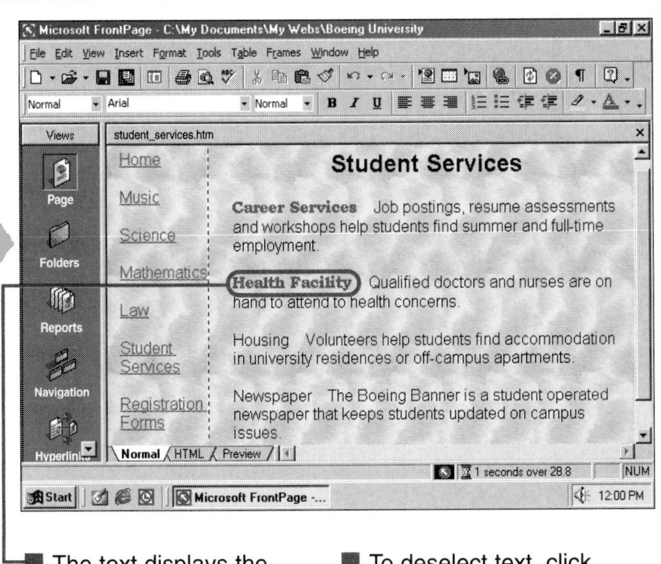

■ The text displays the same formatting.

■ To deselect text, click outside the selected area.

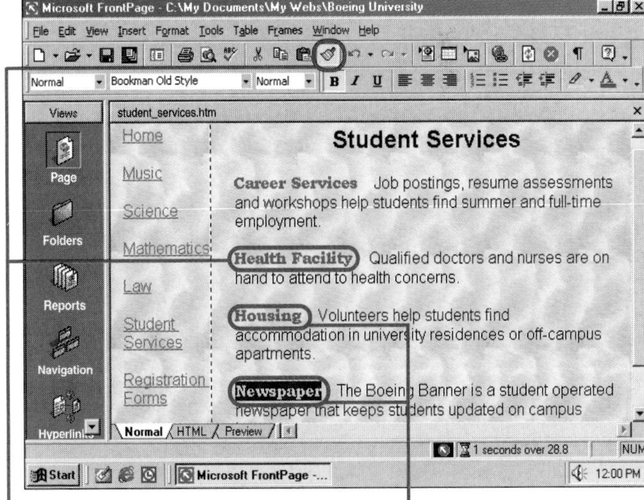

COPY FORMATTING TO SEVERAL AREAS

1 Select the text that displays the formatting you want to copy. To select text, see page 54.

2 Double-click to copy the formatting.

3 Select each area of text you want to display the same formatting.

4 When you finish selecting each area of text, press the Esc key.

INDENT TEXT

You can indent text to make paragraphs on your Web page stand out.

INDENT TEXT

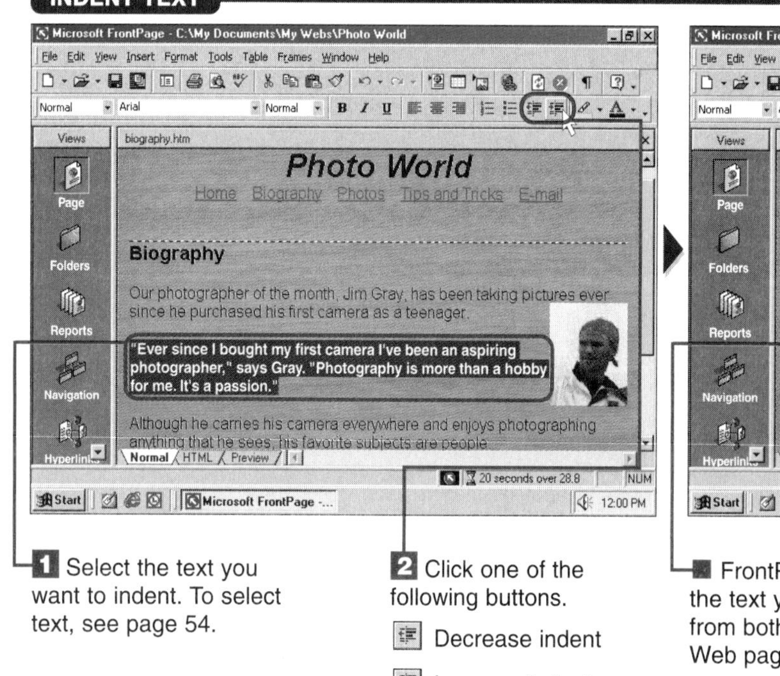

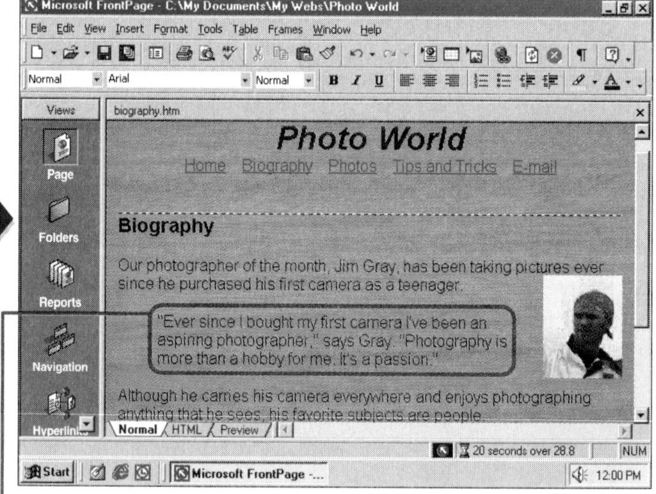

1 Select the text you want to indent. To select text, see page 54.

2 Click one of the following buttons.

- Decrease indent
- Increase indent

■ FrontPage indents the text you selected from both sides of the Web page.

■ You can repeat step **2** to further indent the text.

■ To deselect text, click outside the selected area.

CREATE A DEFINITION LIST

You can create a definition list to display terms and their definitions. This type of list is ideal for a glossary.

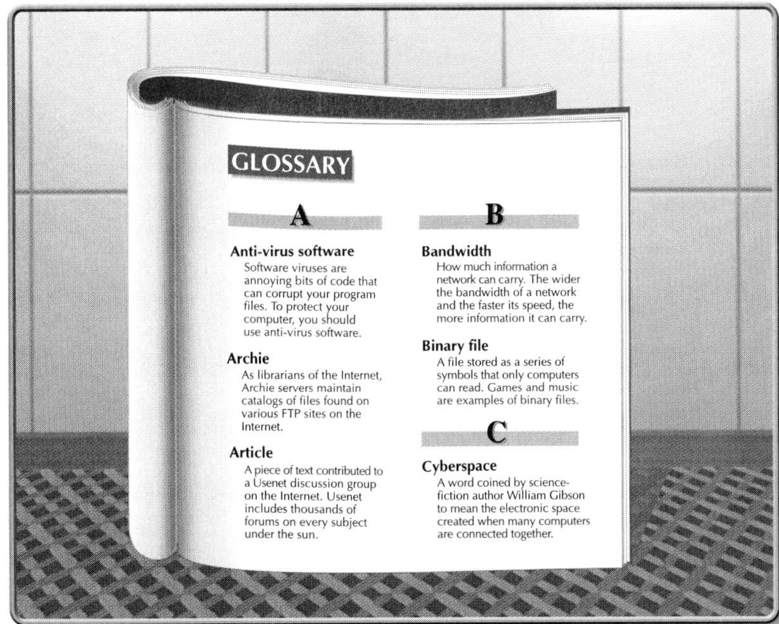

CREATE A DEFINITION LIST

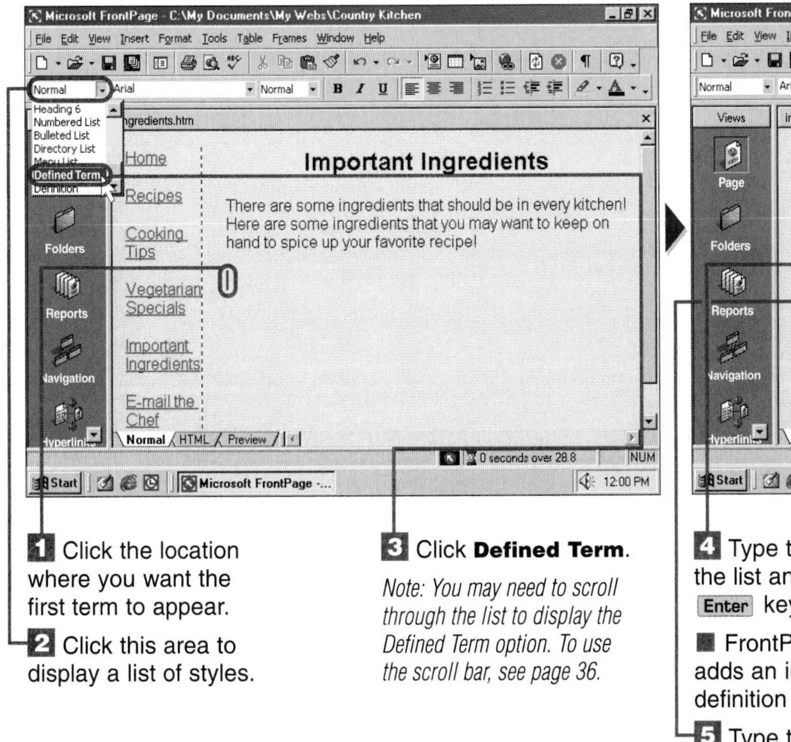

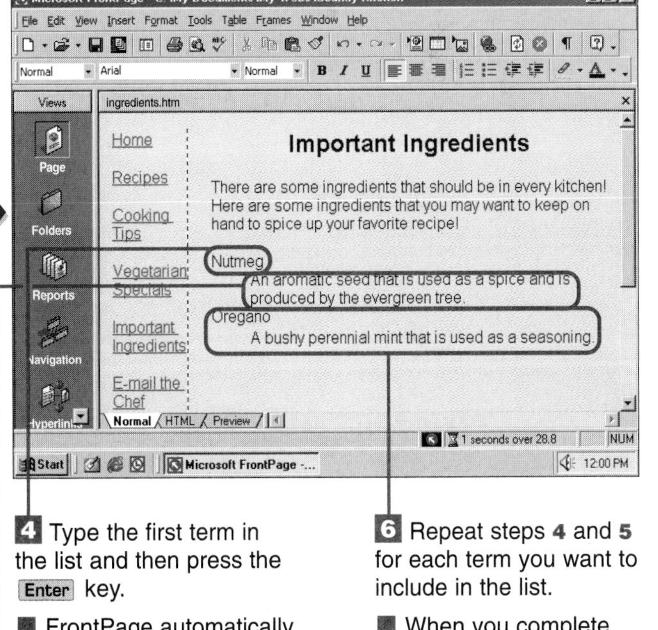

1 Click the location where you want the first term to appear.

2 Click this area to display a list of styles.

3 Click **Defined Term**.

Note: You may need to scroll through the list to display the Defined Term option. To use the scroll bar, see page 36.

4 Type the first term in the list and then press the Enter key.

■ FrontPage automatically adds an indent for the definition of the term.

5 Type the definition of the term and then press the Enter key.

6 Repeat steps **4** and **5** for each term you want to include in the list.

■ When you complete the list, press the Enter key twice.

CREATE A BULLETED OR NUMBERED LIST

You can separate items in a list by beginning each item with a bullet or number.

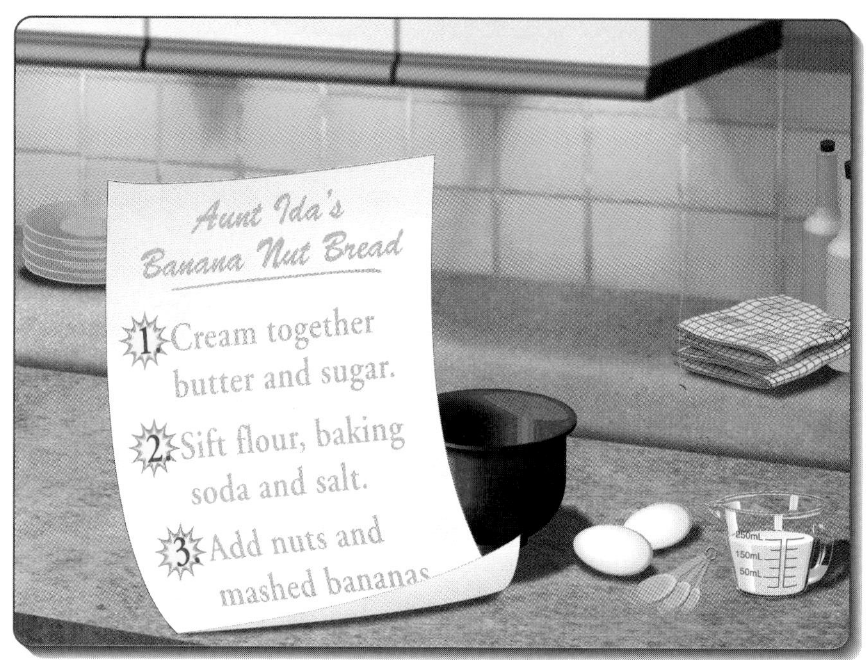

CREATE A BULLETED OR NUMBERED LIST

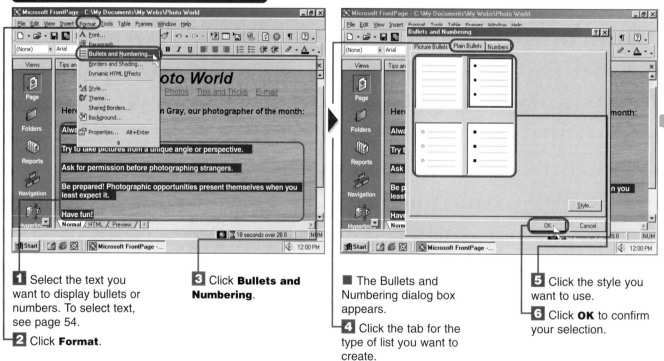

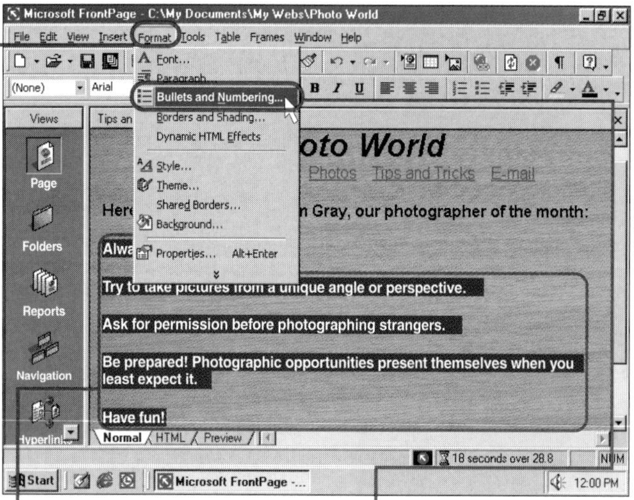

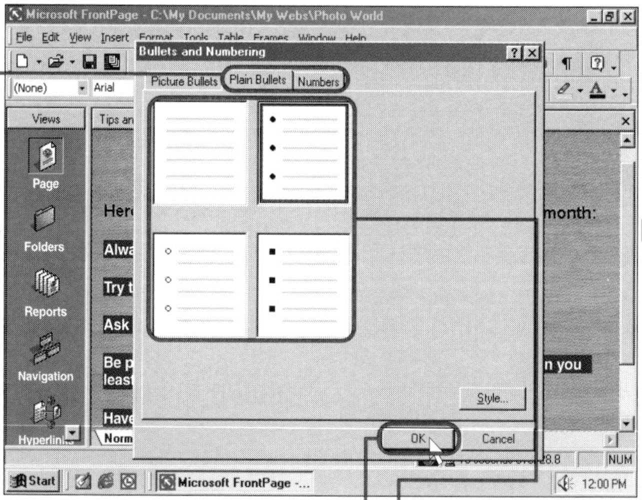

1 Select the text you want to display bullets or numbers. To select text, see page 54.

2 Click **Format**.

3 Click **Bullets and Numbering**.

■ The Bullets and Numbering dialog box appears.

4 Click the tab for the type of list you want to create.

5 Click the style you want to use.

6 Click **OK** to confirm your selection.

What type of list should I create?

Bulleted List

Bulleted lists are useful for items in no particular order, such as a list of products or Web pages. Bulleted lists are also known as unordered lists.

Numbered List

Numbered lists are useful for items in a specific order, such as a set of instructions or a table of contents. Numbered lists are also known as ordered lists.

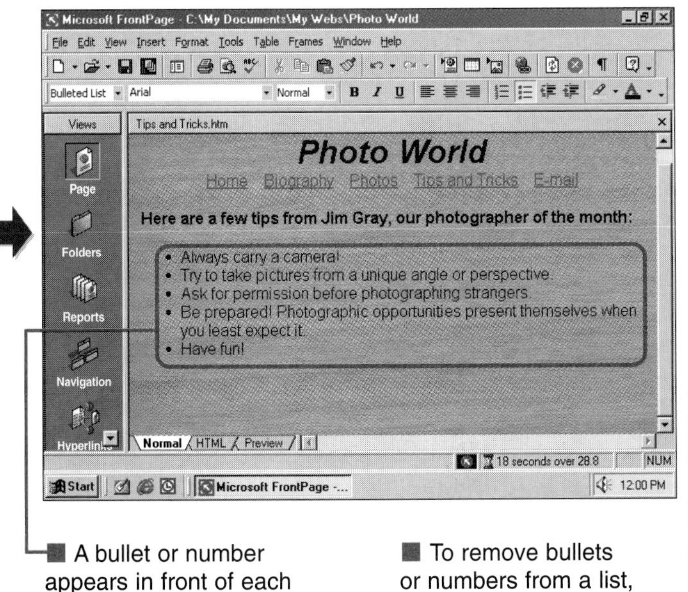

■ A bullet or number appears in front of each item in the list.

■ To deselect text, click outside the selected area.

■ To remove bullets or numbers from a list, repeat steps **1** to **6**, selecting the top left style in step **5**.

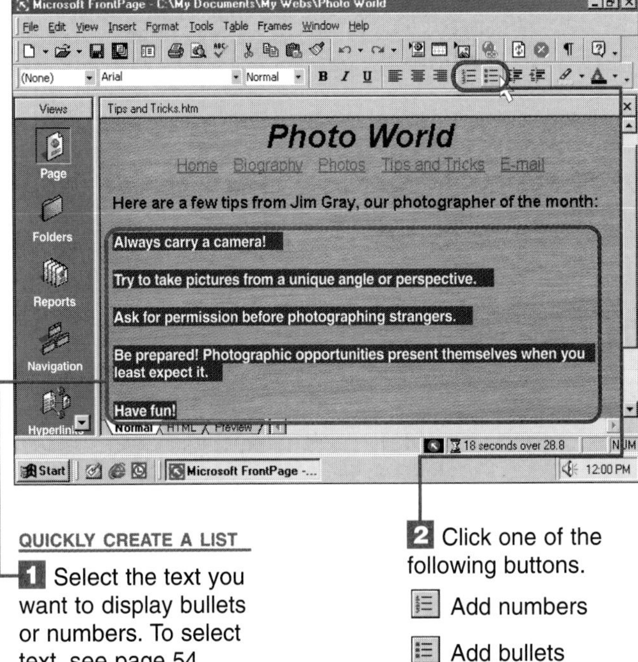

QUICKLY CREATE A LIST

1 Select the text you want to display bullets or numbers. To select text, see page 54.

2 Click one of the following buttons.

- Add numbers
- Add bullets

CREATE A LIST WITH PICTURE BULLETS

You can create an eye-catching list that uses images as bullets on your Web page.

CREATE A LIST WITH PICTURE BULLETS

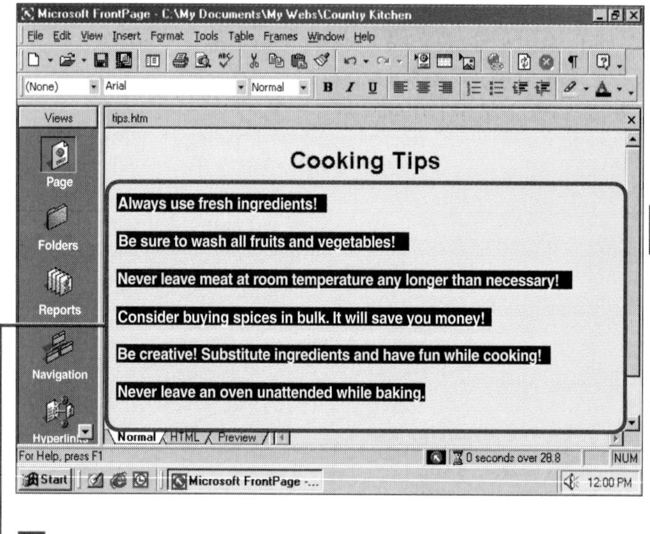

1 Select the text you want to display picture bullets. To select text, see page 54.

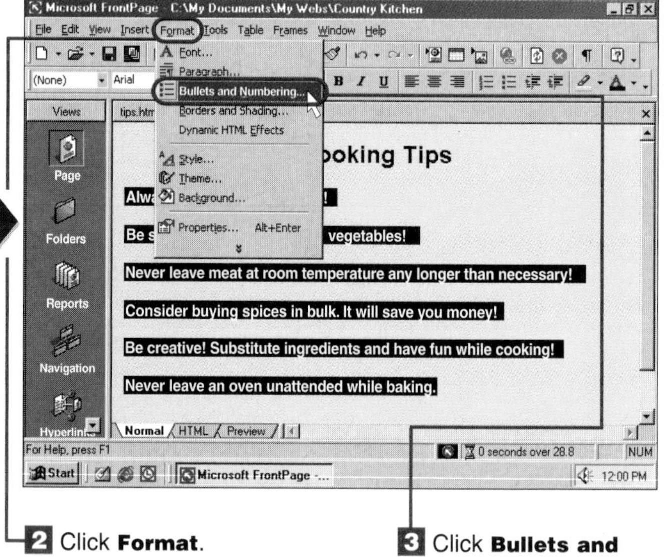

2 Click **Format**.

3 Click **Bullets and Numbering**.

Where can I find images that I can use as bullets in a list?

Many Web sites offer images that you can use as bullets in a list. You can find images you can use as bullets at the following Web sites.

www.grapholina.com/Graphics

www.theshockzone.com

www.abcgiant.com

Is there a faster way to add picture bullets to a list?

When you apply a theme to a Web page, FrontPage will automatically add picture bullets to bulleted lists you create. To create a bulleted list, see page 86. To apply a theme to a Web page, see page 94.

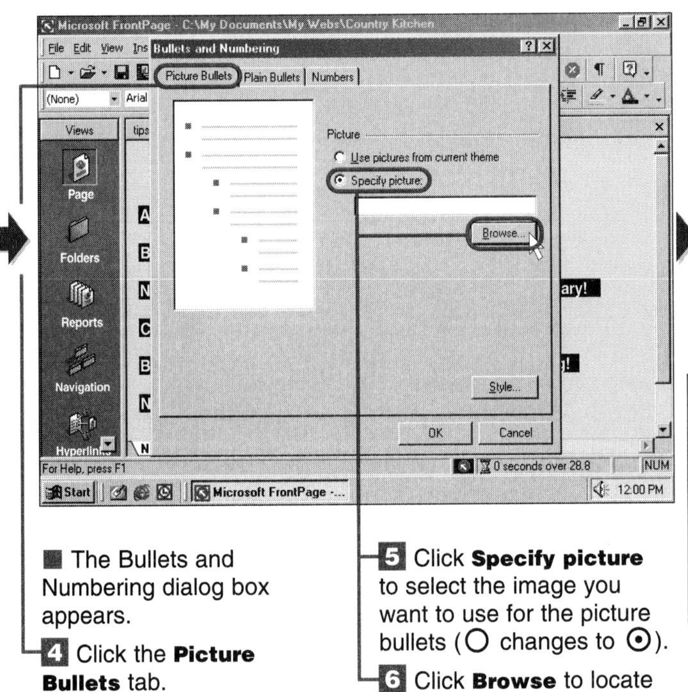

■ The Bullets and Numbering dialog box appears.

4 Click the **Picture Bullets** tab.

5 Click **Specify picture** to select the image you want to use for the picture bullets (○ changes to ⊙).

6 Click **Browse** to locate the image on your computer.

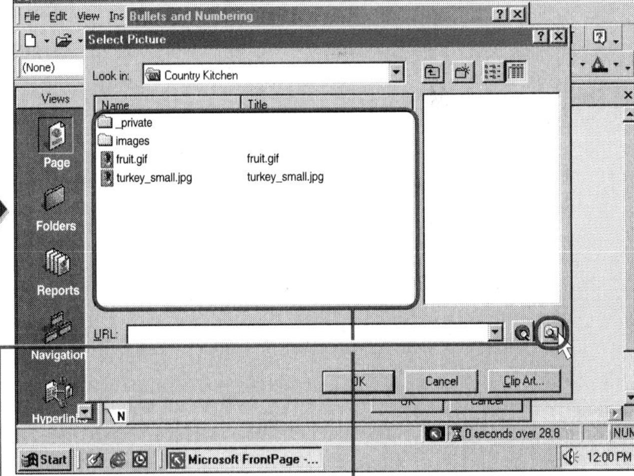

■ The Select Picture dialog box appears.

7 Click the select file button to locate the image on your computer that you want to use.

■ This area displays images you have previously added to your Web site. To use one of these images for the picture bullets, click the image and then press the Enter key. Then skip to step **10**.

CONTINUED

CREATE A LIST WITH PICTURE BULLETS

When creating a list with picture bullets, you should use a small image for the bullets.

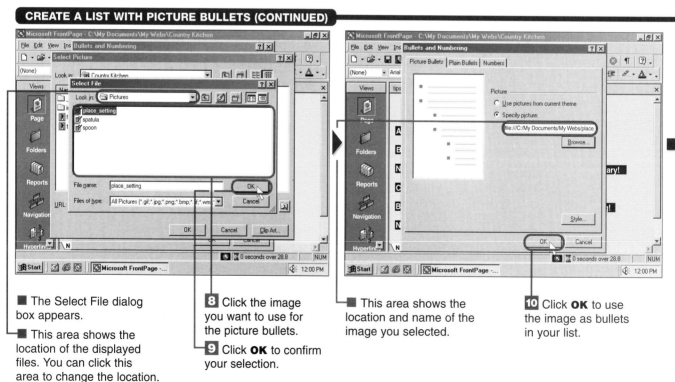

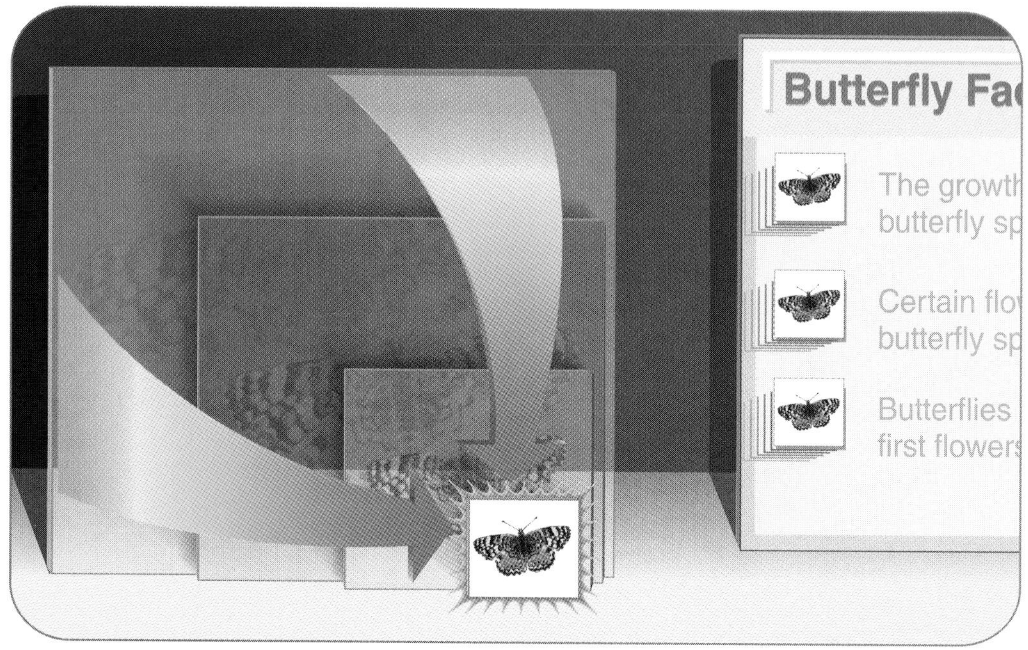

CREATE A LIST WITH PICTURE BULLETS (CONTINUED)

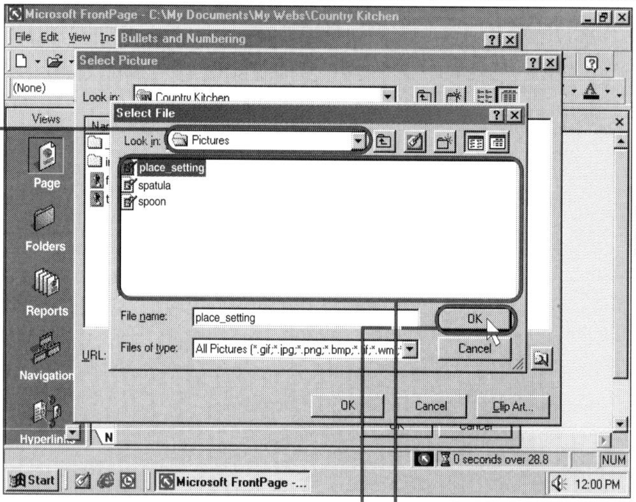

■ The Select File dialog box appears.

■ This area shows the location of the displayed files. You can click this area to change the location.

8 Click the image you want to use for the picture bullets.

9 Click **OK** to confirm your selection.

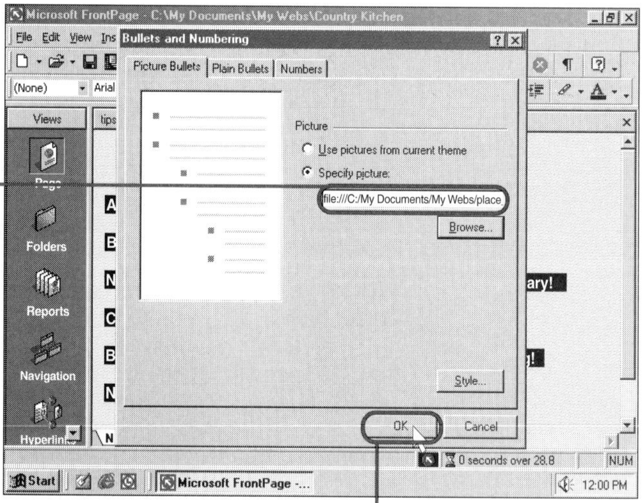

■ This area shows the location and name of the image you selected.

10 Click **OK** to use the image as bullets in your list.

?

After I create a list with picture bullets, can I add a new item to the list?

You can add a new item to a list by performing the following steps.

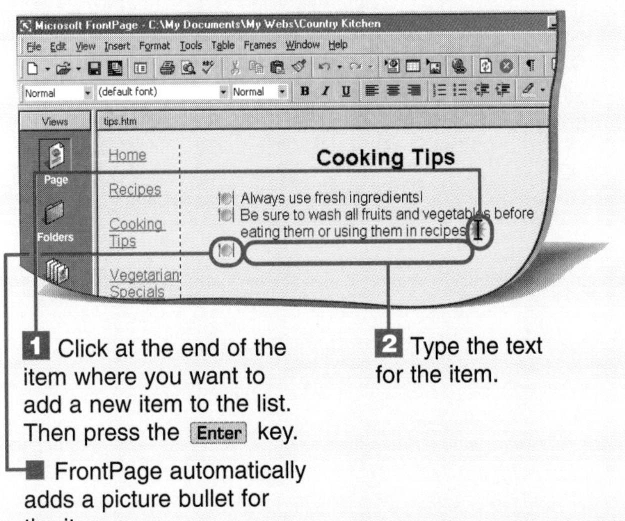

1 Click at the end of the item where you want to add a new item to the list. Then press the Enter key.

■ FrontPage automatically adds a picture bullet for the item.

2 Type the text for the item.

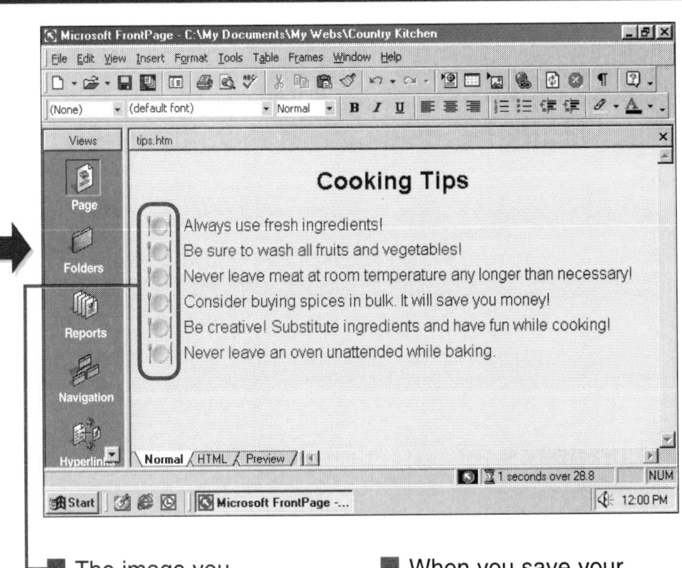

■ The image you specified appears in front of each item in the list.

■ To deselect the text in the list, click outside the selected area.

■ When you save your Web page, FrontPage will ask you to save the image as part of your Web site. To save a Web page, see page 28.

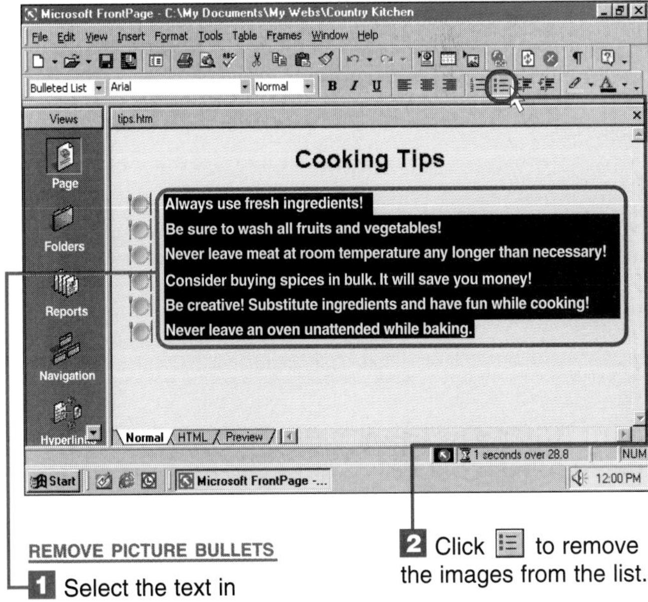

REMOVE PICTURE BULLETS

1 Select the text in the list that displays the picture bullets. To select text, see page 54.

2 Click ☰ to remove the images from the list.

CHANGE BACKGROUND COLOR

You can change the background color of your Web page.

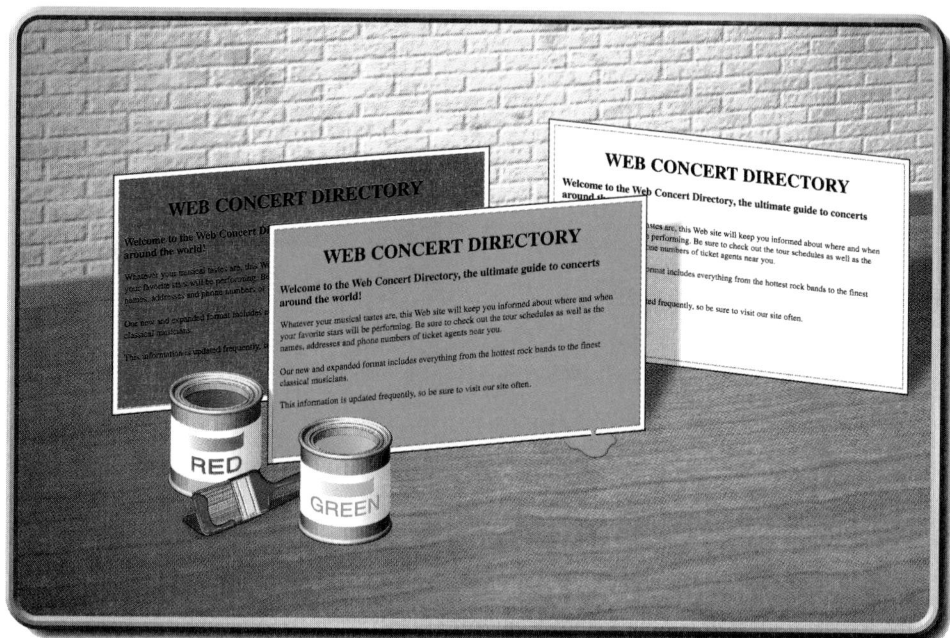

CHANGE BACKGROUND COLOR

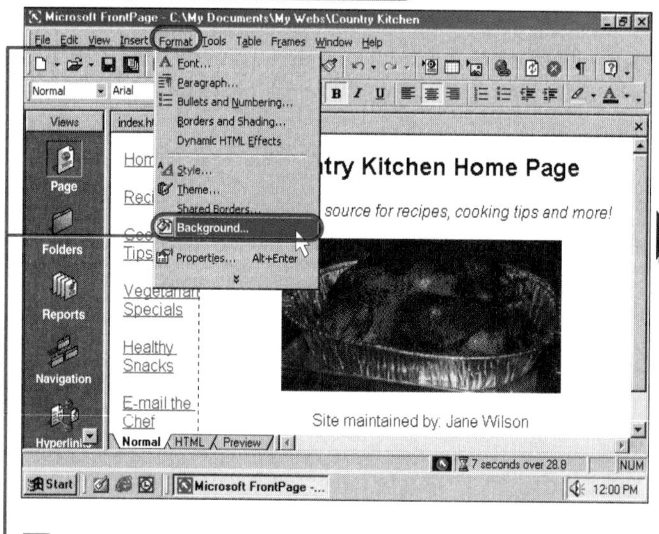

1 Click **Format**.

2 Click **Background**.

Note: If Background does not appear on the menu, position the mouse over the bottom of the menu to display all the menu commands.

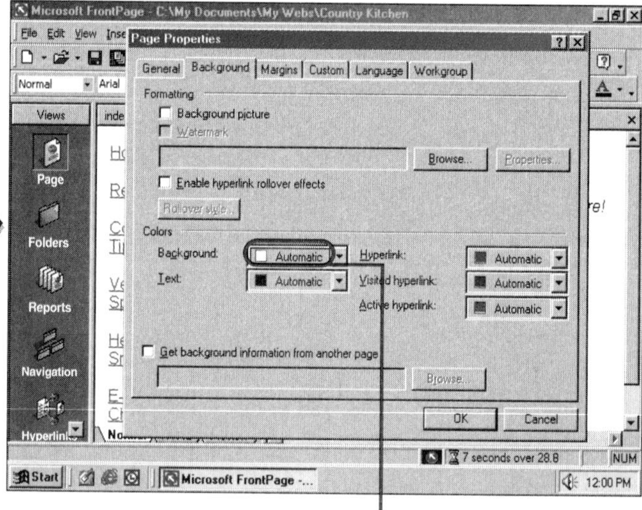

■ The Page Properties dialog box appears.

■ This area displays the current background color of your Web page.

What should I consider when changing the background color of my Web page?

Make sure you select a background color that works well with the color of your text. For example, red text on a blue background can be difficult to read. To help the readability of the text on your Web page, try to use dark text on a light background or light text on a dark background. To change text color, see page 76.

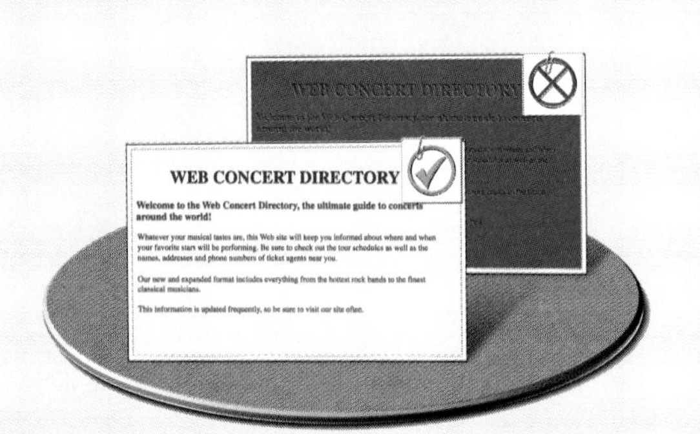

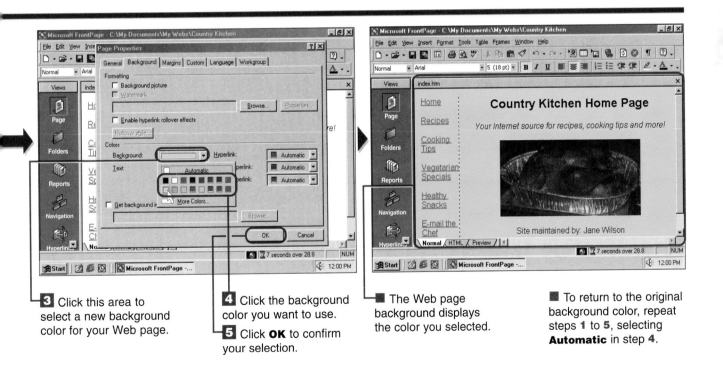

3 Click this area to select a new background color for your Web page.

4 Click the background color you want to use.

5 Click **OK** to confirm your selection.

■ The Web page background displays the color you selected.

■ To return to the original background color, repeat steps **1** to **5**, selecting **Automatic** in step **4**.

APPLY A THEME

FrontPage offers many themes that you can choose from to give your Web pages a professional appearance.

A theme will change the way fonts, colors, bullets and lines appear on your Web pages.

APPLY A THEME

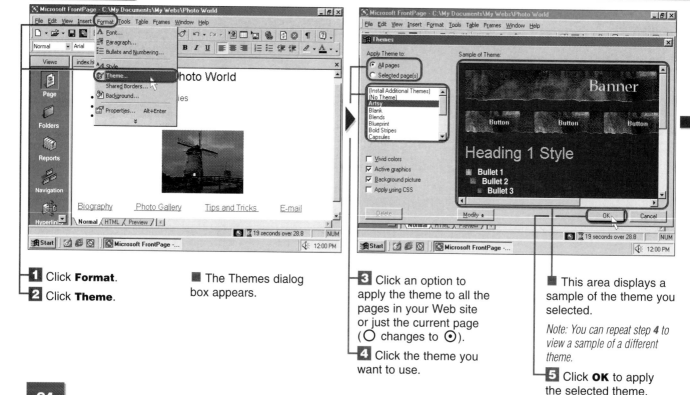

1. Click **Format**.
2. Click **Theme**.

■ The Themes dialog box appears.

3. Click an option to apply the theme to all the pages in your Web site or just the current page (○ changes to ⊙).
4. Click the theme you want to use.

■ This area displays a sample of the theme you selected.

*Note: You can repeat step **4** to view a sample of a different theme.*

5. Click **OK** to apply the selected theme.

?

How can I change the appearance of a theme?

In the Themes dialog box, FrontPage provides additional options you can use to customize themes. You can click an option to turn the option on (☑) or off (☐).

Vivid colors

Use brighter colors.

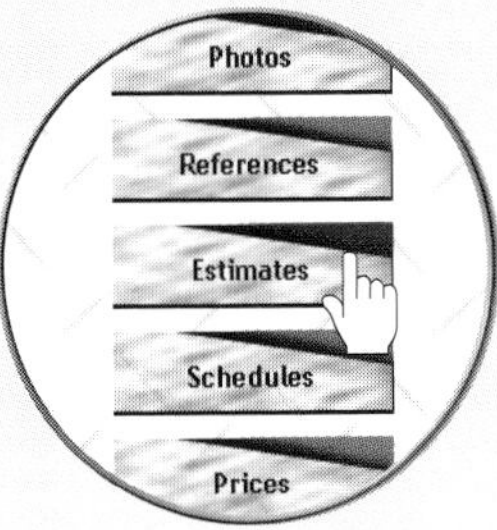

Active graphics

Use animated graphics.

Background picture

Use a background image.

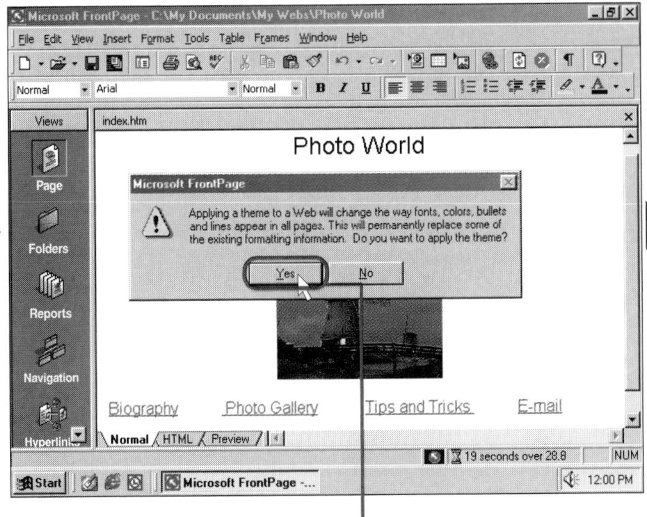

■ A dialog box may appear, stating that applying a theme will change the appearance of your Web pages and replace some of the formatting changes you previously made.

6 Click **Yes** to continue.

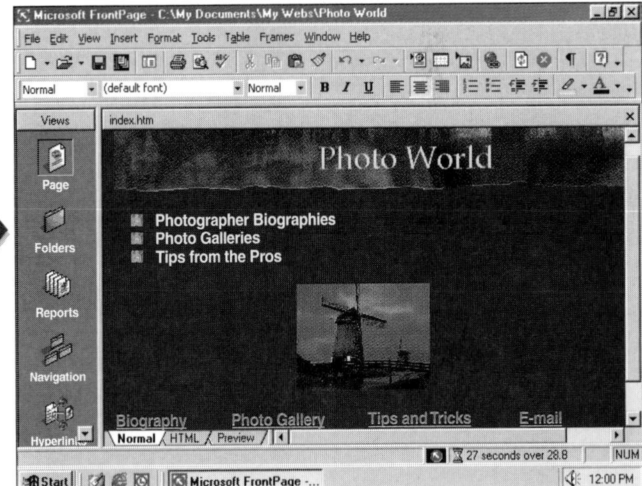

■ The Web page(s) you specified display the theme.

■ To remove a theme from Web pages, repeat steps **1** to **6**, selecting **[No Theme]** in step **4**.

BIRD WATCHERS' HOME PAGE

The page dedicated to people who love to watch birds!

Bird watchers appreciate the beauty and wonder of birds. This month, with summer just around the corner, we will discuss the best spots for bird-watching in the national parks of the northern states. These locations have been recommended by visitors to our page. If you have a new location to add, please e-mail us today!

Popular Sites

Membership Information

Bird

Build
Better B

CHAPTER 6

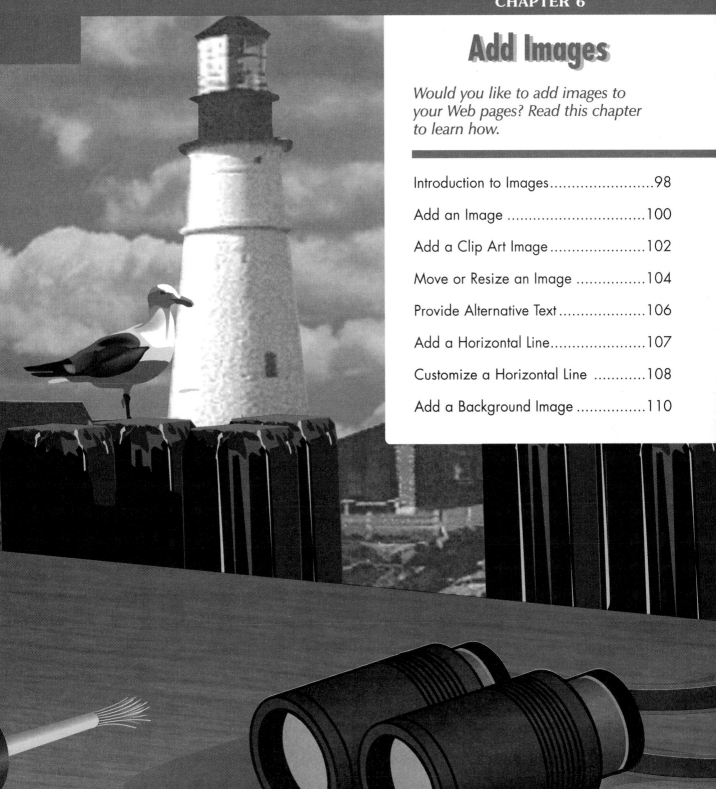

Would you like to add images to your Web pages? Read this chapter to learn how.

REASONS FOR USING IMAGES

GRAPHICS

You can add images to your Web pages to display drawings, paintings and computer-generated art. You can also add images that help illustrate a concept that is difficult to explain with words. For example, you can include a map to give directions, a chart to show financial trends or a diagram to point out essential parts of a product.

PHOTOGRAPHS

You can display photographs of your family, pets or favorite celebrities on your Web pages. Many companies include photographs of their products so people around the world can view the products without having to visit a store or wait for a brochure to arrive in the mail.

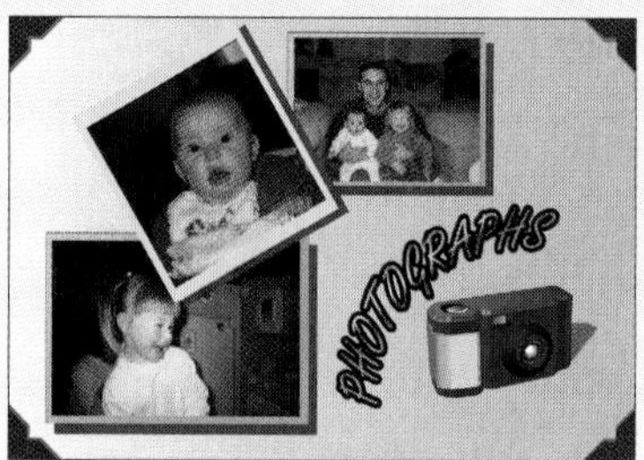

TYPES OF IMAGES

When you save a Web page that contains an image, FrontPage automatically converts the image to the GIF or JPEG format. The GIF and JPEG formats are the most popular image formats on the Web.

GIF

Graphics Interchange Format (GIF) images are limited to 256 colors and are often used for logos, banners and computer-generated art. GIF images have the .gif extension (example: logo.gif).

JPEG

Joint Photographic Experts Group (JPEG) images can have millions of colors and are often used for photographs and very large images. JPEG images have the .jpg extension (example: stonehenge.jpg).

OBTAIN IMAGES

INTERNET

Many Web sites offer images you can use free of charge on your Web pages. Make sure you have permission to use any images you obtain on the Web. You can find images at the following Web sites:

www.allfree-clipart.com

www.bestclipart.com/photographs/photoframes.htm

www.noeticart.com

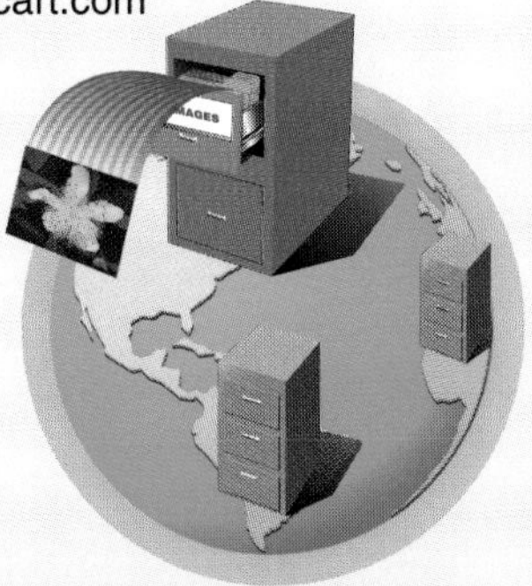

SCAN IMAGES

You can use a scanner to scan images into your computer. You can scan photographs, logos and drawings and then place the scanned images on your Web pages. If you do not have a scanner, many service bureaus will scan images for a fee.

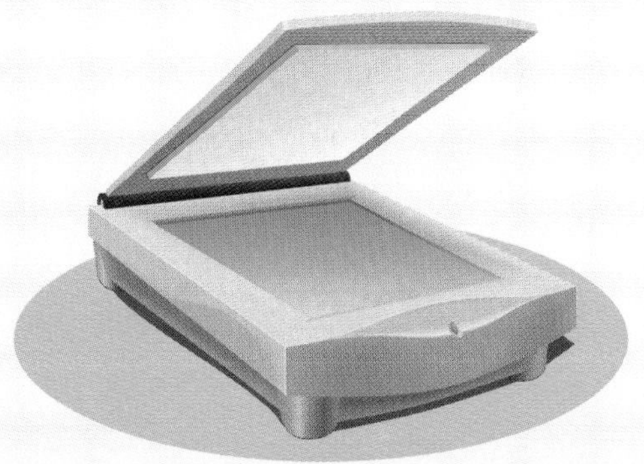

CREATE IMAGES

You can use an image editing program to create your own images. Creating your own images lets you design images that best suit your Web pages. Popular image editing programs include Adobe Photoshop and Paint Shop Pro.

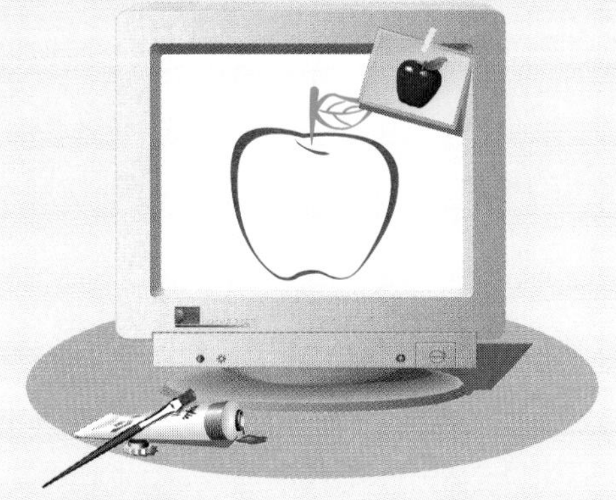

IMAGE COLLECTIONS

You can buy collections of ready-made images at computer stores. Image collections can include cartoons, drawings, photographs or computer-generated art.

ADD AN IMAGE

You can add an image to illustrate a concept or enhance the appearance of your Web page.

ADD AN IMAGE

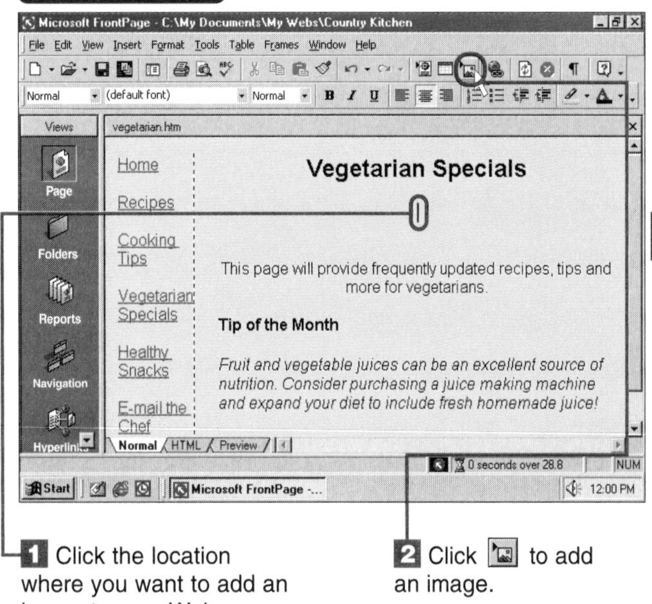

1 Click the location where you want to add an image to your Web page.

2 Click to add an image.

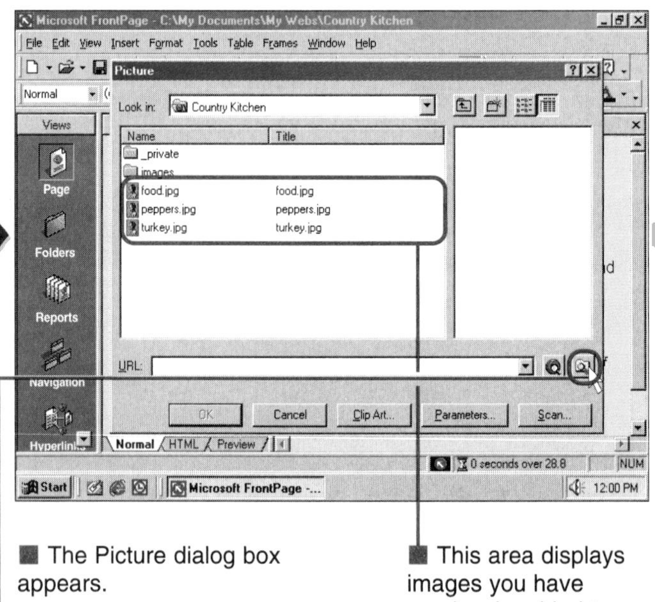

■ The Picture dialog box appears.

3 Click to locate the image on your computer that you want to use.

■ This area displays images you have previously added to your Web site. To add one of these images, click the image. Then press the **Enter** key to add the image.

What should I consider when adding an image to a Web page?

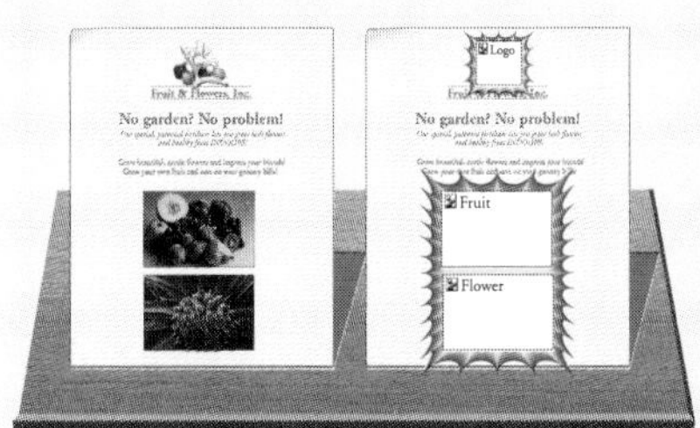

View Web Pages Without Images

Make sure your Web pages will look attractive and make sense if the images are not displayed. Some readers turn off the display of images to browse the Web more quickly, while others use Web browsers that cannot display images.

Image Size

Images increase the time it takes for a Web page to appear on a screen. If a Web page takes too long to appear, readers may lose interest and move to another page. Whenever possible, you should use images with small file sizes since these images will transfer faster.

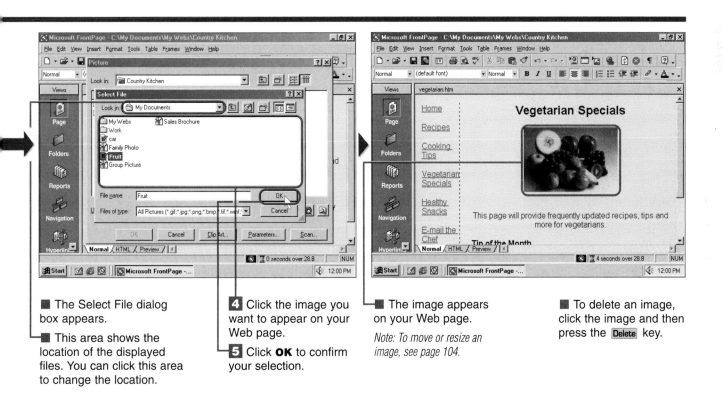

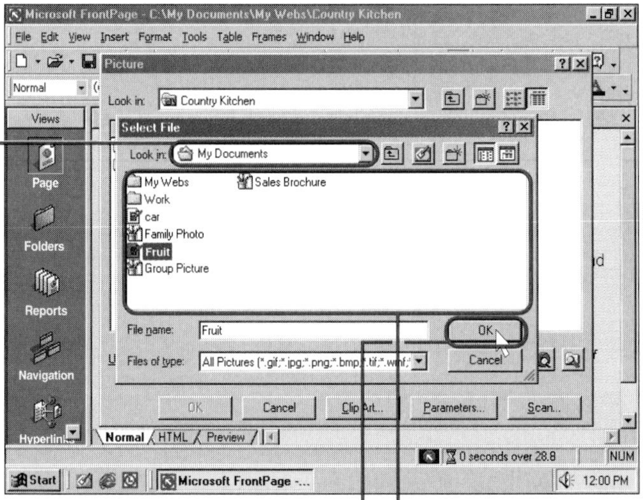

■ The Select File dialog box appears.

■ This area shows the location of the displayed files. You can click this area to change the location.

4 Click the image you want to appear on your Web page.

5 Click **OK** to confirm your selection.

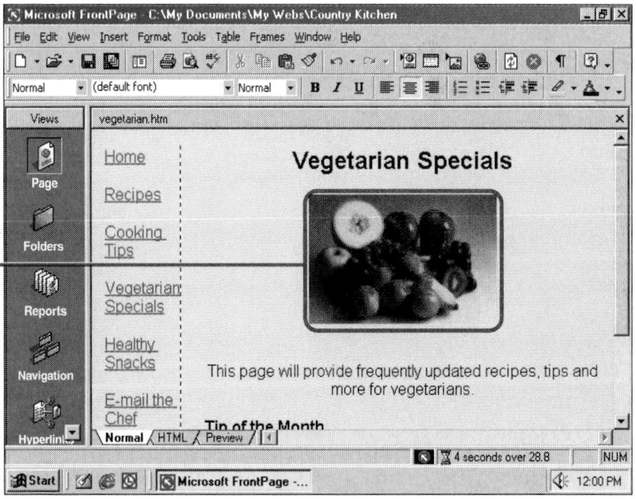

■ The image appears on your Web page.

Note: To move or resize an image, see page 104.

■ To delete an image, click the image and then press the **Delete** key.

ADD A CLIP ART IMAGE

You can add a clip art image to your Web page to illustrate a concept and make your Web page more appealing.

FrontPage organizes clip art images into various categories such as Animals, Business, Entertainment, Nature and Travel.

ADD A CLIP ART IMAGE

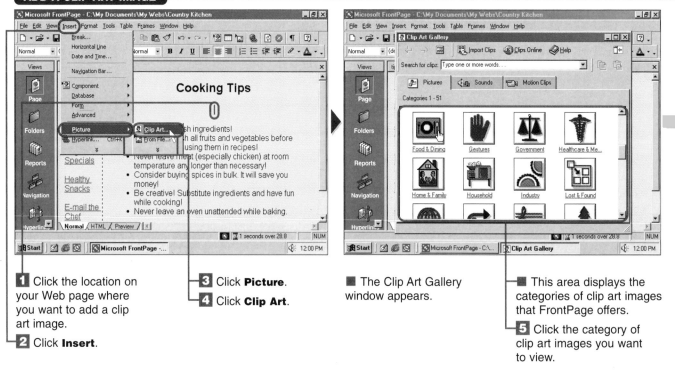

1 Click the location on your Web page where you want to add a clip art image.

2 Click **Insert**.

3 Click **Picture**.

4 Click **Clip Art**.

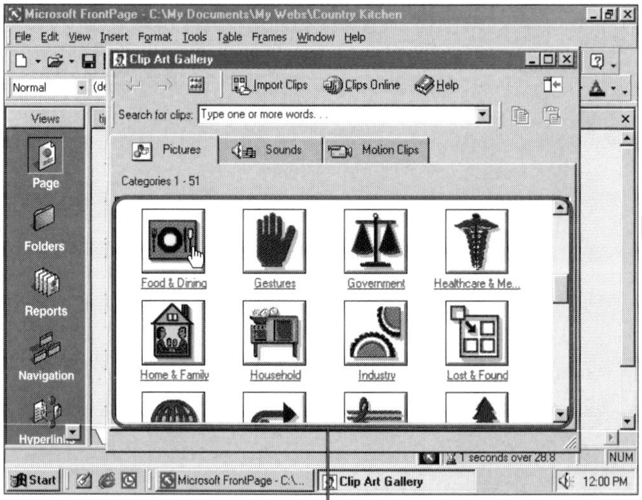

■ The Clip Art Gallery window appears.

■ This area displays the categories of clip art images that FrontPage offers.

5 Click the category of clip art images you want to view.

Where can I find more clip art images?

If you are connected to the Internet, you can visit Microsoft's Clip Gallery Live Web page to find additional clip art images. In the Clip Art Gallery window, click **Clips Online**. In the dialog box that appears, click **OK** to connect to the Web page. You can also purchase additional clip art images for your Web pages at computer stores.

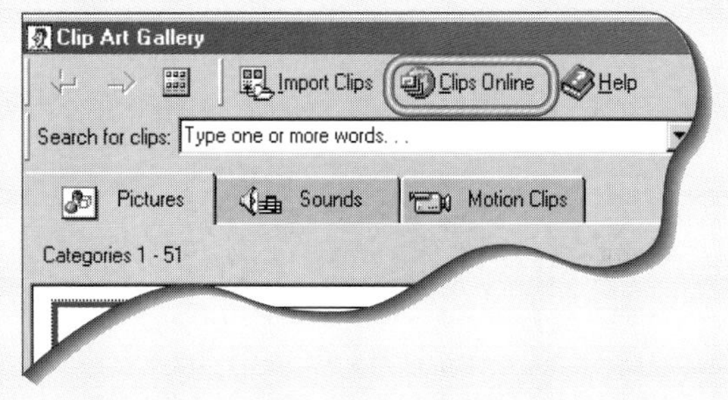

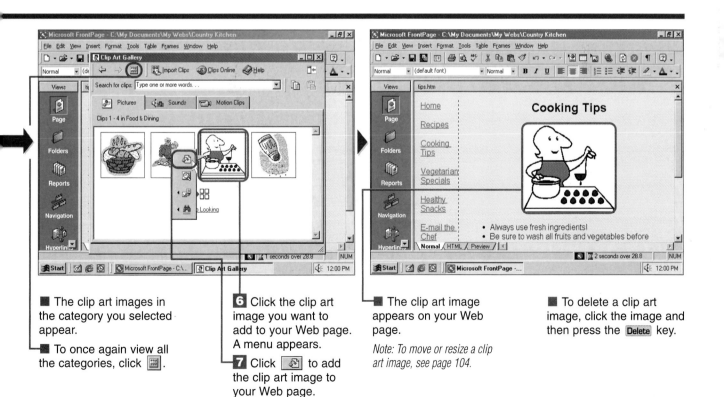

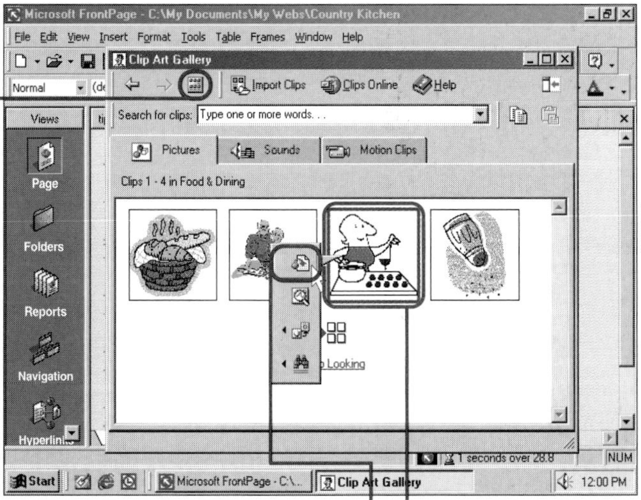

■ The clip art images in the category you selected appear.

■ To once again view all the categories, click [icon].

6 Click the clip art image you want to add to your Web page. A menu appears.

7 Click [icon] to add the clip art image to your Web page.

■ The clip art image appears on your Web page.

Note: To move or resize a clip art image, see page 104.

■ To delete a clip art image, click the image and then press the Delete key.

MOVE OR RESIZE AN IMAGE

You can change the location or size of an image on your Web page.

MOVE
Birds' Nest
One of the easiest ways to enjoy
Bird watching is a very popular hobby in the United States, and it is growing in popularity all the time!
From the tiny hummingbird to the spectacular bald eagle, the opportunities for bird watchers are endless!
Home
Cats' Corner
Birds' Nest
Nature Paradises
RESIZE
The Nature Preserve
Join us for a journey through the World Wide Web!
Home
Cats' Corner
Birds' Nest
Nature Paradises

MOVE AN IMAGE

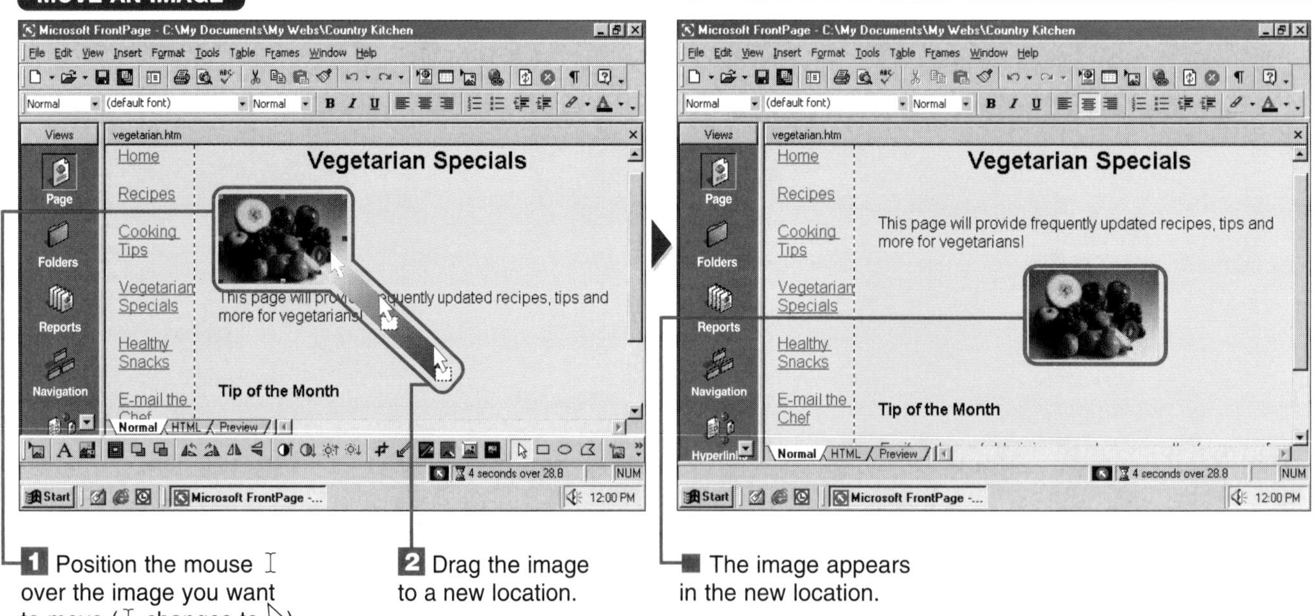

1 Position the mouse I over the image you want to move (I changes to ↖).

2 Drag the image to a new location.

■ The image appears in the new location.

How can I make an image appear less distorted?

After you resize an image, you can use the Resample button ( ) to make the image appear less distorted. To resample an image, click the image and then click the Resample button ( ).

When you resample an image, the file size of the image will change. Keep in mind the file size determines how fast an image transfers and appears on a reader's screen.

RESIZE AN IMAGE

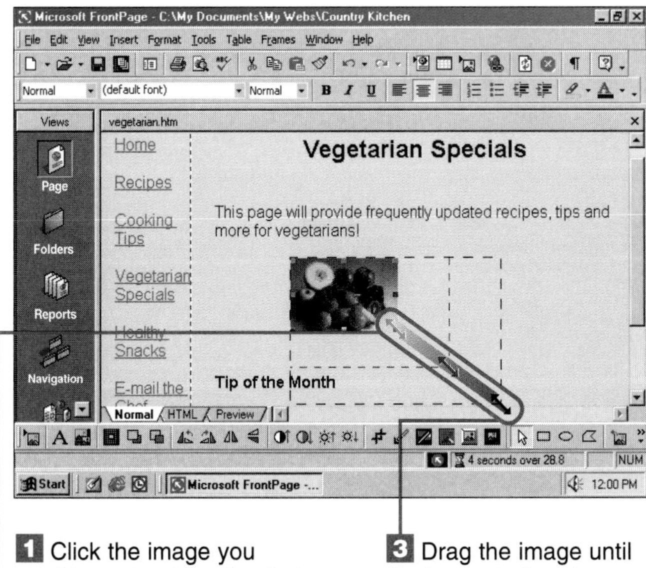

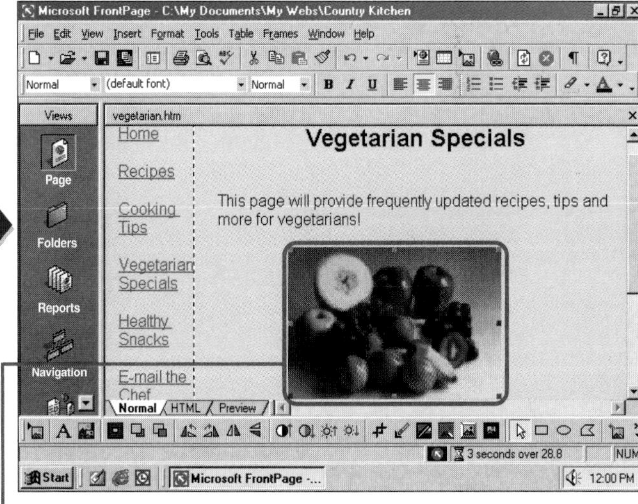

1 Click the image you want to resize. Handles (■) appear around the image.

2 Position the mouse I over one of the handles (I changes to ↘, ↕ or ↔).

3 Drag the image until the image is the size you want.

Note: To keep the image in proportion, drag a corner handle.

■ The image appears in the new size.

Note: If you make an image too large, the image may appear distorted.

PROVIDE ALTERNATIVE TEXT

You can provide text that you want to display if an image on your Web page does not appear. This will give readers who do not see the image information about the missing image.

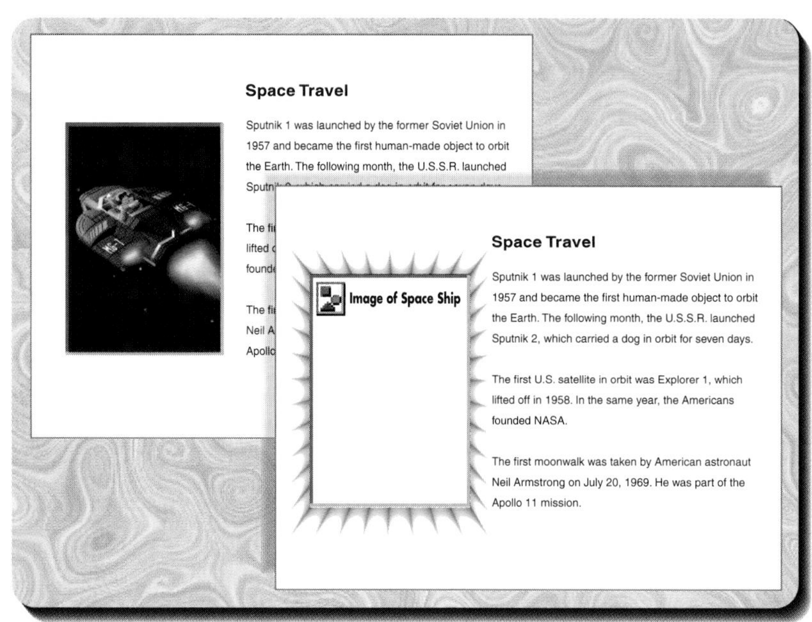

Some readers use Web browsers that cannot display images, while others turn off the display of images to browse the Web more quickly.

PROVIDE ALTERNATIVE TEXT

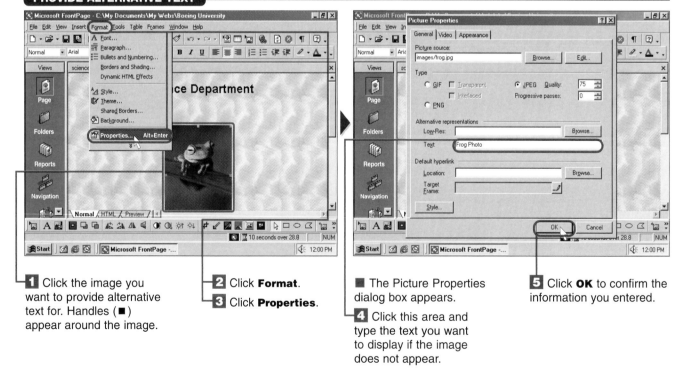

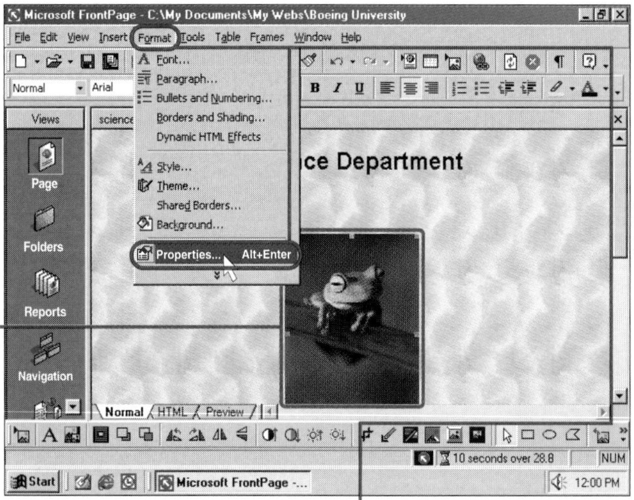

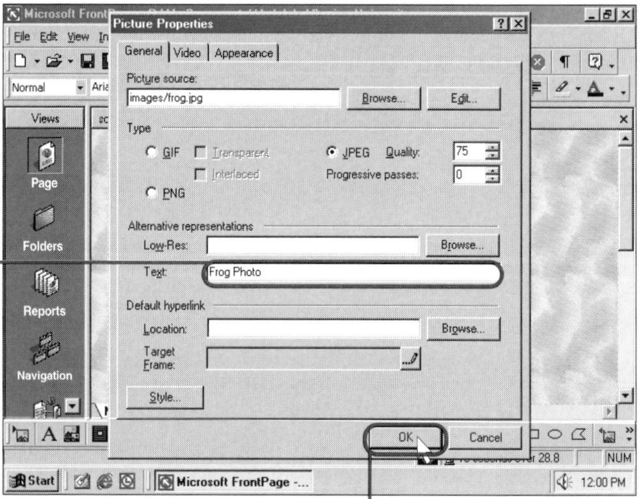

1 Click the image you want to provide alternative text for. Handles (■) appear around the image.

2 Click **Format**.

3 Click **Properties**.

■ The Picture Properties dialog box appears.

4 Click this area and type the text you want to display if the image does not appear.

5 Click **OK** to confirm the information you entered.

ADD A HORIZONTAL LINE

You can add a horizontal line to visually separate sections of your Web page.

Fruit & Flowers, Inc.
No garden? No problem!
Our special, patented fertilizer lets you grow lush flowers and healthy fruit INDOORS!
Grow beautiful, exotic flowers and impress your friends!
Grow your own fruit and save on your grocery bills!
Our fruit selection includes:
• Popular berries such as strawberries, raspberries and blueberries
• Exotic fruit such as mangos, papayas and kiwis
Our flower selection includes:
• Seasonal plants such as poinsettias, holly and mistletoe
• Tropical flowers such as orchids, birds of paradise and yellow jasmine

You should not overuse horizontal lines on your Web page since this can distract your readers and make your Web page difficult to read. Try not to place more than one horizontal line on each screen.

ADD A HORIZONTAL LINE

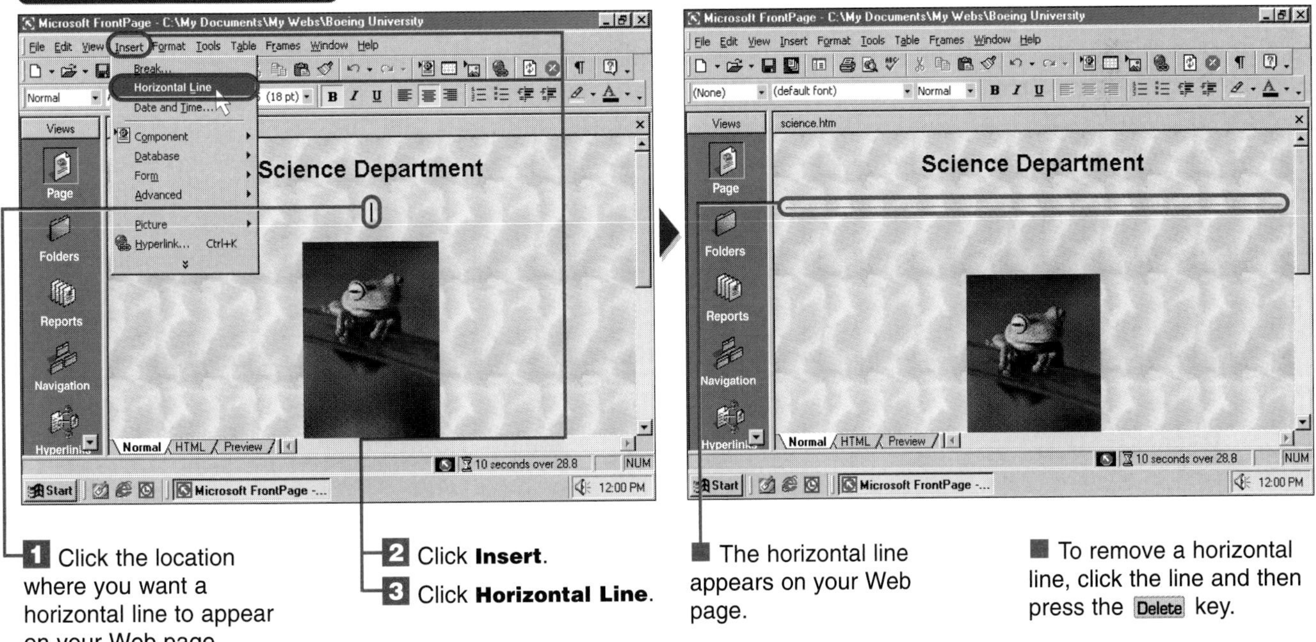

1 Click the location where you want a horizontal line to appear on your Web page.

2 Click **Insert**.

3 Click **Horizontal Line**.

■ The horizontal line appears on your Web page.

■ To remove a horizontal line, click the line and then press the Delete key.

CUSTOMIZE A HORIZONTAL LINE

You can customize the appearance of a horizontal line on your Web page.

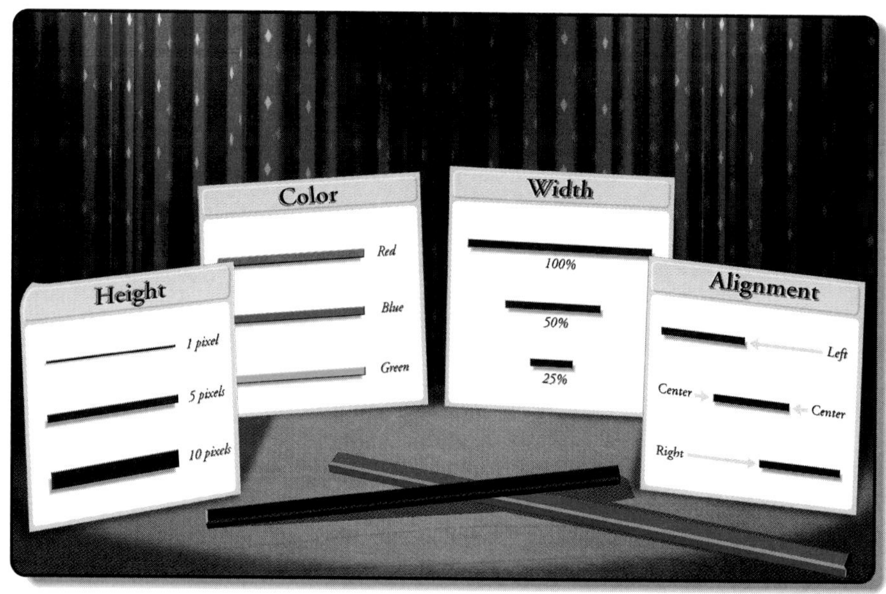

You can change the height, color, width and alignment of a horizontal line.

If you have applied a theme to your Web page, you cannot customize a horizontal line. To apply a theme, see page 94.

CUSTOMIZE A HORIZONTAL LINE

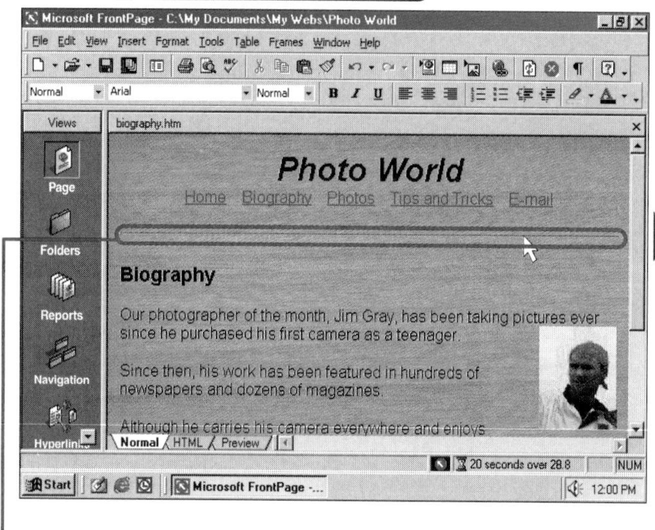

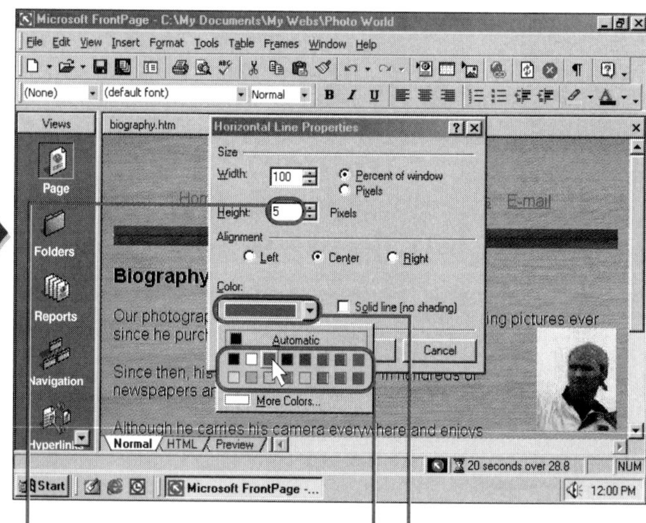

1 Double-click the horizontal line you want to customize.

■ The Horizontal Line Properties dialog box appears.

2 To change the height of the horizontal line, double-click this area and type a number for the height in pixels.

Note: A pixel is a dot on a computer screen.

3 To change the color of the horizontal line, click this area to display the available colors.

4 Click the color you want to use.

How can I add a more elaborate horizontal line to my Web page?

You can use an image instead of a horizontal line to visually separate sections of your Web page. You can create your own horizontal line images in an image editing program or obtain images on the Internet.

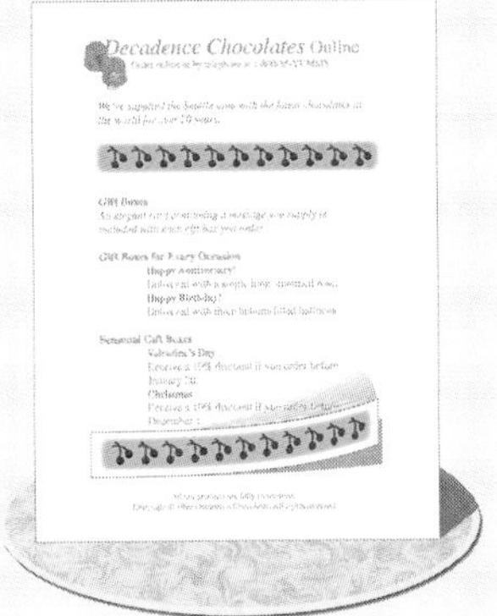

The following Web sites offer images you can use as horizontal lines:

members.xoom.com/SSWebGraphics/lines/lines.htm

www.coolgraphics.com/gallery.shtml

www.theskull.com/hor_rule.html

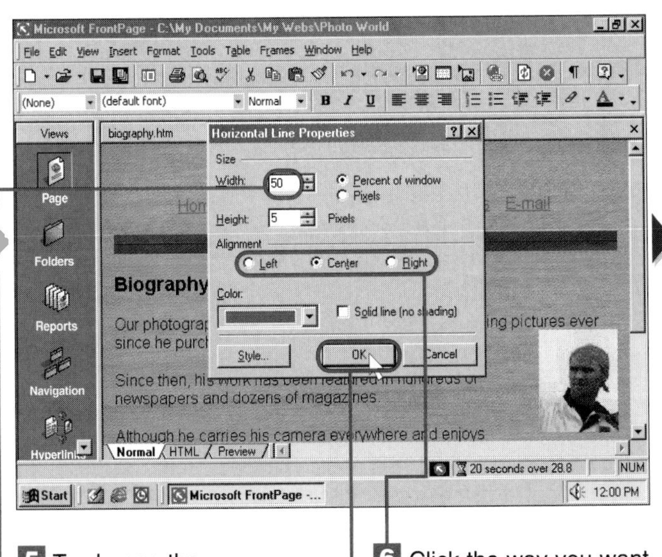

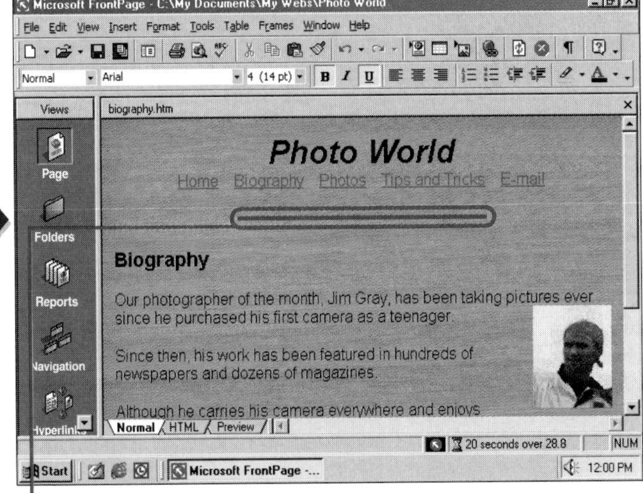

5 To change the percentage of the Web page the horizontal line extends across, double-click this area and type a percentage.

Note: To extend the horizontal line halfway across your Web page, type ***50****.*

6 Click the way you want to align the horizontal line (○ changes to ⊙).

Note: Selecting an alignment will have no effect if the horizontal line width is set at 100.

7 Click **OK**.

■ The appearance of the horizontal line changes.

Note: The Netscape Navigator Web browser will not display a horizontal line in color.

■ To deselect a horizontal line, click outside the horizontal line.

ADD A BACKGROUND IMAGE

You can have a small image repeat to fill an entire Web page. This can add an interesting background design to your Web page.

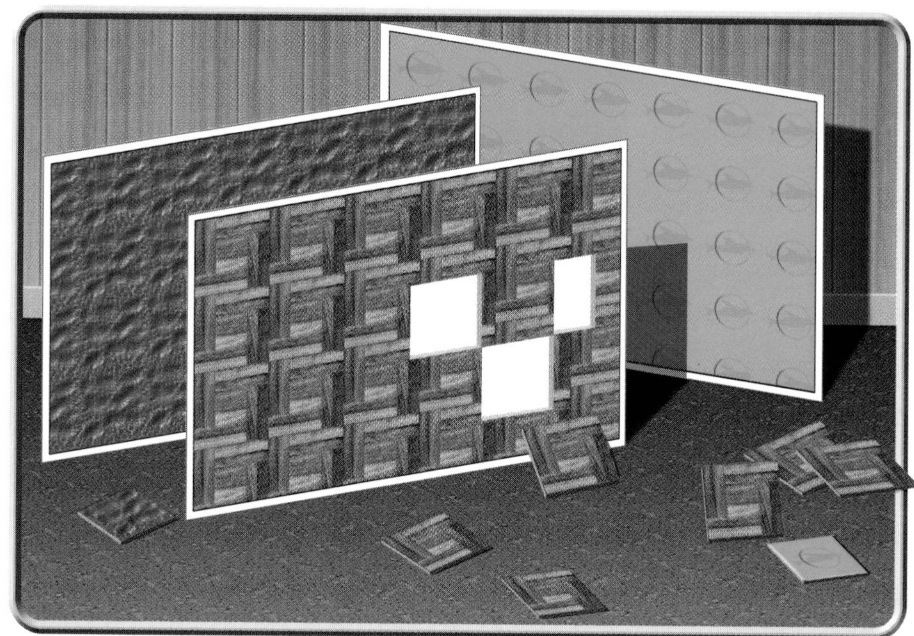

ADD A BACKGROUND IMAGE

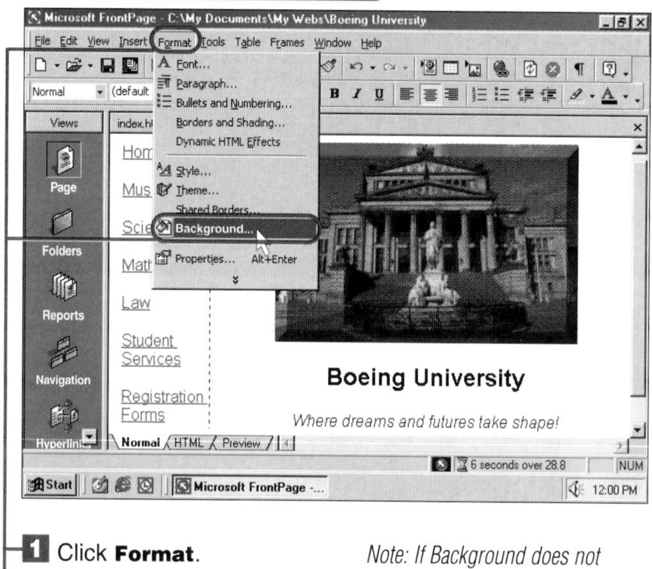

1 Click **Format**.

2 Click **Background**.

Note: If Background does not appear on the menu, position the mouse over the bottom of the menu to display all the menu commands.

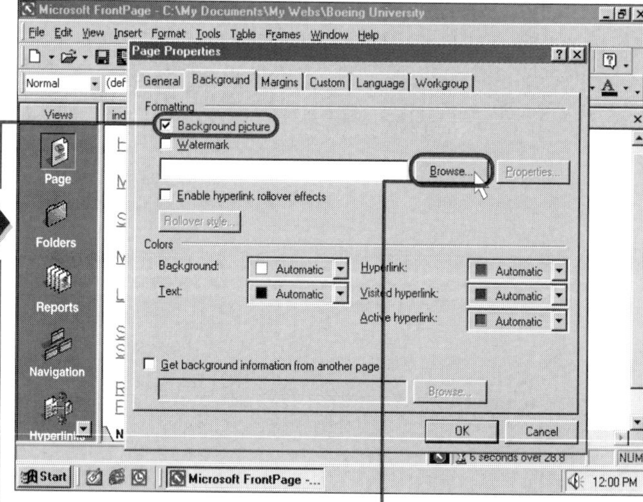

■ The Page Properties dialog box appears.

3 Click **Background picture** to add a background image to your Web page (☐ changes to ☑).

4 Click **Browse** to locate the image you want to use.

Where can I find background images?

Many Web sites offer background images you can use for free on your Web pages. You can find a variety of background images, including marble, stone, wood and water. Since background images increase the time Web pages take to appear on a screen, you should choose images with small file sizes that will transfer faster.

You can find background images at the following Web sites:

imagine.metanet.com

www.ip.pt/webground/main.htm

www.nepthys.com/textures

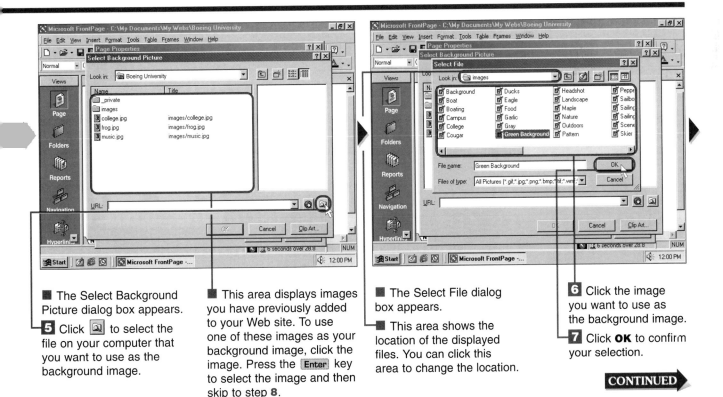

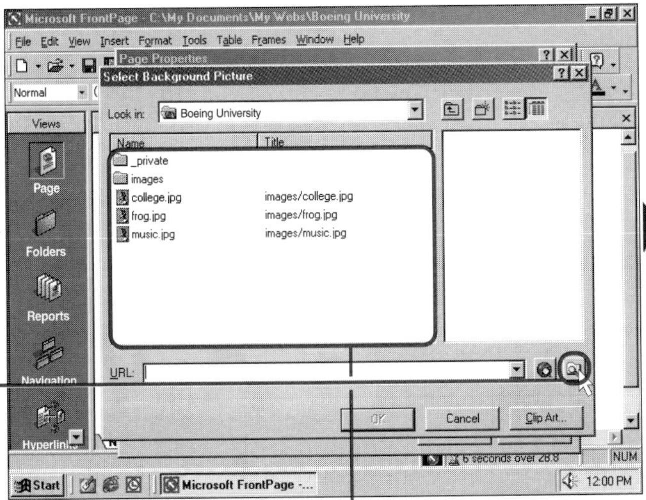

■ The Select Background Picture dialog box appears.

5 Click [icon] to select the file on your computer that you want to use as the background image.

■ This area displays images you have previously added to your Web site. To use one of these images as your background image, click the image. Press the Enter key to select the image and then skip to step **8**.

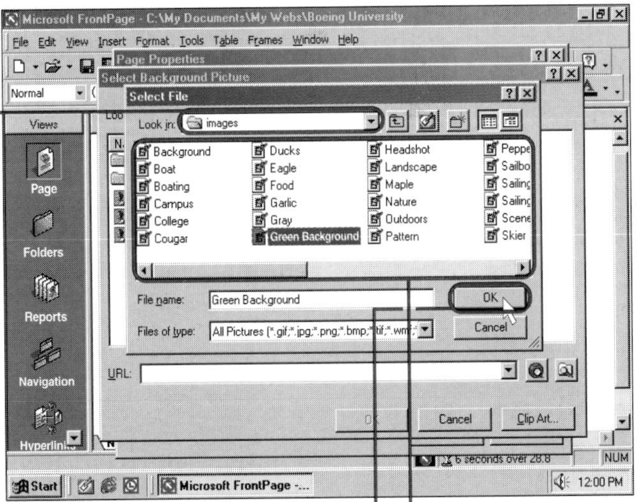

■ The Select File dialog box appears.

■ This area shows the location of the displayed files. You can click this area to change the location.

6 Click the image you want to use as the background image.

7 Click **OK** to confirm your selection.

CONTINUED

ADD A BACKGROUND IMAGE

You should use a background image that creates an interesting design without overwhelming your Web page.

ADD A BACKGROUND IMAGE (CONTINUED)

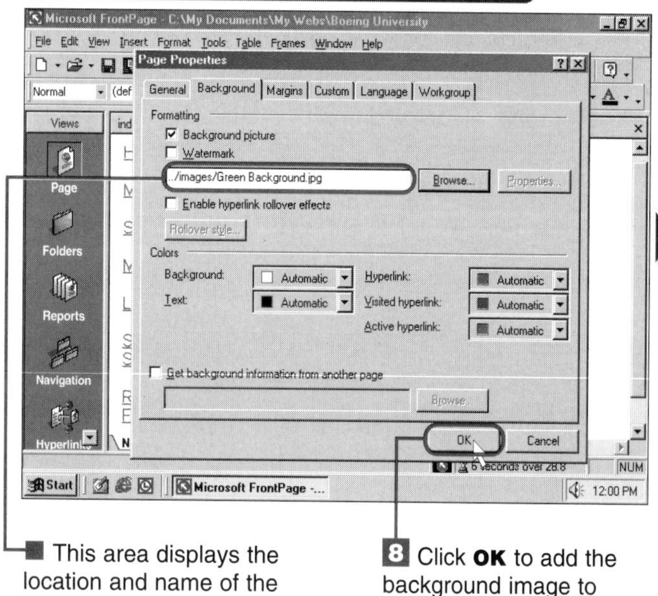

■ This area displays the location and name of the image you selected.

8 Click **OK** to add the background image to your Web page.

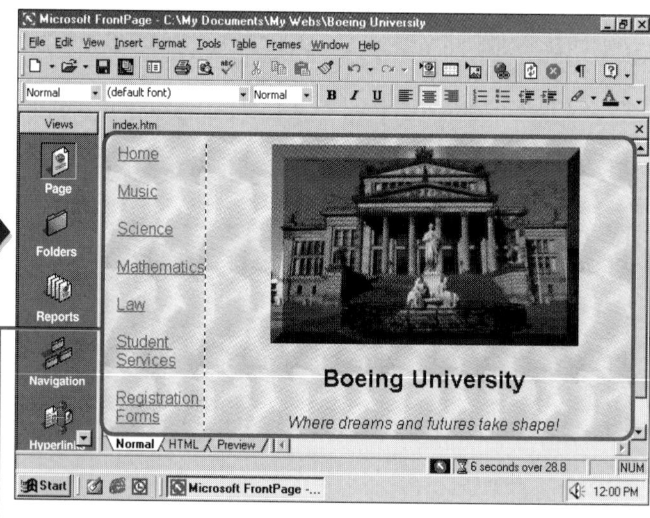

■ The image repeats to fill your entire Web page.

What type of image should I use as a background image?

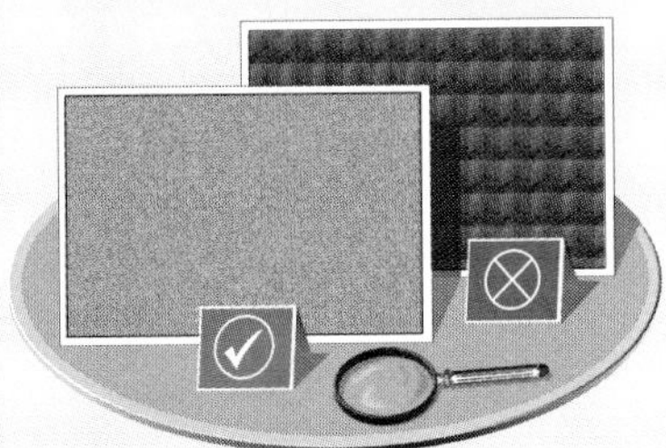

Seamless Background

A good background image should have invisible edges. When the image repeats to fill the Web page, you should not be able to tell where the edges of the images meet.

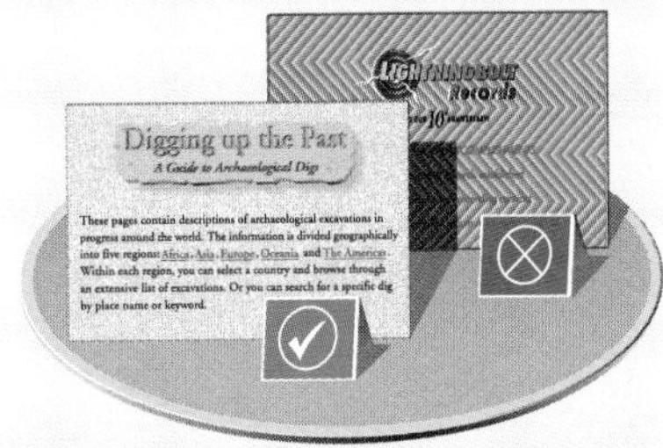

Web Page Readability

Make sure the background image you choose does not affect the readability of your Web page. You may need to change the color of text to make the Web page easier to read. To change the text color, see page 76.

REMOVE A BACKGROUND IMAGE

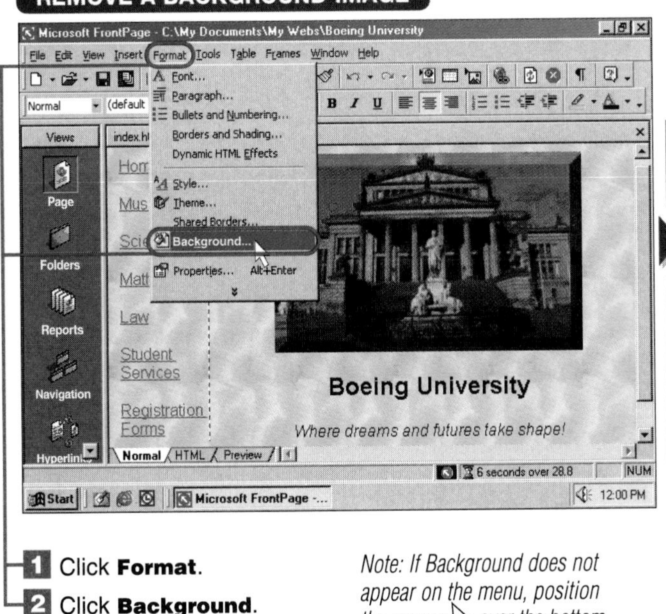

1 Click **Format**.

2 Click **Background**.

Note: If Background does not appear on the menu, position the mouse over the bottom of the menu to display all the menu commands.

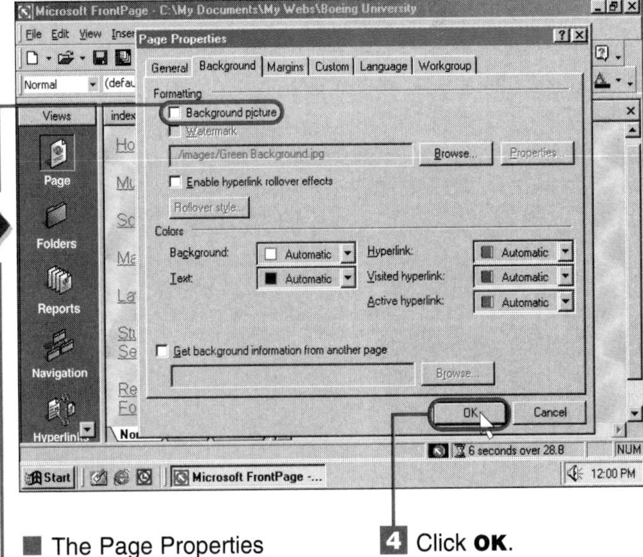

■ The Page Properties dialog box appears.

3 Click **Background picture** to remove the background image from your Web page (☑ changes to ☐).

4 Click **OK**.

■ The background image disappears from your Web page.

BIRD WATCHERS'
Eagle
Popular
Nest Sites
Membership
Information
Building a
Better Birdhouse

CHAPTER 7

Customize Images

Do you want to customize your images? This chapter shows you how to add a border to images, create an image map and more.

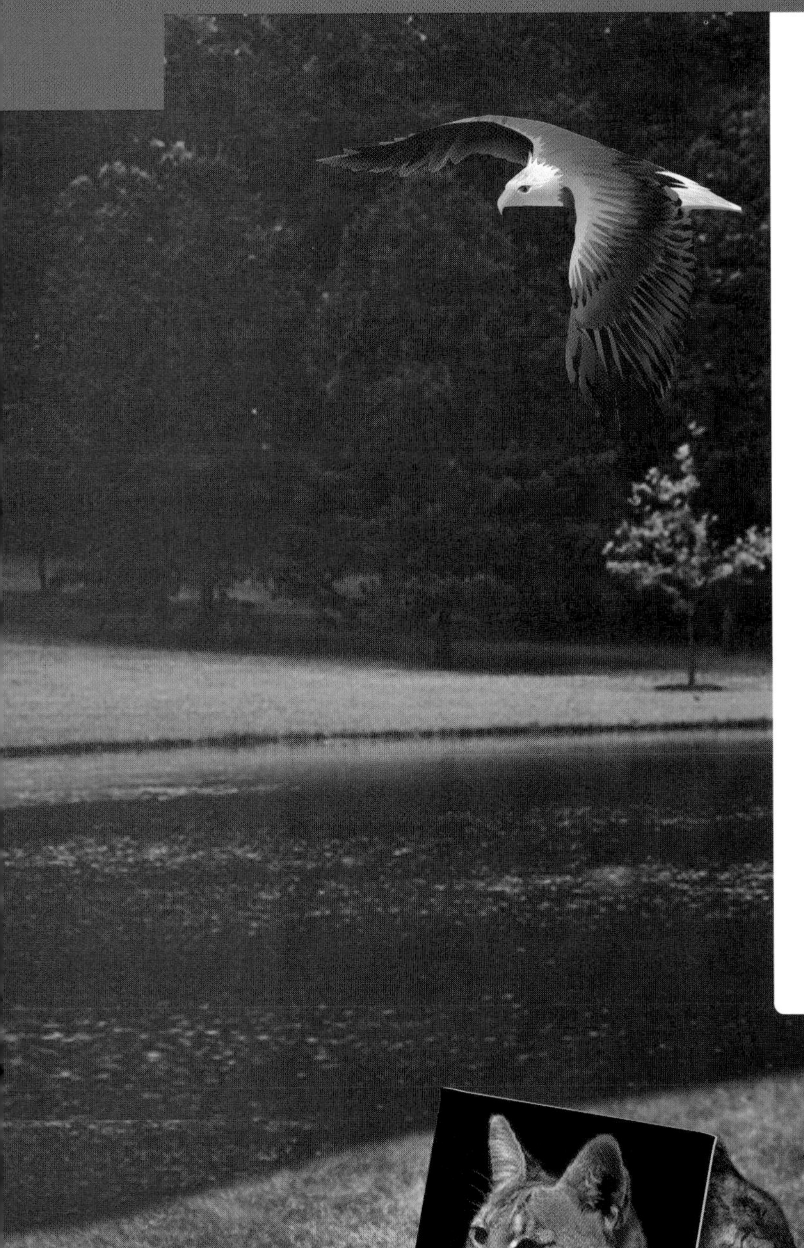

ADD A BORDER TO AN IMAGE

You can add a border to an image on your Web page. This lets you place a frame around the image.

ADD A BORDER TO AN IMAGE

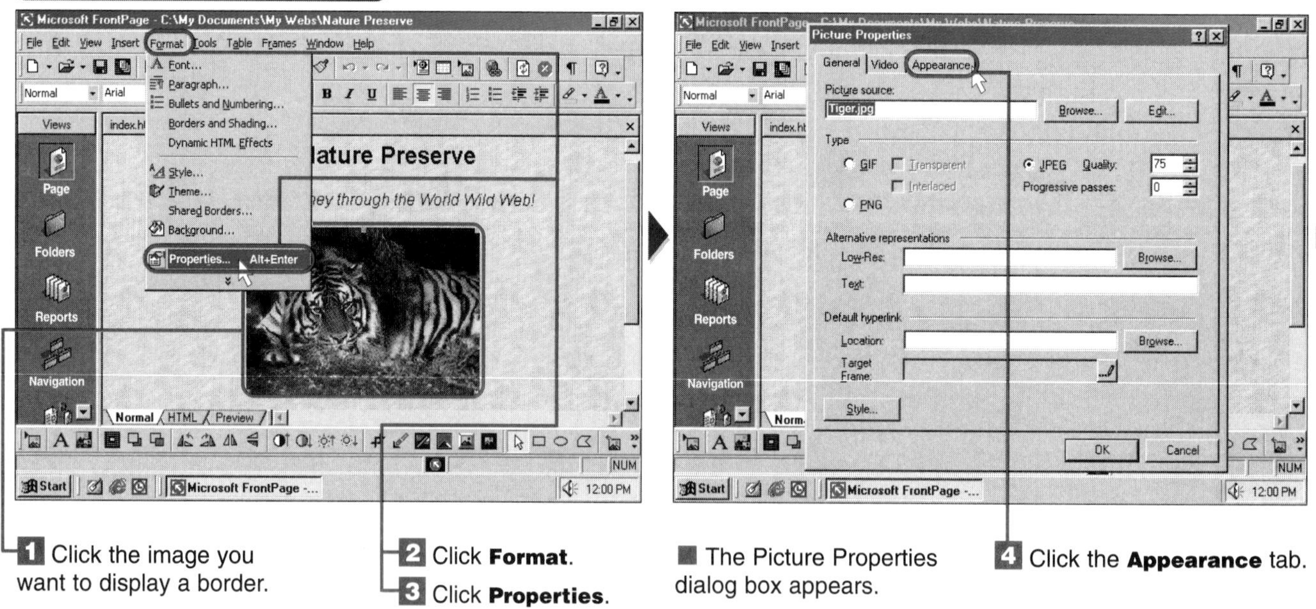

1 Click the image you want to display a border.

2 Click **Format**.

3 Click **Properties**.

■ The Picture Properties dialog box appears.

4 Click the **Appearance** tab.

What color border will appear around an image?

A black border will appear around an image, unless the image is a link. Linked images display a blue border to help people quickly recognize that the image is a link. To create an image link that readers can click to display another Web page, see page 132.

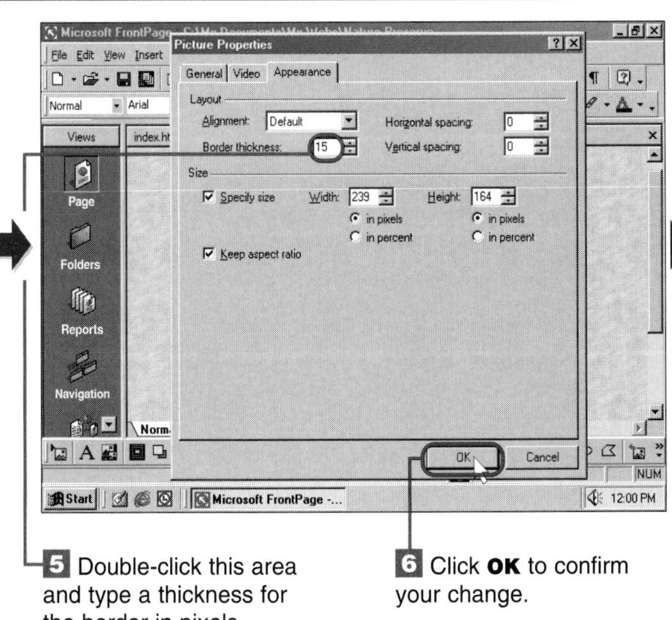

5 Double-click this area and type a thickness for the border in pixels.

Note: A pixel is a dot on a computer screen.

6 Click **OK** to confirm your change.

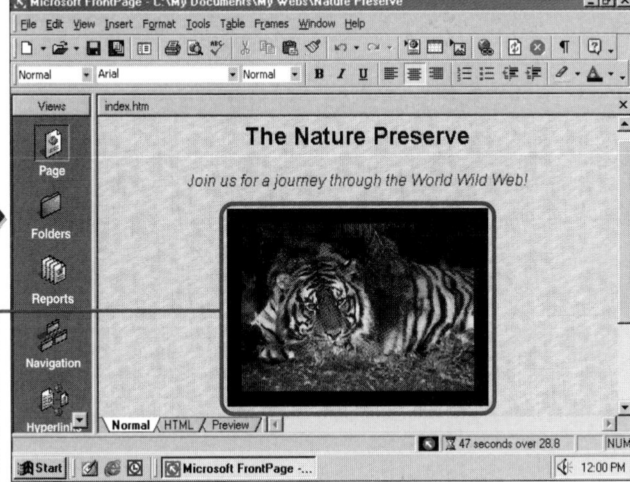

■ A border appears around the image.

■ To deselect an image, click outside the image.

■ To remove a border from an image, repeat steps **1** to **6**, typing **0** in step **5**.

ALIGN AN IMAGE WITH TEXT

You can change the way an image appears in relation to the surrounding text.

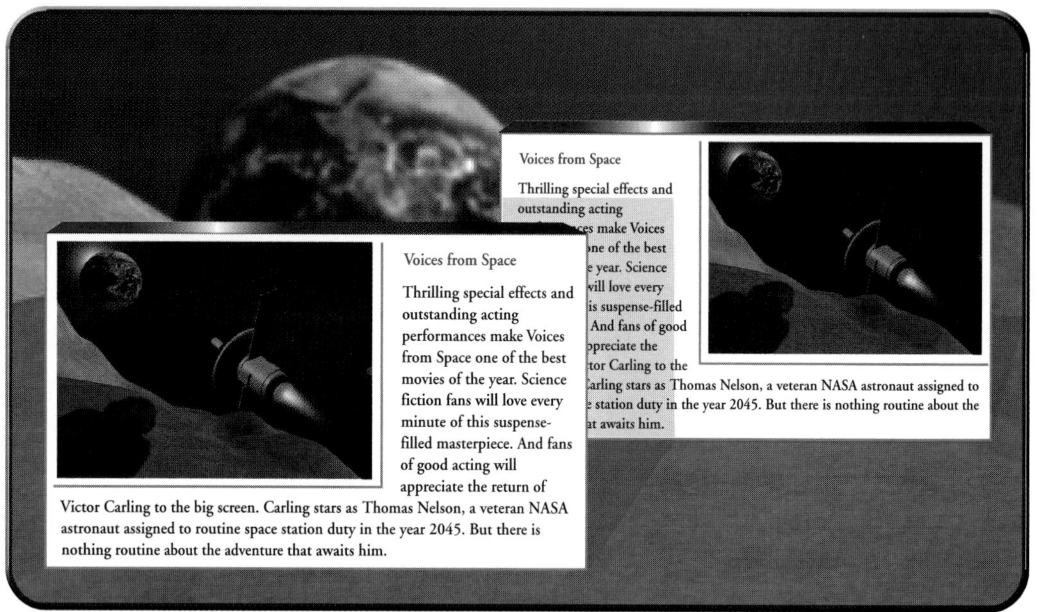

ALIGN AN IMAGE WITH TEXT

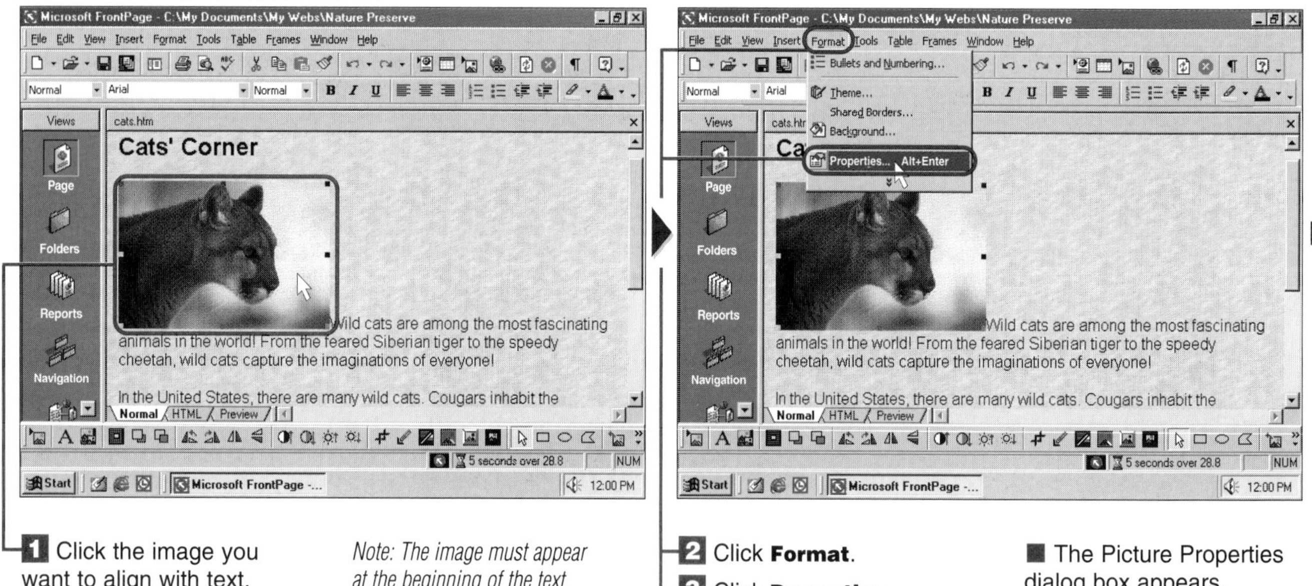

1 Click the image you want to align with text.

Note: The image must appear at the beginning of the text that you want to align with the image. To move an image on your Web page, see page 104.

2 Click **Format**.

3 Click **Properties**.

■ The Picture Properties dialog box appears.

What are some of the alignment options that FrontPage offers?

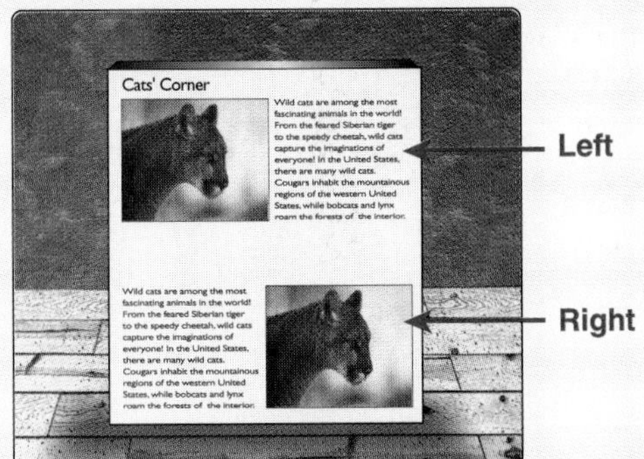

You can use the Left and Right options to wrap a paragraph around an image. The Left option places the image on the left side of the text. The Right option places the image on the right side of the text.

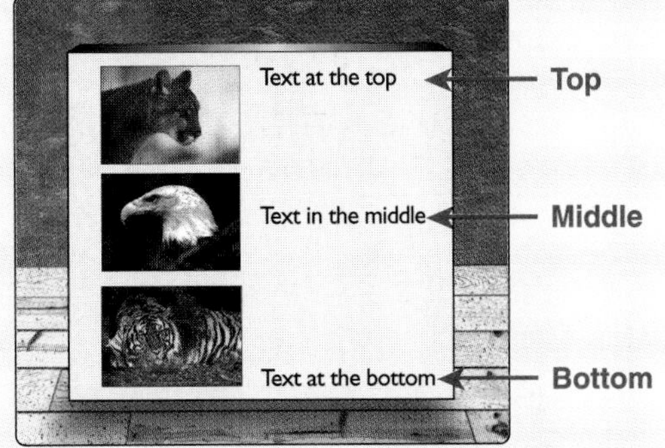

You can use the Top, Middle and Bottom options to vertically align an image with a single line of text.

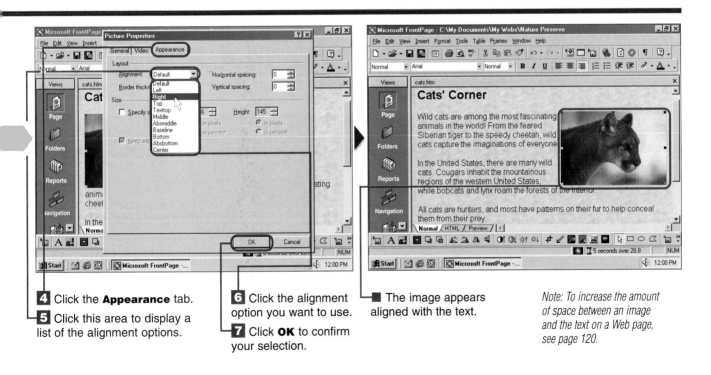

4 Click the **Appearance** tab.

5 Click this area to display a list of the alignment options.

6 Click the alignment option you want to use.

7 Click **OK** to confirm your selection.

■ The image appears aligned with the text.

Note: To increase the amount of space between an image and the text on a Web page, see page 120.

ADD SPACE AROUND AN IMAGE

You can increase the amount of space between an image and other elements on a Web page.

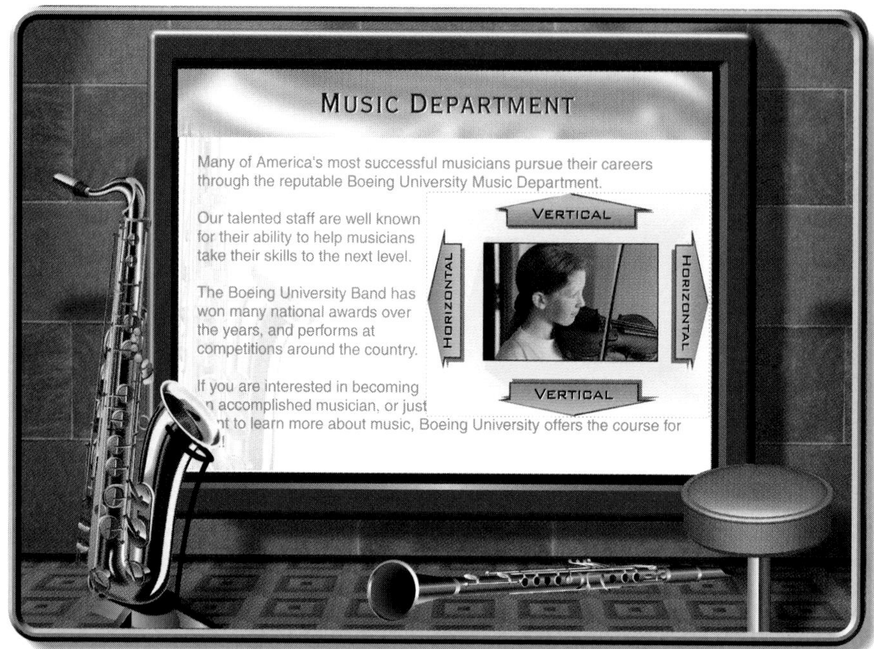

ADD SPACE AROUND AN IMAGE

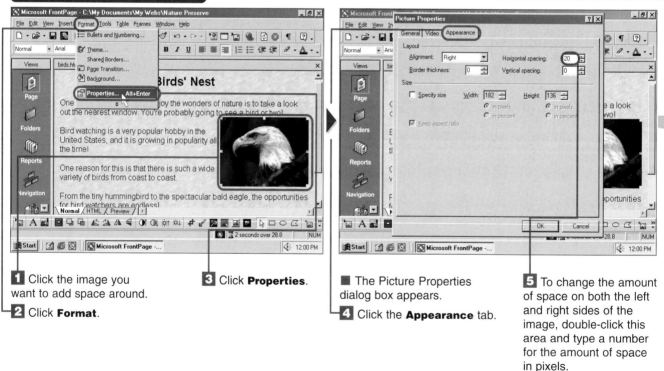

1. Click the image you want to add space around.
2. Click **Format**.
3. Click **Properties**.

■ The Picture Properties dialog box appears.

4. Click the **Appearance** tab.
5. To change the amount of space on both the left and right sides of the image, double-click this area and type a number for the amount of space in pixels.

Can I increase the amount of space on just one side of an image?

No. You cannot specify the amount of space for just one side of an image. The horizontal spacing defines the amount of space for both the left and right sides of an image. The vertical spacing defines the amount of space for both the top and bottom of an image.

How do I specify the amount of space around an image?

You specify the amount of space around an image in pixels. A pixel is a dot on a computer screen. The word "pixel" comes from **pic**ture **el**ement.

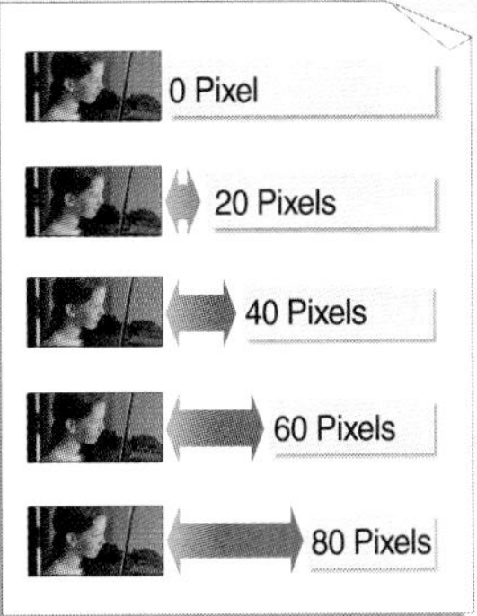

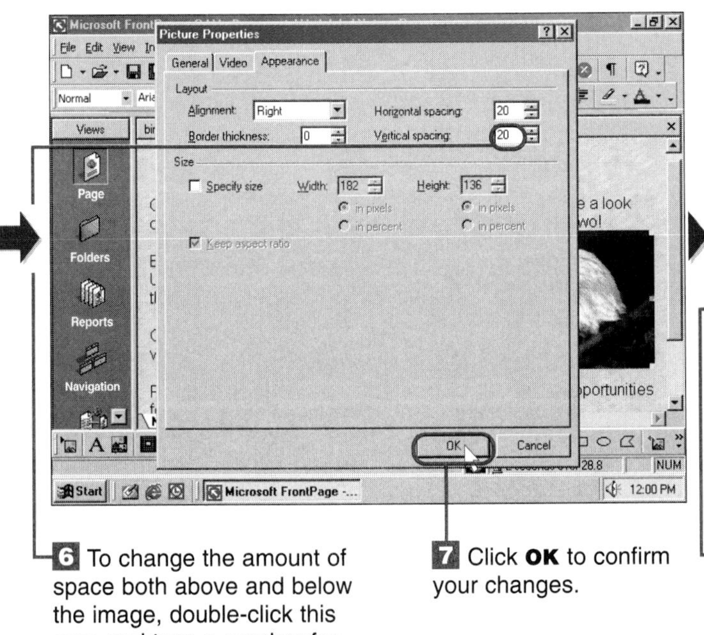

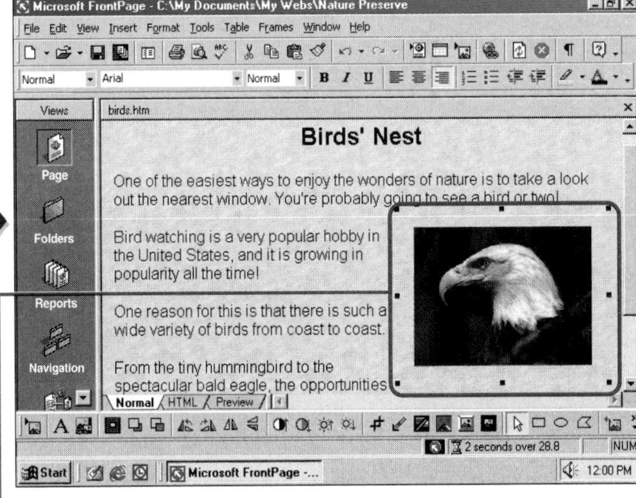

6 To change the amount of space both above and below the image, double-click this area and type a number for the amount of space in pixels.

7 Click **OK** to confirm your changes.

■ The image appears with the spacing you specified.

CROP AN IMAGE

You can crop an image to remove parts of the image you do not need.

CROP AN IMAGE

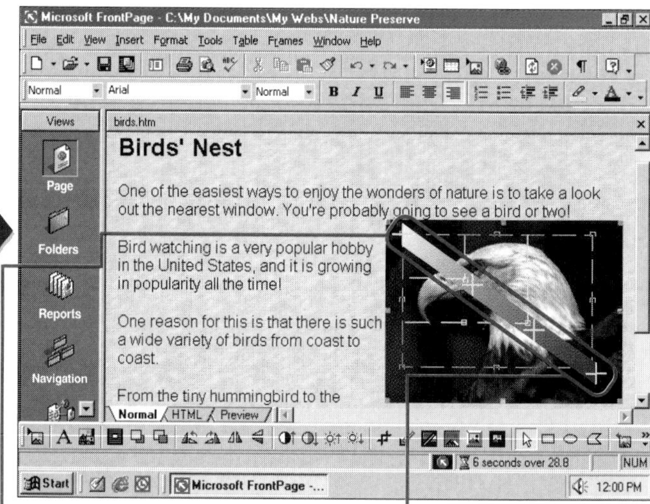

1 Click the image you want to crop.

2 Click [crop button] to crop the image.

Note: If the [crop button] button is not displayed, see page 30 to display the Pictures toolbar.

■ A dashed line appears around the image.

3 Position the mouse + over the top left corner of the part of the image you want to keep.

4 Drag the mouse + over the part of the image you want to keep.

*Note: If you make a mistake when selecting the area, click outside of the image and then repeat steps **1** to **4**.*

Why would I crop an image?

You can crop an image to focus a reader's attention on an important part of the image. Cropping an image also lets you change the proportions of an image so the image fits better on your Web page.

When you crop an image, you reduce the file size of the image. This allows the image to transfer more quickly to a reader's screen.

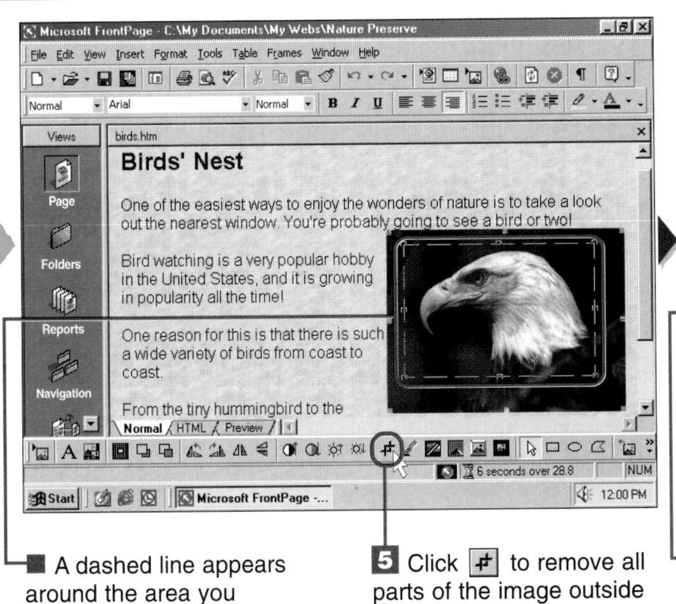

■ A dashed line appears around the area you selected.

5 Click [crop button] to remove all parts of the image outside of the area you selected.

■ All parts of the image outside of the area you selected disappear.

Note: If you previously resized the image, the cropped area will change to the size you specified for the image.

CHANGE ALIGNMENT OF AN IMAGE

You can align images in different ways to enhance the appearance of your Web page.

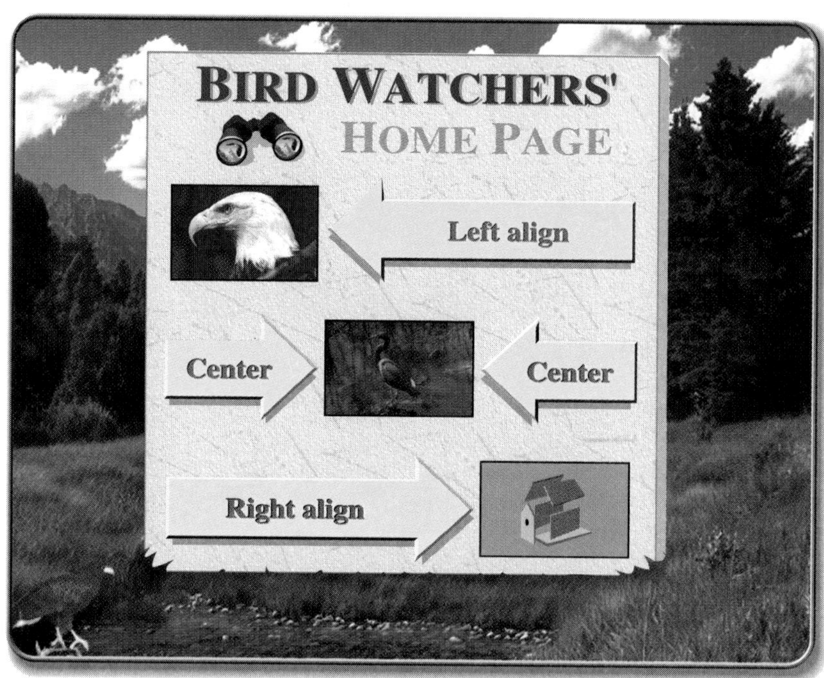

CHANGE ALIGNMENT OF AN IMAGE

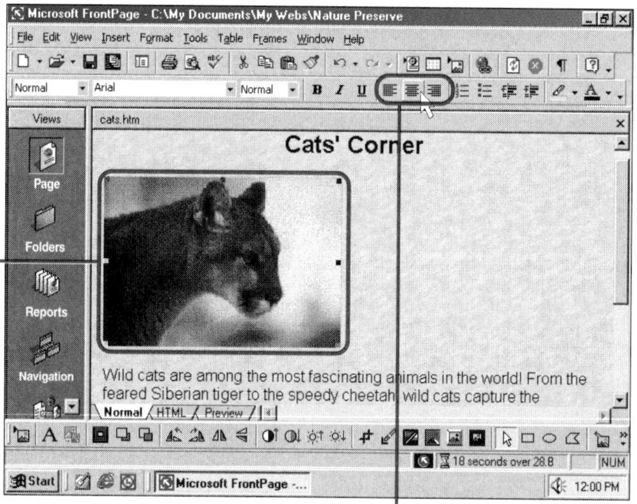

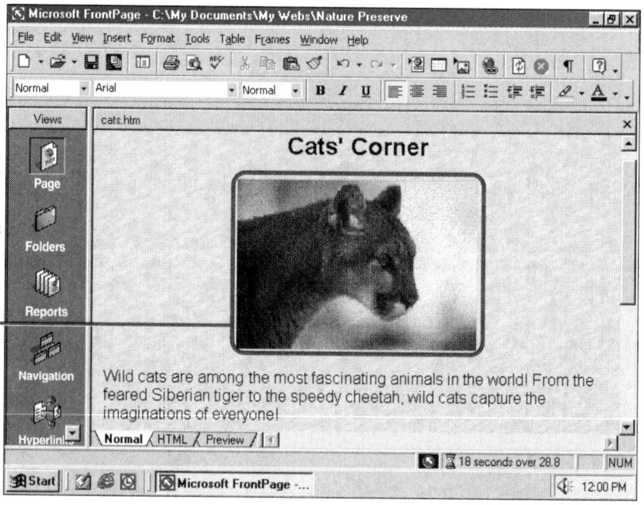

1 Click the image you want to align differently.

2 Click one of the following options.

- Left align
- Center
- Right align

■ The image appears in the new alignment.

■ To deselect the image, click outside the image.

ADD TEXT TO AN IMAGE

You can add text to an image to provide a title or explanation for the image.

You can only add text to a GIF image. For information on GIF images, see page 98.

ADD TEXT TO AN IMAGE

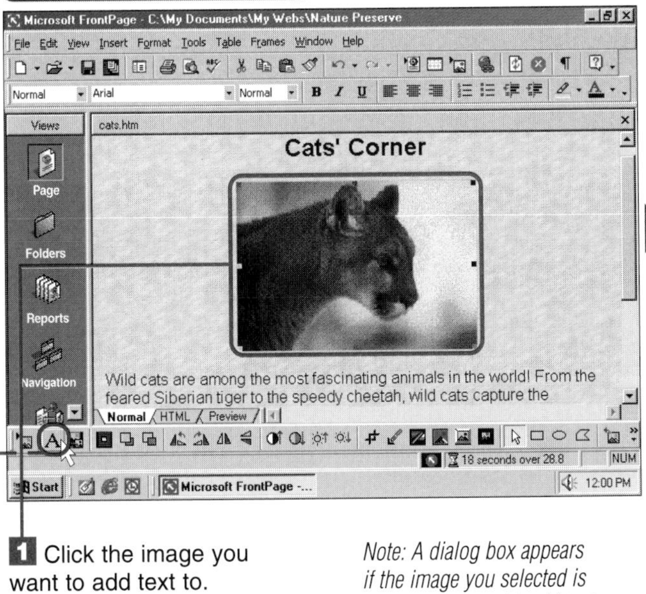

1 Click the image you want to add text to.

2 Click A to add text to the image.

Note: A dialog box appears if the image you selected is not a GIF image. To add text to the image, FrontPage will need to convert the image to a GIF image. Click ***OK*** *to continue.*

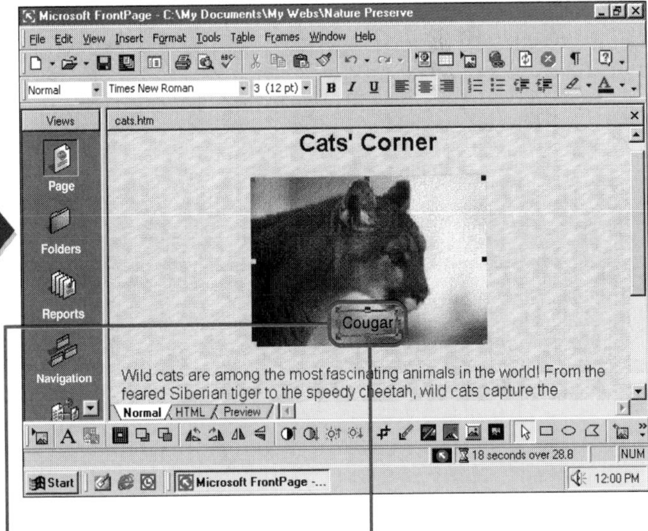

■ A text box appears on the image.

3 Type the text you want to add to the image.

4 When you finish typing the text, click outside the image.

Note: You can move or resize a text box as you would move or resize any image. To move or resize an image, see page 104.

■ To delete the text, click the text and then press the Delete key.

CREATE A THUMBNAIL IMAGE

You can create a thumbnail image on your Web page. A thumbnail image is a small version of an image that readers can select to display a larger version of the image.

Thumbnail images allow readers to quickly view the smaller image and decide if they want to wait to view the larger image. Thumbnail images transfer faster and appear on a reader's screen more quickly.

CREATE A THUMBNAIL IMAGE

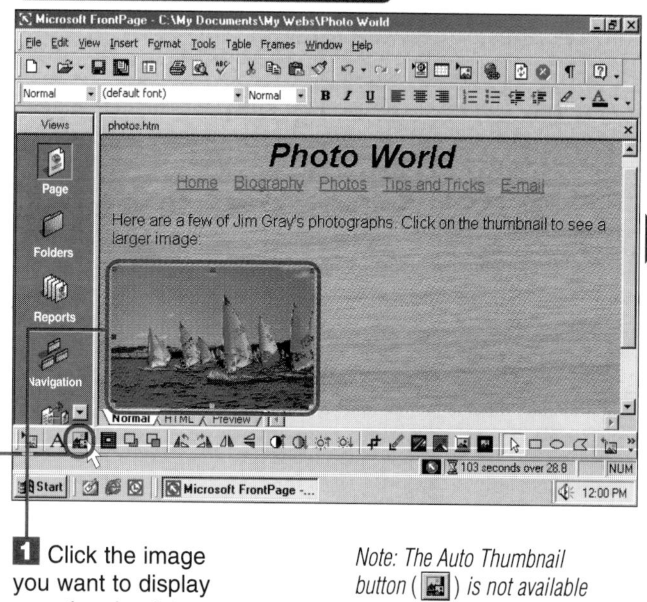

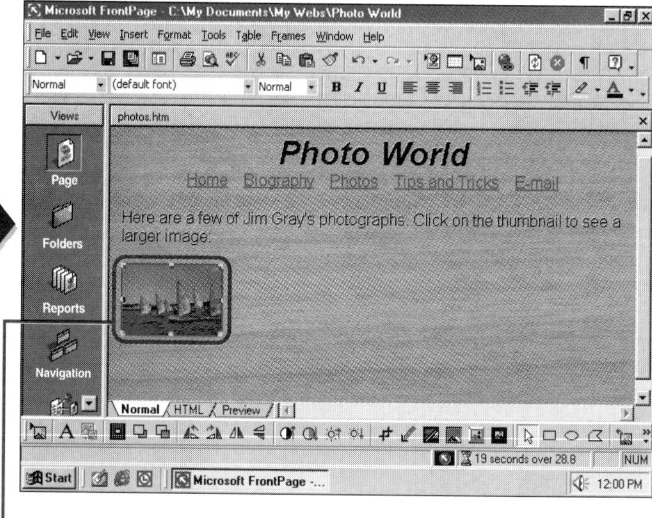

1 Click the image you want to display as a thumbnail image.

2 Click to create a thumbnail image.

Note: The Auto Thumbnail button ( ) is not available if your image is too small to create a thumbnail image or if the image is already a link.

■ A smaller version of the image appears on your Web page.

■ A reader can click the image to view the larger version of the image.

Note: To test the link, you must use the Preview view. For information on the Preview view, see page 42.

■ When you save the Web page, FrontPage will save the new thumbnail image as part of your Web site.

MAKE IMAGE BACKGROUND TRANSPARENT

You can make the background of an image transparent so the background will blend into your Web page.

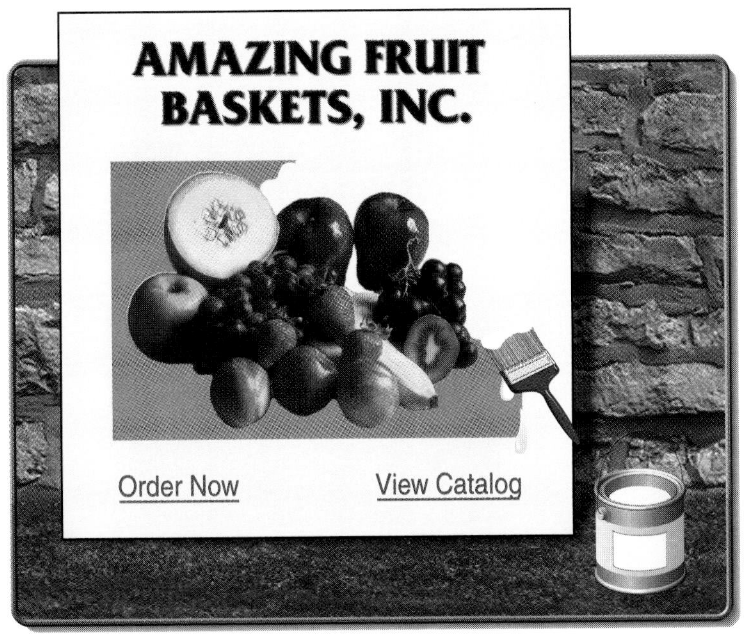

You can make only one color in the background of an image transparent. Every part of the image that displays the color will also become transparent.

You can make only a GIF image transparent. For information on the types of images, see page 98.

MAKE IMAGE BACKGROUND TRANSPARENT

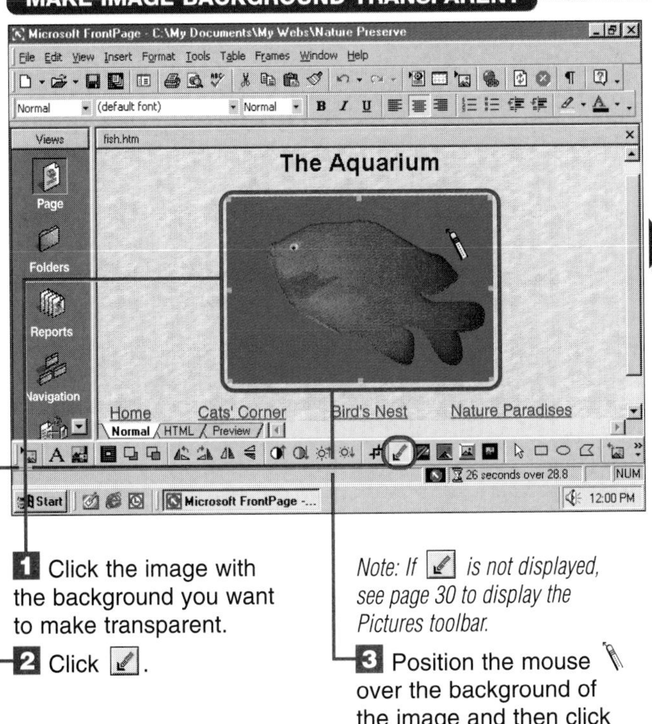

1 Click the image with the background you want to make transparent.

2 Click [icon].

Note: If [icon] is not displayed, see page 30 to display the Pictures toolbar.

3 Position the mouse over the background of the image and then click to select the background color.

■ The image displays a transparent background.

CREATE AN IMAGE MAP

You can create an image map that divides an image into different areas, called hotspots, which each link to a different Web page.

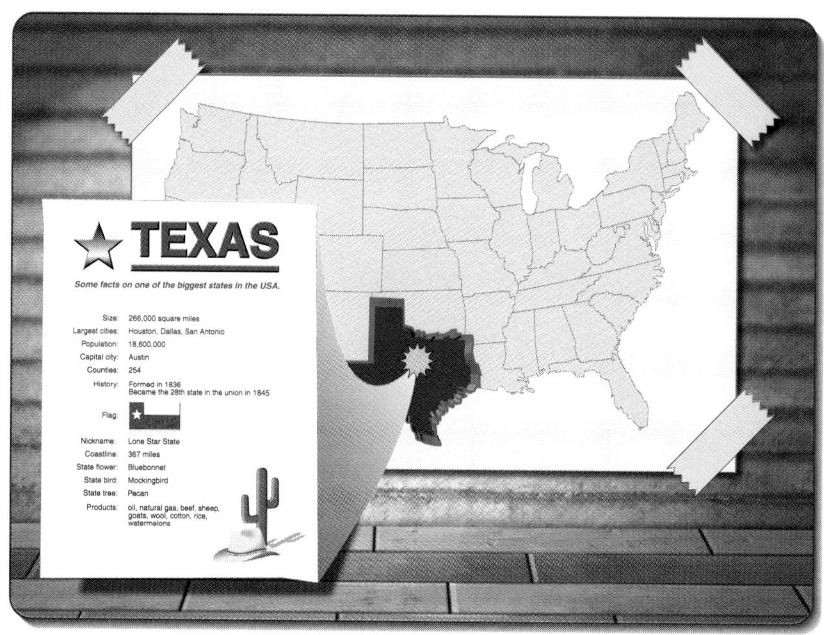

Creating an image map is useful for an image such as a floor plan or map that you want to contain links to different Web pages.

CREATE AN IMAGE MAP

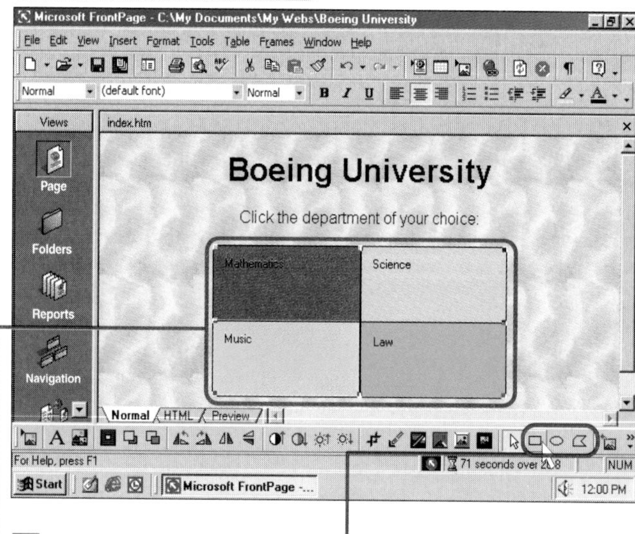

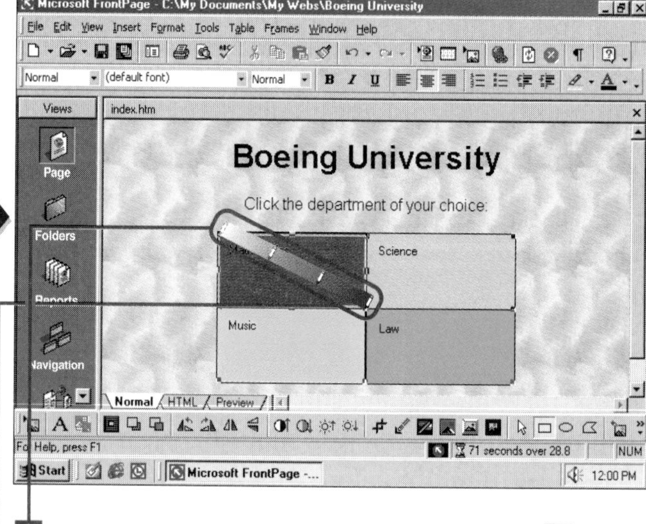

1 Click the image you want to use as an image map. Handles (■) appear around the image. To add an image, see pages 100 to 103.

2 Click the shape you want to use to create a hotspot.

- Rectangle
- Circle
- Irregular shape

Note: If the buttons are not displayed, see page 30 to display the Pictures toolbar.

3 Position the mouse I over the area of the image you want to make a hotspot (I changes to ✎).

4 Drag the mouse ✎ until the shape is the size you want.

■ If you selected the irregular shape in step **2**, repeat steps **3** and **4** until you finish drawing all the lines for the shape. Then double-click the mouse to complete the shape.

Note: A hotspot cannot extend beyond the edge of an image.

What should I consider when choosing an image for an image map?

When creating an image map, you should use an image that has several distinct areas that readers can select. Photographs do not usually make good image maps.

How do I move, resize or delete a hotspot?

You can move or resize a hotspot as you would move or resize any image on your Web page. To move or resize an image, see page 104.

To remove a hotspot, click the hotspot and then press the Delete key.

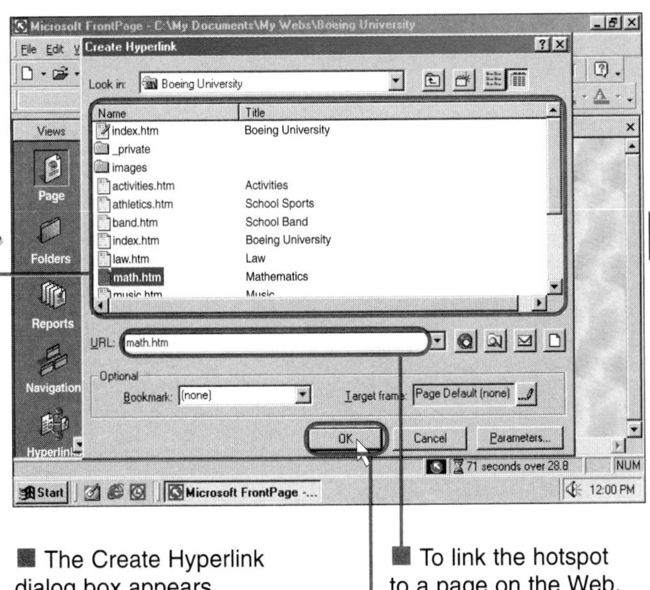

■ The Create Hyperlink dialog box appears.

■ This area displays all the Web pages in your current Web site.

5 To link the hotspot to a Web page in your current Web site, click the Web page.

■ To link the hotspot to a page on the Web, click this area and then type the address of the Web page.

6 Click **OK** to create the link.

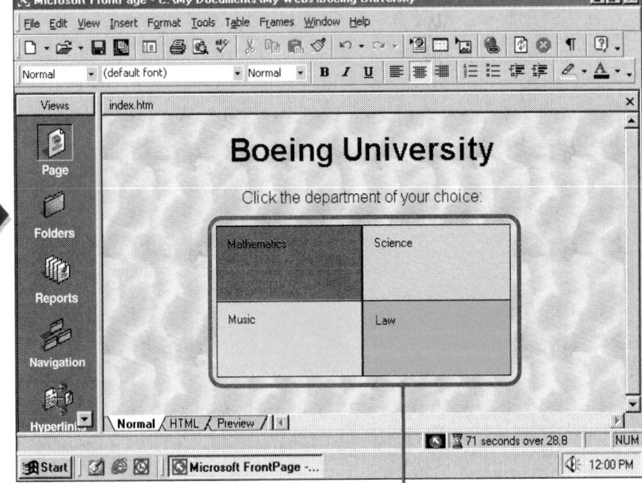

■ You can repeat steps 1 to 6 for each hotspot you want to create.

■ To deselect the image and hide the hotspots, click outside the image.

Note: To once again display the hotspots, click the image.

■ A reader can click a hotspot to display the linked Web page.

Note: To test hotspots, you must use the Preview view. For information on the Preview view, see page 42.

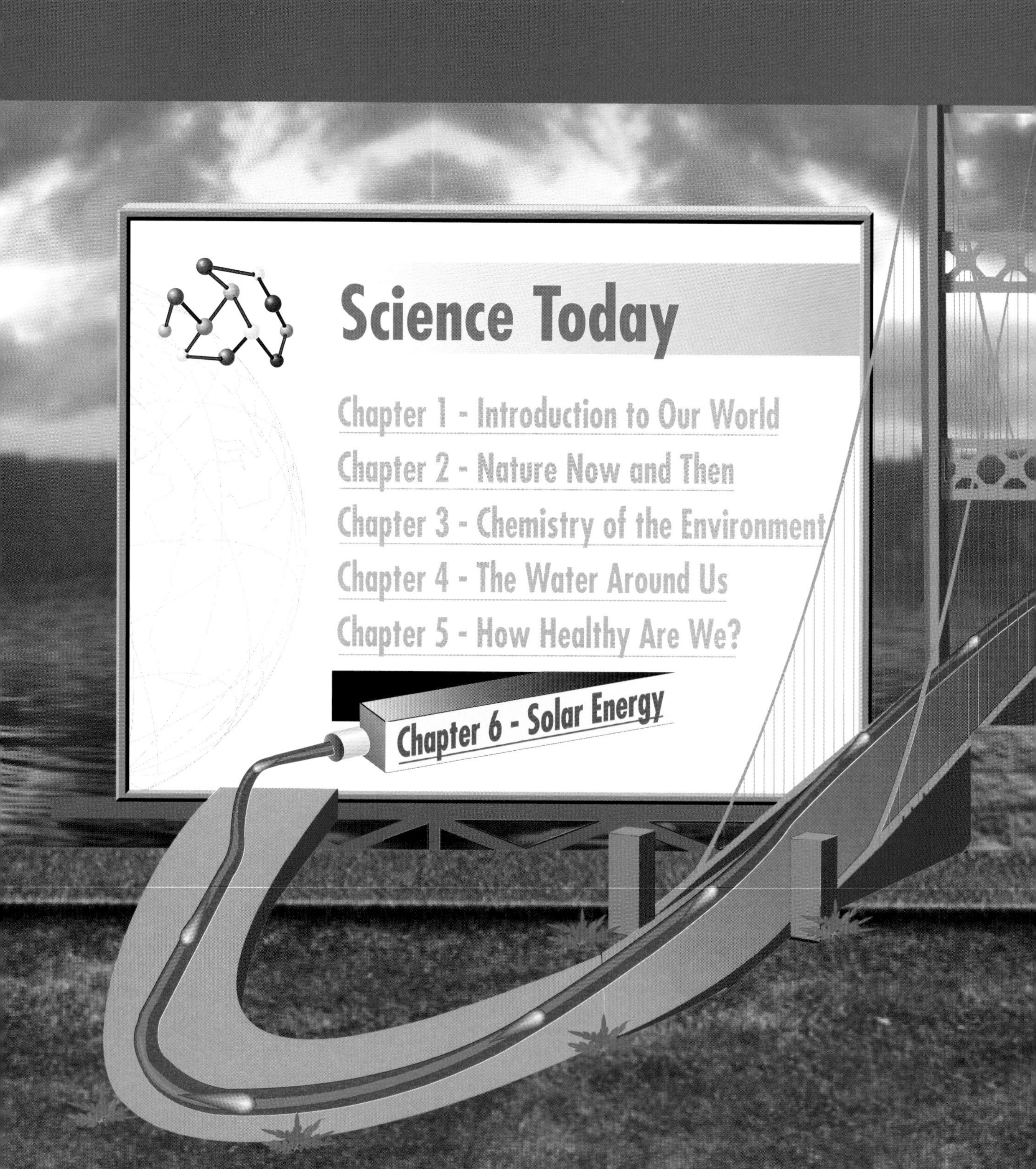

Science Today
Chapter 1 - Introduction to Our World
Chapter 2 - Nature Now and Then
Chapter 3 - Chemistry of the Environment
Chapter 4 - The Water Around Us
Chapter 5 - How Healthy Are We?
Chapter 6 - Solar Energy

hapter 6 - Solar Energy

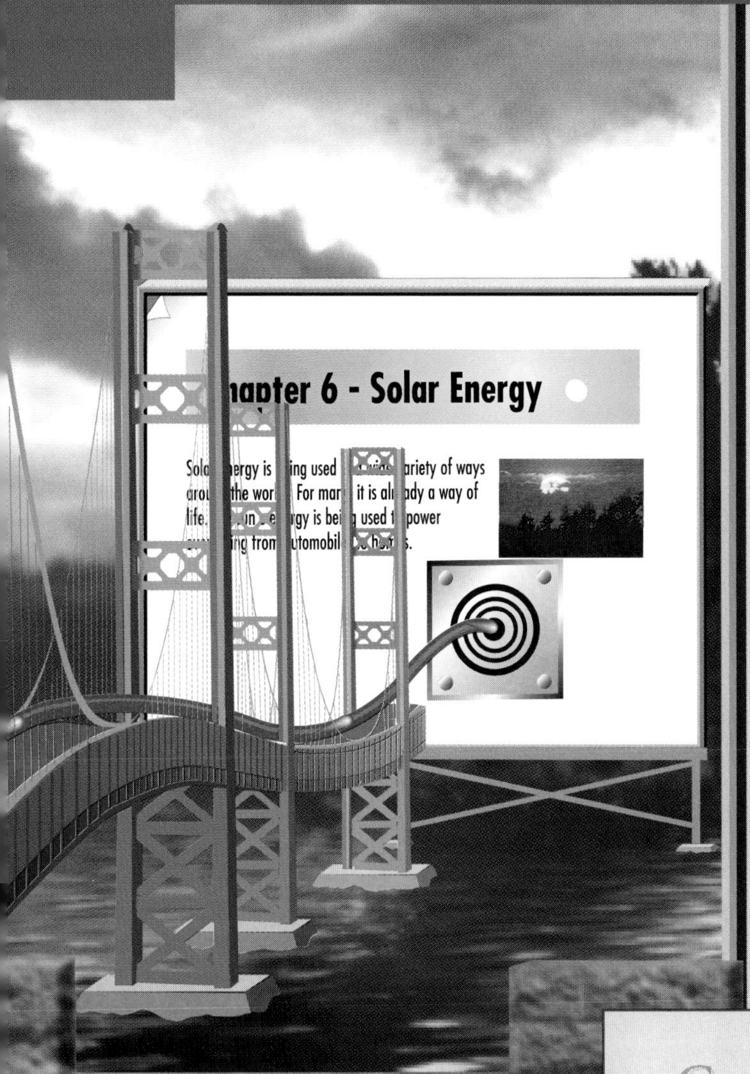

CHAPTER 8

Create Links

Would you like to create links that will connect your Web pages to other information on the Internet? Learn how in this chapter.

Great Web Sites You Can Visit!
1 Bank of America
2 Wal-Mart
3 McDonald's
4 NBC News
5 NFL Football
6 Sunkist
7 Pepsi
8 BMW
Link
Visited link
Active link

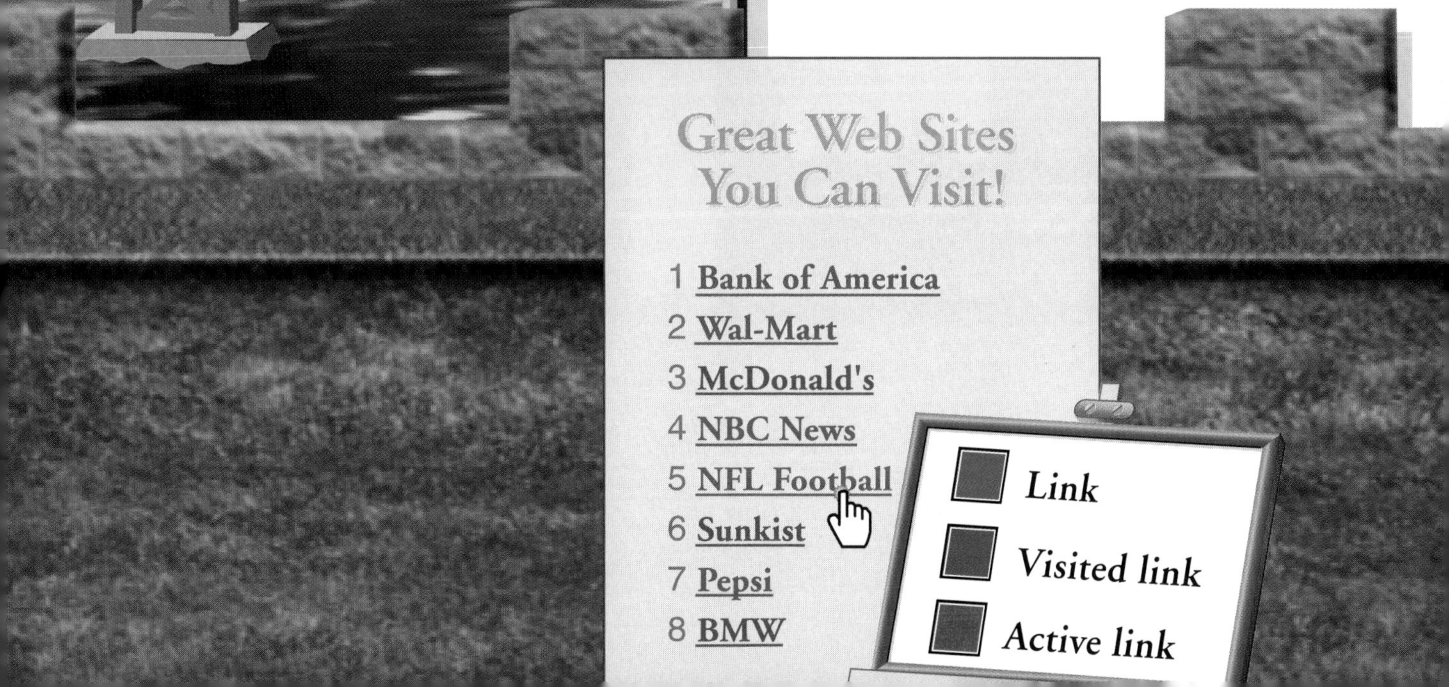

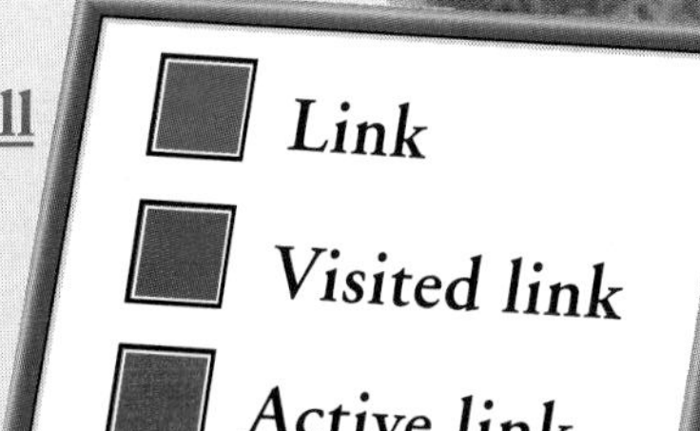

CREATE A LINK TO ANOTHER WEB PAGE

You can create a link to connect a word, phrase or image on your Web page to another page on the Web.

You can create a link to a Web page in your own Web site or to a Web page created by another person or company.

CREATE A LINK TO ANOTHER WEB PAGE

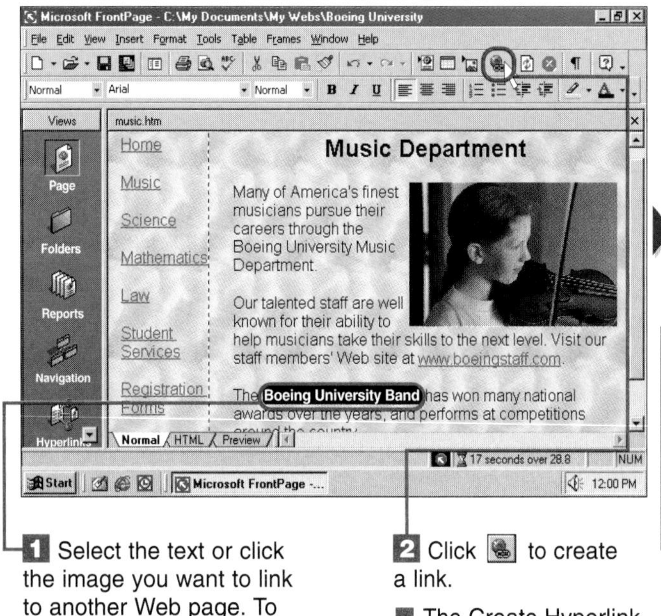

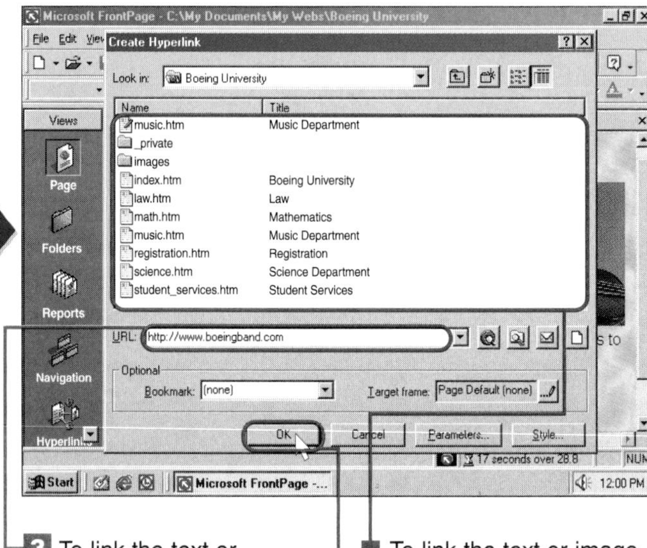

1 Select the text or click the image you want to link to another Web page. To select text, see page 54.

Note: To add an image, see pages 100 to 103.

2 Click 🌐 to create a link.

■ The Create Hyperlink dialog box appears.

3 To link the text or image to a page on the Web, type the address of the Web page.

■ To link the text or image to a Web page in the current Web site, click the Web page in this area. The area displays all the Web pages in the current Web site.

4 Click **OK** to create the link.

What should I consider when creating a link to another Web page?

Be Descriptive

Make sure the text or image you use for a link clearly indicates where the link will take your readers. Do not use the phrase "Click Here" for a link, since this phrase is not very informative.

Check Your Links

When you create a link to a Web page you did not create, you should verify the link on a regular basis. You may frustrate readers if they select a link that no longer contains relevant information or displays an error message.

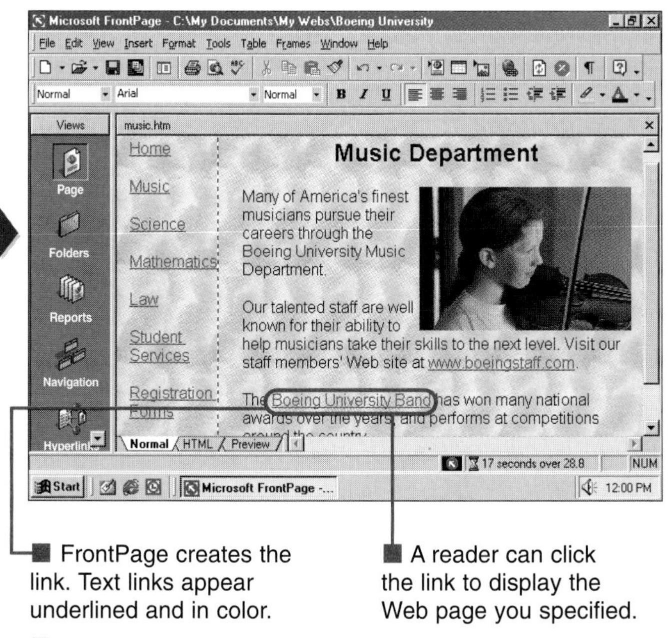

■ FrontPage creates the link. Text links appear underlined and in color.

■ To deselect text, click outside the selected area.

■ A reader can click the link to display the Web page you specified.

Note: To test the link, you must use the Preview view. For information on the Preview view, see page 42.

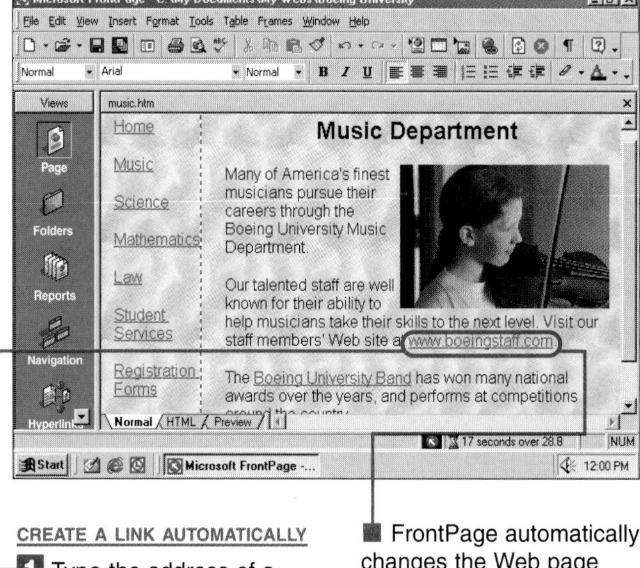

CREATE A LINK AUTOMATICALLY

1 Type the address of a Web page.

2 Press the **Spacebar** or the Enter key.

■ FrontPage automatically changes the Web page address to a link.

CREATE A LINK WITHIN A WEB PAGE

You can create a link that will take readers to a specific area on the same Web page. This helps readers quickly display information of interest.

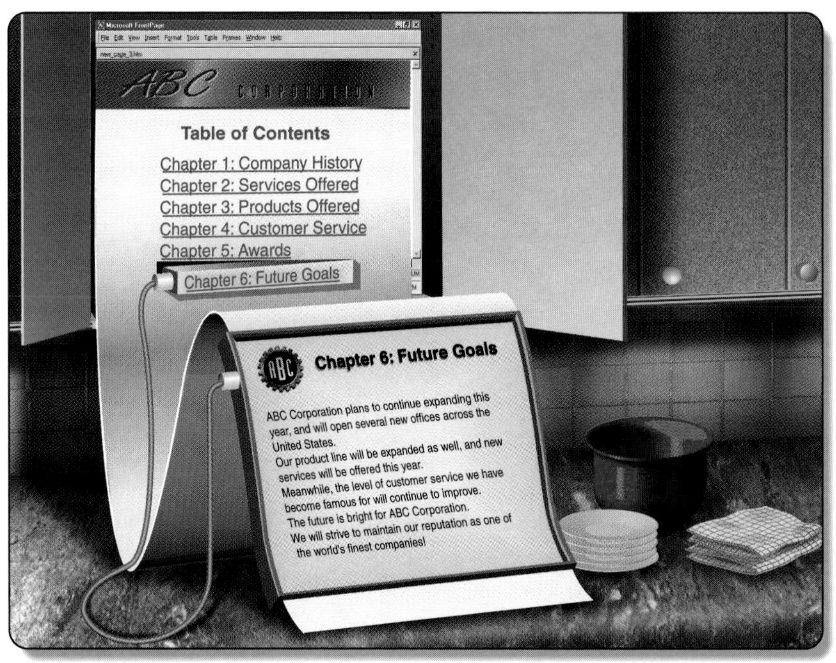

For example, you can create a table of contents at the top of a Web page that contains links to various sections of the page.

CREATE A LINK WITHIN A WEB PAGE

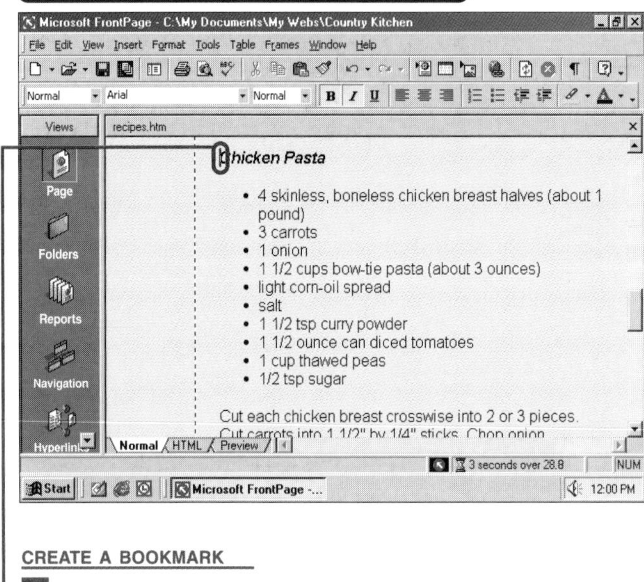

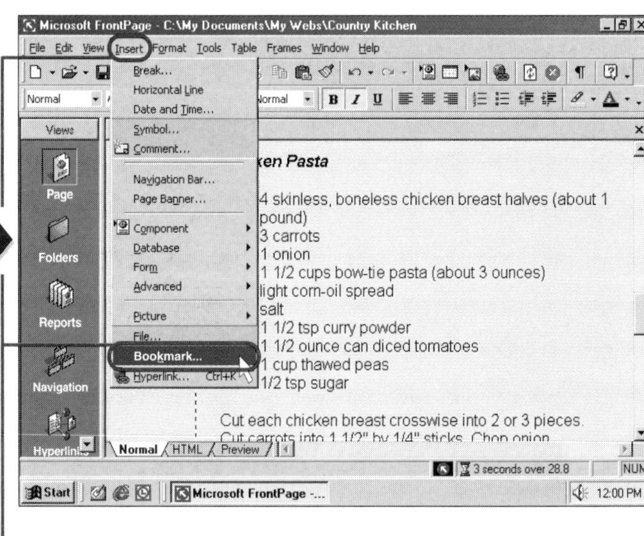

CREATE A BOOKMARK

1 Click the location on the Web page you want readers to be able to quickly display.

2 Click **Insert**.

3 Click **Bookmark**.

Note: If Bookmark does not appear on the menu, position the mouse over the bottom of the menu to display all the menu commands.

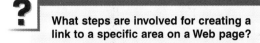

What steps are involved for creating a link to a specific area on a Web page?

Step 1–Create a Bookmark

You must create a bookmark that identifies the area of the Web page you want readers to be able to quickly display.

Step 2–Create a Link to a Bookmark

You must create a link that readers can select to display the area of the Web page you have bookmarked.

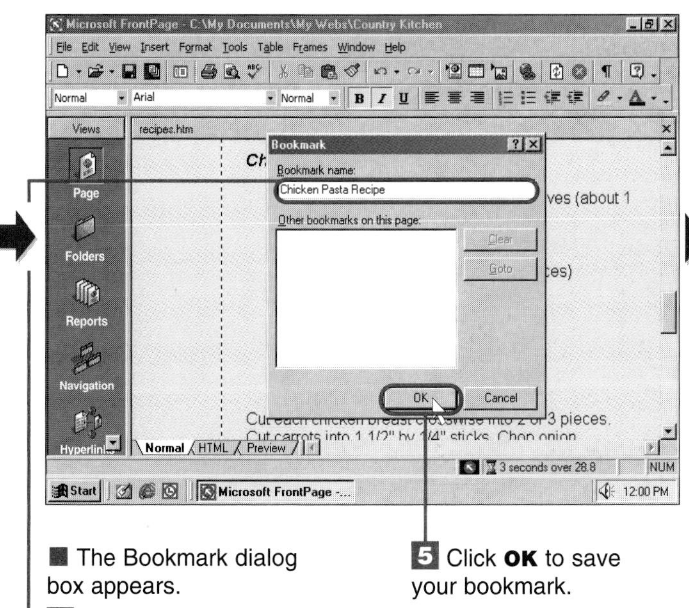

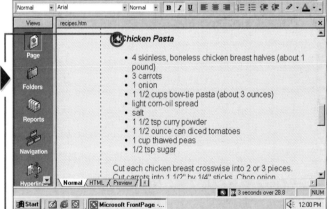

■ The Bookmark dialog box appears.

4 Type a name for the bookmark. Make sure the name clearly describes the Web page area.

5 Click **OK** to save your bookmark.

■ A flag ( ) appears on your Web page. The flag will not appear when you publish your Web page.

■ To delete a bookmark at any time, double-click the flag ( ) and then press the Delete key.

■ You now need to create a link that readers can select to display the area of the Web page you have bookmarked.

CONTINUED

CREATE A LINK WITHIN A WEB PAGE

After you create a bookmark to identify an area of a Web page, you will need to create a link that readers can select to display the area.

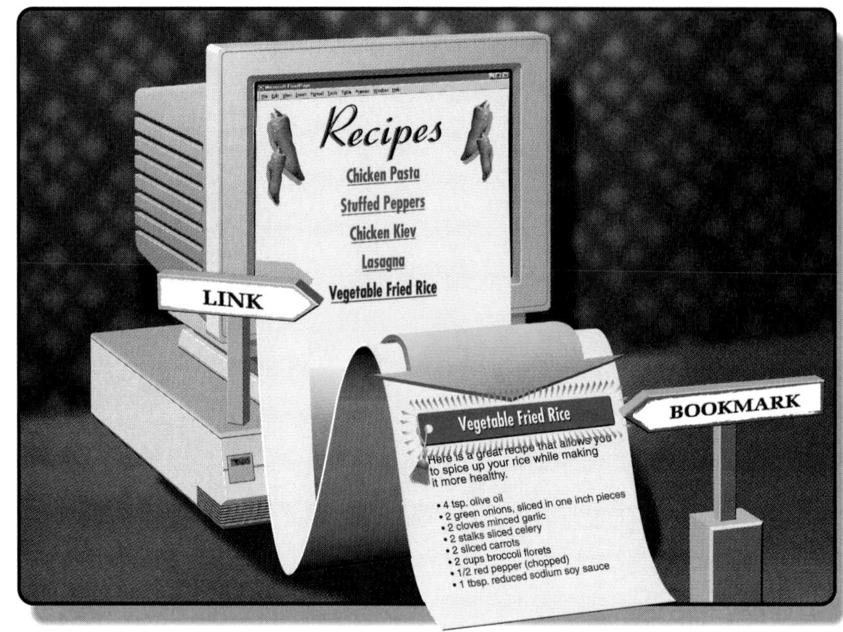

Make sure the text or image you use for the link clearly indicates where the link will take your readers.

CREATE A LINK WITHIN A WEB PAGE (CONTINUED)

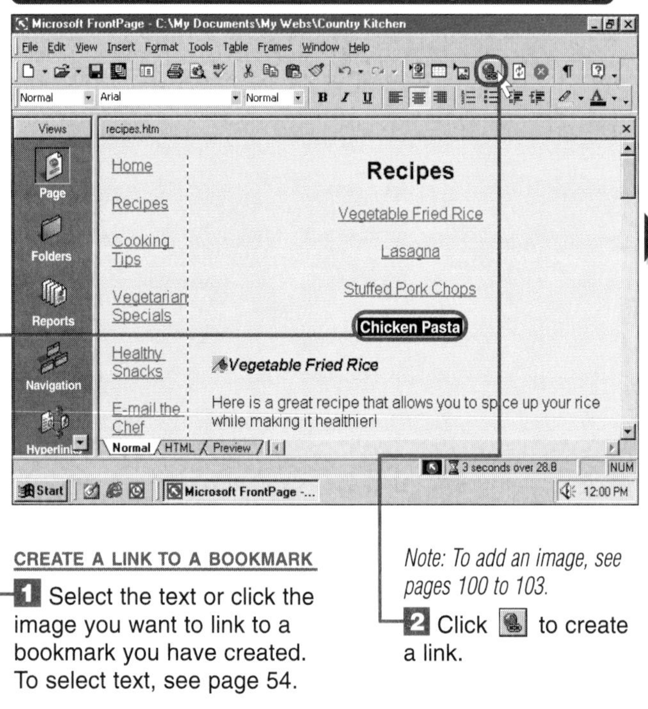

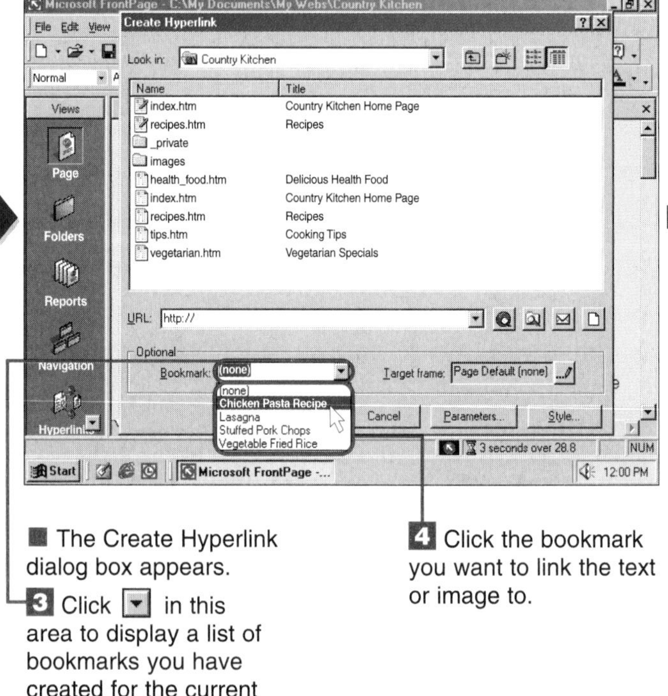

CREATE A LINK TO A BOOKMARK

1 Select the text or click the image you want to link to a bookmark you have created. To select text, see page 54.

Note: To add an image, see pages 100 to 103.

2 Click to create a link.

■ The Create Hyperlink dialog box appears.

3 Click ▼ in this area to display a list of bookmarks you have created for the current Web page.

4 Click the bookmark you want to link the text or image to.

? What should I consider when adding links to my Web page?

Separate Links

Do not place two text links beside each other on your Web page. When two text links appear side by side, readers may see one long link rather than two separate links.

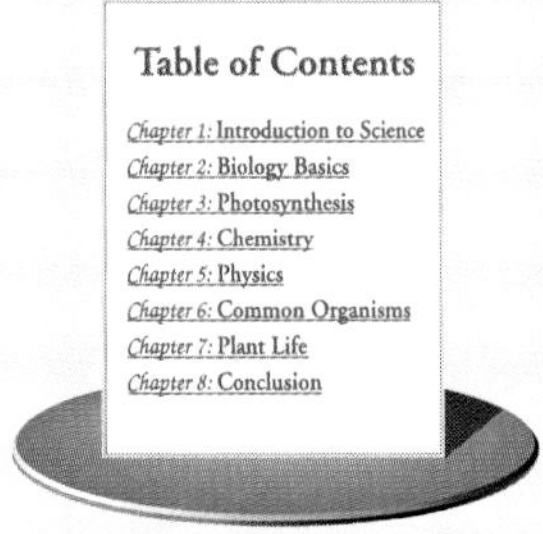

Use Link Menus

If you plan to include many links on your Web page, you should consider displaying the links in a menu format, like a table of contents in a book.

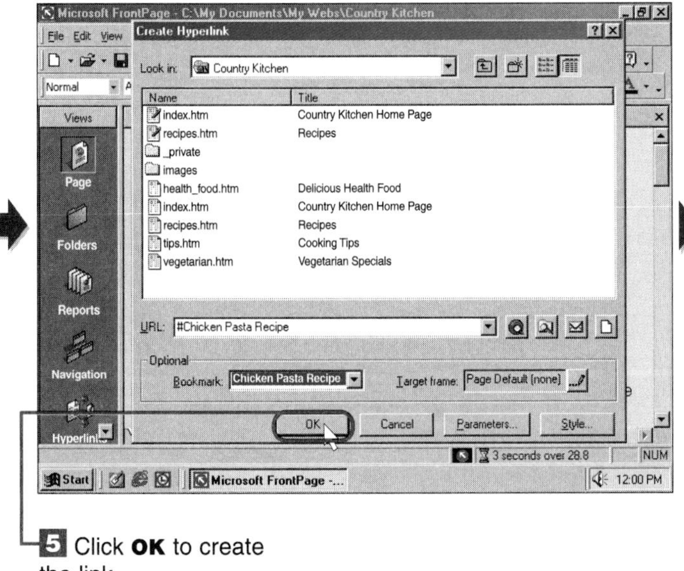

5 Click **OK** to create the link.

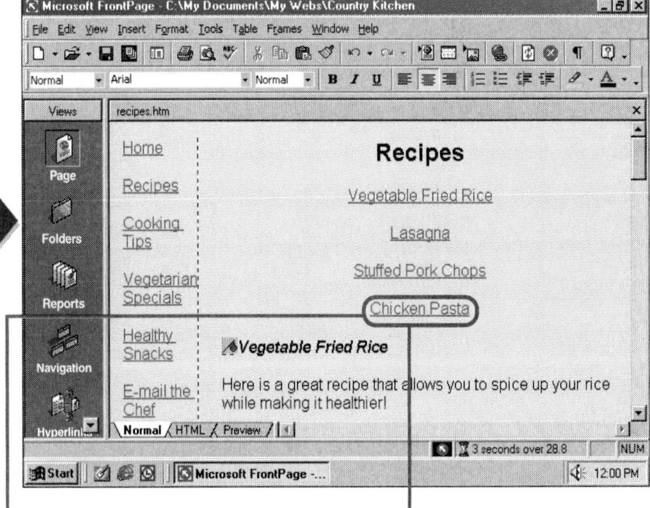

■ FrontPage creates the link. Text links appear underlined and in color.

■ To deselect text, click outside the selected area.

■ A reader can click the link to display the Web page area you specified.

Note: To test the link, you must use the Preview view. *For information on the Preview view, see page 42.*

You can create a link on your Web page that allows readers to quickly send you an e-mail message.

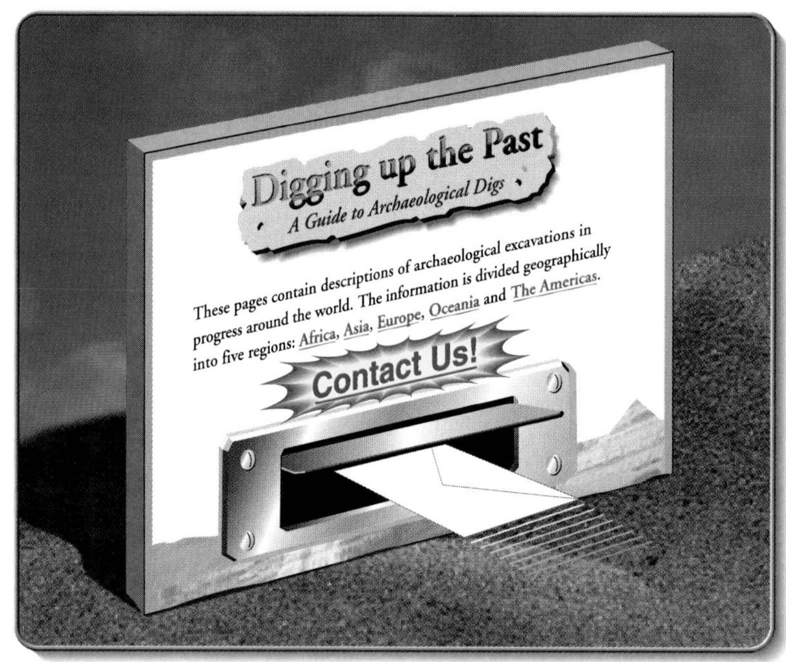

When a reader selects an e-mail link, a blank message addressed to you will appear.

CREATE AN E-MAIL LINK

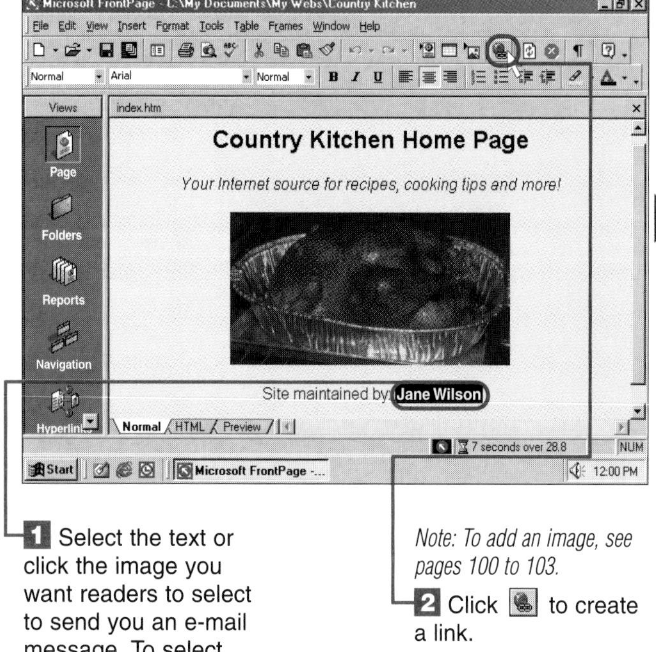

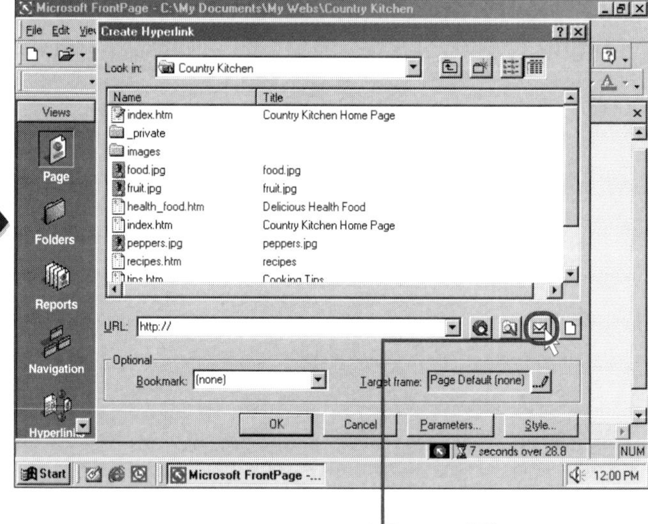

1 Select the text or click the image you want readers to select to send you an e-mail message. To select text, see page 54.

Note: To add an image, see pages 100 to 103.

2 Click [link icon] to create a link.

■ The Create Hyperlink dialog box appears.

3 Click [e-mail icon] to create an e-mail link.

? Why should I include an e-mail link on my Web page?

An e-mail link allows readers to send you questions and comments that can help you improve your Web pages. Many companies include a list of e-mail links that allow you to contact employees in different departments.

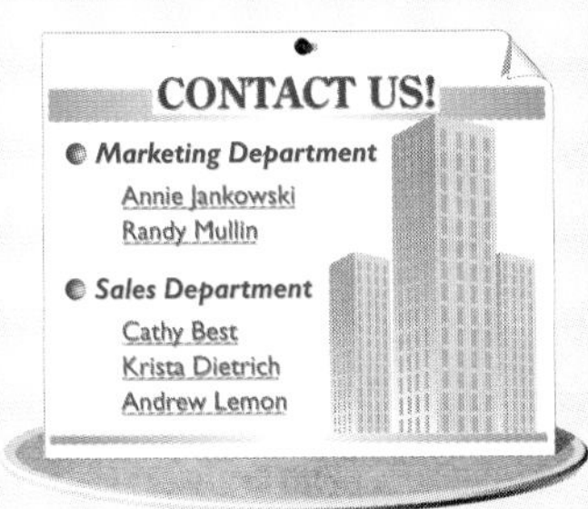

? Can FrontPage automatically create an e-mail link?

When you type an e-mail address on your Web page, FrontPage will automatically change the address to a link for you.

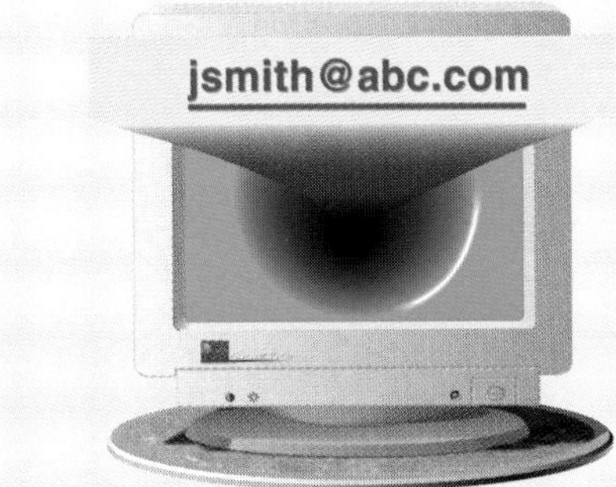

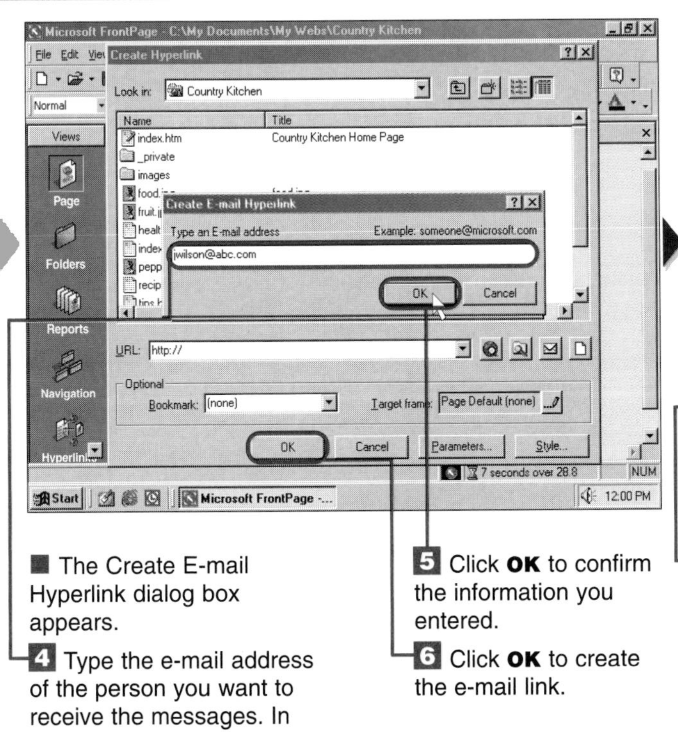

■ The Create E-mail Hyperlink dialog box appears.

4 Type the e-mail address of the person you want to receive the messages. In most cases, you will enter your own e-mail address.

5 Click **OK** to confirm the information you entered.

6 Click **OK** to create the e-mail link.

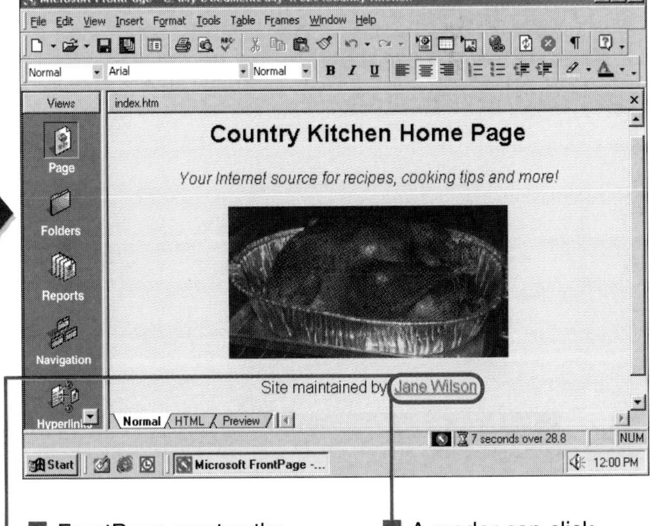

■ FrontPage creates the e-mail link. Text e-mail links appear underlined and in color.

■ To deselect text, click outside the selected area.

■ A reader can click the e-mail link to send a message to the e-mail address you specified.

Note: To test the link, you must use the Preview view. For information on the Preview view, see page 42.

EDIT A LINK

You can change the Web page that will appear when readers select a link.

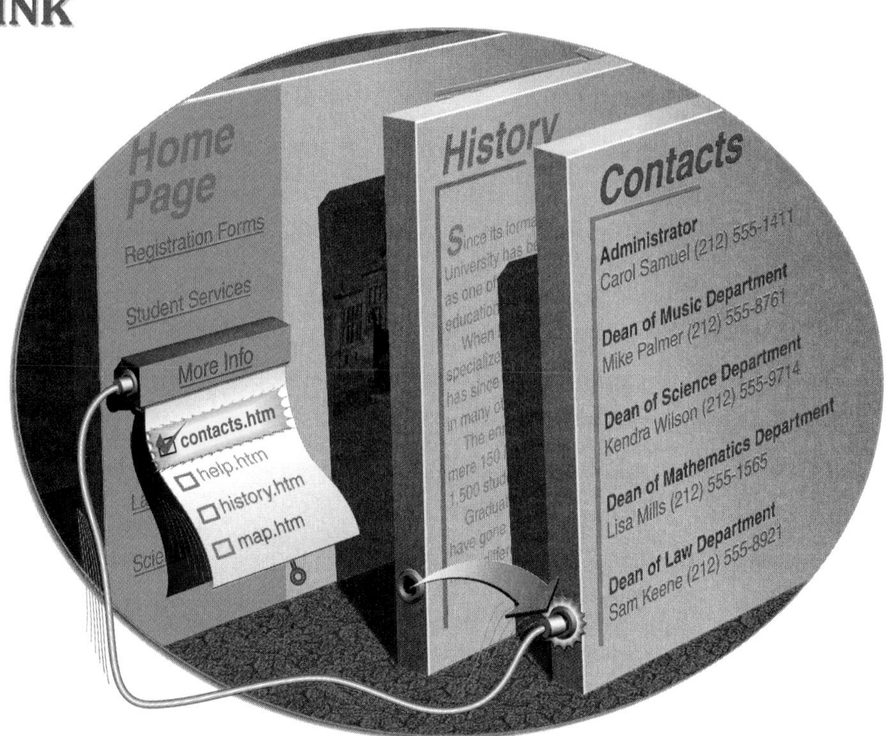

EDIT A LINK

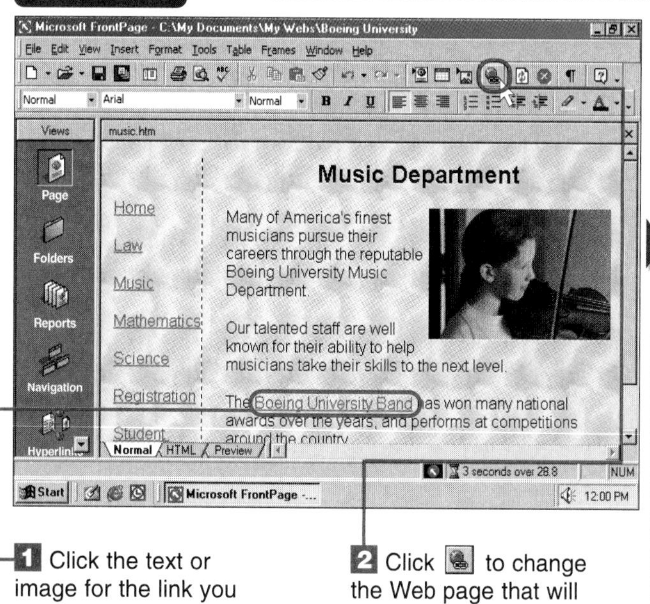

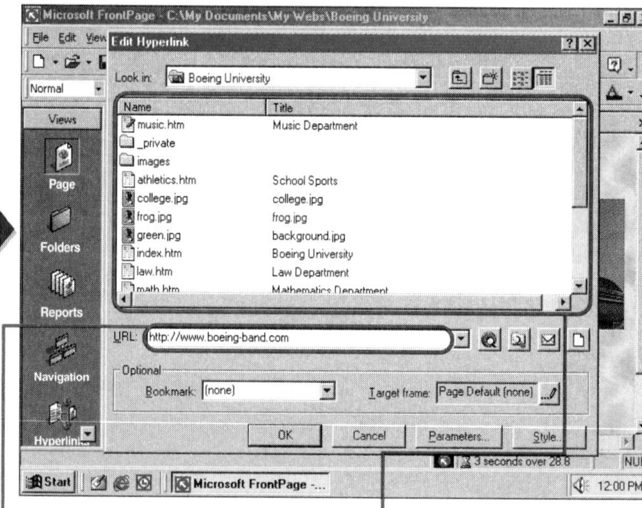

1 Click the text or image for the link you want to edit.

2 Click 🌐 to change the Web page that will appear when readers click the link.

■ The Edit Hyperlink dialog box appears.

3 To link the text or image to a different page on the Web, type the address of the Web page.

■ To link the text or image to a different Web page in the current Web site, click the Web page in this area. This area displays all the Web pages in the current Web site.

When would I need to edit a link?

You may need to edit a link if you typed a Web page address incorrectly when you created the link or if you want a link to connect to a different Web page. You should regularly check links that connect to Web pages you did not create. Companies and individuals often change the content of their Web pages and the content may no longer relate to your Web page.

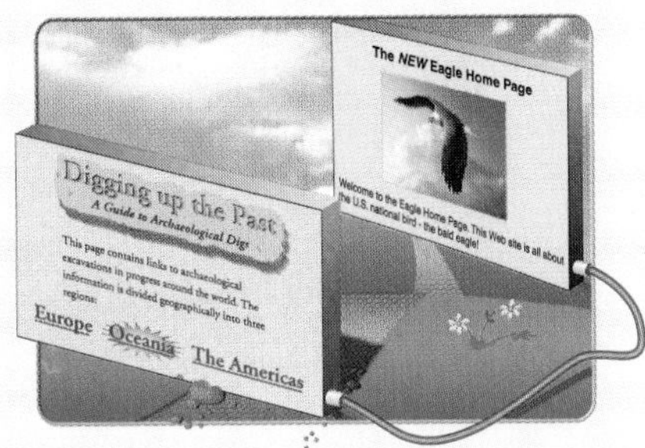

Can I edit the text for a link?

To edit the text for a link, drag the mouse I over the text you want to change until you highlight all the text and then type the new text. For example, you could change "www.maran.com" to "maranGraphics."

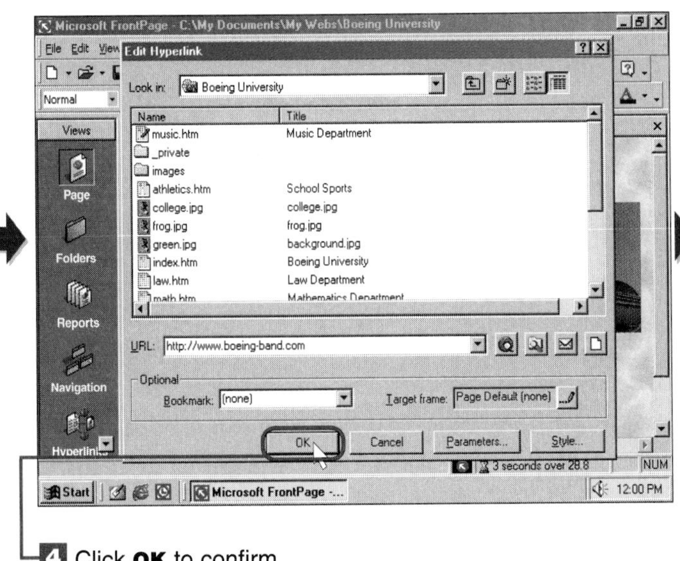

4 Click **OK** to confirm your change.

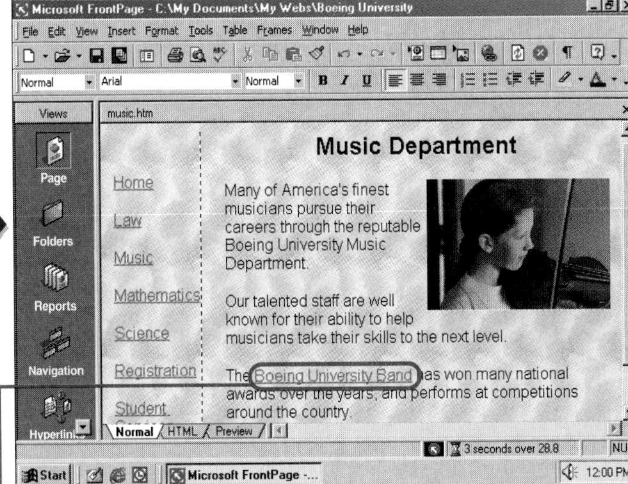

■ When readers click the link, the link will now display the Web page you specified.

■ To deselect the link, click outside the selected area.

Note: To test the link, you must use the Preview view. For information on the Preview view, see page 42.

REMOVE A LINK

You can remove a link from text or an image on your Web page.

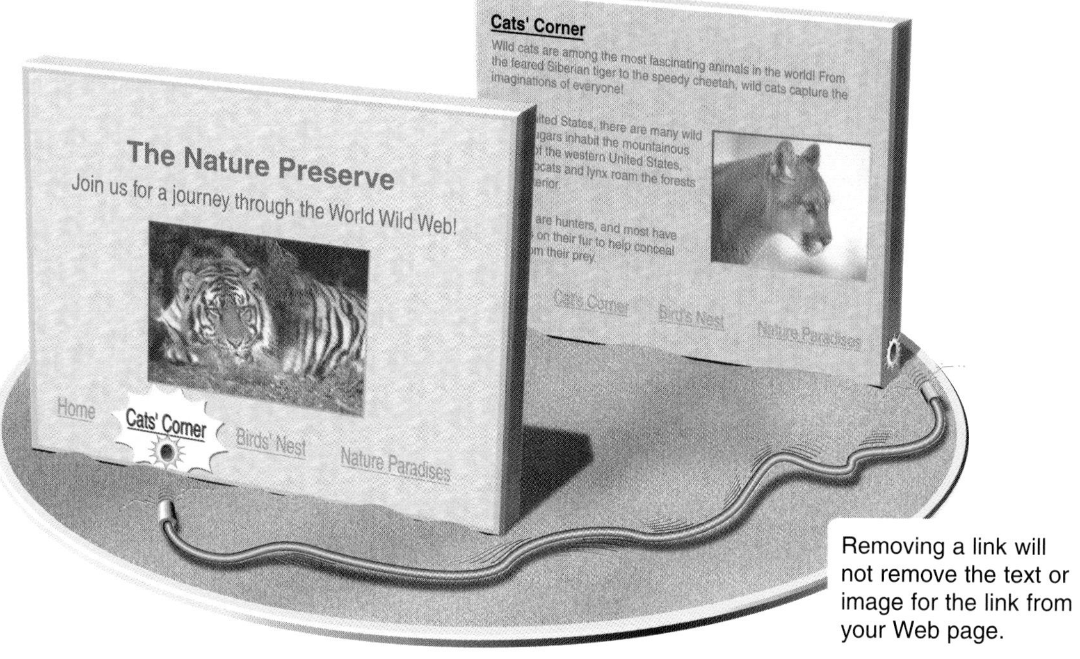

Removing a link will not remove the text or image for the link from your Web page.

REMOVE A LINK

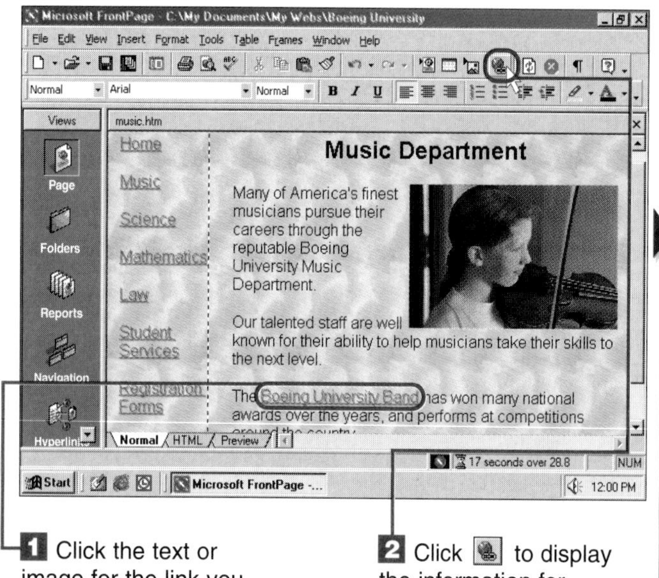

1 Click the text or image for the link you want to remove.

2 Click the hyperlink button to display the information for the link.

■ The Edit Hyperlink dialog box appears.

3 To select the information in this area, drag the mouse I over the text until you highlight all the information.

4 Press the **Delete** key to delete the information.

How do I remove a link as well as the text or image for the link?

To remove a link as well as the text or image for the link, select the text or click the image and then press the Delete key.

You may want to remove a link that takes readers to a Web page that no longer contains relevant information. Many companies and individuals regularly make changes to their Web pages, so you should check your links often and remove links that are no longer useful.

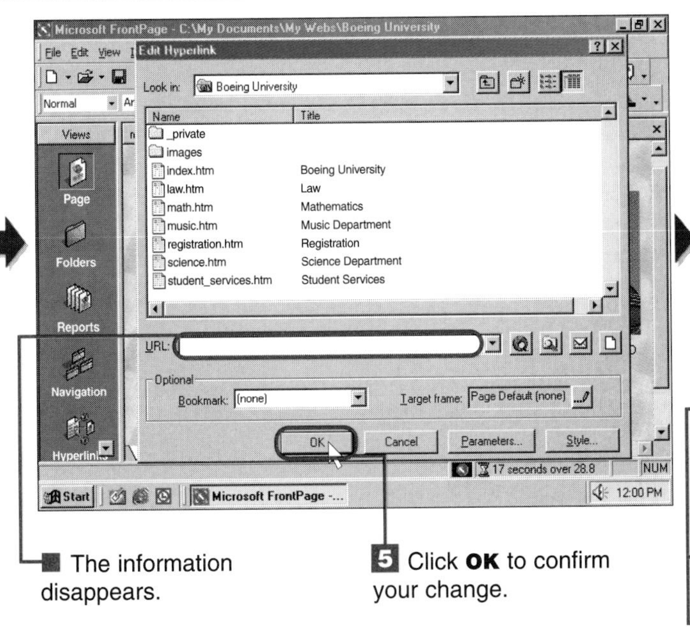

■ The information disappears.

5 Click **OK** to confirm your change.

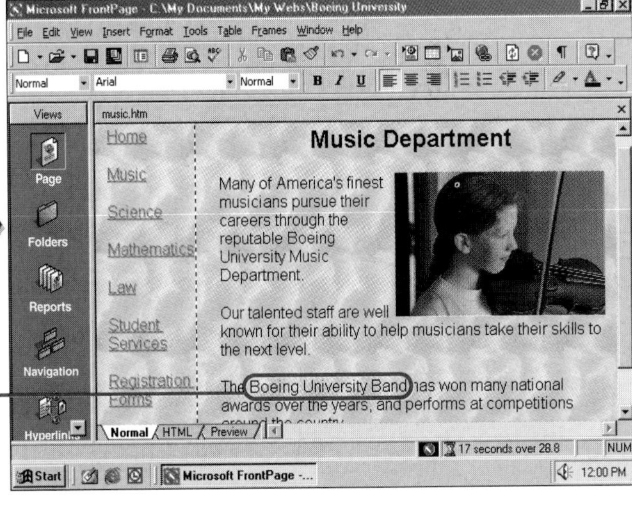

■ FrontPage removes the link from the text or image.

■ Text links no longer appear underlined and in color. The appearance of image links does not change.

■ To deselect text, click outside the selected area.

CHANGE LINK COLORS

You can change the color of links on your Web page.

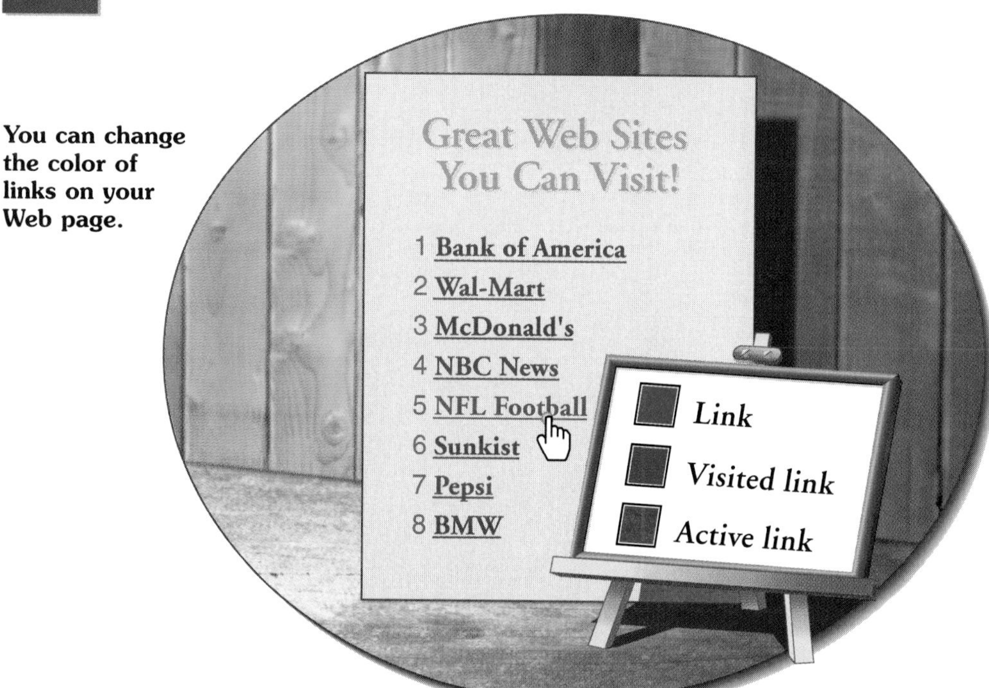

A Web page can contain three types of links.

Link
A link a reader has not previously selected.

Visited link
A link a reader has previously selected.

Active link
A link a reader is currently selecting.

CHANGE LINK COLORS

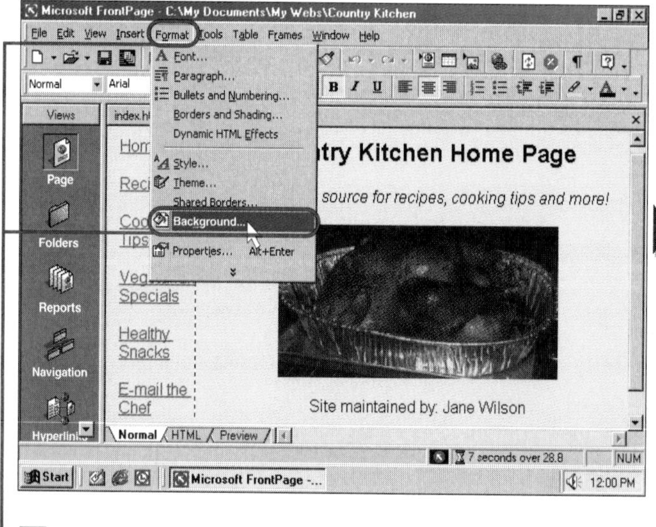

1 Click **Format**.

2 Click **Background**.

Note: If Background does not appear on the menu, position the mouse over the bottom of the menu to display all the menu commands.

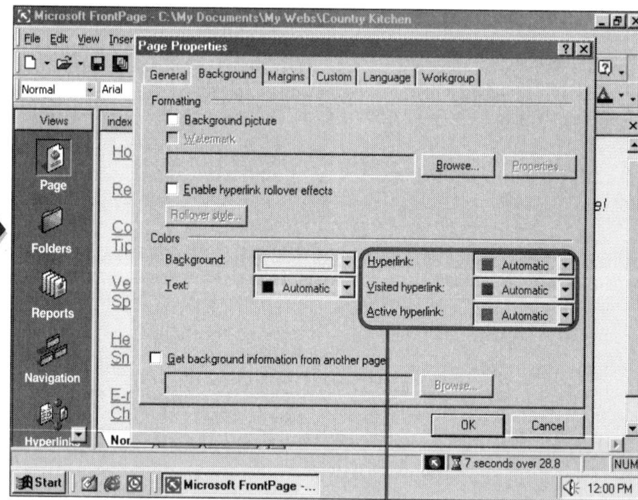

■ The Page Properties dialog box appears.

■ This area displays the colors currently used for links, visited links and active links.

What should I consider when changing the color of links?

Change Only When Necessary

You may confuse some readers if you do not use the standard link colors. You should change link colors only when necessary, such as when the background color you are using makes the links difficult to read.

Choose Different Colors

Make sure you choose different colors for links, visited links and active links so you can clearly distinguish between the types of links. By default, links are blue, visited links are purple and active links are red.

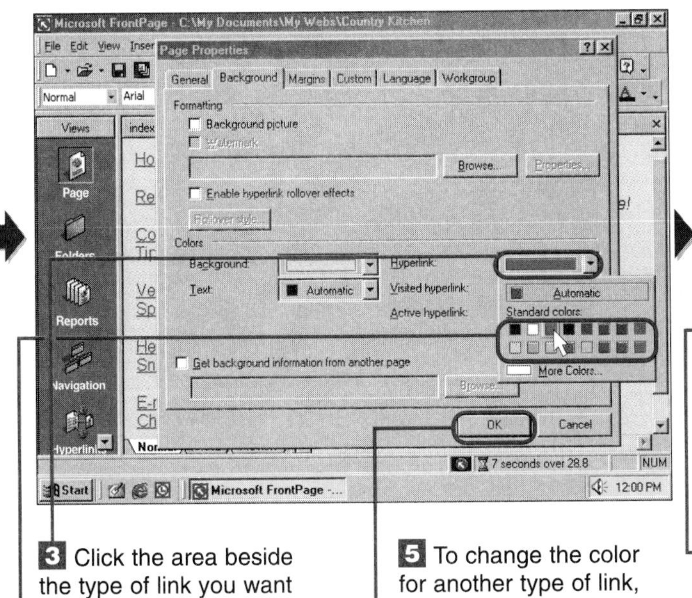

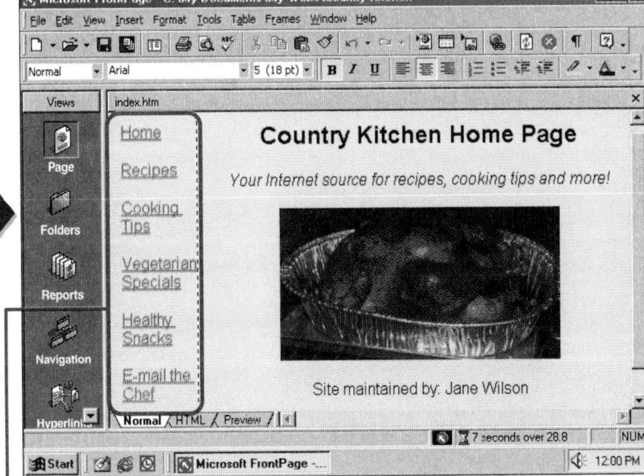

3 Click the area beside the type of link you want to display in a different color.

4 Click the color you want to use.

5 To change the color for another type of link, repeat steps **3** and **4** for each link.

6 Click **OK** to confirm your changes.

- The links on your Web page appear in the colors you selected.

- To return a link to its original color, repeat steps **1** to **6**, selecting **Automatic** in step **4**.

Note: To test a link, you must use the Preview view. For information on the Preview view, see page 42.

USING THE HYPERLINKS VIEW

You can use the Hyperlinks view to display the links that connect each Web page to other pages in your Web site.

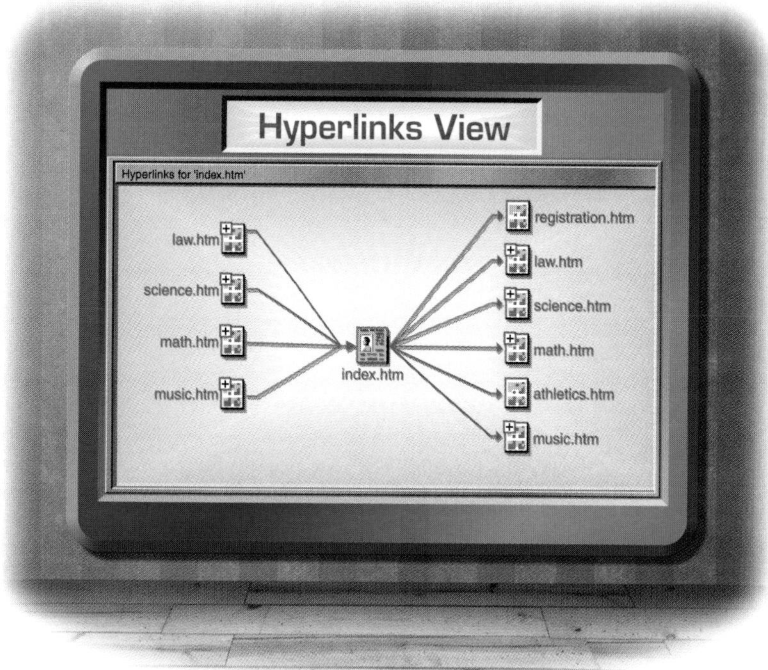

The Hyperlinks view helps you review the links you have added to your Web pages. This can help you determine if you forgot to add links to a Web page.

USING THE HYPERLINKS VIEW

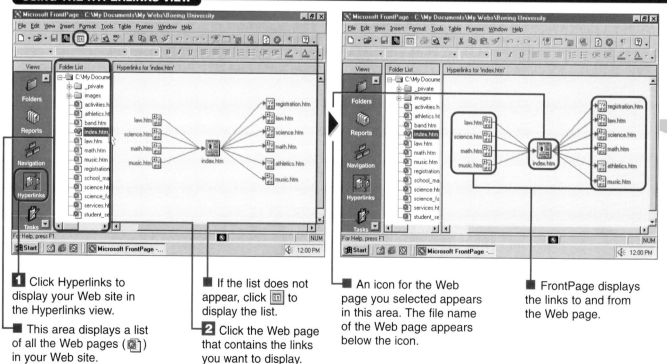

1 Click Hyperlinks to display your Web site in the Hyperlinks view.

■ This area displays a list of all the Web pages in your Web site.

■ If the list does not appear, click the Folder List button to display the list.

2 Click the Web page that contains the links you want to display.

■ An icon for the Web page you selected appears in this area. The file name of the Web page appears below the icon.

■ FrontPage displays the links to and from the Web page.

What does each icon represent in the Hyperlinks view?

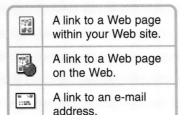

Icon	Meaning
	A link to a Web page within your Web site.
	A link to a Web page on the Web.
	A link to an e-mail address.

Why do links I didn't create appear in my Web site?

When you use a template or wizard to create your Web site, FrontPage may add links to the Web pages for you. To create a Web site using a template or wizard, see page 20.

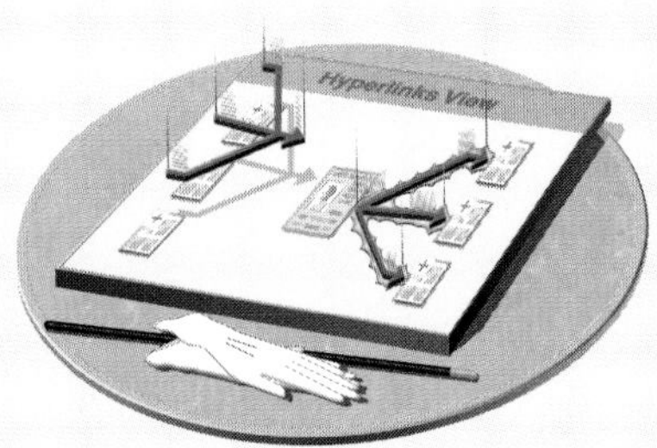

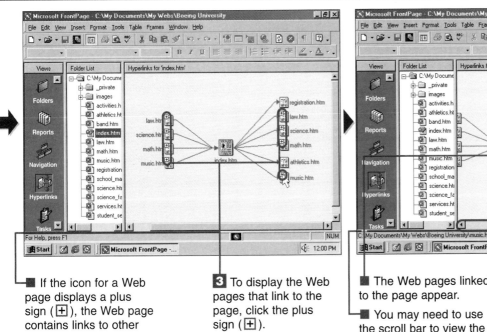

■ If the icon for a Web page displays a plus sign (⊞), the Web page contains links to other pages.

3 To display the Web pages that link to the page, click the plus sign (⊞).

■ The Web pages linked to the page appear.

■ You may need to use the scroll bar to view the linked Web pages.

■ You can click the minus sign (⊟) to once again hide the linked Web pages (⊟ changes to ⊞).

CHECK LINKS

You can check the links in your Web site to determine if the links are working correctly.

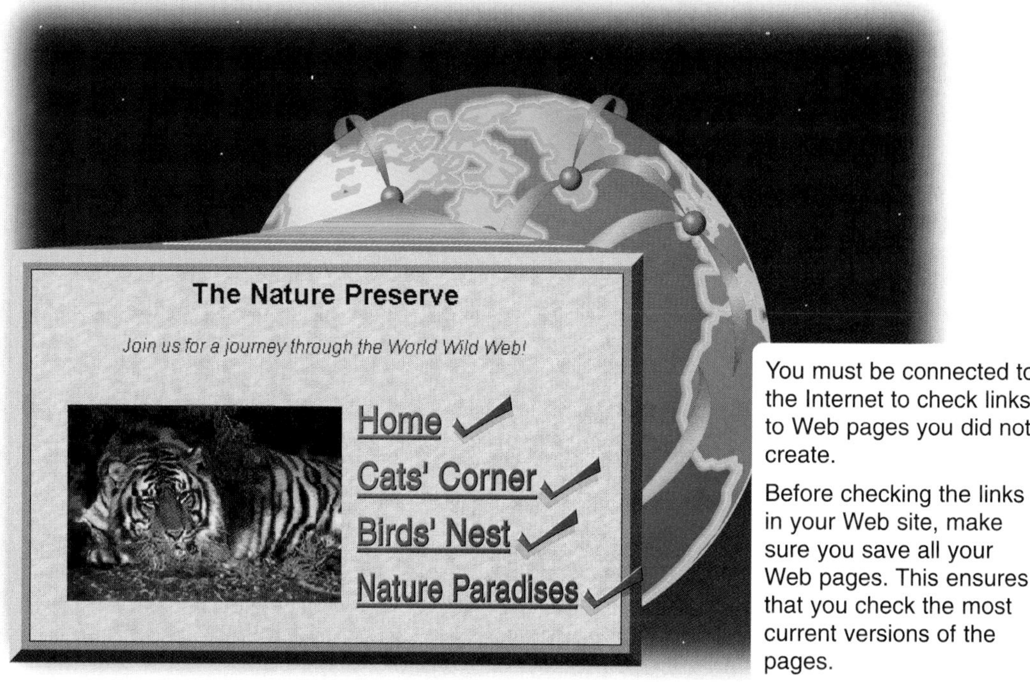

You must be connected to the Internet to check links to Web pages you did not create.

Before checking the links in your Web site, make sure you save all your Web pages. This ensures that you check the most current versions of the pages.

CHECK LINKS

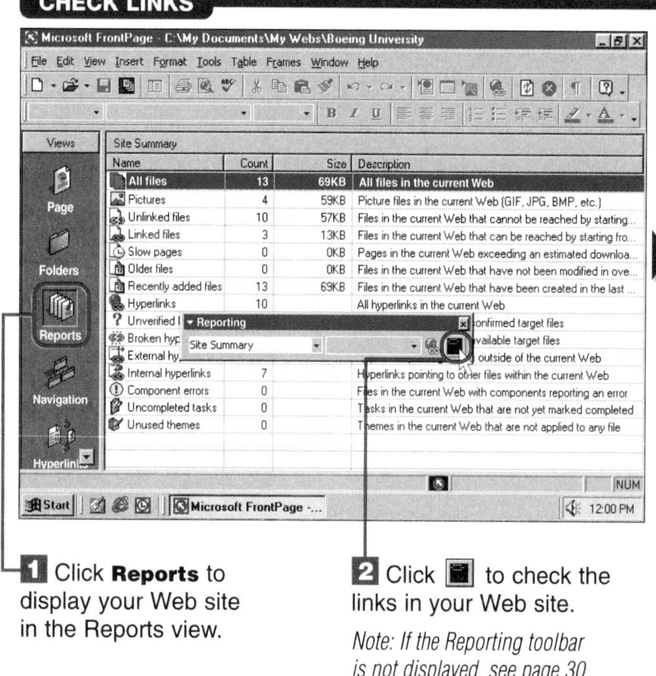

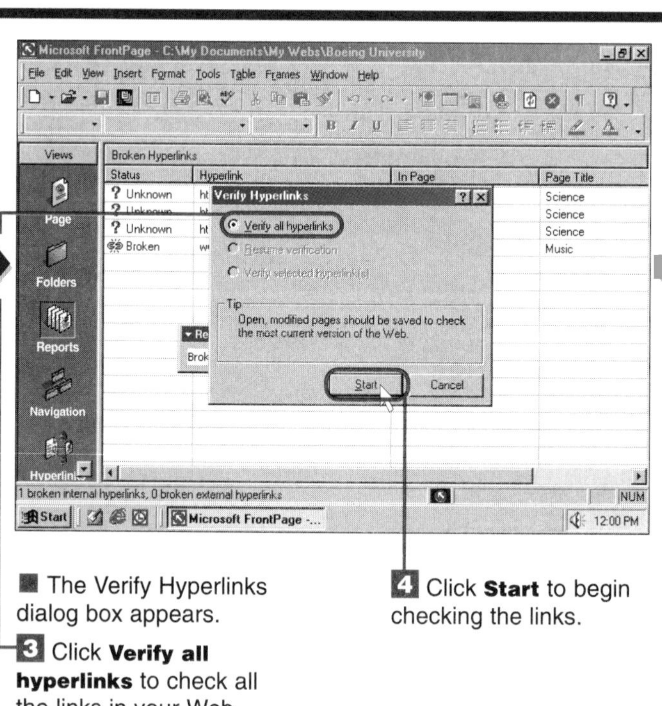

1 Click **Reports** to display your Web site in the Reports view.

2 Click ▣ to check the links in your Web site.

Note: If the Reporting toolbar is not displayed, see page 30 to display the toolbar.

■ The Verify Hyperlinks dialog box appears.

3 Click **Verify all hyperlinks** to check all the links in your Web site (○ changes to ⊙).

4 Click **Start** to begin checking the links.

Why is a link in my Web site broken?

A link that has an incorrect Web page address is called a broken link. When a reader clicks a broken link, an error message will appear. A link may not work for the following reasons:

- You typed the Web page address incorrectly.
- You deleted the Web page the link connects to.
- The Web page was moved or deleted on the Web.

Should I check the links on my Web pages manually?

You should manually check the links that connect to Web pages you did not create. Companies and individuals often change the content of their Web pages and the content may no longer relate to your pages.

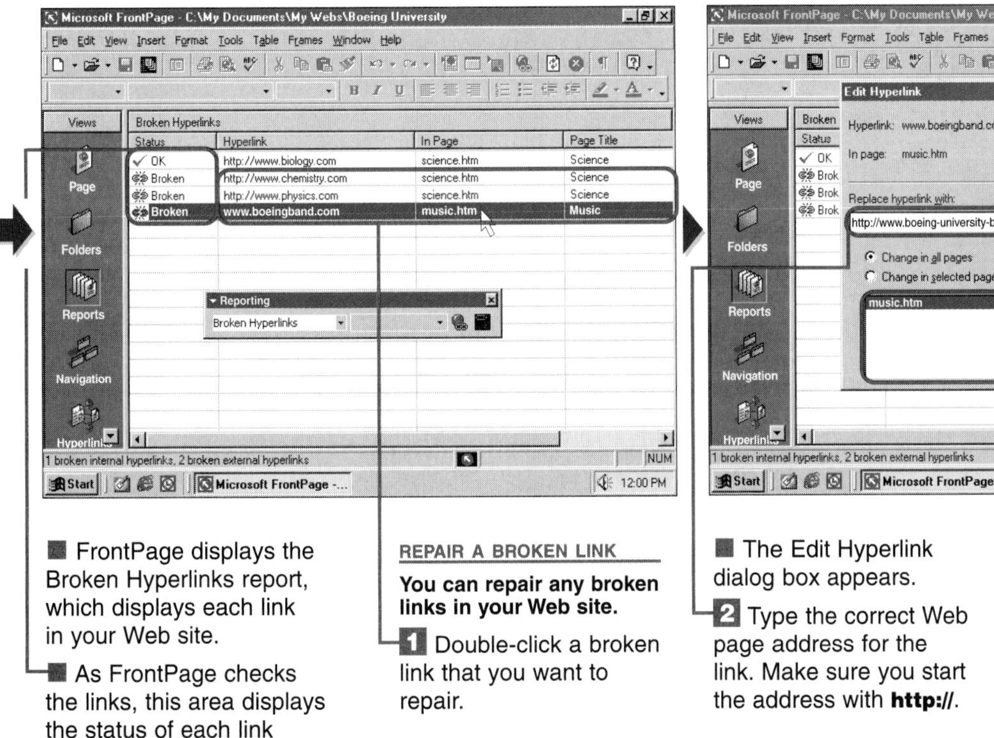

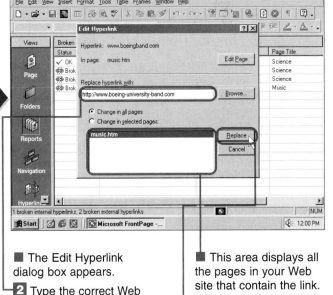

■ FrontPage displays the Broken Hyperlinks report, which displays each link in your Web site.

■ As FrontPage checks the links, this area displays the status of each link (✓ OK, Broken).

REPAIR A BROKEN LINK

You can repair any broken links in your Web site.

1 Double-click a broken link that you want to repair.

■ The Edit Hyperlink dialog box appears.

2 Type the correct Web page address for the link. Make sure you start the address with **http://**.

■ This area displays all the pages in your Web site that contain the link.

3 Click **Replace** to replace every occurrence of the link on your Web pages.

TEAMS
GAMES
WINS
LOSSES
POINTS
Dinos 10 10 0 20
Champs 10 9 1 18
Wizards 10 8 2 16
Pacers 10 6 4 12
Eagles 10 4 6 8
Hawks 10 2 4
Panthers 10 0 10 0
PLAYER
NO.
Jones
Smith
Robinson
33
1
32
Carter 22
Davis 21

CHAPTER 9

Create Tables

Do you want to use tables to help you organize information on your Web pages? Find out how in this chapter.

ADD A TABLE

You can add a table to neatly display a list of information on a Web page.

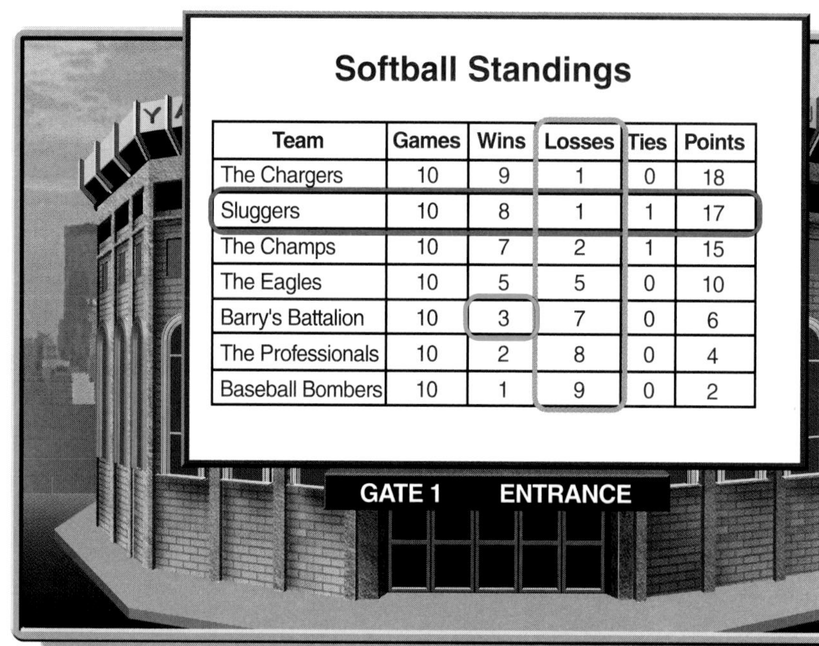

Softball Standings

Team	Games	Wins	Losses	Ties	Points
The Chargers	10	9	1	0	18
Sluggers	10	8	1	1	17
The Champs	10	7	2	1	15
The Eagles	10	5	5	0	10
Barry's Battalion	10	3	7	0	6
The Professionals	10	2	8	0	4
Baseball Bombers	10	1	9	0	2

A table consists of rows, columns and cells.

A **row** is a horizontal line of boxes.

A **column** is a vertical line of boxes.

A **cell** is one box.

ADD A TABLE

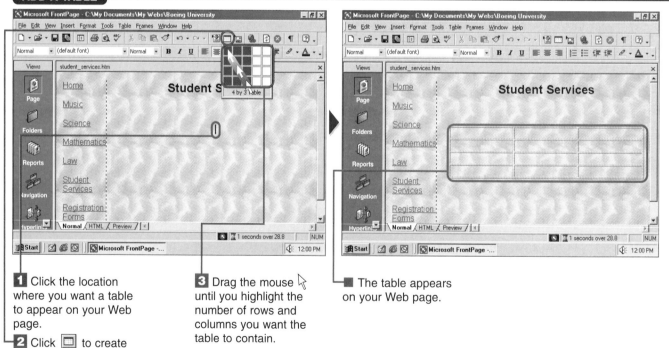

1 Click the location where you want a table to appear on your Web page.

2 Click [table icon] to create a table.

3 Drag the mouse until you highlight the number of rows and columns you want the table to contain.

■ The table appears on your Web page.

What other ways can I use a table on a Web page?

Create Newspaper Columns

You can use tables to present information in columns like those found in a newspaper. To display information in three newspaper columns, you can create a table with one row that contains three cells.

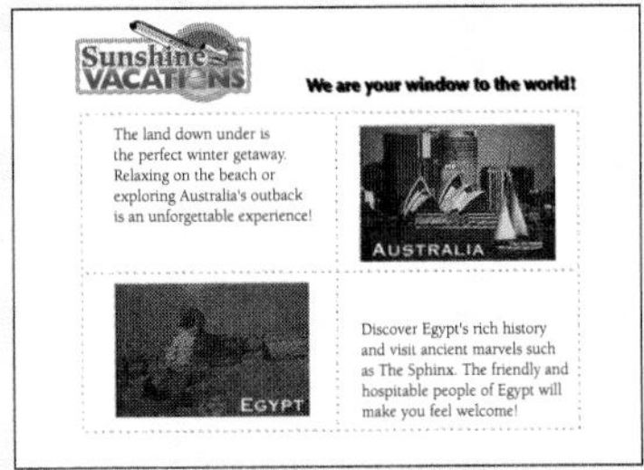

Control Web Page Layout

Tables are useful for controlling the placement of text and images on a Web page. To neatly position two paragraphs and two images, you can create a table with two rows and two columns.

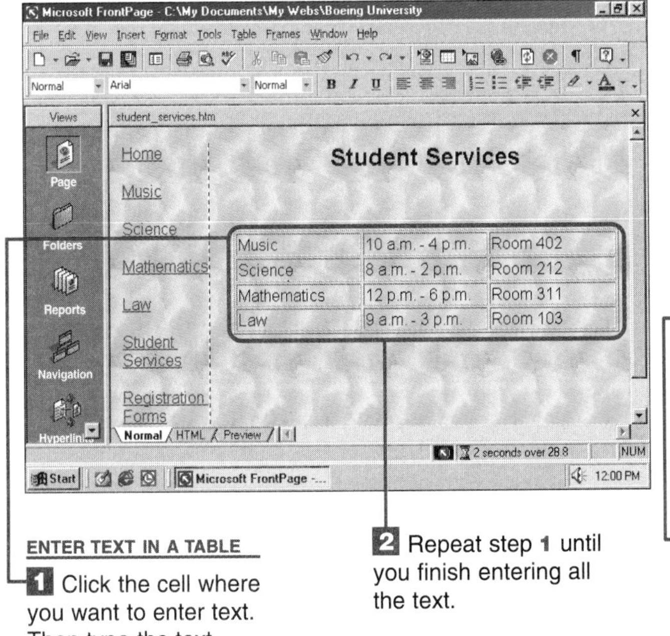

ENTER TEXT IN A TABLE

1 Click the cell where you want to enter text. Then type the text.

2 Repeat step 1 until you finish entering all the text.

DELETE A TABLE

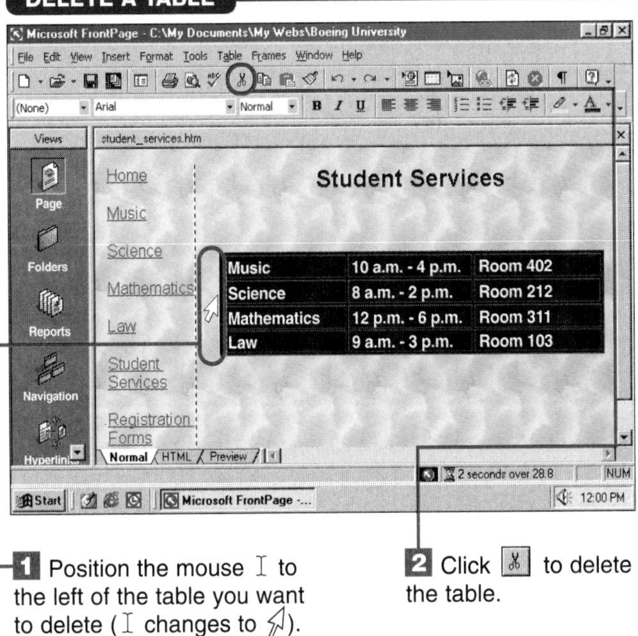

1 Position the mouse I to the left of the table you want to delete (I changes to ↖). Then double-click to select the table.

2 Click ✂ to delete the table.

ADD A ROW OR COLUMN

You can add a row or column to your table to insert additional information.

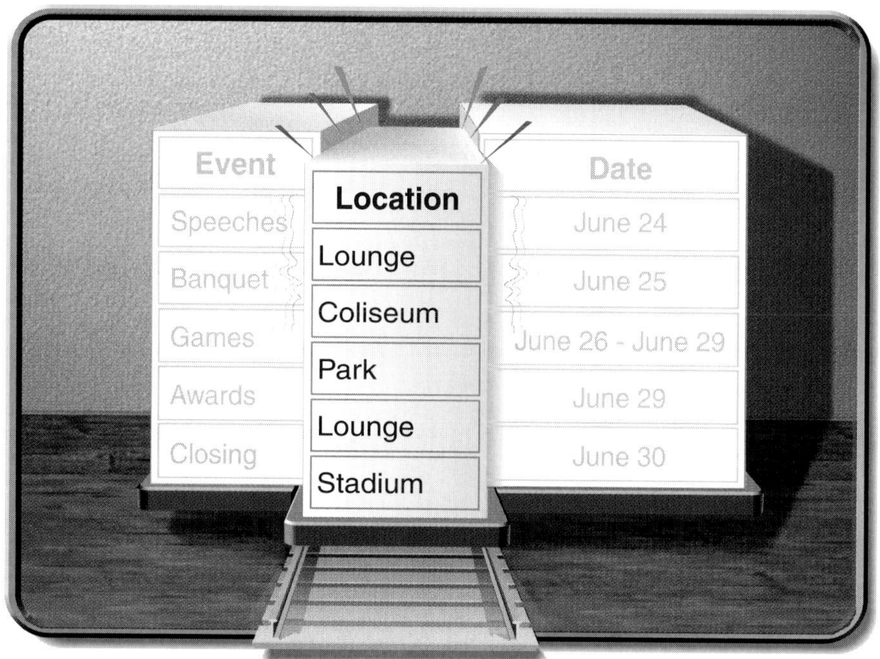

ADD A ROW OR COLUMN

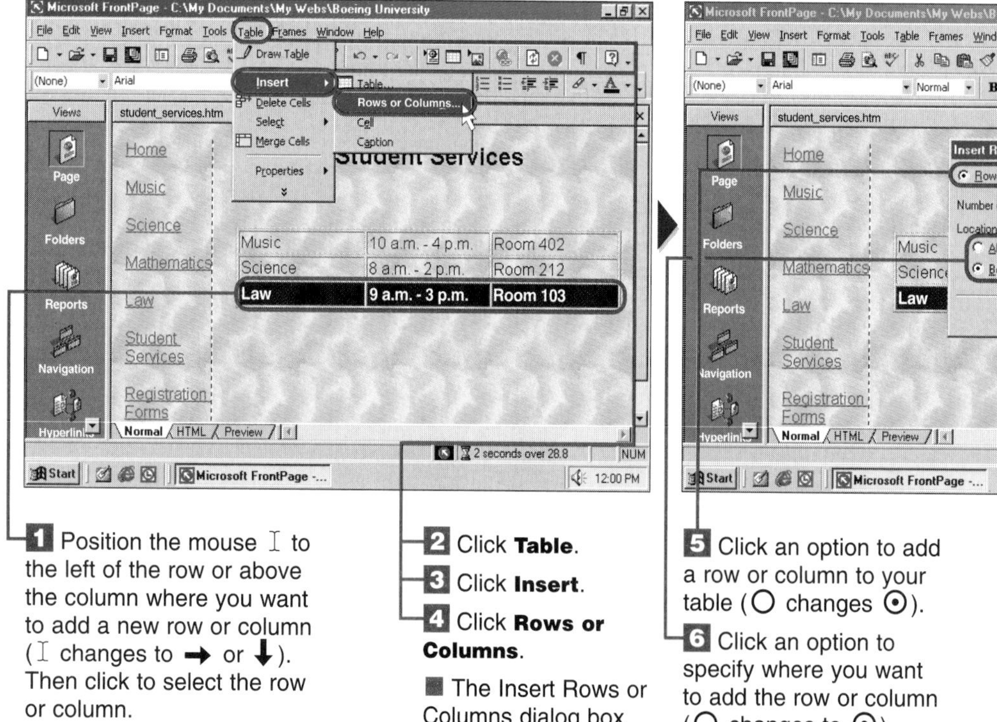

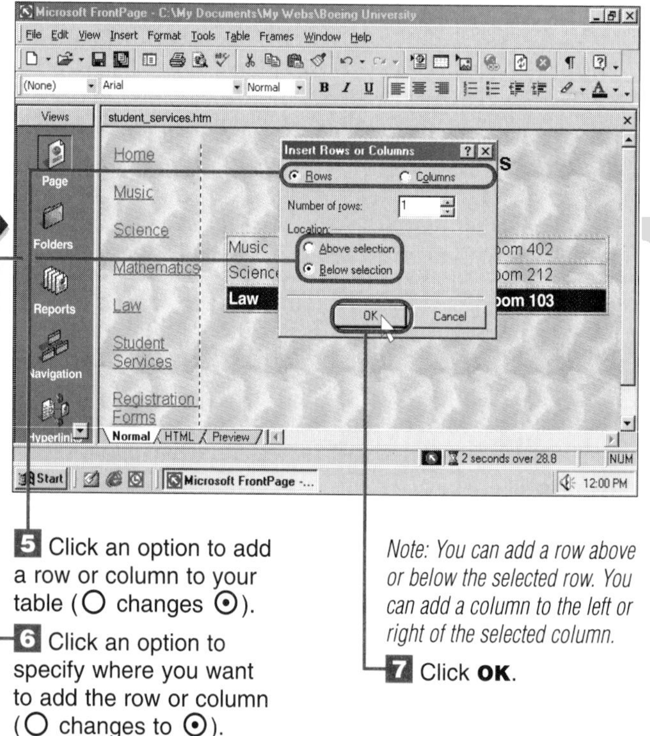

1 Position the mouse I to the left of the row or above the column where you want to add a new row or column (I changes to ➞ or ⬇). Then click to select the row or column.

2 Click **Table**.

3 Click **Insert**.

4 Click **Rows or Columns**.

■ The Insert Rows or Columns dialog box appears.

5 Click an option to add a row or column to your table (○ changes ⊙).

6 Click an option to specify where you want to add the row or column (○ changes to ⊙).

Note: You can add a row above or below the selected row. You can add a column to the left or right of the selected column.

7 Click **OK**.

How can I quickly add a row to the bottom of a table?

To quickly add a row to the bottom of a table, click the bottom right cell in the table. Then press the Tab key.

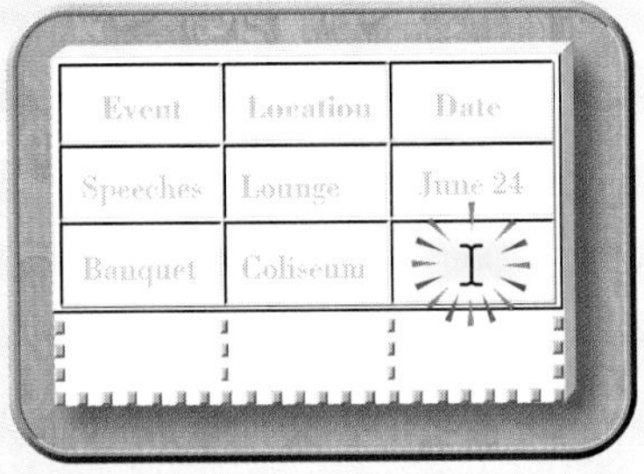

Can I delete the information in a row or column without removing the row or column from a table?

Yes. To select the cells that contain the information you want to delete, drag the mouse I over the cells. Then press the Delete key to remove the information.

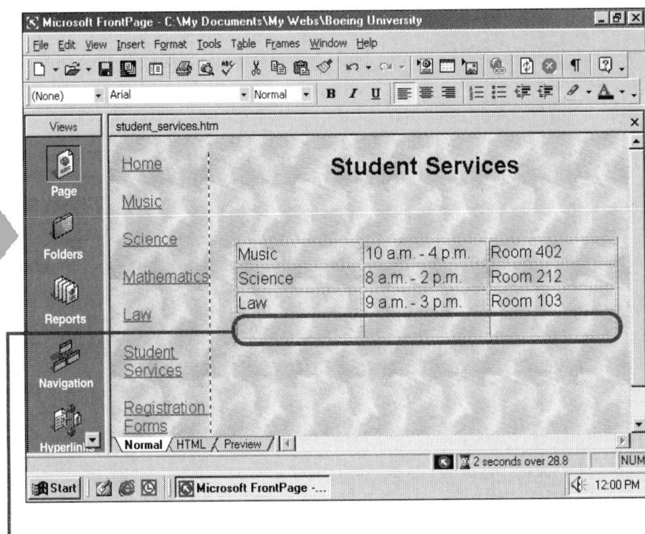

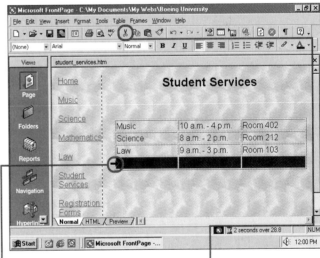

■ The new row or column appears in your table.

■ To deselect a row or column, click outside the table.

DELETE A ROW OR COLUMN

1 Position the mouse I to the left of the row or above the column you want to delete (I changes to → or ↓). Then click to select the row or column.

2 Click ✂ to delete the row or column you selected.

CHANGE ROW HEIGHT OR COLUMN WIDTH

You can change the height of rows and the width of columns to improve the layout of a table.

CHANGE ROW HEIGHT

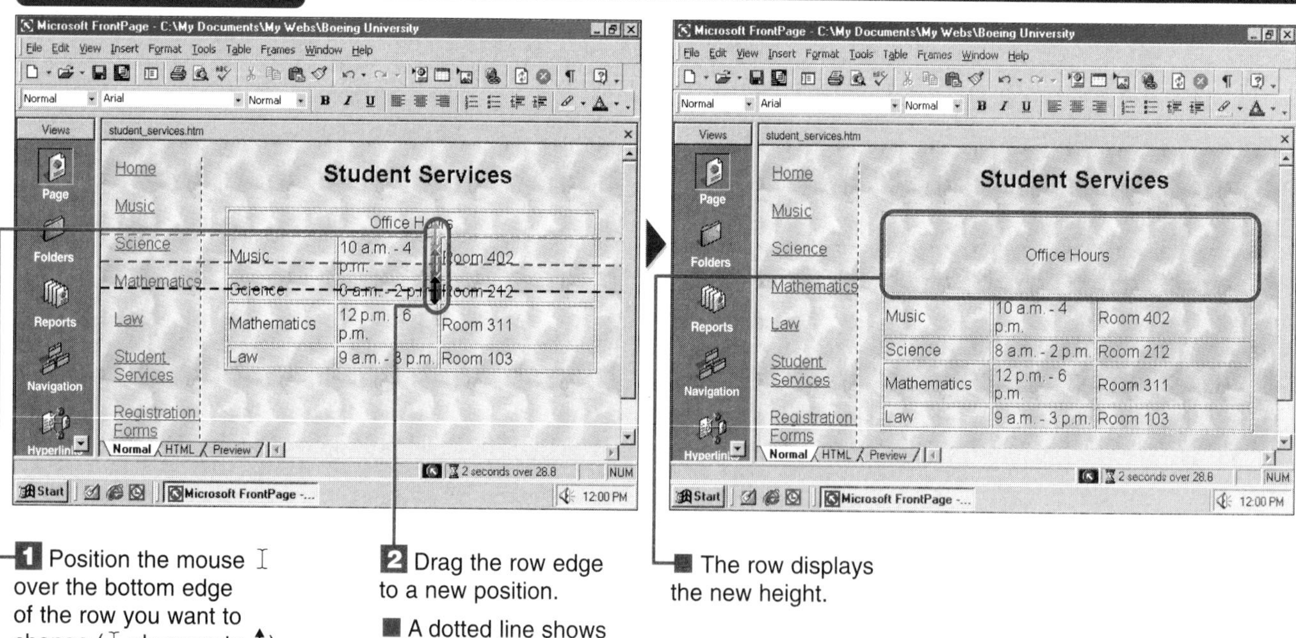

1 Position the mouse I over the bottom edge of the row you want to change (I changes to ↕).

2 Drag the row edge to a new position.

■ A dotted line shows the new position.

■ The row displays the new height.

Will FrontPage ever automatically adjust the row height or column width?

When you enter text in a table, FrontPage automatically increases the row height or column width to accommodate the text you type.

Can I make the row height or column width any size?

You can make the row height or column width any size you want. However, FrontPage will not allow you to make the row or column too small to display the text or image in a cell.

CHANGE COLUMN WIDTH

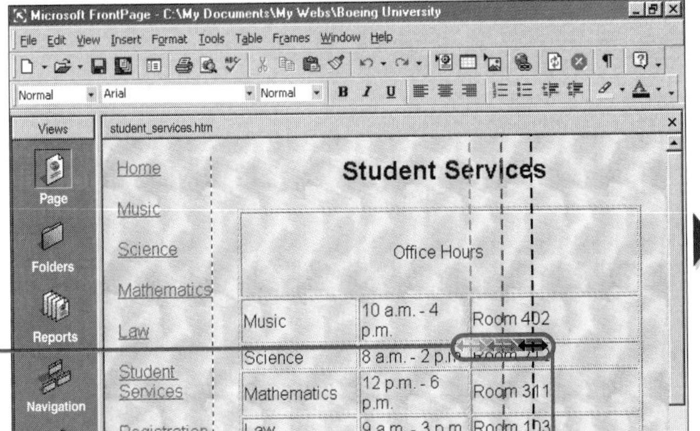

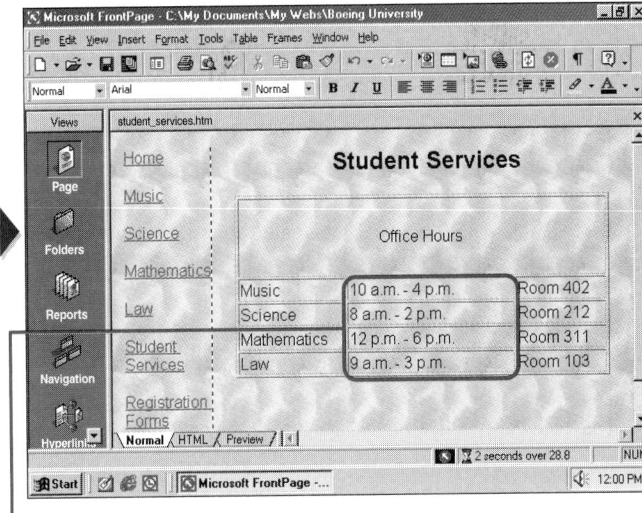

1 Position the mouse I over the right edge of the column you want to change (I changes to ↔).

2 Drag the column edge to a new position.

■ A dotted line shows the new position.

■ The column displays the new width.

Note: When you change the column width for the last column, the width of the entire table changes.

CHANGE ALIGNMENT OF TEXT

You can change the horizontal alignment of text in a table.

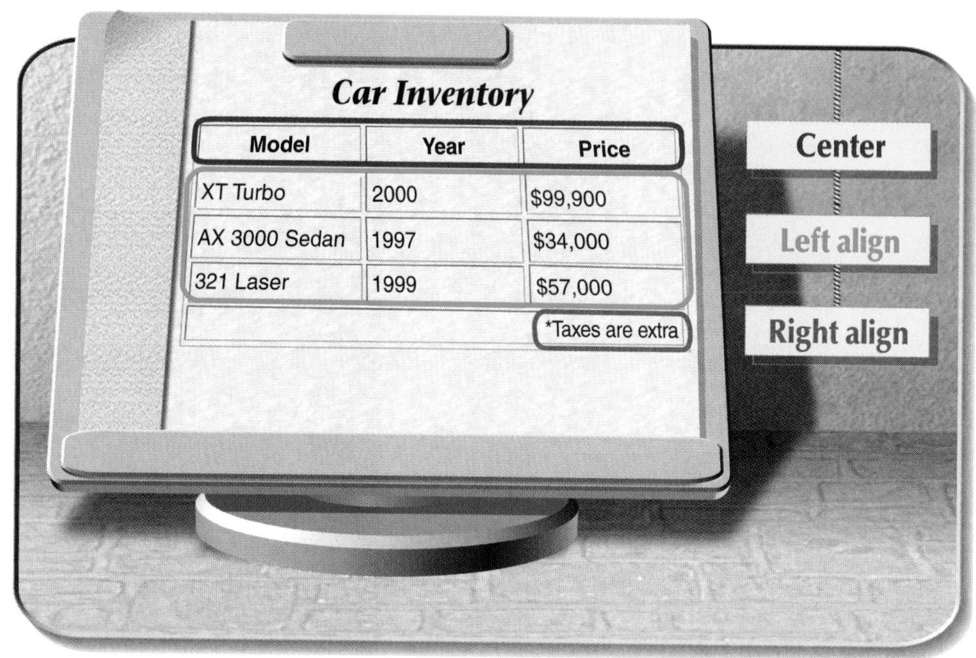

Car Inventory
Model
Year
Price
XT Turbo
2000
$99,900
AX 3000 Sedan
1997
$34,000
321 Laser
1999
$57,000
*Taxes are extra
Center
Left align
Right align

CHANGE ALIGNMENT OF TEXT

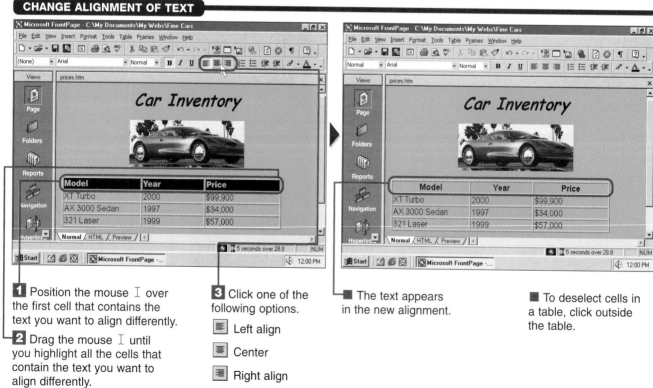

■1 Position the mouse I over the first cell that contains the text you want to align differently.

■2 Drag the mouse I until you highlight all the cells that contain the text you want to align differently.

■3 Click one of the following options.

- Left align
- Center
- Right align

■ The text appears in the new alignment.

■ To deselect cells in a table, click outside the table.

MOVE A TABLE

You can move a table to a new location on your Web page.

MOVE A TABLE

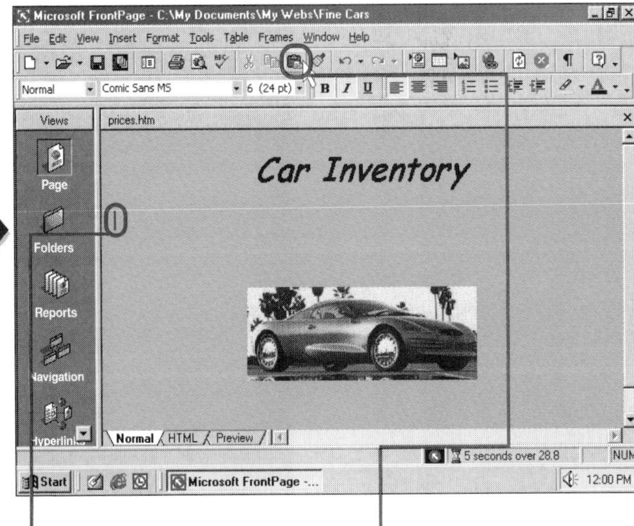

1 Position the mouse I to the left of the table you want to move (I changes to ↖). Then double-click to select the table.

2 Click ✂ to move the table to a new location.

■ The table disappears from your Web page.

3 Click the location where you want to place the table.

4 Click 📋 to place the table in the new location.

■ The table appears in the new location.

ADD A CAPTION TO A TABLE

You can add a caption to summarize the information in a table.

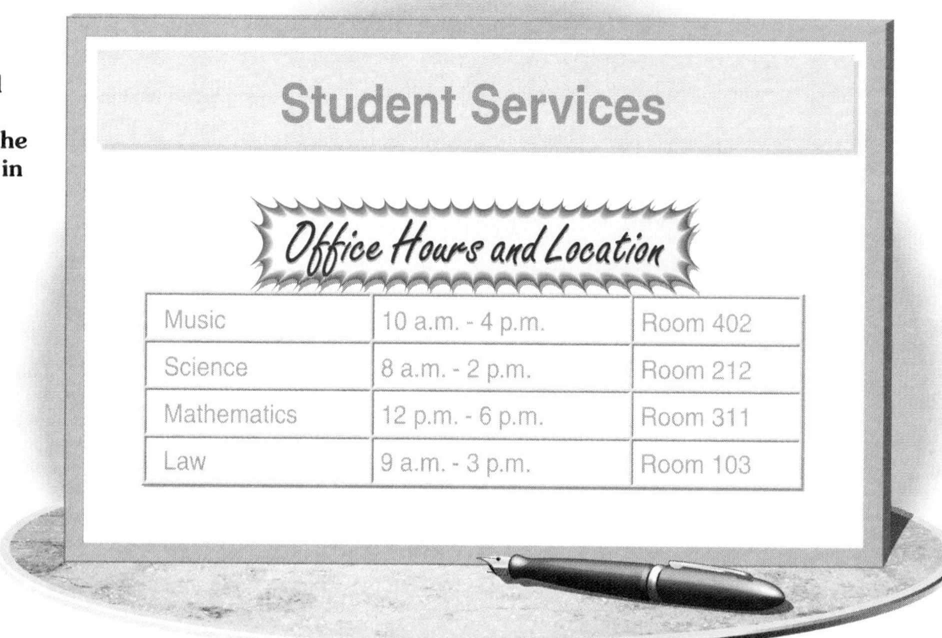

Captions are automatically centered at the top of a table.

ADD A CAPTION TO A TABLE

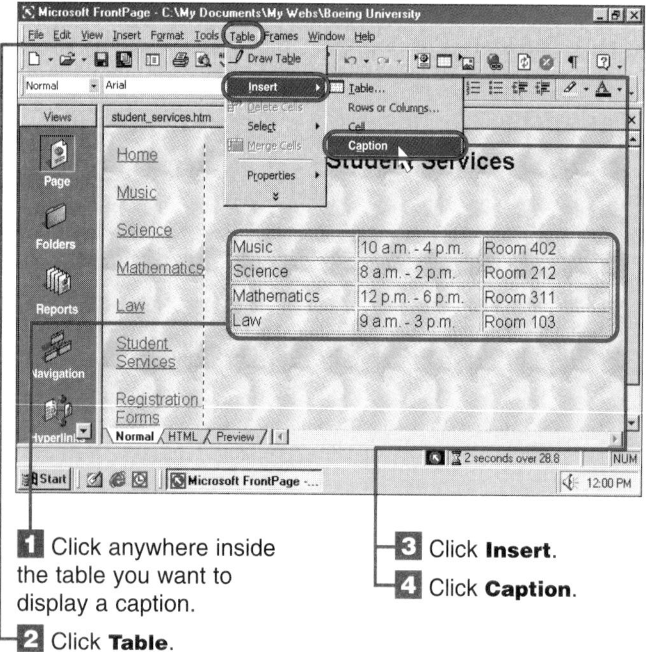

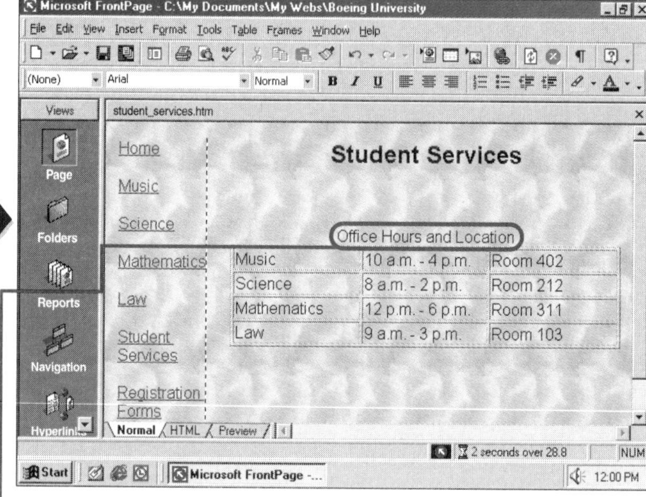

1 Click anywhere inside the table you want to display a caption.

2 Click **Table**.

3 Click **Insert**.

4 Click **Caption**.

■ A flashing insertion point appears above the table.

5 Type the caption you want the table to display.

■ To delete a caption, click to the left of the caption to select the caption. Then press the Delete key.

COMBINE CELLS

You can combine two or more cells in a table to make one large cell. This is useful if you want to display a title across the top or down the side of a table.

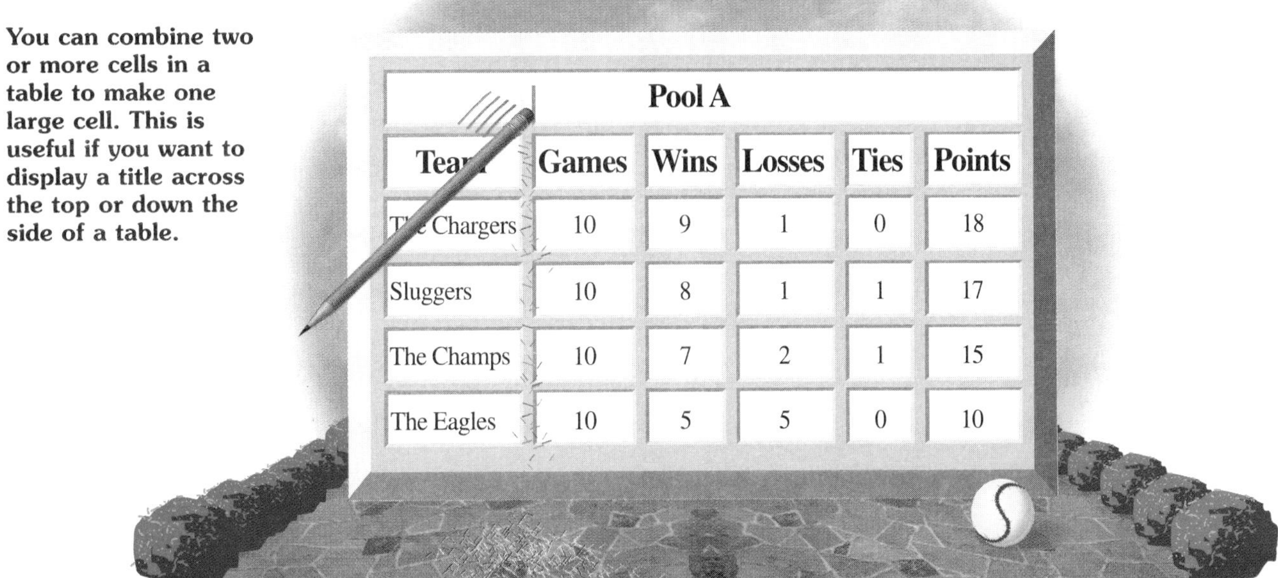

Pool A
Team
Games
Wins
Losses
Ties
Points
The Chargers
10
9
1
0
18
Sluggers
10
8
1
1
17
The Champs
10
7
2
1
15
The Eagles
10
5
5
0
10

COMBINE CELLS

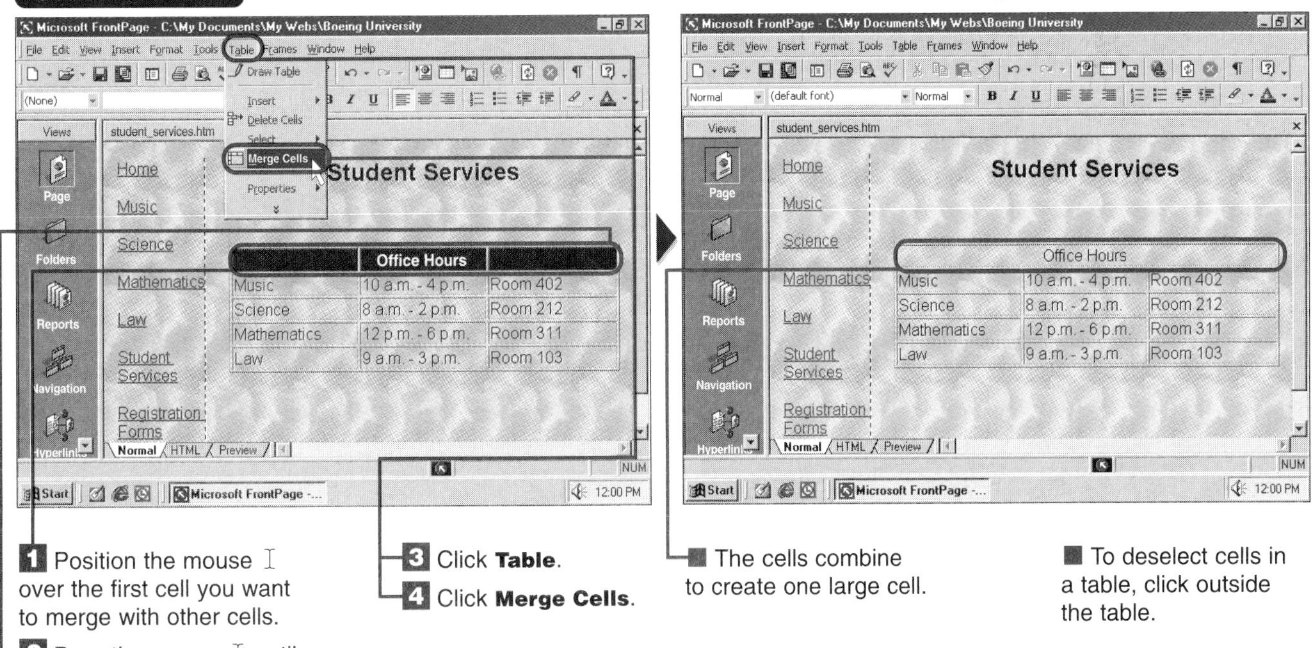

1 Position the mouse I over the first cell you want to merge with other cells.

2 Drag the mouse I until you highlight all the cells you want to merge.

3 Click **Table**.

4 Click **Merge Cells**.

■ The cells combine to create one large cell.

■ To deselect cells in a table, click outside the table.

SPLIT CELLS

You can split one cell in your table into two or more cells.

SPLIT CELLS

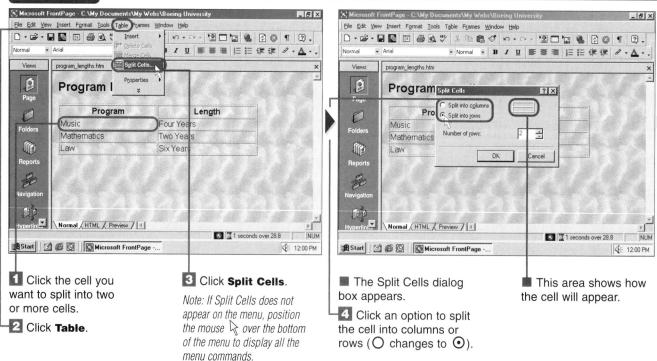

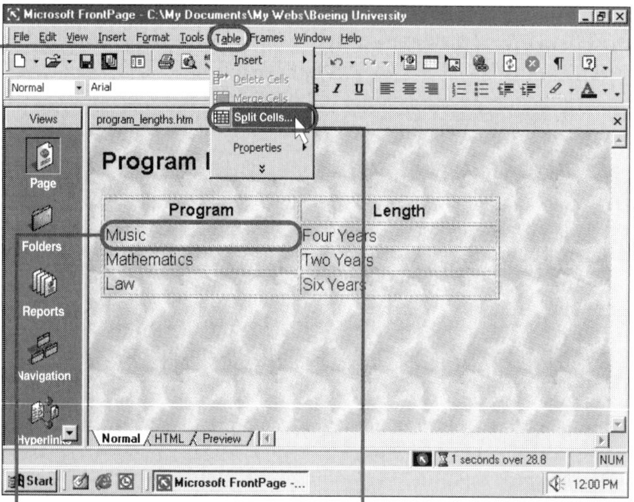

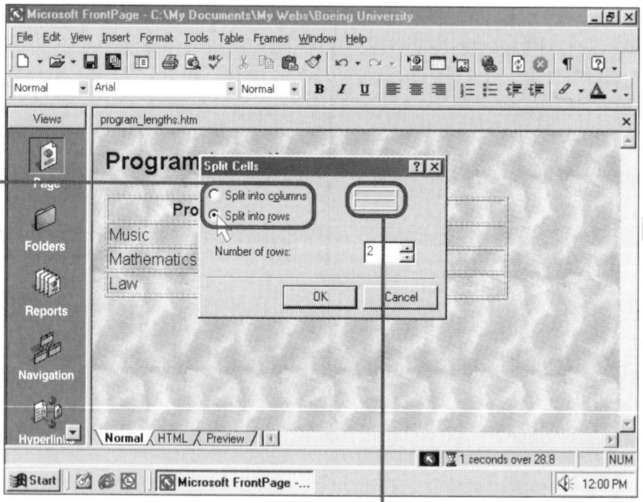

1 Click the cell you want to split into two or more cells.

2 Click **Table**.

3 Click **Split Cells**.

Note: If Split Cells does not appear on the menu, position the mouse over the bottom of the menu to display all the menu commands.

■ The Split Cells dialog box appears.

4 Click an option to split the cell into columns or rows (○ changes to ⊙).

■ This area shows how the cell will appear.

How can I split cells in a table?

You can split cells into columns or rows.

Columns
Splitting a cell into columns does not change the size of any other cells in the table.

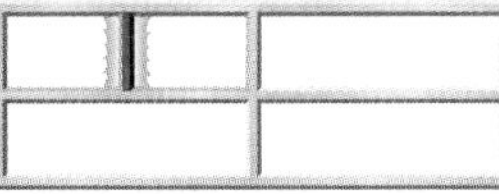

Rows
Splitting a cell into rows increases the height of other cells in the same row.

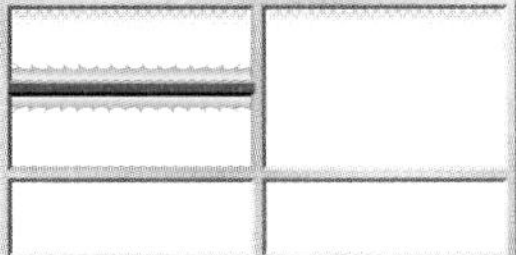

Can I split more than one cell at a time?

Yes. To split more than one cell at a time, drag the mouse over the cells you want to split until you highlight all the cells. Then perform steps **2** to **6** below.

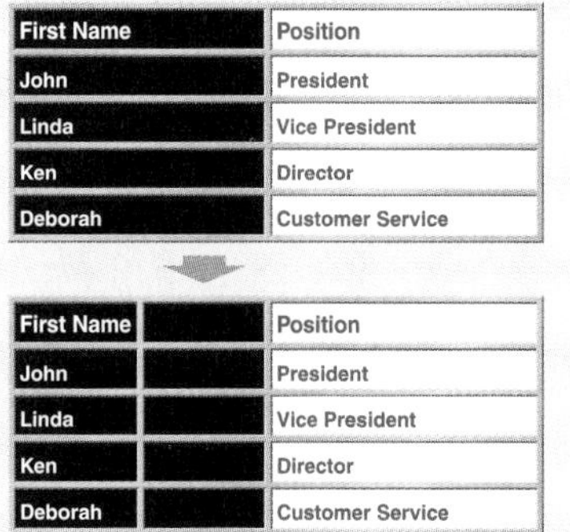

First Name	Position
John	President
Linda	Vice President
Ken	Director
Deborah	Customer Service

First Name		Position
John		President
Linda		Vice President
Ken		Director
Deborah		Customer Service

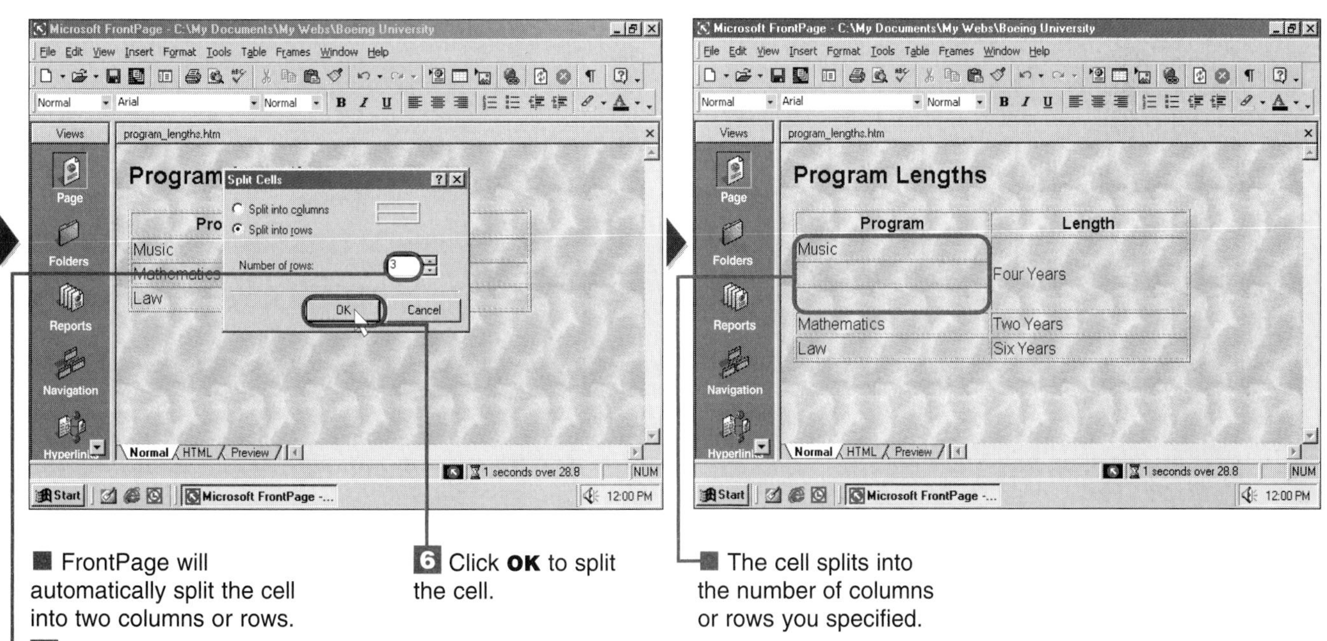

■ FrontPage will automatically split the cell into two columns or rows.

5 To change the number of columns or rows you want to split the cell into, double-click this area and type a new number.

6 Click **OK** to split the cell.

■ The cell splits into the number of columns or rows you specified.

CHANGE TABLE BORDER

You can change the size of the border that surrounds a table. You can also change the color of the border.

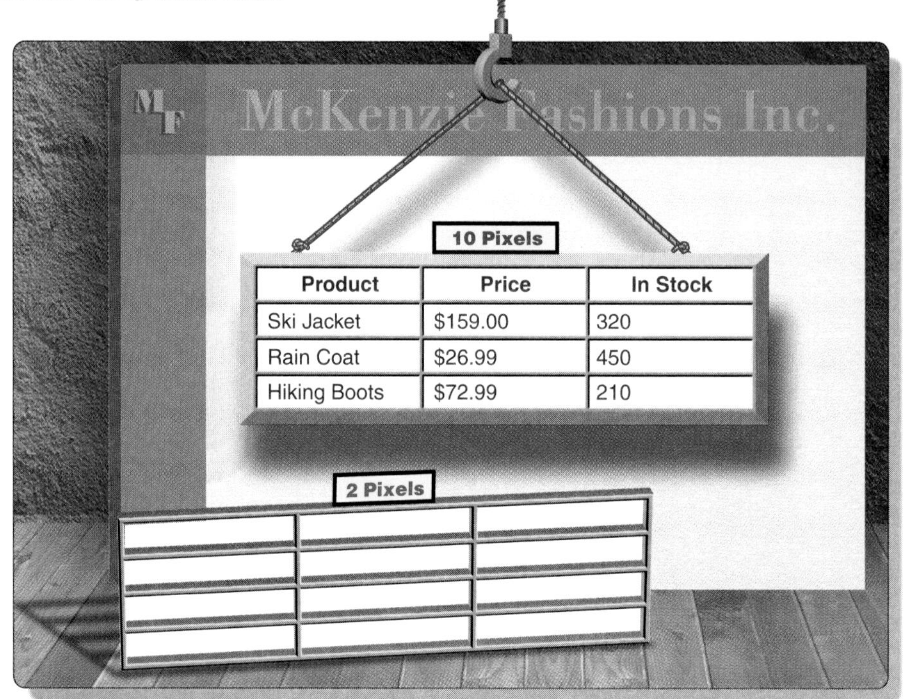

CHANGE TABLE BORDER

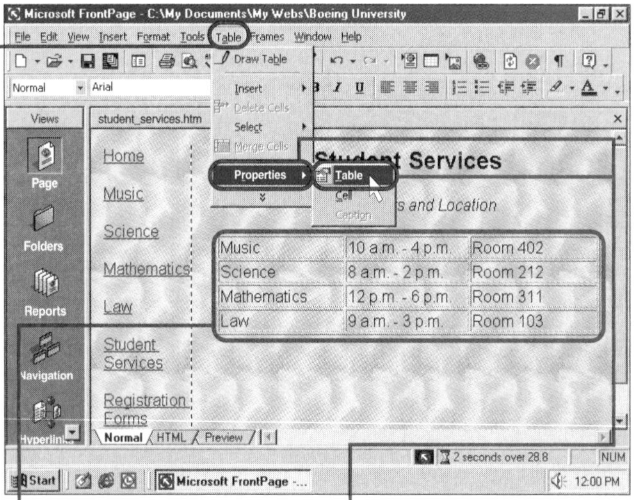

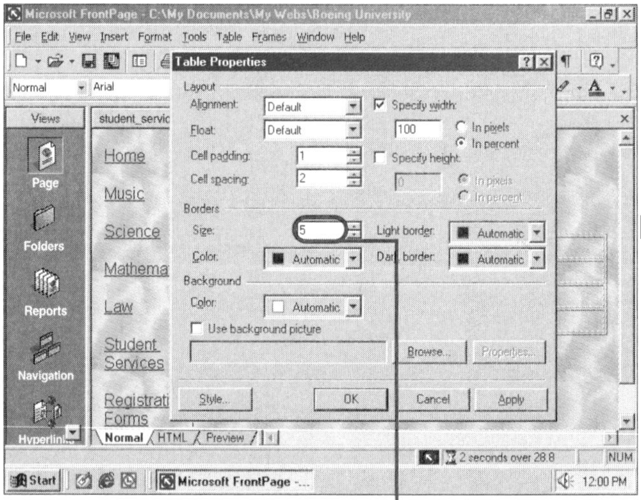

1 Click anywhere in the table that displays the border you want to change.

2 Click **Table**.

3 Click **Properties**.

4 Click **Table**.

■ The Table Properties dialog box appears.

5 Double-click this area and type the size you want to use for the border.

How do I specify the size of a border around a table?

You specify the size of a border around a table in pixels. A pixel is a dot on a computer screen. The word "pixel" comes from **pic**ture **el**ement.

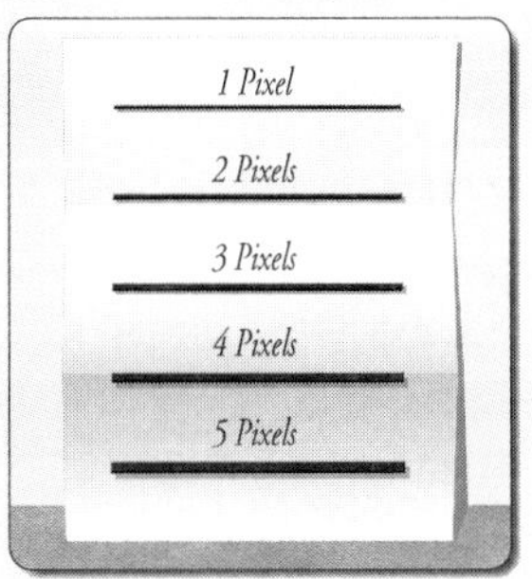

Can I remove a border from a table?

Yes. When you are using a table to organize the information on a Web page, you can remove the border to make the table invisible. To remove the border from a table, use a border size of **0**.

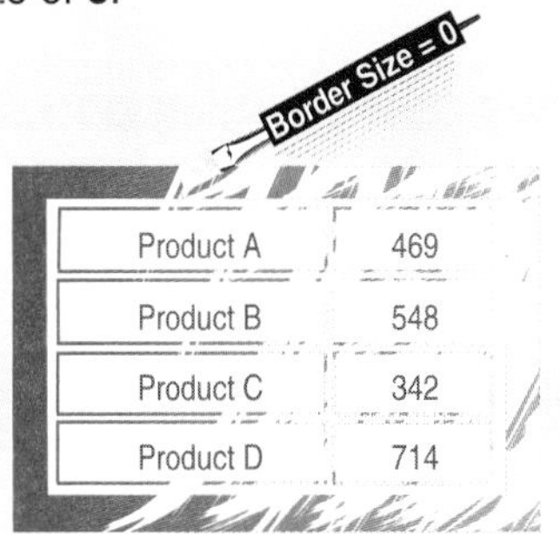

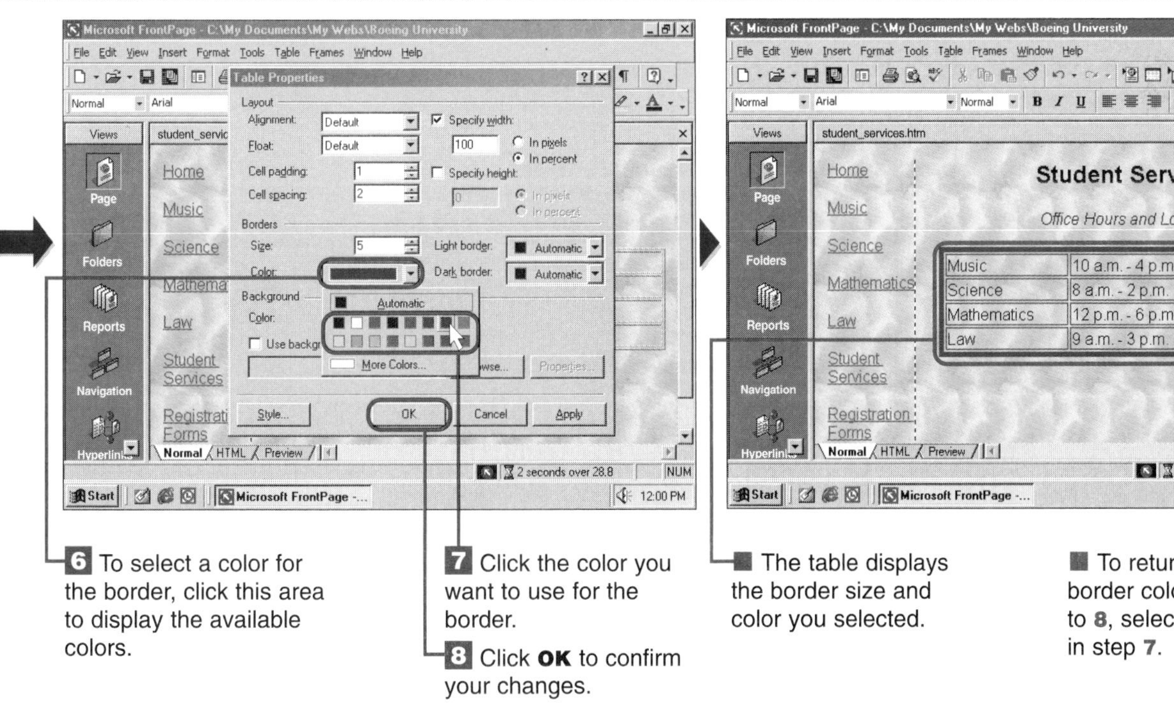

6 To select a color for the border, click this area to display the available colors.

7 Click the color you want to use for the border.

8 Click **OK** to confirm your changes.

■ The table displays the border size and color you selected.

■ To return to the original border color, repeat steps **1** to **8**, selecting **Automatic** in step **7**.

ADD AN IMAGE TO A TABLE

You can add an image to a cell in your table. Tables allow you to control the placement of images and text on your Web page.

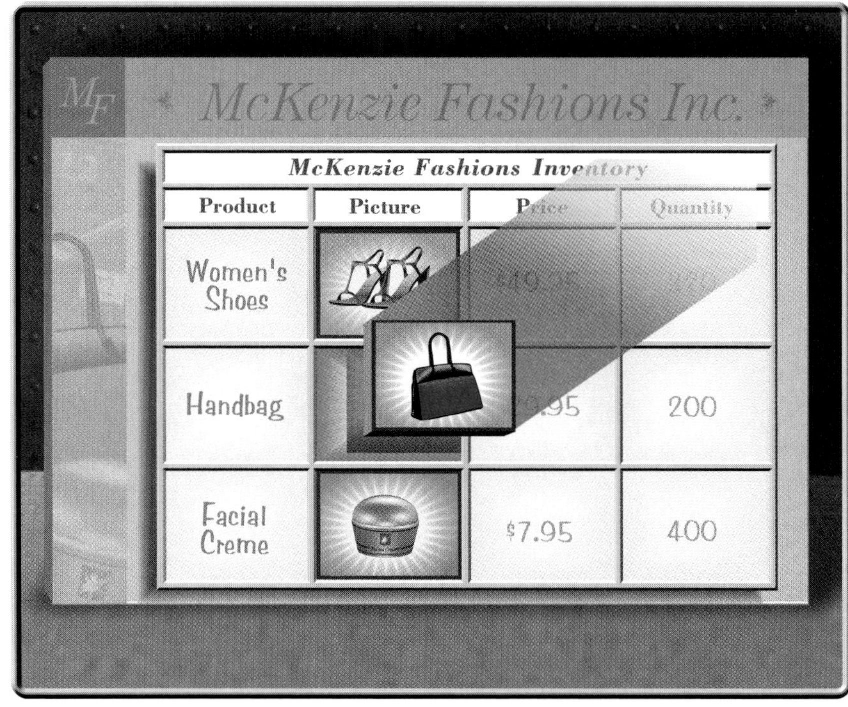

To obtain images that you can add to a table, see page 99.

ADD AN IMAGE TO A TABLE

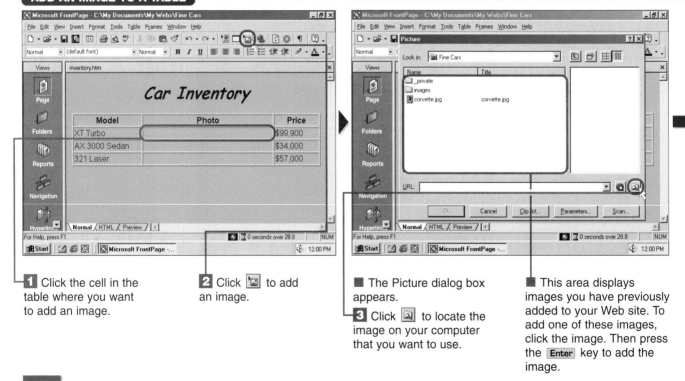

1 Click the cell in the table where you want to add an image.

2 Click [image icon] to add an image.

■ The Picture dialog box appears.

3 Click [icon] to locate the image on your computer that you want to use.

■ This area displays images you have previously added to your Web site. To add one of these images, click the image. Then press the **Enter** key to add the image.

How do tables control the placement of images and text on a Web page?

Tables provide a structure for images and text on a Web page. For example, to neatly position two paragraphs and two images, you can create a table with two rows and two columns.

When you use a table to organize information on a Web page, you may want to remove the border to make the table invisible. To remove the border from a table, see the top of page 165.

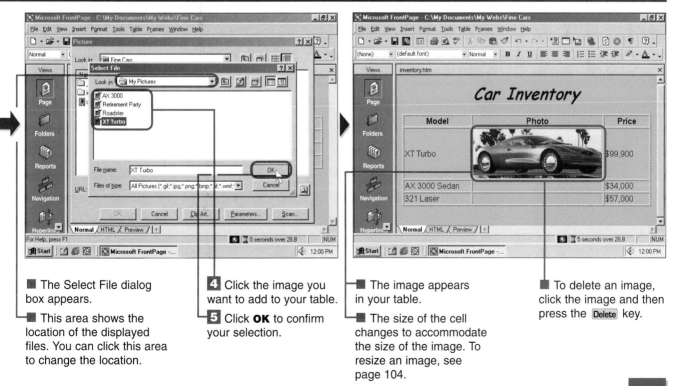

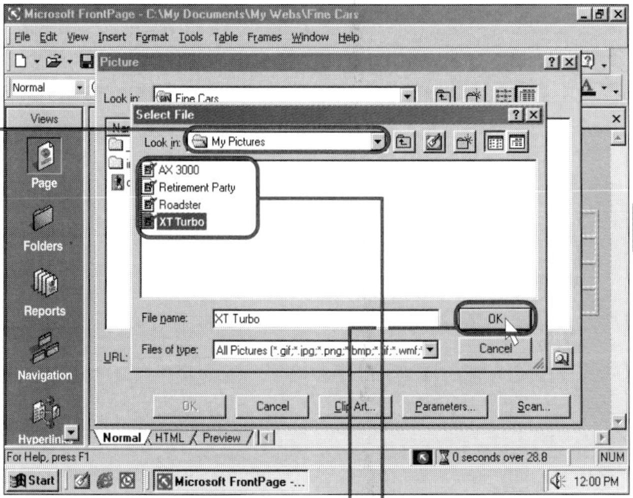

■ The Select File dialog box appears.

■ This area shows the location of the displayed files. You can click this area to change the location.

4 Click the image you want to add to your table.

5 Click **OK** to confirm your selection.

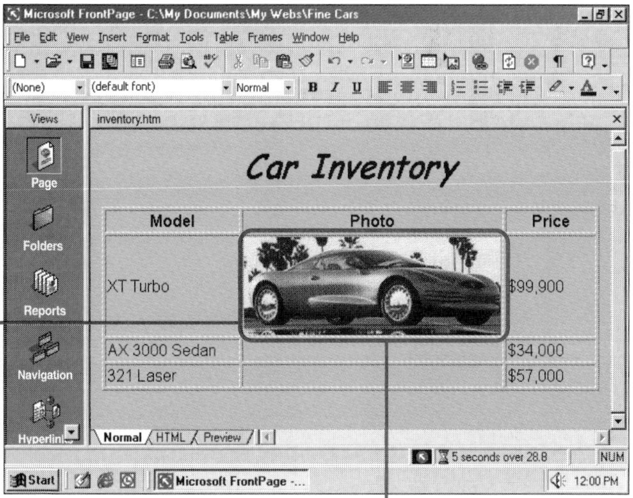

■ The image appears in your table.

■ The size of the cell changes to accommodate the size of the image. To resize an image, see page 104.

■ To delete an image, click the image and then press the Delete key.

ADD A BACKGROUND IMAGE TO A TABLE

You can add a background image to a table to make the table appear more interesting and attractive.

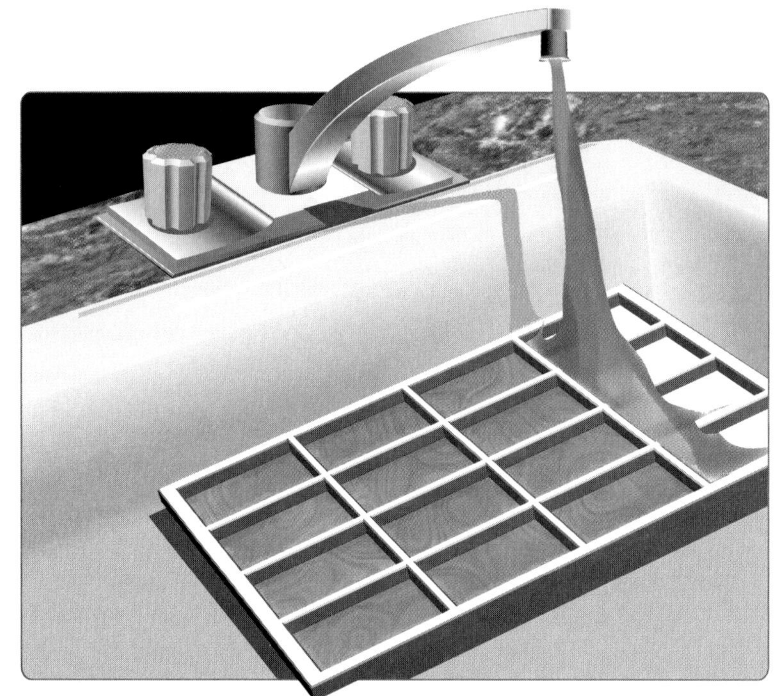

Make sure the background image you choose does not affect the readability of the text in the table.

ADD A BACKGROUND IMAGE TO A TABLE

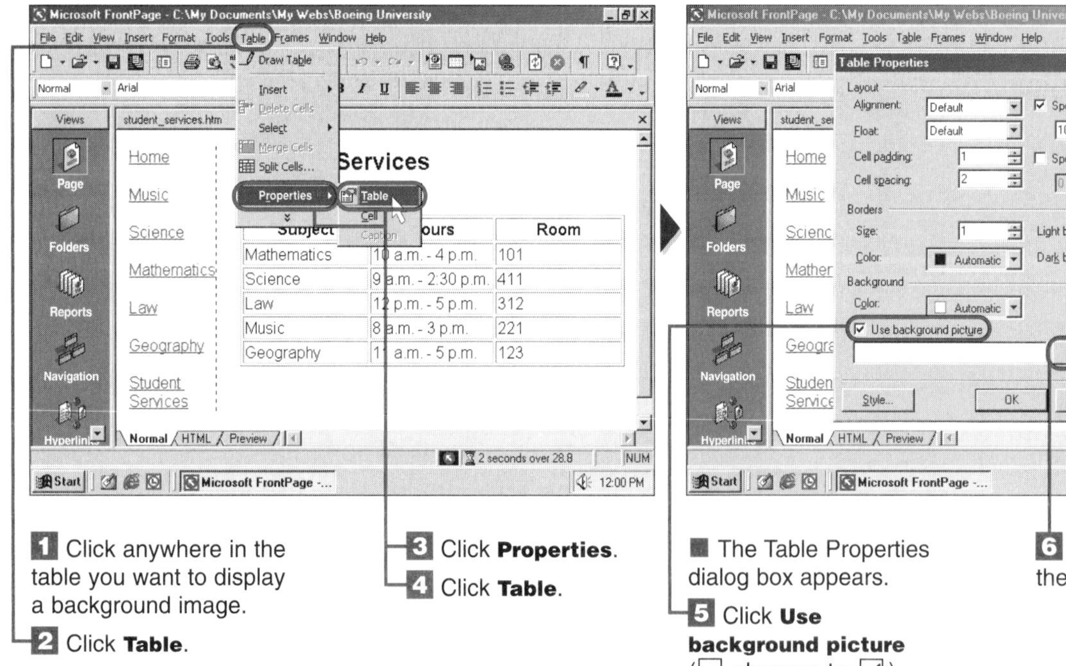

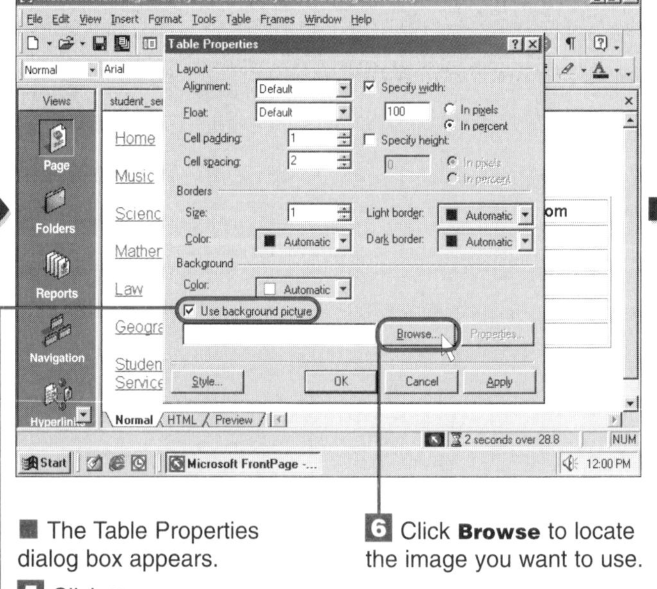

1 Click anywhere in the table you want to display a background image.

2 Click **Table**.

3 Click **Properties**.

4 Click **Table**.

■ The Table Properties dialog box appears.

5 Click **Use background picture** (☐ changes to ☑).

6 Click **Browse** to locate the image you want to use.

Where can I find background images?

Many Web sites offer background images you can use for free on your Web pages. You can find a variety of background images, including marble, stone, wood and water. Since background images increase the time Web pages take to appear on a screen, you should choose images with small file sizes that will transfer faster.

You can find background images at the following Web sites:

imagine.metanet.com

www.ip.pt/webground/main.htm

www.nepthys.com/textures

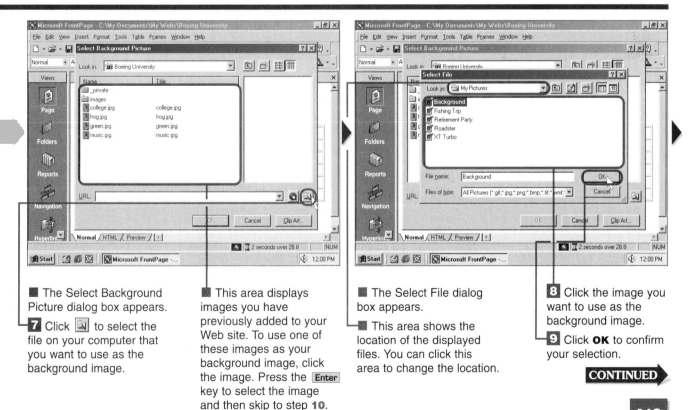

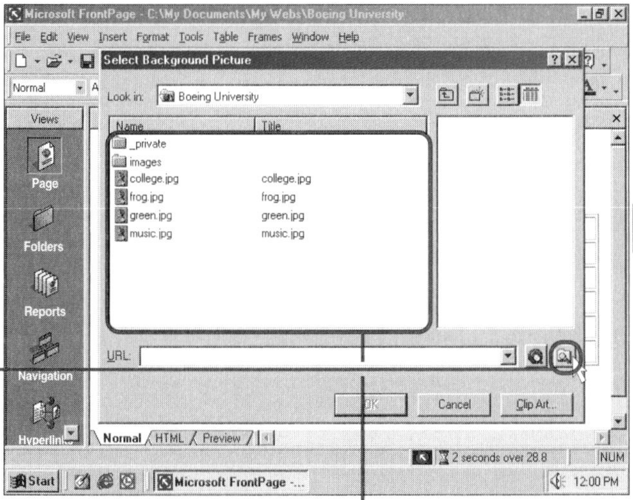

■ The Select Background Picture dialog box appears.

7 Click to select the file on your computer that you want to use as the background image.

■ This area displays images you have previously added to your Web site. To use one of these images as your background image, click the image. Press the **Enter** key to select the image and then skip to step **10**.

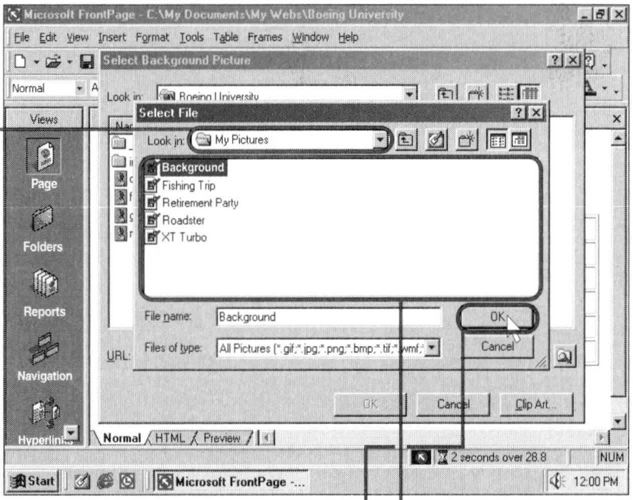

■ The Select File dialog box appears.

■ This area shows the location of the displayed files. You can click this area to change the location.

8 Click the image you want to use as the background image.

9 Click **OK** to confirm your selection.

CONTINUED

ADD A BACKGROUND IMAGE TO A TABLE

When you add a background image to a table, Web browsers will display the background image in different ways.

Microsoft Internet Explorer will repeat the background image to fill the entire table.

Netscape Navigator will repeat the background image in each cell in the table.

ADD A BACKGROUND IMAGE TO A TABLE (CONTINUED)

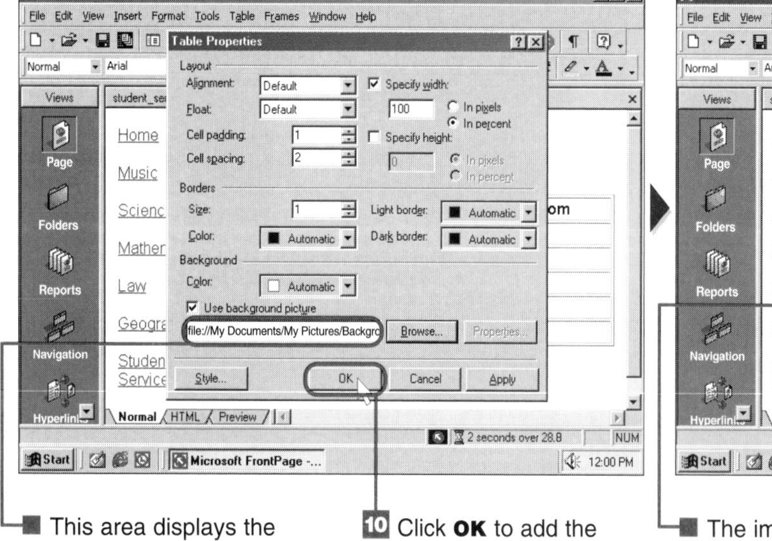

■ This area displays the location and name of the image you selected.

10 Click **OK** to add the background image to your table.

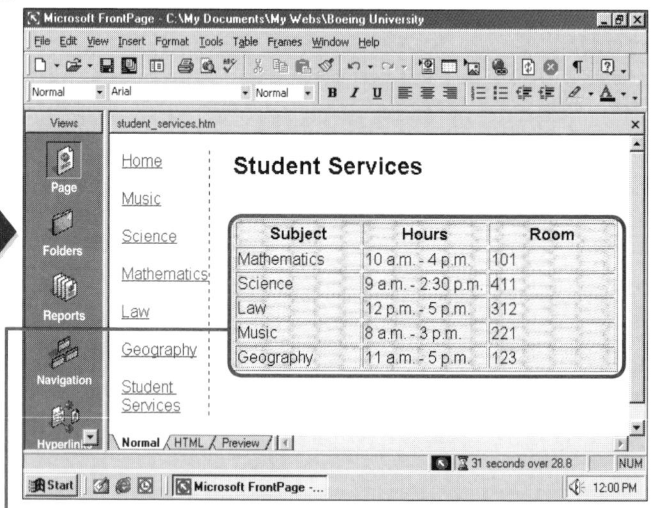

■ The image repeats to fill your entire table.

■ To remove a background image from a table, repeat steps **1** to **5** (☑ changes to ☐ in step **5**). Then press the **Enter** key.

ADD COLOR TO CELLS

You can add a background color to cells in a table to enhance the appearance of the table.

To change the color of text in a table, see page 76.

ADD COLOR TO CELLS

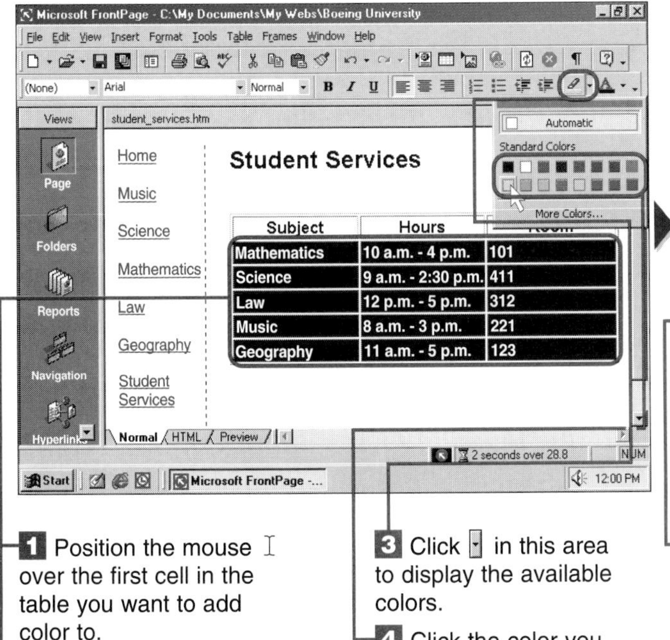

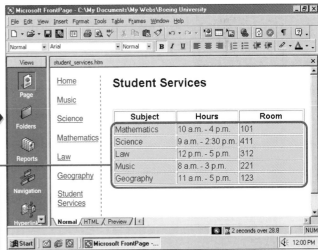

1 Position the mouse I over the first cell in the table you want to add color to.

2 Drag the mouse I until you highlight all the cells you want to add color to.

3 Click ▾ in this area to display the available colors.

4 Click the color you want to use.

■ The cells in the table display the color you selected.

■ To deselect cells in a table, click outside the table.

■ To remove color from cells in a table, repeat steps **1** to **4**, selecting **Automatic** in step **4**.

CHANGE CELL PADDING AND SPACING

You can change the amount of space around the contents of cells and between cells in a table.

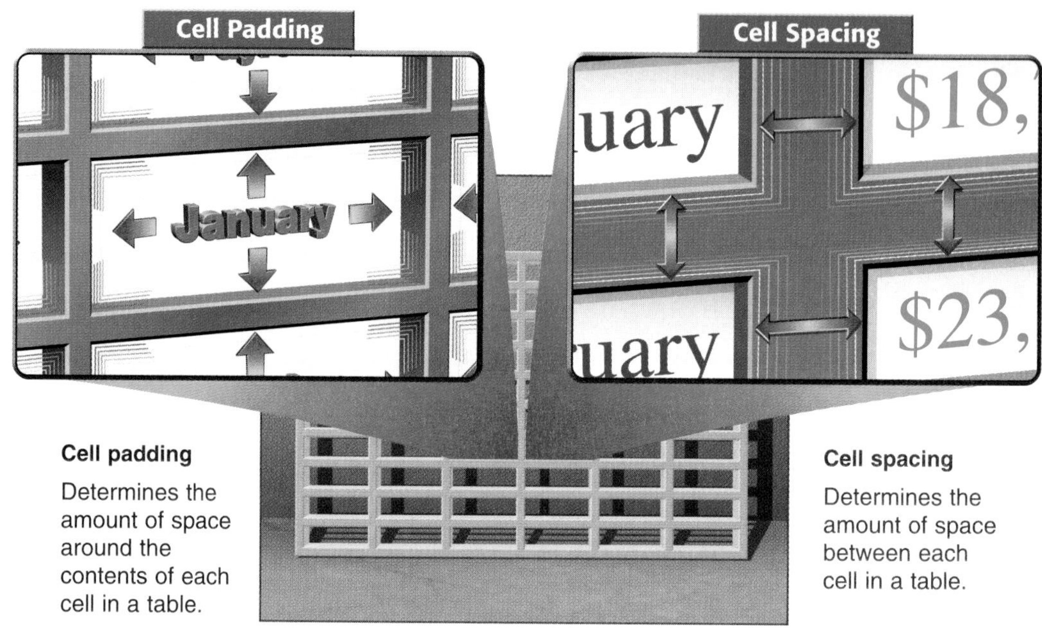

Cell padding

Determines the amount of space around the contents of each cell in a table.

Cell spacing

Determines the amount of space between each cell in a table.

CHANGE CELL PADDING AND SPACING

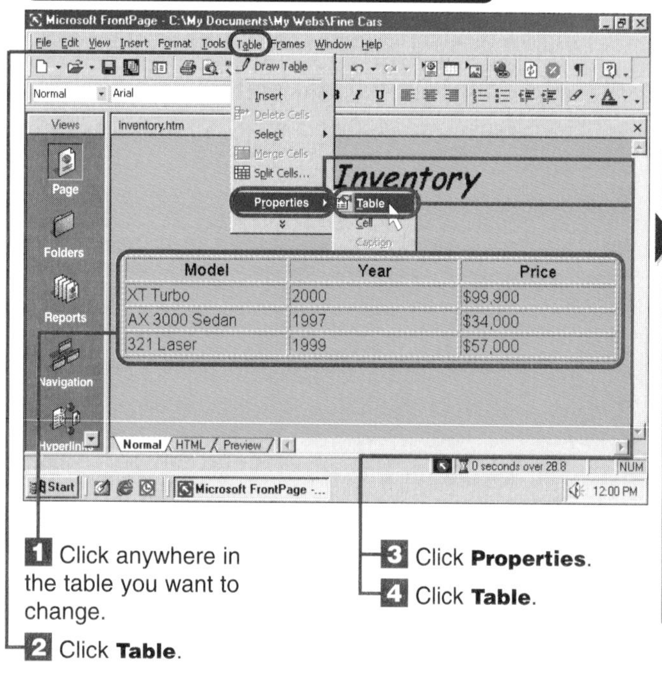

1 Click anywhere in the table you want to change.

2 Click **Table**.

3 Click **Properties**.

4 Click **Table**.

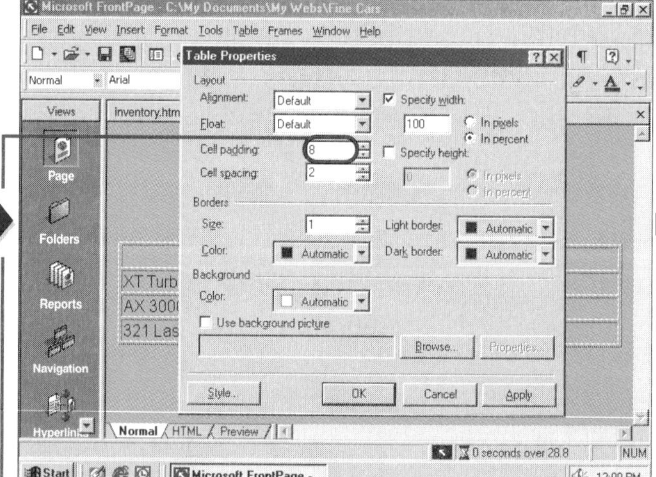

■ The Table Properties dialog box appears.

5 To change the amount of space around the contents of each cell, double-click this area and type a number for the amount of space in pixels.

Note: You can set the cell padding to 0 to remove the space around the contents of each cell.

When would I change the cell padding and spacing in a table to zero (0)?

You can change the cell padding and spacing to 0 pixels if you want to remove the space between the contents of cells in a table. This is useful when you want to make two or more images appear as one large image.

Can I change the cell padding or spacing for one cell?

No. When you change the cell padding or spacing in a table, FrontPage changes every cell in the table. You cannot change the cell padding or spacing for just one cell.

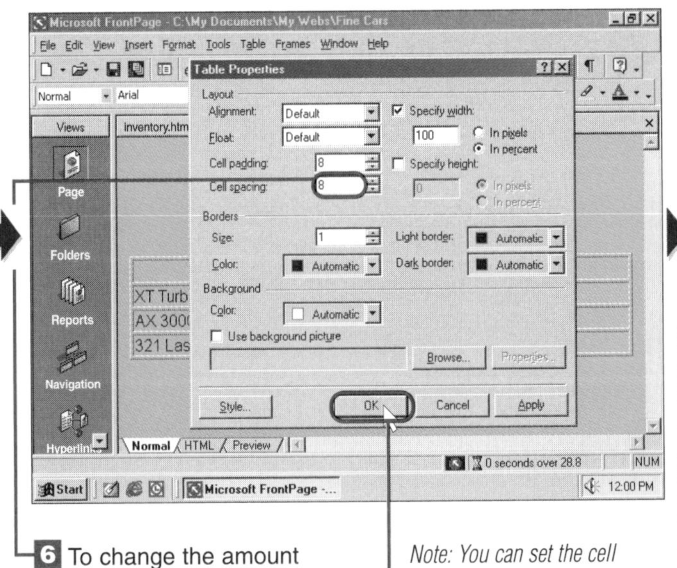

6 To change the amount of space between each cell, double-click this area and type a number for the amount of space in pixels.

Note: You can set the cell spacing to 0 to remove the space between each cell.

7 Click **OK** to confirm your changes.

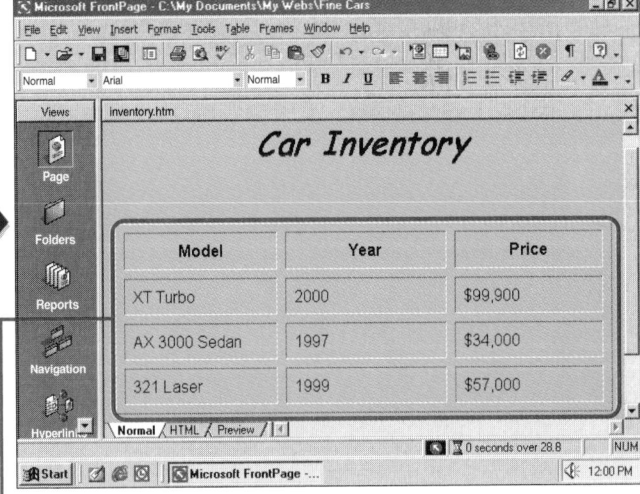

■ The table displays the cell padding and spacing you specified.

NAVIGATION VIEW

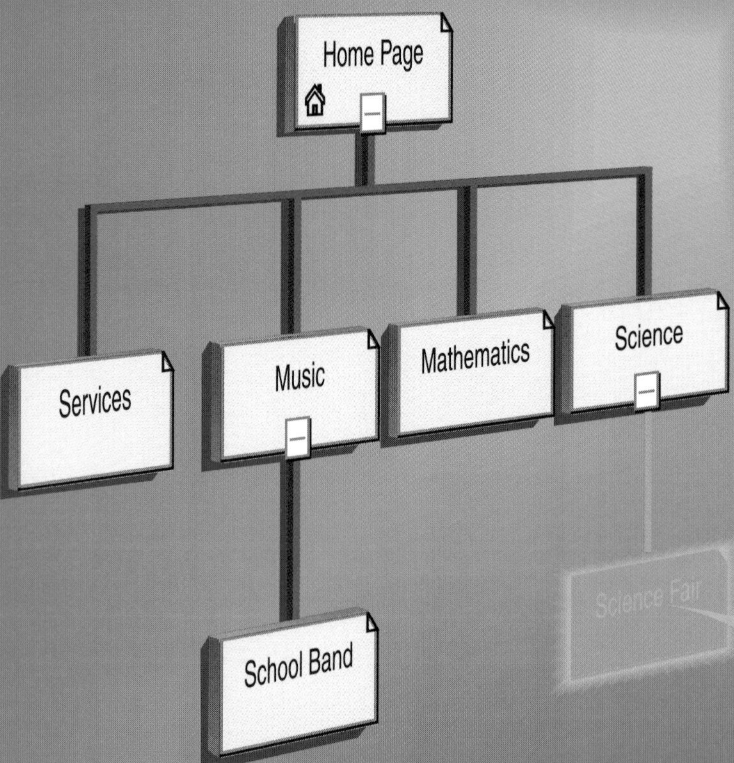
Home Page
Services
Music
Mathematics
Science
School Band
Science Fair
Navigation Buttons to Appear on Web Pages

CHAPTER 10

Work With Navigational Structure

Are you wondering how to arrange the Web pages in your Web site? This chapter shows you how to build the structure of your Web site.

Science Fair

USING THE NAVIGATION VIEW

You can use the Navigation view to work with the navigational structure of your Web site.

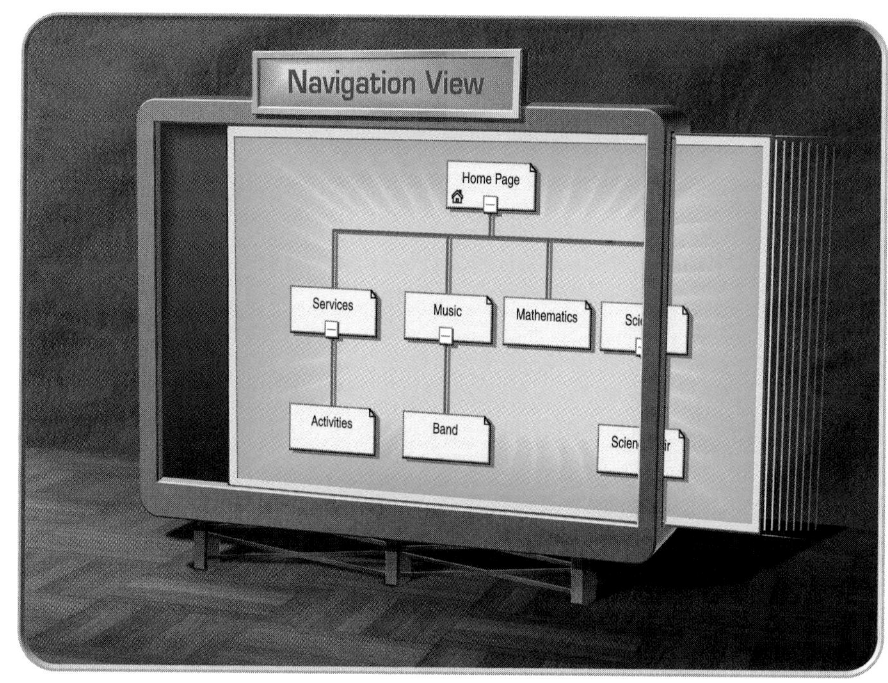

The Navigation view shows how the pages in your Web site are related.

USING THE NAVIGATION VIEW

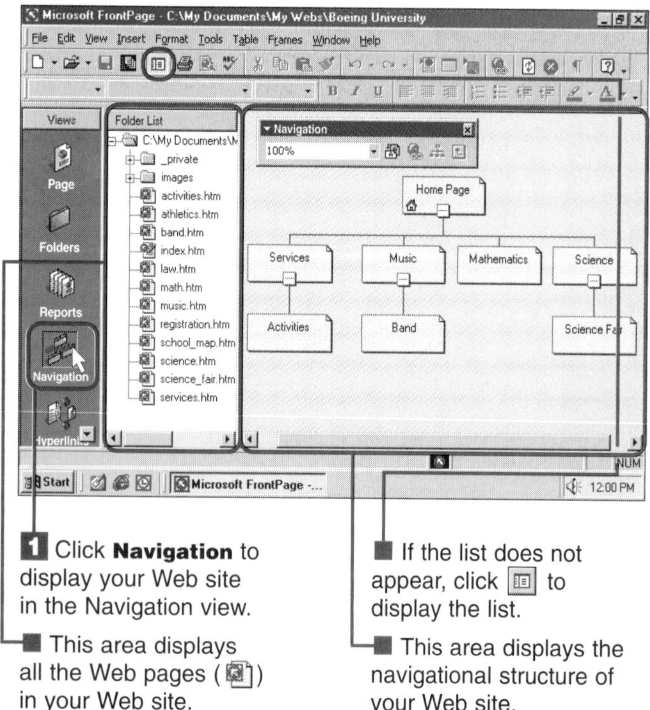

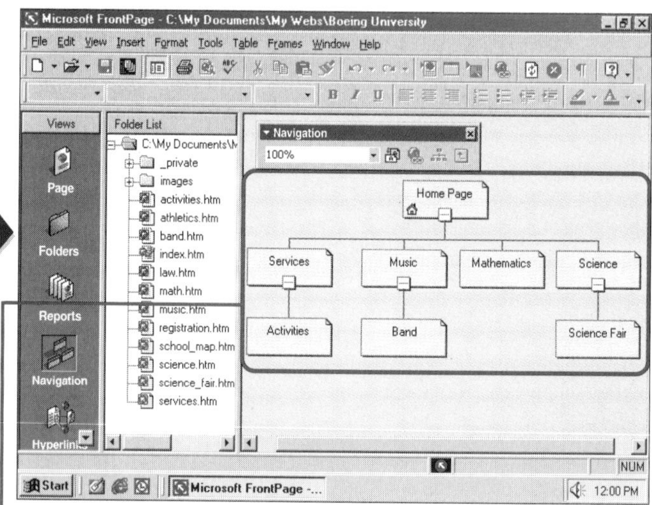

1 Click **Navigation** to display your Web site in the Navigation view.

■ This area displays all the Web pages ( ) in your Web site.

■ If the list does not appear, click to display the list.

■ This area displays the navigational structure of your Web site.

■ Each box represents one Web page. The title of the Web page appears in the box.

■ Lines between the boxes indicate how the Web pages are related.

Note: FrontPage may automatically set up the navigational structure for the Web site when you create the Web site. If the area appears blank, you need to add Web pages to the navigational structure. To add Web pages, see page 178.

Why should I work with the navigational structure of my Web site?

The navigational structure of your Web site determines which navigation buttons appear on your Web pages. Navigation buttons are links readers can select to move through the pages in your Web site. When you change the navigational structure of your Web site, FrontPage automatically updates the navigation buttons for you. To change the navigational structure of your Web site, see pages 178 to 181. To add navigation buttons to your Web pages, see page 182.

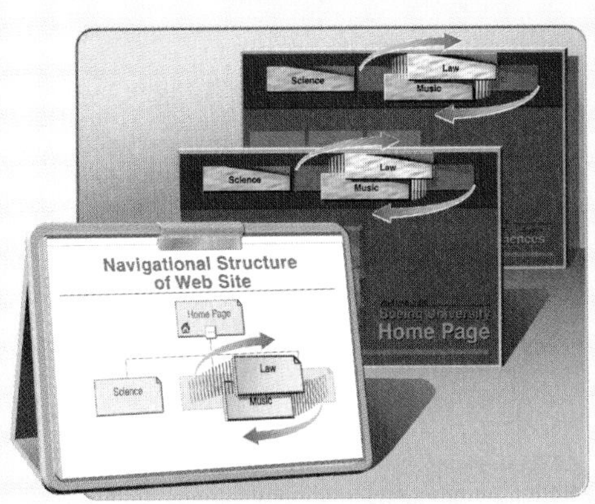

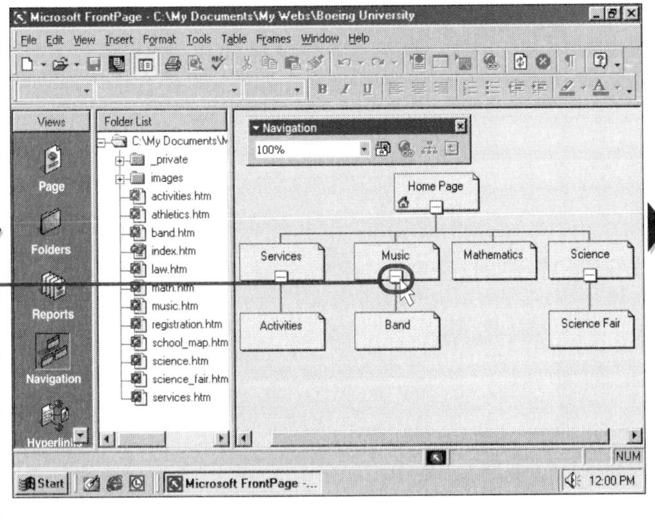

■ If the box for a Web page displays a minus sign (⊟), one or more pages appear below the page.

2 To hide the Web pages below a page, click the minus sign (⊟).

Note: Hiding Web pages allows you to hide pages that are currently not of interest so you can focus on other pages.

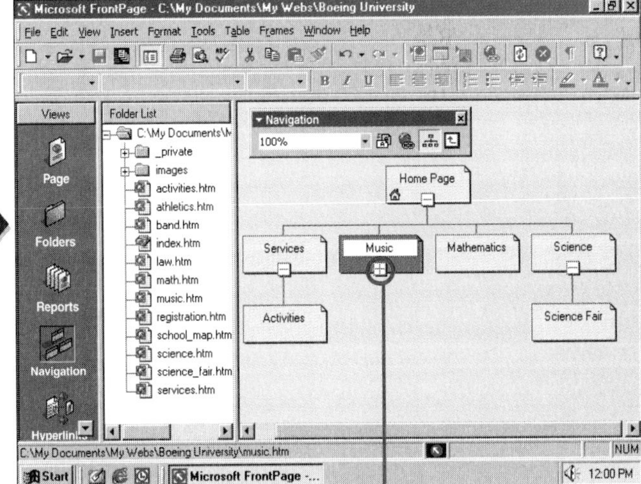

■ The Web pages are hidden from view.

■ You can click the plus sign (⊞) to once again display the Web pages below the page (⊞ changes to ⊟).

ADD A WEB PAGE TO THE WEB SITE STRUCTURE

You can add Web pages in the Navigation view to build the navigational structure of your Web site.

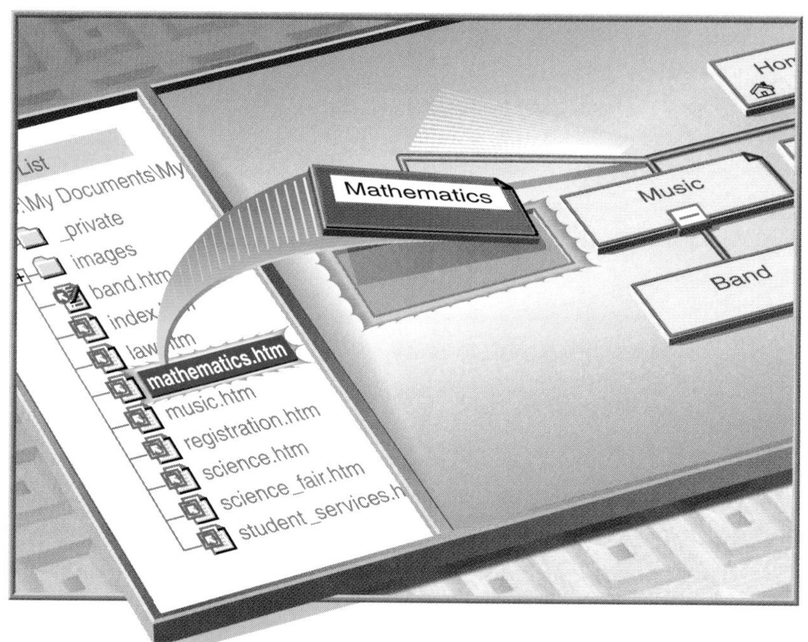

When you add navigation buttons to your Web pages, any Web pages you add to the navigational structure will appear as navigation buttons on your Web pages. To add navigation buttons to your Web pages, see page 182.

ADD A WEB PAGE TO THE WEB SITE STRUCTURE

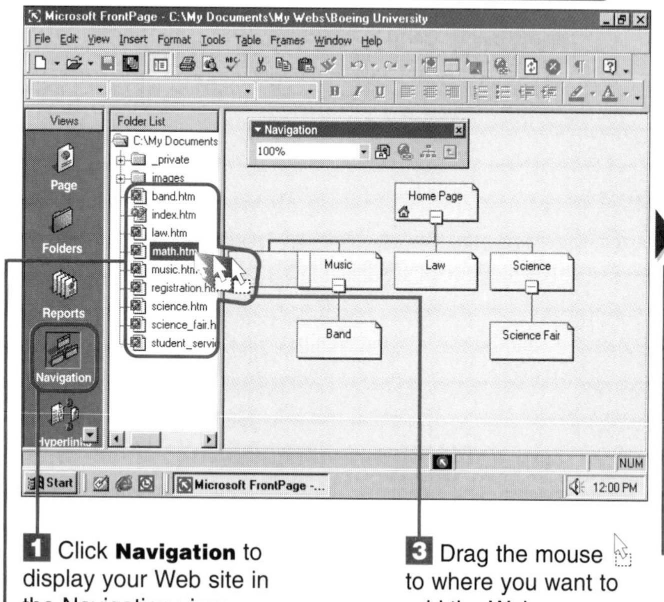

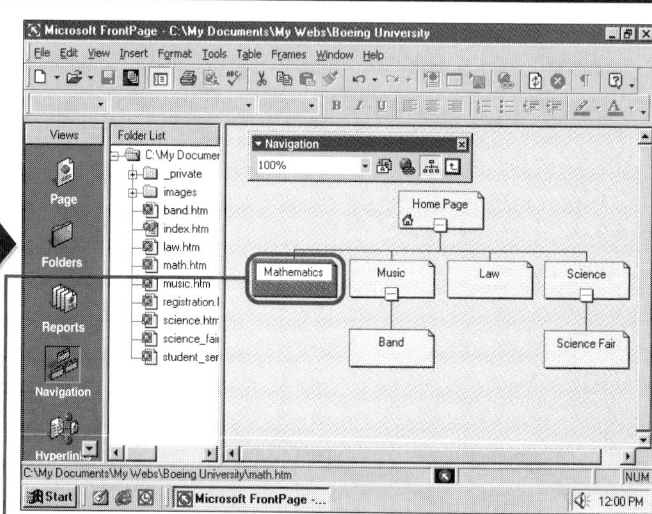

1 Click **Navigation** to display your Web site in the Navigation view.

2 Position the mouse over the Web page you want to add to the navigational structure of your Web site.

3 Drag the mouse to where you want to add the Web page.

Note: A gray outline shows where the Web page will appear.

■ The Web page appears in the navigational structure of your Web site.

■ You can repeat steps **2** and **3** for each Web page you want to add.

REMOVE A WEB PAGE FROM THE WEB SITE STRUCTURE

You can remove a Web page from the navigational structure of your Web site.

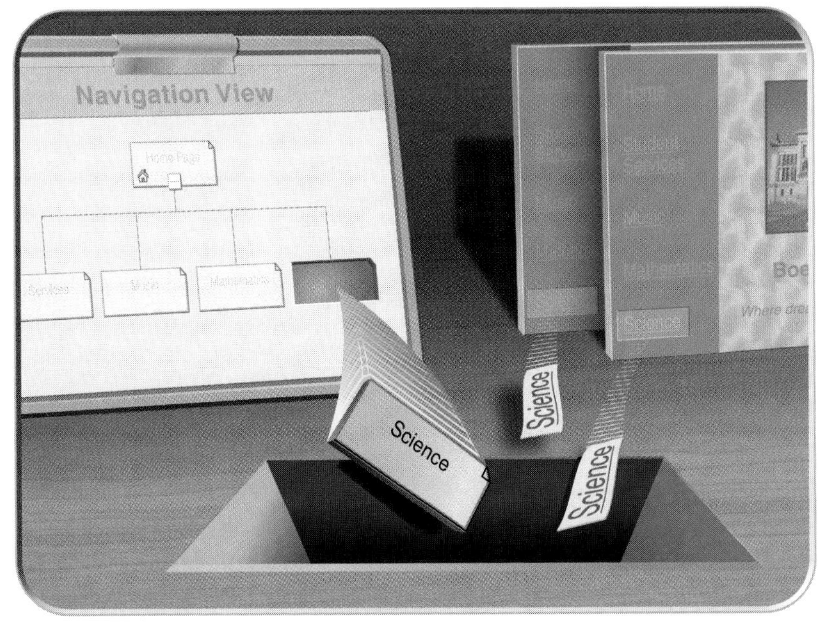

When you add navigation buttons to your Web pages, any Web pages you remove from the navigational structure will no longer appear as navigation buttons on your Web pages. To add navigation buttons to your Web pages, see page 182.

REMOVE A WEB PAGE FROM THE WEB SITE STRUCTURE

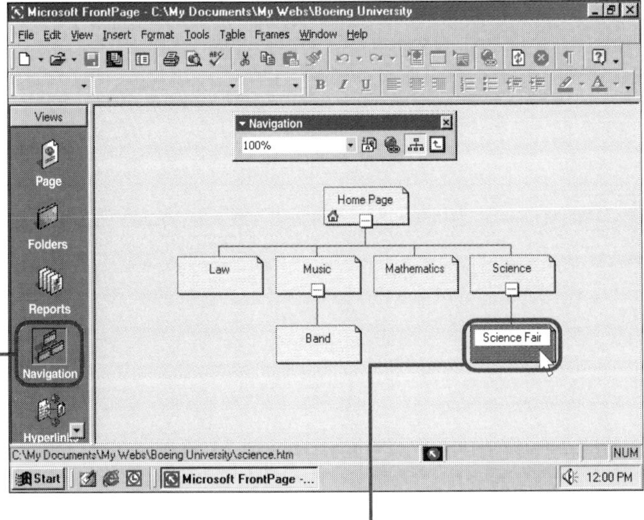

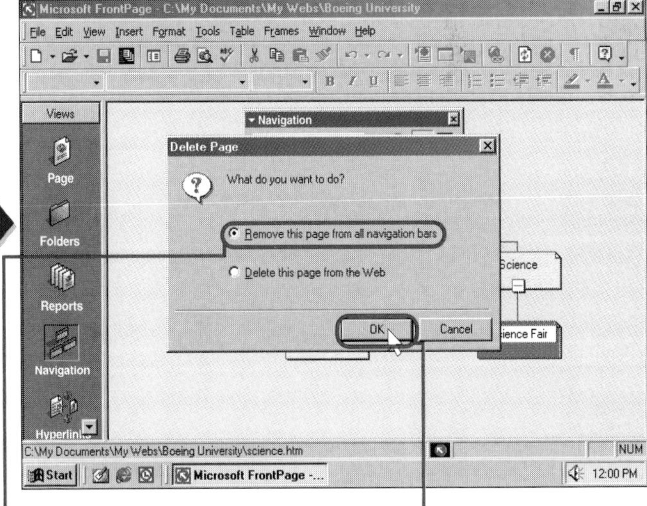

1 Click **Navigation** to display your Web site in the Navigation view.

2 Click the Web page you want to remove from the navigational structure of your Web site.

3 Press the Delete key to remove the Web page.

■ The Delete Page dialog box appears.

4 Click this option to delete the Web page from the navigational structure of your Web site (○ changes to ⊙).

5 Click **OK**.

Note: When you delete a Web page from the navigational structure of your Web site, you do not delete the page from your Web site.

MOVE A WEB PAGE IN THE WEB SITE STRUCTURE

You can rearrange Web pages to better organize the information in your Web site.

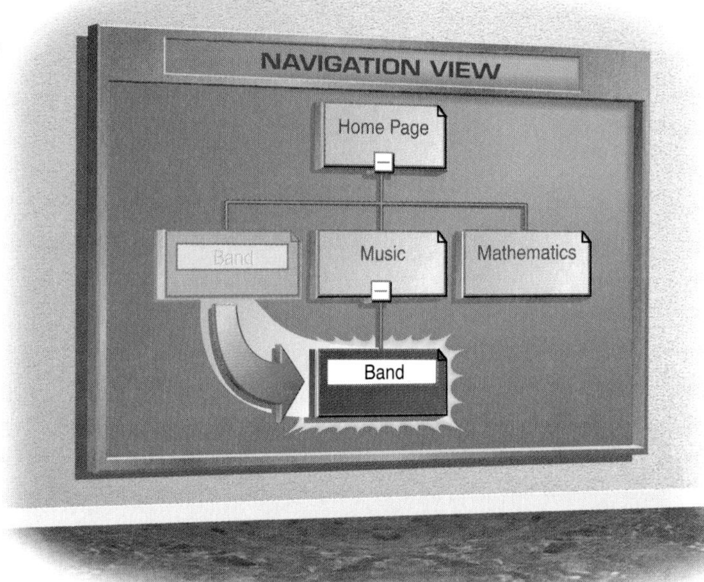

When you add navigation buttons to your Web pages, rearranging Web pages in the navigational structure will change which navigation buttons appear on your Web pages and the order of the navigation buttons. To add navigation buttons to your Web pages, see page 182.

MOVE A WEB PAGE IN THE WEB SITE STRUCTURE

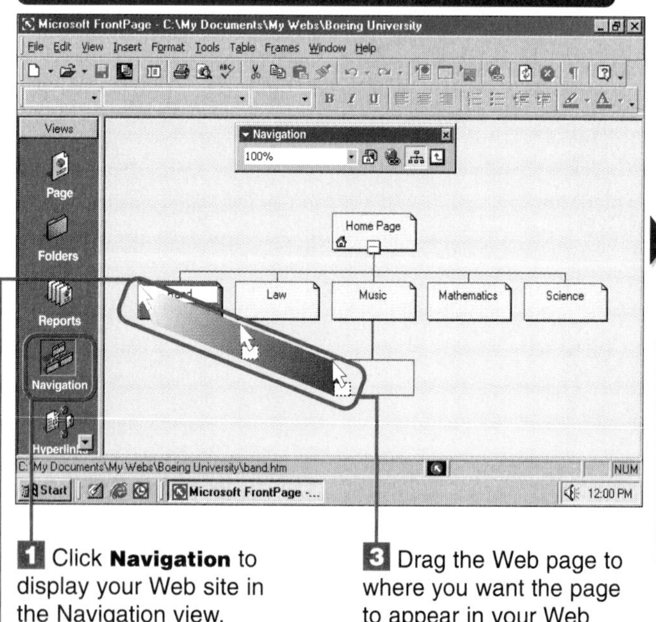

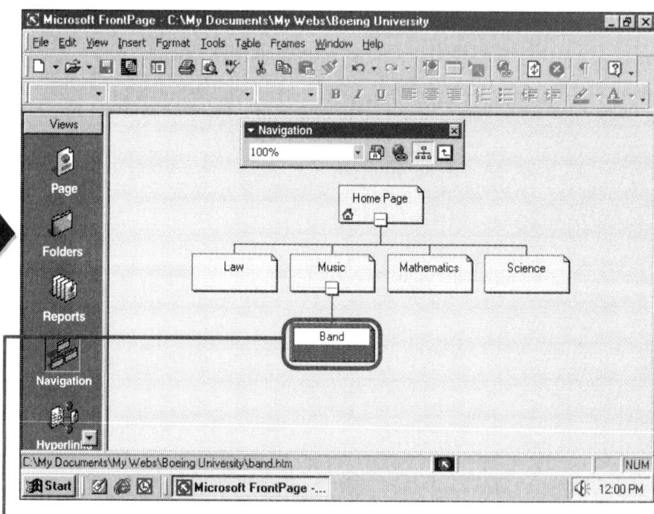

1 Click **Navigation** to display your Web site in the Navigation view.

2 Position the mouse over the Web page you want to move.

3 Drag the Web page to where you want the page to appear in your Web site structure.

Note: A gray outline shows where the Web page will appear.

■ The Web page appears in the new location.

CHANGE A WEB PAGE TITLE IN THE WEB SITE STRUCTURE

You can change the title of a Web page to better describe the contents of the page.

Changing the titles of Web pages will only change the labels for navigation buttons on your Web pages. To add navigation buttons to your Web pages, see page 182.

Changing the title of a Web page in the Navigation view will not change the title that appears at the top of a Web browser window when the page appears on the Web. To change this title, see page 49.

CHANGE A WEB PAGE TITLE IN THE WEB SITE STRUCTURE

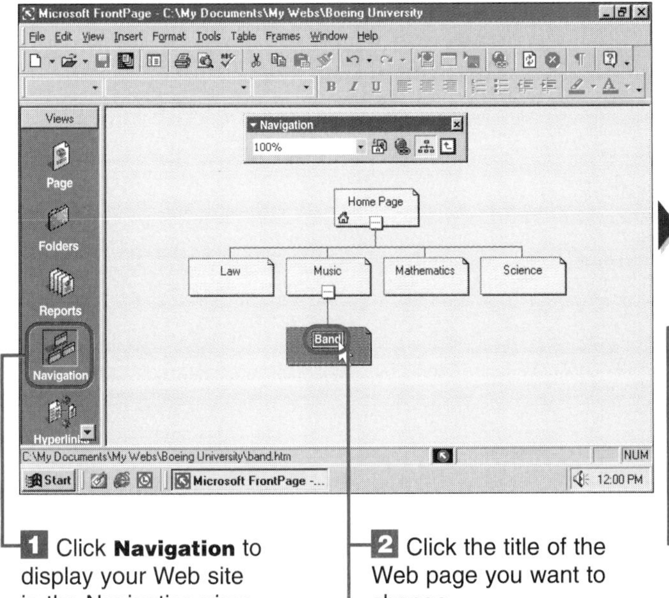

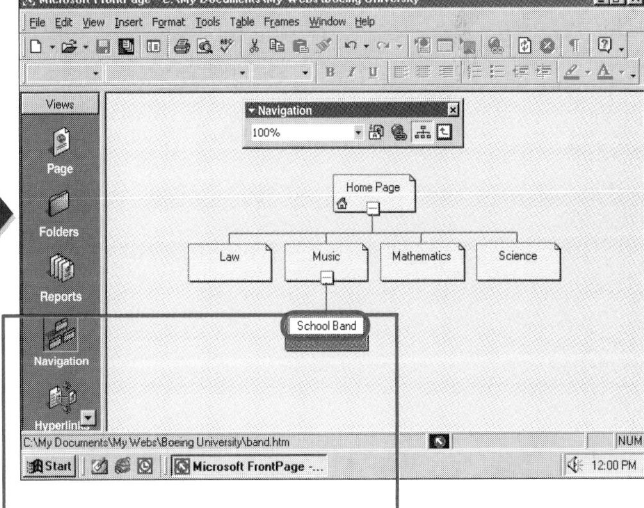

1 Click **Navigation** to display your Web site in the Navigation view.

2 Click the title of the Web page you want to change.

3 Wait a moment and then click the title of the Web page again.

■ The title of the Web page appears in a box.

4 Type a new title for the Web page and then press the Enter key.

ADD SHARED BORDERS

You can add shared borders to every page in your Web site. Shared borders allow you to display the same information on every Web page.

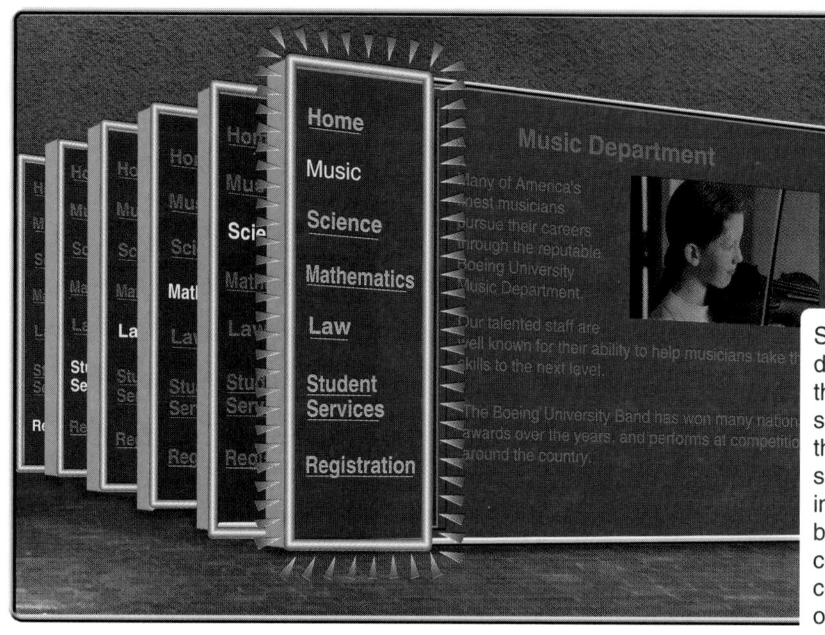

Shared borders can display navigation buttons that are links readers can select to move through the pages in your Web site. You can also add information to shared borders such as images, contact numbers, copyright information or a company logo.

ADD SHARED BORDERS

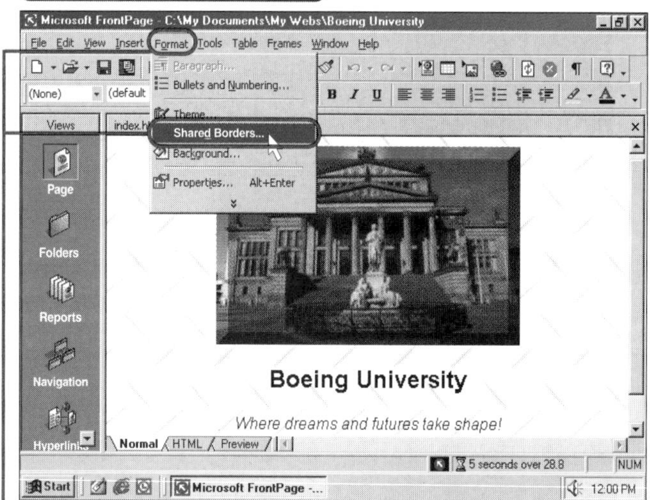

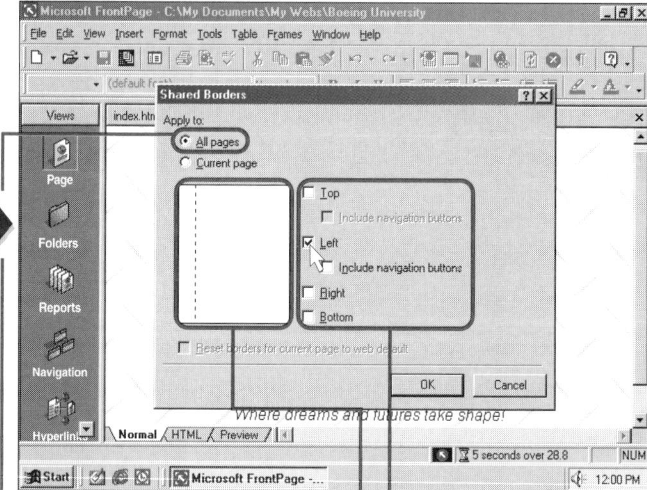

1 Click **Format**.

2 Click **Shared Borders**.

Note: If Shared Borders does not appear on the menu, position the mouse over the bottom of the menu to display all the menu commands.

■ The Shared Borders dialog box appears.

3 Click **All pages** to add a shared border to every Web page in your Web site (○ changes to ⊙).

4 Click an option to specify where you want the shared border to appear on every Web page (☐ changes to ☑).

■ A dashed line indicates where the shared border will appear on your Web pages.

How does FrontPage determine which navigation buttons to place on my Web pages?

FrontPage sets up navigation buttons based on the structure of your Web site in the Navigation view. To use the Navigation view, see pages 176 to 181.

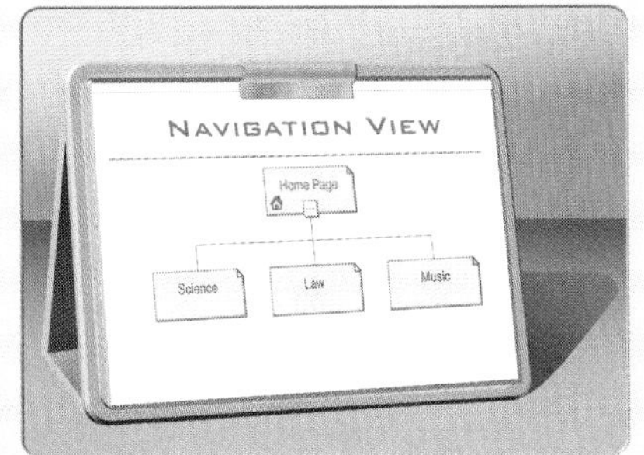

What labels will FrontPage use for navigation buttons?

The titles of your Web pages determine the labels for navigation buttons. To change the title of a Web page, see page 181.

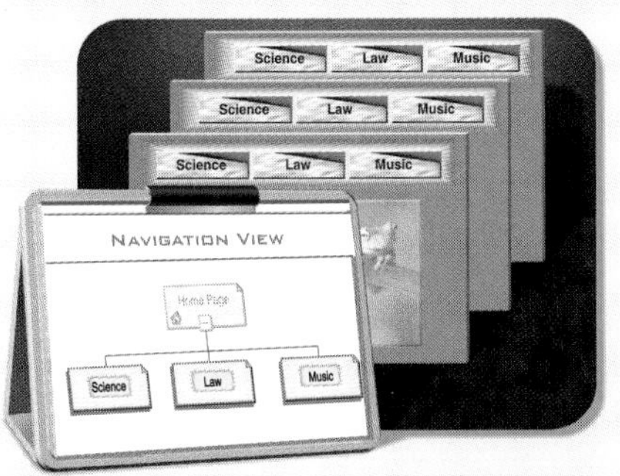

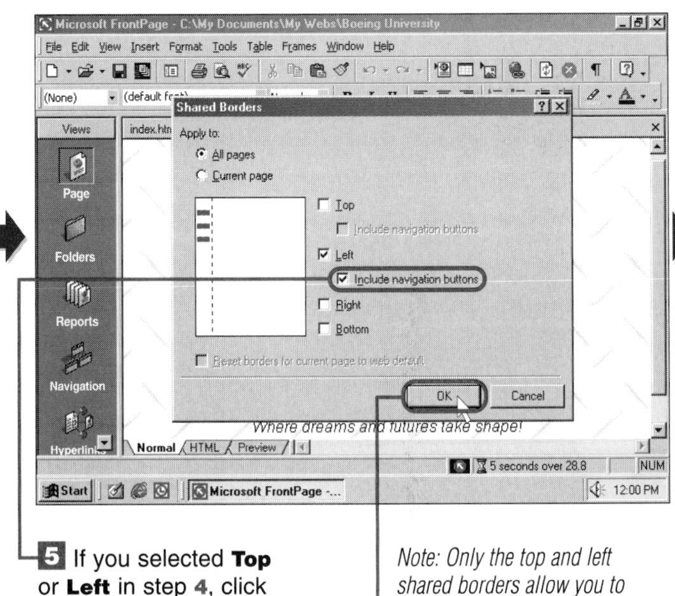

5 If you selected **Top** or **Left** in step **4**, click **Include navigation buttons** to display navigation buttons on your Web pages (☐ changes to ☑).

Note: Only the top and left shared borders allow you to display navigation buttons.

6 Click **OK** to save your changes.

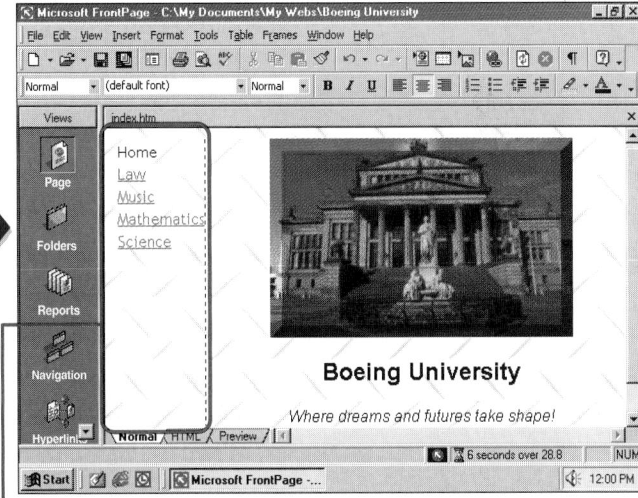

■ All the Web pages in your Web site display the shared border.

■ If you chose to include navigation buttons in step **5**, the buttons will appear in the shared border.

■ You need to apply a theme to your Web page to display graphical navigation buttons. To apply a theme, see page 94.

■ To remove a shared border from all the pages in your Web site, repeat steps **1** to **4** (☑ changes to ☐ in step **4**). Then perform step **6**.

CHANGE NAVIGATION BUTTONS IN SHARED BORDERS

Once you add navigation buttons to your Web pages, you can specify which navigation buttons you want to appear on the pages. You can also change the orientation and appearance of the navigation buttons.

Navigation buttons are links readers can select to move through the pages in your Web site. To add navigation buttons to your Web pages, see page 182.

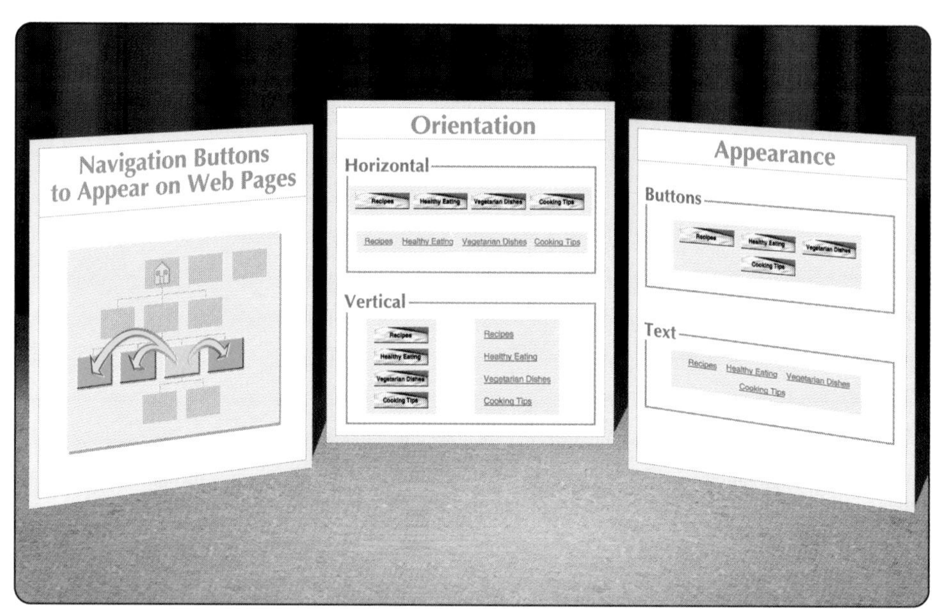

CHANGE NAVIGATION BUTTONS IN SHARED BORDERS

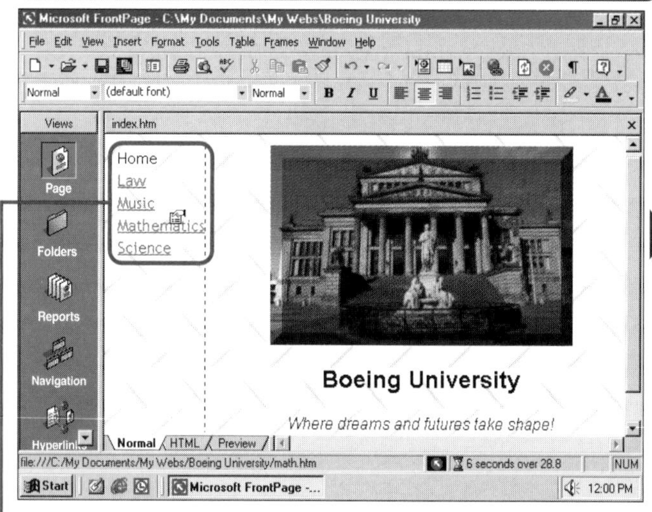

1 Double-click a navigation button on a Web page.

Note: If your Web page does not display navigation buttons, double-click the text that appears in the navigation button area.

■ The Navigation Bar Properties dialog box appears.

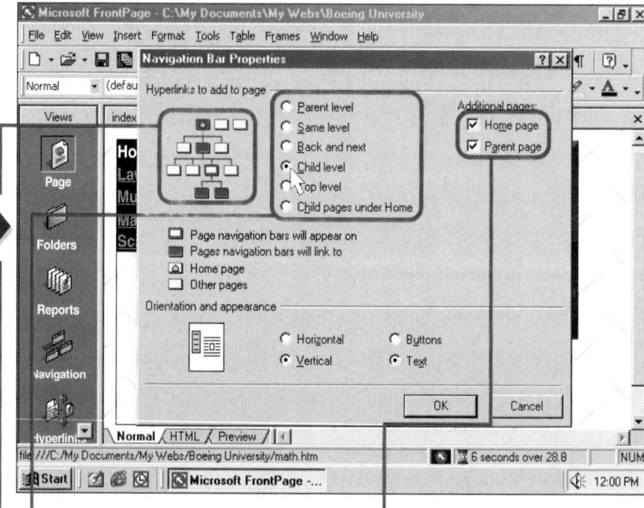

2 Click an option to specify which links you want to appear on your Web pages (○ changes to ⊙).

■ This area shows the links that will appear on your Web pages.

■ These options add links to the home page and the page above the current page. If you do not want to display these links, click an option to turn the option off (☑ changes to ☐).

? What navigation buttons can I add to my Web pages?

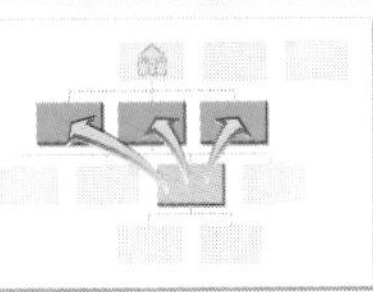

Parent level

Include links to pages directly above the current page.

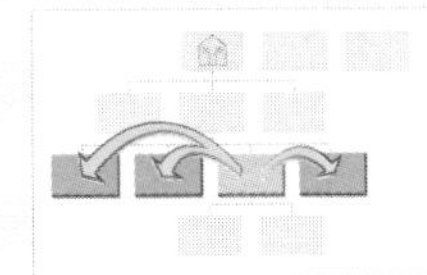

Same level

Include links to pages on the same level as the current page.

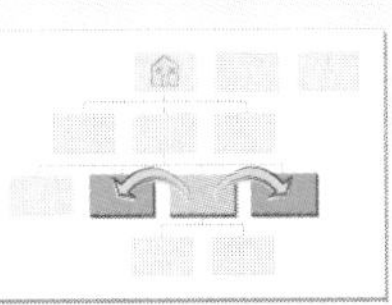

Back and next

Include links to pages beside the current page.

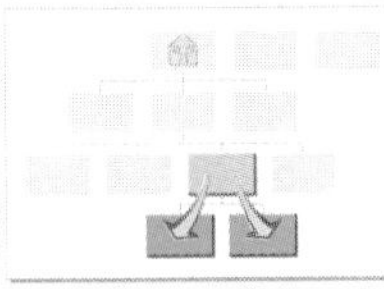

Child level

Include links to pages directly below the current page.

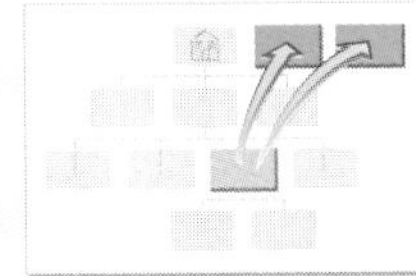

Top level

Include links to pages on the same level as the home page.

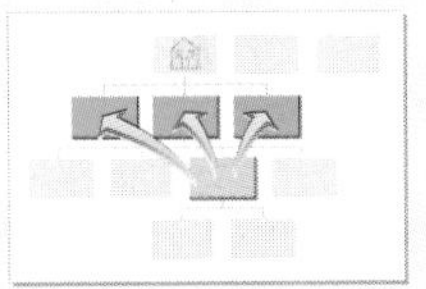

Child pages under Home

Include links to pages directly below the home page.

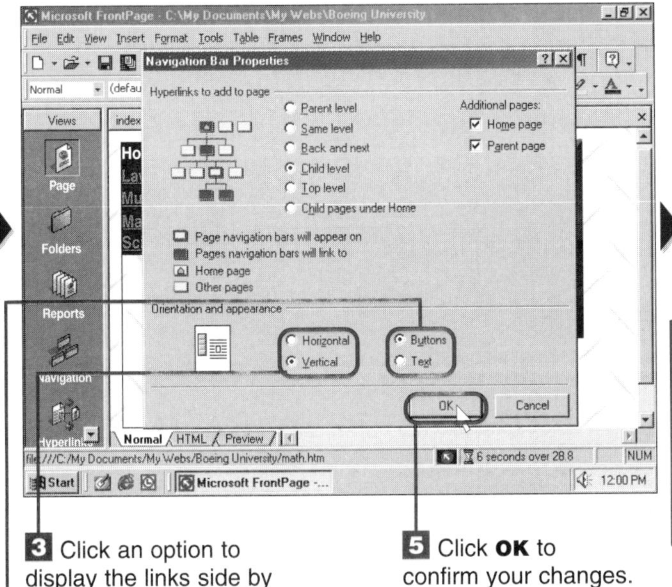

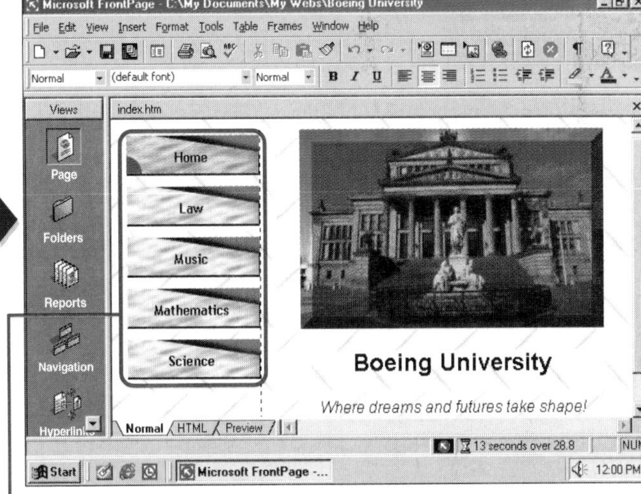

3 Click an option to display the links side by side (Horizontal) or in a list (Vertical) (○ changes to ⊙).

4 Click an option to display the links as graphical buttons or as text (○ changes to ⊙).

5 Click **OK** to confirm your changes.

■ The navigation buttons display the changes.

■ If you selected **Buttons** in step **4**, you need to apply a theme to your Web page to display graphical navigation buttons. To apply a theme, see page 94.

Reservations
Schedules
Travel Tips
Arrivals
Departures
Sunshine VACATIONS
Plan Your Vacation With Us
At Sunshine Vacations, we make all your vacations memorable ones. Call us today to plan your next trip!

CHAPTER 11

Create Frames

Would you like to display your Web pages in frames? This chapter teaches you how to create and work with frames.

CREATE FRAMES

You can create frames to divide a Web browser window into sections. Each section will display a different Web page.

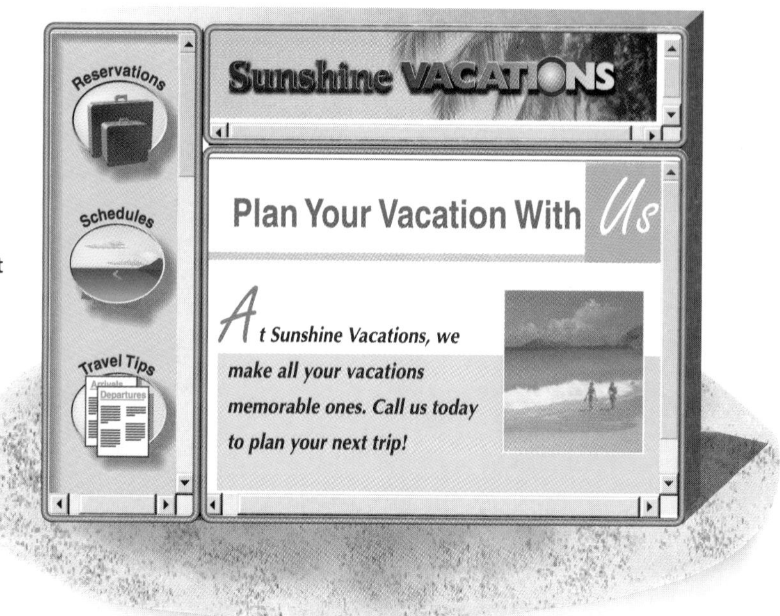

To create frames, you must create a frames page. A frames page provides the structure for displaying several Web pages at the same time.

FrontPage offers several ready-to-use templates that you can choose from to quickly create frames.

CREATE FRAMES

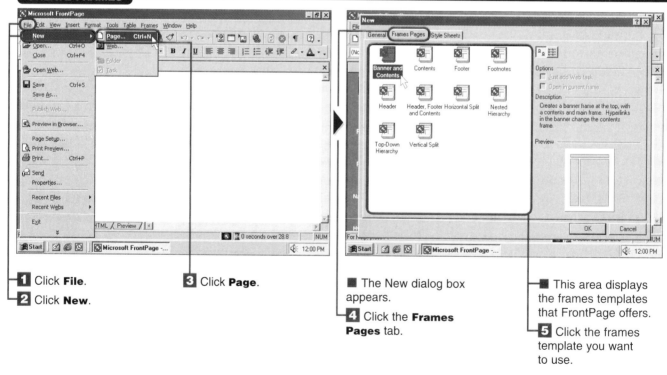

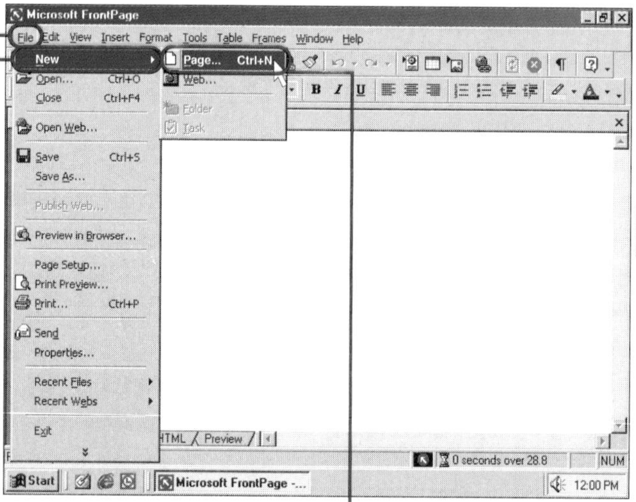

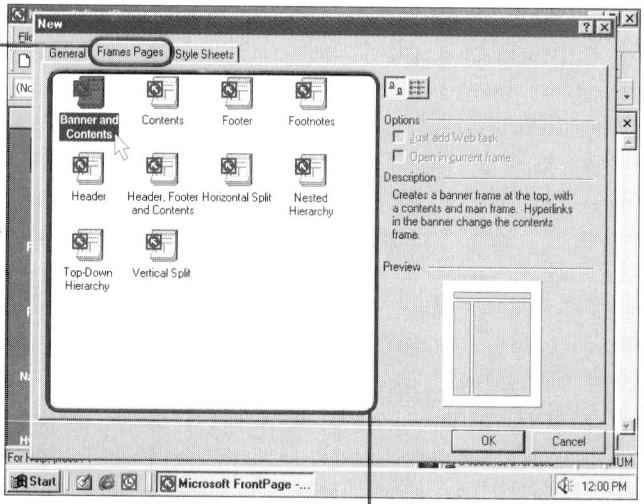

1 Click **File**.

2 Click **New**.

3 Click **Page**.

■ The New dialog box appears.

4 Click the **Frames Pages** tab.

■ This area displays the frames templates that FrontPage offers.

5 Click the frames template you want to use.

Why would I use frames?

Frames allow you to display information on a Web page that will remain on the screen while readers browse through your Web pages.

Banners

Frames can display information such as an advertisement, a warning message or a company logo.

Navigation

Frames can display a table of contents or navigational tools to help readers move through your Web pages and find information of interest.

Supporting Information

Frames can display supporting information such as copyright notices or footnotes.

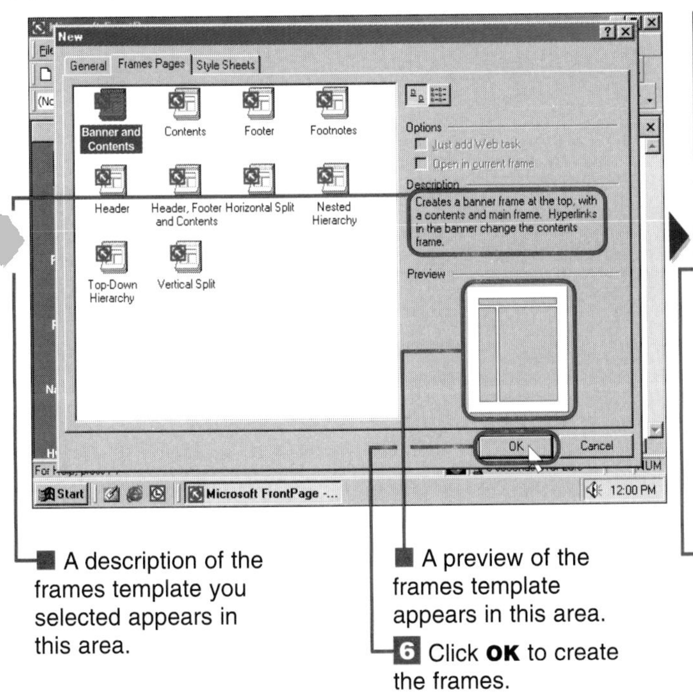

■ A description of the frames template you selected appears in this area.

■ A preview of the frames template appears in this area.

6 Click **OK** to create the frames.

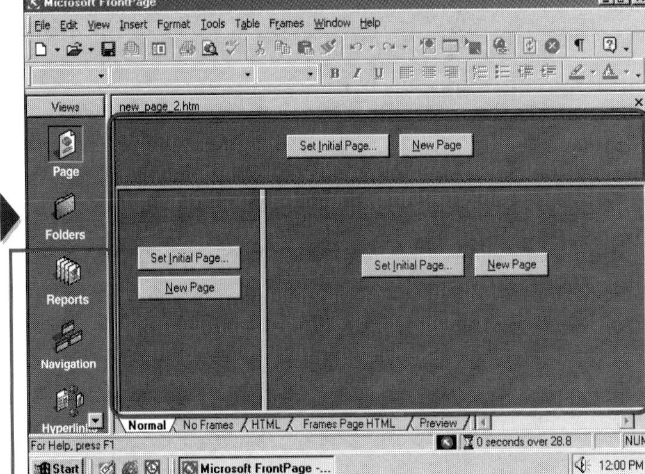

■ A blank frames page based on the template you selected appears.

■ You can now specify which Web page you want to appear in each frame. To add a Web page to a frame, see pages 190 to 192.

ADD AN EXISTING WEB PAGE TO A FRAME

You can add a Web page you previously created to a frame.

ADD AN EXISTING WEB PAGE TO A FRAME

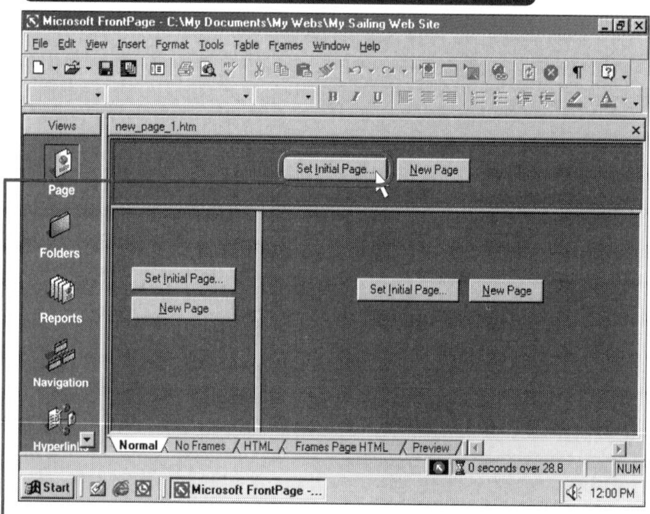

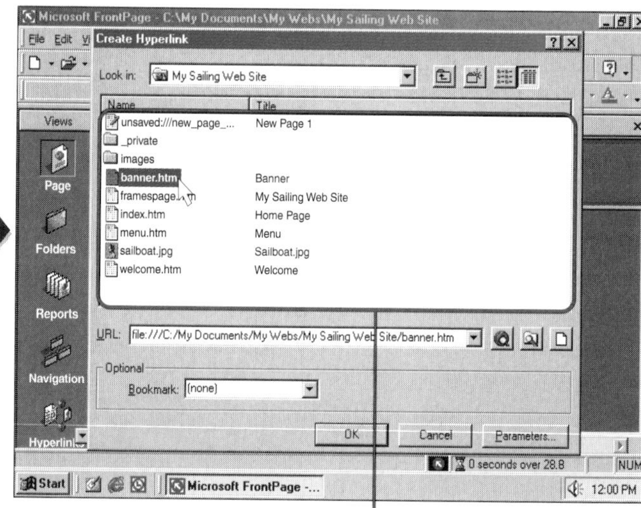

1 Click **Set Initial Page** to add a Web page you previously created to a frame.

Note: If the Set Initial Page button is not displayed, see page 188 to create frames.

■ The Create Hyperlink dialog box appears.

■ This area displays all the Web pages in your current Web site.

2 Click the Web page you want to appear in the frame.

What should I consider when adding Web pages to frames?

You should check how the Web pages displayed in your frames appear on computers with monitors using different resolutions. The resolution of a monitor determines the amount of information that will appear in each frame. Monitors using lower resolutions will show less information in each frame. For example, a heading or image may not fully appear in a frame on monitors using lower resolutions.

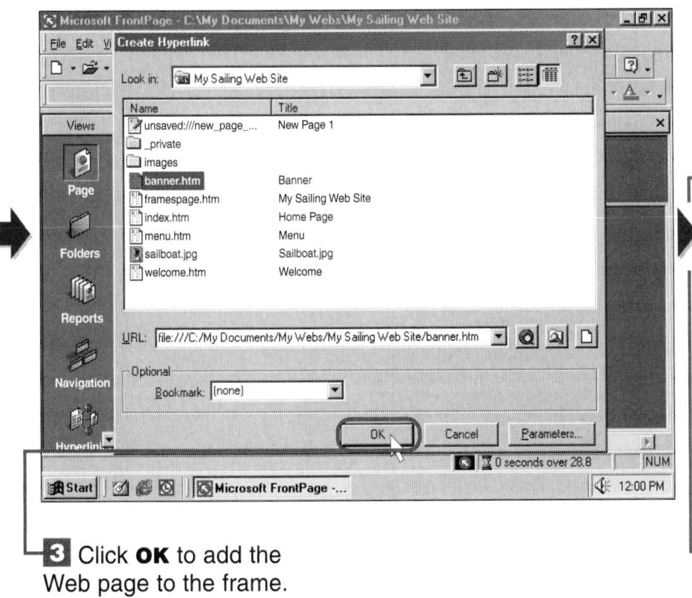

3 Click **OK** to add the Web page to the frame.

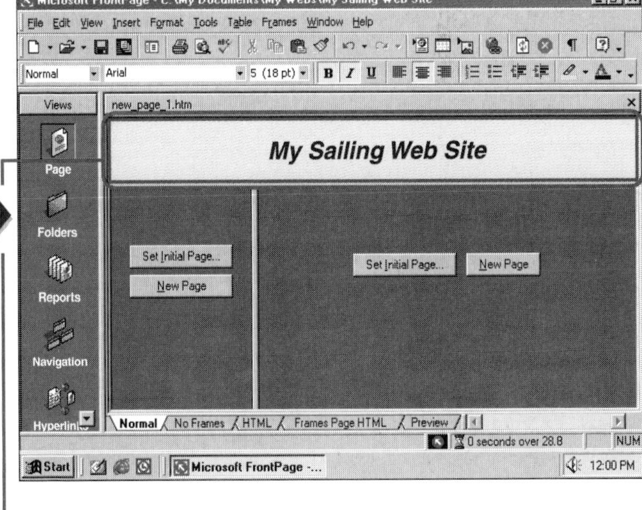

■ The Web page appears in the frame.

■ You can repeat steps **1** to **3** for each frame you want to display a Web page you previously created.

ADD A NEW WEB PAGE TO A FRAME

Once you create frames, you can add a new Web page to a frame.

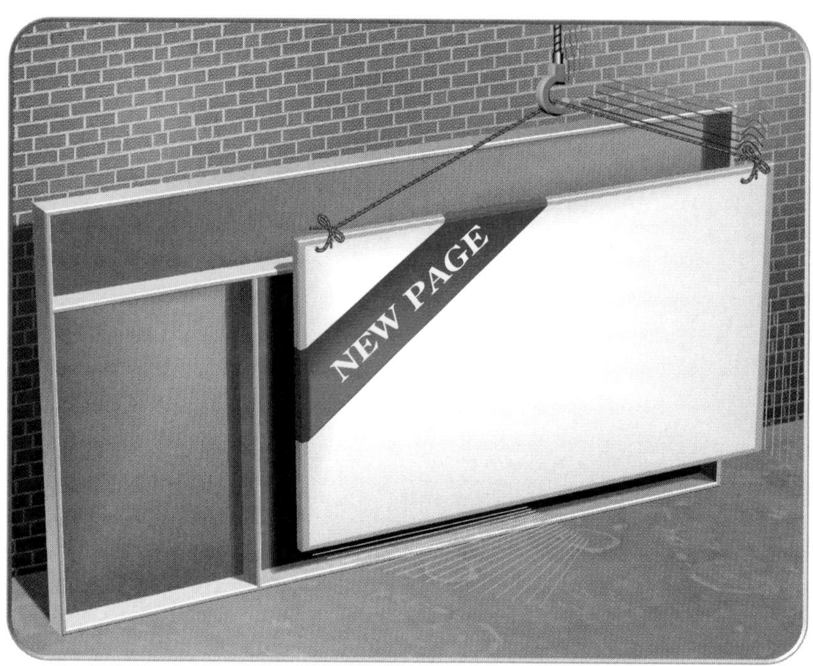

ADD A NEW WEB PAGE TO A FRAME

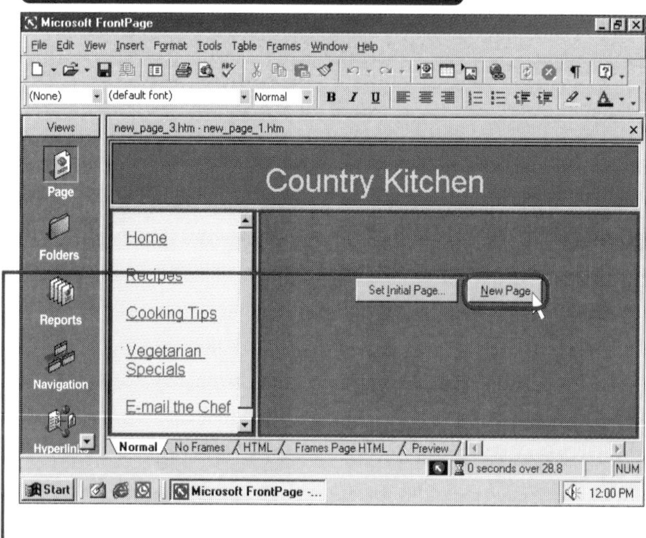

1 Click **New Page** to add a new Web page to a frame.

Note: If the New Page button is not displayed, see page 188 to create frames.

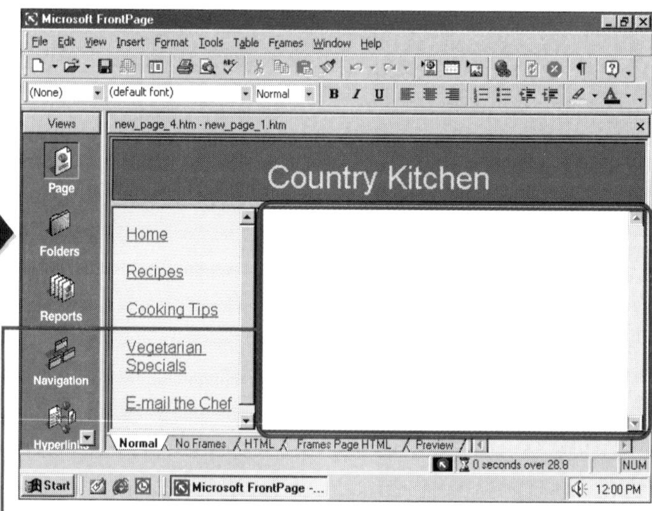

■ A new Web page appears in the frame.

■ You can immediately add information to the Web page.

RESIZE A FRAME

You can easily change the size of a frame.

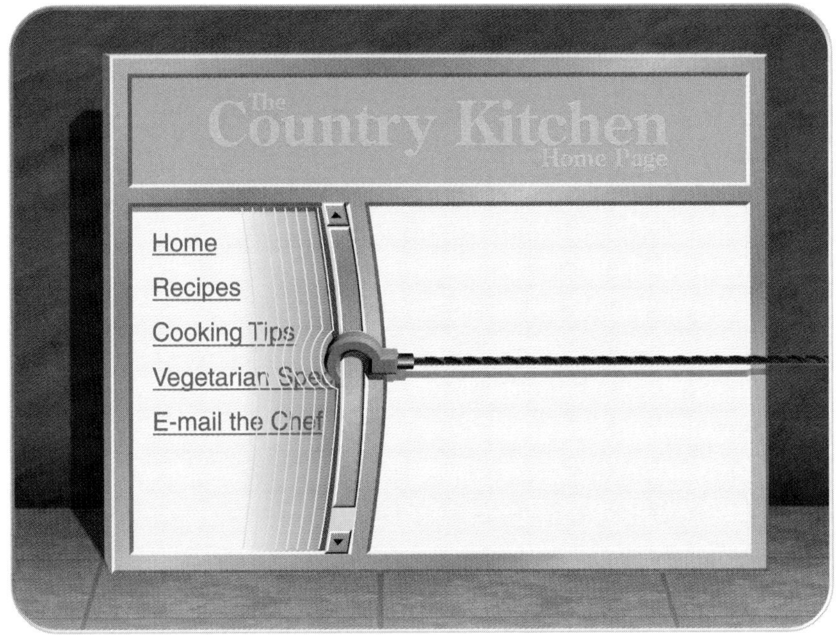

Resizing a frame will not affect the information displayed in the frame. Resizing a frame only changes how much information the frame displays.

RESIZE A FRAME

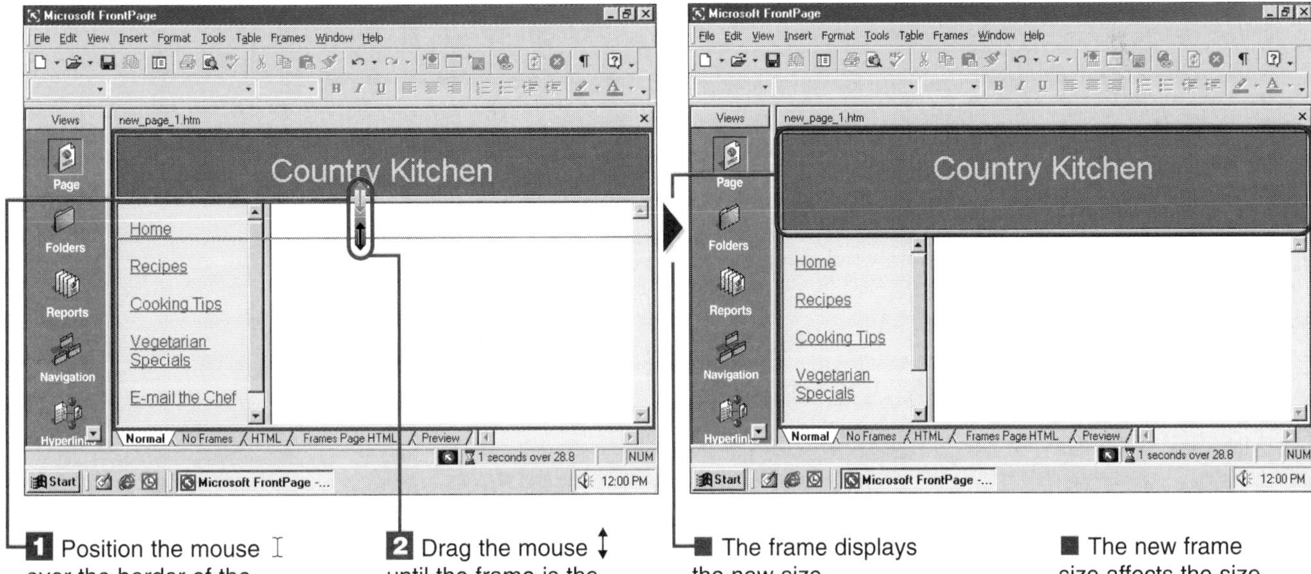

1 Position the mouse I over the border of the frame you want to resize (I changes to ↕ or ↔).

2 Drag the mouse ↕ until the frame is the size you want.

■ The frame displays the new size.

■ The new frame size affects the size of adjacent frames.

SAVE FRAMES

You should save your frames to store the frames for future use. This lets you later review and edit the Web pages displayed in the frames.

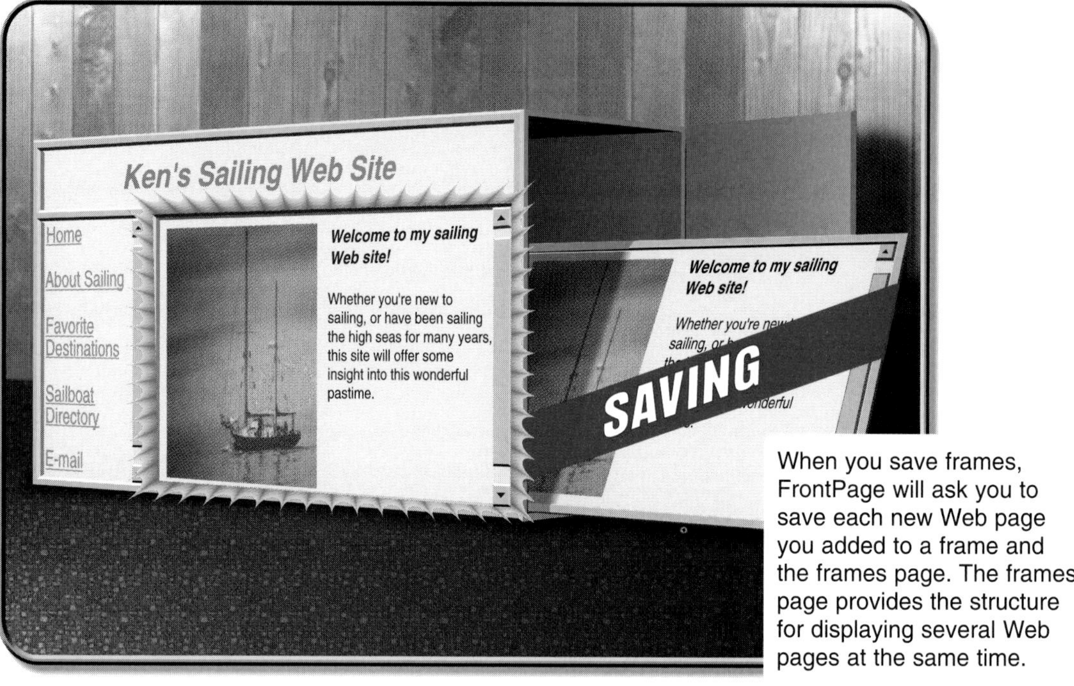

When you save frames, FrontPage will ask you to save each new Web page you added to a frame and the frames page. The frames page provides the structure for displaying several Web pages at the same time.

SAVE FRAMES

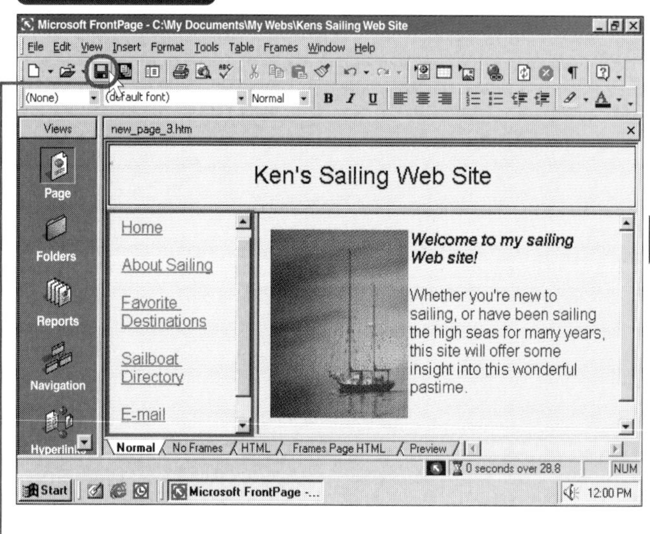

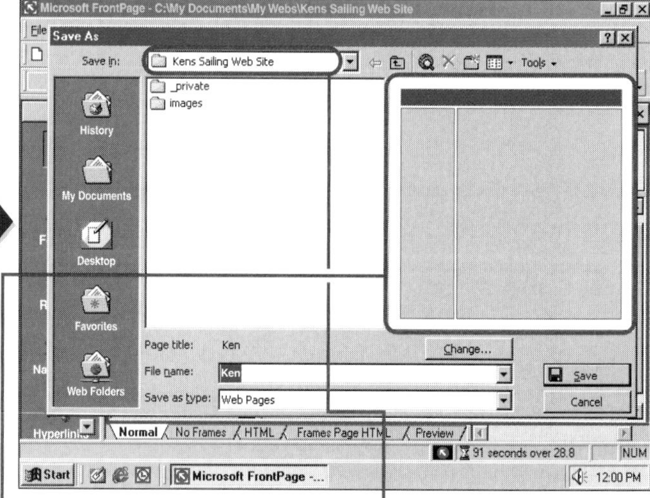

1 Click 💾 to save your frames.

■ The Save As dialog box appears.

■ This area displays the layout of the frames. If you added a new Web page to a frame, the frame appears highlighted.

*Note: If you did not add a new Web page to a frame, skip to step **5**.*

■ This area shows the location where FrontPage will store the new Web page.

Note: FrontPage will automatically store your Web page in the folder for the current Web site.

? Why does the Save Embedded Files dialog box appear when I save my frames?

If you added an image to a Web page displayed in a frame, you need to save the image as part of your Web site. A copy of the image will be stored in the same folder that stores all the Web pages for your Web site. This ensures the image will transfer with your Web site when you publish your Web pages.

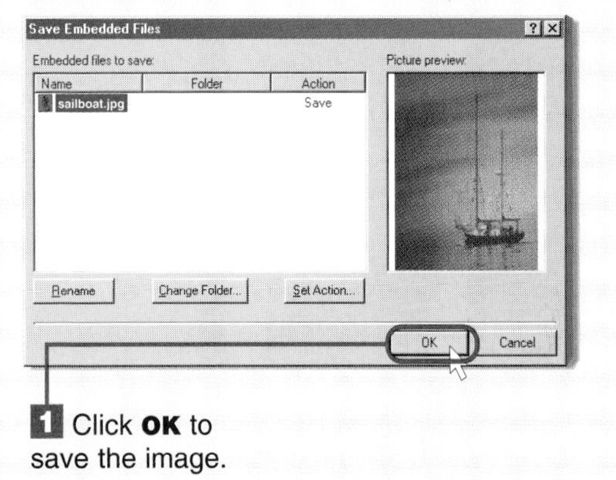

1 Click **OK** to save the image.

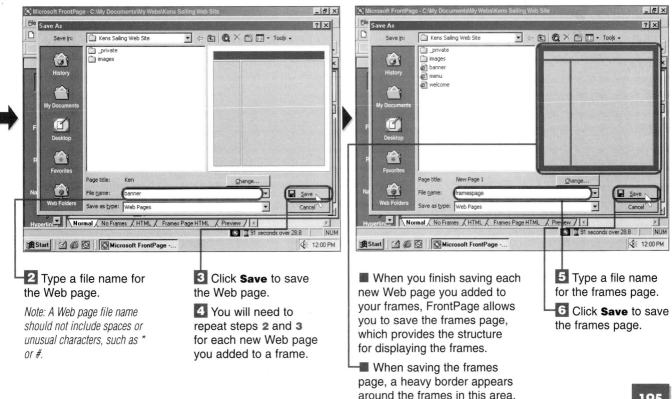

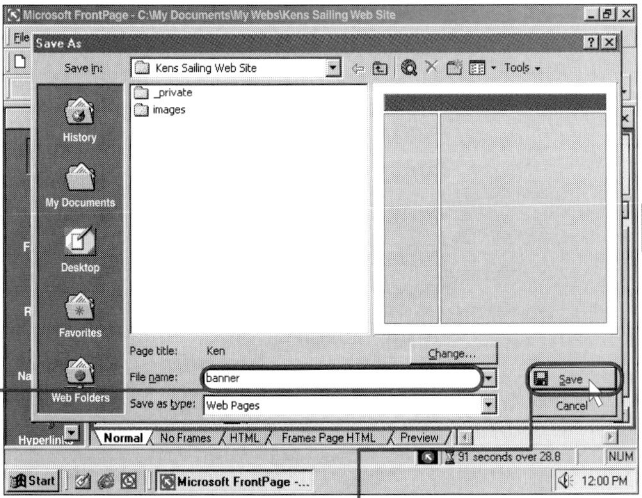

2 Type a file name for the Web page.

*Note: A Web page file name should not include spaces or unusual characters, such as * or #.*

3 Click **Save** to save the Web page.

4 You will need to repeat steps **2** and **3** for each new Web page you added to a frame.

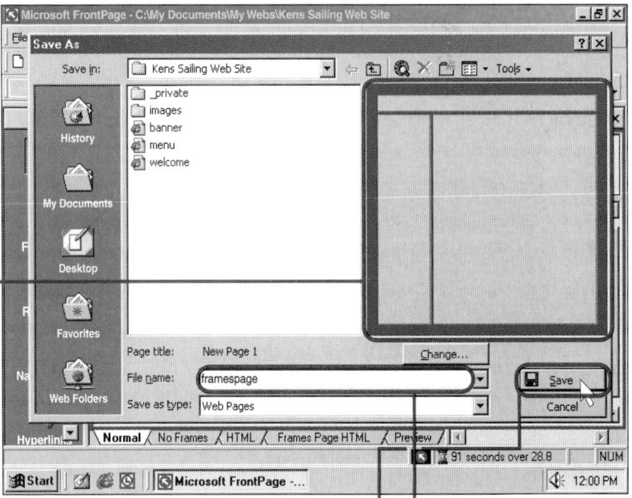

■ When you finish saving each new Web page you added to your frames, FrontPage allows you to save the frames page, which provides the structure for displaying the frames.

■ When saving the frames page, a heavy border appears around the frames in this area.

5 Type a file name for the frames page.

6 Click **Save** to save the frames page.

CREATE A LINK TO A FRAME

You can create a link on a Web page that readers can select to display a Web page in another frame.

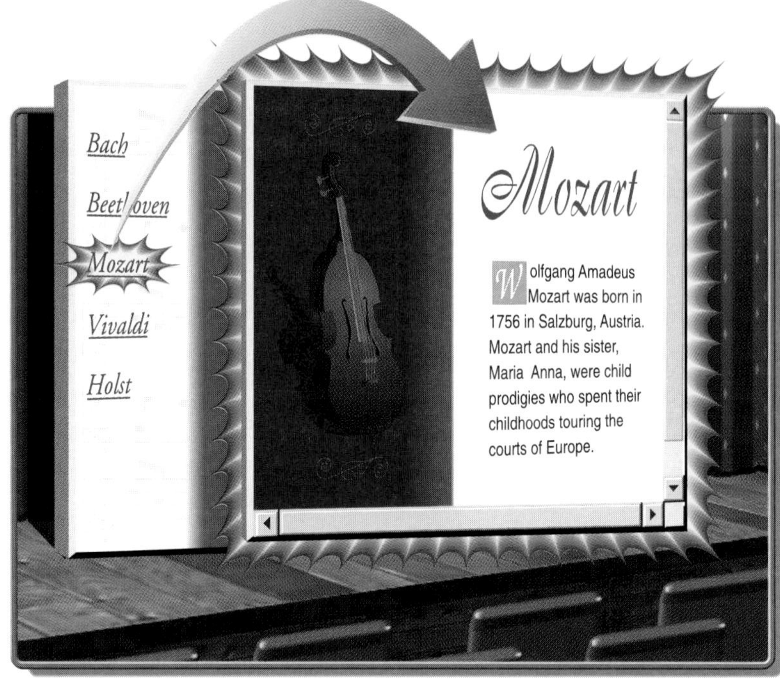

Creating a link to a frame is useful when you place a table of contents, navigational tools or search tools in one frame and you want the linked Web pages to appear in another frame.

CREATE A LINK TO A FRAME

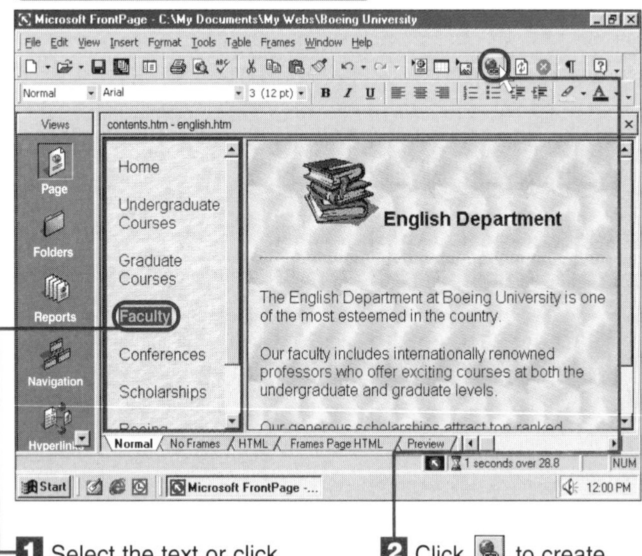

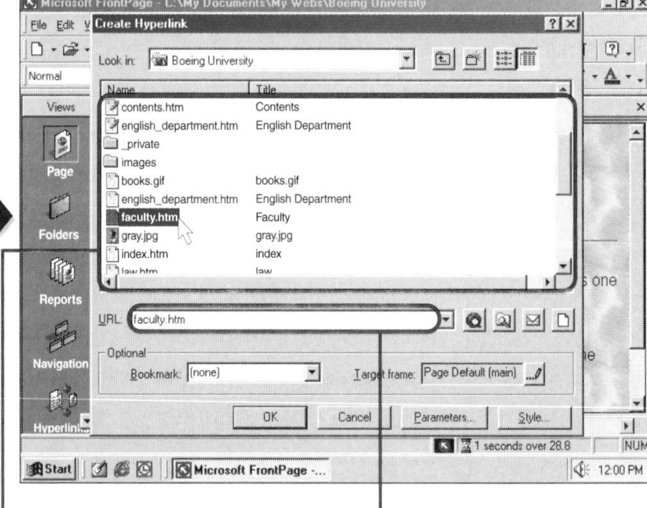

1 Select the text or click the image you want readers to select to display a Web page in another frame. To select text, see page 54.

Note: To add an image, see pages 100 to 103.

2 Click to create a link.

■ The Create Hyperlink dialog box appears.

■ This area displays all the Web pages in your current Web site.

3 To link the text or image to a Web page in your current Web site, click the Web page in this area.

■ To link the text or image to a page on the Web, click this area and type the address of the Web page.

What should I consider when creating a link to another frame?

Make sure the text or image you use for a link clearly indicates where the link will take your readers. Do not use the phrase "Click Here" for a link, since this phrase is not very informative.

When a reader selects a link, which frame will display the linked Web page?

When you create frames, FrontPage will automatically set up one frame to display links and another frame that will display the linked Web pages. In most cases, linked Web pages will appear in the largest frame.

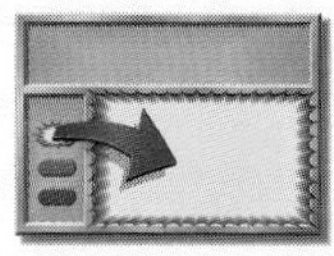

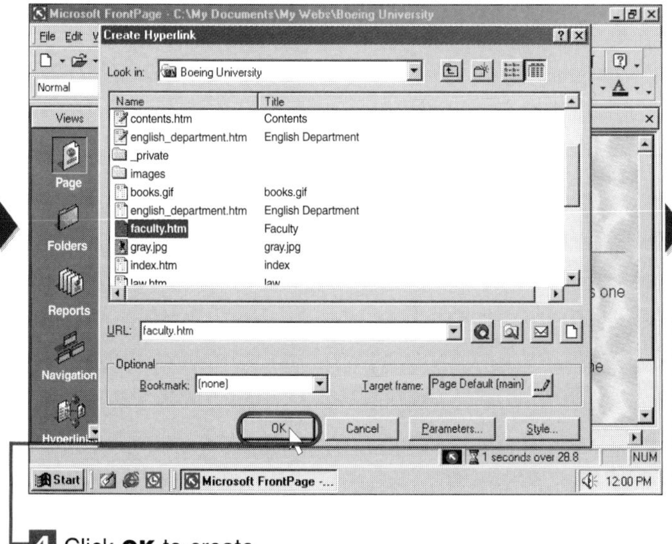

4 Click **OK** to create the link.

■ FrontPage creates the link. Text links appear underlined and in color.

■ To deselect text, click outside the selected area.

■ A reader can click the link to display the linked Web page in another frame.

Note: To test the link, you must use the Preview view. For information on the Preview view, see page 42.

CHANGE THE TARGET FRAME

You can change the frame that will display a Web page when readers select a link. The frame you select is called the target frame.

When you create frames, FrontPage will automatically set up one frame to display links and another frame that will display the linked Web pages.

CHANGE THE TARGET FRAME

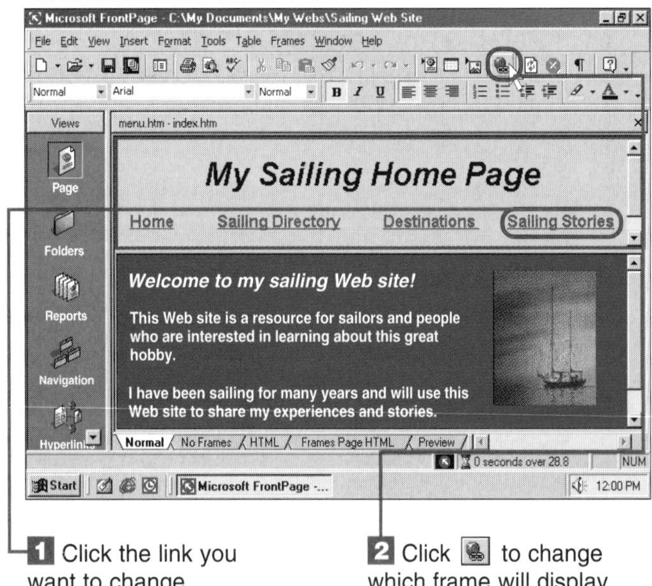

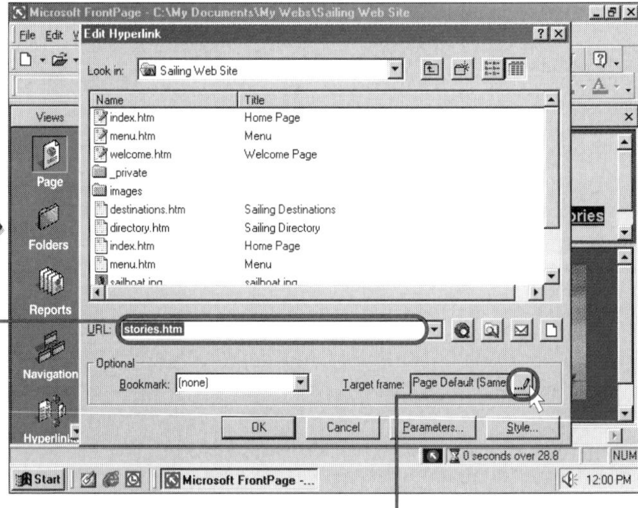

1 Click the link you want to change.

Note: To create a link, see page 196.

2 Click [icon] to change which frame will display the linked Web page.

■ The Edit Hyperlink dialog box appears.

■ This area displays the Web page that will appear when readers select the link.

3 Click [icon] to specify which frame you want to display the linked Web page.

What are some targets that I can use to display a linked Web page?

Page Default

The Web page will appear in the frame that FrontPage automatically sets up to display the linked Web page.

Same Frame

The Web page will appear in the same frame that contains the link.

Whole Page

The Web page will replace all the frames with a single Web page.

New Window

The Web page will appear in its own Web browser window.

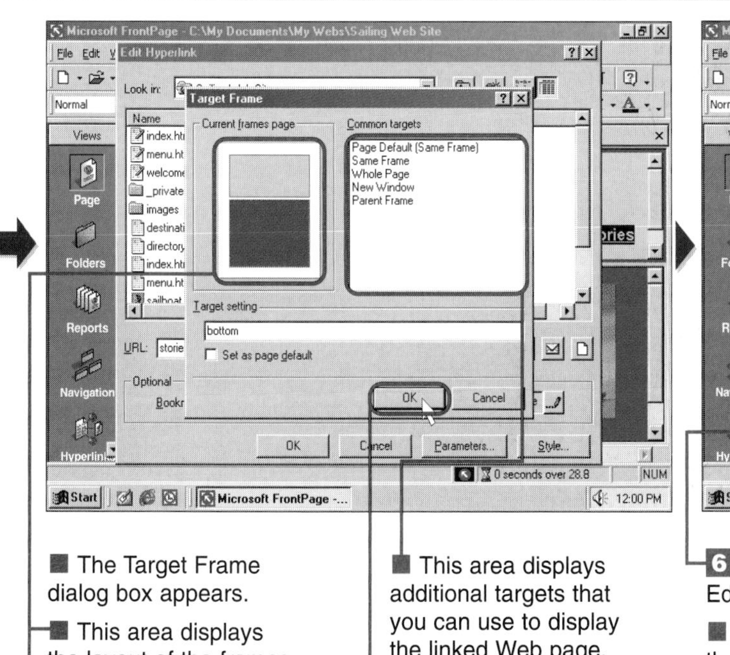

■ The Target Frame dialog box appears.

■ This area displays the layout of the frames.

4 Click the frame you want to display the linked Web page. The frame appears highlighted.

■ This area displays additional targets that you can use to display the linked Web page. Instead of performing step **4**, you can click the target you want to use.

5 Click **OK**.

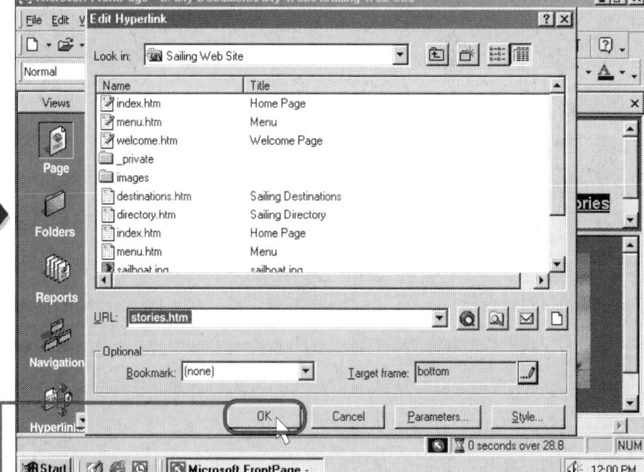

6 Click **OK** to close the Edit Hyperlink dialog box.

■ When a reader clicks the link, the linked Web page will appear in the frame you specified.

Note: To test the link, you must use the Preview view. For information on the Preview view, see page 42.

CHANGE FRAME MARGINS

You can change the margins of a frame to adjust the amount of space between the frame contents and the borders of the frame.

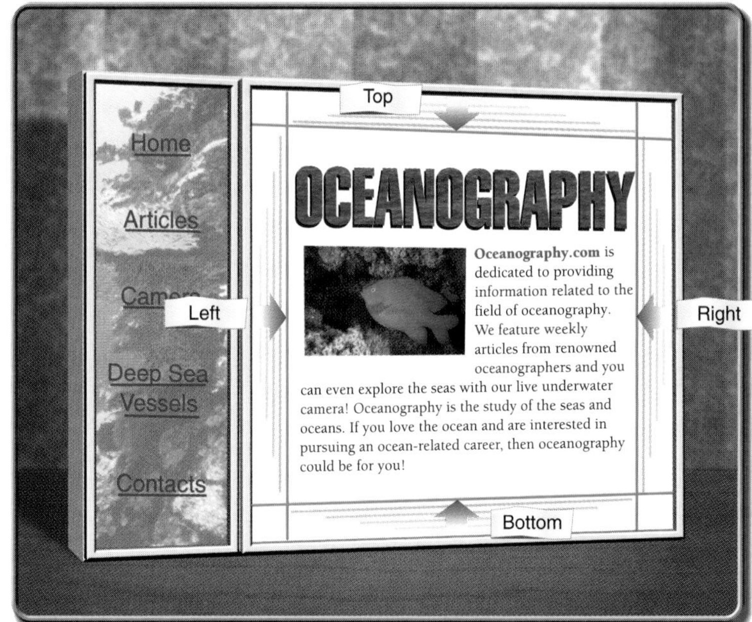

Width

Determines the amount of space between the contents of the frame and the left and right frame borders.

Height

Determines the amount of space between the contents of the frame and the top and bottom frame borders.

CHANGE FRAME MARGINS

1 Click anywhere inside the frame you want to change.

2 Click **Frames**.

3 Click **Frame Properties**.

■ The Frame Properties dialog box appears.

4 To change the left and right margins for the frame, double-click this area and type a number for the amount of space in pixels.

Can I set the frame margins to zero (0)?

Yes. You can set the margins of a frame to 0 pixels if you want the contents of the frame to appear directly beside the borders of the frame. By default, the left and right margins are set at 12 pixels. The top and bottom margins are set at 16 pixels.

Can I change the margin for one side of a frame?

No. You cannot change the left, right, top or bottom margins separately. You can only change both the left and right margins or both the top and bottom margins at the same time.

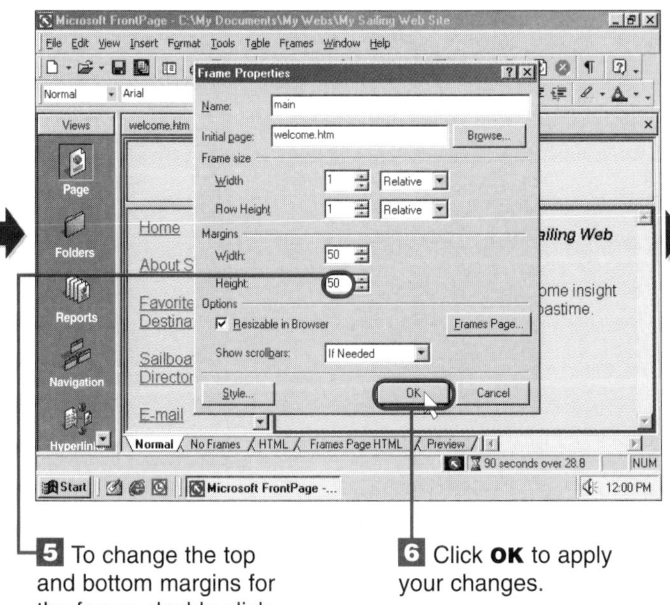

5 To change the top and bottom margins for the frame, double-click this area and type a number for the amount of space in pixels.

6 Click **OK** to apply your changes.

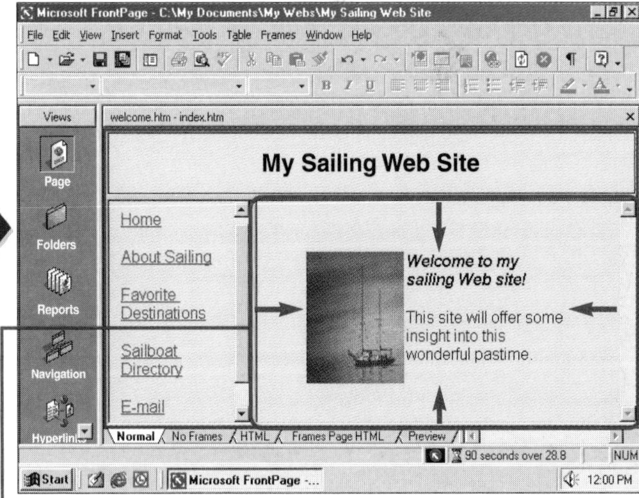

■ The frame displays the margins you specified.

HIDE FRAME BORDERS

You can hide the borders between your frames to make the frames invisible. When you hide the frame borders, the contents of the frames will appear as one Web page.

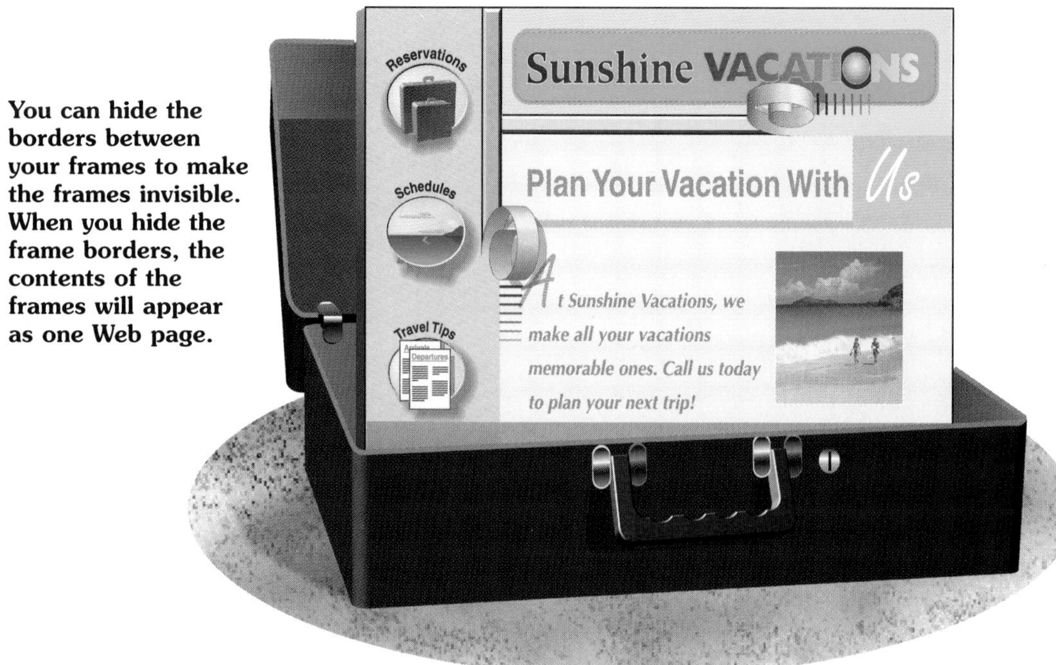

Hiding the frame borders allows information in one frame, such as an advertisement, company logo or table of contents, to appear as part of another frame.

HIDE FRAME BORDERS

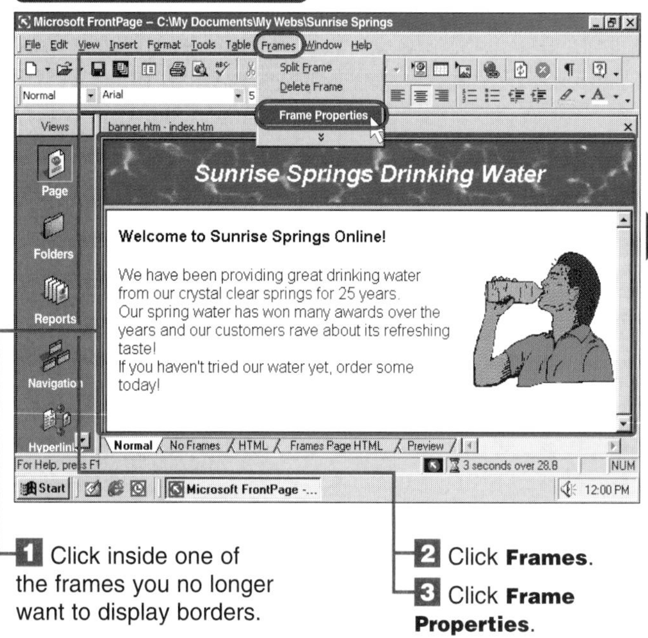

1 Click inside one of the frames you no longer want to display borders.

2 Click **Frames**.

3 Click **Frame Properties**.

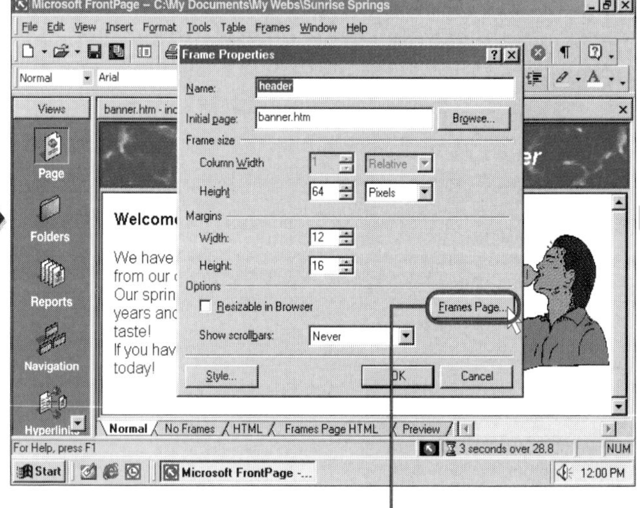

■ The Frame Properties dialog box appears.

4 Click **Frames Page** to change the properties of all the frames.

When I hide the frame borders, why does FrontPage change the amount of space between the frames to zero (0)?

When you hide the frame borders, FrontPage automatically changes the amount of space between the frames from 2 pixels to 0 pixels. If the frames display a background color or image, a white border may appear between the frames if the amount of space is not set to 0 pixels.

After hiding the frame borders, why do scroll bars still appear?

When a reader views the frames in a Web browser, scroll bars will appear if a frame contains more information than can fit in the frame. To hide scroll bars in a frame, see page 206.

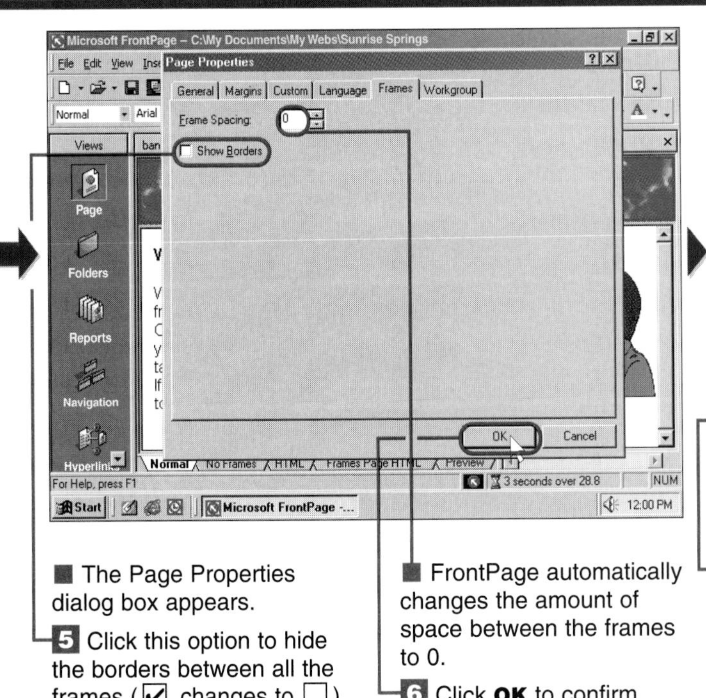

■ The Page Properties dialog box appears.

5 Click this option to hide the borders between all the frames (☑ changes to ☐).

■ FrontPage automatically changes the amount of space between the frames to 0.

6 Click **OK** to confirm your change.

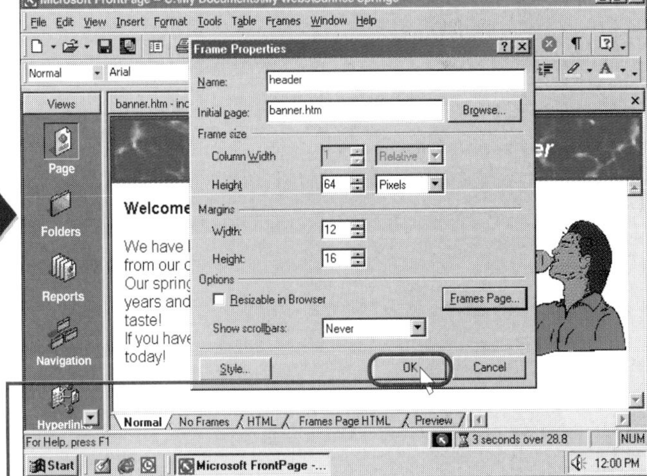

7 Click **OK** to close the Frame Properties dialog box.

■ FrontPage hides the borders between all the frames.

Note: To see how the frames will appear in a Web browser, you must use the Preview view. For information on the Preview view, see page 42.

SPLIT A FRAME

You can quickly add another frame by splitting an existing frame into two frames.

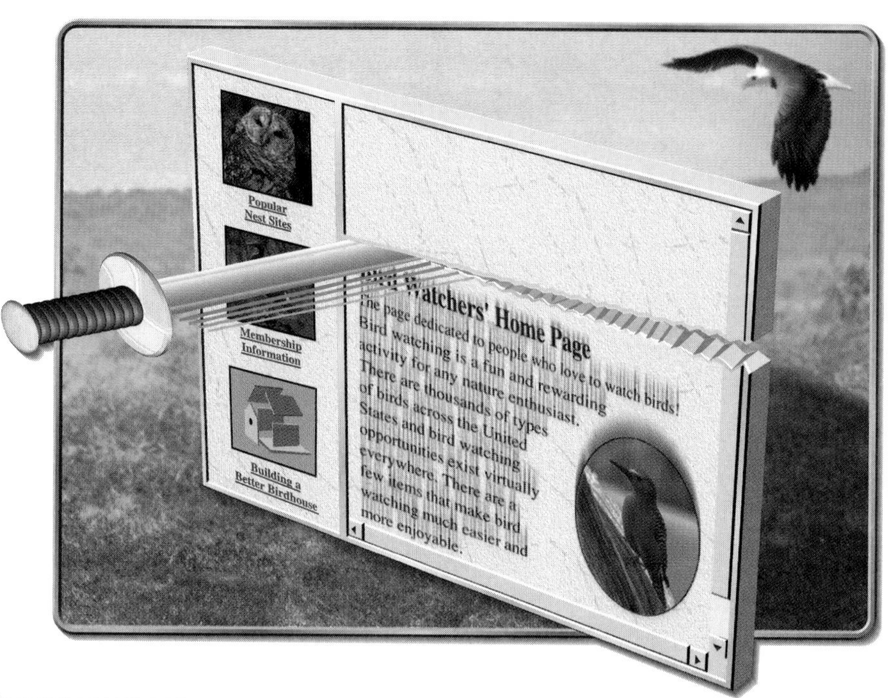

SPLIT A FRAME

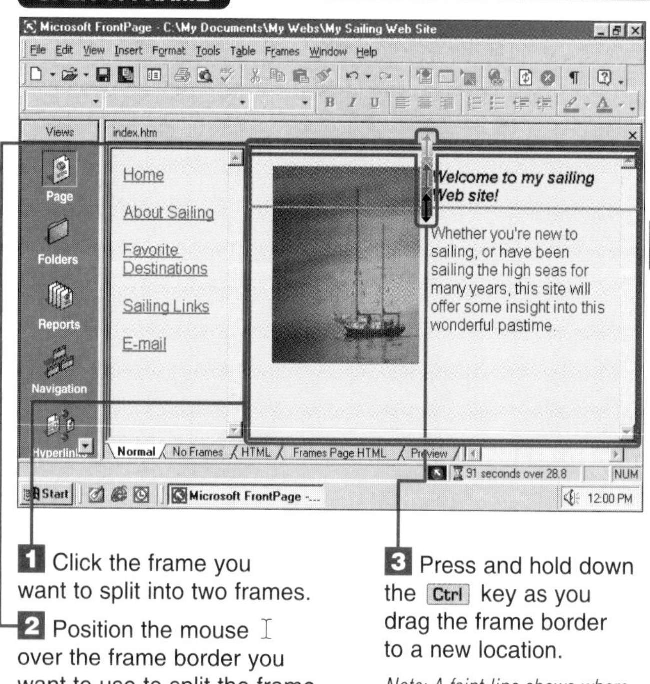

1 Click the frame you want to split into two frames.

2 Position the mouse I over the frame border you want to use to split the frame (I changes to ↖, ↕ or ↔).

3 Press and hold down the Ctrl key as you drag the frame border to a new location.

Note: A faint line shows where the frame will split into two frames.

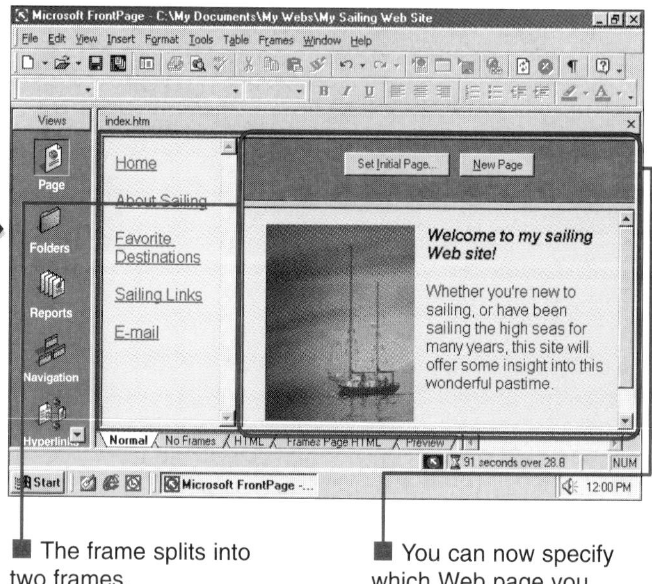

■ The frame splits into two frames.

■ You can now specify which Web page you want to appear in the new frame. To add a Web page to the new frame, see pages 190 to 192.

DELETE A FRAME

You can delete a frame if your frames page contains more frames than you need.

DELETE A FRAME

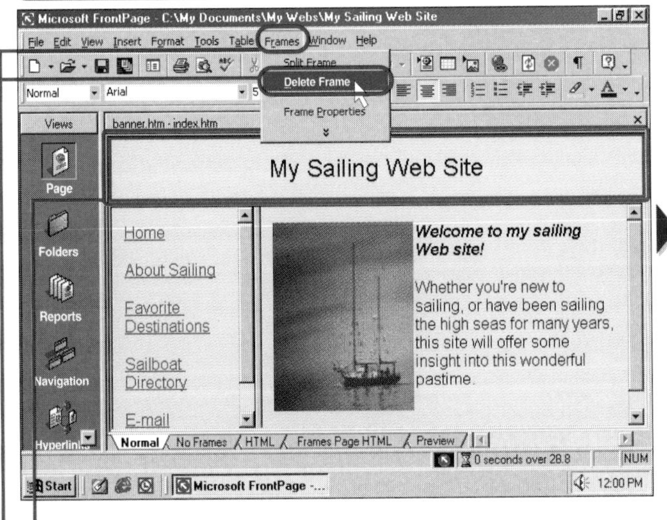

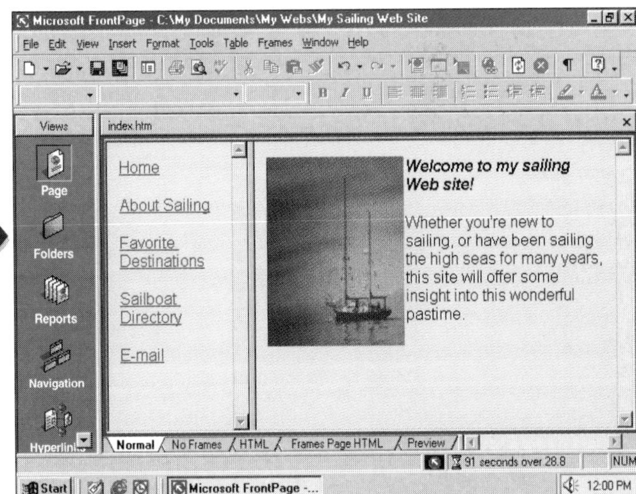

1 Click inside the frame you want to delete.

2 Click **Frames**.

3 Click **Delete Frame**.

*Note: A dialog box may appear, asking you to save your changes. Click **Yes** to save your changes. For more information on saving a Web page, see page 28.*

■ The frame disappears.

Note: Deleting a frame does not delete the Web page displayed in the frame.

HIDE OR DISPLAY SCROLL BARS IN A FRAME

You can hide or display the scroll bars in a frame. Scroll bars allow readers to browse through the information displayed in a frame.

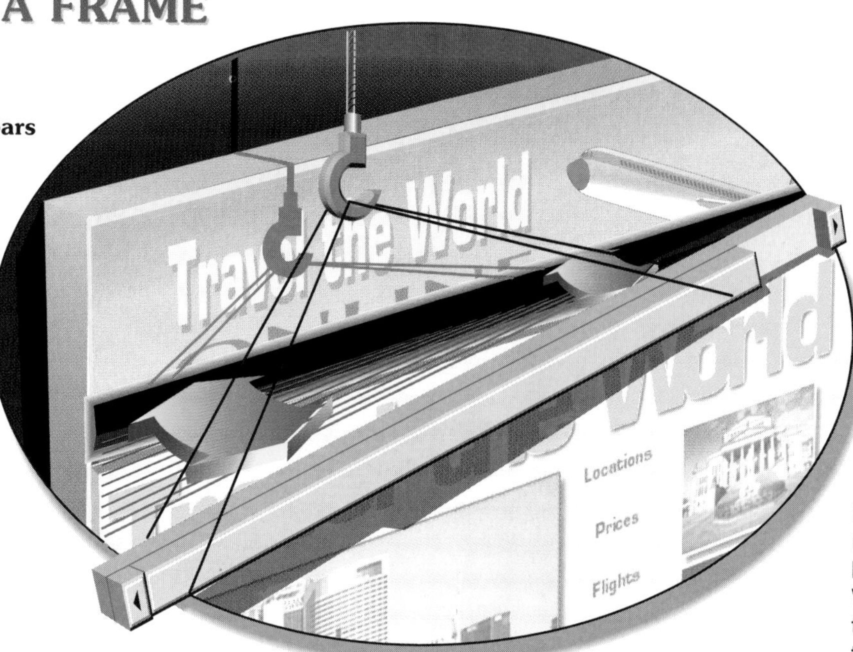

Most frames are set up to display scroll bars only when a Web page contains too much information to fit in the frame.

HIDE OR DISPLAY SCROLL BARS IN A FRAME

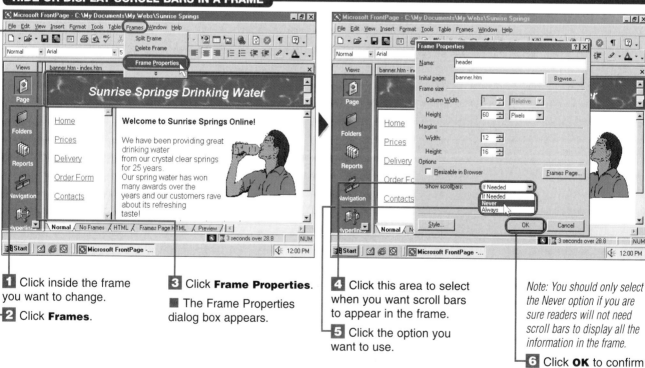

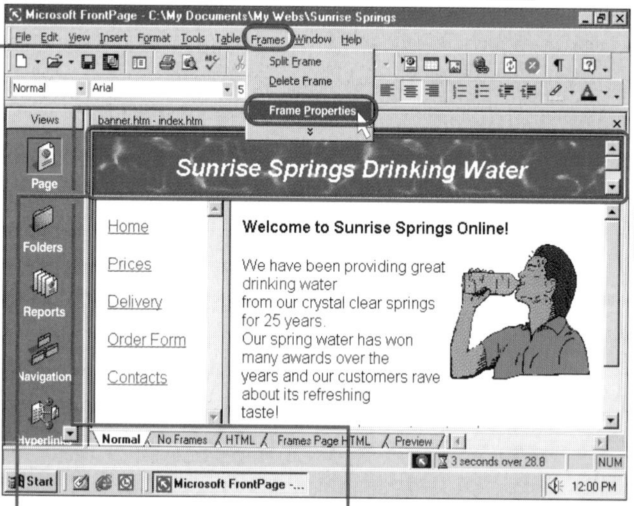

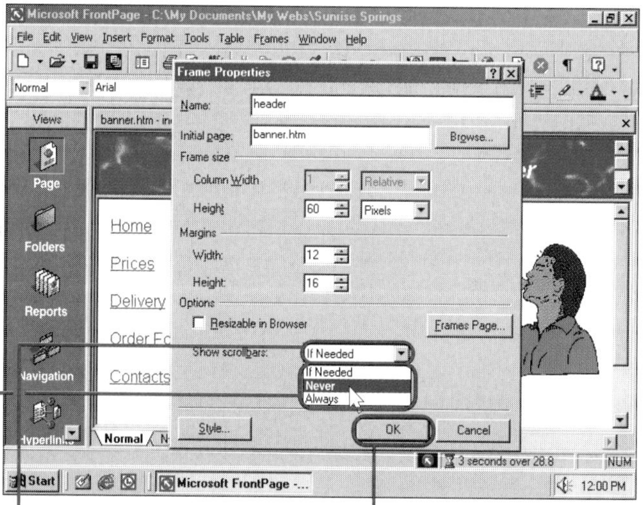

1 Click inside the frame you want to change.

2 Click **Frames**.

3 Click **Frame Properties**.

■ The Frame Properties dialog box appears.

4 Click this area to select when you want scroll bars to appear in the frame.

5 Click the option you want to use.

Note: You should only select the Never option if you are sure readers will not need scroll bars to display all the information in the frame.

6 Click **OK** to confirm your selection.

PREVENT READERS FROM RESIZING A FRAME

You can prevent readers from resizing a frame. This is useful when you do not want the layout of your frames to change.

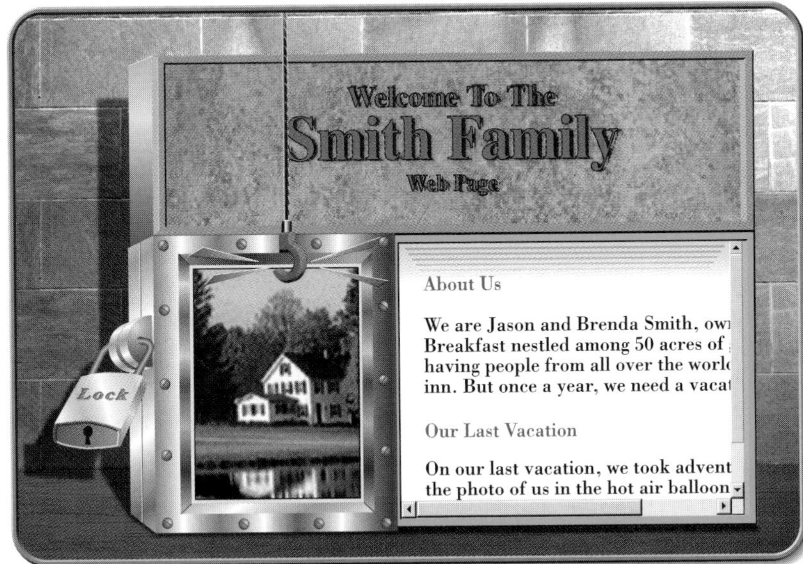

Readers may want to change the size of a frame to display more information in the frame.

FrontPage automatically prevents readers from resizing some frames, such as a frame displaying a banner.

PREVENT READERS FROM RESIZING A FRAME

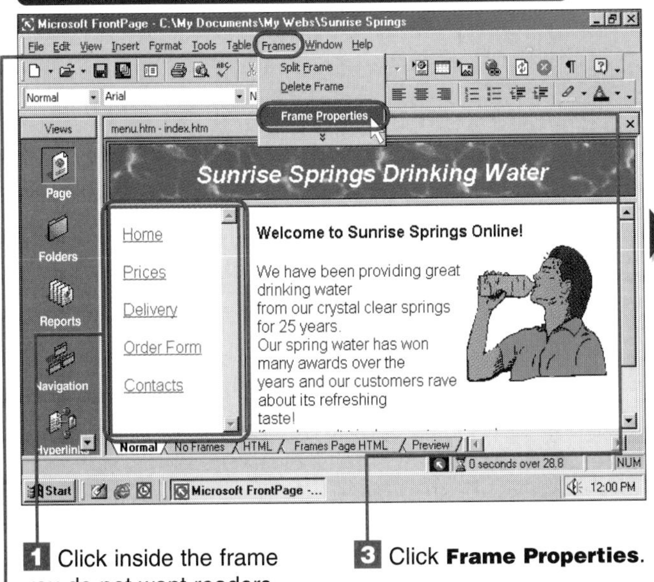

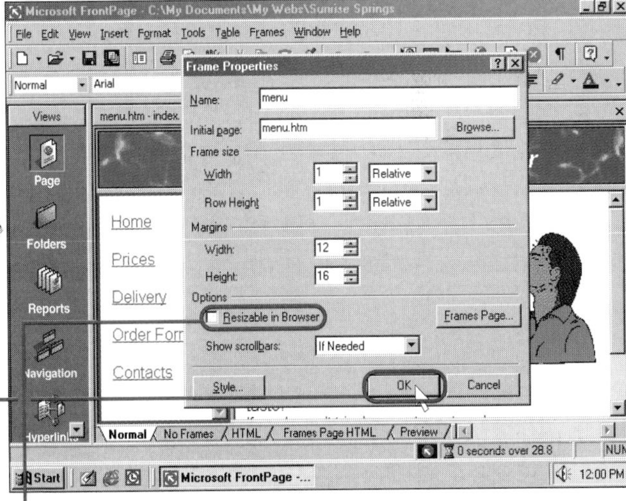

1 Click inside the frame you do not want readers to be able to resize.

2 Click **Frames**.

3 Click **Frame Properties**.

■ The Frame Properties dialog box appears.

4 Click this option if you do not want readers to be able to resize the frame (☑ changes to ☐).

5 Click **OK**.

Note: When you prevent readers from resizing a frame, they will not be able to use the frame borders to resize neighboring frames.

■ To once again allow readers to resize the frame, repeat steps **1** to **5** (☐ changes to ☑ in step **4**).

PROVIDE ALTERNATIVE TEXT FOR FRAMES

You can provide text that you want to appear if a Web browser cannot display frames. This will give readers information about the missing frames.

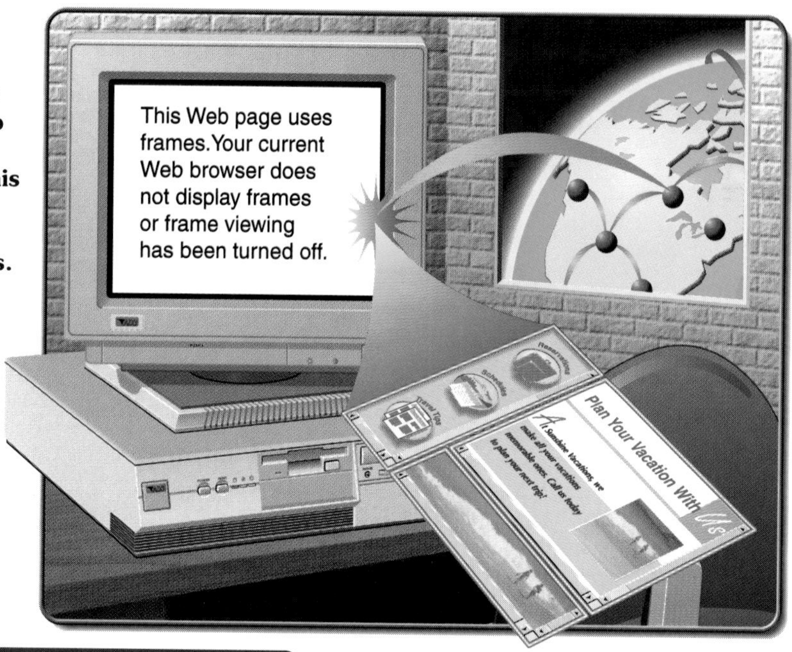

FrontPage automatically provides text that will appear on your Web page if a Web browser cannot display frames. You can change the text that FrontPage provides.

PROVIDE ALTERNATIVE TEXT FOR FRAMES

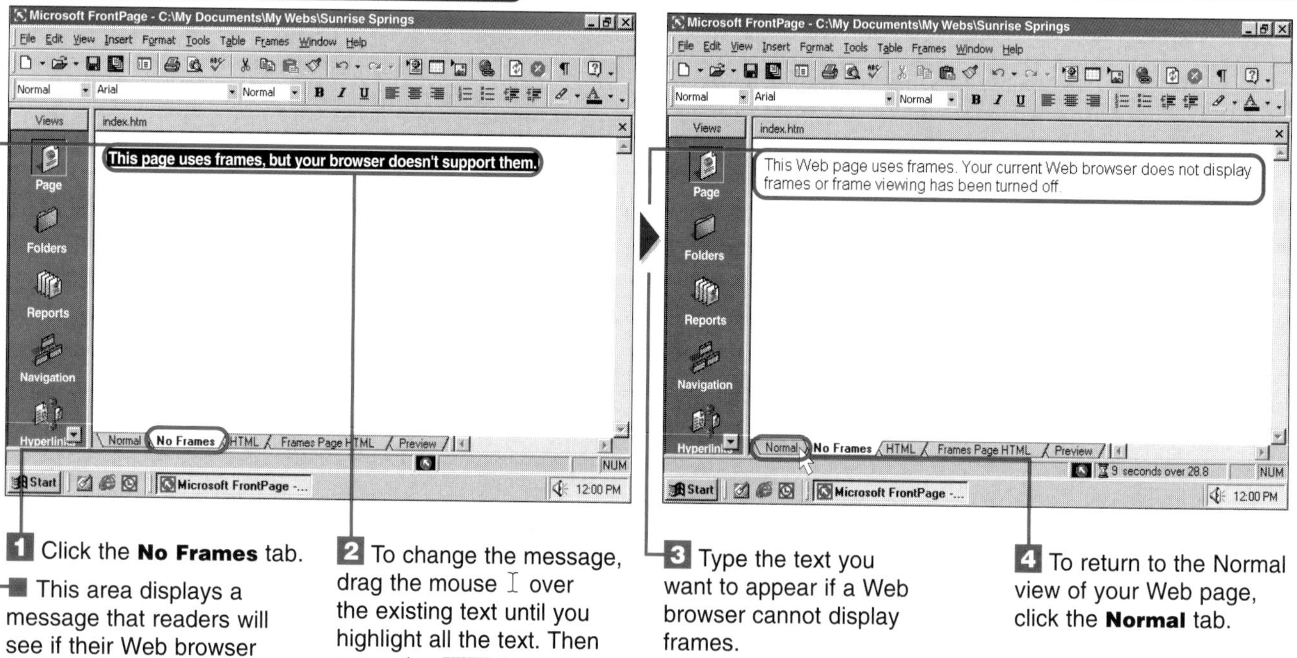

1 Click the **No Frames** tab.

■ This area displays a message that readers will see if their Web browser cannot display frames.

2 To change the message, drag the mouse I over the existing text until you highlight all the text. Then press the **Delete** key.

3 Type the text you want to appear if a Web browser cannot display frames.

4 To return to the Normal view of your Web page, click the **Normal** tab.

SET A FRAMES PAGE AS YOUR HOME PAGE

You can set a frames page as your home page. The home page is the main Web page in a Web site and is the first page people will see when they visit a Web site.

When you create a Web site, FrontPage automatically names your home page index.htm.

SET A FRAMES PAGE AS YOUR HOME PAGE

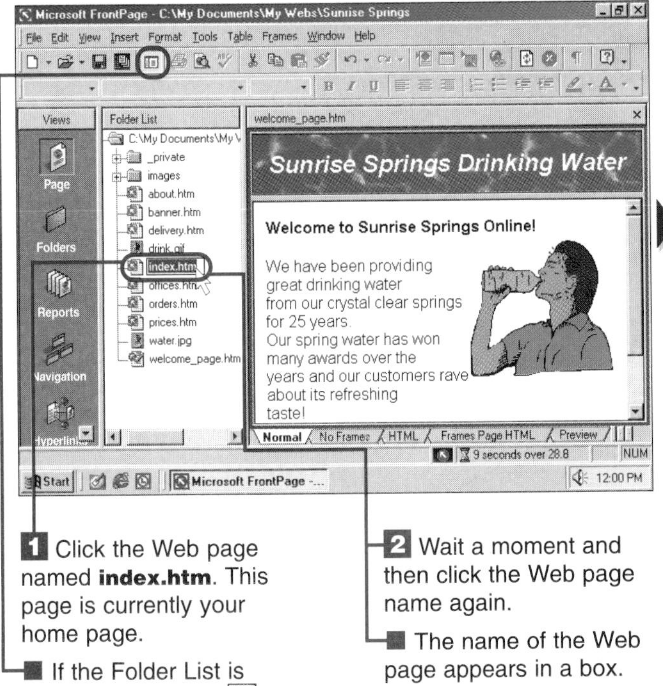

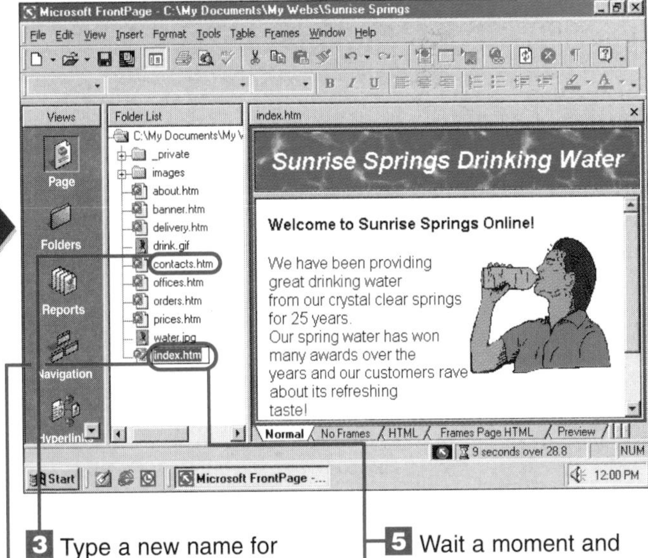

1 Click the Web page named **index.htm**. This page is currently your home page.

■ If the Folder List is not displayed, click to display the list.

2 Wait a moment and then click the Web page name again.

■ The name of the Web page appears in a box.

3 Type a new name for the Web page and then press the Enter key. Make sure you add the .htm extension to the end of the Web page name.

4 Click the frames page you want to set as your home page.

5 Wait a moment and then click the frames page name again.

6 Type **index.htm** to set the frames page as your home page and then press the Enter key.

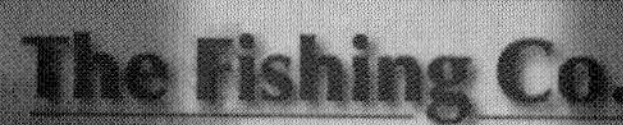
The Fishing Co.

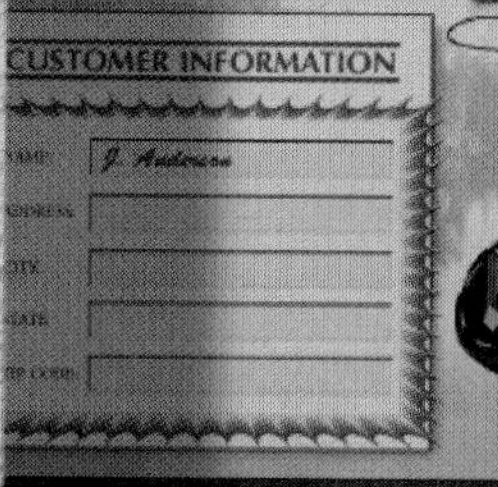
CUSTOMER INFORMATION

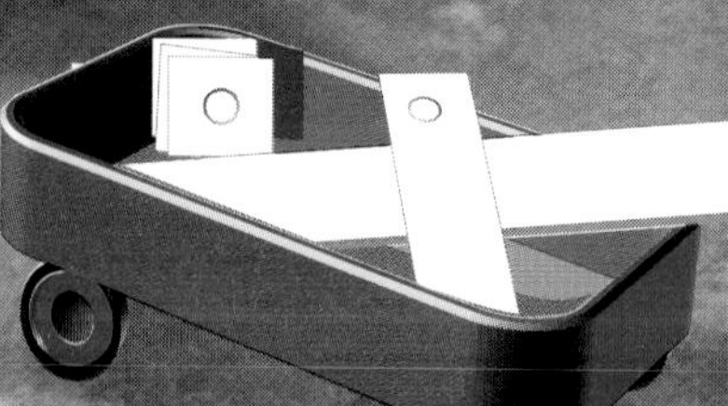

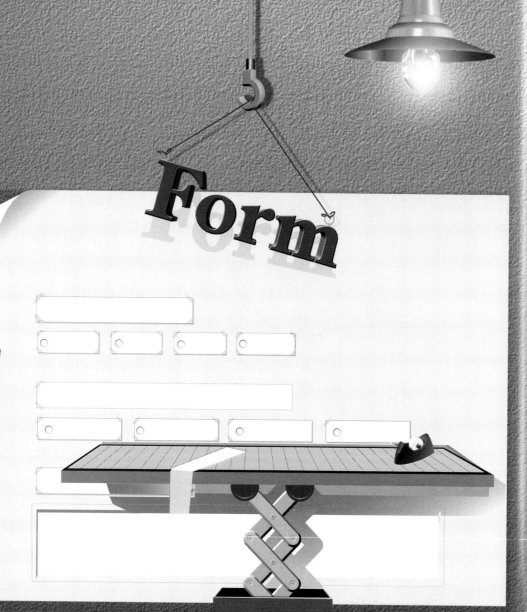

CHAPTER 12

Create Forms

Would you like to create forms that readers can use to send you information? Find out how in this chapter.

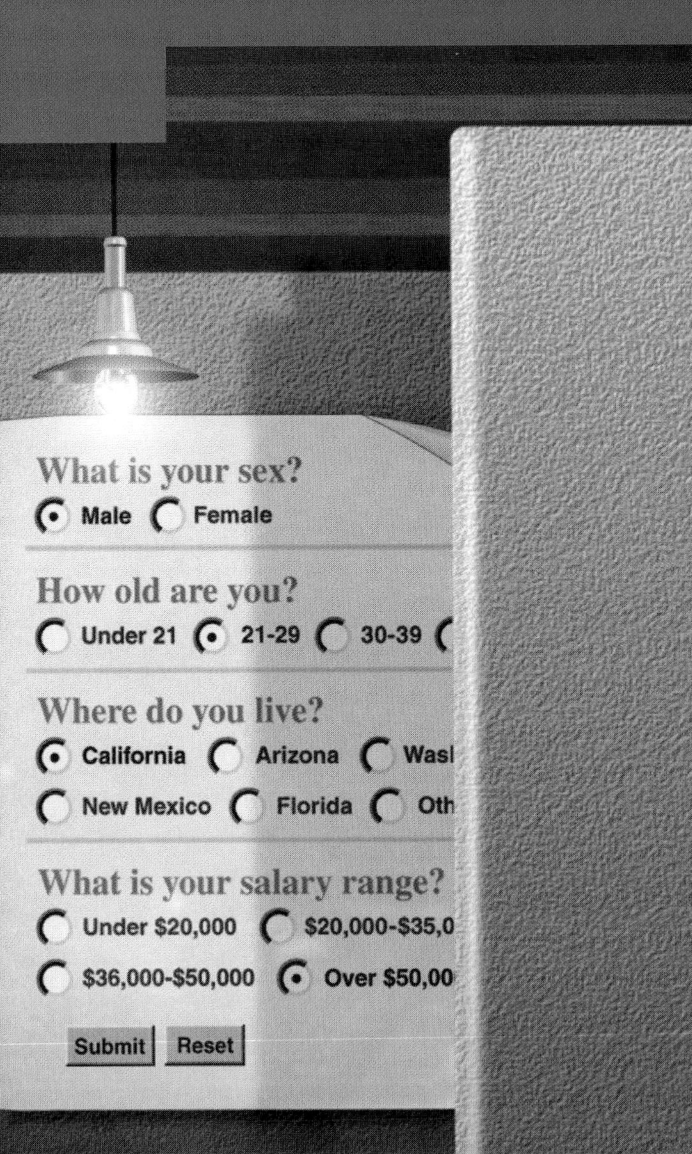

What is your sex?
Male
Female
How old are you?
Under 21
21-29
30-39
Where do you live?
California
Arizona
New Mexico
Florida
What is your salary range?
Under $20,000
$36,000-$50,000
Submit
Reset

DIGGING UP THE PAST
A GUIDE TO ARCHAEOLOGICAL DIGS
"We provide the most comprehensive, educational and informative resource on archaeological studies. Digging up the past to uncover the future."
These pages contain descriptions of archaeological excavations in progress around the world. Professional archaeologists can use our pages to stay on top of the latest archaeological finds. Amateurs can research topics of interest and find out which digs accept volunteers.
The information is divided geographically into five regions: Africa, Asia, Europe, Oceania and The Americas. Within each region, you can select a country and browse through an extensive list of excavations. Or you can search for a specific dig by place name or keyword.
Africa
Asia
Europe
Oceania
The Americas

SET UP A FORM

Forms allow you to gather information from readers who visit your Web pages. You must set up a form before you can add information to the form.

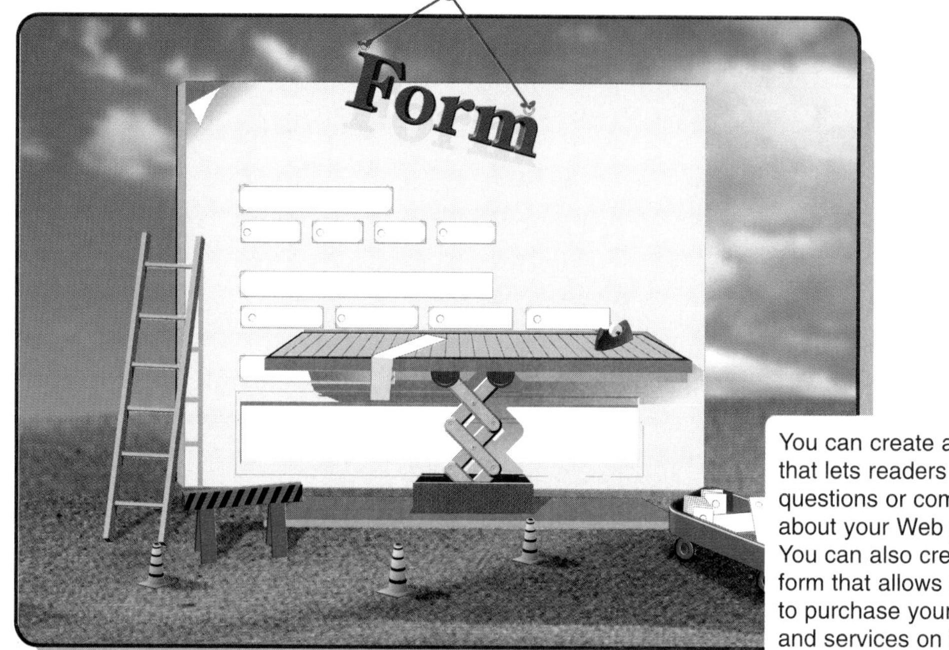

You can create a form that lets readers send you questions or comments about your Web pages. You can also create a form that allows readers to purchase your products and services on the Web.

SET UP A FORM

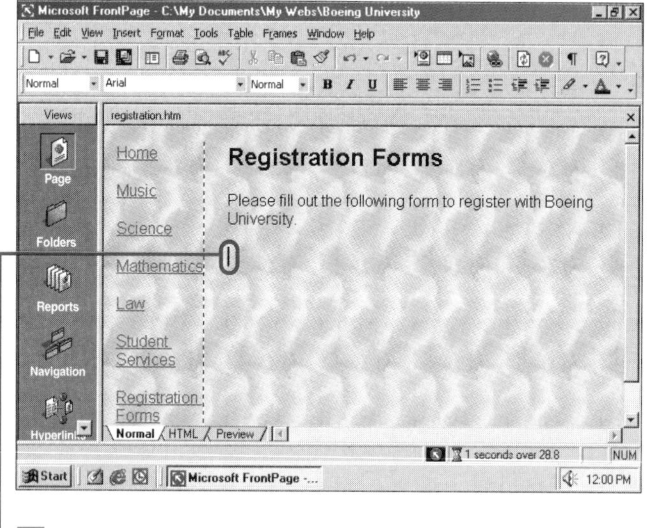

1 Click the location where you want the form to appear on your Web page.

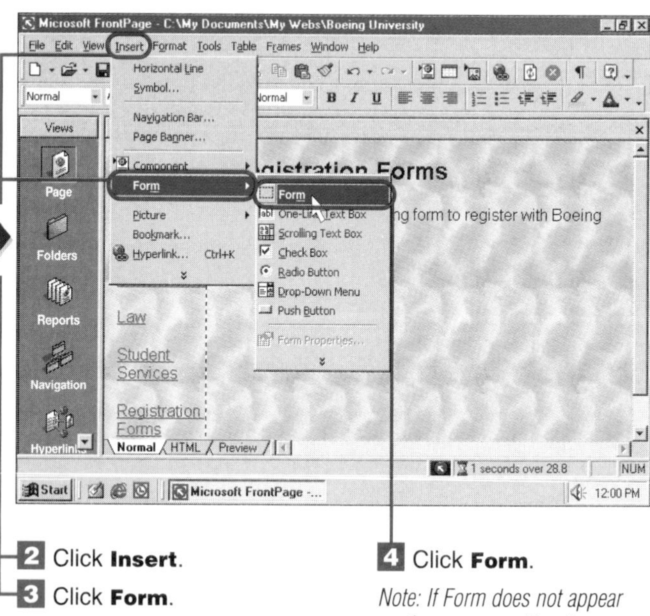

2 Click **Insert**.

3 Click **Form**.

4 Click **Form**.

Note: If Form does not appear on the menu, position the mouse over the bottom of the menu to display all the menu commands.

What should I consider before I set up a form on my Web page?

Before you set up a form on your Web page, make sure FrontPage Server Extensions are installed on your Web server. You can determine if your Web server uses FrontPage Server Extensions by asking the company that will make your Web pages available on the Web.

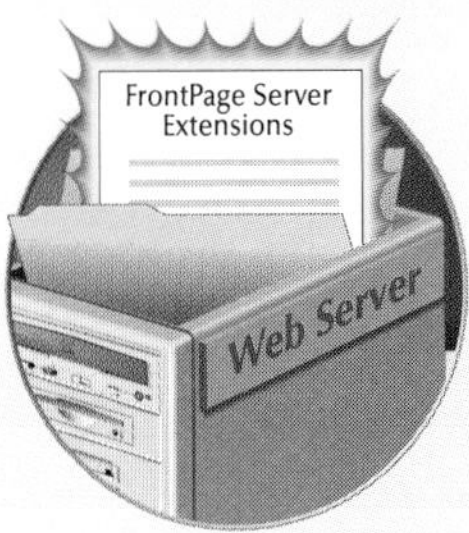

How do forms work?

A reader can enter information and select options on a form. When a reader clicks the Submit button, the information transfers to your Web server.

When your Web server receives information from a form, the server processes the information. By default, the results of a form are stored in a text file on your Web server. To change how you access the results of a form, see page 228.

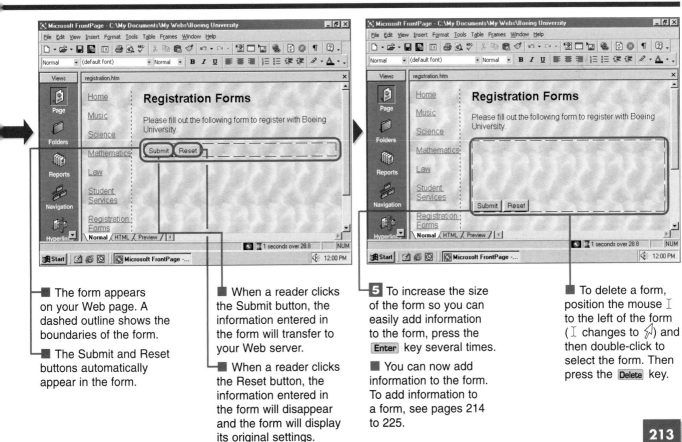

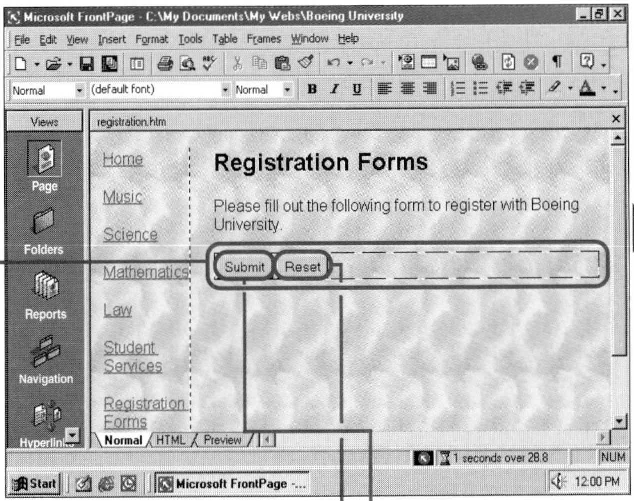

■ The form appears on your Web page. A dashed outline shows the boundaries of the form.

■ The Submit and Reset buttons automatically appear in the form.

■ When a reader clicks the Submit button, the information entered in the form will transfer to your Web server.

■ When a reader clicks the Reset button, the information entered in the form will disappear and the form will display its original settings.

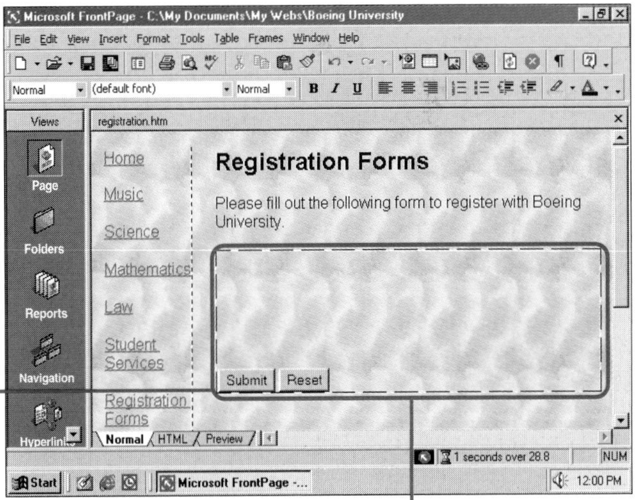

5 To increase the size of the form so you can easily add information to the form, press the Enter key several times.

■ You can now add information to the form. To add information to a form, see pages 214 to 225.

■ To delete a form, position the mouse I to the left of the form (I changes to ↗) and then double-click to select the form. Then press the Delete key.

ADD A ONE-LINE TEXT BOX

You can add a one-line text box that allows readers to enter a line of text.

One-line text boxes are commonly used for entering names and addresses.

ADD A ONE-LINE TEXT BOX

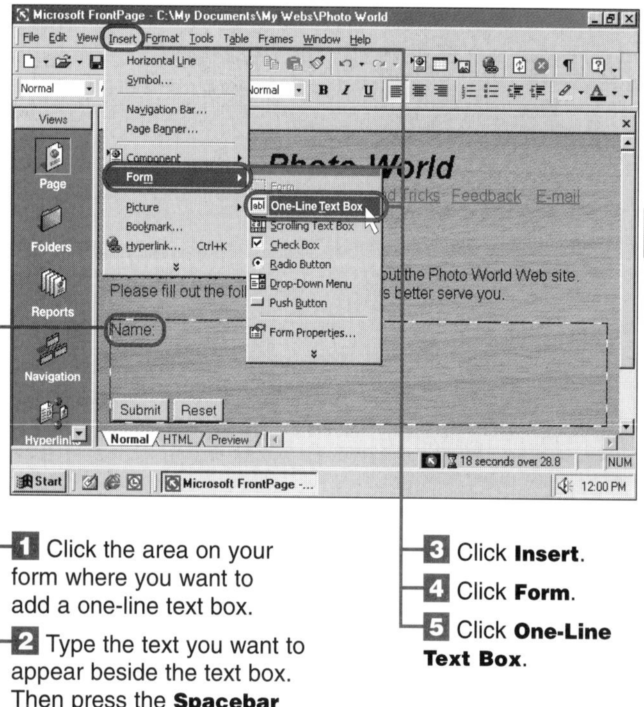

1 Click the area on your form where you want to add a one-line text box.

2 Type the text you want to appear beside the text box. Then press the **Spacebar** to add a blank space.

3 Click **Insert**.

4 Click **Form**.

5 Click **One-Line Text Box**.

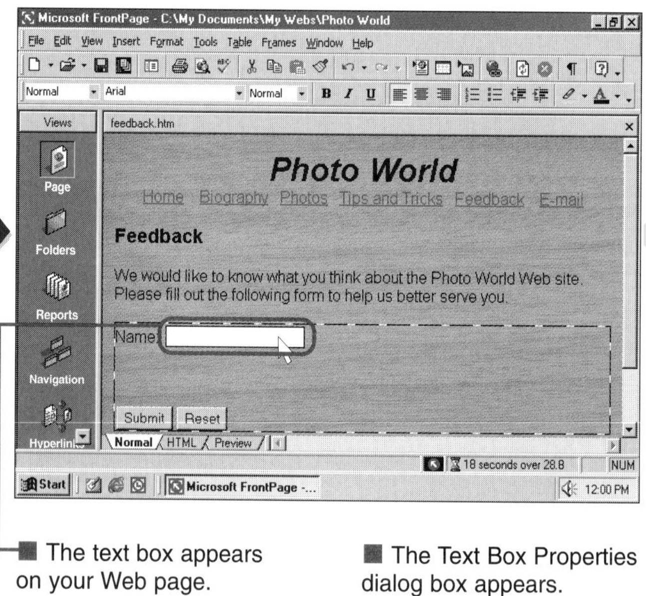

■ The text box appears on your Web page.

6 Double-click the text box to change the properties of the text box.

■ The Text Box Properties dialog box appears.

Can I create a one-line text box that hides information that readers enter?

You can create a one-line text box that displays an asterisk (*) for each character a reader types. This is known as a password box. A password box lets readers enter confidential information, such as a password or credit card number, without other people viewing the information. To create a password box, click **Yes** beside Password field in the Text Box Properties dialog box (○ changes to ⊙).

Will the width of a one-line text box affect the number of characters readers can enter in the text box?

No. The width of a text box only determines the size of the text box on your Web page. If readers enter more characters than the text box can display, the existing text moves to the left to make room for the new text.

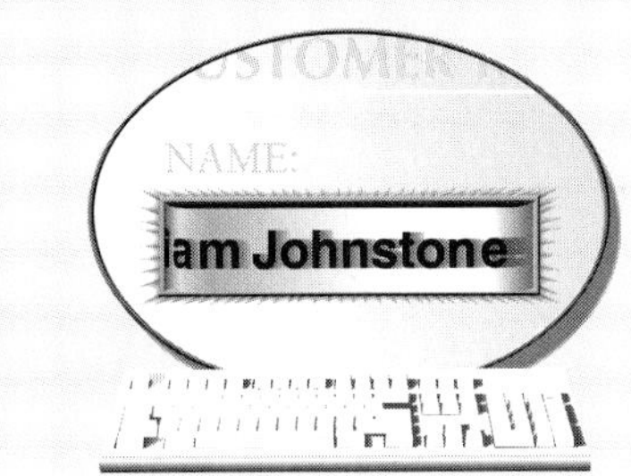

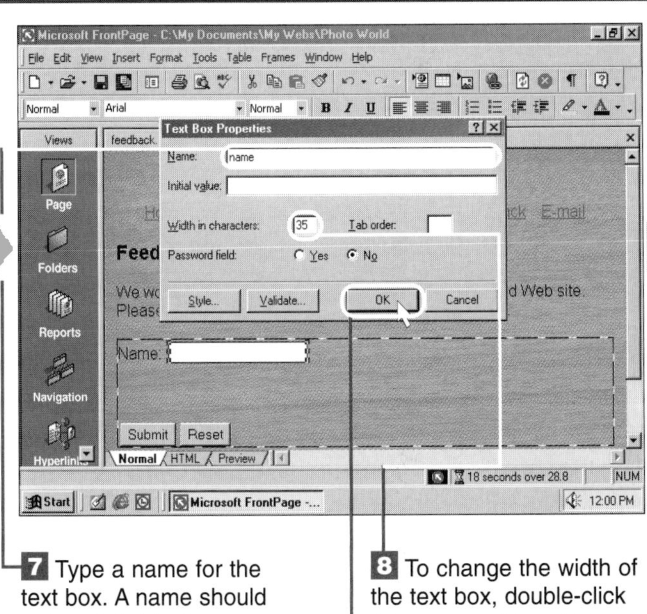

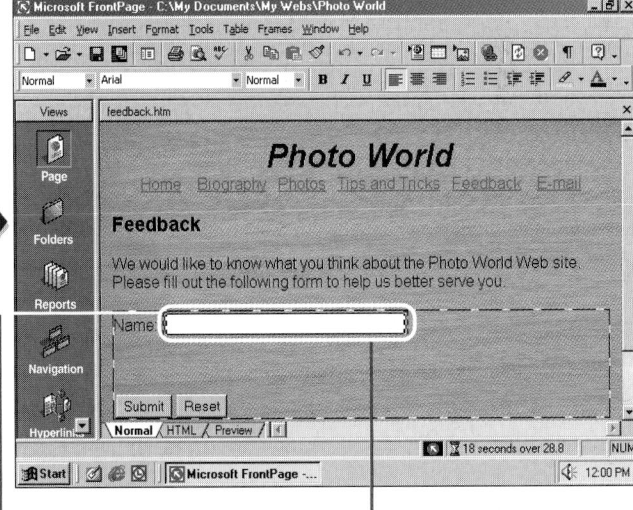

7 Type a name for the text box. A name should not contain blank spaces.

Note: The name you enter will not appear on your Web page. The name helps you identify the information readers enter in the text box when you view the form results.

8 To change the width of the text box, double-click this area and type the width you want to use in characters.

9 Click **OK**.

■ The text box displays the new width.

■ A reader can click in the text box and type the requested information.

Note: To test the text box, you must use the Preview view. For information on the Preview view, see page 42.

■ To delete a one-line text box, click the text box and then press the Delete key.

ADD A SCROLLING TEXT BOX

You can add a scrolling text box that allows readers to enter several lines or paragraphs of text.

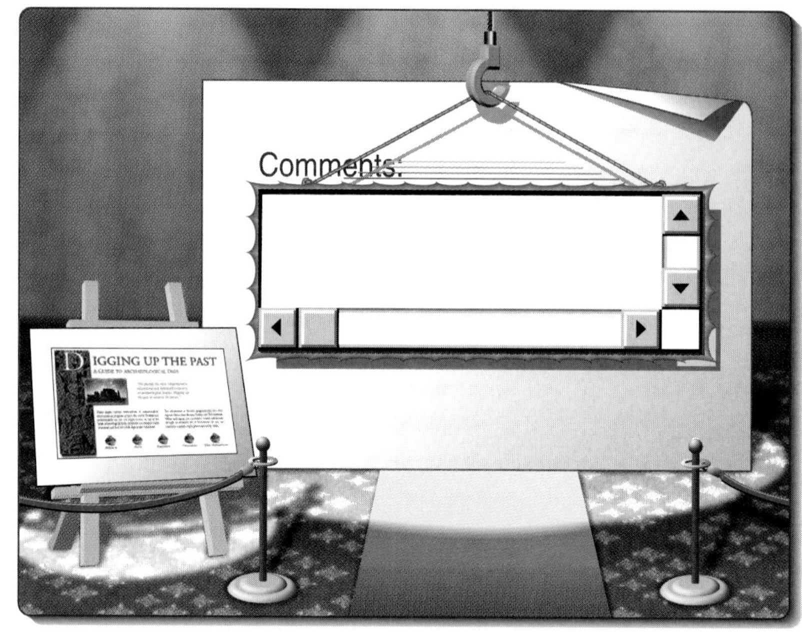

A scrolling text box is ideal for gathering comments or questions from your readers.

ADD A SCROLLING TEXT BOX

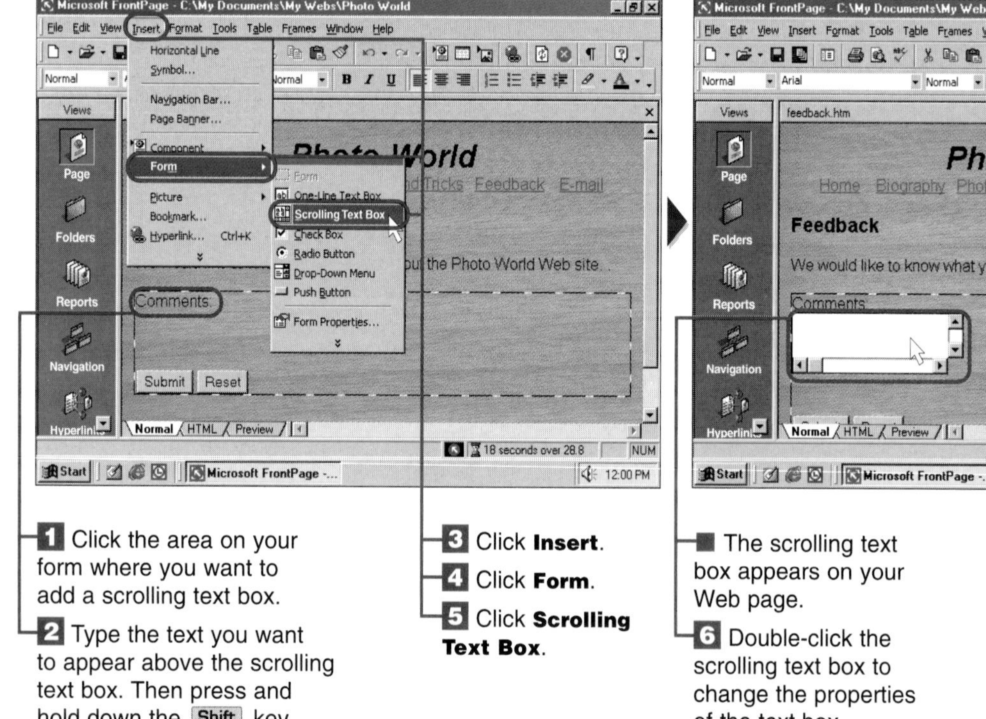

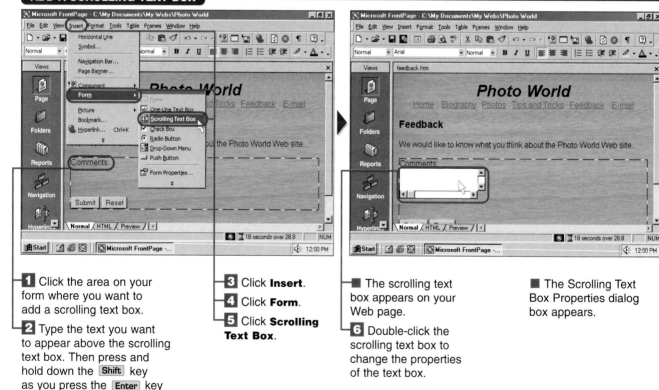

1 Click the area on your form where you want to add a scrolling text box.

2 Type the text you want to appear above the scrolling text box. Then press and hold down the **Shift** key as you press the **Enter** key to start a new line.

3 Click **Insert**.

4 Click **Form**.

5 Click **Scrolling Text Box**.

■ The scrolling text box appears on your Web page.

6 Double-click the scrolling text box to change the properties of the text box.

■ The Scrolling Text Box Properties dialog box appears.

Can I change the size of a scrolling text box?

You can change the size of a scrolling text box as you would change the size of an image on your Web page. When you change the size of a scrolling text box, you should make sure the text box will clearly display the text readers type. If the text readers type does not fit in the text box, readers can use the scroll bar to scroll through the text. To change the size of an image, see page 104.

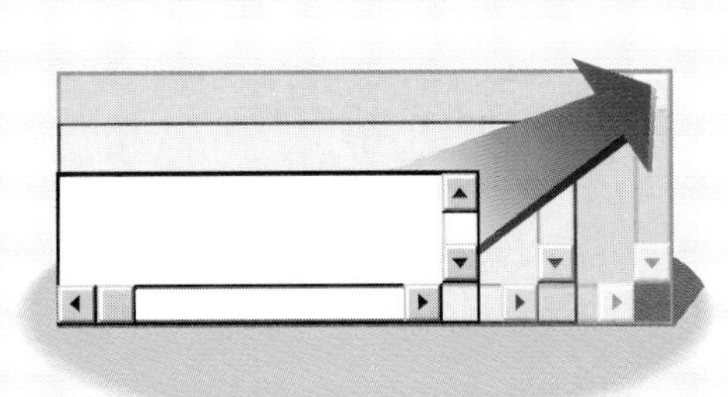

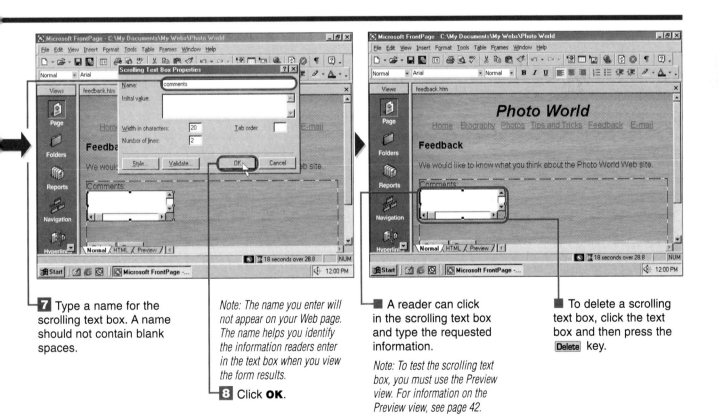

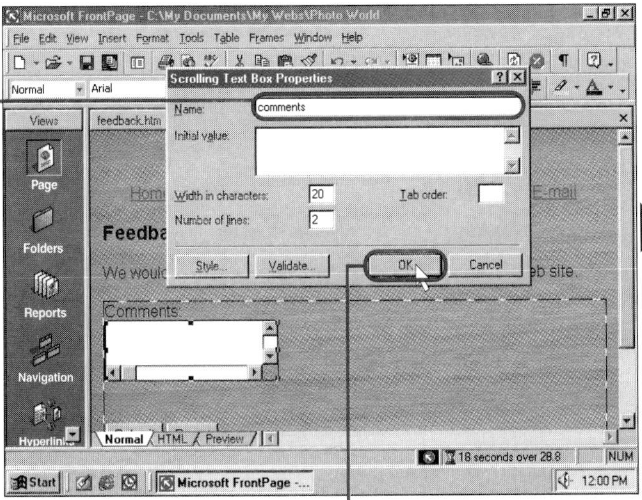

7 Type a name for the scrolling text box. A name should not contain blank spaces.

Note: The name you enter will not appear on your Web page. The name helps you identify the information readers enter in the text box when you view the form results.

8 Click **OK**.

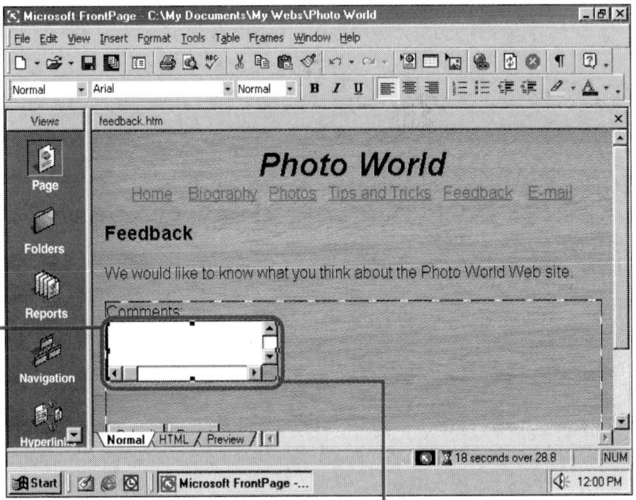

■ A reader can click in the scrolling text box and type the requested information.

Note: To test the scrolling text box, you must use the Preview view. For information on the Preview view, see page 42.

■ To delete a scrolling text box, click the text box and then press the Delete key.

ADD CHECK BOXES

You can include check boxes on a form if you want readers to be able to select one or more options.

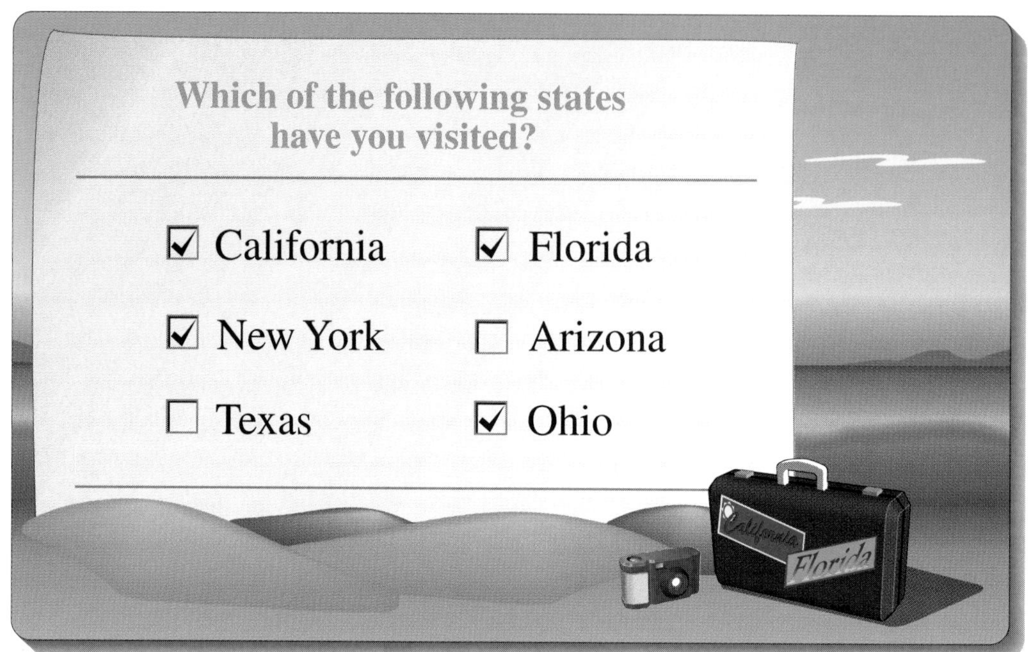

Which of the following states have you visited?
California
Florida
New York
Arizona
Texas
Ohio
California
Florida

ADD CHECK BOXES

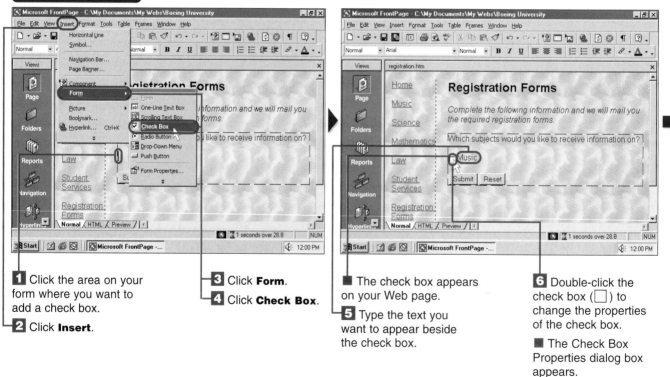

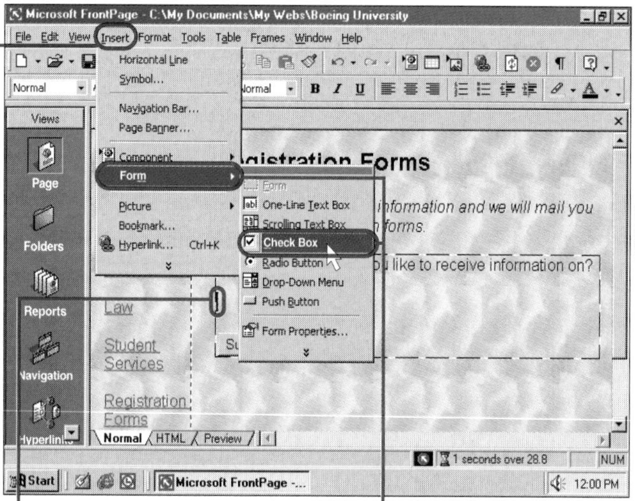

1 Click the area on your form where you want to add a check box.

2 Click **Insert**.

3 Click **Form**.

4 Click **Check Box**.

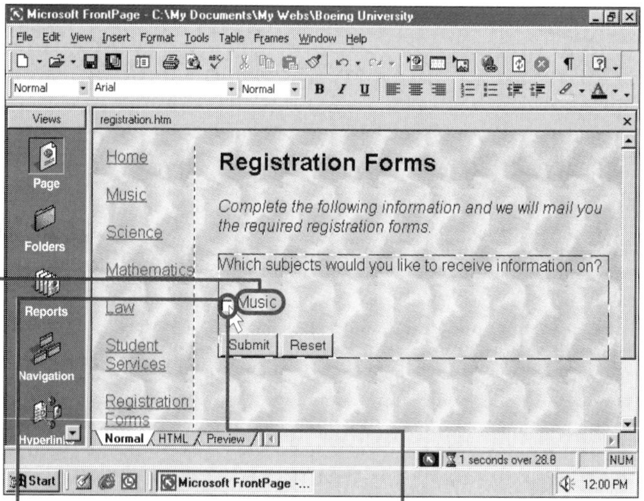

■ The check box appears on your Web page.

5 Type the text you want to appear beside the check box.

6 Double-click the check box (☐) to change the properties of the check box.

■ The Check Box Properties dialog box appears.

? **What information do I need to specify when creating check boxes?**

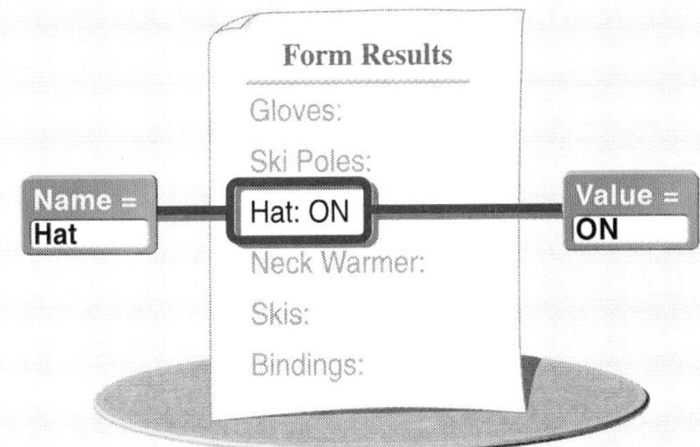

Name

You need to specify a name that describes the check box. The name identifies the check box when you view the results of the form.

Value

You need to specify a value for the check box. When you view the results of the form, the value appears with the name of the check box to indicate the check box was selected.

Initial state

You need to specify if you want the check box to appear checked or not checked on your form. If most people will select the option, you should choose to have the check box appear checked.

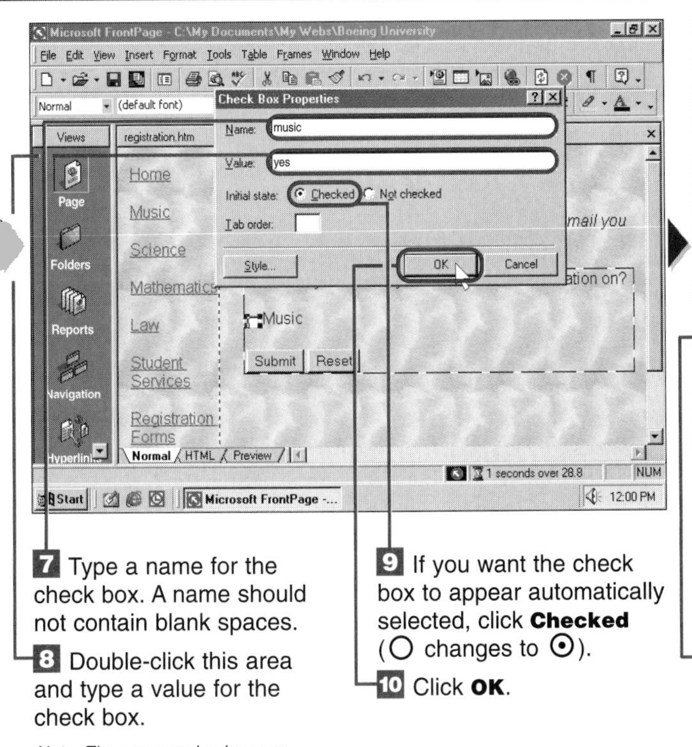

7 Type a name for the check box. A name should not contain blank spaces.

8 Double-click this area and type a value for the check box.

Note: The name and value you enter will not appear on your Web page.

9 If you want the check box to appear automatically selected, click **Checked** (○ changes to ⊙).

10 Click **OK**.

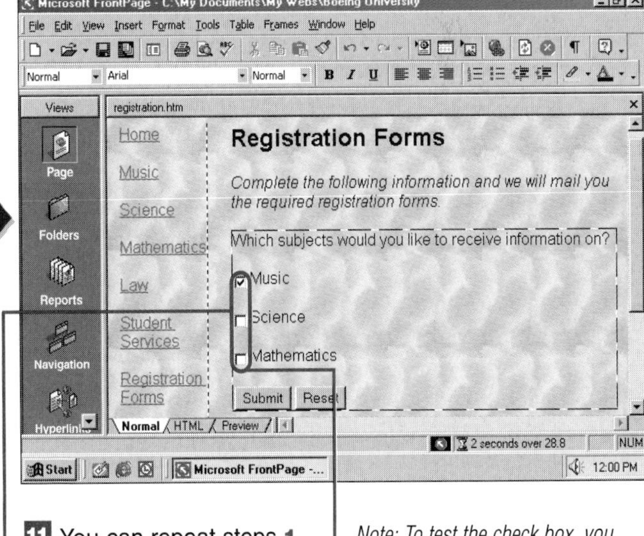

11 You can repeat steps **1** to **10** for each check box you want to add.

■ A reader can click the check box for each option they want to select (☐ changes to ☑).

Note: To test the check box, you must use the Preview view. For information on the Preview view, see page 42.

■ To delete a check box, click the check box (☐) and then press the Delete key.

ADD RADIO BUTTONS

You can include a group of radio buttons on a form if you want readers to select only one of several options.

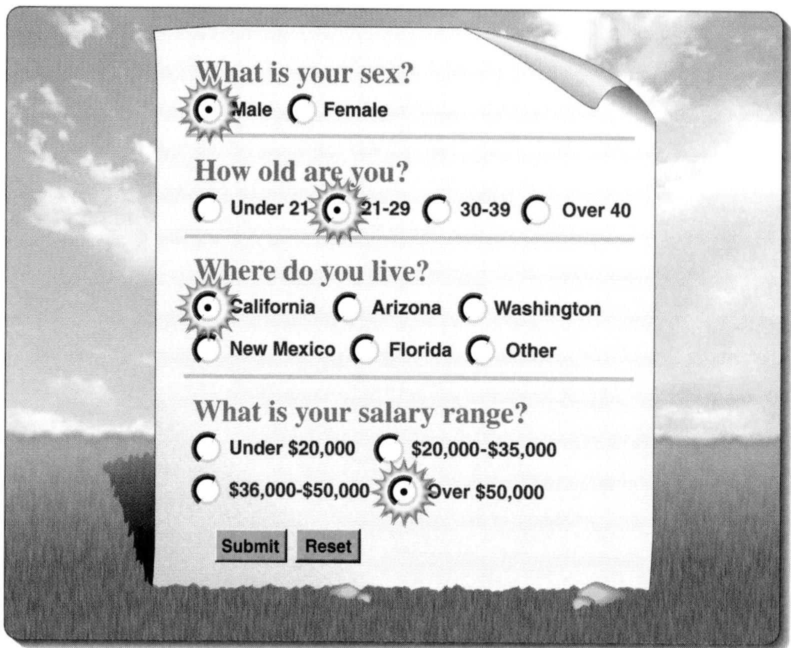

ADD RADIO BUTTONS

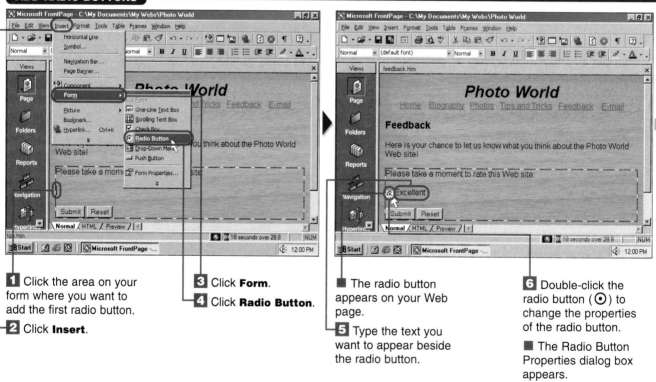

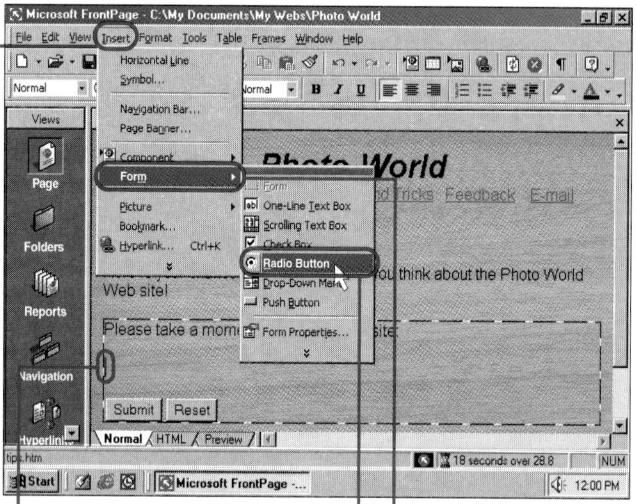

1 Click the area on your form where you want to add the first radio button.

2 Click **Insert**.

3 Click **Form**.

4 Click **Radio Button**.

■ The radio button appears on your Web page.

5 Type the text you want to appear beside the radio button.

6 Double-click the radio button (⊙) to change the properties of the radio button.

■ The Radio Button Properties dialog box appears.

What information do I need to specify when creating radio buttons?

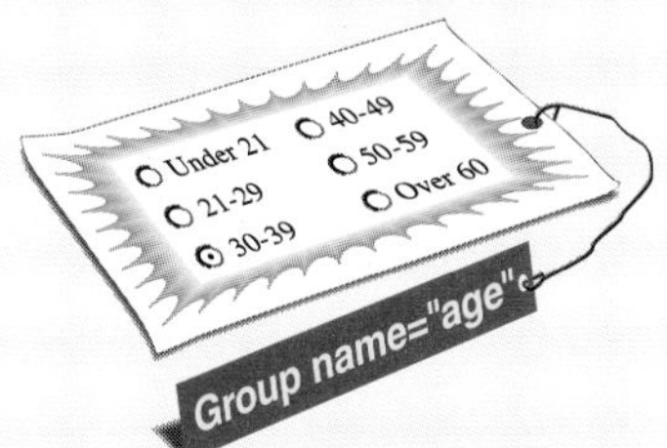

Group name

You need to specify a name that describes the group of radio buttons. The name identifies the group of radio buttons when you view the results of the form.

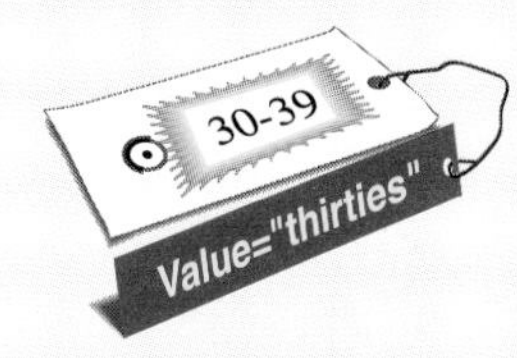

Value

You need to specify a value that describes each radio button. The value identifies the selected radio button when you view the results of the form.

Initial state

You need to specify if you want a radio button to appear selected or not selected on your form. Only one radio button in a group can appear selected.

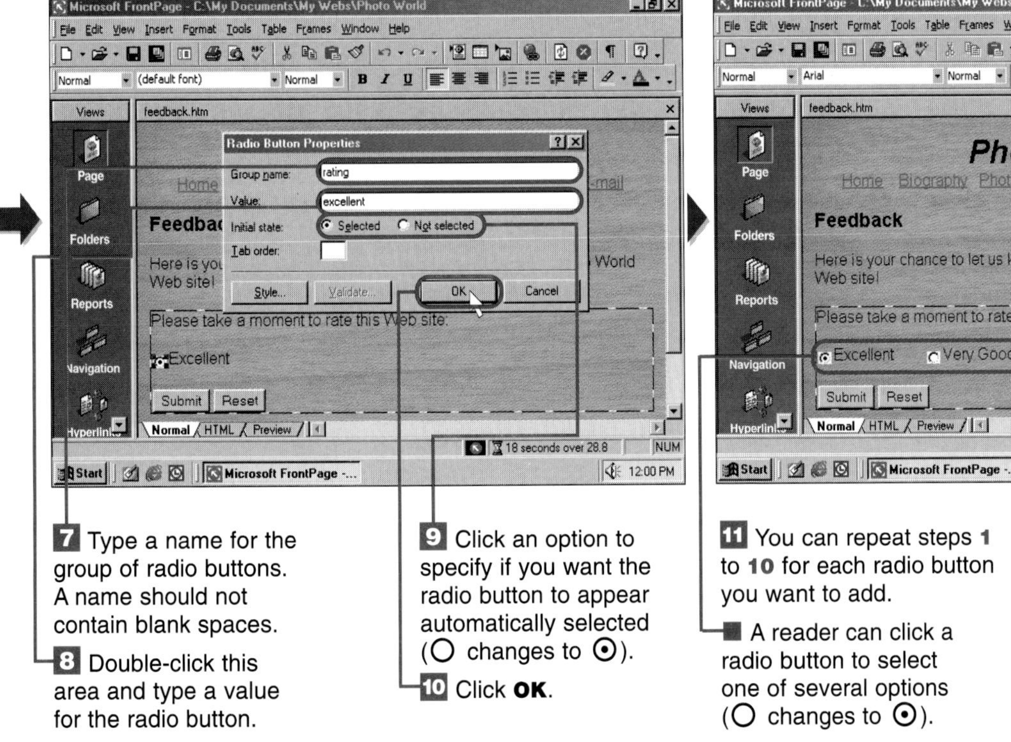

7 Type a name for the group of radio buttons. A name should not contain blank spaces.

8 Double-click this area and type a value for the radio button.

Note: The name and value you enter will not appear on your Web page.

9 Click an option to specify if you want the radio button to appear automatically selected (○ changes to ⊙).

10 Click **OK**.

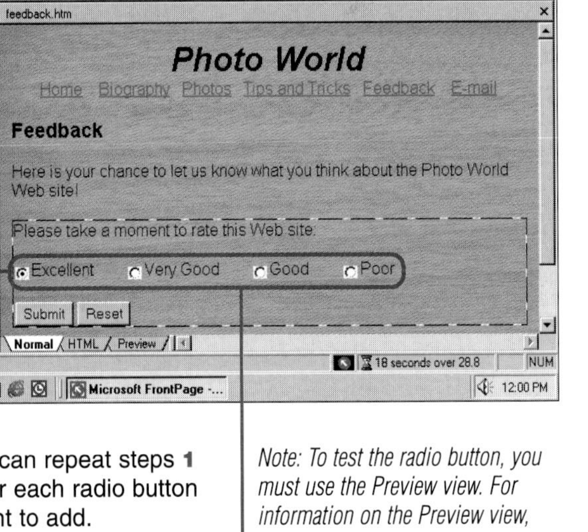

11 You can repeat steps **1** to **10** for each radio button you want to add.

■ A reader can click a radio button to select one of several options (○ changes to ⊙).

Note: To test the radio button, you must use the Preview view. For information on the Preview view, see page 42.

■ To delete a radio button, click the radio button (○) and then press the Delete key.

ADD A DROP-DOWN MENU

You can add a drop-down menu to provide a list of items that readers can choose from.

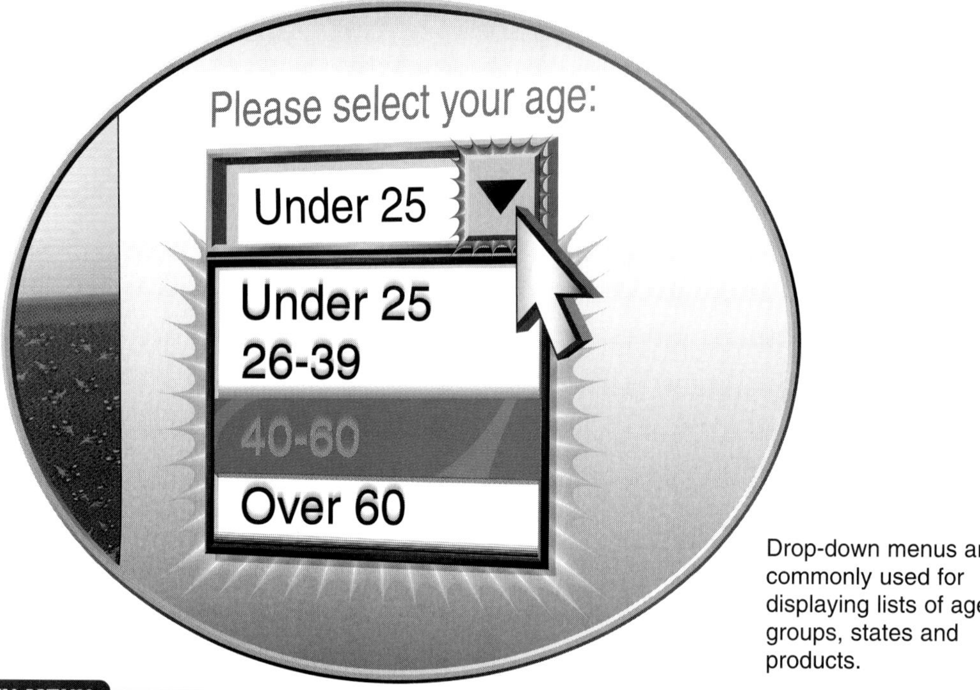

Drop-down menus are commonly used for displaying lists of age groups, states and products.

ADD A DROP-DOWN MENU

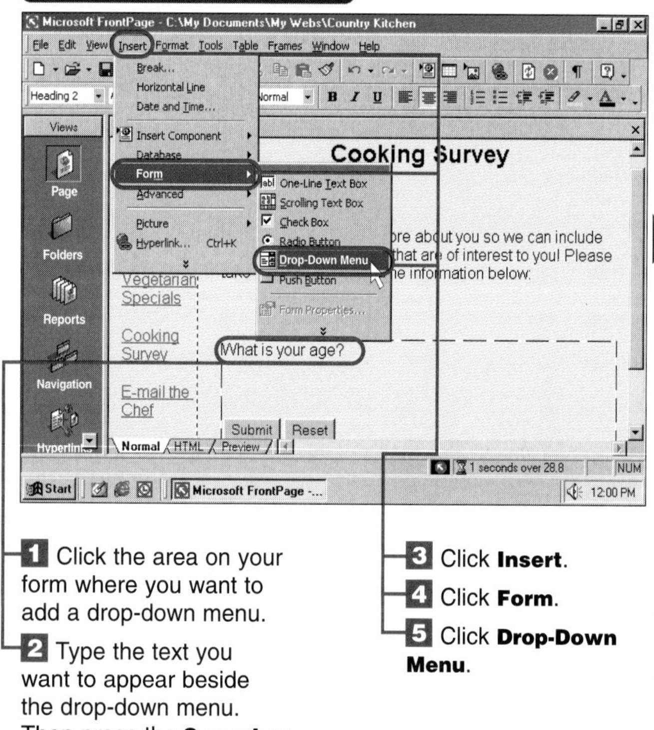

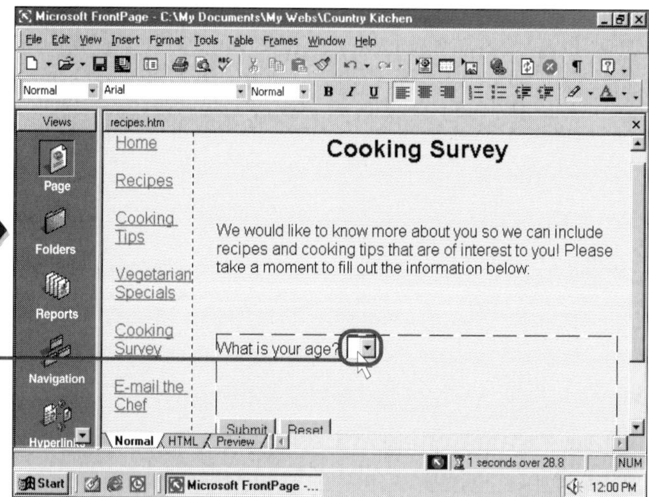

1 Click the area on your form where you want to add a drop-down menu.

2 Type the text you want to appear beside the drop-down menu. Then press the **Spacebar** to add a blank space.

3 Click **Insert**.

4 Click **Form**.

5 Click **Drop-Down Menu**.

■ The drop-down menu appears on your Web page. The menu appears empty.

6 Double-click the drop-down menu to add items to the menu.

■ The Drop-Down Menu Properties dialog box appears.

What information do I need to specify when creating a drop-down menu?

Name

You need to specify a name that describes the drop-down menu. The name identifies the drop-down menu when you view the results of the form.

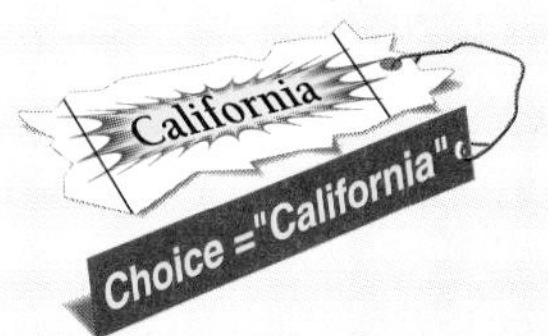

Choice

You need to specify the text you want to appear for each item in the drop-down menu.

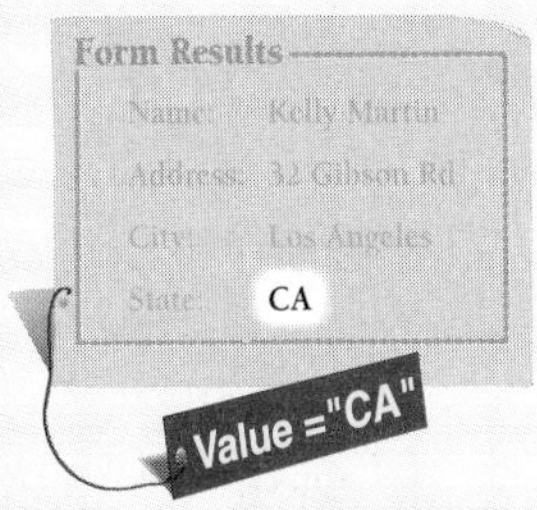

Value

You can specify a value for each item in the drop-down menu. When you view the results of the form, the value identifies the menu item a reader selected. The value can be the same as the text displayed in the menu or you can use different text. For example, you can use a more specific or shorter name, such as CA for California.

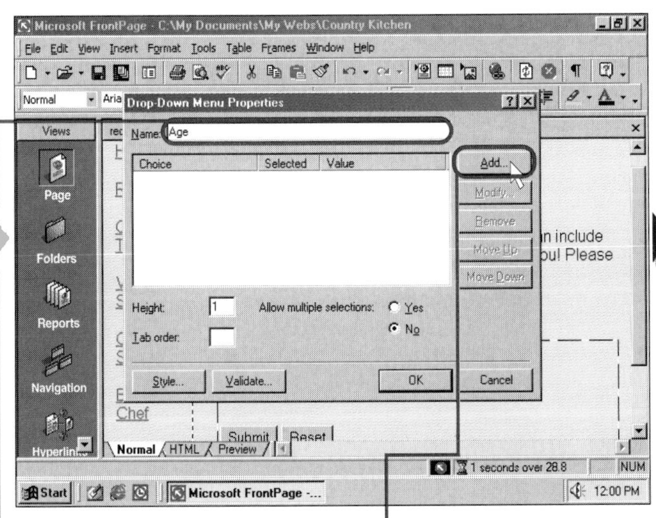

7 Type a name to describe the drop-down menu. A name should not contain blank spaces.

Note: The name you enter will not appear on your Web page. The name helps you identify the drop-down menu when you view the form results.

8 Click **Add** to add an item to the drop-down menu.

■ The Add Choice dialog box appears.

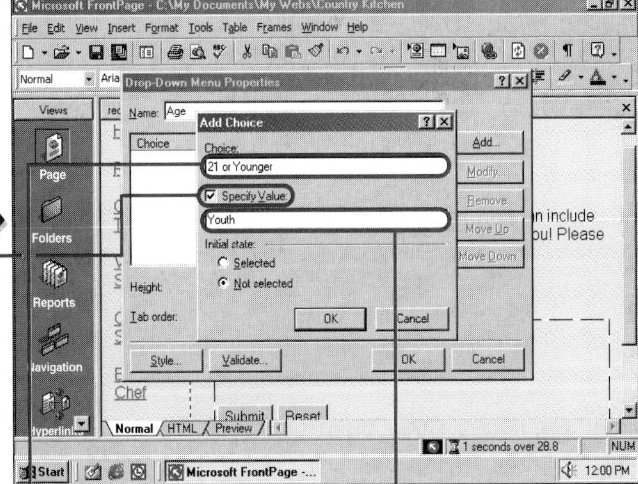

9 Type the first item you want to appear in the menu.

10 To specify a value for the item, click **Specify Value** (☐ changes to ☑).

■ By default, the text you typed in step **9** appears as the value.

11 To use a different value, drag the mouse over the text in this area until you highlight all the text. Then type the value you want to use.

CONTINUED

ADD A DROP-DOWN MENU

You can have a drop-down menu item appear automatically selected on your form. This is useful if most people will select the item.

ADD A DROP-DOWN MENU (CONTINUED)

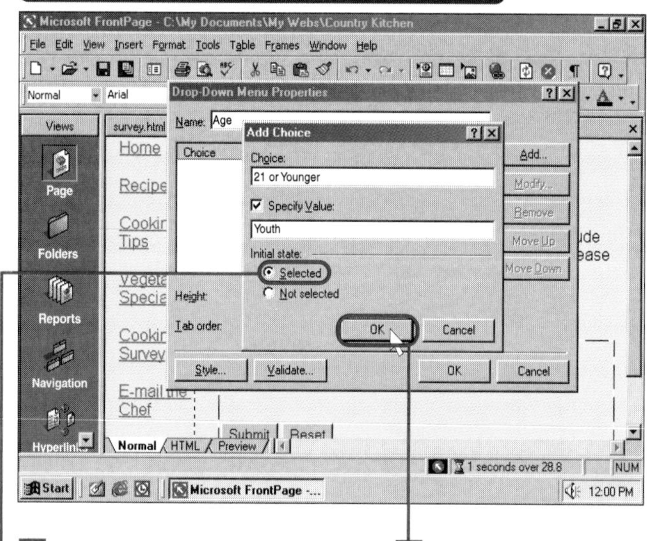

12 If you want the menu item to appear automatically selected, click **Selected** (○ changes to ⊙). You can have only one menu item appear automatically selected.

13 Click **OK** to add the menu item.

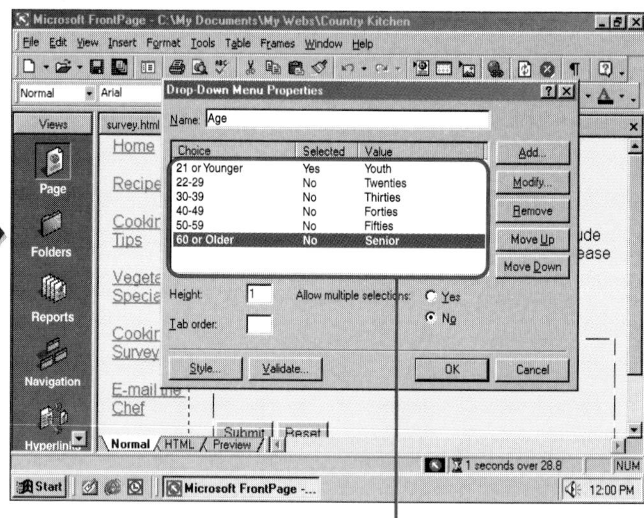

■ You can repeat steps **8** to **13** for each item you want to add to the drop-down menu.

■ Each menu item you add appears in this area.

Why would I change the number of items readers initially see in a drop-down menu?

To save space on your form, FrontPage initially sets up a drop-down menu to show only the first item in the menu. Readers can click the arrow to display all the menu items.

If you have a short list of items, you may want a drop-down menu to display all the items. For example, if your drop-down menu contains three items, you can set the height at 3 to display all three items on your form.

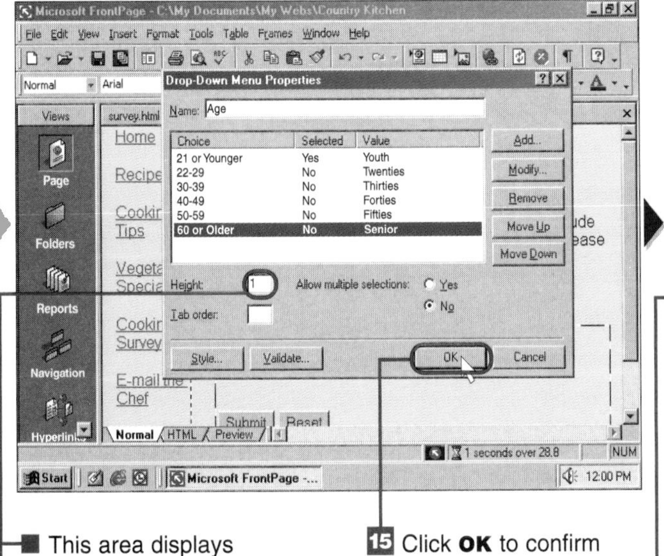

■ This area displays the number of items that readers will initially see in the drop-down menu.

14 To change the number of items that readers will initially see, double-click this area and type a new number.

15 Click **OK** to confirm all of your changes.

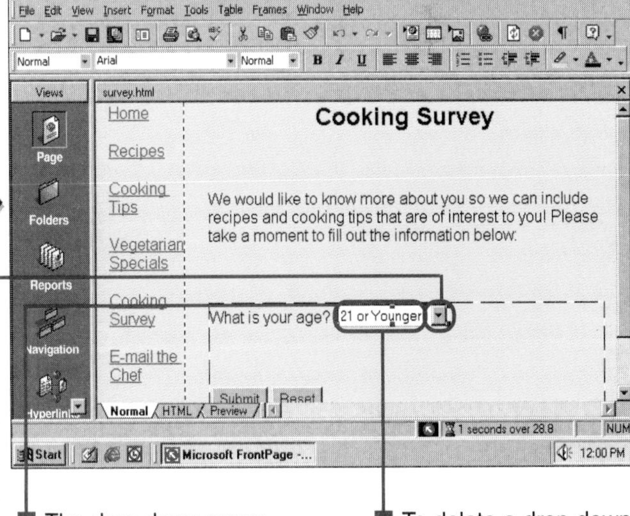

■ The drop-down menu displays your changes.

■ A reader can click the arrow to display the menu items.

Note: To test the drop-down menu, you must use the Preview view. For information on the Preview view, see page 42.

■ To delete a drop-down menu, click the menu and then press the Delete key.

CREATE A FEEDBACK FORM

You can quickly create a feedback form that collects comments from readers about your Web pages, products or company.

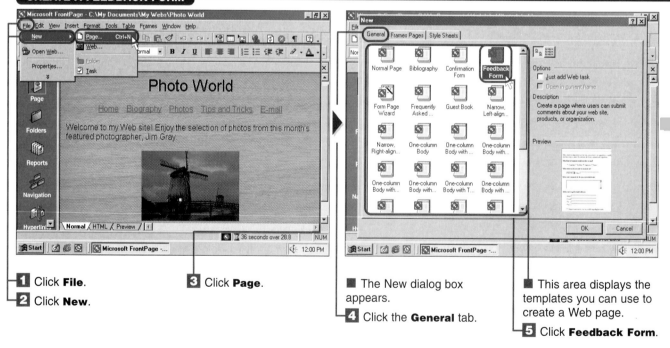

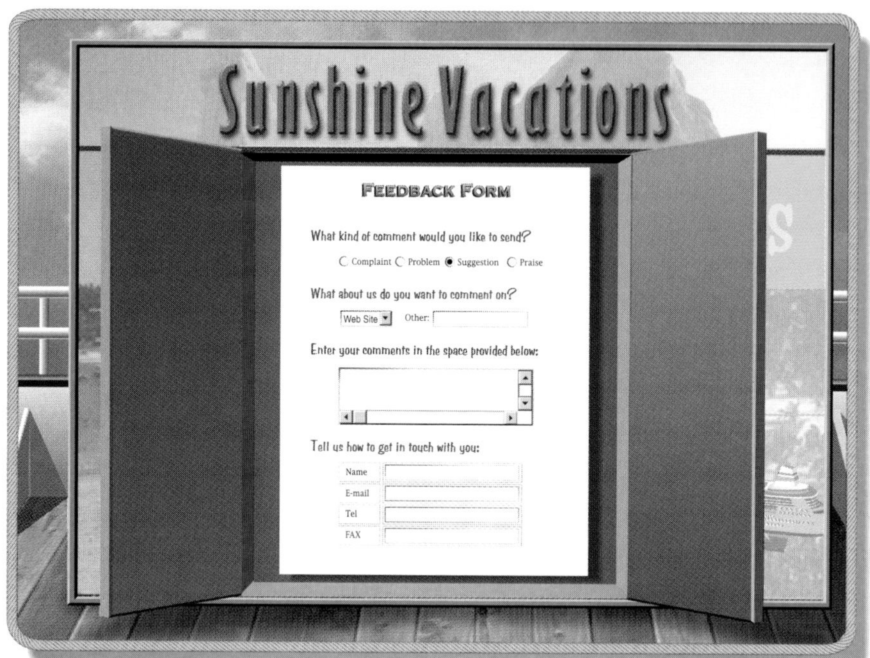

CREATE A FEEDBACK FORM

1 Click **File**.

2 Click **New**.

3 Click **Page**.

■ The New dialog box appears.

4 Click the **General** tab.

■ This area displays the templates you can use to create a Web page.

5 Click **Feedback Form**.

Is there another way that FrontPage can help me create a form?

Yes. FrontPage provides a wizard that will ask you a series of questions about the type of form you want to create and then use your answers to create a customized form. To create a form using the wizard, perform steps **1** to **6** below, selecting **Form Page Wizard** in step **5**.

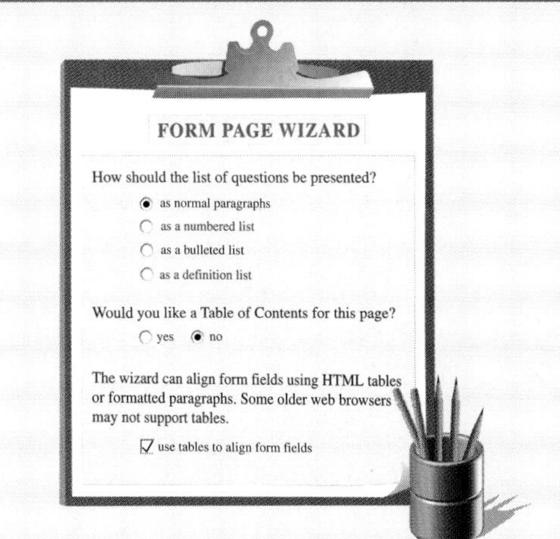

FORM PAGE WIZARD
How should the list of questions be presented?
as normal paragraphs
as a numbered list
as a bulleted list
as a definition list
Would you like a Table of Contents for this page?
yes
no
The wizard can align form fields using HTML tables or formatted paragraphs. Some older web browsers may not support tables.
use tables to align form fields

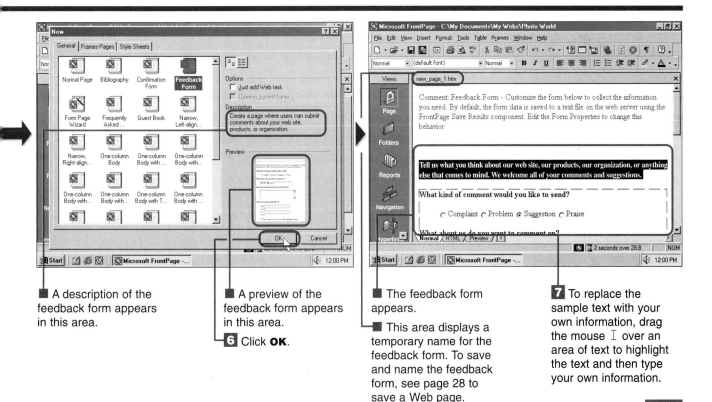

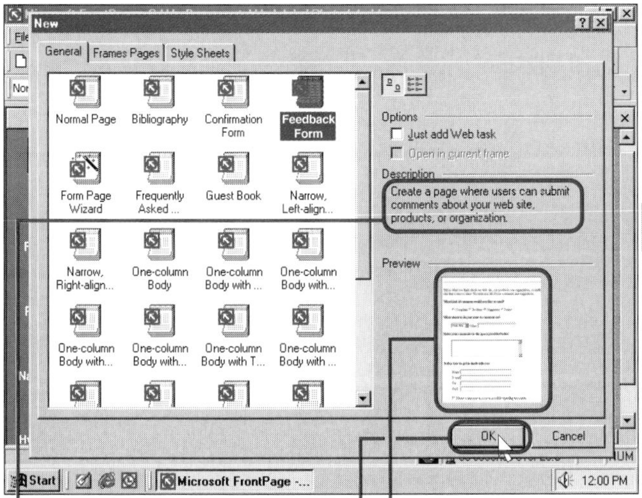

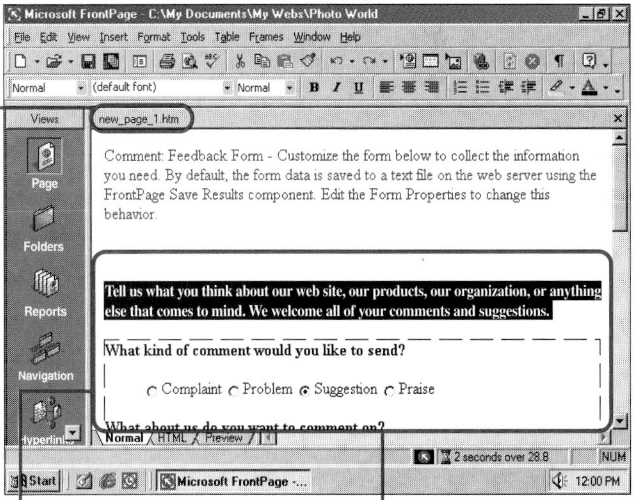

■ A description of the feedback form appears in this area.

■ A preview of the feedback form appears in this area.

6 Click **OK**.

■ The feedback form appears.

■ This area displays a temporary name for the feedback form. To save and name the feedback form, see page 28 to save a Web page.

7 To replace the sample text with your own information, drag the mouse I over an area of text to highlight the text and then type your own information.

ACCESS FORM RESULTS

After you create a form, you need to specify how you want to access the results of the form.

ACCESS FORM RESULTS

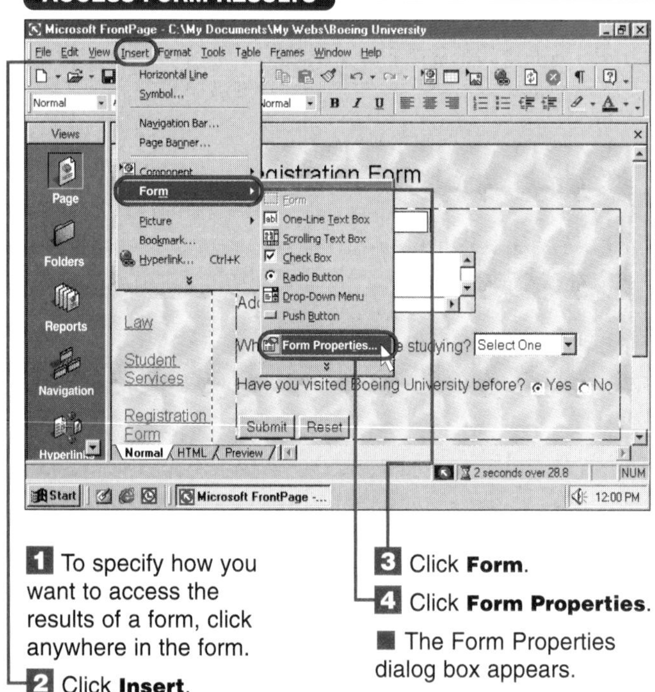

1 To specify how you want to access the results of a form, click anywhere in the form.

2 Click **Insert**.

3 Click **Form**.

4 Click **Form Properties**.

■ The Form Properties dialog box appears.

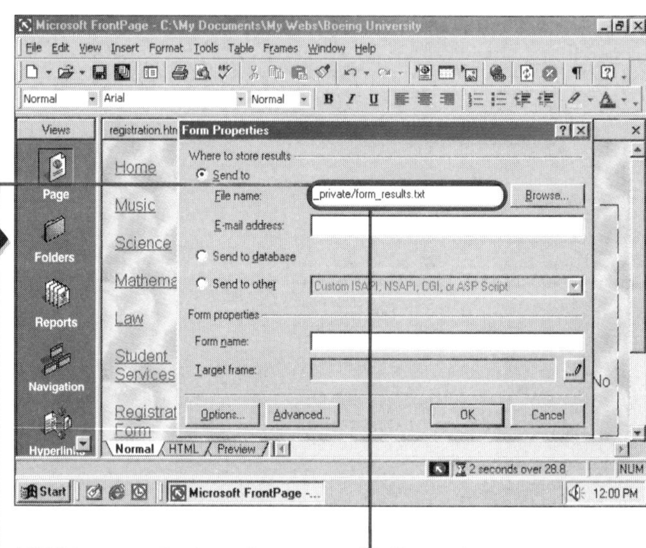

■ This area displays the location and name of the file on your Web server where the results of your form will be stored.

■ If you do not want to store the results of the form in a file on your Web server, drag the mouse I over the text in this area until you highlight all the information. Then press the Delete key to remove the information.

How can I access the results of a form?

Store form results in a file on the Web server

You can store the form results in a file on the Web server that stores your Web pages. When a reader enters information into a form, the information will be added to the file.

Send form results in an e-mail message

You can send the form results in an e-mail message addressed to you. When a reader enters information into a form, the information will be sent to your e-mail address. To use this feature, your Web server must be set up to send the results of forms in e-mail messages.

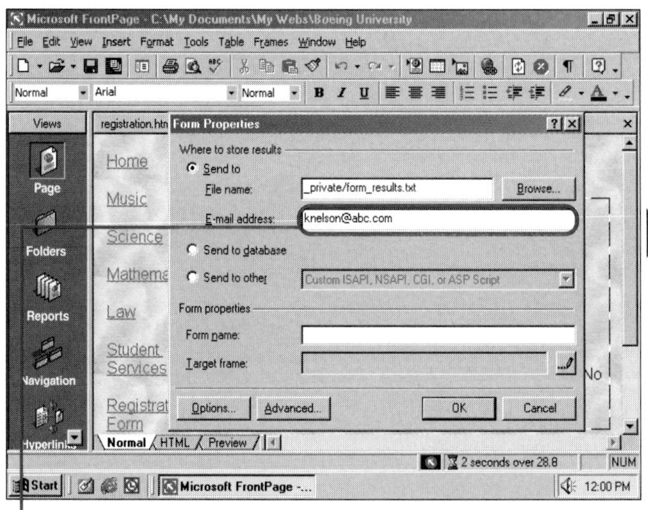

5 To send the results of the form in an e-mail message, click this area and then type your e-mail address.

Note: You can store the results of the form in a file on your Web server as well as send the results of the form in an e-mail message.

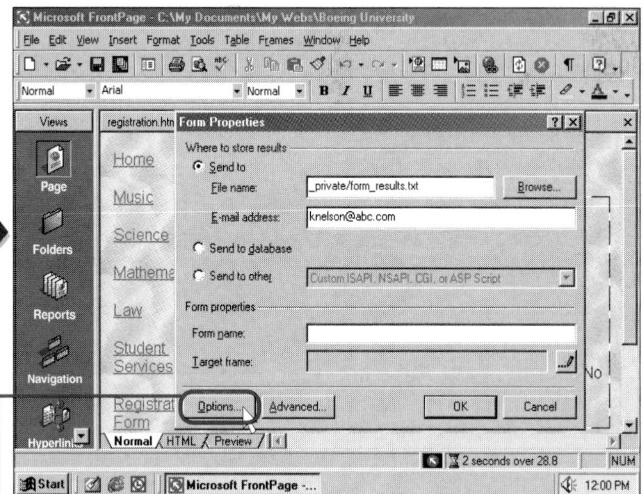

6 Click **Options** if you want to change the options for the file stored on your Web server or an e-mail message containing the form results.

■ The Options for Saving Results of Form dialog box appears.

CONTINUED

ACCESS FORM RESULTS

If you will access the results of the form from a file on your Web server, you can choose a format for the file.

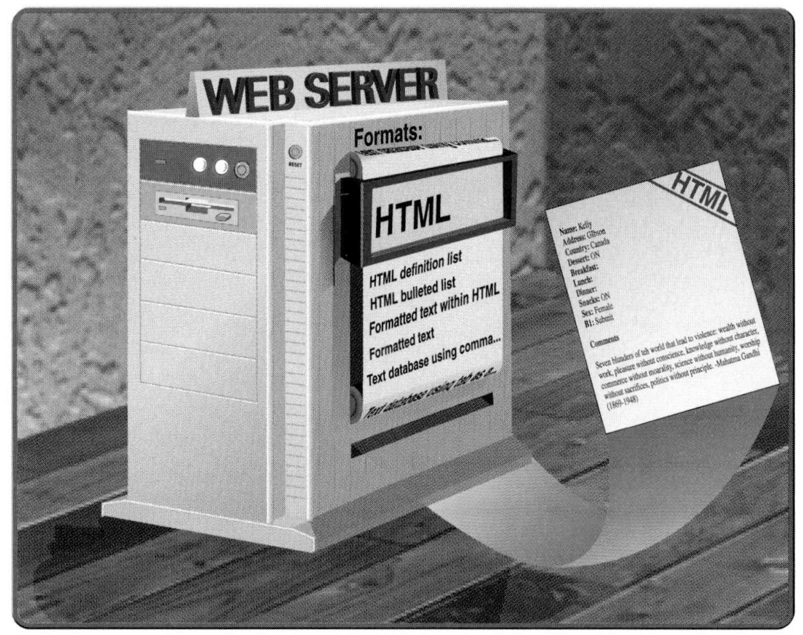

You should choose a file format based on the way you plan to use the form results. HTML file formats are useful if you want to view the information on the Web. The other formats are useful if you plan to use the form results in a spreadsheet or database program.

ACCESS FORM RESULTS (CONTINUED)

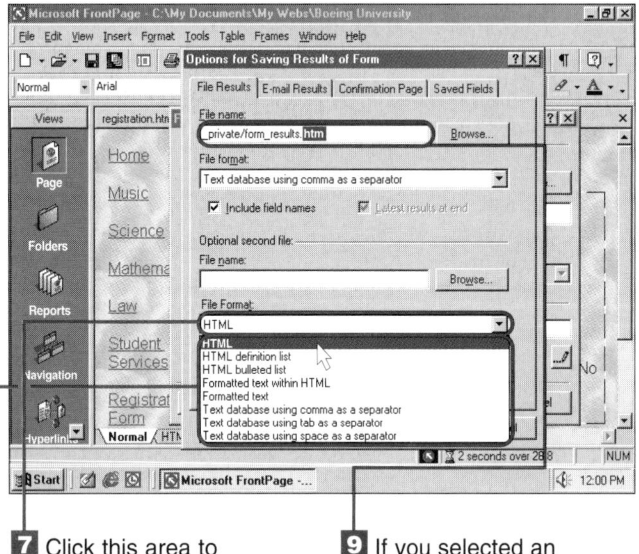

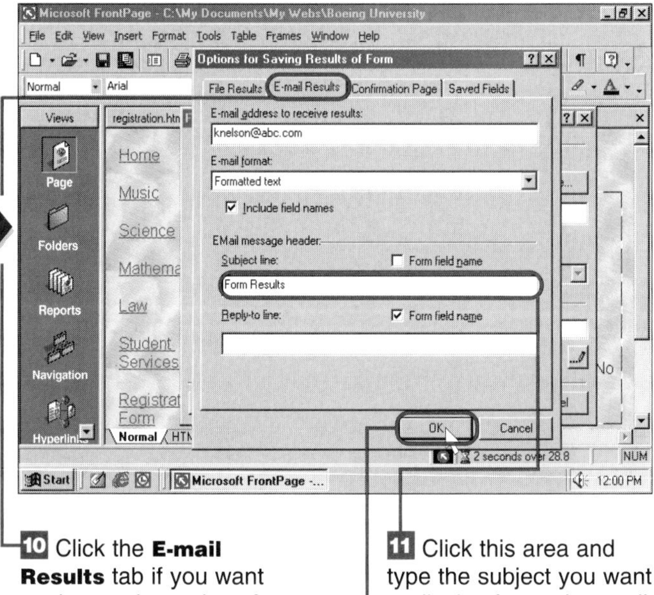

7 Click this area to display a list of the available file formats.

8 Click the file format you want to use.

9 If you selected an HTML option in step **8**, drag the mouse I over the **txt** extension in this area until you select the text. Then type the **htm** extension.

Note: Changing the file extension from txt to htm allows Web browsers to properly display the file containing the form results.

10 Click the **E-mail Results** tab if you want to change the options for sending the form results in an e-mail message.

11 Click this area and type the subject you want to display for each e-mail message you receive.

12 Click **OK**.

How do I view the results of a form on my Web server?

You can view the results of a form in your Web browser. FrontPage stores the results of the form in the _private folder, which is a hidden folder on your Web server. Readers browsing through your Web pages cannot view the contents of this folder.

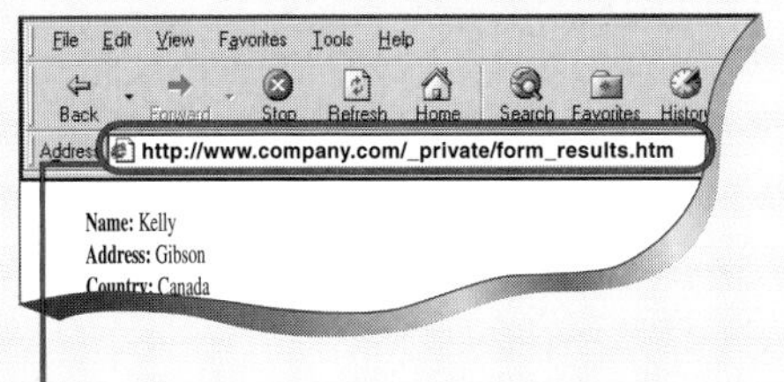

You will need to enter your user name and password supplied by your Web presence provider to access the form results.

1 Click this area and type the address of the Web server where you published your Web pages followed by **/_private/form_results.txt** or **/_private/form_results.htm**. The file name you type depends on whether you changed the file name in step **9**.

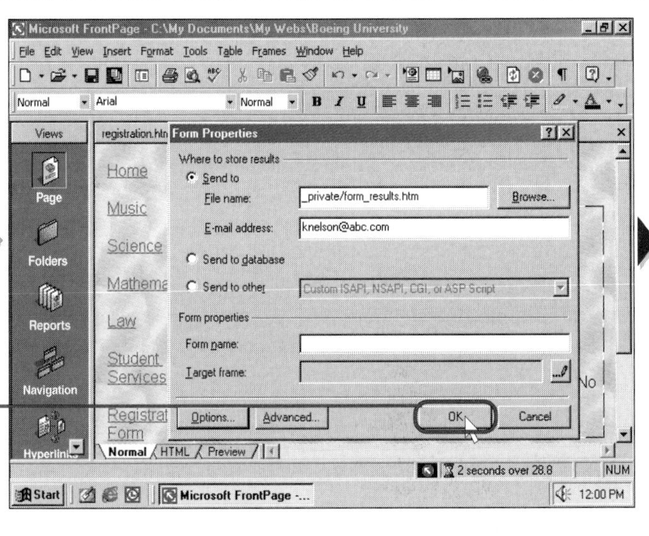

13 Click **OK** to confirm all your changes.

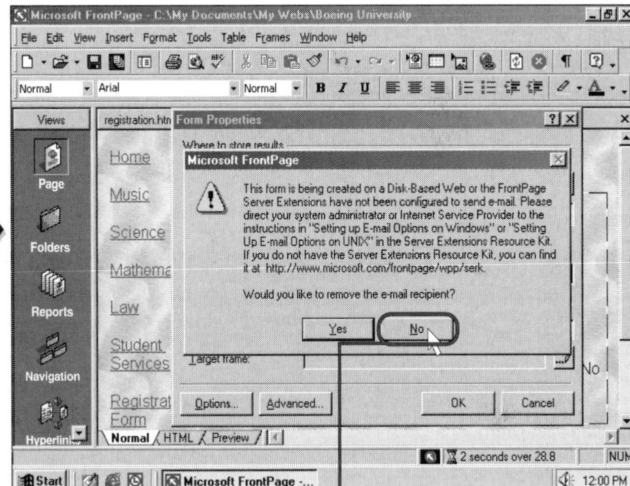

■ If you entered an e-mail address in step **5**, a dialog box appears, stating that your computer is not set up to send the results of your form in an e-mail message.

Note: This dialog box only applies to people who will use their own computer to publish their Web pages. If you are using a Web presence provider to publish your Web pages, you can ignore this message.

14 Click **No** to keep the e-mail address you specified.

CREATE A CONFIRMATION PAGE

You can create a confirmation page that will appear after readers submit a form. A confirmation page allows readers to review the information they entered in a form.

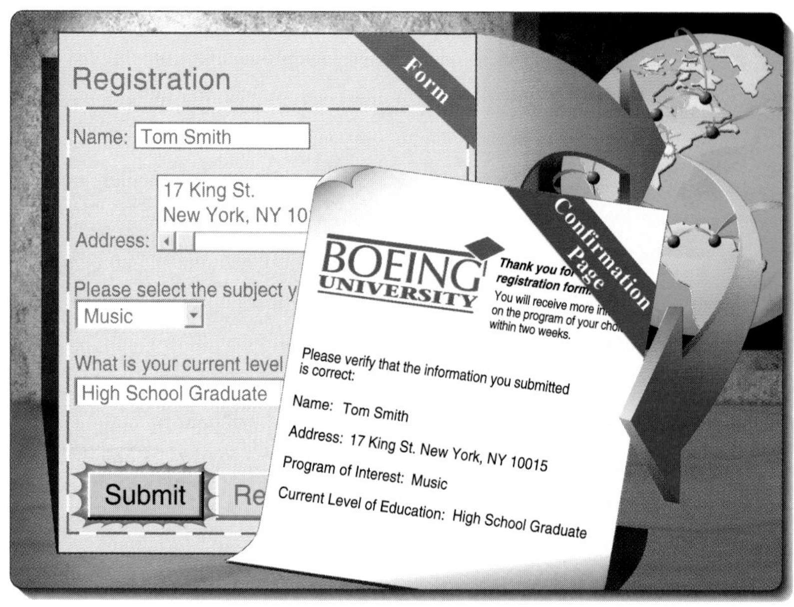

If you do not create a confirmation page, FrontPage will automatically display a basic confirmation page that lists all of the information readers entered in the form.

CREATE A CONFIRMATION PAGE

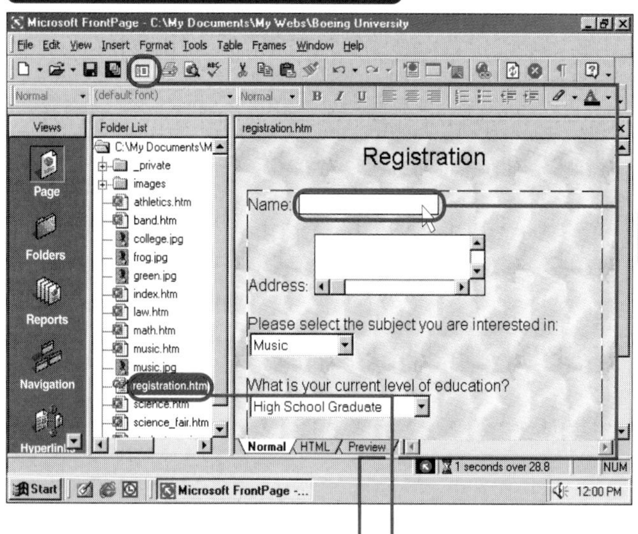

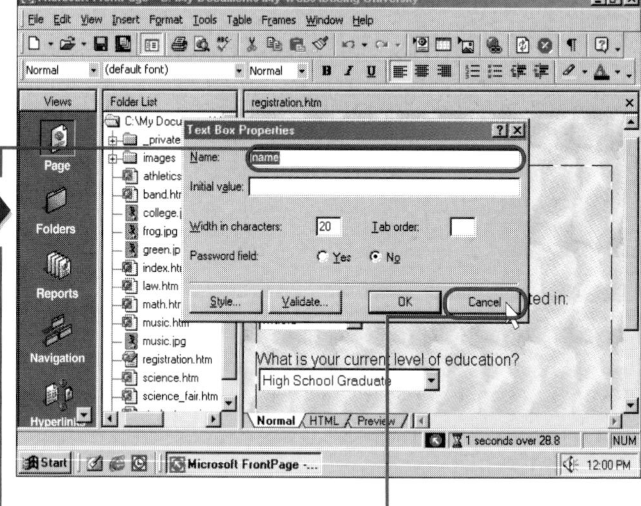

DETERMINE NAMES OF ITEMS ON A FORM

■ Before you can create a confirmation page for a form, you need to write down the name you assigned to each item on the form.

1 Double-click the Web page that contains the form you want to use the confirmation page.

■ If the Folder List is not displayed, click ▣ to display the list.

2 Double-click an item on the form.

■ A Properties dialog box appears.

■ This area displays the name you assigned to the item.

3 Write down the name of the item on a piece of paper.

4 Click **Cancel** to close the dialog box.

5 Repeat steps **2** to **4** for each item on the form.

What should I consider when creating a confirmation page?

Make sure your confirmation page uses a layout that clearly shows the information that readers enter in a form. You should place each item that readers enter on a different line. You may also want to add a background color or image to the confirmation page to differentiate the page from the Web page that contains the form.

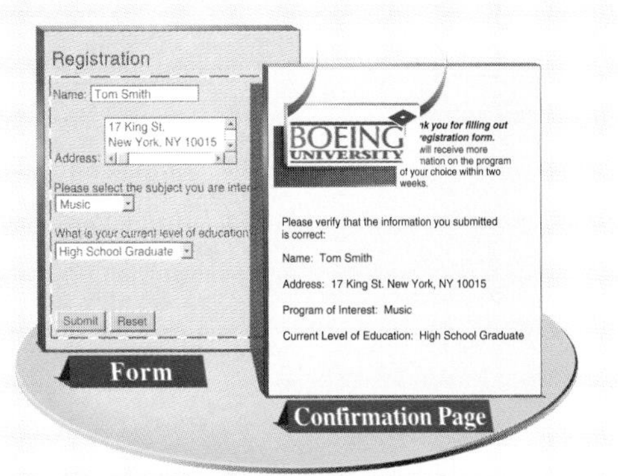

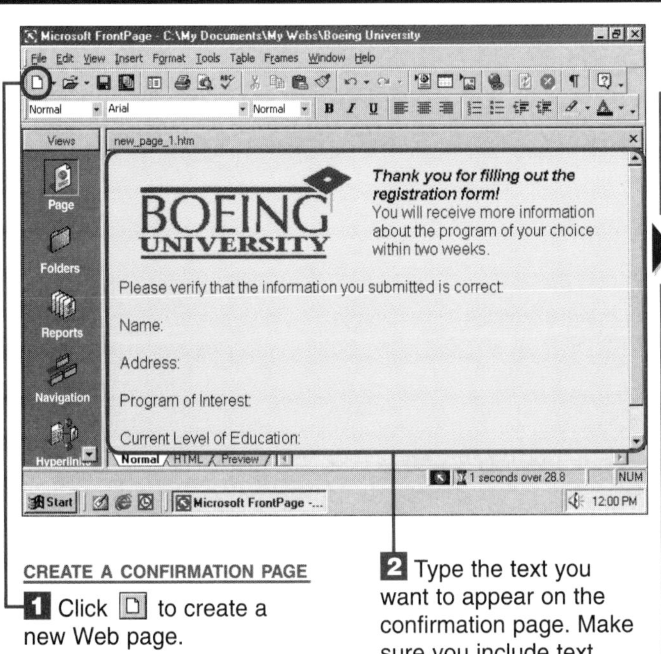

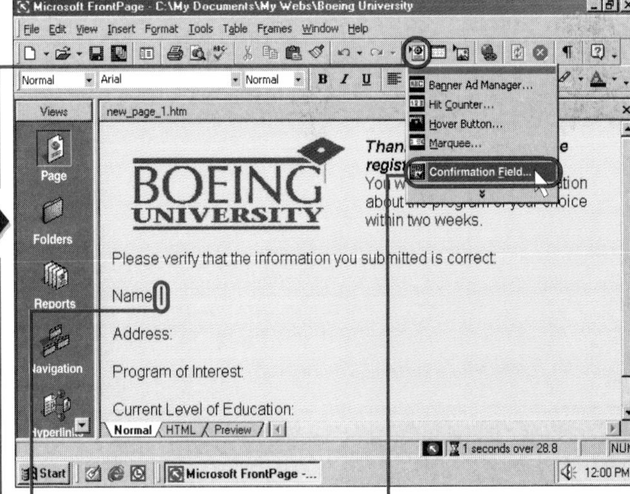

CREATE A CONFIRMATION PAGE

1 Click [new page icon] to create a new Web page.

Note: Make sure you create the new Web page in the same Web site that contains the form.

2 Type the text you want to appear on the confirmation page. Make sure you include text that describes each item that readers will enter in the form.

3 Click beside an area of text that describes an item that readers will enter in the form.

4 Click [component icon] to display a list of components you can add to your Web page.

5 Click **Confirmation Field.**

Note: If Confirmation Field does not appear on the menu, position the mouse [pointer icon] over the bottom of the menu to display all the menu commands.

CONTINUED

CREATE A CONFIRMATION PAGE

When creating a confirmation page, you need to enter the name you assigned to each item on the form. FrontPage will replace the name with the information readers enter in the form.

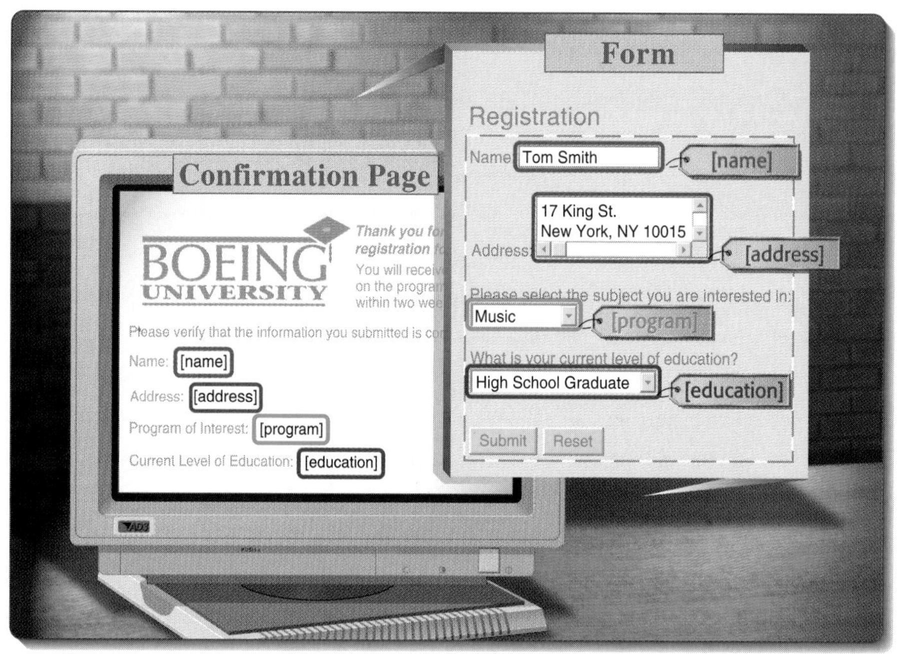

CREATE A CONFIRMATION PAGE (CONTINUED)

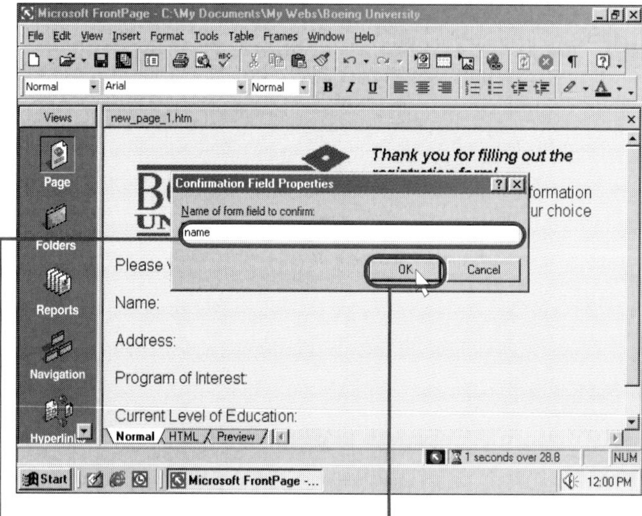

■ The Confirmation Field Properties dialog box appears.

6 Type the name you assigned to the item on the form. Make sure you enter the name exactly.

7 Click **OK** to confirm the information you entered.

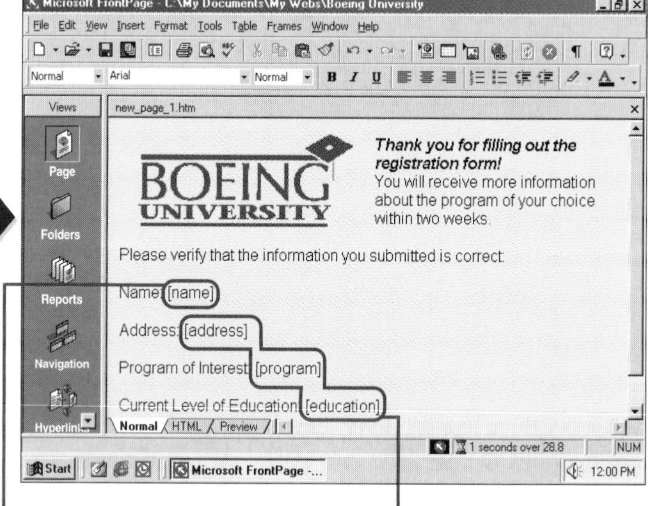

■ The name of the item appears in brackets on your Web page.

■ FrontPage will replace the name with the information readers enter in the form.

8 Repeat steps **3** to **7** for each area of text that describes an item that readers will enter in the form.

■ Make sure you save the Web page. To save a Web page, see page 28.

How can I quickly create a confirmation page?

FrontPage includes a template that allows you to quickly create a confirmation page. The Confirmation Form template provides you with the layout and design for a confirmation page. You can add your personalized information to the appropriate areas. To create a confirmation page using the Confirmation Form template, see page 26.

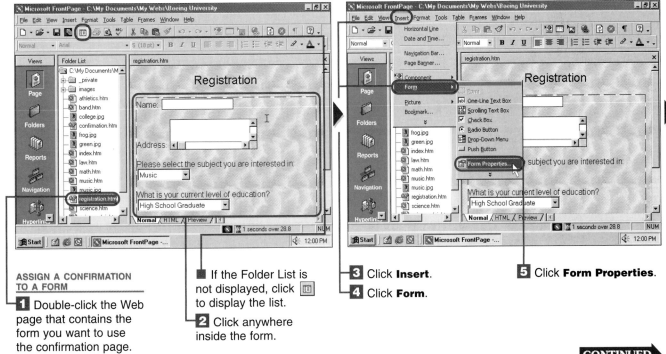

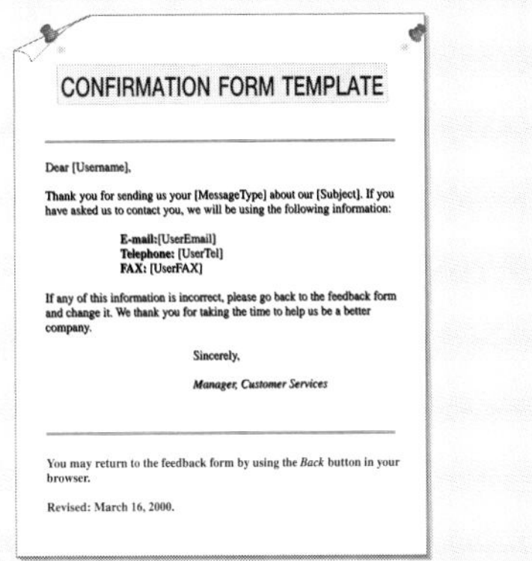

CONFIRMATION FORM TEMPLATE

Dear [Username],

Thank you for sending us your [MessageType] about our [Subject]. If you have asked us to contact you, we will be using the following information:

E-mail:[UserEmail]
Telephone: [UserTel]
FAX: [UserFAX]

If any of this information is incorrect, please go back to the feedback form and change it. We thank you for taking the time to help us be a better company.

Sincerely,

Manager, Customer Services

You may return to the feedback form by using the *Back* button in your browser.

Revised: March 16, 2000.

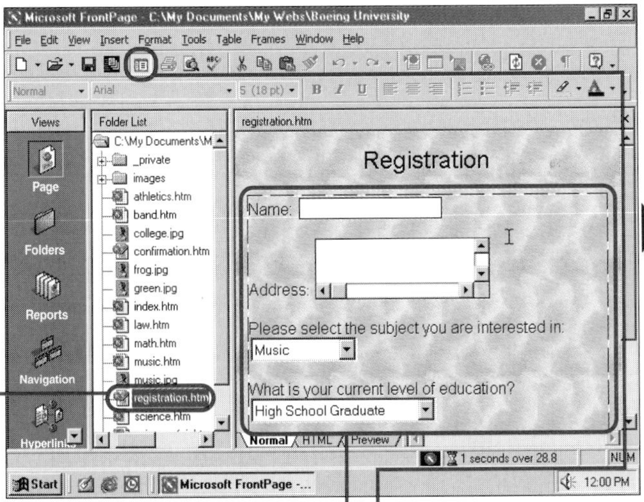

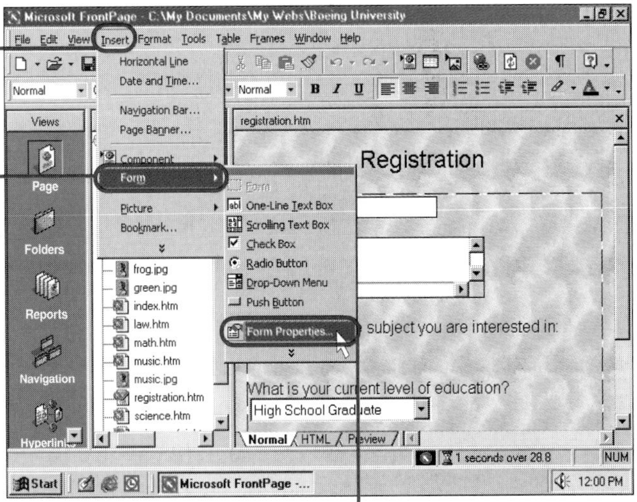

ASSIGN A CONFIRMATION TO A FORM

1 Double-click the Web page that contains the form you want to use the confirmation page.

■ If the Folder List is not displayed, click ▥ to display the list.

2 Click anywhere inside the form.

3 Click **Insert**.

4 Click **Form**.

5 Click **Form Properties**.

CONTINUED

CREATE A CONFIRMATION PAGE

After you assign a confirmation page to a form, the page will appear when readers submit the form.

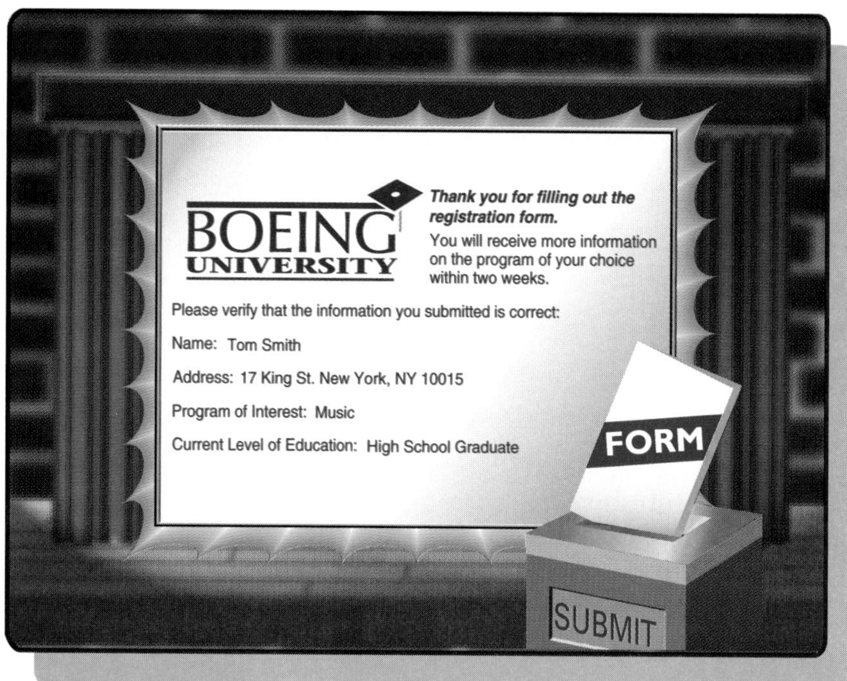

BOEING UNIVERSITY
Thank you for filling out the registration form.
You will receive more information on the program of your choice within two weeks.
Please verify that the information you submitted is correct:
Name: Tom Smith
Address: 17 King St. New York, NY 10015
Program of Interest: Music
Current Level of Education: High School Graduate
FORM
SUBMIT

CREATE A CONFIRMATION PAGE (CONTINUED)

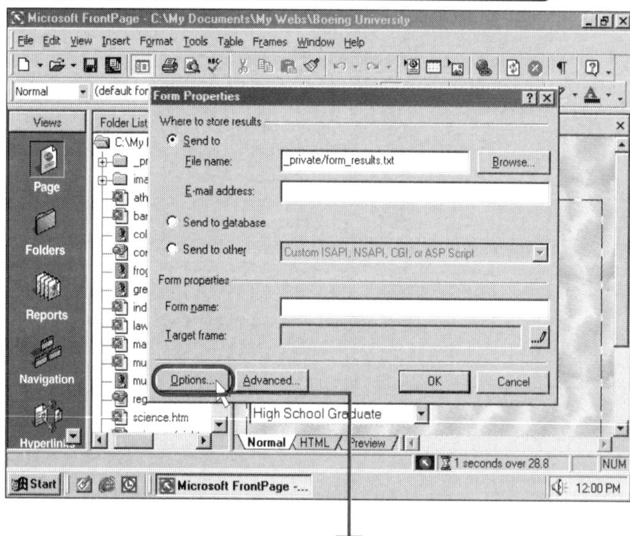

■ The Form Properties dialog box appears.

6 Click **Options** to specify the confirmation page you want to assign to the form.

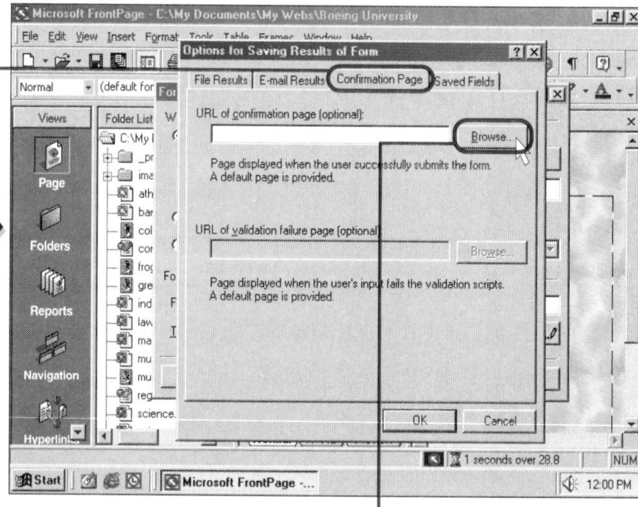

■ The Options for Saving Results of Form dialog box appears.

7 Click the **Confirmation Page** tab.

8 Click **Browse** to locate the confirmation page that you want to use.

?

I no longer want a form to use the confirmation page I created. What can I do?

If you no longer want a form to use the confirmation page you created, you need to remove the connection between the form and the confirmation page. The form will once again use the basic confirmation page that FrontPage provides.

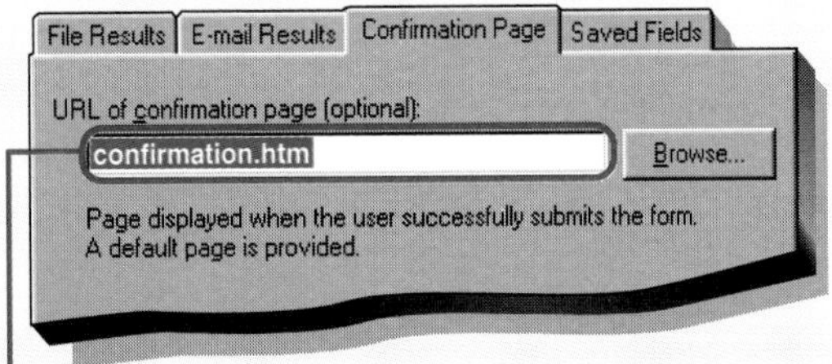

1 Perform steps 1 to 7 starting on page 235.

2 Double-click this area and then press the Delete key to remove the connection between the form and the confirmation page.

3 Perform steps 11 and 12 below to confirm your change.

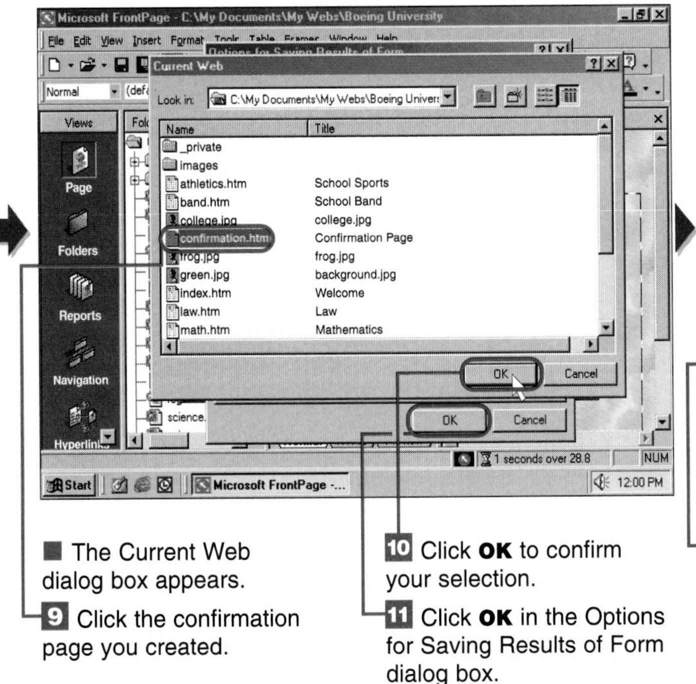

■ The Current Web dialog box appears.

9 Click the confirmation page you created.

10 Click **OK** to confirm your selection.

11 Click **OK** in the Options for Saving Results of Form dialog box.

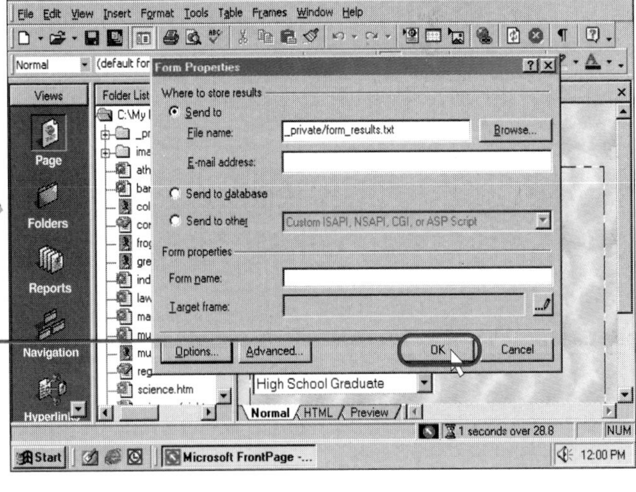

12 Click **OK** in the Form Properties dialog box.

■ When readers submit the form, the confirmation page you specified will now appear.

Note: To test the confirmation page, you must publish your Web pages. To publish your Web pages, see page 290.

DIGGING UP THE PAST
A GUIDE TO ARCHAEOLOGICAL DIGS

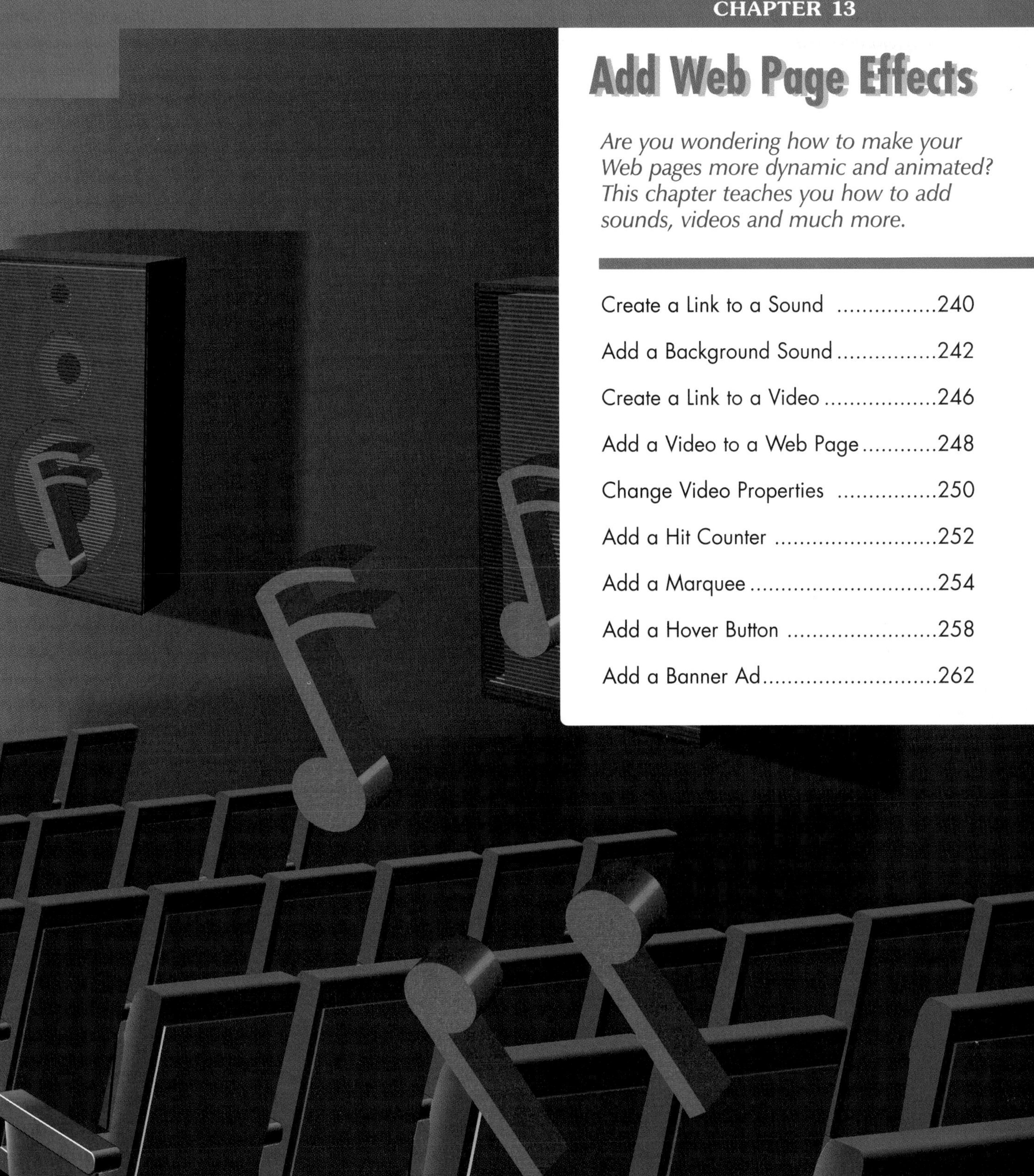

CHAPTER 13

Add Web Page Effects

Are you wondering how to make your Web pages more dynamic and animated? This chapter teaches you how to add sounds, videos and much more.

CREATE A LINK TO A SOUND

You can create a link on your Web page that readers can select to play a sound.

You can provide entertaining sound clips from television shows, movies and famous speeches. You can also add sound clips to provide samples of your products, such as music CDs or audiotapes.

The most common types of sounds on the Web are MIDI, MPEG, RealAudio and Wave.

CREATE A LINK TO A SOUND

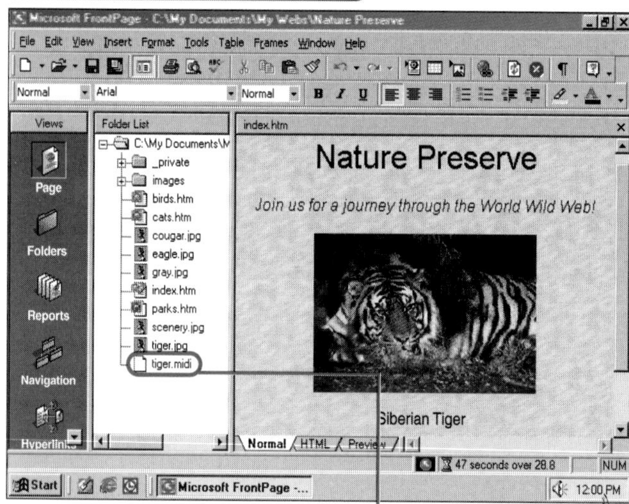

■ Before you can create a link to a sound on your Web page, you must add the sound file to the folder that stores all the Web pages for your Web site. For more information, see the top of page 241.

■ The sound file you add to the folder will appear in the Folder List.

Note: If the sound file does not appear in the Folder List, click the Folder List area and then press the F5 key to refresh the list.

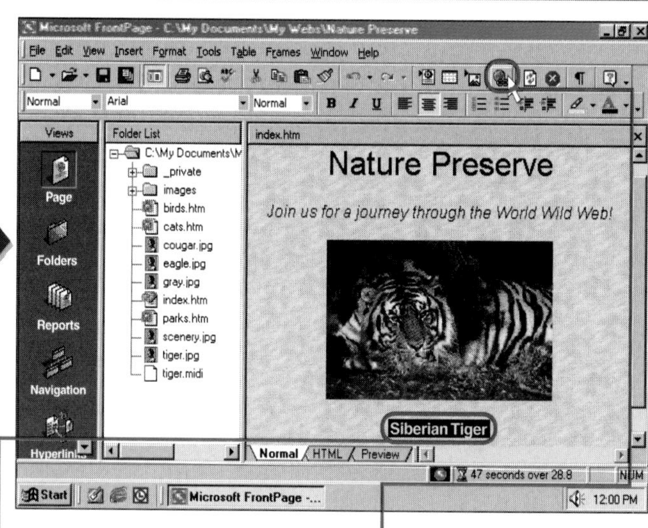

1 Select the text or click the image you want readers to select to play the sound. To select text, see page 54.

Note: To add an image, see pages 100 to 103.

2 Click [icon] to create a link.

What do I need to do before I can create a link to a sound on my Web page?

You need to place a copy of the sound file in the same folder that stores all the Web pages for your Web site. This ensures the sound file will transfer with your Web site when you publish your Web pages. If you do not copy the sound file, people will not be able to play the sound.

Each Web site you create has its own folder in the My Webs folder. The My Webs folder is stored in the My Documents folder on your C drive.

Where can I obtain sounds?

You can purchase collections of sounds at computer stores and also obtain sounds on the Internet. You can find sounds at the following Web sites.

earthstation1.com
wavcentral.com
soundamerica.com

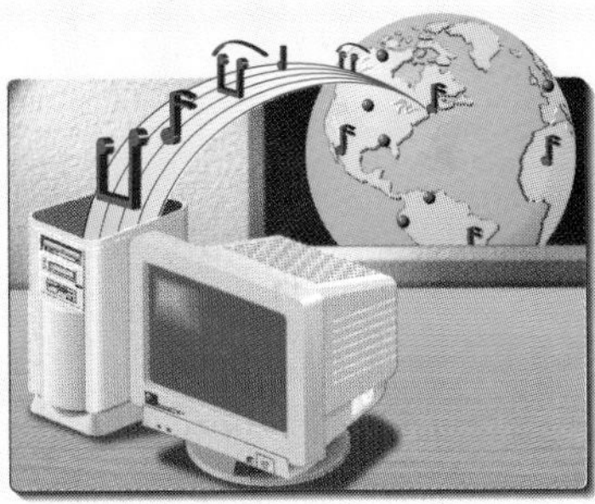

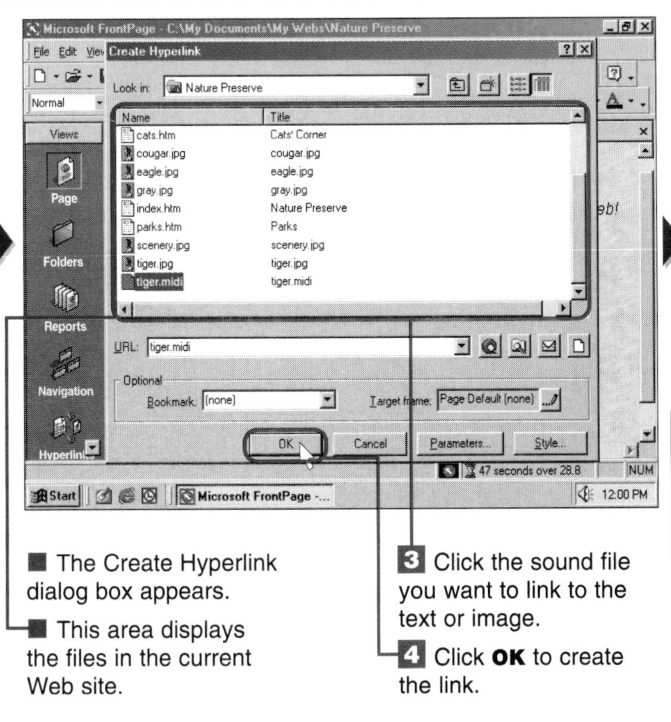

■ The Create Hyperlink dialog box appears.

■ This area displays the files in the current Web site.

3 Click the sound file you want to link to the text or image.

4 Click **OK** to create the link.

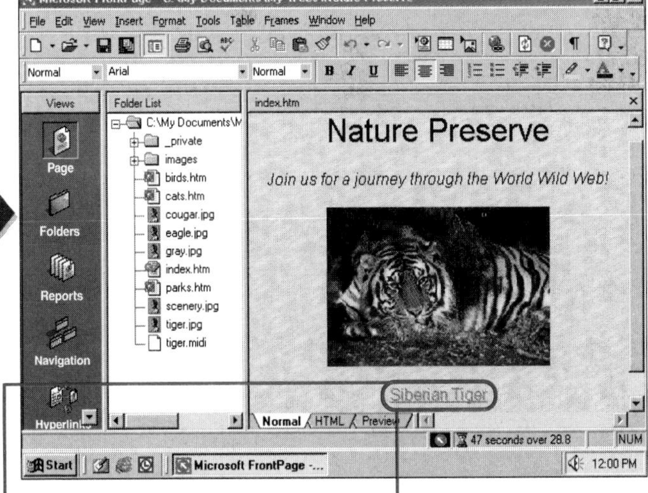

■ FrontPage creates the link. Text links appear underlined and in color.

■ To deselect text, click outside the selected area.

■ When a reader selects the sound link, the sound will transfer to their computer and play.

Note: To test the link, you must use the Preview view. For information on the Preview view, see page 42.

ADD A BACKGROUND SOUND

You can add a background sound to a Web page. When a reader displays the Web page, the sound will automatically play.

By default, the Netscape Navigator Web browser will not play a background sound you add to a Web page.

ADD A BACKGROUND SOUND

1 Click **File**.

2 Click **Properties**.

Note: If Properties does not appear on the menu, position the mouse over the bottom of the menu to display all the menu commands.

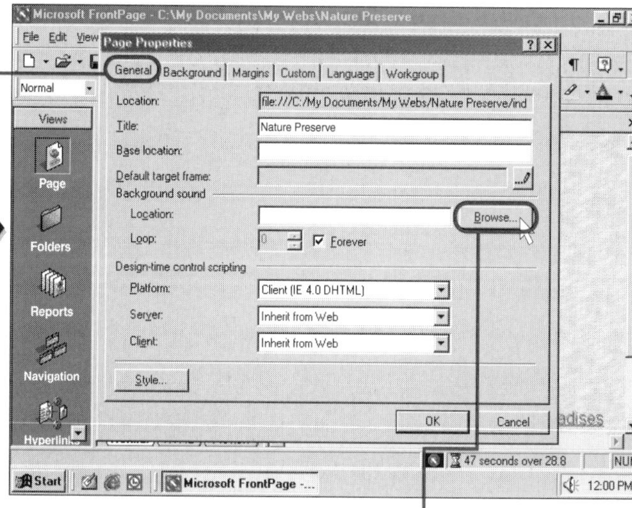

■ The Page Properties dialog box appears.

3 Click the **General** tab.

4 Click **Browse** to locate the sound file you want to use.

Where can I obtain sounds?

You can purchase collections of sounds at computer stores and also obtain sounds on the Internet. Make sure you have permission to use any sounds you obtain on the Internet. You can find sounds at the following Web sites.

earthstation1.com

soundamerica.com

wavcentral.com

What type of background sounds can I add to a Web page?

You can add several types of background sounds to a Web page. The most popular type of background sound is MIDI. You can determine the type of a sound by the characters that appear after the period in the sound file name (example: birdchirp.wav).

Type of Sound	Extension
AU	.au
MIDI	.mid
WAVE	.wav

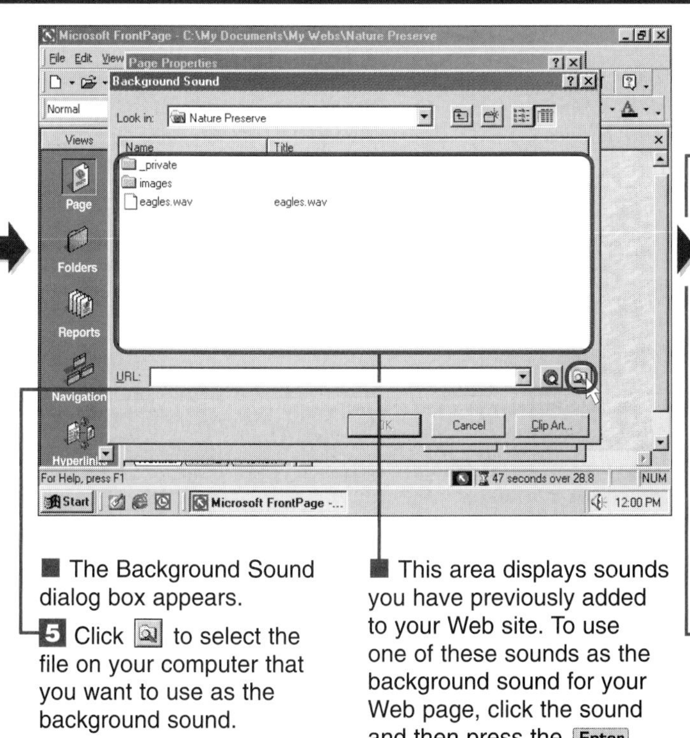

■ The Background Sound dialog box appears.

5 Click [icon] to select the file on your computer that you want to use as the background sound.

■ This area displays sounds you have previously added to your Web site. To use one of these sounds as the background sound for your Web page, click the sound and then press the Enter key. Then skip to step **10**.

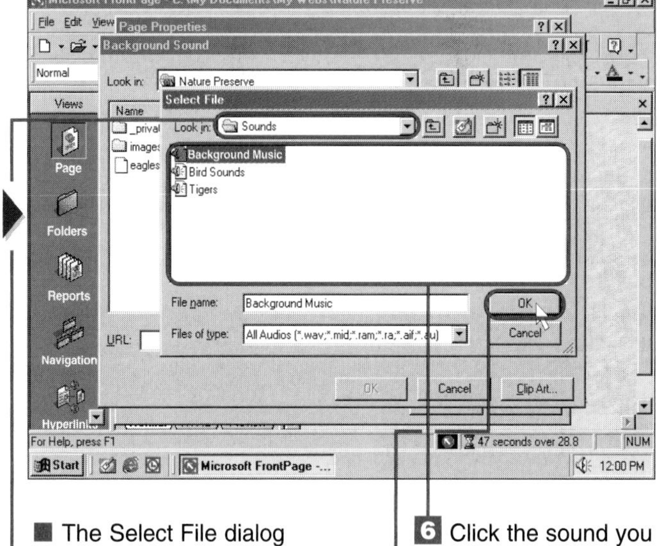

■ The Select File dialog box appears.

■ This area shows the location of the displayed files. You can click this area to change the location.

6 Click the sound you want to use as the background sound.

7 Click **OK** to confirm your selection.

CONTINUED

ADD A BACKGROUND SOUND

You can choose to play a background sound continuously or a specific number of times when a reader displays your Web page.

Playing a background sound continuously may annoy readers who visit your Web page. Readers may turn off their speakers or leave your Web page.

ADD A BACKGROUND SOUND (CONTINUED)

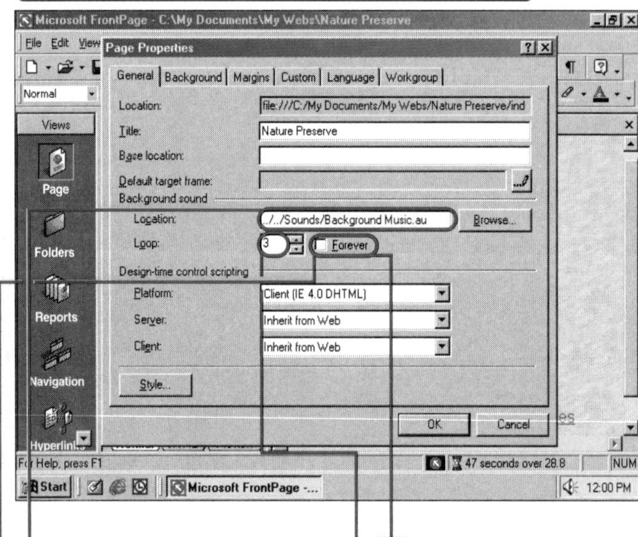

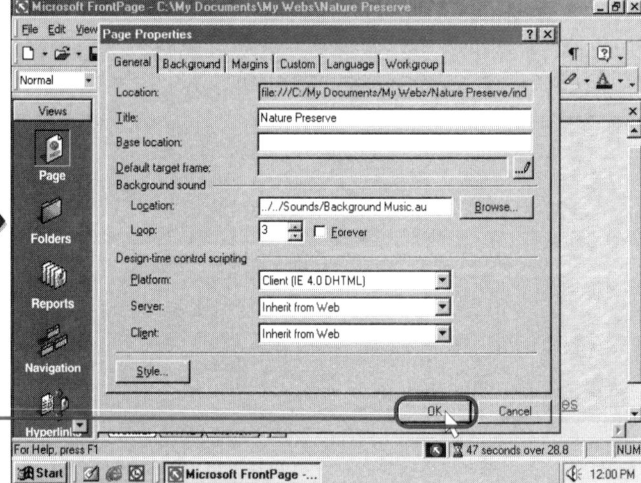

■ This area displays the location and name of the sound file you selected.

■ This option plays the sound continuously while the Web page is displayed.

8 To play the sound a specific number of times, click this option (☑ changes to ☐).

9 If you turned off the option in step **8**, double-click this area and type the number of times you want to play the sound.

10 Click **OK** to add the background sound to your Web page.

Note: To test the background sound, you must use the Preview view. For information on the Preview view, see page 42.

■ When you save the Web page, FrontPage will ask you to save the sound file as part of your Web site.

What should I consider before adding a background sound to a Web page?

Sounds increase the time it takes for a Web page to appear on a screen. If a Web page takes too long to appear, readers may lose interest and move to another page. Whenever possible, you should use sounds with small file sizes since these sounds will transfer faster to a reader's computer.

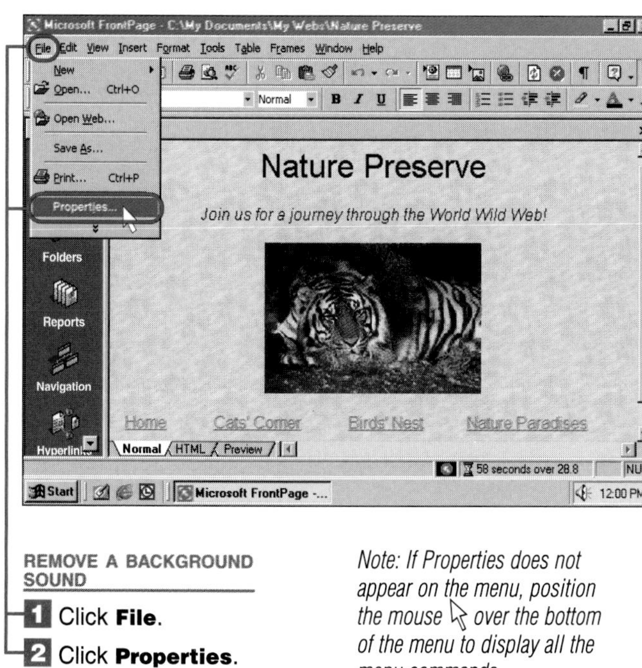

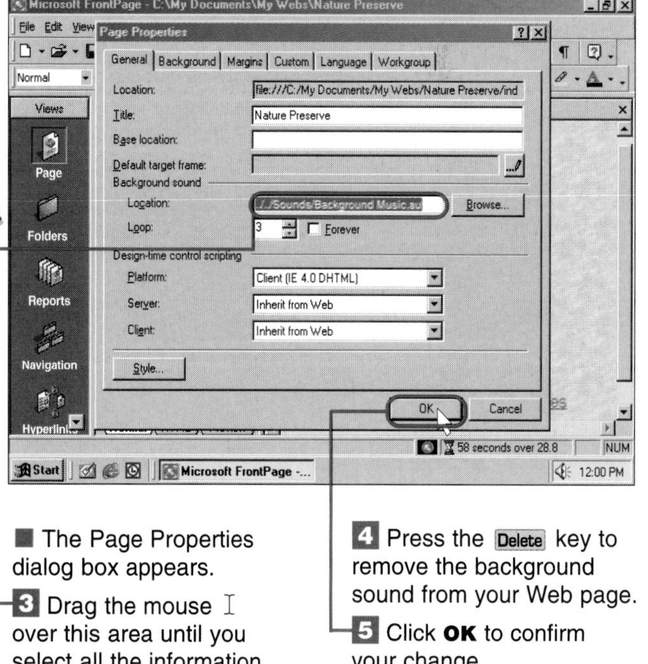

REMOVE A BACKGROUND SOUND

1 Click **File**.

2 Click **Properties**.

Note: If Properties does not appear on the menu, position the mouse over the bottom of the menu to display all the menu commands.

■ The Page Properties dialog box appears.

3 Drag the mouse over this area until you select all the information.

4 Press the Delete key to remove the background sound from your Web page.

5 Click **OK** to confirm your change.

CREATE A LINK TO A VIDEO

You can create a link on your Web page that readers can select to play a video.

You can provide entertaining videos such as visual effects, movie clips, animation and home videos. You can also add videos to provide information about your company, organization or topic of interest.

The most common types of videos on the Web are AVI, MPEG, QuickTime and RealVideo.

CREATE A LINK TO A VIDEO

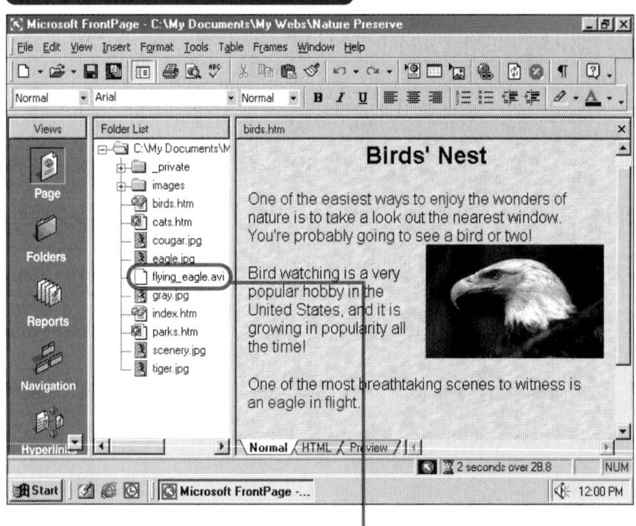

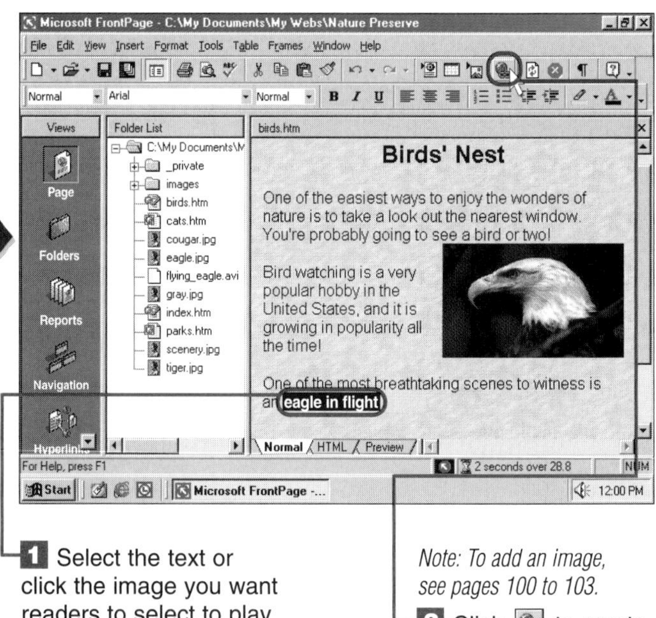

■ Before you can create a link to a video on your Web page, you must add the video file to the folder that stores all the Web pages for your Web site. For more information, see the top of page 247.

■ The video file you add to the folder will appear in the Folder List.

Note: If the video file does not appear in the Folder List, click the Folder List area and then press the F5 key to refresh the list.

1 Select the text or click the image you want readers to select to play the video. To select text, see page 54.

Note: To add an image, see pages 100 to 103.

2 Click to create a link.

What do I need to do before I can create a link to a video on my Web page?

You need to place a copy of the video file in the same folder that stores all the Web pages for your Web site. This ensures the video file will transfer with your Web site when you publish your Web pages. If you do not copy the video file, people will not be able to play the video.

Each Web site you create has its own folder in the My Webs folder. The My Webs folder is stored in the My Documents folder on your C drive.

Where can I obtain videos?

You can purchase collections of videos at computer stores and also obtain videos on the Internet. You can find videos at the following Web sites.

www.jurassicpunk.com

www.nasa.gov/gallery/video

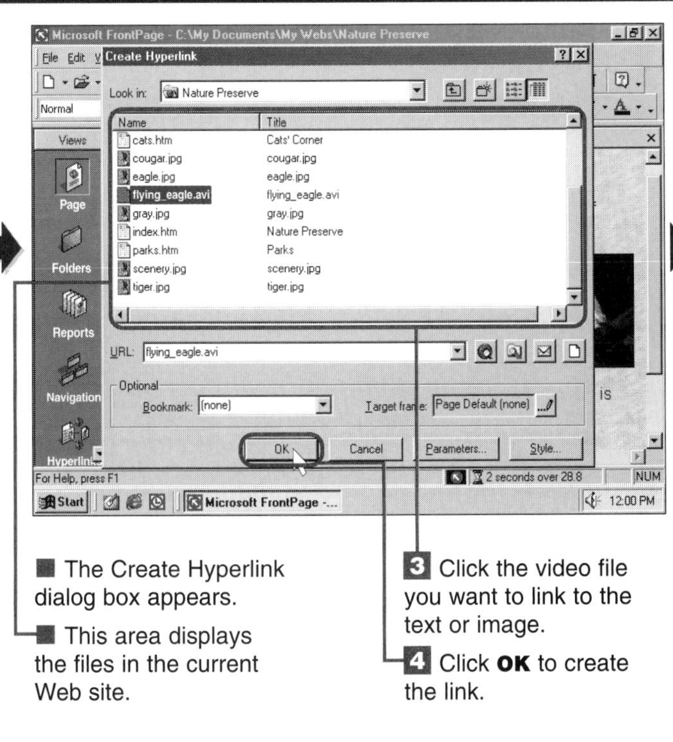

■ The Create Hyperlink dialog box appears.

■ This area displays the files in the current Web site.

3 Click the video file you want to link to the text or image.

4 Click **OK** to create the link.

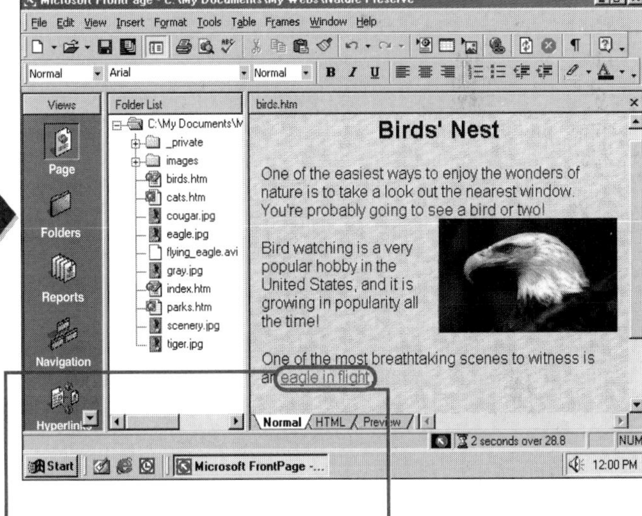

■ FrontPage creates the link. Text links appear underlined and in color.

■ To deselect text, click outside the selected area.

■ When a reader selects the video link, the video will transfer to their computer and play.

Note: To test the link, you must use the Preview view. For information on the Preview view, see page 42.

ADD A VIDEO TO A WEB PAGE

You can add a video that will play automatically on a Web page when a reader displays the page.

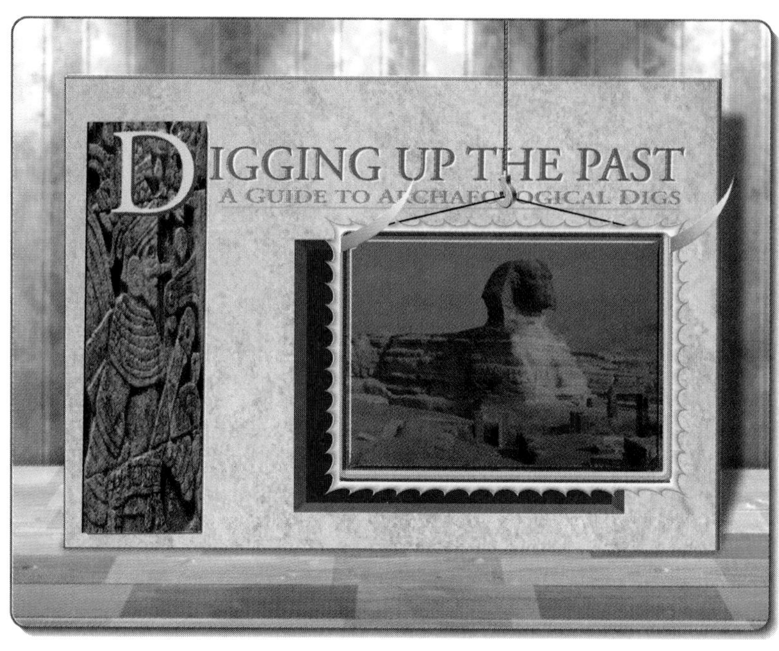

When adding a video that will play automatically on a Web page, you should use AVI videos.

By default, the Netscape Navigator Web browser will not play a video automatically on a Web page.

ADD A VIDEO TO A WEB PAGE

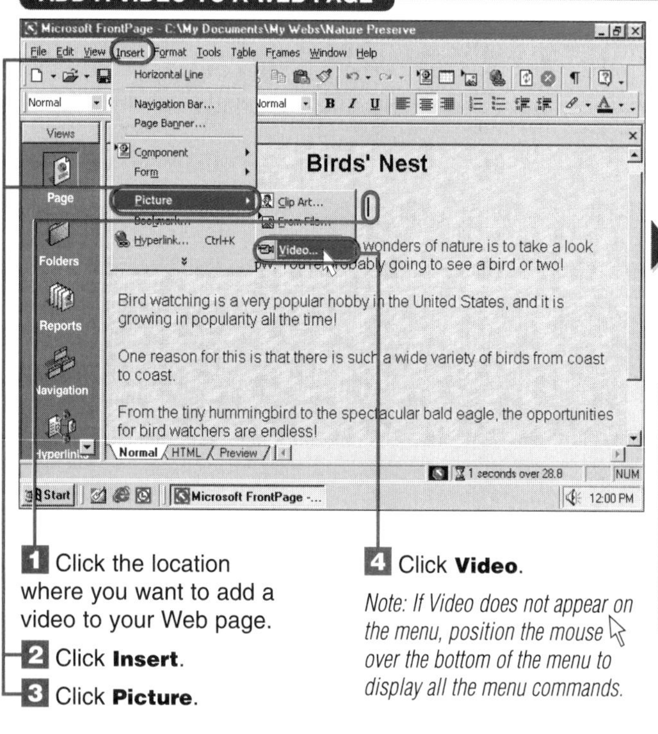

1 Click the location where you want to add a video to your Web page.

2 Click **Insert**.

3 Click **Picture**.

4 Click **Video**.

Note: If Video does not appear on the menu, position the mouse over the bottom of the menu to display all the menu commands.

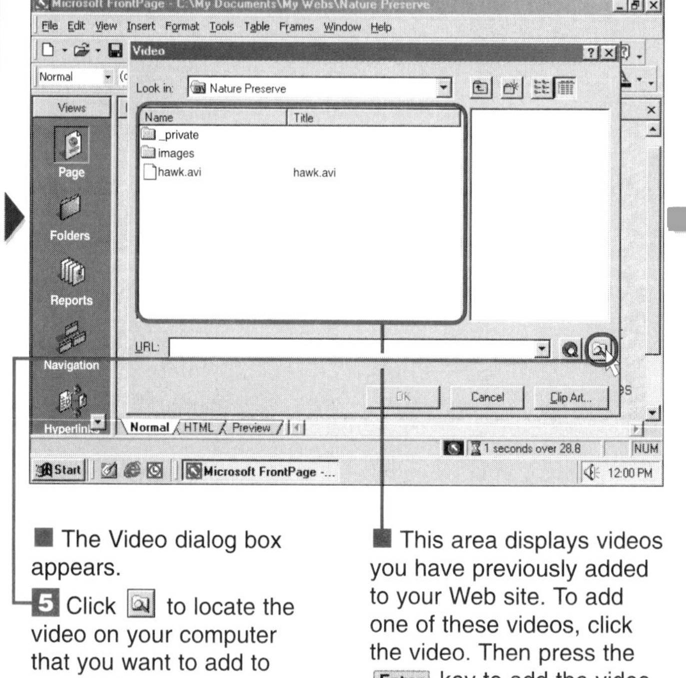

■ The Video dialog box appears.

5 Click the browse button to locate the video on your computer that you want to add to your Web page.

■ This area displays videos you have previously added to your Web site. To add one of these videos, click the video. Then press the Enter key to add the video.

What should I consider when adding a video to a Web page?

Video files tend to be the largest files on the Web. Videos with large file sizes can take a long time to transfer to a computer. Whenever possible, you should use videos with small file sizes.

Where can I obtain videos?

You can purchase collections of videos at computer stores. You can also obtain videos on the Internet, such as at the www.jurassicpunk.com Web site.

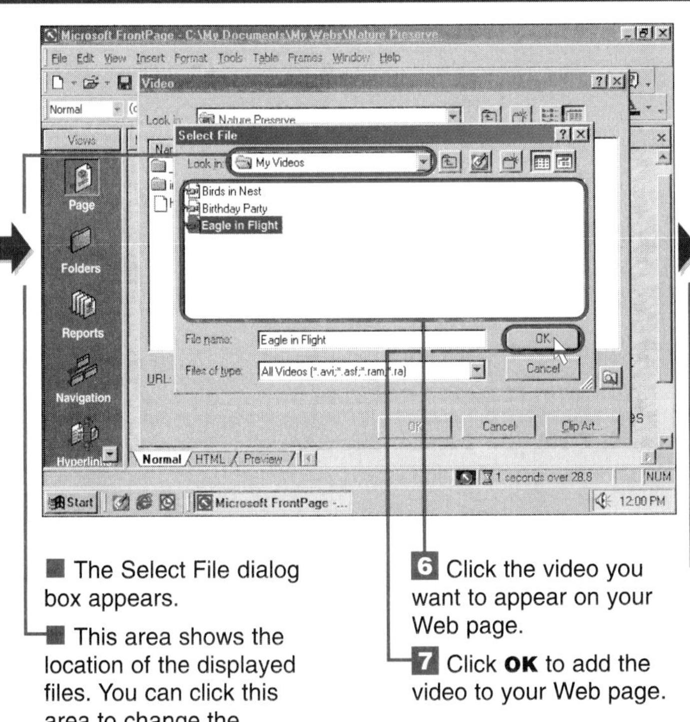

■ The Select File dialog box appears.

■ This area shows the location of the displayed files. You can click this area to change the location.

6 Click the video you want to appear on your Web page.

7 Click **OK** to add the video to your Web page.

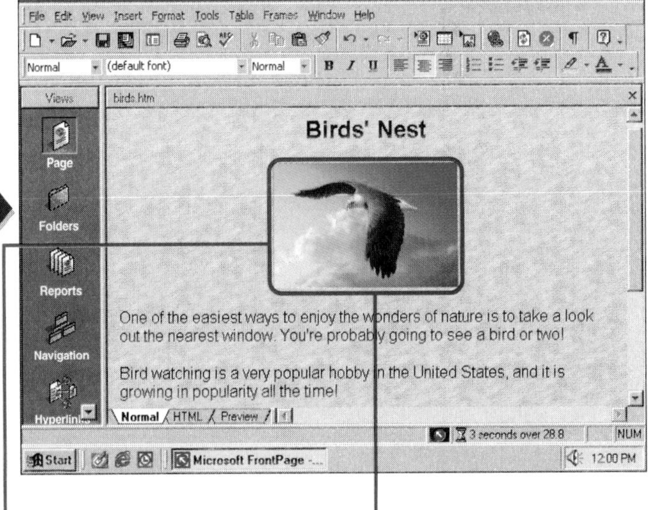

■ The video appears on your Web page.

■ When you save the Web page, FrontPage will ask you to save the video file as part of your Web site.

Note: To test the video, you must use the Preview view. *For information on the Preview view, see page 42.*

■ To delete a video, click the video and then press the Delete key.

CHANGE VIDEO PROPERTIES

You can change the properties of a video, such as the number of times a video will play and when a video will begin to play.

CHANGE VIDEO PROPERTIES

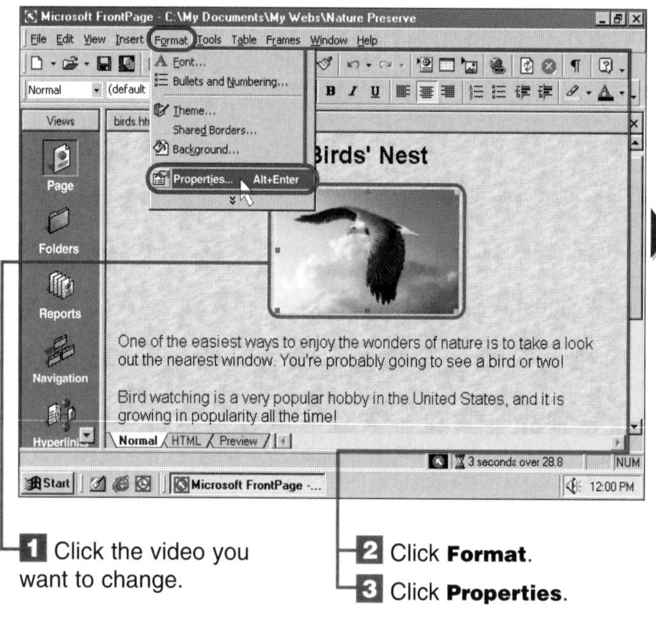

1 Click the video you want to change.

2 Click **Format**.

3 Click **Properties**.

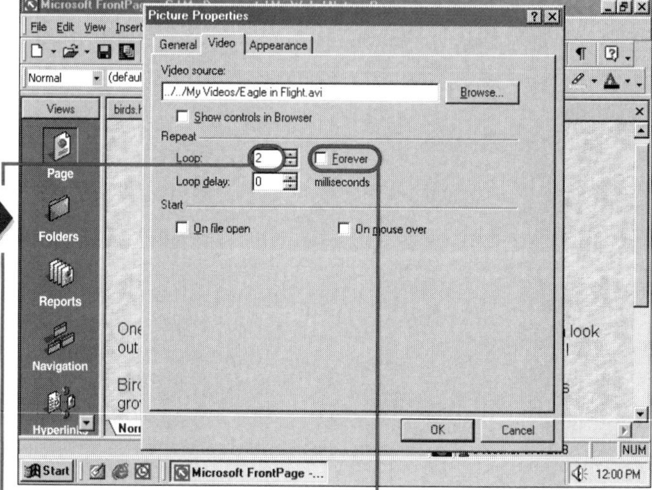

■ The Picture Properties dialog box appears.

4 Double-click this area and type the number of times you want the video to play.

■ If you want the video to play continuously while the Web page is displayed, click this option (☐ changes to ☑).

Note: Playing a video continuously may annoy readers. Readers may turn off their speakers or leave your Web page.

What happens if a Web browser cannot play a video?

If a Web browser cannot play a video, a box will appear where the video should appear on the Web page. If you provide text for the video in step **7** below, the text will appear in the box. This text will provide information about the missing video for readers who do not see the video.

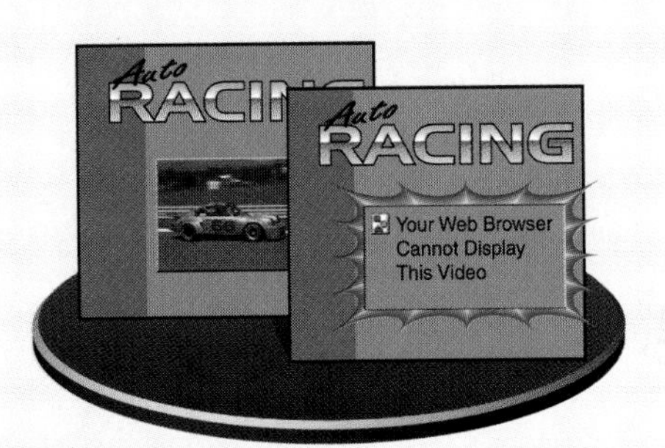

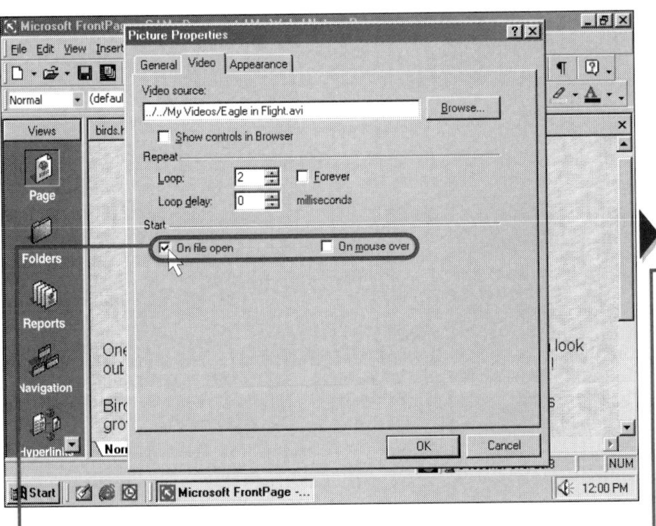

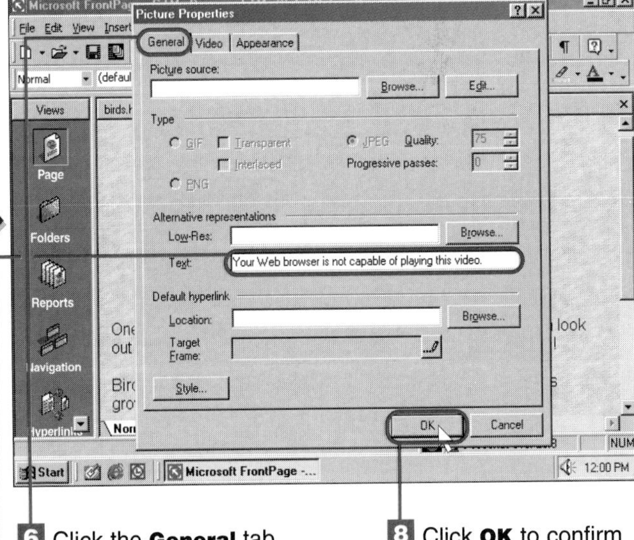

5 To specify when the video plays on your Web page, click an option to turn the option on (☑) or off (☐).

On file open

The video plays when a reader first displays the Web page.

On mouse over

The video plays when a reader moves the mouse over the video.

6 Click the **General** tab.

7 Click this area and type the text you want to appear if a Web browser cannot play the video.

8 Click **OK** to confirm your changes.

ADD A HIT COUNTER

You can add a hit counter to your Web page to keep track of the number of people who have visited the page.

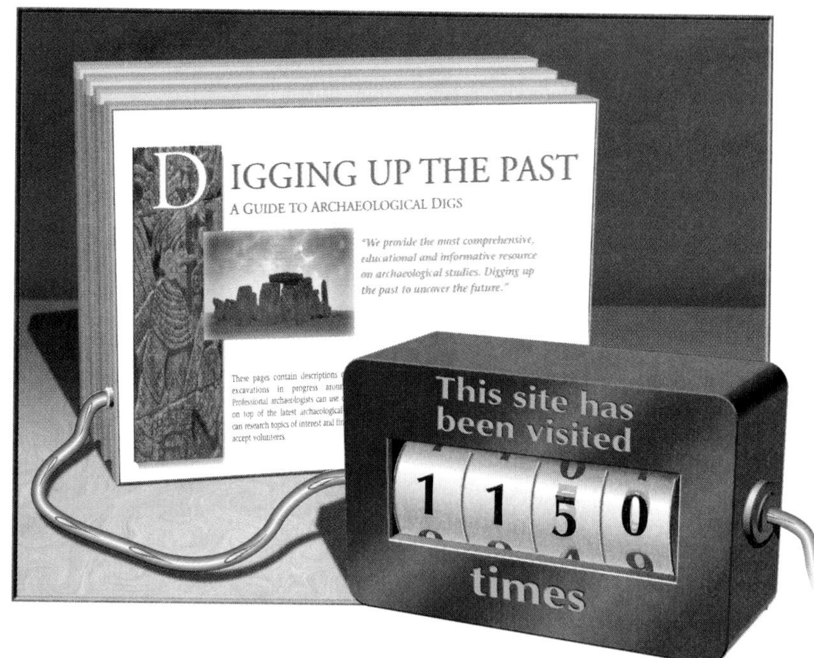

A hit counter displays the number of times a Web page has been viewed. For example, a hit counter will display "50" if one person displays the Web page 50 times or if 50 people view the Web page once.

ADD A HIT COUNTER

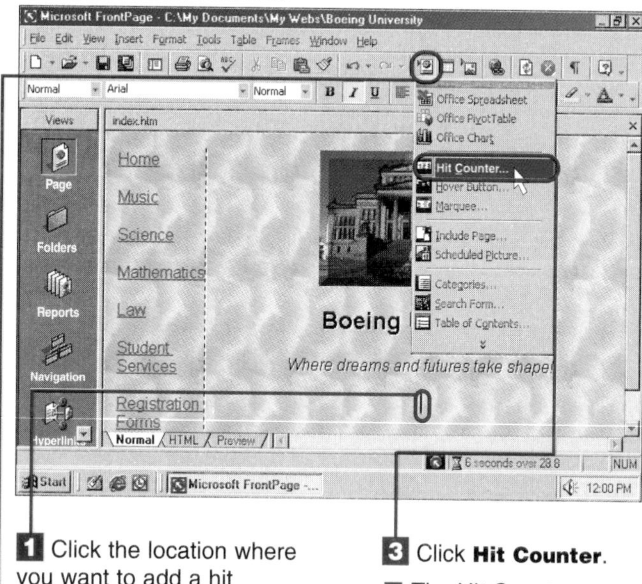

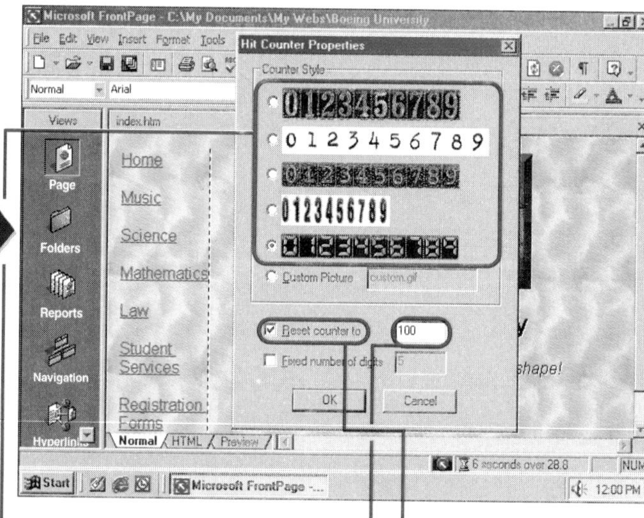

1 Click the location where you want to add a hit counter to your Web page.

2 Click [icon] to display a list of components that you can add to your Web page.

3 Click **Hit Counter**.

■ The Hit Counter Properties dialog box appears.

4 Click the style of hit counter you want to use (○ changes to ⊙).

■ When you add a hit counter to your Web page, the hit counter automatically starts at zero.

5 To start the hit counter at a specific number, click this option (☐ changes to ☑).

6 Double-click this area and type the starting number you want to use.

What should I consider before adding a hit counter to my Web page?

To use a hit counter, your Web server must use FrontPage Server Extensions. You can determine if your Web server uses FrontPage Server Extensions by asking the company that will make your Web pages available on the Web.

Which Web page should I add a hit counter to?

Most people add a hit counter to their home page since this is the first page people will see when they visit the Web site. The home page is named index.htm. You can also add hit counters to other Web pages to determine which pages are the most popular.

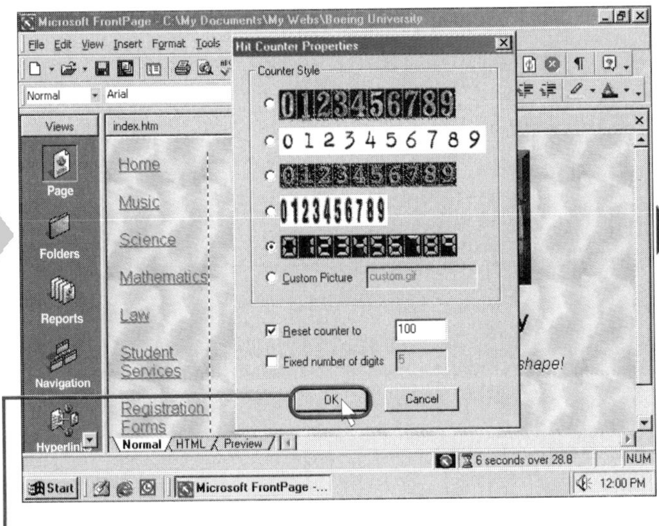

7 Click **OK** to create the hit counter.

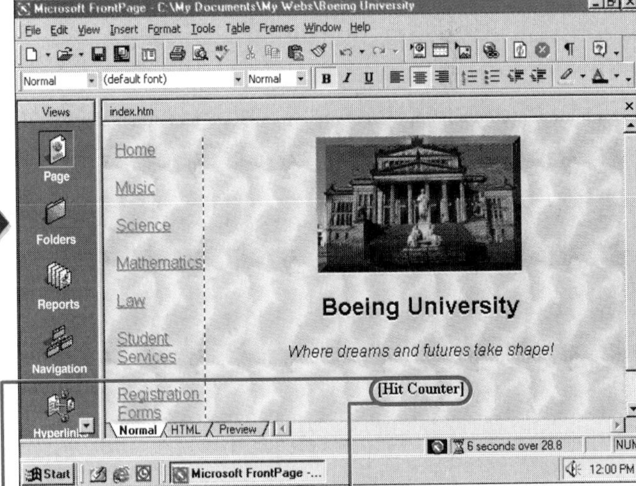

■ The text **[Hit Counter]** appears on your Web page.

■ The hit counter will replace the text when you publish the Web page.

Note: You must publish your Web page before you can view a hit counter.

■ To remove a hit counter, click **[Hit Counter]** and then press the Delete key.

ADD A MARQUEE

You can add a marquee that displays text that moves across a Web page.

The Netscape Navigator Web browser cannot display a marquee properly. The Web browser will display the marquee text, but the text will not move across the Web page.

ADD A MARQUEE

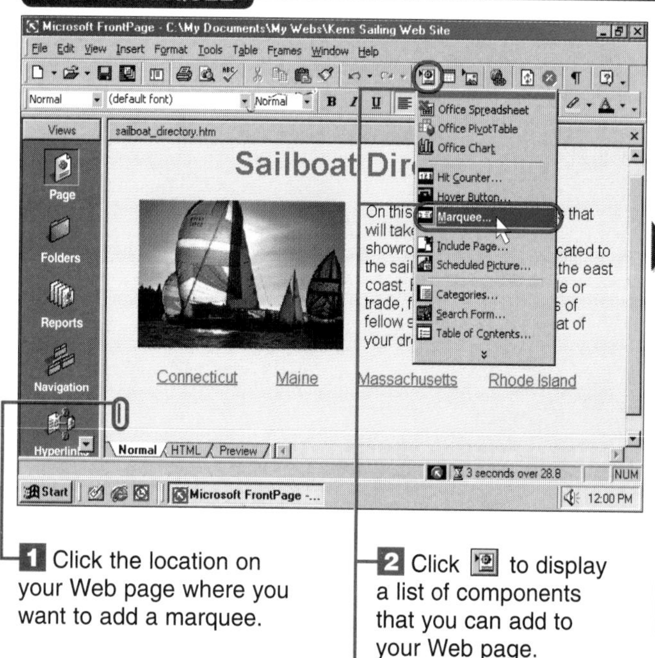

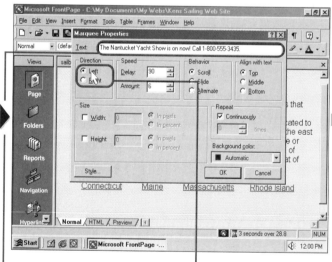

1 Click the location on your Web page where you want to add a marquee.

2 Click [icon] to display a list of components that you can add to your Web page.

3 Click **Marquee**.

■ The Marquee Properties dialog box appears.

4 Type the text you want the marquee to display.

5 Click an option to move the text towards the left or right side of the Web page (○ changes to ⊙).

How can I move a marquee across a Web page?

Scroll

The text appears from one side of the Web page, moves across the screen and then disappears on the other side of the page.

Slide

The text appears from one side of the Web page, moves across the screen and then stops at the other side of the page.

Alternate

The text bounces back and forth between the left and right sides of the Web page.

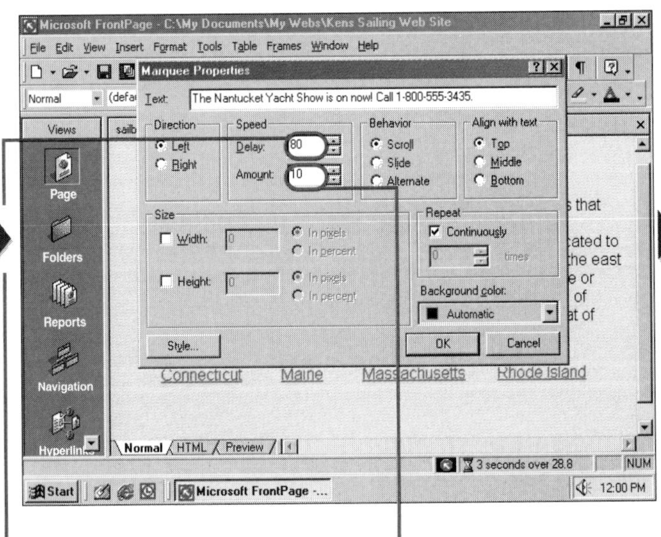

6 Double-click this area and type the number of milliseconds you want to pass between each movement of the marquee across the Web page.

Note: To move the marquee more quickly across the Web page, use smaller numbers.

7 Double-click this area and type the distance in pixels you want the marquee to move each time it moves across the Web page.

Note: To move the marquee more quickly across the Web page, use larger numbers.

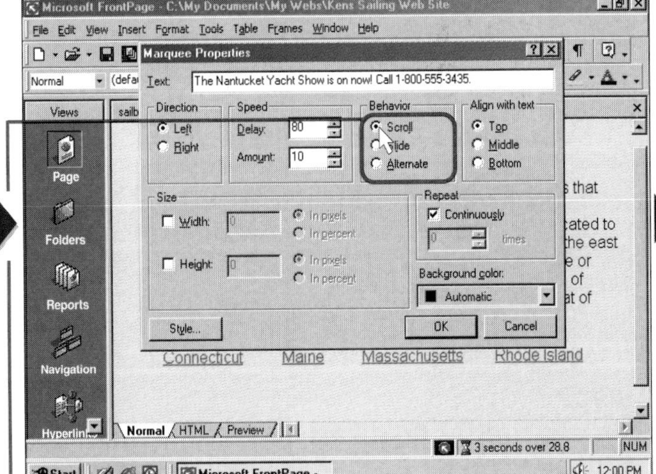

8 Click the way you want to move the marquee across the Web page (○ changes to ⊙).

Note: For information on how you can move the marquee across the Web page, see the top of this page.

CONTINUED

ADD A MARQUEE

You can select a background color that you want to display behind the text for a marquee.

ADD A MARQUEE (CONTINUED)

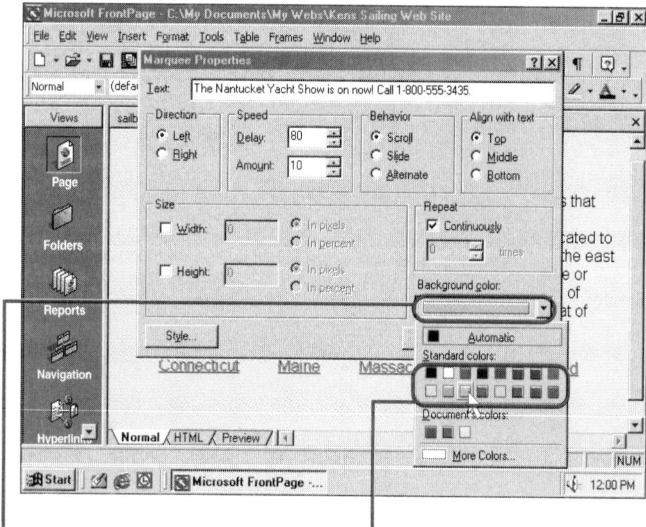

9 Click this area to select the background color you want to display behind the text for the marquee.

10 Click the background color you want to use.

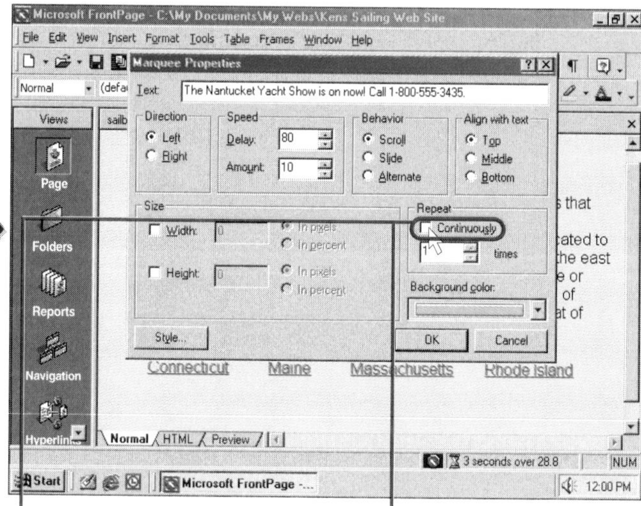

■ This option moves the marquee continuously across the Web page while the page is displayed.

*Note: If you selected Slide in step **8**, this option will not move the marquee continuously across the Web page.*

11 To move the marquee a specific number of times, click this option (☑ changes to ☐).

How do I change or resize a marquee?

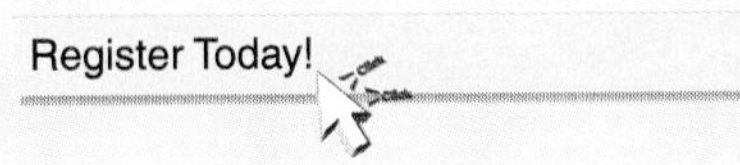

Change a Marquee

To make changes to a marquee, double-click the marquee to redisplay the Marquee Properties dialog box. Then perform steps **4** to **13** starting on page 254 to make changes to the marquee.

Resize a Marquee

You can resize a marquee as you would resize an image on a Web page. To resize an image, see page 104.

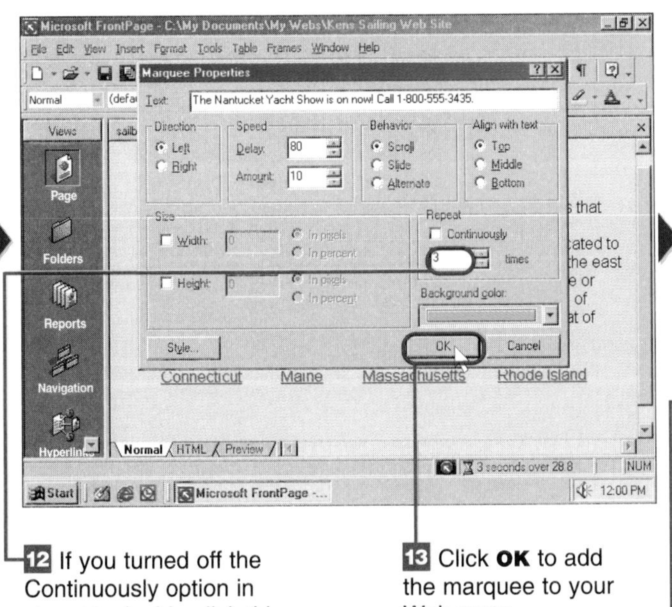

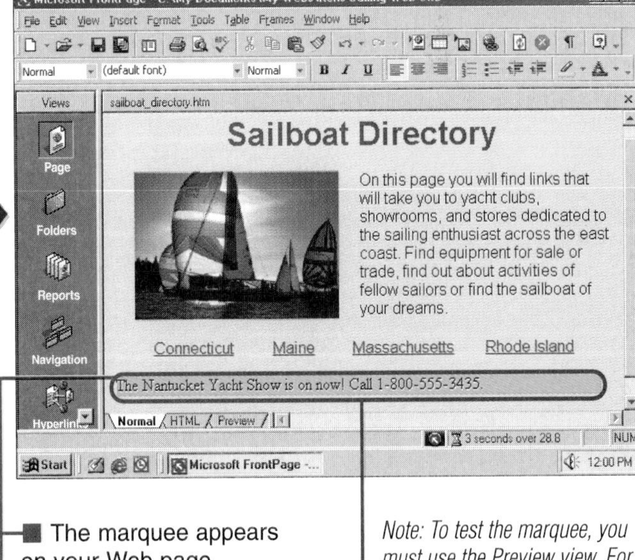

12 If you turned off the Continuously option in step **11**, double-click this area and then type the number of times you want the marquee to move across your Web page.

13 Click **OK** to add the marquee to your Web page.

■ The marquee appears on your Web page.

■ When a reader displays the Web page, the marquee text will move across the page.

Note: To test the marquee, you must use the Preview view. For information on the Preview view, see page 42.

■ To delete a marquee, click the marquee and then press the Delete key.

ADD A HOVER BUTTON

You can create a button that will change appearance when a reader moves the mouse over the button. This is called a hover button.

A hover button is a link that readers can select to display another Web page.

ADD A HOVER BUTTON

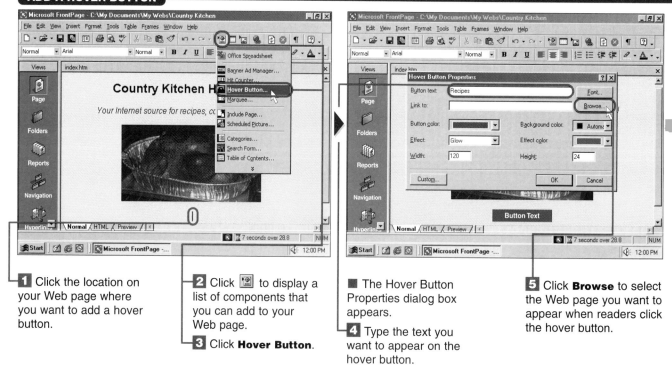

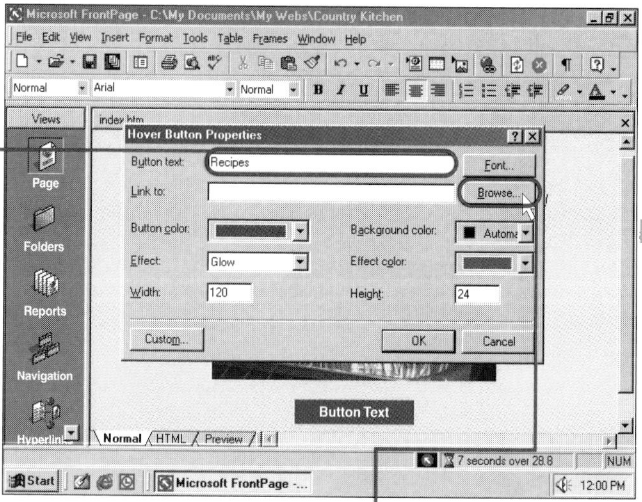

1 Click the location on your Web page where you want to add a hover button.

2 Click [icon] to display a list of components that you can add to your Web page.

3 Click **Hover Button**.

■ The Hover Button Properties dialog box appears.

4 Type the text you want to appear on the hover button.

5 Click **Browse** to select the Web page you want to appear when readers click the hover button.

?

When would I use a hover button?

Hover buttons are useful when you want to make your Web pages more interactive. For example, you can create a hover button for each item in a menu. When a reader moves the mouse over a menu item, the appearance of the item will change. This can help readers determine which menu item they are selecting.

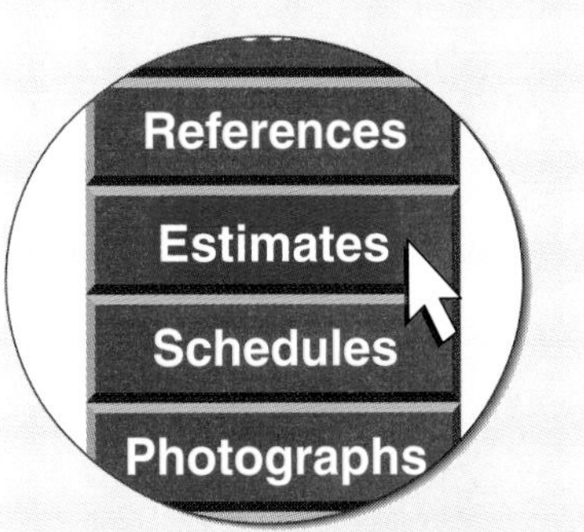

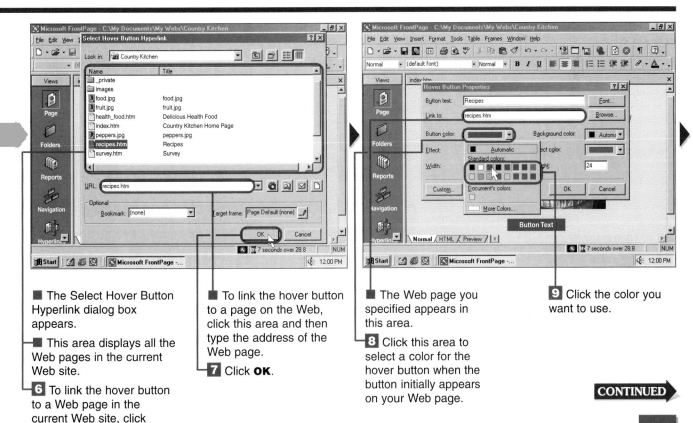

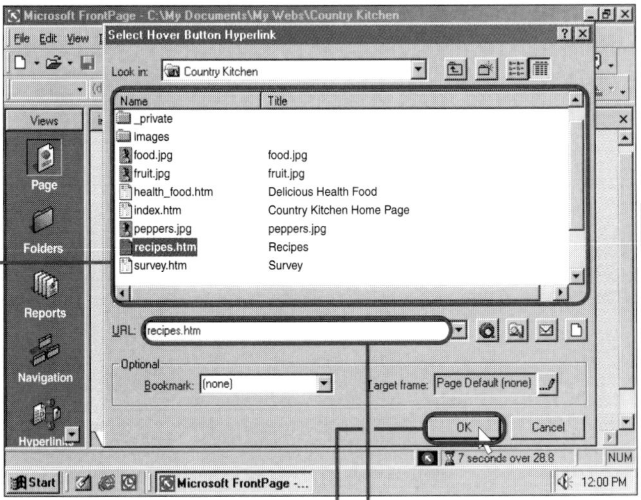

■ The Select Hover Button Hyperlink dialog box appears.

■ This area displays all the Web pages in the current Web site.

6 To link the hover button to a Web page in the current Web site, click the Web page in this area.

■ To link the hover button to a page on the Web, click this area and then type the address of the Web page.

7 Click **OK**.

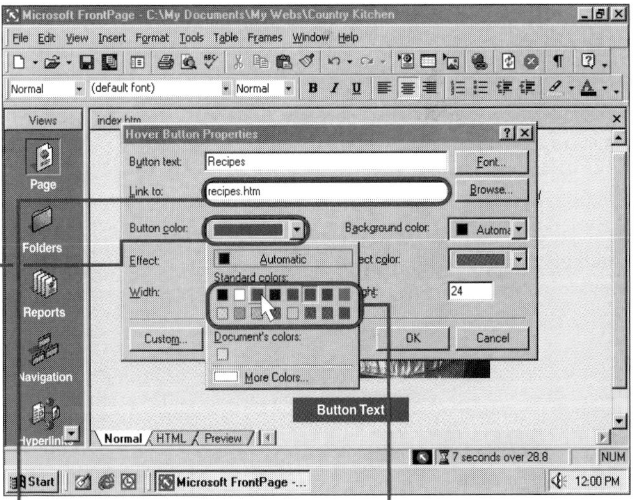

■ The Web page you specified appears in this area.

8 Click this area to select a color for the hover button when the button initially appears on your Web page.

9 Click the color you want to use.

CONTINUED

ADD A HOVER BUTTON

FrontPage allows you to choose from several effects that can occur when a reader moves the mouse over the hover button.

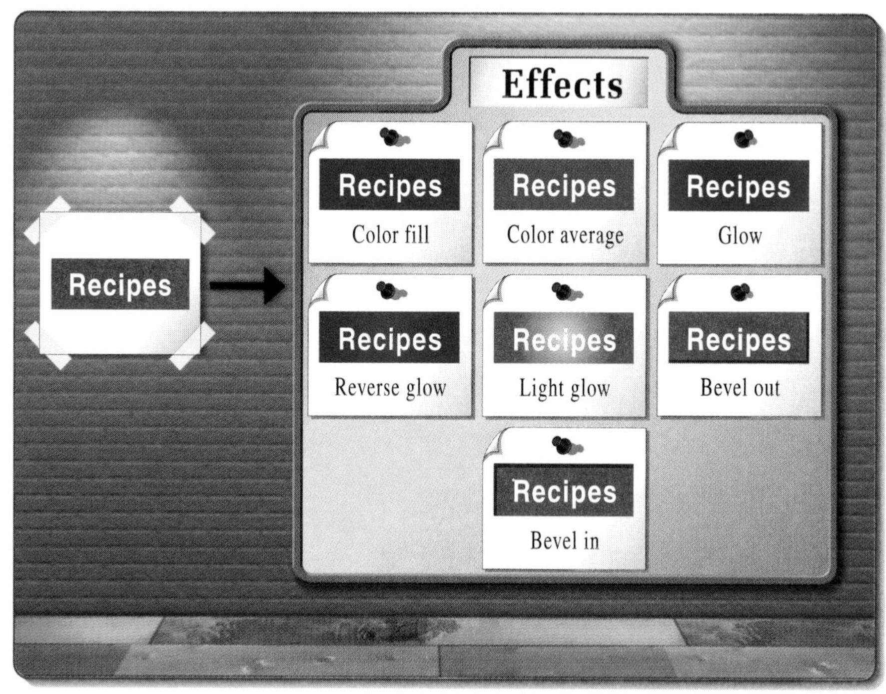

ADD A HOVER BUTTON (CONTINUED)

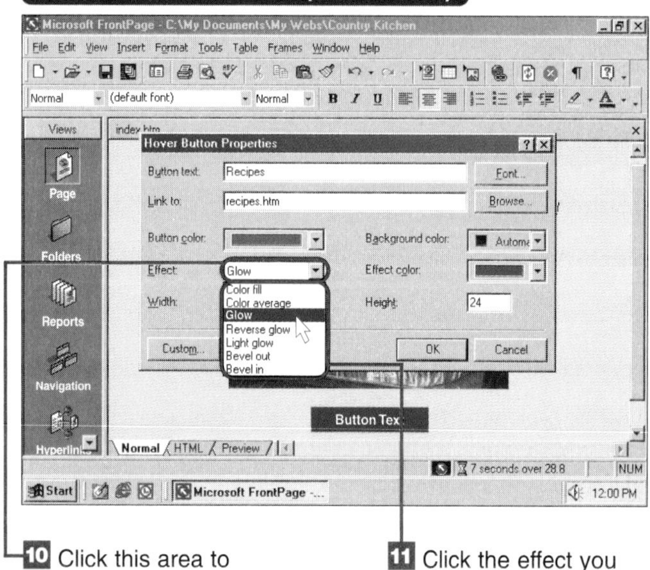

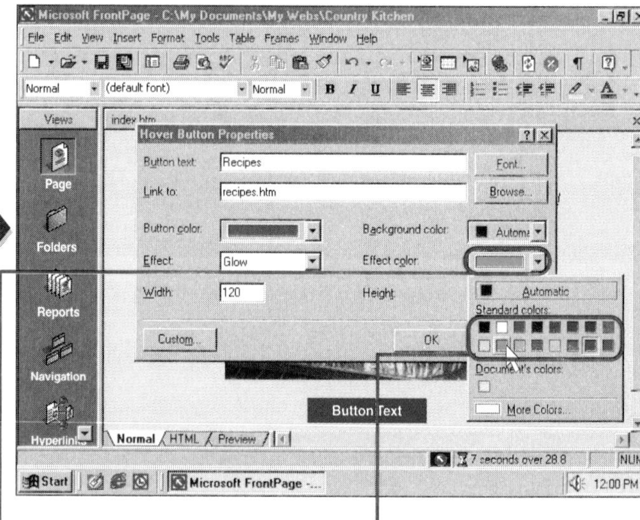

10 Click this area to select the effect you want to occur when a reader moves the mouse over the hover button.

11 Click the effect you want to use.

12 Click this area to select a color for the effect.

*Note: You only need to select a color if you chose the Color fill, Color average, Glow or Reverse glow effect in step **11**.*

13 Click the color you want to use for the effect. Make sure you choose a different color than the color you selected in step **9**.

How do I change, resize or delete a hover button?

Change a Hover Button

To make changes to a hover button, double-click the button to redisplay the Hover Button Properties dialog box. Then perform steps **4** to **14** starting on page 258 to make changes to the button.

Resize a Hover Button

You may need to resize a hover button if the button is not large enough to display the text for the button. You can resize a hover button as you would resize any image on your Web page. To resize an image, see page 104.

Delete a Hover Button

To delete a hover button, click the hover button and then press the Delete key.

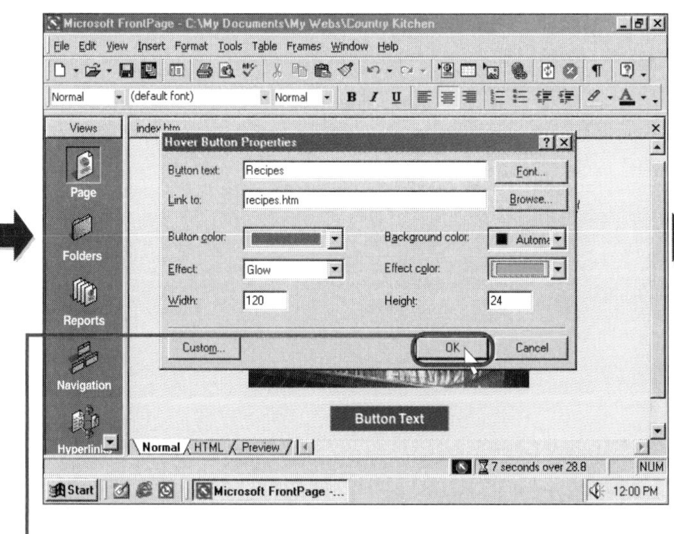

14 Click **OK** to confirm your selections.

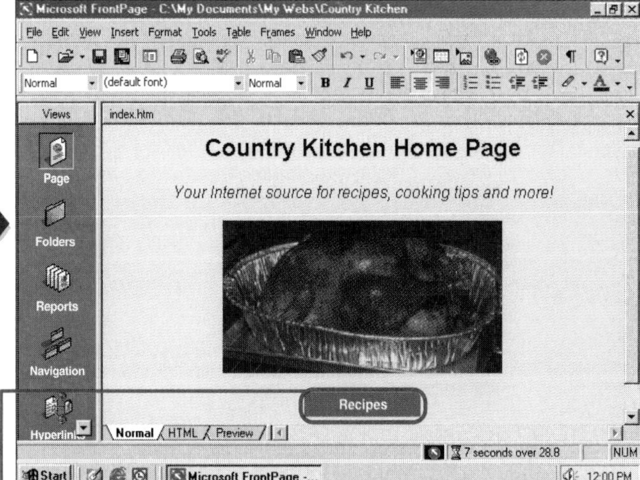

■ When a reader moves the mouse over the hover button, the appearance of the button will change. A reader can click the hover button to display the Web page you specified.

Note: To test the hover button, you must save your Web page and then use the Preview view. To save your Web page, see page 28. For information on the Preview view, see page 42.

ADD A BANNER AD

You can add a banner ad that continuously rotates to display different images on a Web page.

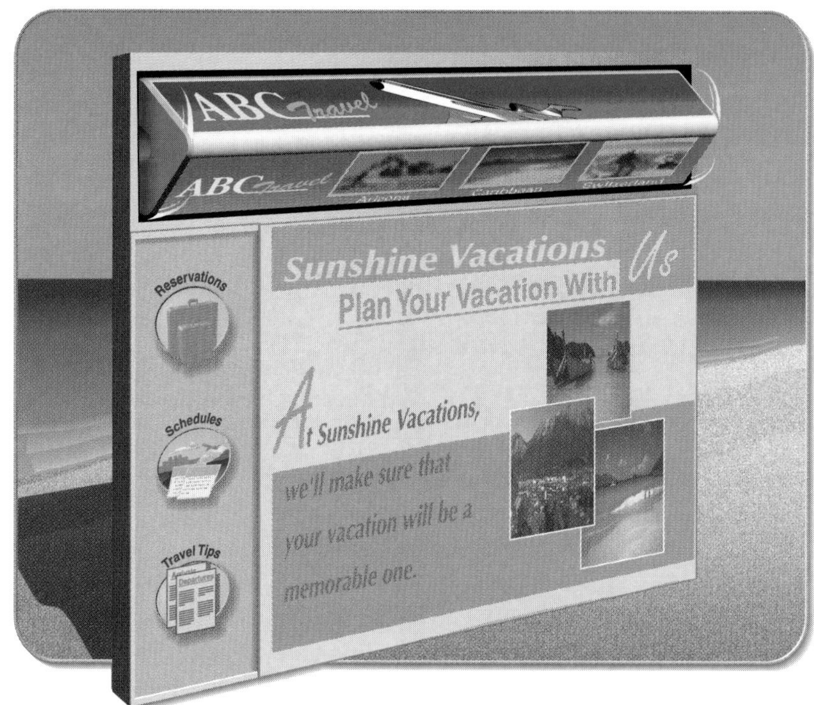

When adding a banner ad, you should use images that are approximately the same size.

ADD A BANNER AD

1 Click the location on your Web page where you want to add a banner ad.

2 Click to display a list of components that you can add to your Web page.

3 Click **Banner Ad Manager**.

Note: If Banner Ad Manager does not appear on the menu, position the mouse over the bottom of the menu to display all the menu commands.

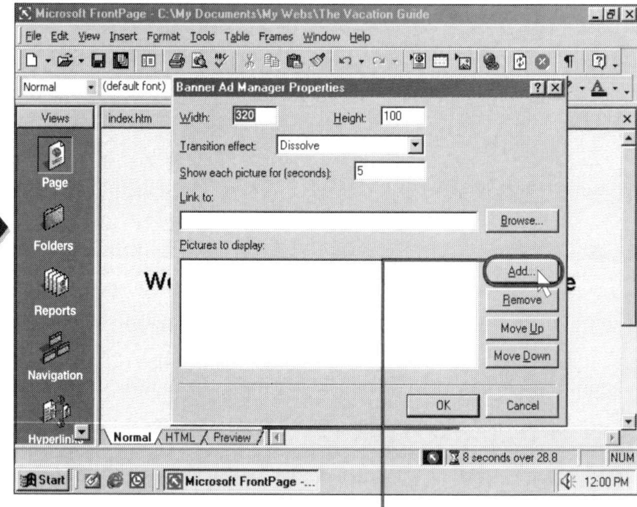

■ The Banner Ad Manager Properties dialog box appears.

4 Click **Add** to select an image that you want to appear on the banner ad.

How can I use a banner ad?

Banner ads are often used to display advertisements on a Web page. Many companies earn money by offering space for advertisements on their Web pages. If another page on the Web discusses ideas related to your Web pages, you can ask the author to include an advertisement for your Web pages if you will do the same. For example, if you are an artist, you can contact the Web sites of local galleries.

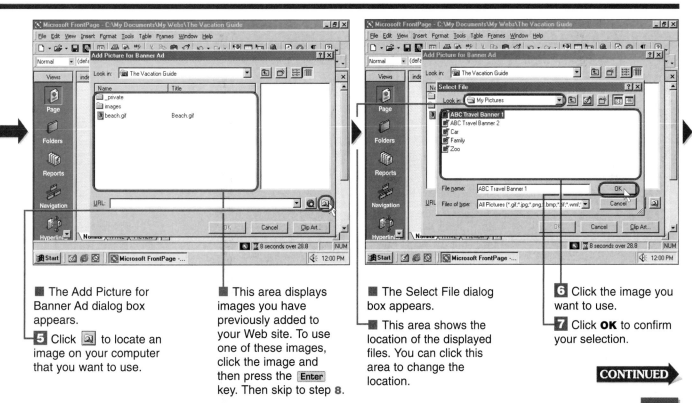

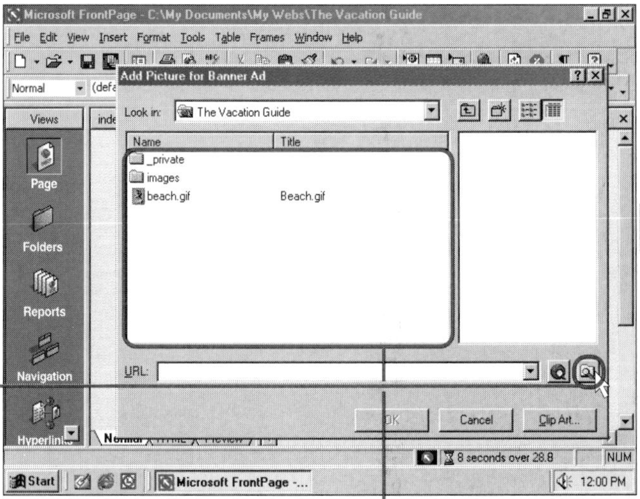

■ The Add Picture for Banner Ad dialog box appears.

5 Click [icon] to locate an image on your computer that you want to use.

■ This area displays images you have previously added to your Web site. To use one of these images, click the image and then press the Enter key. Then skip to step 8.

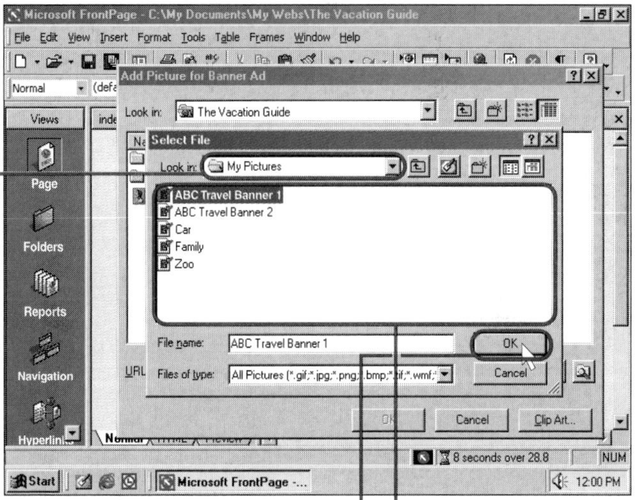

■ The Select File dialog box appears.

■ This area shows the location of the displayed files. You can click this area to change the location.

6 Click the image you want to use.

7 Click **OK** to confirm your selection.

CONTINUED

ADD A BANNER AD

You can create a link to connect a banner ad on a Web page to another page on the Web. When a reader clicks the banner ad, the Web page you specify will appear.

You cannot link each image displayed in a banner ad to a different Web page. Each image must link to the same Web page.

ADD A BANNER AD (CONTINUED)

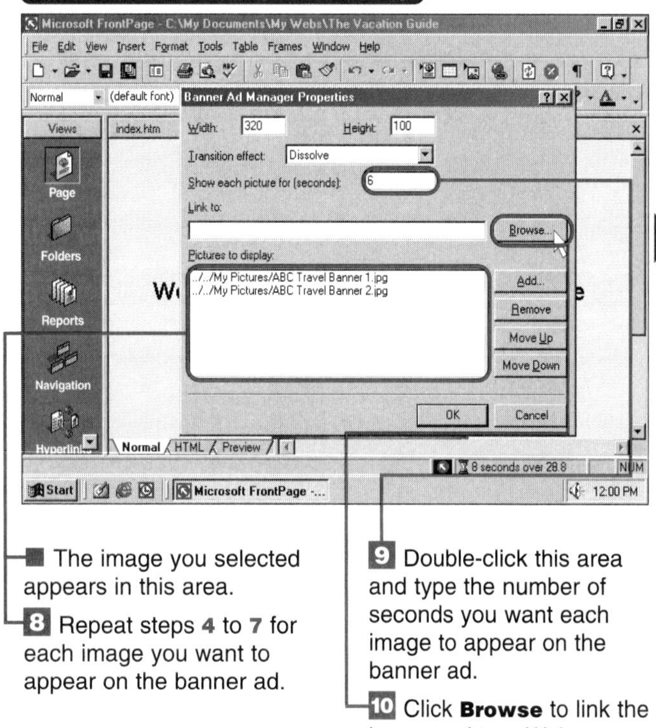

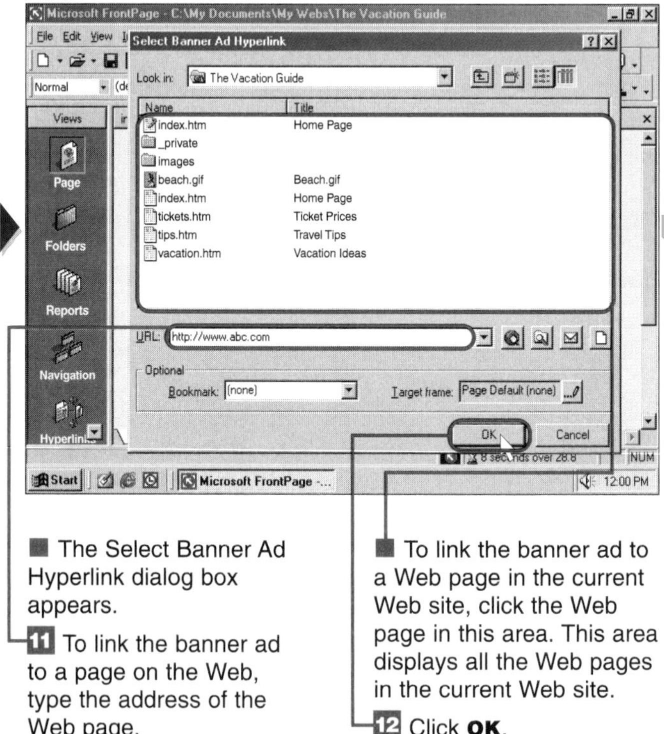

■ The image you selected appears in this area.

8 Repeat steps **4** to **7** for each image you want to appear on the banner ad.

9 Double-click this area and type the number of seconds you want each image to appear on the banner ad.

10 Click **Browse** to link the banner ad to a Web page.

*Note: If you do not want to link the banner ad to a Web page, skip to step **13**.*

■ The Select Banner Ad Hyperlink dialog box appears.

11 To link the banner ad to a page on the Web, type the address of the Web page.

■ To link the banner ad to a Web page in the current Web site, click the Web page in this area. This area displays all the Web pages in the current Web site.

12 Click **OK**.

What is a transition effect?

A transition effect determines how one image moves to the next image on your banner ad. FrontPage offers the Blinds Horizontal, Blinds Vertical, Dissolve, Box In and Box Out transition effects.

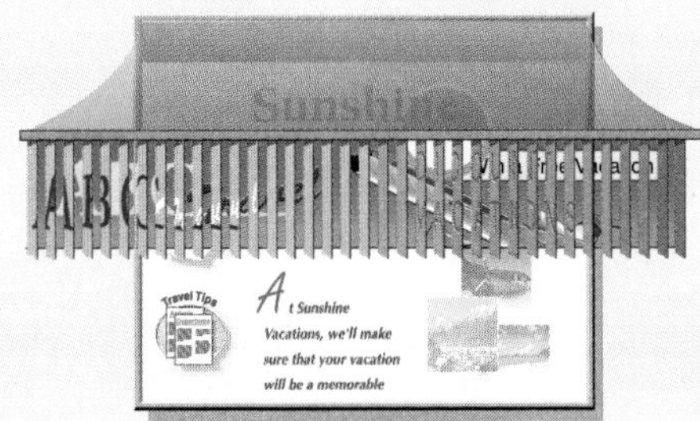

Blinds Vertical

How do I change or resize a banner ad?

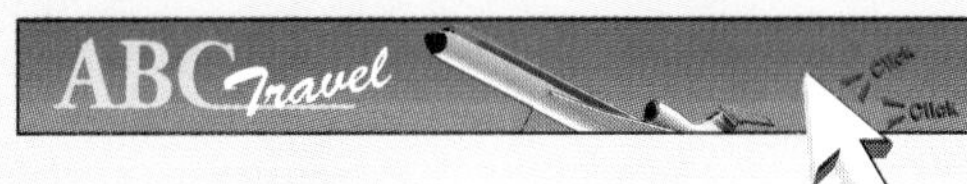

Change a Banner Ad

To make changes to a banner ad, double-click the banner ad to redisplay the Banner Ad Manager Properties dialog box. Then perform steps **9** to **15** below to make changes to the banner ad.

Resize a Banner Ad

You can resize a banner ad as you would resize any image on your Web page. To resize an image, see page 104.

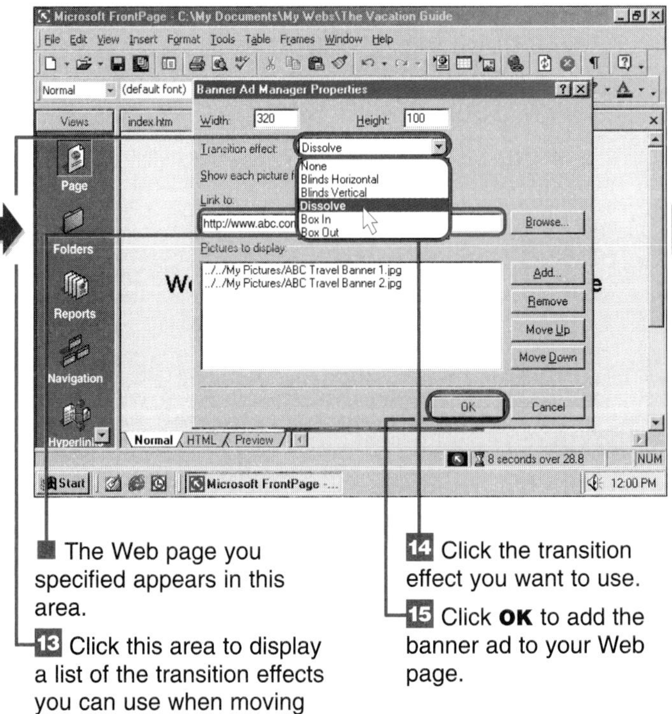

- The Web page you specified appears in this area.

13 Click this area to display a list of the transition effects you can use when moving from one image to another.

14 Click the transition effect you want to use.

15 Click **OK** to add the banner ad to your Web page.

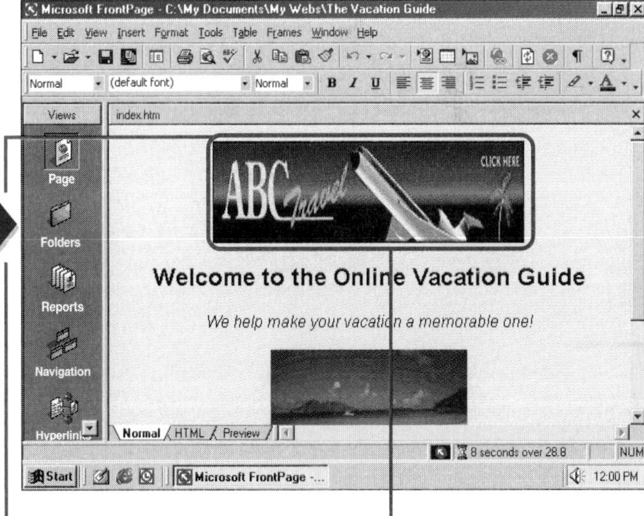

- The banner ad appears on your Web page.

Note: To test the banner ad, you must display the Web page in a Web browser. To display a Web page in a Web browser, see page 44.

- To delete a banner ad, click the banner ad and then press the Delete key.

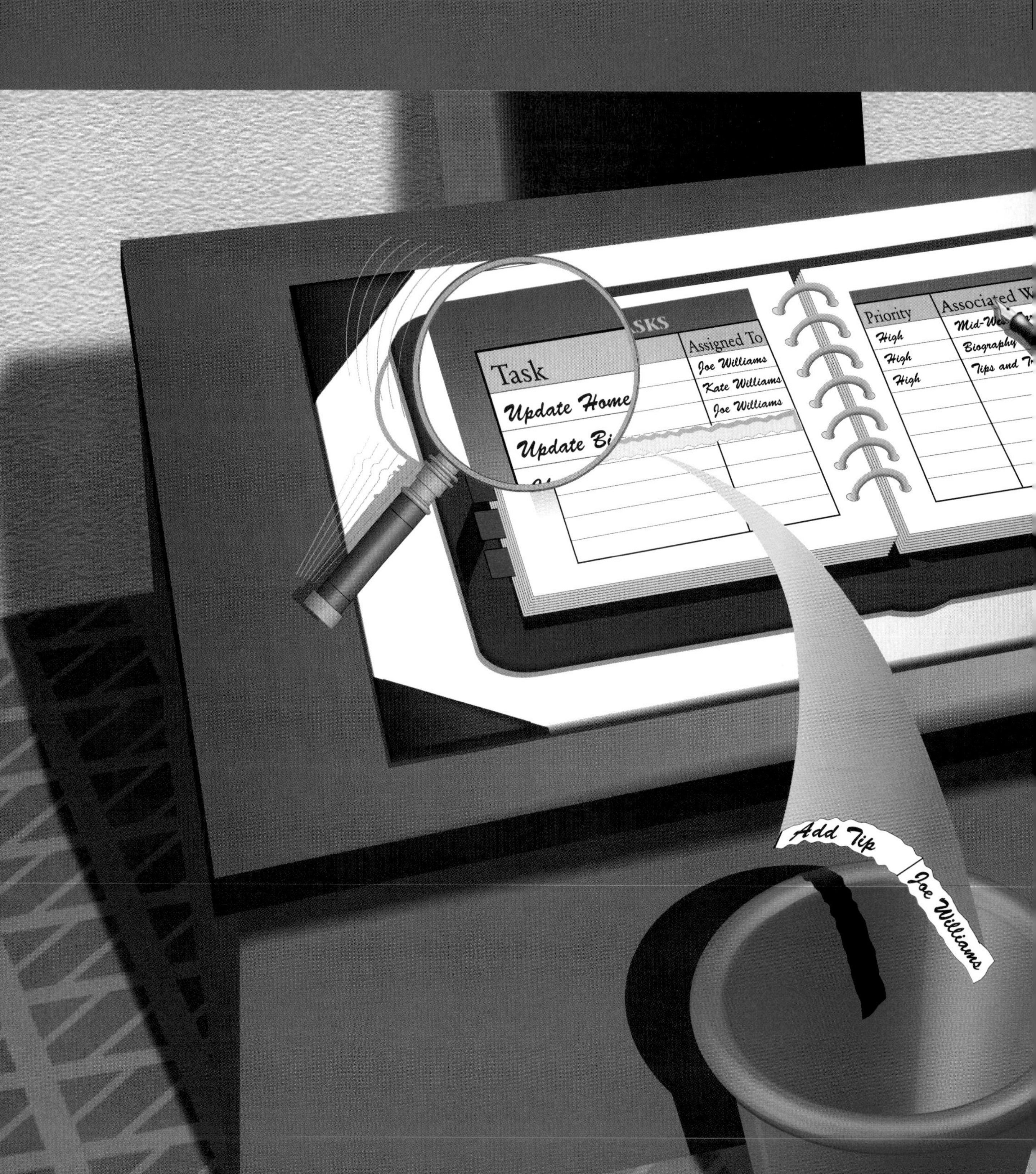

Task
Update Home
Assigned To
Joe Williams
Kate Williams
Joe Williams
Priority
High
High
High
Biography
Add Tip
Joe Williams

CHAPTER 14

Manage Web Pages

Do you want to keep track of your Web site's progress? This chapter shows you how to create and work with tasks, use reports and more.

CREATE A NEW FOLDER

You can create a new folder to help you organize the files in your Web site.

For example, you can create a folder named multimedia to store all your sounds and videos.

FrontPage automatically creates the private and images folders for you. The private folder stores files you do not want readers to view. The images folder can be used to store images.

CREATE A NEW FOLDER

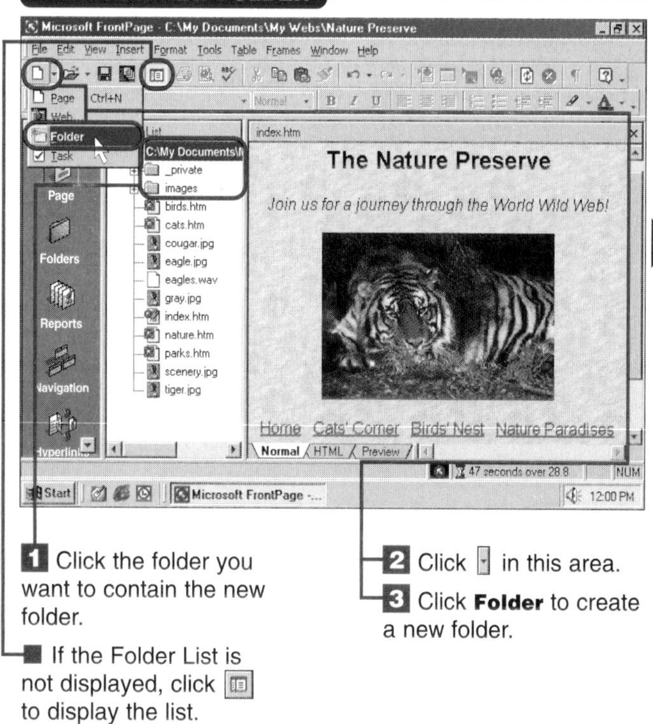

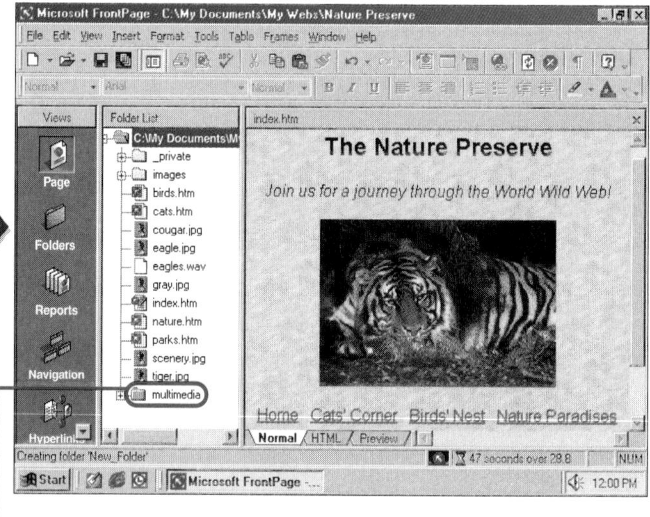

1 Click the folder you want to contain the new folder.

■ If the Folder List is not displayed, click ▤ to display the list.

2 Click ▾ in this area.

3 Click **Folder** to create a new folder.

■ The new folder appears. Folders display the ▭ symbol.

4 Type a name for the new folder and then press the Enter key.

*Note: To delete a folder you created, click the folder and then press the Delete key. A dialog box will appear to confirm the deletion. Click **Yes** to delete the folder.*

MOVE A FILE TO A FOLDER

You can move a file to a folder in your Web site. This allows you to place related files in the same location.

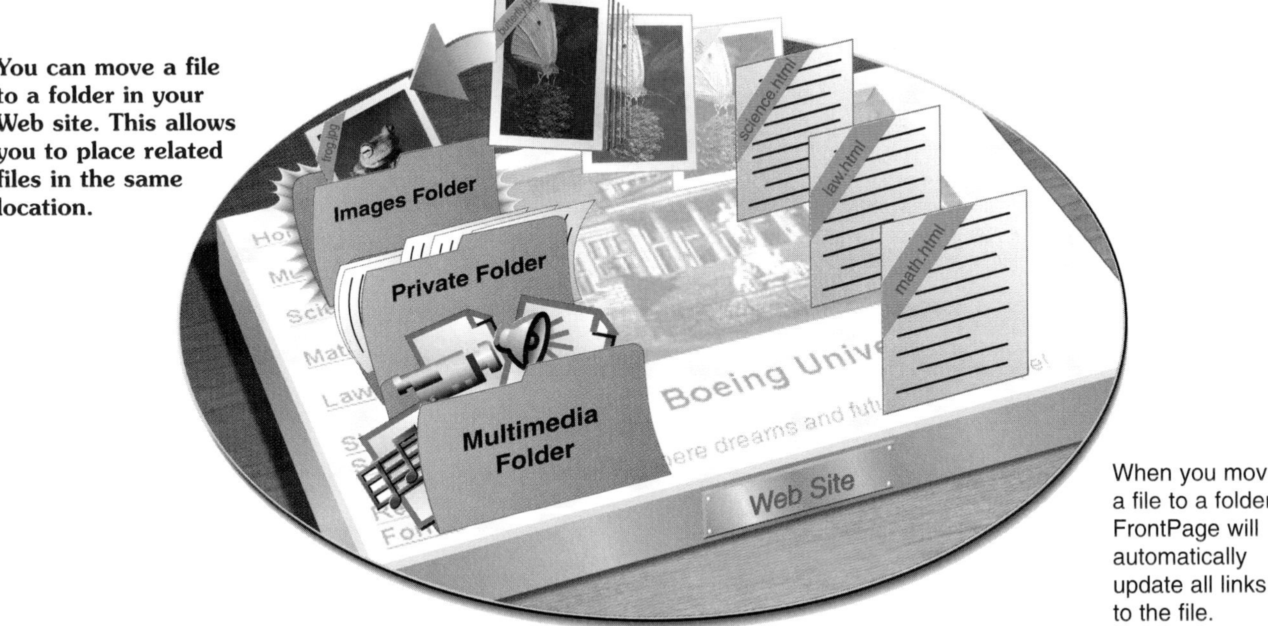

When you move a file to a folder, FrontPage will automatically update all links to the file.

MOVE A FILE TO A FOLDER

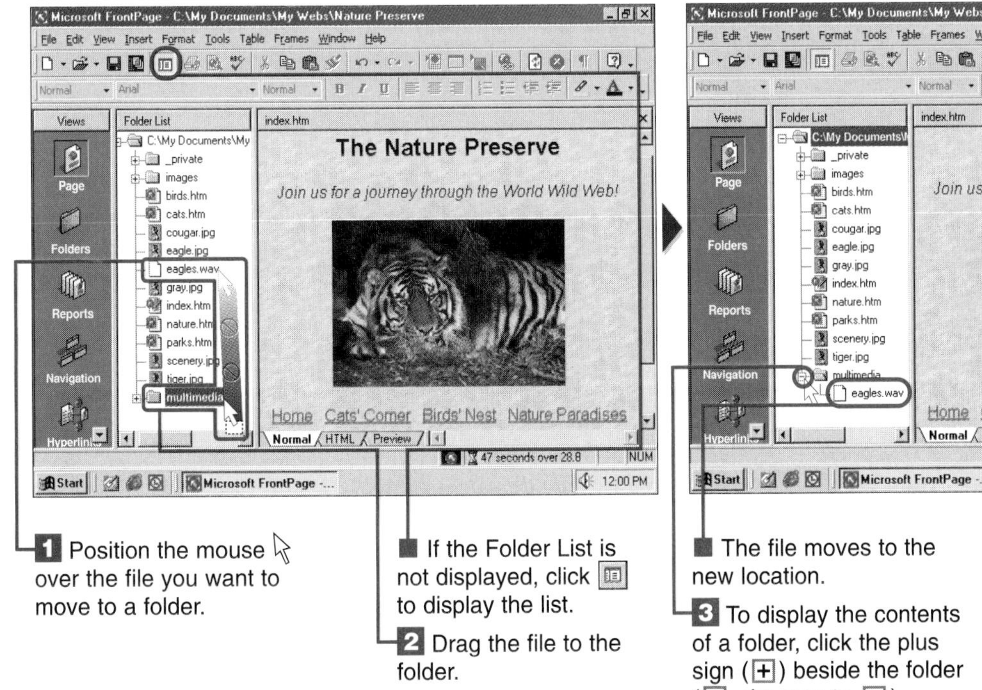

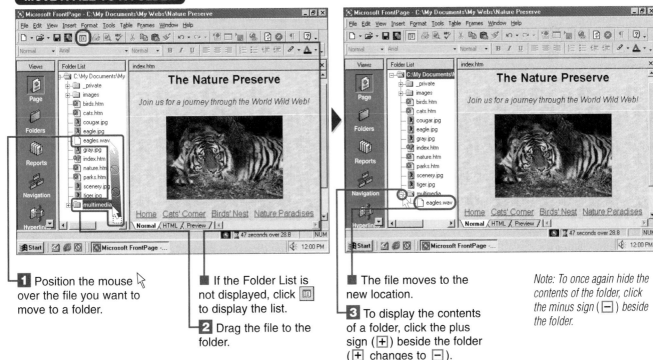

1 Position the mouse over the file you want to move to a folder.

■ If the Folder List is not displayed, click ▣ to display the list.

2 Drag the file to the folder.

■ The file moves to the new location.

3 To display the contents of a folder, click the plus sign (⊞) beside the folder (⊞ changes to ⊟).

Note: To once again hide the contents of the folder, click the minus sign (⊟) beside the folder.

ADD A TASK

You can create a to-do list to keep track of Web pages you need to work on.

You can add a task to remind you to add, update, review or confirm information on a Web page at a later time.

You can associate each task you add with a specific Web page.

ADD A TASK

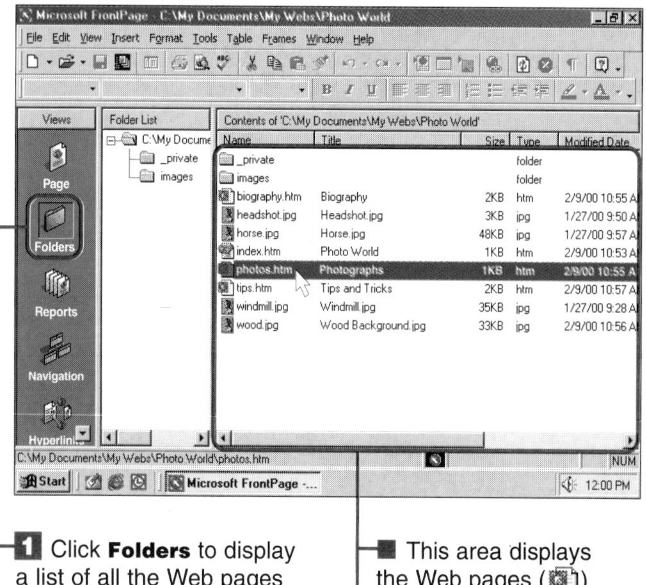

1 Click **Folders** to display a list of all the Web pages in your Web site.

■ This area displays the Web pages ( ) and images ( ) in your Web site.

2 Click the Web page you want to associate with a task.

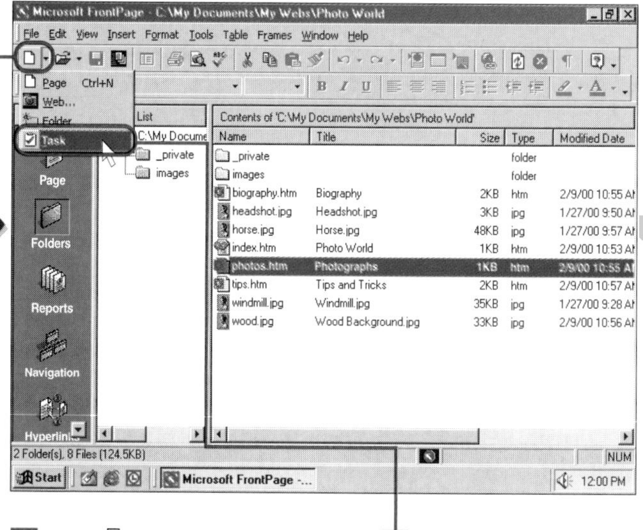

3 Click in this area.

4 Click **Task**.

Can I add a task that is not associated with a specific Web page?

Yes. This is useful if you have a task that relates to more than one Web page, such as a task for verifying all of the phone numbers that appear on your Web pages.

To add a task that is not associated with a specific Web page, click the **Tasks** icon and then perform steps **3** to **8** below.

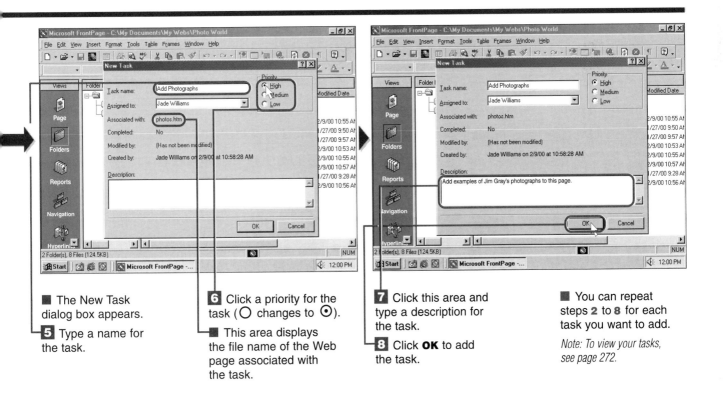

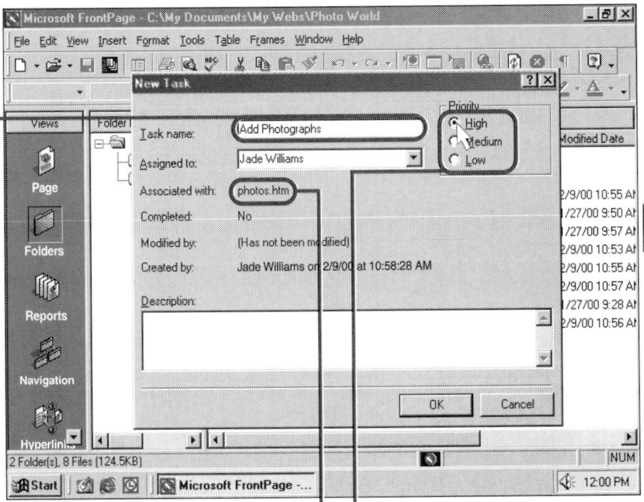

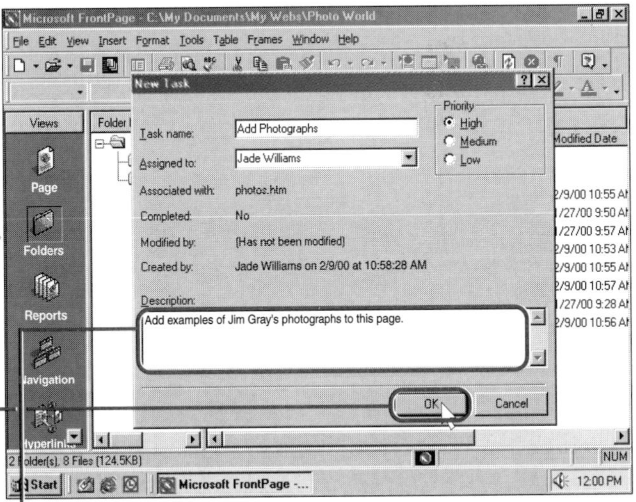

■ The New Task dialog box appears.

5 Type a name for the task.

6 Click a priority for the task (○ changes to ⊙).

■ This area displays the file name of the Web page associated with the task.

7 Click this area and type a description for the task.

8 Click **OK** to add the task.

■ You can repeat steps **2** to **8** for each task you want to add.

Note: To view your tasks, see page 272.

VIEW TASKS

You can view a list of all the tasks you have added to your Web site. Tasks help you keep track of Web pages you need to work on.

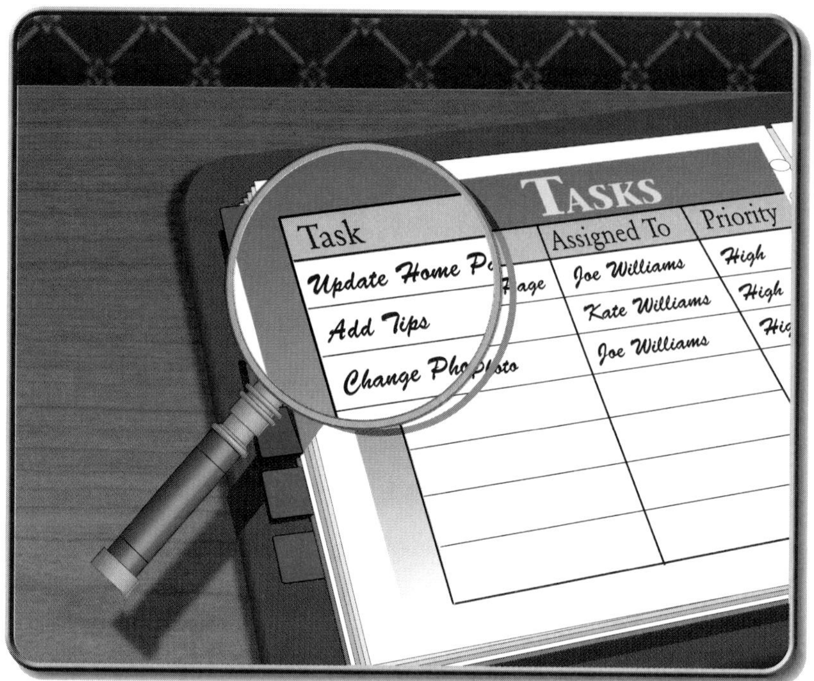

VIEW TASKS

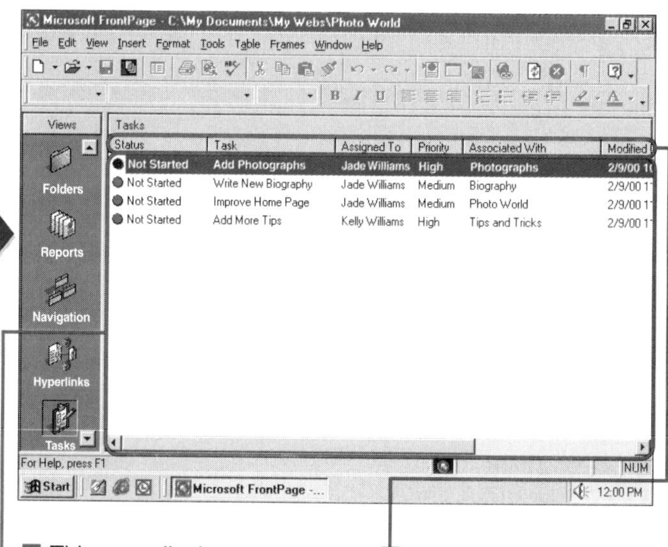

1 Click **Tasks** to view the tasks you have added to your Web site.

■ If the Tasks icon is not displayed, click ▾ to display the icon.

■ This area displays information about each task, such as the name, priority and Web page associated with the task.

■ To view the tasks in a different order, click the heading of the column you want to use to sort the tasks.

Note: You can click the heading of the column again to sort the tasks in the opposite order.

EDIT A TASK

You can change the information you specified for a task, such as providing a more accurate name or more detailed description for the task.

EDIT A TASK

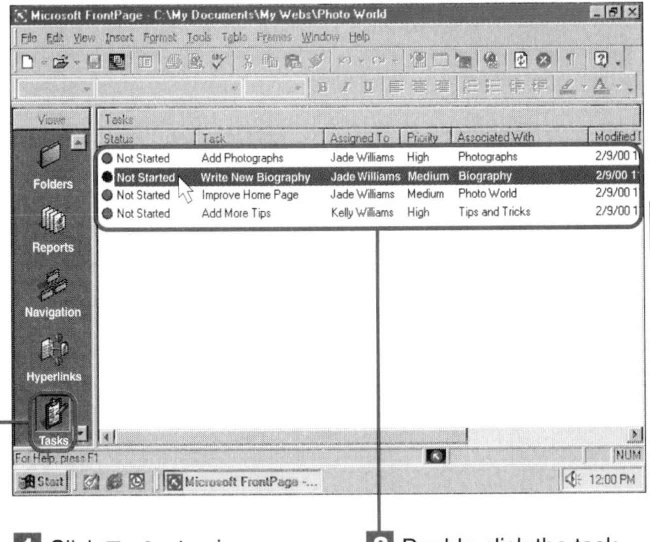

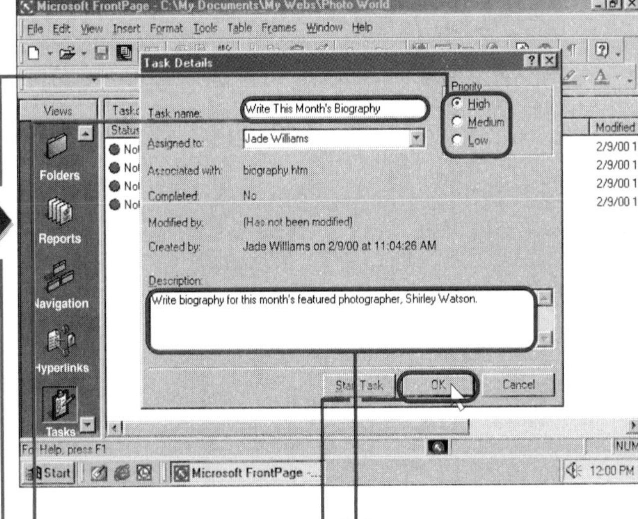

1 Click **Tasks** to view the tasks you have added to your Web site.

2 Double-click the task you want to change.

■ The Task Details dialog box appears.

3 To change the name of the task, type a new name.

4 To change the priority of the task, click a different priority (○ changes to ⊙).

5 To change the description of the task, drag the mouse I over the existing text until you highlight the text. Then type a new description.

6 Click **OK** to save your changes.

START A TASK

You can start a task that you associated with a specific Web page.

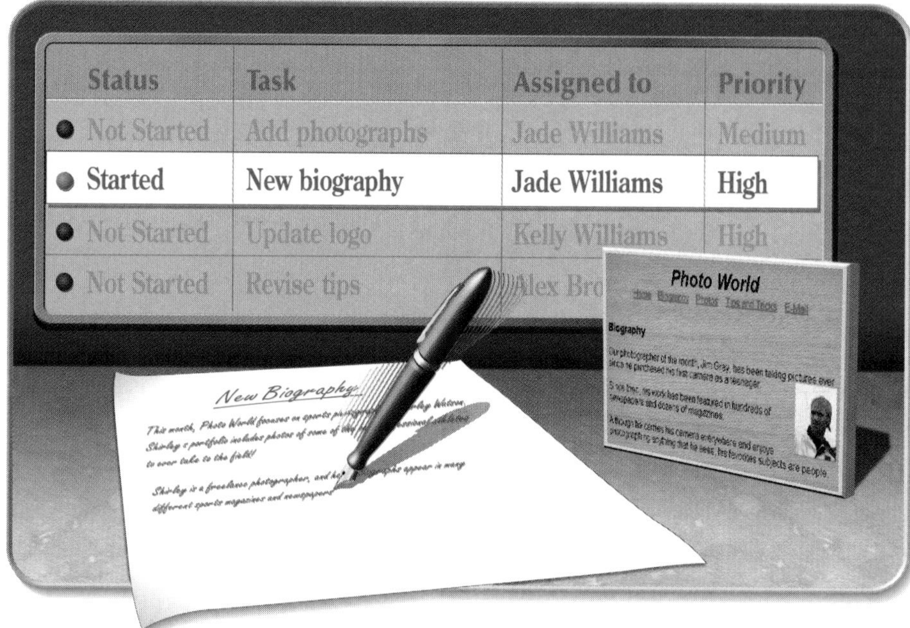

Status
Task
Assigned to
Priority
Not Started
Add photographs
Jade Williams
Medium
Started
New biography
Jade Williams
High
Not Started
Update logo
Kelly Williams
High
Not Started
Revise tips
Photo World
Biography
New Biography

You cannot start a task that you did not associate with a specific Web page.

START A TASK

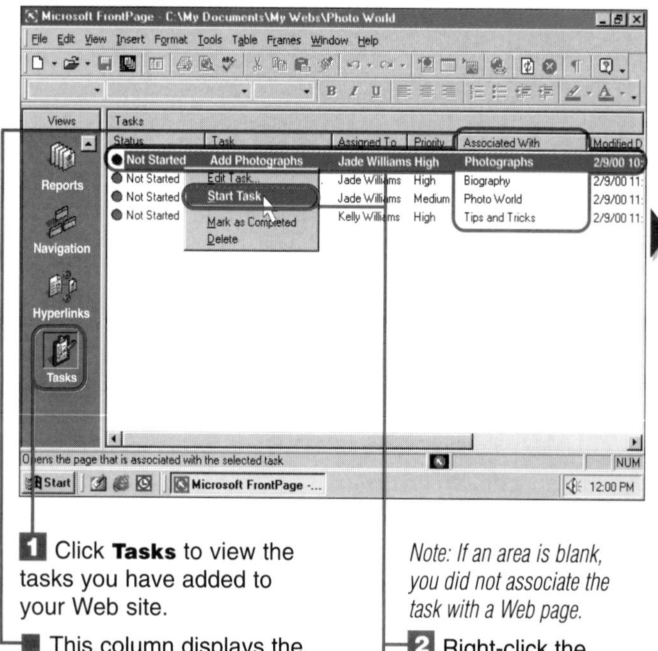

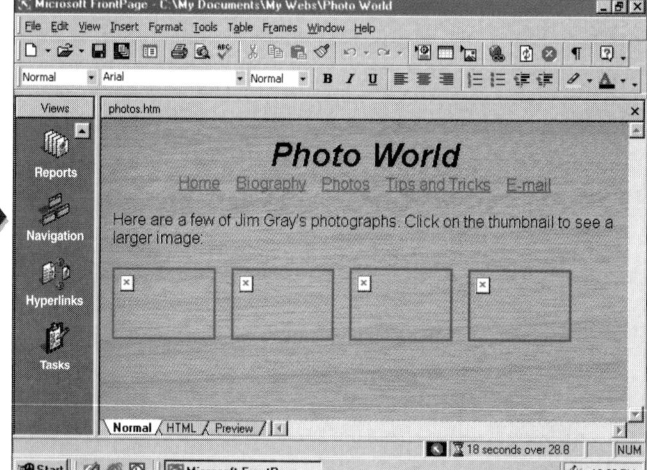

1 Click **Tasks** to view the tasks you have added to your Web site.

■ This column displays the Web page you associated with each task.

Note: If an area is blank, you did not associate the task with a Web page.

2 Right-click the task you want to start. A menu appears.

3 Click **Start Task**.

■ The Web page associated with the task appears in the Page view.

■ You can now work on the task.

DELETE A TASK

You can delete a task you have completed to keep your list of tasks up to date.

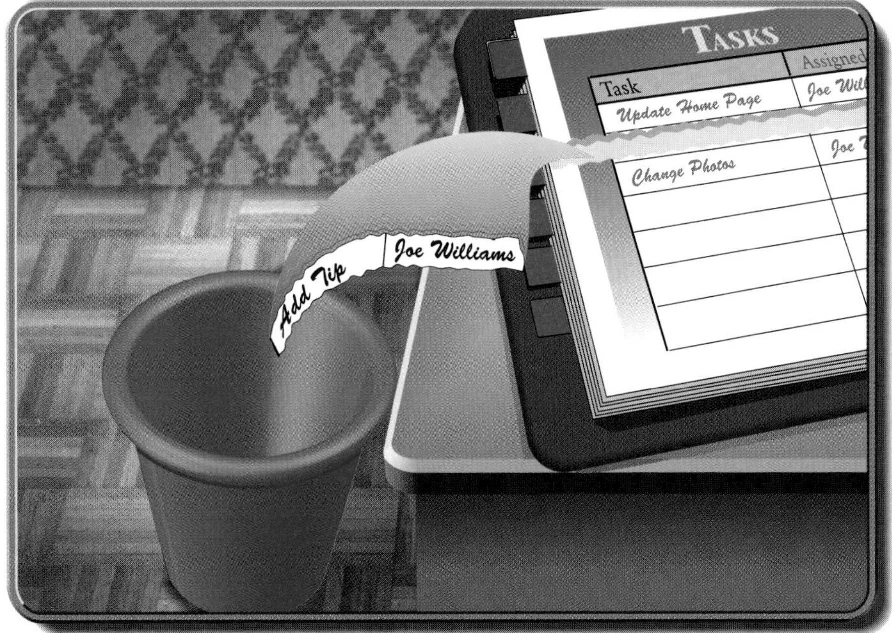

DELETE A TASK

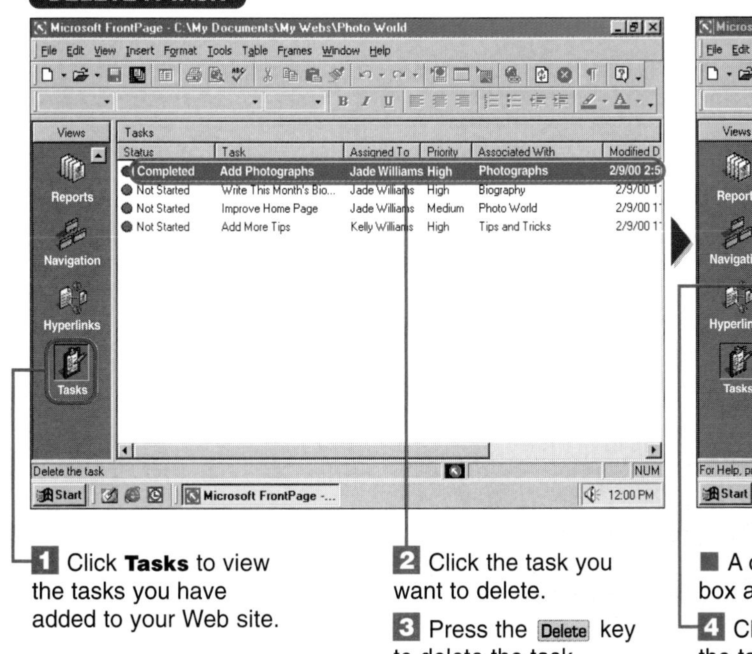

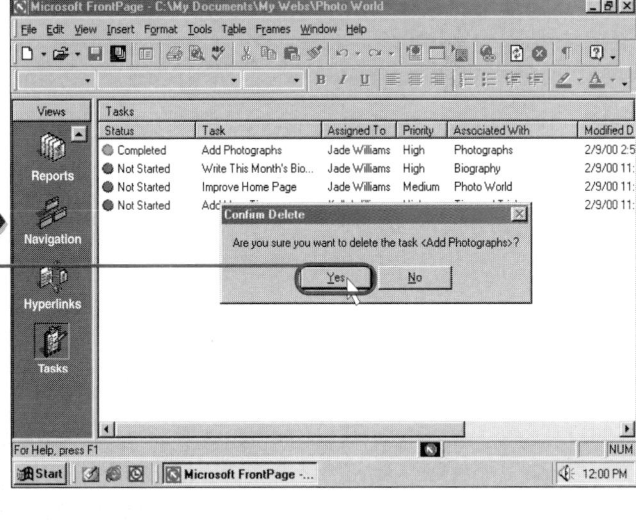

1 Click **Tasks** to view the tasks you have added to your Web site.

2 Click the task you want to delete.

3 Press the Delete key to delete the task.

■ A confirmation dialog box appears.

4 Click **Yes** to delete the task.

■ The task disappears from the list of tasks.

USING REPORTS

You can use the Reports view to display various reports that analyze and summarize information about your Web site.

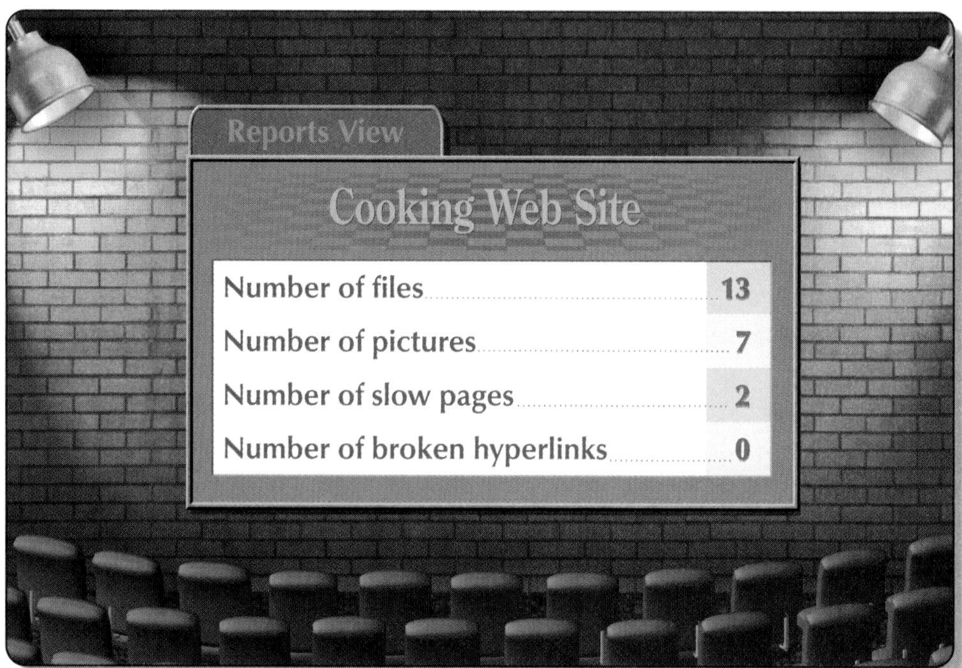

USING REPORTS

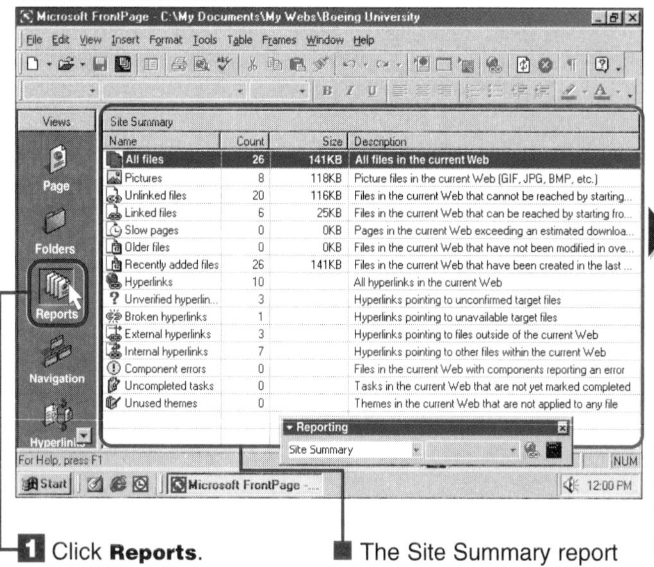

1 Click **Reports**.

■ The Site Summary report appears in this area. This report provides an overview of your Web site, including the total size of all the files in the Web site and the total number of images in the Web site.

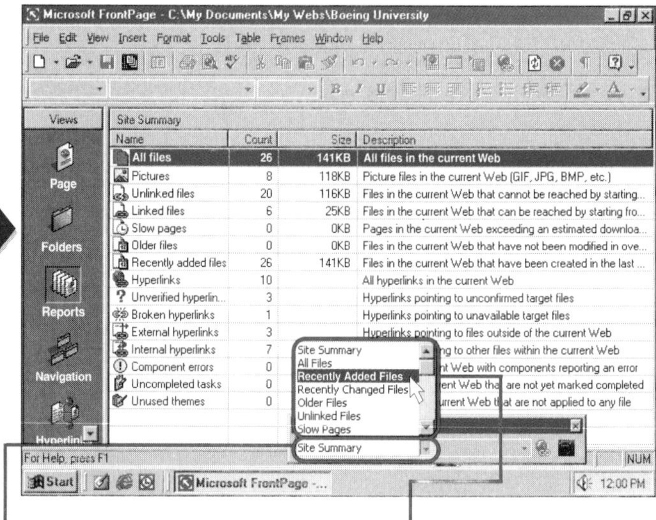

2 To display a different report, click this area.

Note: If the Reporting toolbar is not displayed, see page 30 to display the toolbar.

3 Click the report you want to display.

Note: You may need to scroll through the list to find the report you want to display.

What reports does FrontPage offer?

Here are some reports that FrontPage offers to help you review and analyze the information in your Web site.

Report	Description
Site Summary	Provides an overview of your Web site.
All Files	Displays information about each file in your Web site.
Recently Added Files	Displays files created in the last 30 days.
Recently Changed Files	Displays files changed in the last 30 days.
Older Files	Displays files you have not changed in the last 72 days.
Unlinked Files	Displays files you cannot access from your home page.
Slow Pages	Displays Web pages that may take at least 1 second to download when using a 28.8 Kb/s modem.
Broken Hyperlinks	Displays the status of the links in your Web site.

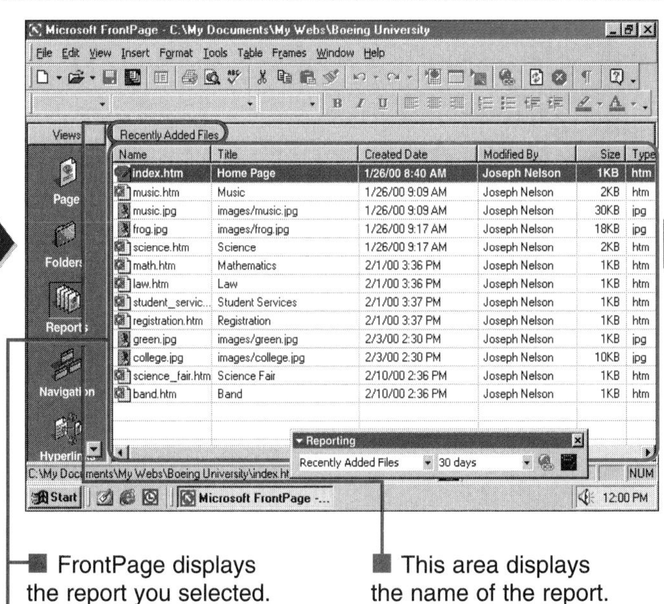

■ FrontPage displays the report you selected.

■ In this example, the Recently Added Files report appears. This report shows information about the files you created in the last 30 days.

■ This area displays the name of the report.

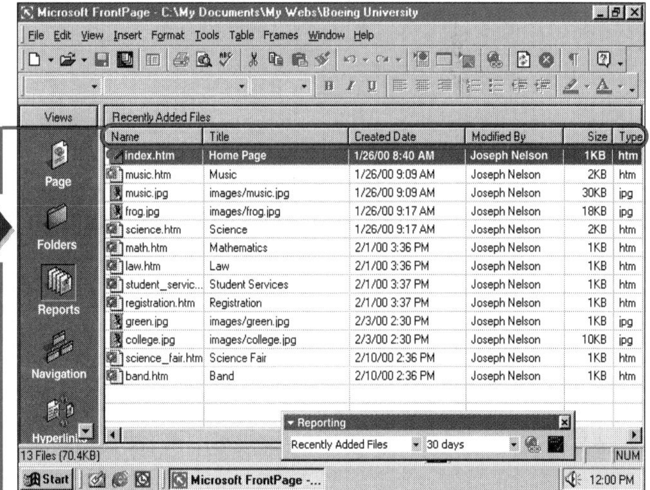

■ To view the files in a different order, click the heading of the column you want to use to sort the files.

Note: You can click the heading of the column again to sort the files in the opposite order.

Welcome To The
SMITH FAMILY
Web Page
Our Latest Addition
We are pleased to announce there's a new addition to our family. His name is Jack and he was born nine months ago! He is our first child and has brought us nothing but happiness since he arrived.
About Us
We are Jason & Brenda Smith, owners of a 50 acre horse farm. We breed thoroughbred horses and enjoy showing them at national horse shows.
E-mail
ISP INTERNET SERVICE PROVIDER
Service Provider
ISP

CHAPTER 15

Publish Web Pages

Are you ready to publish your Web pages? This chapter will show you how.

INTRODUCTION TO WEB PRESENCE PROVIDERS

Web presence providers are companies that store Web pages and make them available on the Web.

Web presence providers store Web pages on computers called Web servers. Web servers store, monitor and control access to Web pages.

INTERNET SERVICE PROVIDERS

Internet service providers are companies that offer people access to the Internet. Most Internet service providers offer space on their Web servers where customers can publish their Web pages free of charge.

COMMERCIAL ONLINE SERVICES

Commercial online services such as America Online will publish Web pages created by customers for free. Many commercial online services offer easy-to-use programs to help people create and publish Web pages.

FREE WEB PRESENCE PROVIDERS

Many companies on the Web will publish your Web pages for free. These companies offer a limited amount of storage space and may place advertisements on your Web pages.

You can find companies that will publish your Web pages for free at the following Web sites:

geocities.yahoo.com

www.tripod.lycos.com

xoom.com

DEDICATED WEB PRESENCE PROVIDERS

Dedicated Web presence providers are companies that specialize in publishing Web pages for a fee. Dedicated Web presence providers are flexible and offer features that other Web presence providers do not offer.

You can find dedicated Web presence providers at the following Web sites:

www.dreamhost.com

www.hostess.com

www.pair.com

YOUR OWN WEB SERVER

Purchasing your own Web server is the most expensive way to publish Web pages and requires a full-time connection to the Internet. Setting up and maintaining your own Web server is difficult but will give you the greatest amount of control over your Web pages.

CHOOSE A WEB PRESENCE PROVIDER

You should consider several factors when choosing a Web presence provider to publish your Web pages.

TECHNICAL SUPPORT

A Web presence provider should have a technical support department to answer your questions. You should be able to contact the department by telephone or e-mail. A good technical support department will respond to questions you send by e-mail within a day.

TRAFFIC LIMIT

When readers view your Web pages, information transfers from the Web server to their computers. The amount of information that transfers depends on the number of people that view your Web pages and the file size of your pages.

Most Web presence providers limit the amount of information that can transfer in one day. If more information transfers, you may have to pay extra. You should choose a Web presence provider that allows at least 50 MB (megabytes) of information to transfer in one day.

RELIABILITY

Make sure the Web presence provider you choose is reliable. A Web presence provider should be able to tell you how often their Web servers shut down. You may want to ask a Web presence provider for customer references that you can contact. You should take into consideration that all Web presence providers occasionally shut down their Web servers for maintenance and upgrades.

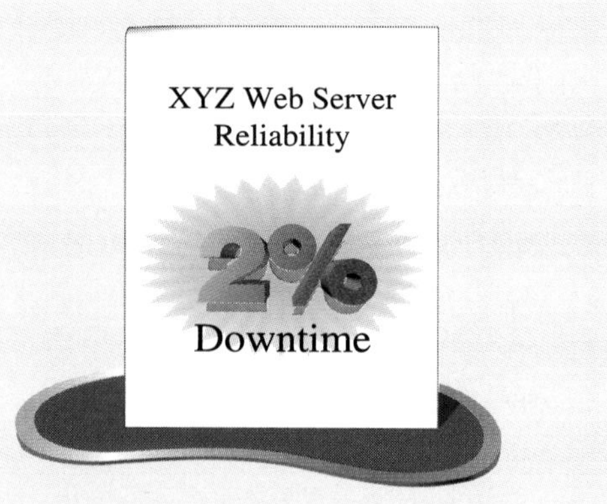

STORAGE SPACE

Most Web presence providers limit the amount of space you can use to store your Web pages. Choose a Web presence provider that allows you to store at least 5 MB (megabytes) of information.

ACCESS LOGS

A good Web presence provider will supply you with statistics about your Web pages, such as which Web pages are the most popular and where your readers are from. You may also be able to view any error messages readers may see when viewing your Web pages, such as "Page Not Found." Access logs can help you determine if you need to make changes to your Web pages.

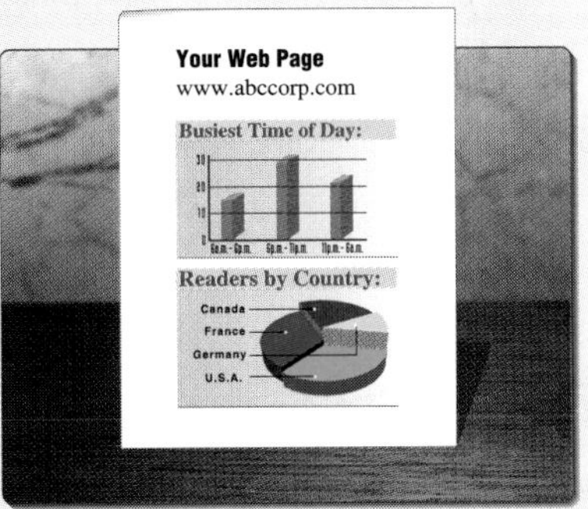

DOMAIN NAME REGISTRATION

For a fee, you can choose the address, or domain name, that people type to access your Web pages. A personalized domain name is easy for people to remember and will not change if you switch to another Web presence provider. Most Web presence providers will register your domain name for a fee.

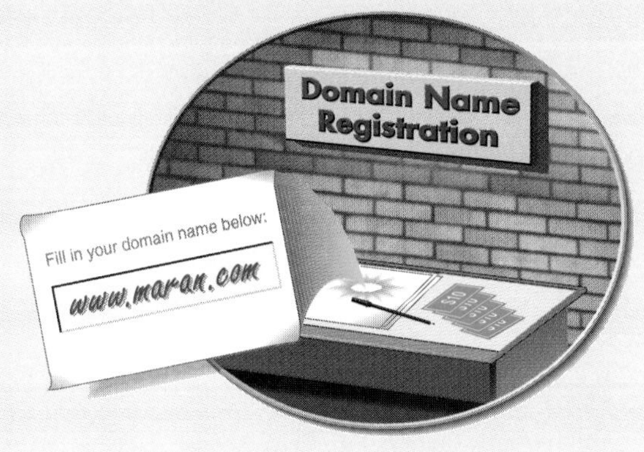

FRONTPAGE SERVER EXTENSIONS

Your Web presence provider must have FrontPage Server Extensions installed on their Web server for some advanced Web page features to work. For example, you will need FrontPage Server Extensions to use forms and some components, such as hit counters, on your Web pages.

SPECIFY KEYWORDS FOR A WEB PAGE

You can specify keywords to help search tools catalog your Web pages.

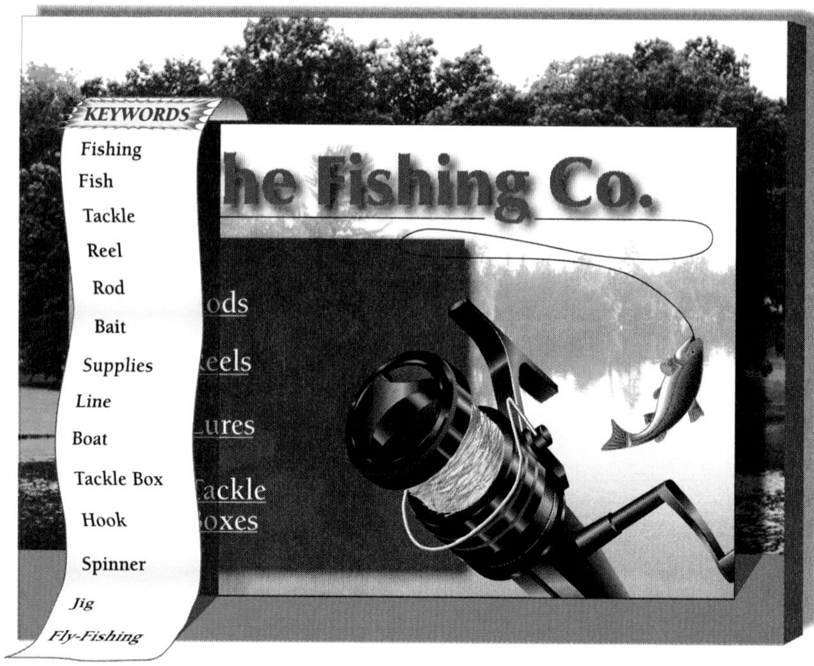

Search tools help people find Web pages that discuss information of interest. Popular search tools include AltaVista, Lycos and Yahoo!.

When readers enter words in a search tool that match your keywords, your Web page will more likely appear in the search results.

SPECIFY KEYWORDS FOR A WEB PAGE

1 Click **File**.

2 Click **Properties**.

Note: If Properties does not appear on the menu, position the mouse over the bottom of the menu to display all the menu commands.

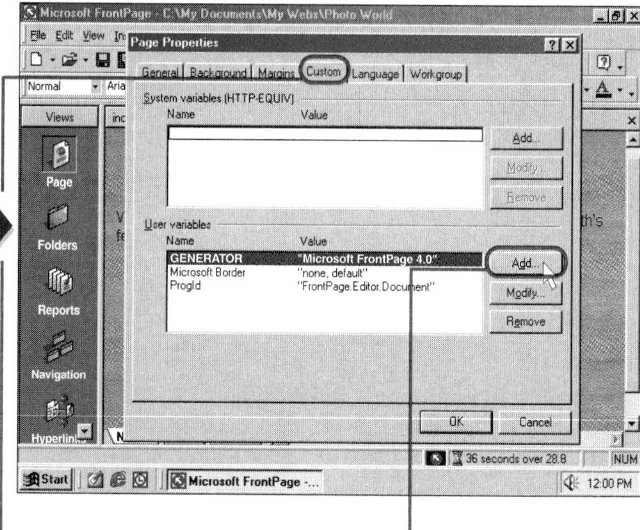

■ The Page Properties dialog box appears.

3 Click the **Custom** tab.

4 Click **Add** to specify keywords for your Web page.

Will the keywords I entered appear on my Web page?

Readers will not see the keywords you entered when viewing your Web page. Keywords appear in the HTML code for the Web page. To view the HTML code for a Web page, see page 42.

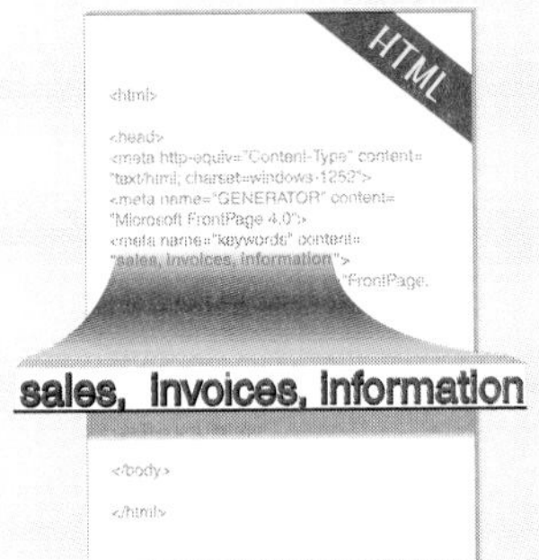

What words should I specify as keywords?

You should use both general and specific words to describe your Web page. For example, if your Web page contains information about corvettes, use the keywords "car" and "corvette." You may also want to include misspelled words that people may type, such as "corvete."

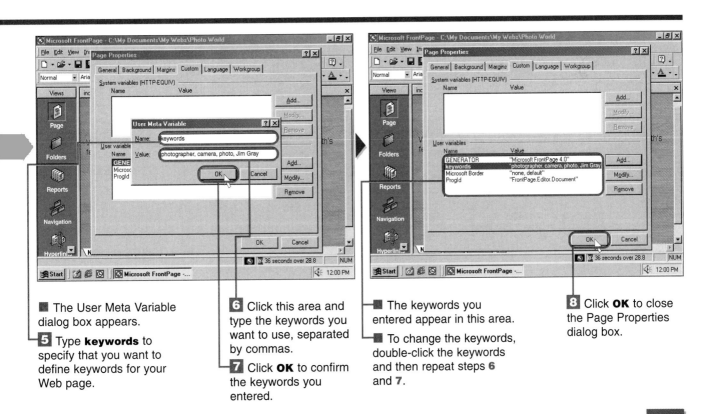

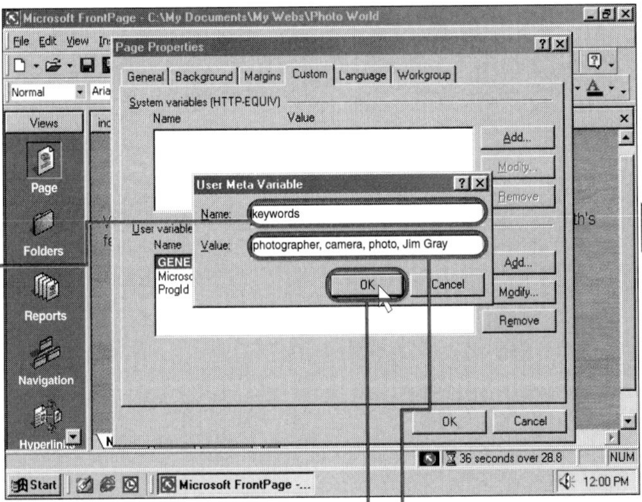

■ The User Meta Variable dialog box appears.

5 Type **keywords** to specify that you want to define keywords for your Web page.

6 Click this area and type the keywords you want to use, separated by commas.

7 Click **OK** to confirm the keywords you entered.

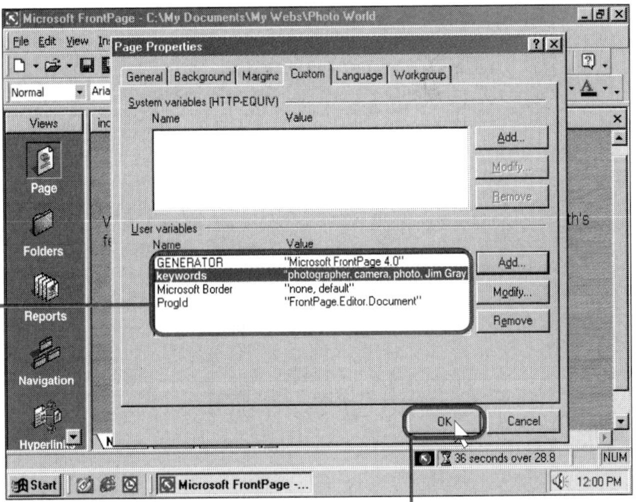

■ The keywords you entered appear in this area.

■ To change the keywords, double-click the keywords and then repeat steps **6** and **7**.

8 Click **OK** to close the Page Properties dialog box.

PREVENT ROBOTS FROM INDEXING A WEB PAGE

Many search tools use programs called robots to find new pages on the Web. You can prevent most robots from indexing your Web page.

Search tools index Web pages to help people find Web pages that discuss information of interest. Popular search tools include AltaVista, Lycos and Yahoo!.

You may want to prevent robots from indexing a Web page you created for just your family, friends or organization.

PREVENT ROBOTS FROM INDEXING A WEB PAGE

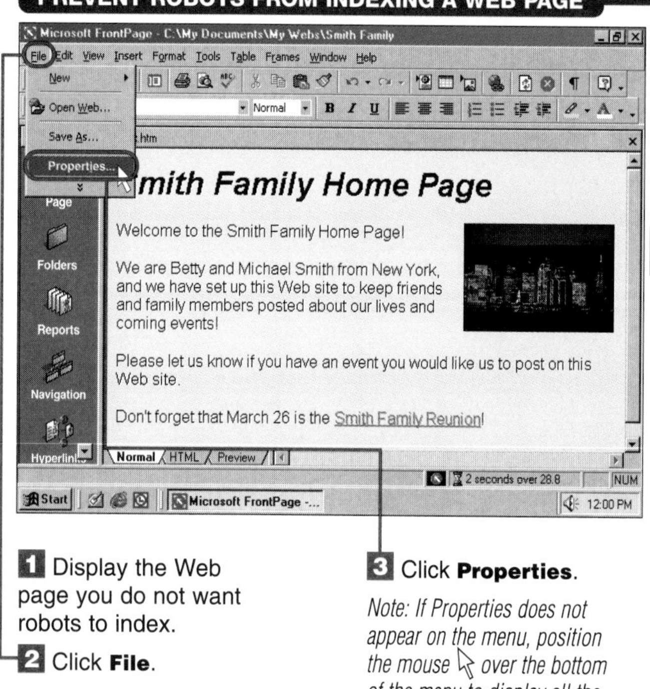

1 Display the Web page you do not want robots to index.

2 Click **File**.

3 Click **Properties**.

Note: If Properties does not appear on the menu, position the mouse over the bottom of the menu to display all the menu commands.

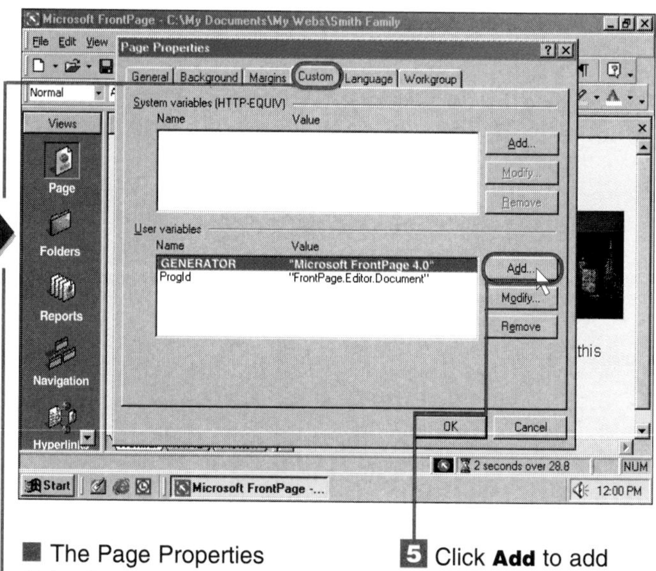

■ The Page Properties dialog box appears.

4 Click the **Custom** tab.

5 Click **Add** to add information that will prevent robots from indexing the Web page.

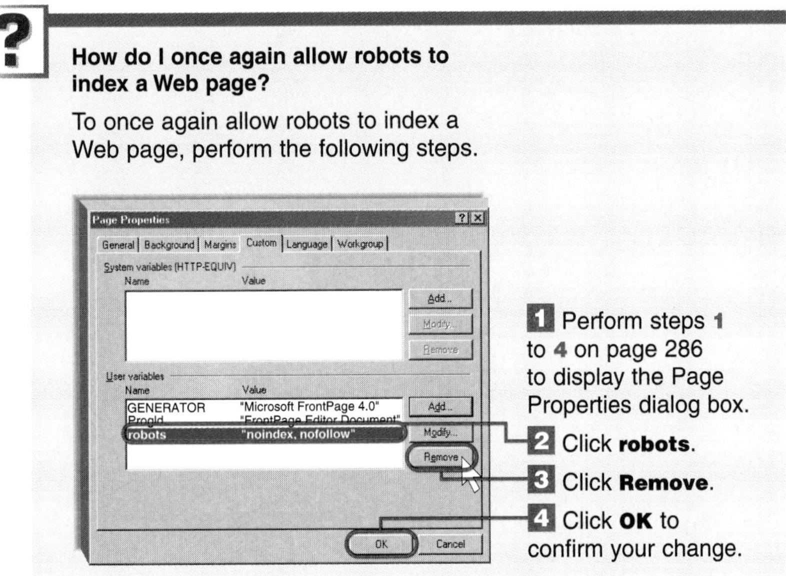

How do I once again allow robots to index a Web page?

To once again allow robots to index a Web page, perform the following steps.

1 Perform steps 1 to 4 on page 286 to display the Page Properties dialog box.

2 Click **robots**.

3 Click **Remove**.

4 Click **OK** to confirm your change.

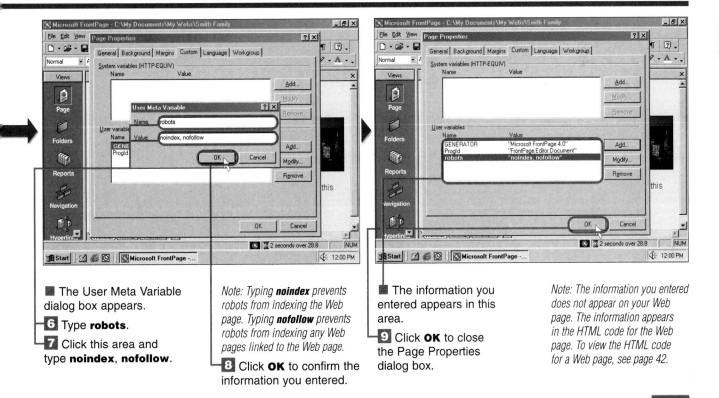

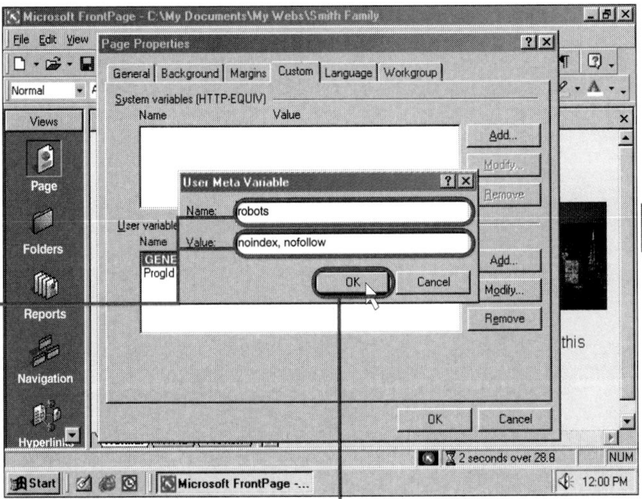

■ The User Meta Variable dialog box appears.

6 Type **robots**.

7 Click this area and type **noindex**, **nofollow**.

*Note: Typing **noindex** prevents robots from indexing the Web page. Typing **nofollow** prevents robots from indexing any Web pages linked to the Web page.*

8 Click **OK** to confirm the information you entered.

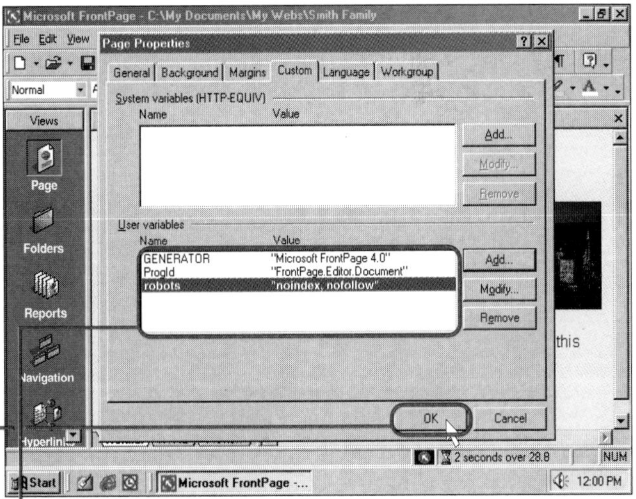

■ The information you entered appears in this area.

9 Click **OK** to close the Page Properties dialog box.

Note: The information you entered does not appear on your Web page. The information appears in the HTML code for the Web page. To view the HTML code for a Web page, see page 42.

SELECT A WEB PAGE NOT TO PUBLISH

When you publish your Web pages, you can choose not to publish a specific Web page in your Web site.

SELECT A WEB PAGE NOT TO PUBLISH

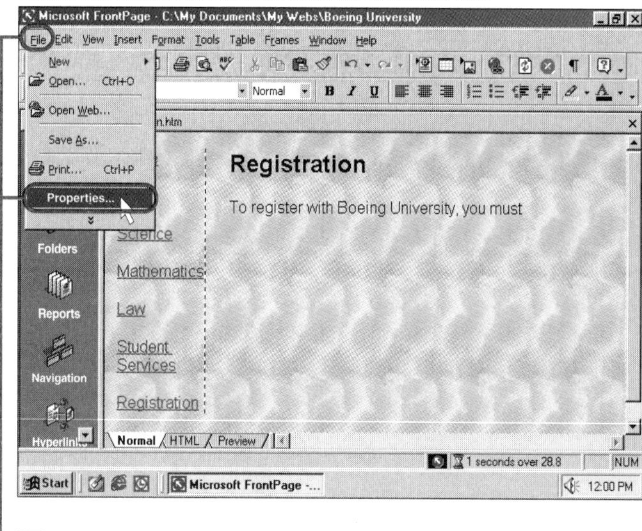

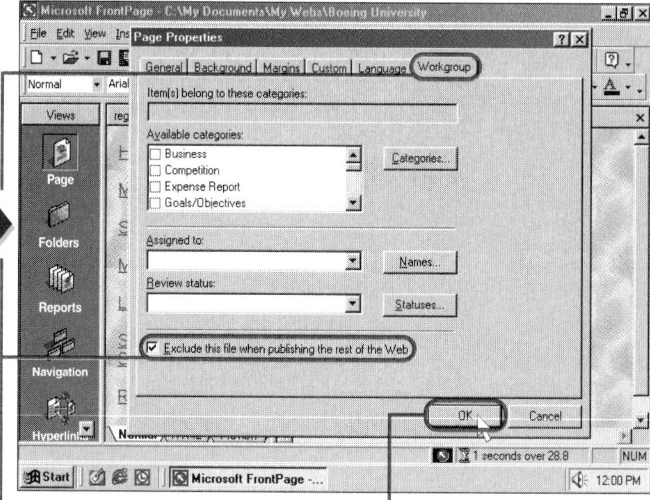

1 Display the Web page you do not want to publish.

2 Click **File**.

3 Click **Properties**.

Note: If Properties does not appear on the menu, position the mouse over the bottom of the menu to display all the menu commands.

■ The Page Properties dialog box appears.

4 Click the **Workgroup** tab.

5 Click this option to exclude the Web page when you publish the rest of your Web pages (☐ changes to ☑).

6 Click **OK**.

■ To once again include the Web page when you publish the rest of your Web pages, repeat steps **1** to **6** (☑ changes to ☐ in step **5**).

Why would I choose not to publish a Web page?

FrontPage will automatically publish all of the Web pages in your Web site. If your Web site includes a Web page you have not yet completed, you can publish the rest of your Web pages without the incomplete Web page.

Does FrontPage offer other reports that I can use?

FrontPage offers many reports that can help you analyze and summarize information about your Web site. For example, you can display a report that shows the status of all the links in your Web site. For more information on using reports, see page 276.

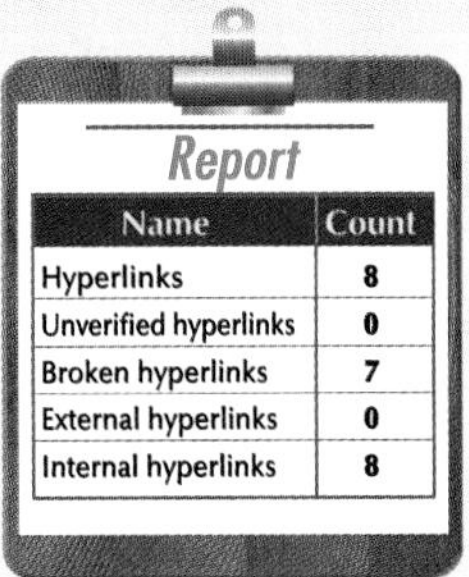

Report

Name	Count
Hyperlinks	8
Unverified hyperlinks	0
Broken hyperlinks	7
External hyperlinks	0
Internal hyperlinks	8

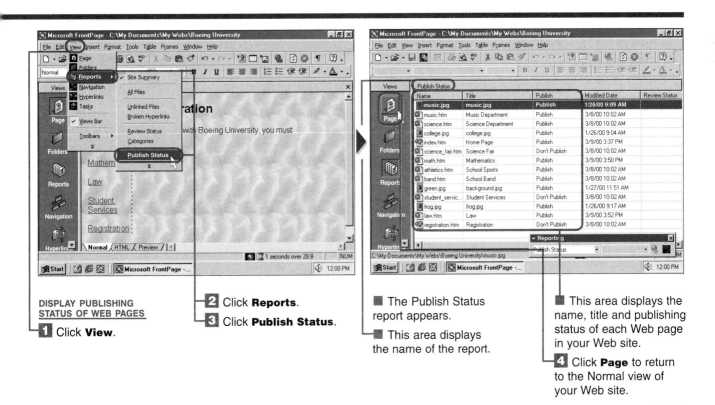

DISPLAY PUBLISHING STATUS OF WEB PAGES

1 Click **View**.

2 Click **Reports**.

3 Click **Publish Status**.

■ The Publish Status report appears.

■ This area displays the name of the report.

■ This area displays the name, title and publishing status of each Web page in your Web site.

4 Click **Page** to return to the Normal view of your Web site.

TRANSFER WEB PAGES TO WEB SERVER

When you finish creating your Web pages, you can transfer the pages to a Web server to make the pages available on the Web.

Before you can transfer your Web pages to a Web server, you must choose a Web presence provider that will publish your Web pages. For information on Web presence providers, see pages 280 to 283.

TRANSFER WEB PAGES TO WEB SERVER

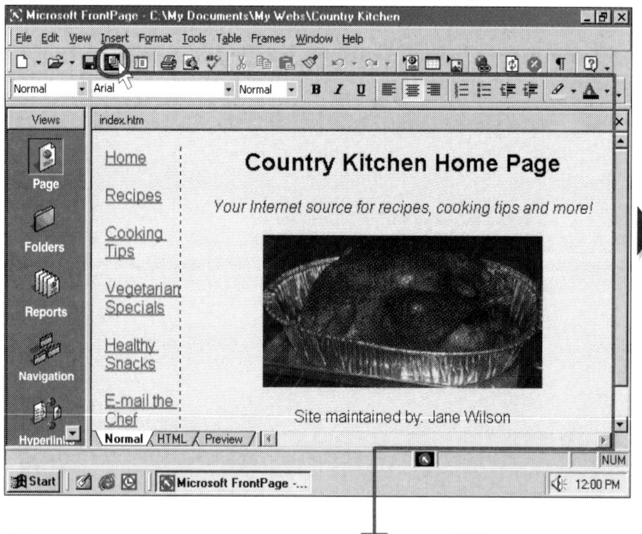

■ You need to connect to the Internet before you can transfer your Web pages to a Web server.

1 Click [icon] to publish your Web pages.

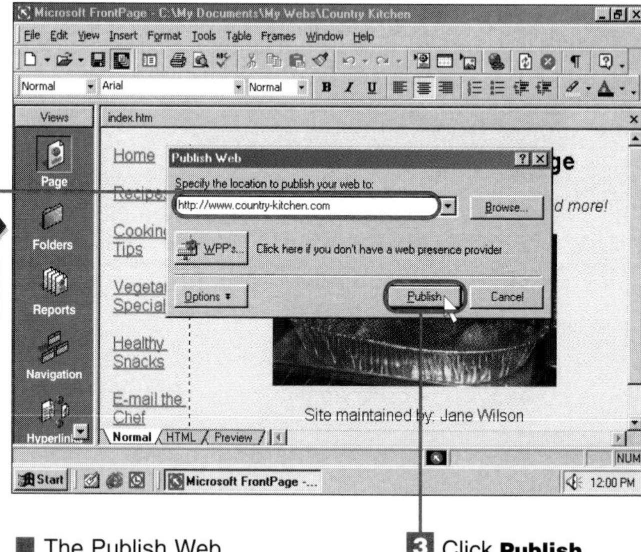

■ The Publish Web dialog box appears.

2 Click this area and type the address of the Web server where you want to publish your Web pages.

3 Click **Publish**.

What information do I need to transfer my Web pages to a Web server?

You will need the following information to transfer your Web pages to a Web server. If you do not know the information, ask your Web presence provider.

Web server address

User name

Password

How do I update my Web pages on the Web server?

If you make changes to Web pages on your computer, you must transfer the updated pages to the Web server. The updated Web pages will replace the old Web pages on the Web server. To transfer the updated Web pages to the Web server, click 🖫.

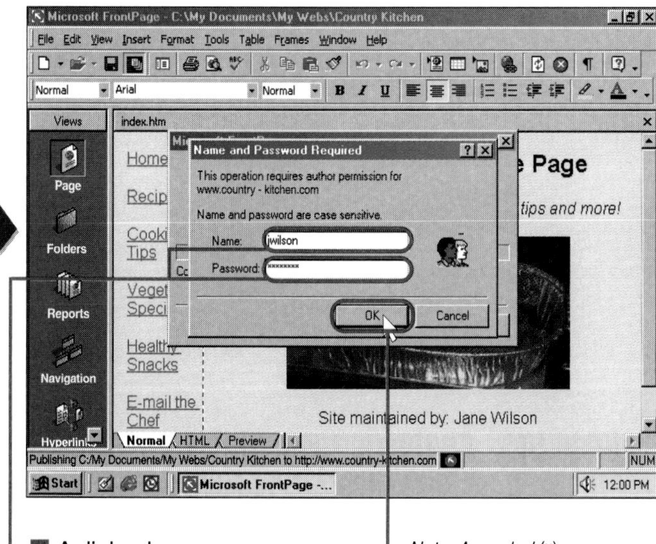

■ A dialog box appears, asking for your user name and password.

4 Type your user name.

5 Click this area and type your password.

Note: A symbol (x) appears for each character you type to prevent others from seeing your password.

6 Click **OK**.

■ FrontPage copies your Web pages to the Web server.

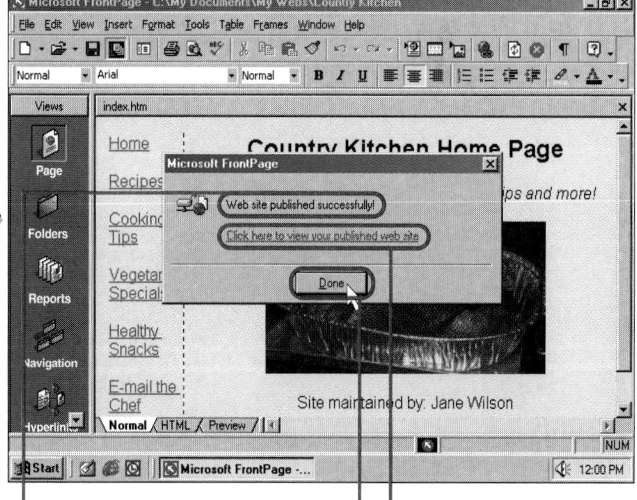

■ This message appears when your Web pages have been published successfully.

■ You can click this option to view your published Web pages on the Web.

7 Click **Done** to close the dialog box.

PUBLICIZE WEB PAGES

After you publish your Web pages, there are several ways you can let people know about the pages.

MAIL ANNOUNCEMENTS

You can mail an announcement about your Web pages to family, friends, colleagues and clients. You can also mail information about your Web pages to local newspapers and magazines that may be interested in your Web pages.

E-MAIL MESSAGES

Most e-mail programs include a feature, called a signature, that allows you to add the same information to the end of every e-mail message you send. You can use a signature to include information about your Web pages in all your e-mail messages.

EXCHANGE LINKS

If another page on the Web discusses ideas related to your Web pages, you can ask the author to include a link to your pages if you do the same. This allows people reading the other Web page to easily visit your Web pages.

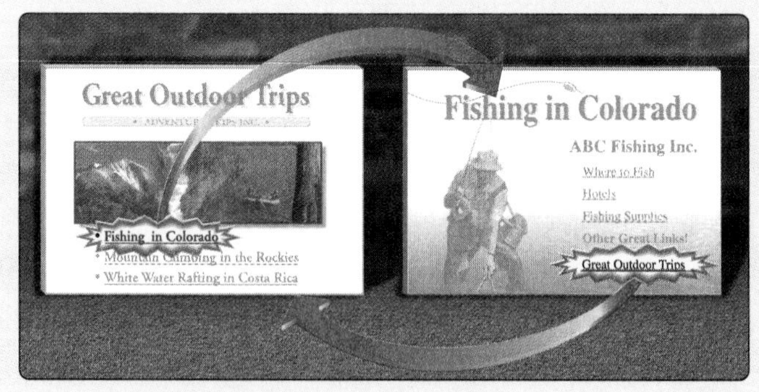

WEB PAGE ADVERTISEMENTS

Many companies set aside areas on their Web pages where you can advertise your Web pages. You can use the LinkExchange to advertise your Web pages free of charge. The LinkExchange is located at the adnetwork.bcentral.com Web site.

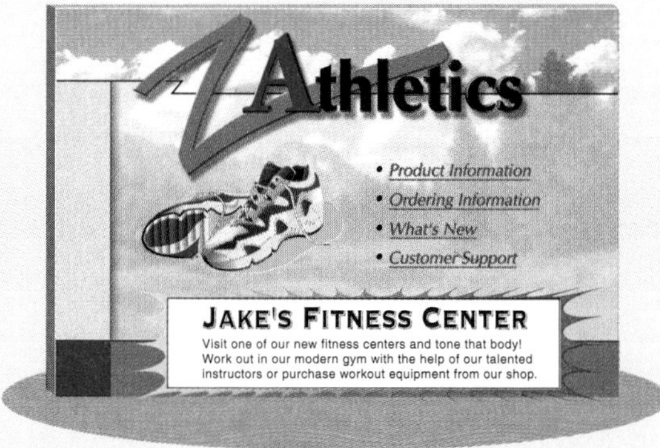

NEWSGROUPS

You can send an announcement about your Web pages to discussion groups on the Internet called newsgroups. Make sure you choose newsgroups that discuss topics related to your Web pages. You can announce new or updated Web pages to the comp.infosystems.www.announce newsgroup.

MAILING LISTS

You can send an announcement to carefully selected mailing lists on the Internet. A mailing list is a discussion group that communicates through e-mail. You should read the messages in a mailing list for a week before sending an announcement to make sure the mailing list members would be interested in your Web pages. You can find a directory of mailing lists at the www.liszt.com Web site.

SEARCH TOOLS

Search tools help people quickly find information on the Web. You can add your Web pages to various search tools so people can easily find your Web pages. Some popular search tools include:

AltaVista	www.altavista.com
Lycos	www.lycos.com
Yahoo!	www.yahoo.com

You can add your Web pages to many search tools at once at the www.submit-it.com Web site.

INDEX

C

D

G

H

I

J

K

L

M

N

O

P

R

S

U

V

W

OVER 8 MILLION

OTHER 3-D Visual SERIES

SIMPLIFIED SERIES

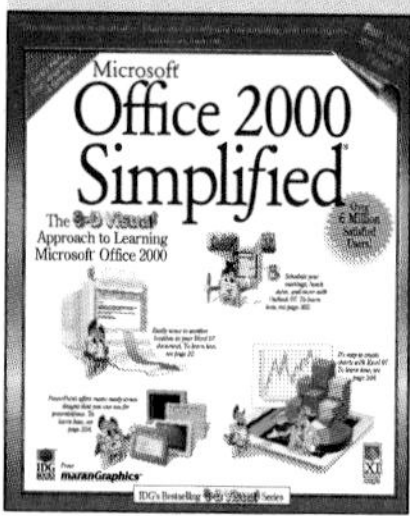

Microsoft Office 2000 Simplified

ISBN 0-7645-6052-2
$29.99 USA/£28.99 UK
$39.99 CAN

Microsoft Word 2000 Simplified

ISBN 0-7645-6054-9
$24.99 USA/£23.99 UK
$32.99 CAN

Microsoft Excel 2000 Simplified

ISBN 0-7645-6053-0
$24.99 USA/£23.99 UK
$32.99 CAN

Microsoft Access 2000 Simplified

ISBN 0-7645-6058-1
$24.99 USA/£23.99 UK
$32.99 CAN

Internet and World Wide Web Simplified, 3rd Edition

ISBN 0-7645-3409-2
$24.99 USA/£23.99 UK
$32.99 CAN

Computers Simplified, 4th Edition

ISBN 0-7645-6042-5
$24.99 USA/£23.99 UK
$32.99 CAN

PC Upgrade and Repair Simplified

ISBN 0-7645-6049-2
$24.99 USA/£23.99 UK
$32.99 CAN

Word For Windows 95 Simplified

ISBN 1-56884-681-9
$19.99 USA/£18.99 UK
$29.99 CAN

Word 6 For Windows Simplified

ISBN 1-56884-660-6
$19.99 USA/£18.99 UK
$29.99 CAN

WordPerfect 6.1 For Windows Simplified

ISBN 1-56884-665-7
$19.99 USA/£18.99 UK
$29.99 CAN

POCKETGUIDES

The Proven 3-D Visual Approach To Learning Computers In A Handy Pocket Size.

Windows 98 Visual PocketGuide

ISBN 0-7645-6035-2
$16.99 USA/£15.99 UK
$23.99 CAN

Windows 95 Visual PocketGuide

ISBN 1-56884-661-4
$14.99 USA/£13.99 UK
$21.99 CAN

ALSO AVAILABLE:

Windows 3.1 Visual PocketGuide

ISBN 1-56884-650-9
$14.99 USA/£13.99 UK
$21.99 CAN

...Visit our Web site at **www.maran.com**